DATE DUE / DATE DE RETOUR

CANADA YEAR BOOK

Published by authority of the Minister
responsible for Statistics Canada
© Minister of Industry, 1996

The 1997 *Canada Year Book*
is published both in CD-ROM
and print format.
Both versions are available from:

Operations and Integration Division
Circulation Management
Statistics Canada
120 Parkdale Avenue
Ottawa, Ontario
K1A 0T6
Internet: order@statcan.ca

All rights reserved. No part of this publication may be reproduced, stored in a retrieval system or transmitted in any form or by any means, electronic, mechanical, photocopying, recording or otherwise without prior written permission from Licence Services, Marketing Division, Statistics Canada, Ottawa, Ontario, Canada K1A 0T6.

Every attempt has been made to identify and credit sources for photographs. We would appreciate receiving information as to any inaccuracies in the credits for subsequent editions.

Catalogue No. 11-402-XPE/1997
ISBN 0-660-16494-9

The *Canada Year Book* is edited and prepared in the Communications Division of Statistics Canada.

Production and composition: Dissemination Division, Statistics Canada
Printing: Friesens Corporation, Altona, Manitoba
Cover and book design: Rachel Penkar
Art Direction: John MacCraken
Design Production: Danielle Baum
Graphic Production: Renée Saumure
Cover photography: John de Visser/Masterfile
Richard Desmarais/Desmarais Photography Inc.

The Cover

On the front cover, the ineffable beauty of the Rocky Mountains at dawn is captured by photographer John de Visser on a trip along the Hope–Princeton Highway, in British Columbia. On the back cover, Richard Desmarais' photo conveys the eternal mystery of the Atlantic Ocean, taken at Fort Louisbourg, Cape Breton Island, at sunset.

Both photographs are compelling. They are peaceful and quiet, conveying a sense of the majesty of Canada, and the passage of time. Much like the *Canada Year Book* itself, first published in 1867, they remind us of the stability of the country and the peace and progress of its citizens.

Note of Appreciation

Canada owes the success of its statistical system to a long-standing co-operation involving Statistics Canada, the citizens of Canada, its businesses, governments and other institutions. Accurate and timely statistical information could not be produced without their continued co-operation and goodwill.

The paper used in this publication meets the minimum requirements of the American National Standard for Information Sciences – Permanence of Paper for Printed Library Materials, ANSI Z39.48 – 1984.
Printed in Canada

FOREWORD

t Statistics Canada, we have a mandate to collect information about life in Canada, and present it in a way that all Canadians may find accessible and useful.

The *Canada Year Book* offers us a unique opportunity to carry out this task. More than just a collection of statistics, this publication has historically offered readers an in-depth picture of the forces shaping our social and economic life.

In the 1997 edition, we have enlarged this picture, aligning the contents of the *Canada Year Book* with the many changes we are experiencing as a people and a nation. As a result, the *Year Book* gives us a sense of what is going on in Canada today, of the major trends and issues, of the story behind the numbers.

I am pleased to recommend it to all our readers.

Ivan P. Fellegi
Chief Statistician of Canada

ACKNOWLEDGEMENTS

The 1997 *Canada Year Book* is a story of commitment, fun and creative thinking. Above all, it has been an inspiration to collaborate with the *Year Book* team, all of whom have consistently pushed the boundaries of excellence in their work.

I am especially happy to signal the contribution of Krista Campbell, who, as production manager for the 1997 *Canada Year Book*, brought a sense of grace and humour to the project. Together with Ms. Campbell and Wayne Smith, Director of Communications and a constant and supportive mentor of this project, I am honoured to thank all who have worked with us.

My special thanks go to an inspiring group of writers and editors who helped us turn the numbers into readable and interesting prose. On the English team, headed by Krista Campbell as Senior Editor, were: Steve Aplin, Patricia Buchanan (indexer), Brian Cameron, Amélie Crosson-Gooderham, Jenefer Curtis, Josephine Dyrkton, Marla Fletcher, Liz Hart, Jocelyn Harvey, Sarah Hubbard, Steve Hunt, Laurel Hyatt, Susan Lightstone, Bruce Nesbitt, Jody Proctor, Jim Reil, Barbara Riggs, David Scrimshaw, Alan Sharpe, Keane Shore and Julie Swettenham. A special thanks also to David Gonczol, principal researcher for the project.

On the French team, under the inspired management of Senior Editor Nathalie Turcotte, were Nicole Castéran, Nancy Fontaine, Christiane Melançon and Jean-Charles Merleau. Special appreciation is also extended to Denis Bernard and Christian Carbonneau, for their collaboration at project's end and many thanks must also go to Official Languages for translation services.

To revise and update the more than 250 tables featured in the *Canada Year Book*, a talented group of editors was assembled within Communications Division. Appreciation is extended to the "Tables Committee," and especially to Valerie Peters, David Scrimshaw, Colleen Bolger, Nancy Fontaine and Jody Proctor. Also, a special word of thanks must go to the Systems and Production team, headed by Diane Leblanc and supervised by Lynda Verreault, and including Sandra Boivin, Elaine Brassard, Chantal Chalifoux, Danielle Fournier and Loui Massicotte. A special thanks to Andrew Neish for daily assistance.

Within the Dissemination Division, two managers supervised the production of the *Canada Year Book* from start to finish. Special appreciation is extended both to John

MacCraken and Johanne Beauseigle for their intelligent and committed attention to the many details of production. Many thanks also to Lynne Durocher and Francine Simoneau, who formed a superb team of typesetters, headed by Louise Demers, and with assistance from Suzanne Beauchamp. A very special word of thanks also to Danielle Baum, Special Advisor on systems integration and table design, for her commitment and hard work.

Many thanks to Rachel Penkar who, as the book designer, faced and met the challenge of providing a new, innovative and exciting look for the *Year Book*. Much appreciation is extended to John MacCraken for skilled art direction and to Renée Saumure, who as design production manager provided effective stewardship of the design project. Thanks also to Jean-Marie Lacombe for his creative work on the graphics.

For yet again a superb job in handling the printing liaison for the *Canada Year Book*, thanks to Jacques Téssier. For creative marketing initiatives, special thanks to Kathryn Bonner and Mary Rigby. Many thanks also to Sandra Dyck for researching a collection of photographs that infuse the book with both life and spirit.

We are grateful to the many experts both internal and external to Statistics Canada who act as referees for the *Year Book*. We wish to especially signal the contributions made by Ken Bennett, Mary Cromie, Philip Cross, Jean Dumas, Pierre Gauthier, Gerry Gravel, Lucie Laliberté, Craig McKie, François Miranda, Henry Puderer, George Sciadas, Claude Simard and Philip Smith.

Last, but not least, we extend our appreciation to the librarians at Statistics Canada, who hold the key to treasures of knowledge and inspiration, and who have supported our efforts with unfailing courtesy and diligence.

Jonina Wood
Editor-in-Chief
Canada Year Book

WELCOME TO THE 1997 CANADA YEAR BOOK

Life in Canada is changing. With the arrival of the Internet, globalization, our greater integration in international economies, a frustrating run of recessions throughout much of the 1980s and 1990s, the crunching of government budgets and even the dramatic changes in our concept of family life, many of our established and traditional ways of living are radically altering.

The mirror to much of this activity, since Canada was founded in 1867, has been the *Canada Year Book.* But, as life in Canada alters, so must the *Year Book.* The 1997 *Canada Year Book* has been redesigned to provide a more consistent and comprehensive view of Canadian society, and to mirror, as faithfully as possible, many of the major trends and shifts currently taking place in our economic and social lives.

How to use this Year Book

If you are a habitual user of the *Year Book,* this brief guide will let you know of several key changes to this latest edition. If you are a new user, the following instructions should be helpful in guiding you to the information you require.

A good starting point is the Index which has been extended to direct you more effectively to a relevant area either in the text, or in the statistical tables at the end of each chapter. For a more general overview, the Table of Contents will direct you to the book's 16 chapters grouped under four main headings: The Environment, The People, The Economy and The Nation.

Although the format of the 1997 *Canada Year Book* is smaller, the basic contents are the same. A more streamlined text offers perspectives on the environment, the land, our social and economic sectors, our demography, our labour force, our government and the legal system. The *Year Book* continues to offer a phalanx of tables at the end of each chapter, and they now better reflect the great range of information available through Statistics Canada.

Indeed, this edition of the *Canada Year Book* features more than 250 tables, with information on everything from population counts to the way Canadians spend their spare time. To preserve the reference value of the *Year Book*, we continued to update the tables, even after the text had been finalized. Should there be discrepancies, readers may rely on the data presented in the tables. Tables are located at the end of each chapter, as are the legends which explain the meaning of symbols used. In addition, the Sources sections at the end of each chapter list major contributors, either from within Statistics Canada, or from other government departments or agencies.

As in past issues of the *Year Book*, each chapter presents a number of charts and graphs which are designed to stand alone in telling the "story" of major trends and changing patterns. Our practice of including short feature articles on the slightly offbeat and interesting side of Canadian life also continues. We are pleased to offer an entirely new collection devoted to a wide variety of topics, from the story of the northern lights to sales of maple syrup.

Last, but not least, are the more than 95 photographs which appear in this *Year Book*. In colour and black and white, they are drawn from the work of Canadian photographers and artists. Detailed information is offered on selected photos in Appendix C, specifically the cover photos, as well as those which begin each of the sections and chapters, and those which are found on the first page of each chapter. All other photos carry the credits and relevant information directly beneath them.

There are three other appendices. Appendix A provides a complete listing of all Statistics Canada Regional Reference Centres. Appendix B lists a table on metric/imperial conversions. Appendix D provides copyright details for quotations and literary excerpts.

The Canada Year Book on CD-ROM

The 1997 *Canada Year Book* is also available on CD-ROM, with an enhanced and expanded collection of tables. While the CD-ROM remains faithful to the form and content of the *Year Book*, it also features multi-media accessories to enrich and highlight areas of the text. For further information on the CD-ROM, please call 1-800-267-6677.

An invitation to all readers

We would like to extend an invitation to all readers to write to us, if you have any comments or suggestions for the improvement of this book. At Statistics Canada, we regard the *Canada Year Book* as an ongoing chronicle of life in Canada, and therefore one of the most important reference resources available. We welcome your opinion in the development of this information treasure.

We can be reached at the following address:

Canada Year Book 1997
Communications Division
Statistics Canada
R.H. Coats Building
Tunney's Pasture
Ottawa, Canada
KIA 0T6

TABLE OF CONTENTS

SECTION 1

THE ENVIRONMENT

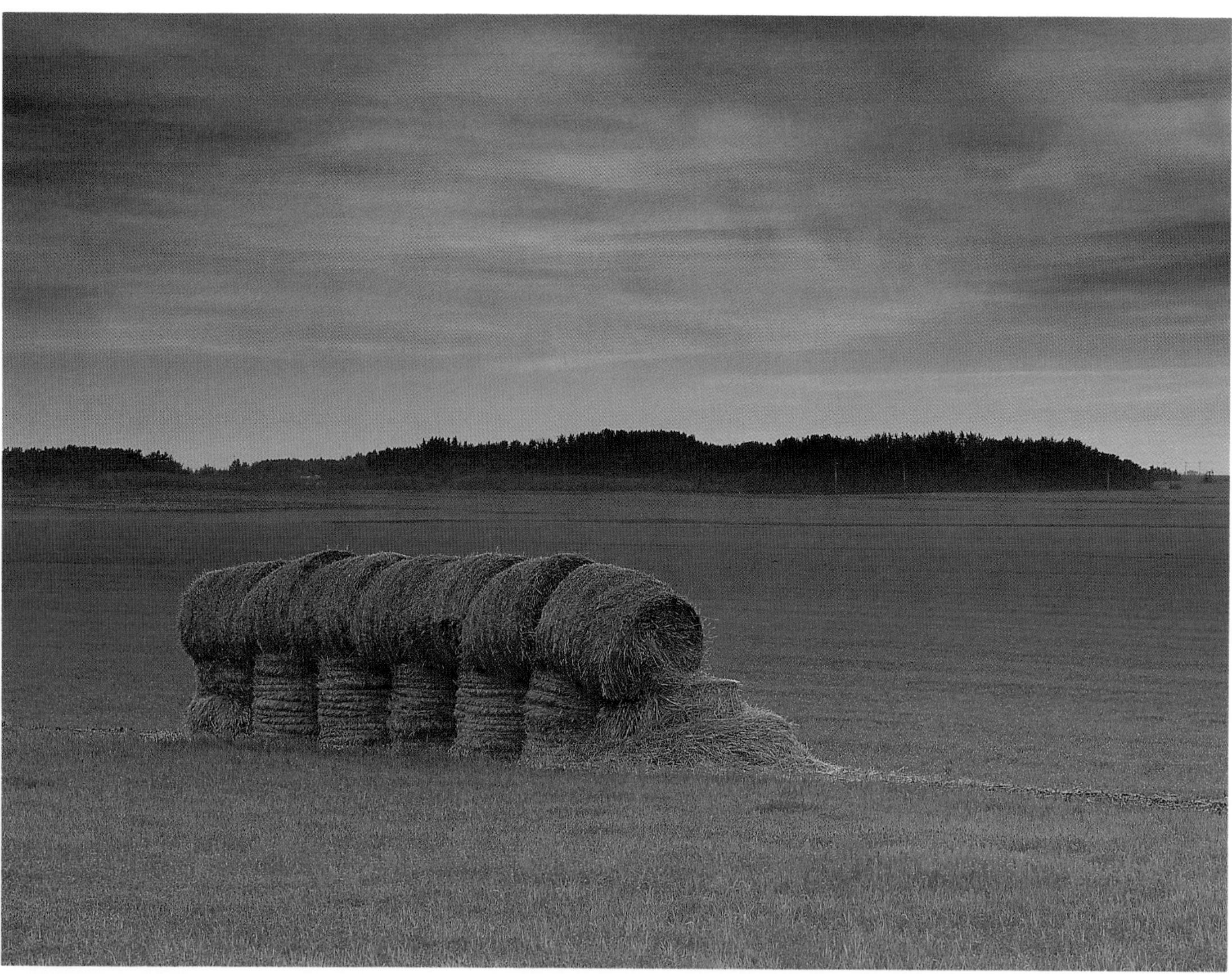

DARWIN WIGGETT, FIRST LIGHT

Chapter 1

THE LAND

J. David Andrews, Dynamic Light Productions

"It's a big country, Canada," Canadian novelist Antonine Maillet has said. "To find its equal, you would have to go a very long way. To see it all, you would have to look down on it from a very great height."

Indeed, Canada dwarfs most other countries. It has the world's longest coastline—the equivalent of circling the globe six times. It has an Arctic island twice the size of Great Britain, but with fewer than 9,000 permanent inhabitants.

The Mackenzie River drains an area three times the size of France. The 3,790 kilometre-long St. Lawrence Seaway–Great Lakes Waterway is the world's longest inland shipping lane. And with the United States, Canada shares the Great Lakes, which hold one-quarter of the world's fresh water in lakes.

The distance from the Yukon–Alaska border to Cape Spear, Newfoundland, on the Atlantic coast is 5,500 kilometres. If you were to fly that far from Newfoundland towards Europe, you would land in Warsaw, Poland.

The distance from south to north is almost as great: 4,600 kilometres from Middle Island in Lake Erie to Ellesmere Island in the High Arctic. The same distance south from Lake Erie takes you to Quito, the capital of Ecuador.

Most of Canada's 10 million square kilometres are uninhabited. Indeed, about three in four Canadians live in a widely-spaced string of cities close to the border with the United States. To travel north from these cities is to enter uninhabited forests or plains; wilderness remains always at our back door.

The North

For many Canadians, the North is the last frontier of a frontier nation. As Canadian poet Ralph Gustafson puts it: "In Europe, you can't move without going down into history. Here, all is a beginning . . . ."

Magazine editor and journalist Robert Fulford describes the North as "the geographic location of the Canadian unconscious." The North, he says, "sits heavily on top of the Canadian imagination—the place of mystery and magic and romance."

Together, Yukon and the Northwest Territories total 3.9 million square kilometres—40% of Canada's area. Yet in early 1996, only about 97,000 people were residents of the North—that's about 0.3% of Canada's population. Mostly, these people live in 75 or so communities. Whitehorse, capital of Yukon, is the largest, with a population of 18,000 in 1991.

Despite the North's reputation for cold weather, there's actually less snowfall in the Arctic than in many other regions of Canada. Indeed, some Arctic areas have as little precipitation as the Egyptian capital of Cairo; a whole winter may bring as little snow as falls in Montreal during a single day.

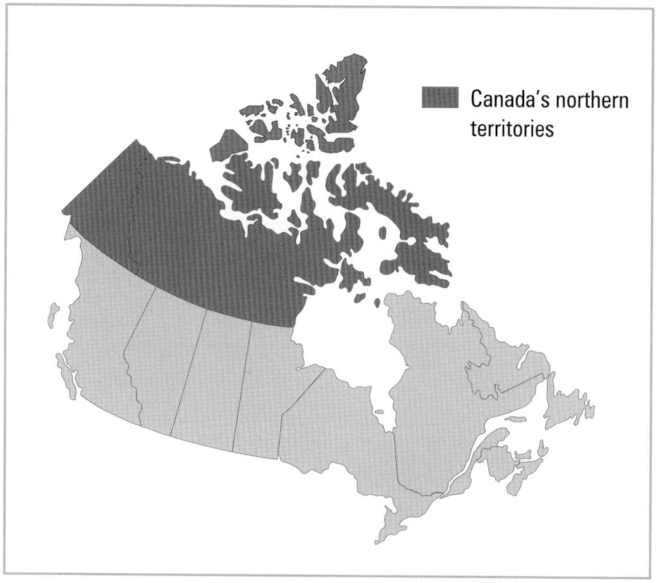

Canada's northern territories

But make no mistake about it, the North can be very cold. Indeed, Canada's all-time lowest temperature was recorded at Snag, in the Yukon Territory, on February 3, 1947; on that day, the mercury dipped to –63°C. In the Arctic, the average temperature is below –10°C for six months of the year or more.

The Precambrian Shield

"This land stares at the sun in huge silence," has written the Canadian poet F.R. Scott, "endlessly repeating something we cannot hear." What we cannot hear finds its echo in the vastness of the North, from the mountainous, ice-buried Arctic Islands to the flat, treeless plains of the Mackenzie River delta.

Canada's North is dominated by the Precambrian Shield, a sheet of rock covering more than half of the Northwest Territories, as well as most of Quebec, Ontario and Labrador, and the northern sections of Manitoba and Saskatchewan. Shaped like a horseshoe, with Hudson Bay at its centre, the Shield features two distinct landscapes.

Across its southern half are exposed rocks, low-lying swamps, countless lakes and a sea of trees—one of the world's largest forests, extending thousands of kilometres from Newfoundland to Yukon. Beavers, bears, weasels, foxes, porcupines, wolves and squirrels are just some of the mammals living in these forests of fir, pine, spruce, cedar, tamarack, birch and aspen.

Across its northern half is the tundra—a vast plain beyond the tree line carpeted with mosses, lichens and hardy dwarf willows. The tundra is permanently frozen to depths of up to almost half a kilometre. Yet in the very brief summers, more than 800 kinds of flowering plants and ferns grow here. Plants such as the Arctic poppy, for example, take less than a month to flower and produce seeds.

Despite the cold, wildlife thrives on the tundra: polar bears, lemmings, muskox, Arctic foxes, large white hares and

Art Wolfe, Tony Stone Images

Arctic hares in territorial dispute.

hundreds of thousands of caribou. Lake trout and Arctic char are found in the lakes and rivers, and in the sea are whales, walruses and seals.

About 75 species of birds fly in great numbers to tundra breeding grounds. These include the Arctic tern, which migrates to Ellesmere Island from as far south as Antarctica—a round trip each year of 40,000 kilometres and possibly the longest migration of any bird in the world.

At the Shield's centre is the Hudson Bay Lowlands, Canada's largest wetland. The lowlands are 300,000 square kilometres of forest and vast muskeg swamps. With the exception of a few people in small settlements along Hudson Bay's southern shore, no one lives here.

On the Shield's western edge are the North's largest lakes, including Great Slave Lake—at 614 metres, Canada's deepest lake. The Shield's eastern edge is the Atlantic coast of Labrador.

The Shield is ancient; indeed, the oldest rocks on earth are found near the eastern shore of Great Bear Lake in the Northwest Territories. These few square kilometres of rock are about four billion years old.

With its long geological history—including the rise of mountains and their subsequent erosion—it's not surprising that the Shield is a storehouse of valuable minerals. Since around the turn of the century, Canadians have mined its rich deposits of gold, silver, copper, nickel, lead, uranium and other minerals.

On the other hand, the Shield has little potential as farming land: most of its soil was scraped away during the ice ages. As well, it's both difficult and expensive to cut roads and railways through the region's swamps and hard rocks.

"She would explode into a lake of candled ice with millions and trillions of little flickering lights that would rise up and sink down, bunch up, or scatter wherever the water and the currents carried them," wrote Canadian author Jacques Ferron in his storybook description of the aurora borealis, also known as the northern lights.

For thousands of years, the aurora borealis has entertained and mystified viewers. A cascade of red, green, purple and white across the sky, it pulsates, shimmers, or simply stands still. Taking on many forms, the aurora can be seen as an arc across the horizon, a ray of light, or simply a coloured curtain blanketing the stars.

Because Canada is an ideal location for viewing this spectacle, familiarity has spawned a number of other "auroral" myths among its inhabitants. The Dogrib people thought the moving lights were their departed hero, Ithenhiela, beckoning them to join him in the sky. French–Canadian ancestors saw the aurora as a series of dancing marionettes. The Iroquois thought that beyond the light existed the Land of the Souls. The Alaskan Eskimo imagined the souls of their favourite animals dancing in the heights above.

Auroral legends have arisen beyond Canada's borders, too. In Finland, the lights were "fire foxes" who lit the sky up with their shining fur. The Scots, on the other hand, saw the lights as merry dancers, and the Swedes saw a kind of folk dance. A tale from Estonia had it that the glow of the lights came from a celestial wedding, in which guests and their horse-drawn sleds all gave off a kind of mysterious radiance.

Even today, notions of the aurora's power still persist. For example, Japanese newlyweds come to Canada's North in the belief that the presence of the aurora blesses the conception of their children-to-be.

Early scientists thought the aurora was caused by light reflecting off ice crystals in the sky. But they have since attributed the phenomenon to a blazing solar wind that sends charged particles—at speeds of up to three million kilometres per hour—into the Earth's magnetic field. These particles slam into the upper atmosphere 100 kilometres off the Earth's surface. There, they excite elements of oxygen and nitrogen which release some of their energy as light. This release of energy is what then gives the aurora its beautiful colouring.

The aurora's visual splendour is equalled by its power. It releases an average 50 gigawatts of power, which is about the same as the combined total power Ontario and British Columbia might use in a year. Because it is so great, this power sometimes interferes with human technology, disturbing compass needles and disrupting radio waves, particularly during magnetic storms. These storms can also bring about power failure. An auroral storm on March 13, 1989, left six million eastern Canadians in darkness for nine hours when it knocked out power at Hydro–Québec.

The Shield's surface is strewn with hundreds of thousands of lakes. From the air, the lake regions are as geometrical as a chess board; both rivers and lakes flow in parallel lines and at sharp right angles as they follow faults and fractures in the Earth's surface. For thousands of years, Native peoples travelled in birchbark canoes along these rivers and lakes. In the 1700s, European fur traders and explorers crossed the continent along the same routes.

Beyond the Shield

North of the Precambrian Shield is a land of frozen seas and ice-covered islands, the largest of which are Baffin and Ellesmere. This is Canada's eastern Arctic. Its scale is immense: Baffin Island alone is twice the size of Great Britain, yet in 1991, it had a permanent population of only 8,850.

Ellesmere Island, on the other hand, provides us with our furthest point north; indeed, its northern cape is closer to the geographic North Pole than any other point on the map. Ellesmere also has the eastern Arctic's highest peaks—some rising more than 2,700 metres.

Of these Arctic Islands, much has been written and much of it poetic. From the American writer Barry Lopez, we hear that "the beauty here is a beauty you feel in your flesh. You feel it physically, and that is why it is sometimes terrifying to approach. Other beauty takes only the heart, or the mind."

Yet another source of Northern power is the great Mackenzie River system, Canada's longest. Winding more than 4,000 kilometres from its source in Alberta's Rocky Mountains to the Arctic Ocean, the Mackenzie is more than a mile wide in many places. Unlike most northern rivers, the Mackenzie has no major rapids or waterfalls; ships can navigate almost its entire length, making it an important transportation route. Many of the Northwest Territories' major settlements are located on or near the Mackenzie.

Even further west, the Yukon Territory covers almost half a million square kilometres between the Mackenzie Mountains and Alaska. The mountain ranges and high plateaus of the Cordillera mountain system occupy almost all of Yukon. Canada's highest peak, Mount Logan at 5,959 metres, is in western Yukon.

Most Yukoners live along the banks of the Yukon River. About one-third of the river's 3,000-kilometre length lies in the Yukon; the rest is in Alaska. The Yukon River has few rapids and is navigable from its mouth to Whitehorse, a distance of 2,860 kilometres.

"Underground" Economy

The North's greatest bounty is in its underground, which contains several kinds of minerals and huge stores of oil and gas.

The most northerly mine in the world is the Polaris lead and zinc mine on Little Cornwallis Island in the Northwest Territories; in 1992, this community of 200 had Canada's highest median income, at $92,800.

Northwest Territory miners also work in a zinc and lead mine at Nanisivik on Baffin Island, and in the Lupin and Colomac gold mines on the mainland. Plants near Fort Liard extract and process natural gas, and there are oil wells at Norman

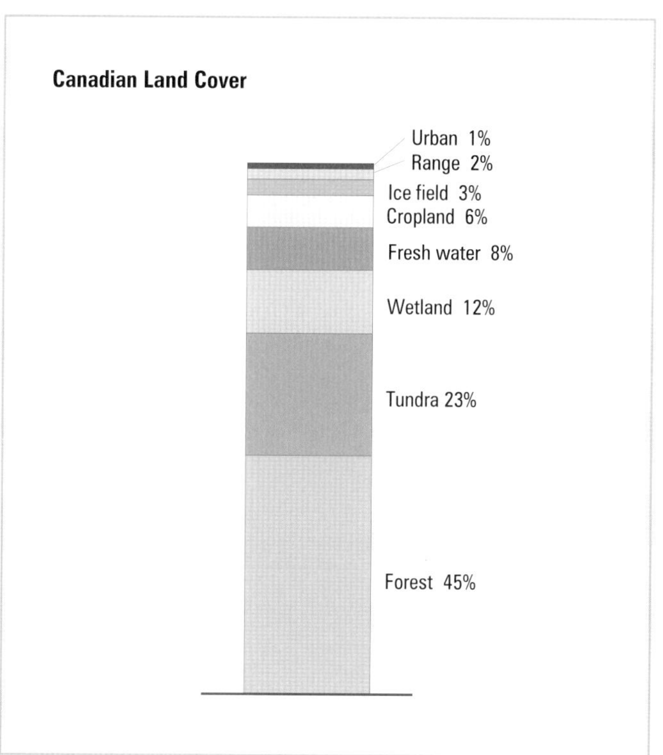

CANADIAN PHYSICAL FACTS

Most northerly point: Cape Columbia, Ellesmere Island, Northwest Territories.

Most southerly point: Middle Island in Lake Erie, Ontario.

Most easterly point: Cape Spear, Newfoundland.

Most westerly point: Yukon–Alaska boundary, along 141° West longitude.

Greatest east–west distance: 5,959 kilometres.

Greatest north–south distance: 4,634 kilometres.

Highest mountain: Mount Logan, Yukon, 5,951 metres.

Largest lake wholly in Canada: Great Bear Lake, Northwest Territories, 31,328 square kilometres.

Longest river: Mackenzie River, (to head of Finlay River in British Columbia), 4,241 kilometres.

Largest island: Baffin Island, Northwest Territories, 507,451 square kilometres.

Longest mountain range: Coast Mountains, British Columbia and Yukon Territory, I,500 kilometres.

Wells on the Mackenzie River. Two mines operate in Yukon—one is a base metal mill and the other is a small jade mill.

With oil reserves already discovered in the Beaufort Sea, the Mackenzie Delta, the Arctic Islands and Hudson Bay, the North's petroleum potential is enormous. Since 1985, oil has been transported by a special ice-breaking tanker from Cameron Island in the Arctic to southern ports such as Montreal during the very short shipping season. However, building additional Arctic Ocean ports or pipelines to transport the oil to southern markets would affect the North's very fragile environment and cost billions of dollars—an investment current world oil prices do not justify.

The Atlantic Region

The Atlantic region includes the provinces of New Brunswick, Nova Scotia and Prince Edward Island, and the island of Newfoundland. The province of Newfoundland also includes the northern mainland territory of Labrador.

Newfoundland's first premier, Joey Smallwood, once described the island, defined as it is by sea and rock, as "this poor bald rock." Novelist E. Annie Proulx writing of the Atlantic provinces in general, said that they are "haunted by lost ships, fishermen [and] explorers [that have] gurgled down into sea holes as black as a dog's throat."

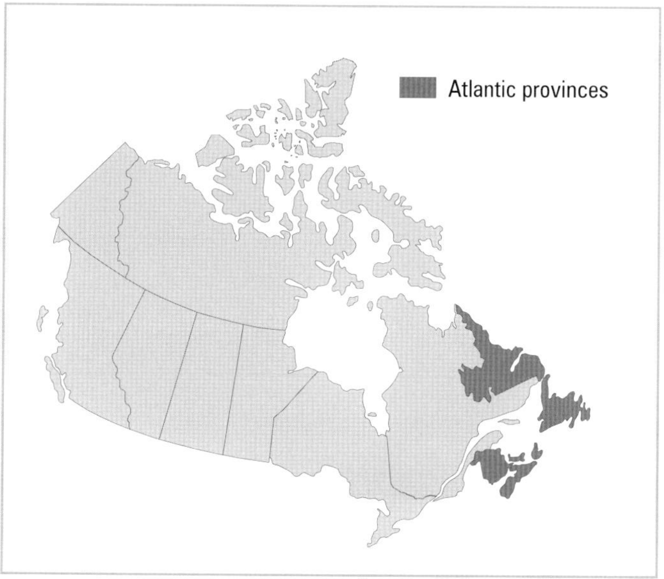

Along the Atlantic coast, storms from the St. Lawrence River valley meet storms from the New England coast. As a result, St. John's in Newfoundland gets the most fog, freezing rain, and wind of any Canadian city. Argentia, on Newfoundland's southwest coast, is Canada's most fog-bound community, with 206 foggy days every year. This cool, damp weather is partly caused by the cold Labrador Current, which in some years brings drifting icebergs past the entrance to St. John's harbour.

Excluding Labrador, the Atlantic region stretches 1,300 kilometres from east to west, and 900 kilometres from south to north. At its heart are three ocean ports that dominate their provinces: Saint John in New Brunswick, Halifax in Nova Scotia, and St. John's in Newfoundland.

These ports are far from southern Quebec and Ontario, Canada's industrial heartland, however. As a result, Atlantic Canada has not become as industrialized as other regions. The region's population of 2.4 million was slightly more than half that of Toronto in 1994. Unemployment tends to be high, and for generations many Atlantic Canadians have migrated to the United States or to the cities of Ontario and the western provinces.

Away from the coasts, most of the land is mountainous. Over millions of years, rain, wind and glaciers have worn these ranges down to rolling, flat-topped hills from 150 to about 800 metres high. These plateaus or highlands include the Central and Caledonian in New Brunswick; the Atlantic, Cape Breton, Cobequid and Antigonish in Nova Scotia; and the various plateaus of Newfoundland. Soils on these uplands are poor, and the terrain can be rough. In particularly rugged uplands, such as those of central New Brunswick, rough logging roads are the only sign that people have been here.

The lowlands along the Atlantic coast are almost entirely submerged under the Gulf of St. Lawrence. Parts that rise above the sea include Prince Edward Island, central and

John Sylvester, First Light

Sunrise over lake, near New Glasgow, P.E.I.

eastern New Brunswick, north-central Nova Scotia, and the St. George's Lowland of Newfoundland. Along with the Annapolis River valley, these are the region's only farming areas.

Atlantic Ways

For centuries, hundreds of Atlantic coast communities have lived off the fisheries. The Grand Banks, a rocky ledge off Newfoundland's south and east coasts, has been the world's most extensive breeding grounds for fish.

In the late 1980s, however, cod stocks began to disappear. The decline became so serious that in 1992, the federal government banned most commercial cod fishing off Labrador and northern Newfoundland for two years. In the following years, the cod stocks in the Gulf of St. Lawrence and the northeastern Scotian Shelf were also closed to fishing. The bans were later extended through 1996.

Nobody knows when any of these fishing grounds will re-open, but it will likely be many years before the Grand Banks again teems with cod.

Atlantic Canadians continue to harvest the ocean, however. They dig for clams and catch lobsters, giant bluefin tuna, Atlantic salmon, shrimps and crab off the coasts of all four provinces. Prince Edward Island is famous for its Malpeque oysters, New Brunswick for its sardines and Nova Scotia for Digby scallops.

Atlantic Canadians have made the most of their limited farming land. Prince Edward Islanders, for example, have turned their iron-rich red soil into Canada's most important potato-growing region. Together with New Brunswick, Prince Edward Island produces 90% of Canada's seed potatoes, and most of its potato exports. Prince Edward Island is by far Canada's smallest province, with an area of only 5,660 square kilometres. Quebec, the largest province, is 272 times as large.

The fertile marsh soils around the Bay of Fundy in Nova Scotia and New Brunswick have been farmed since the early 1600s—longer than any other part of Canada. The area's original French-speaking settlers built dikes to protect their low-lying land from the Bay of Fundy's famous tides—the world's highest—sometimes reaching 16 metres.

Primary Industries

Farmers in New Brunswick's Saint John River valley grow potatoes and pasture livestock. Nova Scotia's Annapolis Valley is famous for its fruit, particularly apples.

Forestry—mostly for the pulp and paper industry—employs substantial numbers of Atlantic Canadians everywhere except in Prince Edward Island. Forests cover almost 90% of New Brunswick, a higher percentage than in any other Canadian province. The rivers of New Brunswick include the Restigouche and the Miramichi, used for generations to drive logs downstream to sawmills and pulp plants. Western Newfoundland's forests supply the pulp and paper mill at Corner Brook, which was the world's largest when it was built in 1925.

Minerals also fuel the Atlantic economy. New Brunswickers mine for zinc, lead and copper near Bathurst, for antimony outside Fredericton and for potash (used to make chemical fertilizers) near Sussex. Newfoundlanders mine iron ore, nickel, zinc and asbestos; Nova Scotians mine coal, gypsum and salt. Labrador's Precambrian Shield rocks have so far yielded deposits of iron ore, nickel, copper, gold and other minerals.

The Atlantic region's greatest mineral bonanza, however, may still be on the horizon. By December 1997, the massive Hibernia drilling platform will have pumped the first of more than 600 million barrels of oil from an ocean-bed reservoir 315 kilometres east of St. John's. Up to 5,000 Newfoundlanders have worked on the construction phase of the $16 billion project, and as of March 31, 1996, local suppliers and workers had been paid about $2.07 billion.

The Hibernia oil fields are only the most promising of several offshore Newfoundland reservoirs discovered since the 1970s. If Hibernia proves profitable, it could be the first step in building a major petrochemical industry in Newfoundland.

Central Canada

If you were to ride the half kilometre it takes to get to the top of Toronto's CN Tower—the world's tallest free-standing structure—you would be gazing out at roughly a third of Canada's very best agricultural land. But instead of farmland, you'd see a huge city and a busy network of highways linking

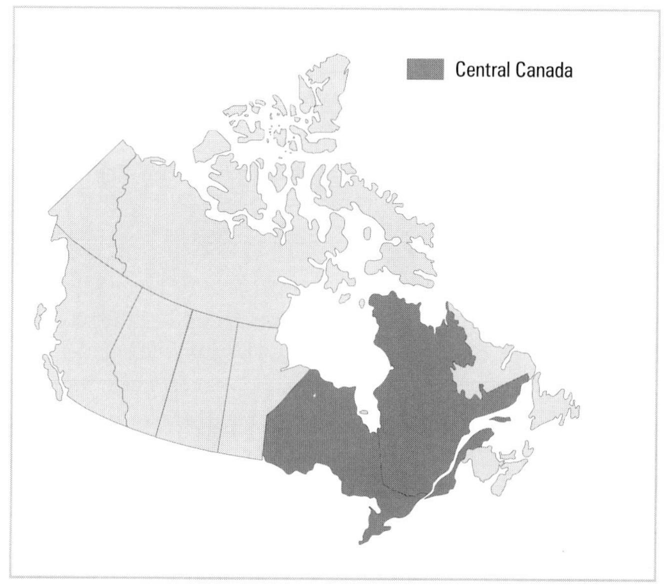

far-flung suburbs. Indeed, Toronto is at the centre of Canada's largest concentration of population—about 15 million people in a corridor from Quebec City to Windsor.

In this region, which includes the provinces of Quebec and Ontario, the pattern of settlement owes much to ice. Twenty thousand years ago, the region was buried under a glacier up to three kilometres thick—six times the height of the CN Tower. When this ice melted 6,000 or 7,000 years ago, it left a covering of finely crushed rocks and soils scraped from the Precambrian Shield. The result today is one of Canada's most important belts of good agricultural land, stretching 1,000 kilometres from Quebec City west to the shores of Lake Huron.

The glaciers also gouged out the beds of the Great Lakes. Over thousands of years, they cut so deeply that the bottom of Lake Superior is up to 200 metres below sea level. The Great Lakes allow Central Canadians to transport goods cheaply by ship. They also slowly release heat through the winter, giving areas close to them a mild climate—by Canadian standards.

With these advantages, it's not surprising that about half of Canadians live in this region, on only 5% of the nation's land. Indeed, before Confederation in 1867, Canada referred only to southern Quebec and the lowlands between the Great Lakes.

With easy access to a major market of millions of consumers around the Great Lakes, the region accounts for three-quarters of Canada's manufacturing, led by transportation equipment for the U.S. market. The region's agricultural production almost equals that of the Prairies.

Although the Quebec City–Windsor corridor is the heartland of Quebec and Ontario, most of the area of both provinces is occupied by the Precambrian Shield. The Shield has given Central Canada raw materials important to building an industrial economy: minerals for manufacturing, trees for pulp and paper, and fast-flowing rivers for generating hydroelectric power.

The Shield also gives weekend and holiday respite to the millions of people living in Montreal, Toronto and other cities along Lake Ontario. In districts such as Muskoka, Haliburton and the Laurentians, the Shield's countless lakes are crowded with summer cottages and resorts.

The Appalachian mountain system of Atlantic Canada extends into a small part of Quebec—the Gaspé Peninsula and the Estrie district (formerly the Eastern Townships). The highest Canadian section of the Appalachians, in Gaspé's Shickshock plateau, stands about 1,200 metres—high enough to be as cold and treeless as Arctic tundra.

Lowlands, Locks and Lakes

Reaching from the Atlantic coast into the heart of North America, the 3,790-kilometre St. Lawrence Seaway–Great Lakes Waterway is the world's longest inland waterway open to ocean shipping. Completed in 1959, the St. Lawrence Seaway links the St. Lawrence River to the Great Lakes via a series of locks.

In the early 1990s, the locks at Sault Ste. Marie were busier than the Panama Canal. Along with manufacturers and mineral producers, Prairie farmers use the Seaway to ship their grain to markets across the Atlantic Ocean. Thunder Bay, on Lake Superior, with 11 dockside terminal grain elevators, is one of the world's largest grain-handling ports. In recent years, demand for Prairie grains and oil seeds has been strongest in Pacific markets, and Vancouver and Prince Rupert have taken over Thunder Bay's shipping prominence.

On the excellent soils of the St. Lawrence–Great Lakes lowlands, farmers grow soybeans, and sweet corn and other vegetables destined for city markets. Dairy farmers and cheese and butter producers cluster in the southeast corner of Ontario and around Montreal. Indeed, Quebec has 40% of Canada's dairy cows and supplies many parts of Ontario with processed dairy products. The Niagara Peninsula, on the southwest shore of Lake Ontario, is one of Canada's most important fruit and grape-growing areas.

Between the Great Lakes in southern Ontario, the landscape is strewn with features created by the glaciers, including thousands of drumlins. Shaped like the backs of whales, these hills can be up to 1,500 metres long and 25 metres high.

Around Peterborough and other southern Ontario cities, farmers grow a range of crops on their fertile tops.

Like Canada's northern plains, southern Ontario is criss-crossed by eskers, which are narrow ridges deposited by glaciers. Some are tens of kilometres long and up to 30 metres high. Once, settlers used them as horse and wagon routes through marshy land; today their sand and gravel are used as construction materials.

At the ends and sides of the glaciers, ridges of gravel and sand called "moraines" were formed. Some moraines are vast; for example, Denmark is the tip of a moraine that is submerged under the Atlantic Ocean. Much smaller moraines are common in southern Ontario. One of these, the Oak Ridges Moraine northeast of Toronto, is more than 100 kilometres long.

"Central" Shield

Drawing on its Precambrian Shield region, Ontario leads Canada in non-fuel mineral production. It also holds several world mineral records: the largest uranium deposits near Elliot Lake, the richest vein of silver (discovered at Cobalt in 1903), and the largest nickel deposits, in the Sudbury Basin. Ontario ranks third in forestry behind British Columbia and Quebec, as it does in hydroelectric generation.

Quebec's Precambrian Shield region has also delivered the goods: one of the world's largest aluminum production centres at Jonquière, and the biggest hydroelectric project at James Bay. The James Bay project's eight dams and 198 dikes hold back five reservoirs that cover 11,900 square kilometres—half the size of Lake Ontario.

Half of Quebec's vast forests are suitable for forest products, and the province's mills produce about one-third of Canada's pulp and paper, including newsprint—12% of the world trade. Only British Columbia produces forestry products with a greater value.

The Prairies

The Prairie provinces—Manitoba, Saskatchewan and Alberta—may look and feel perfectly flat, but in fact, western

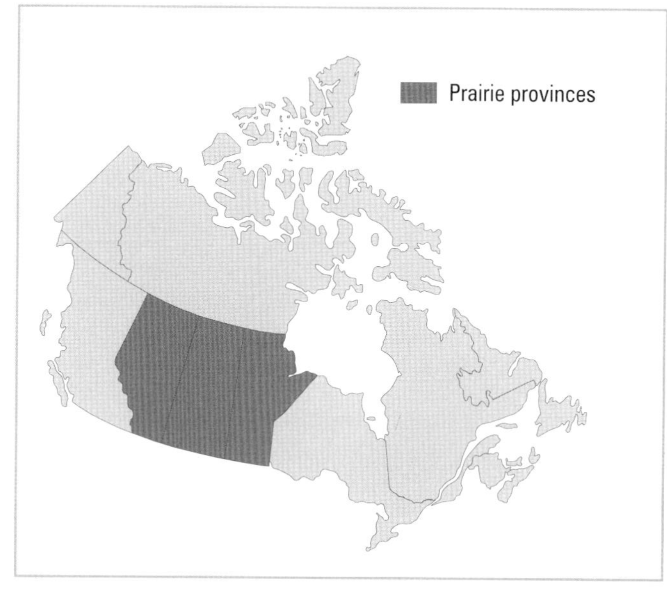

Alberta is a kilometre higher than eastern Manitoba. The Prairies support thousands of grain farmers, mixed-crop farmers, dairy farmers and cattle ranchers. Indeed, if all the grain grown by Prairie farmers in 1993 were loaded onto a single train, that train would have to be 18,000 kilometres long.

Canada's longest continuous belt of settlement, covering 6% of the country, winds through the south of the Prairies. Farmers occupy most of this settled belt, but it also includes the major Prairie urban centres: Winnipeg, Regina, Saskatoon, Calgary and Edmonton.

For centuries, before the Canadian Pacific Railroad was built across the Prairies in the 1880s, people travelled mostly by river. As a result, the major cities are all on riverbanks. Calgary, for example, developed on the banks of the Bow River at the eastern edge of the Rocky Mountain foothills as a regional centre for surrounding farms and cattle ranches; hence, its traditional nickname, "Cowtown."

At the end of the last ice age, most of southern Manitoba and parts of east-central Saskatchewan were covered by a glacial lake, Lake Agassiz, which was larger than all of the Great Lakes combined. Around Winnipeg, the former bed of this

The Aboriginal peoples who visited their lush, sloping forests centuries ago named them "the Thunder Breeding Hills," convinced that they mysteriously created the weather. French travellers mistook the pines that grow there for cypress trees, hence the name Cypress Hills.

Cypress Hills Provincial Park stretches almost 130 kilometres across the southern parts of Saskatchewan and Alberta and forms the highest point of land between Labrador and the Rocky Mountains. Here, a rich ecosystem combines prairie and mountain vegetation, and is home to a large number of animals, birds and plants. The Cypress Hills are a natural time capsule; during the last ice age, their peaks remained above the glaciers and today they provide reminders of that icebound time.

In fact, the Cypress Hills are often called "the hills that shouldn't be" since, despite the mighty glacial force that bulldozed around them, they remained intact. A modern-day site of discovery, the hills have surrendered fossils of more than 40 mammals from 40 million years ago, the only skeletons of this period found anywhere in Canada.

The Hills are populated with turkeys, such predators as lynx, bobcat, and red fox, and muskrats and beavers. About 207 species of birds live here, including the poorwill, one of the rarest breeds in Canada.

Plants are also abundant. It is believed that much of the vegetation has remained unchanged during the past 2,000 years. The rare and beautiful orchid grows wild in the forests, which are largely white spruce, aspen and lodgepole pine. In fact, there are more than 18 species of orchids and about 30 rare and endangered plant species still growing in the Cypress Hills.

The earliest humans to arrive here, some 8,000 years ago, were likely the Fluted Point people, who were named for the style of the stone arrowheads they shaped and who hunted mammoth and mastodon. In recent centuries, the Blackfoot, Assiniboine and Plains Cree have all visited the hills. American whisky traders followed after the American Civil War, plying their wares across the Prairies. Canadian Mounties arrived during the late 1800s to make the West safe for settlers. Today, ranchers, hunters and tourists share the rich geological and biological history of Canada's prairie oasis with the creatures that dwell there.

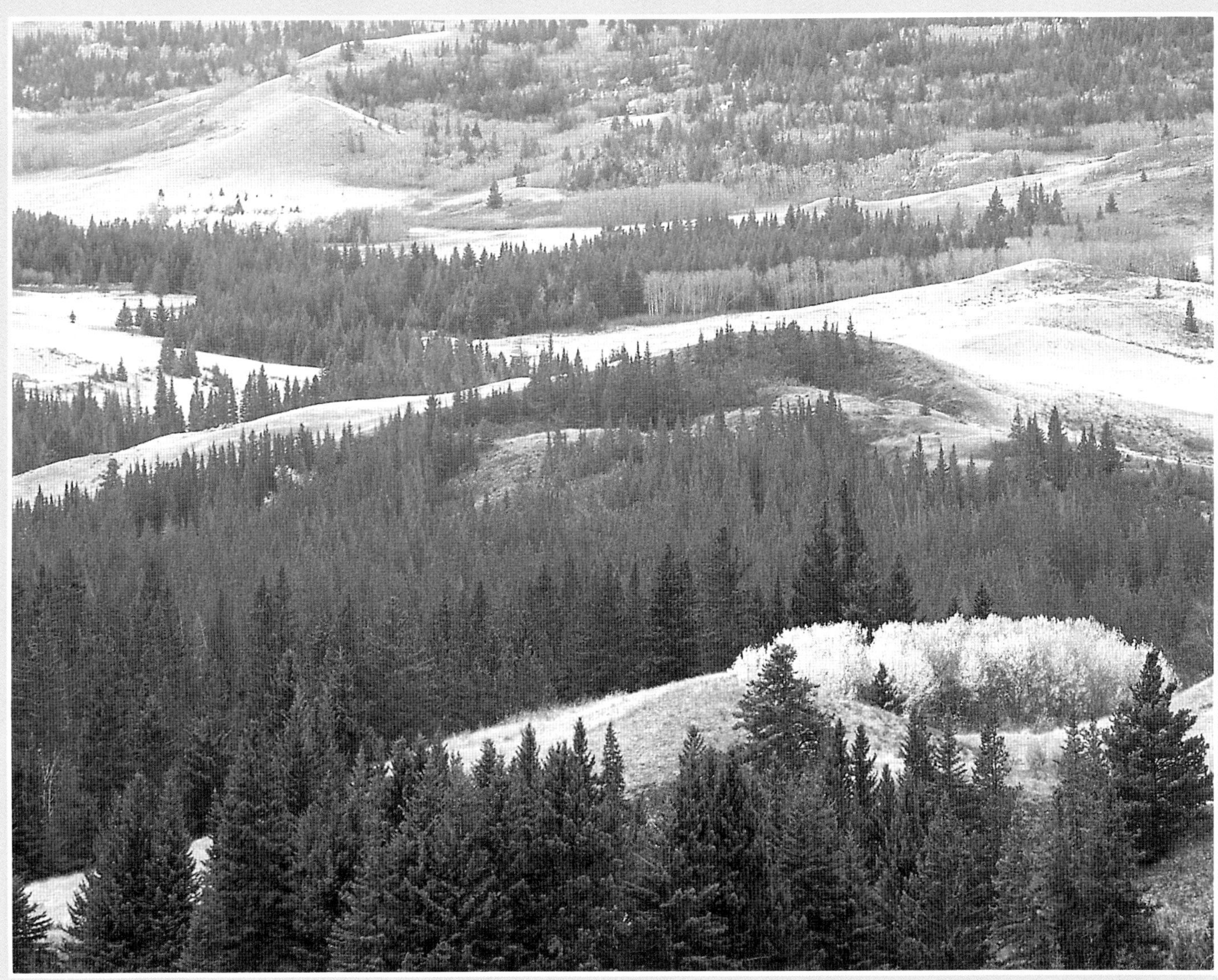

Thomas Kitchin, First Light

Cypress Hills Provincial Park, Saskatchewan.

ancient lake is now flat, rich farmland stretching to the horizon in all directions.

In 1905, police corporal J.G. Donkin wrote of the "hush of an eternal silence hanging over these far-stretching plains . . . no tree or bush relieves the aching eye. There is nothing but the dim fading grey ring of the horizon all around."

During and after glaciation, rivers eroded many of the valleys of the southern prairies. In the South Saskatchewan River and Red Deer River valleys, for example, they carved canyons and ridges through the bedrock. A spectacular example of this is Alberta's Red Deer Badlands near Drumheller, with its mushroom-shaped rock formations called Hoodoos. The Badlands include Dinosaur Provincial Park, the world's richest area of dinosaur fossils.

Prairie Harvest

The Prairie climate can bring long, cold winters and hot, dry summers. Winnipeg is the coldest of major Canadian cities: the average temperature in January is –18.3 C. The desert-like sweep of short grasses in the southern portion of the Prairies is too dry to grow crops, so here beef cattle range by the hundreds of thousands. Farmers irrigate their crops along the Saskatchewan River system, which winds through the dry southern portions of all three Prairie provinces.

Before human settlement, at least 63 varieties of grass grew on the Prairies, including four wild members of the wheat grass family. Domesticated wheat now occupies several million hectares. Other major crops include lentils, dry peas, flax and canola, grown for the oil from its seeds.

Between the dry southwest and the Prairies' barren northern regions is a grain-growing belt with relatively high precipitation. The millions of small ponds called sloughs in this belt are breeding grounds for half of North America's ducks, geese, swans and pelicans. The most populous prairie mammal—and the least popular with farmers—is the Prairie gopher, a type of ground squirrel with a rapacious appetite for grain.

Black Gold

Agriculture still dominates Prairie landscapes, but the chief reason for the region's post-war prosperity is made plain by a 1970s nickname for Calgary—"Oil Town." Alberta's first oil strike was made in 1947, at a well named Leduc No. 1.

In the mid-1970s, when Arab oil-producing countries raised their prices substantially, world demand for Alberta oil soared. By the 1980s, the province had more than 20,000 oil and gas wells. In 1994, the province had 60% of Canada's oil reserves, and produced more than three-quarters of its oil and 83% of its natural gas. Altogether, Alberta accounts for half the value of oil, gas and minerals extracted in Canada.

The other Prairie provinces also have substantial mineral reserves. Saskatchewan has almost half of the world's supply of potash. At current rates of world consumption, this reserve is enough to last more than 1,500 years. Saskatchewan also produces crude oil and natural gas on a more modest scale than Alberta, as well as uranium in its northern Precambrian

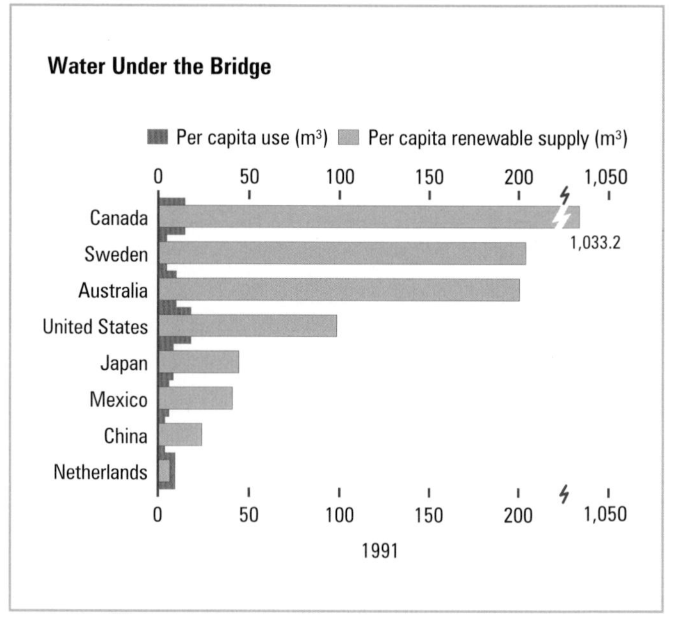

Shield region. Manitobans mine mainly minerals such as nickel, copper and zinc.

British Columbia

Canada's Pacific province seems designed to impress. In 1908, British writer Rudyard Kipling described the capital with an enthusiasm shared by most visitors: "To realize Victoria you must take all that the eye admires most in Bournemouth, Torquay, the Isle of Wight, the Happy Valley of Hong Kong . . . add reminiscences of the Thousand Islands, and arrange the whole round the Bay of Naples, with some Himalayas for the background."

British Columbians value their province's mild climate as much as its spectacular setting. Warmed by ocean currents, southern British Columbia holds many Canadian climate records. These include highest yearly average temperature (Vancouver, at 9.9°C), longest annual frost-free period (233 days, again for Vancouver), and the least annual average snowfall (47 centimetres in Victoria). With the mild weather, however, comes rain. Henderson Lake gets an average of about 6.6 metres of rain every year, making it the rainiest place in Canada.

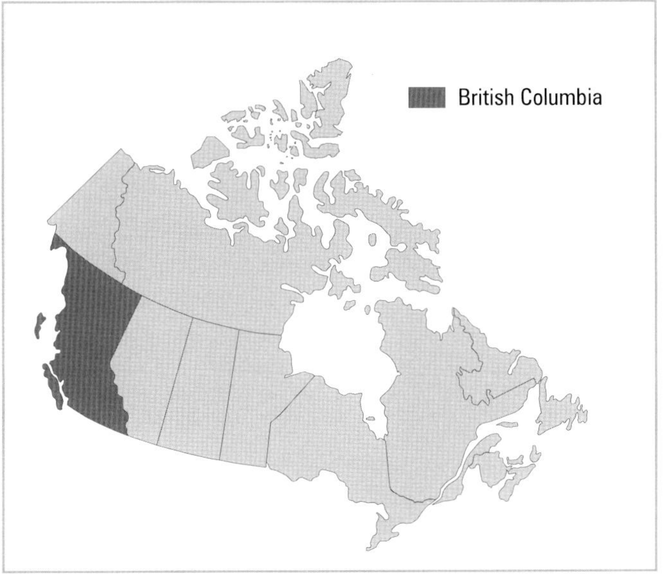

The Big Quake?

For millions in the lower Fraser Valley and on Vancouver Island, expecting the "Big Quake" is just part of daily life. Scientists aren't certain when—or even if—such an earthquake will occur. But they do know that very large earthquakes have occurred in five of six similar zones on the Pacific coast.

If it comes, the quake will be caused by the movements of tectonic plates—huge masses of rock that underlie the continents and the ocean floor. There are 15 such tectonic plates in the earth. From 70 to 100 kilometres thick, they float like rafts on a sea of molten rock.

Offshore of Vancouver Island, a small portion of the so-called Pacific Ocean plate has been pushing sideways against the North American plate for millions of years. If they should someday break apart, the result would be violently destructive shock waves for hundreds of kilometres in every direction.

In 1960, an earthquake in a similar geologic zone off the coast of Chile was the largest ever recorded, 9.5 on the Richter scale. The quake caused parts of coastal Chile to drop by up to two metres.

Louis Hennepin, National Library of Canada, NL5304

Buffalo, **etching, 1697.**

British Columbia's economy is growing more quickly than that of any other province. With access to strong Pacific Rim economies such as those of Japan and South Korea, Vancouver is Canada's busiest port, handling more than 60 million tonnes from some 9,000 cargo ships in 1993. British Columbia manufacturers are benefiting from the Pacific Rim economic boom; in 1993, they produced 8.7% of Canadian manufactured goods.

Most of British Columbia is covered by the Cordillera, a chain of mountain ranges that also covers Yukon, Alaska, and parts of Alberta and the Northwest Territories. Stretching 2,400 kilometres from the 49th parallel to the Arctic Ocean, these mountains tower over towns and cities on the province's coastal plains and narrow river valleys.

"Fraser's Pass"

Engineers have pierced the mountains with highways and railways in only a few places. These include the Roger's Pass in the Selkirk Mountains, where up to 15 metres of snow fall each winter, and the Fraser River canyon, one of the world's most spectacular river gorges. Simon Fraser, the man the river is named after, described his voyage through the canyon in 1808: "Our lives hung by a thread. We had to pass where no human being should venture."

The Rocky Mountains form the eastern edge of the Cordillera. Geologically young compared with the Precambrian Shield, these are high, sharp-edged peaks, many with alpine glaciers and year-round snow cover. Several of Canada's national parks are in the Rockies, where wild sheep, mountain goats, and black and grizzly bears live in the forests and rocky uplands.

Between the Rocky Mountains and the Coast Range is a belt of low mountains, rolling hills, plateaus deeply cut by rivers, and flat plains that were once the beds of glacial lakes. From 330 to 800 kilometres wide, this belt has three major regions:

the Fraser Plateau, the Stikine Plateau, and a rugged central section.

The most densely populated of these is the Fraser Plateau, extending 800 kilometres from the United States border to Prince George. It is cut in the south by canyons and by valleys with rich soils deposited by glacial lakes. Fruit and other crops are grown here, particularly in the Okanagan and Thompson valleys. A zigzag pattern of railways and roads links most of these valleys.

The high, rugged Coast Mountain Range is about 160 kilometres wide and extends the entire Pacific coast. Wide, steep-walled fiords such as Howe Sound north of Vancouver cut from 80 to 160 kilometres into the range.

The last of the Cordillera's ranges is the Insular chain. These mountains are submerged under the Strait and Gulf of Juan de Fuca, except where they rise above the ocean on Vancouver Island and the Queen Charlotte Islands.

Natural Wealth

Canada's Banana Belt—that's what many British Columbians call the lower Fraser River valley and the southern tip of Vancouver Island. Not surprisingly, most of the province's residents live in this temperate, wet region.

The interior of the province, on the other hand, is dry, and cold in winter. As warm, moist air blows from the ocean over the Coast Mountains, it cools rapidly, releasing rain on the lower mountain slopes and snow at higher altitudes. By the time the air has crossed into the interior, it is dry.

Climate has given British Columbia Canada's most valuable forest resources: dense coastal rain forests crowded with Douglas fir, Western Red cedar and other prized species. Indeed, with only 17% of Canada's forest area, British Columbia produces more than half of Canada's sawn lumber, most of its plywood and one-third of its pulp.

Offshore is another form of natural wealth—about 300 species of fish, plus clams, oysters and crab. The province has Canada's largest fishery, although stocks of the industry's mainstay, Pacific salmon, have dropped to disturbingly low levels in recent years.

British Columbia is second only to Ontario in non-fuel mineral production. British Columbia's main mining district, the Kootenays, has major deposits of lead, zinc and silver, and also some of North America's largest reserves of soft coal. In the Highland Valley near Kamloops, miners produce 90% of Canada's molybdenum (used to strengthen steel) and 40% of its copper. Natural gas and oil are extracted from the Peace River district.

British Columbia's many fast-flowing mountain rivers are superb for generating hydro-electricity. The largest hydro project, the W.A.C. Bennet Dam on the Peace River, generates 30% of the province's hydro power.

Most of British Columbia is too mountainous for agriculture; indeed, only in Newfoundland is a smaller proportion of the land suitable for crops. Despite this, British Columbia's farmers account for about 5% of Canada's agricultural production, largely due to a long growing season and the rich soils of the lower Fraser River valley. The valley's farmers supply dairy products and vegetables to Vancouver and its neighbouring urban areas.

Outside the Fraser valley, farming land is limited but highly productive. The mild, sunny Okanagan region on the southwestern Kamloops Plateau produces large quantities of wine grapes and tree fruits. Most of the province's grain crop is grown in the Peace River district. On the Cariboo, the province's great interior plain, ranchers graze cattle.

Weather Bound

"[Canada's] winter is a long night that forgets to stay dark," notes Quebec novelist Roch Carrier. In fact, Canada's climate is more extreme than in parts of Europe at the same latitudes. Mostly, this is because Canada has no Gulf Stream to soften the climate of its northern latitude, as do Britain, the Scandinavian countries and western Europe.

Canadians Chill

Canada's northern chill has sparked many lucrative Canadian inventions: the snowblower, the snowplough, frozen fish, highly efficient insulation, underground shopping malls, winter fuels and lubricants, kerosene, the foghorn, and all-weather asphalt.

And let's not forget that a national passion for hockey grew out of our long Canadian winters and frozen waterways as did our enthusiasm for downhill and cross-country skiing, skating, tobagganing and curling.

On the other hand, Canada's climate is expensive. One-third of the energy consumed is used to overcome the cost of climate, to counter cold, excessive heat, humidity, ice and wind. We spend an estimated $660 million on snow and ice removal every year, and $25 million on keeping airplanes and runways free of ice.

As well, cold Arctic air masses move more easily over water than over land; as a result, Hudson Bay and James Bay allow this cold air to intrude as much as 15 degrees latitude south of the Arctic Circle, into the heart of Central Canada. The Russian port of Murmansk is open throughout the year although it lies within the Arctic Circle, while in winter the Great Lakes—at the same latitude as Rome—are ice-bound.

Nonetheless, despite our colder climate, Canada holds no world weather records; it is always colder, snowier, windier, wetter or hotter someplace else.

Still, Canada has it all, climatically speaking. We have the cold and snow of Siberia, the humid summer heat of the Caribbean, the fog of Britain, the temperateness of the Mediterranean, even the desert and rain forest.

This diversity of climate is partly a result of sheer size—Canada stretches across six time zones and occupies almost one-quarter of the Western Hemisphere. Vancouver is closer to Mexico City than to Halifax, and St. John's is as far from Moscow as from Dawson City in Yukon.

Climate tells humans what they can and cannot do. In Canada, our northern temperatures severely limit the kinds of crops we can grow: only a few regions—such as the Okanagan Valley in British Columbia and Ontario's Niagara Peninsula—are mild enough to grow grapes, and even these favoured spots are too cold for oranges and other citrus fruits.

Even on the Prairies, where about 80% of Canada's farmland is found, agriculture was not viable on a large scale until the turn of the century, when hardy spring wheat and a range of domesticated varieties were introduced, along with dry farming techniques that conserve barely adequate moisture. However, what was once a limitation is now an advantage; the Prairies' short, hot, dry growing season produces a superior quality of grain with more protein than most wheat grown in the United States.

As well, this climate has created the conditions for Canada's vast forests of coniferous trees ideal for timber and wood pulp, for the huge populations of fur-bearing mammals that first drew Europeans into the heart of the continent, and for the fish and other marine animals that breed so profusely in our coastal and inland waters.

SOURCES

Environment Canada
Geomatics Canada
Statistics Canada

FOR FURTHER READING

Selected publications from other sources

- **Canada: A Celebration**. Robert Fulford. 1983.
- **Canada: A Geographical Interpretation**. Canadian Association of Geographers. 1968.
- **Canada: A Land of Superlatives**, *Canadian Geographic* map. Geomatics Canada.
- **The Canadian Encyclopedia Plus, (CD-ROM)**. McClelland & Stewart. 1995.

Legend

–	nil or zero	..	not available	x	confidential
--	too small to be expressed	...	not applicable or not appropriate		*(Certain tables may not add due to rounding)*

1.1 LAND AND FRESHWATER AREA

	Total area	Land	Freshwater	% of total area
		km²		
Canada	9,970,610	9,215,430	755,180	100.0
Newfoundland	405,720	371,690	34,030	4.1
Prince Edward Island	5,660	5,660	–	0.1
Nova Scotia	55,490	52,840	2,650	0.6
New Brunswick	73,440	72,090	1,350	0.7
Quebec	1,540,680	1,356,790	183,890	15.5
Ontario	1,068,580	891,190	177,390	10.7
Manitoba	649,950	548,360	101,590	6.5
Saskatchewan	652,330	570,700	81,630	6.5
Alberta	661,190	644,390	16,800	6.6
British Columbia	947,800	929,730	18,070	9.5
Yukon	483,450	478,970	4,480	4.8
Northwest Territories	3,426,320	3,293,020	133,300	34.4

Source: Natural Resources Canada, Canada Centre for Remote Sensing, GeoAccess.

1.2 WEATHER CONDITIONS IN CAPITAL AND MAJOR CITIES

	Average temperature						Annual				
	Coldest month			Warmest month			Average temperature		Snowfall	Total	Wet
	Month	High	Low	Month	High	Low	High	Low		precipitation	days
		degrees Celsius				degrees Celsius			cm	mm	number
St. John's	February	-1.4	-8.7	July	20.2	10.5	8.6	0.8	322.1	1,482	217
Charlottetown	January	-3.4	-12.2	July	23.1	13.6	9.5	0.8	338.7	1,201	177
Halifax	February	-1.5	-10.6	July	23.4	13.2	10.7	1.4	261.4	1,474	170
Fredericton	January	-4.0	-15.4	July	25.6	12.9	11.0	-0.6	294.5	1,131	156
Quebec City	January	-7.7	-17.3	July	24.9	13.2	9.0	-1.0	337.0	1,208	178
Montreal	January	-5.8	-14.9	July	26.2	15.4	10.9	1.2	214.2	940	162
Ottawa	January	-6.3	-15.5	July	26.4	15.1	10.7	0.8	221.5	911	159
Toronto	January	-1.3	-7.9	July	26.5	17.6	12.6	5.2	135.0	819	139
Winnipeg	January	-13.2	-23.6	July	26.1	13.4	8.1	-3.4	114.8	504	119
Regina	January	-11.0	-22.1	July	26.3	11.9	8.9	-3.8	107.4	364	109
Edmonton	January	-8.2	-17.0	July	23.0	12.0	8.7	-1.5	129.6	461	123
Calgary	January	-3.6	-15.7	July	23.2	9.5	10.3	-2.6	135.4	399	111
Vancouver	January	5.7	0.1	August	21.7	12.9	13.5	6.1	54.9	1,167	164
Victoria	January	6.5	0.3	July	21.8	10.7	13.9	5.1	46.9	858	153
Whitehorse	January	-14.4	-23.2	July	20.3	7.6	4.1	-6.2	145.2	269	122
Yellowknife	January	-23.9	-32.2	July	20.8	12.0	-0.8	-9.7	143.9	267	118

Source: Environment Canada, *Climate Normals 1961-1990*.

1.3 PRINCIPAL HEIGHTS

	Elevation
	m
Newfoundland	
Torngat Mountains	
Mt. Caubvick[1] (highest point in Nfld.) (on Nfld.–Que. boundary)	1,652
Cirque Mountain	1,568
Mt. Cladonia	1,453
Mt. Eliot	1,356
Mt. Tetragona	1,356
Quartzite Mountain	1,186
Blow Me Down Mountain	1,183
Mealy Mountains	
Unnamed peak (53°37' 58°33')	1,176
Kaumajet Mountains	
Bishops Mitre	1,113
Long Range Mountains	
Lewis Hills	814
Gros Morne	806
Prince Edward Island	
Highest point	
Queen's County (46°20' 63°25')	142
Nova Scotia	
Highest point	
Cape Breton Highlands (46°42' 60°36')	532
New Brunswick	
Mt. Carleton (highest point in N.B.)	817
Wilkinson Mountain	785
Quebec	
Monts Torngat	
Mont D'Iberville[1] (highest point in Que.) (on Que.– Nfld. boundary)	1,652
Les Appalaches	
Mont Jacques-Cartier	1,268
Mont Gosford	1,192
Mont Richardson	1,185
Mont Mégantic	1,105
Les Laurentides	
Unnamed peak (47°19' 70°50')	1,166
Mont Tremblant	968
Mont Sainte-Anne	800
Mont Sir-Wilfrid	783
Monts Otish	
Unnamed peak (52°19' 71°27')	1,135
Collines Montérégiennes	
Mont Brome	533
Ontario	
Ishpatina Ridge (highest point in Ont.)	693
Ogidaki Mountain	665
Batchawana Mountain	653
Tip Top Mountain	640
Niagara Escarpment	
Blue Mountains	541
Osler Bluff	526
Caledon Mountain	427
Manitoba	
Baldy Mountain (highest point in Man.)	832
Highest point in Porcupine Hills	823
Riding Mountain	610
Saskatchewan	
Cypress Hills (highest point in Sask.)	1,468
Wood Mountain	1,013
Vermilion Hills	785
Alberta	
Rocky Mountains	
Mt. Columbia (highest point in Alta.) (on Alta.–B.C. boundary)	3,747
North Twin	3,733
Mt. Alberta	3,620
Mt. Assiniboine (on Alta.–B.C. boundary)	3,618
Mt. Forbes	3,612
South Twin	3,581
Mt. Temple	3,547
Mt. Brazeau	3,525
Snow Dome (on Alta.–B.C. boundary)	3,520
Mt. Lyell (on Alta.–B.C. boundary)	3,504
Hungabee Mountain (on Alta.–B.C. boundary)	3,492
Mt. Athabasca	3,491
Mt. King Edward (on Alta.–B.C. boundary)	3,490
Mt. Kitchener	3,490
British Columbia	
St. Elias Mountains	
Fairweather Mountain (highest point in B.C.) (on Alaska–B.C. boundary)	4,663
Mt. Quincy Adams (on Alaska–B.C. boundary)	4,133
Mt. Root (on Alaska–B.C. boundary)	3,901
Coast Mountains	
Mt. Waddington	4,016
Mt. Tiedemann	3,848
Combatant Mountain	3,756
Asperity	3,716
Serra Peaks	3,642
Monarch Mountain	3,459
Rocky Mountains	
Mt. Robson	3,954
Mt. Columbia (on Alta.–B.C. boundary)	3,747
Mt. Clemenceau	3,642
Mt. Assiniboine (on Alta.–B.C. boundary)	3,618
Mt. Goodsir: North Tower	3,581
Mt. Goodsir: South Tower	3,520
Snow Dome (on Alta.–B.C. boundary)	3,520
Mt. Bryce	3,507
Selkirk Mountains	
Mt. Sir Sandford	3,522
Cariboo Mountains	
Mt. Sir Wilfrid Laurier	3,520
Purcell Mountains	
Mt. Farnham	3,481
Monashee Mountains	
Torii Mountain	3,429
Yukon	
St. Elias Mountains	
Mt. Logan (highest point in Canada)	5,959
Mt. St. Elias (on Alaska–Yukon boundary)	5,489
Mt. Lucania	5,226
King Peak	5,173
Mt. Steele	5,067
Mt. Wood	4,838
Mt. Vancouver (on Alaska–Yukon boundary)	4,785
Mt. Macaulay	4,663
Mt. Slaggard	4,663
Mt. Hubbard (on Alaska–Yukon boundary)	4,577
Northwest Territories	
Mackenzie Mountains	
Unnamed peak (61°52' 127°42') (highest point in N.W.T.)	2,773
Mt. Sir James MacBrien	2,762
Ellesmere Island	
Barbeau Peak	2,616
Axel Heiberg Island	
Outlook Peak	2,210
Baffin Island	
Mt. Odin	2,147
Devon Island	
Summit Devon Ice Cap	1,920
Franklin Mountains	
Cap Mountain	1,577
Mt. Clark	1,462
Pointed Mountain	1,405
Nahanni Butte	1,396
Melville Island	
Unnamed peak (75°25' 114°47')	776
Banks Island	
Durham Heights	732
Victoria Island	
Unnamed peak	655

1. Mount Caubvick is also known as Mont D'Iberville in Quebec.

Source: Natural Resources Canada, Canada Centre for Remote Sensing, GeoAccess.

1.4 THE GREAT LAKES

	Elevation	Length	Breadth	Maximum depth	Total area	Area on Canadian side of boundary
	m	km	km	m	km²	km²
Superior	184	563	257	405	82,100	28,700
Michigan	176	494	190	281	57,800	–
Huron	177	332	295	229	59,600	36,000
Erie	174	388	92	64	25,700	12,800
Ontario	75	311	85	244	18,960	10,000

Source: Natural Resources Canada, Canada Centre for Remote Sensing, GeoAccess.

1.5 PRINCIPAL LAKES[1]

	Elevation	Area in Canadian territory
	m	km²
Newfoundland		
Smallwood Reservoir	471	6,527
Melville Lake	tidal	3,069
Nova Scotia		
Bras d'Or Lake	tidal	1,099
Quebec		
Lac Mistassini	372	2,335
Réservoir Manicouagan	360	1,942
Réservoir Gouin	404	1,570
Lac à l'Eau-Claire	241	1,383
Lac Bienville	426	1,249
Lac Saint-Jean	98	1,003
Réservoir Pipmuacan	396	978
Lac Minto	168	761
Réservoir Cabonga	361	677
Ontario		
Lake Nipigon	260	4,848
Lake of the Woods[2] (total 4,472 km²)	323	3,150
Lac Seul	357	1,657
Lake Abitibi[2]	265	931
Lake Nipissing	196	832
Lake Simcoe	219	744
Rainy Lake (total 932 km²)	338	741
Big Trout Lake	213	661
Lake St. Clair (total 1,210 km²)	175	490
Manitoba		
Lake Winnipeg	217	24,387
Lake Winnipegosis	254	5,374
Lake Manitoba	248	4,624
Southern Indian Lake	254	2,247
Cedar Lake	253	1,353
Island Lake	227	1,223
Gods Lake	178	1,151
Cross Lake	207	755
Playgreen Lake	217	657

1.5 PRINCIPAL LAKES[1] (concluded)

	Elevation	Area in Canadian territory
	m	km²
Saskatchewan		
Lake Athabasca[2]	213	7,935
Reindeer Lake[2]	337	6,650
Wollaston Lake	398	2,681
Cree Lake	487	1,434
Lac La Rouge	364	1,413
Peter Pond Lake	421	778
Doré Lake	459	640
Alberta		
Lake Clair	213	1,436
Lesser Slave Lake	577	1,168
British Columbia		
Williston Lake	671	1,761
Atlin Lake[2]	668	775
Yukon		
Kluane Lake	409	781
Northwest Territories		
Great Bear Lake[3]	156	31,328
Great Slave Lake	156	28,568
Nettilling Lake	30	5,542
Dubawnt Lake	236	3,833
Amadjuak Lake	113	3,115
Nueltin Lake[2]	278	2,279
Baker Lake	2	1,887
Lac la Martre	265	1,776
Yathkyed Lake	140	1,449
Kasba Lake	336	1,341
Aberdeen Lake	80	1,100
Napaktulik Lake	381	1,080
MacKay Lake	431	1,061
Garry Lake	148	976
Contwoyto Lake	564	957
Hottah Lake	180	918
Aylmer Lake	375	847
Nonacho Lake	354	784
Clinton–Colden Lake	375	737
Selwyn Lake	398	717
Point Lake	375	701
Ennadai Lake	311	681
Wholdaia Lake	364	678
Tulemalu Lake	279	668
Kamilukuak Lake	266	638
Lac de Gras	396	633
Buffalo Lake	265	612
Kaminak Lake	53	600

1. Lakes with total area of 600 km² or greater except the Great Lakes.
2. Spans provincial or territorial boundary. Listed under province or territory containing larger portion.
3. Largest lake wholly in Canada.

Source: Natural Resources Canada, Canada Centre for Remote Sensing, GeoAccess.

1.6 PRINCIPAL RIVERS AND THEIR TRIBUTARIES

Drainage basin and river	Drainage area	Length
	km²	km
Flowing into the Pacific Ocean		
Yukon (mouth to head of Nisutlin)	..	3,185
(International boundary to head of Nisutlin)	323,800	1,149
Porcupine	61,400	721
Stewart	51,000	644
Pelly	51,000	608
Teslin	35,500	393
White	38,000	265
Columbia (mouth to head of Columbia Lake)	..	2,000
(International boundary to head of Columbia Lake)	102,800	801
Kootenay	37,700	780
Kettle (to head of Holmes Lake)	4,700	336
Okanagan (to head of Okanagan Lake)	21,600	314
Fraser	232,300	1,370
Thompson (to head of North Thompson)	55,400	489
North Thompson	20,700	338
South Thompson (to head of Shuswap)	17,800	332
Nechako (to head of Eutsuk Lake)	47,100	462
Stuart (to head of Driftwood)	16,200	415
Skeena	54,400	579
Stikine	49,800	539
Nass	21,100	380
Flowing into the Arctic Ocean		
Mackenzie (to head of Finlay)	1,805,200	4,241
Peace (to head of Finlay)	302,500	1,923
Smoky	51,300	492
Athabasca	95,300	1,231
Pembina	12,900	547
Liard	277,100	1,115
South Nahanni	36,300	563
Fort Nelson (to head of Sikanni Chief)	55,900	517
Petitot	..	404
Hay	48,200	702
Peel (mouth of west Channel to head of Ogilvie)	73,600	684
Arctic Red	..	499
Slave (from Peace River to Great Slave Lake)	616,400	415
Fond du Lac (to outlet of Wollaston Lake)	66,800	277
Back (to outlet of Muskox Lake)	106,500	974
Coppermine	..	845
Anderson	..	692
Horton	..	618
Flowing into Hudson Bay and Hudson Strait		
Nelson (to head of Bow)	892,300	2,575
(to outlet of Lake Winnipeg)	802,900	644
Saskatchewan (to head of Bow)	334,100	1,939
South Saskatchewan (to head of Bow)	144,300	1,392
Red Deer	45,100	724
Bow	26,200	587
Oldman	26,700	362
North Saskatchewan	12,800	1,287
Battle (to head of Pigeon Lake)	30,300	570
Red (to head of Sheyenne)	138,600	877
Assiniboine	160,600	1,070
Winnipeg (to head of Firesteel)	106,500	813
English	52,300	615
Fairford (to head of Manitoba Red Deer)	80,300	684
Churchill (to head of Churchill Lake)	281,300	1,609
Beaver (to outlet of Beaver Lake)	..	491
Severn (to head of Black Birch)	102,800	982
Albany (to head of Cat)	135,200	982
Thelon	142,400	904
Dubawnt	57,500	842
La Grande-Rivière (Fort George River)	97,600	893
Koksoak (to head of Caniapiscau)	133,400	874
Nottaway (via Bell to head of Mégiscane)	65,800	776
Rupert (to head of Témiscamie)	43,400	763
Eastmain	46,400	756
Attawapiskat (to head of Bow Lake)	50,500	748
Kazan (to head of Ennadai Lake)	71,500	732
Grande rivière de la Baleine	42,700	724
George	41,700	565
Moose (to head of Mattagami)	108,500	547
Abitibi (to head of Louis Lake)	29,500	547
Mattagami (to head of Minisinakwa Lake)	37,000	443
Missinaibi	23,500	426
Harricana/Harricanaw	29,300	533
Hayes	108,000	483
aux Feuilles	42,500	480
Winisk	67,300	475
Broadback	20,800	450
à la Baleine	31,900	428
de Povungnituk	28,500	389
Innuksuac	11,400	385
Petite rivière de la Baleine	15,900	380
Arnaud	49,500	377
Nastapoca	13,400	360
Kogaluc	11,600	304
Flowing into the Atlantic Ocean		
St. Lawrence River	839,200	3,058
Nipigon (to head of Ombabika)	25,400	209
Spanish	14,000	338
Trent (to head of Irondale)	12,400	402
Ottawa River	146,300	1,271
Gatineau	23,700	386
du Lièvre	..	330
Saguenay (to head of Péribonca)	88,000	698
Péribonca	28,200	451
Mistassini	21,900	298
Chamouchouane	..	266
Saint-Maurice	43,300	563
Manicouagan (to head of Mouchalagane)	45,800	560
aux Outardes	19,000	499
Romaine	14,350	496
Betsiamites (to head of Manouanis)	18,700	444
Moisie	19,200	410
St-Augustin	9,900	233
Richelieu (to mouth of Lake Champlain)	3,800	171
Churchill (to head of Ashuanipi)	79,800	856
Saint John	35,500	673
Little Mecatina	19,600	547
Natashquan	16,100	410

Source: Natural Resources Canada, Canada Centre for Remote Sensing, GeoAccess.

1.7 WEATHER RECORDS FOR CANADA, UNITED STATES AND THE WORLD

	Canada	United States	World
Highest maximum air temperature	45.0°C Midale and Yellowgrass, Sask. (July 5, 1937)	56.7°C Death Valley, California (July 10, 1913)	58.0°C Al'azizyah, Libya (September 13, 1922)
Lowest minimum air temperature	-63.0°C Snag, Y.T. (February 3, 1947)	-62.1°C Prospect Creek Camp, Alaska (January 23, 1971)	-89.6°C Vostok, Antarctica (July 21, 1983)
Coldest month	-47.9°C Eureka, N.W.T. (February 1979)	..	..
Highest sea-level pressure	107.96 kPa Dawson, Y.T. (February 2, 1989)	107.86 kPa Northway, Alaska (January 31, 1989)	108.38 kPa Agata, Siberia, Russia (December 31, 1968)
Lowest sea-level pressure	94.02 kPa St. Anthony, Nfld. (January 20, 1977)	89.23 kPa Matecumbe Key, Florida (September 2, 1935)	87.00 kPa In eye of Typhoon Tip in the Pacific Ocean, 17°N, 138°E (October 12, 1979)
Greatest precipitation in 24 hours	489.2 mm Ucluelet Brynnor Mines, B.C. (October 6, 1967)	1,090 mm Alvin, Texas (July 28, 1979)	1,869.9 mm Cilaos, La Réunion Island (March 15, 1952)
Greatest precipitation in one month	2,235.5 mm Swanson Bay, B.C. (November 1917)	2,717.8 mm Kukui, Hawaii (March 1942)	9,300 mm Cherrapunji, India (July 1861)
Greatest precipitation in one year	8,122.4 mm Henderson Lake, B.C. (1931)	17,902.7 mm Kukui, Hawaii (1982)	26,461.2 mm Cherrapunji, India (August 1860 to July 1861)
Greatest average annual precipitation	6,655 mm Henderson Lake, B.C.	11,684 mm Mt. Waialeaie, Kauai, Hawaii	11,684 mm Mt. Waialeaie, Kauai, Hawaii
Least annual precipitation	12.7 mm Arctic Bay, N.W.T. (1949)	0.0 mm Bagdad, California (October 3, 1912 to November 8, 1914)	0.0 mm Arica, Chile—no rain for 14 years
Greatest average annual snowfall	1,433 cm Glacier Mt. Fidelity, B.C.	1,460.8 cm Rainer Paradise Ranger Station, Washington	
Greatest snowfall in one season	2,446.5 cm Revelstoke/Mt. Copeland, B.C. (1971-72)	2,850 cm Rainer Paradise Ranger Station, Washington (1971-72)	..
Greatest snowfall in one month	535.9 cm Haines Apps. No. 2, B.C. (December 1959)	990.6 cm Tamarack, California (January 1911)	..
Greatest snowfall in one day	118.1 cm Lakelse Lake, B.C. (January 17, 1974)	193.0 cm Silver Lake, Colorado (April 14–15, 1921)	..
Highest average annual number of thunderstorm days	34 days London, Ont.	96 days Fort Meyers, Florida	322 days Bogor, Indonesia
Heaviest hailstone	290 g Cedoux, Sask. (August 27, 1973)	758 g Coffeyville, Kansas (September 3, 1970)	5,000 g Guangxi region of China (May 1, 1986)
Highest average annual wind speed	36 km/h Cape Warwick, Resolution Island, N.W.T.	56.3 km/h Mt. Washington, New Hampshire	..
Highest hourly wind speed	201.1 km/h Cape Hopes Advance (Quaqtaq), Que. (November 18, 1931)	372.0 km/h Mt. Washington, New Hampshire (April 12, 1934)	..
Highest average hours of fog	1,890 hrs. Argentia, Nfld.	2,552 hrs. Cape Disappointment, Washington	..

Source: Environment Canada, Canadian Meteorological Centre.

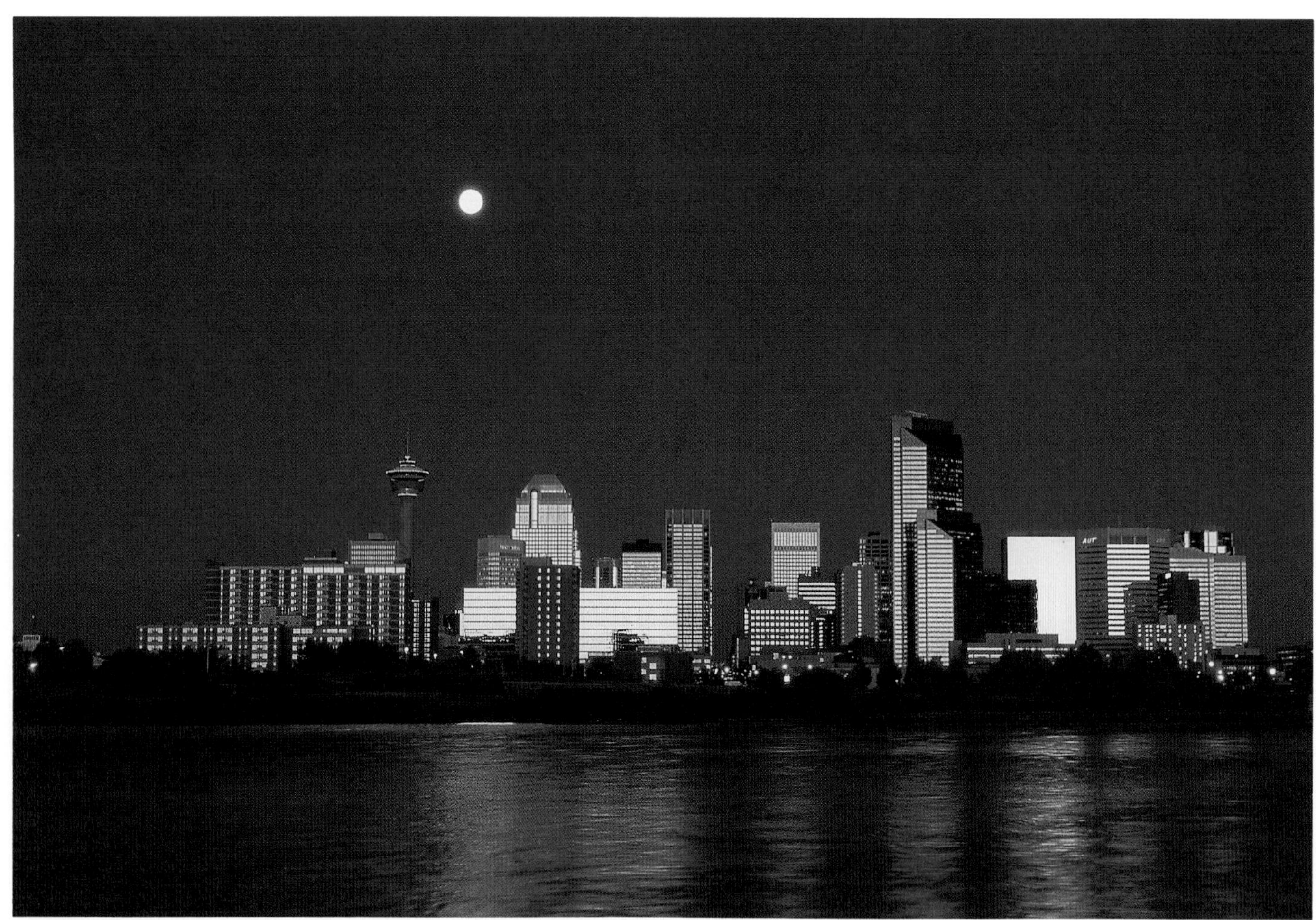

THOMAS KITCHIN, FIRST LIGHT

Chapter 2

THE LEGACY OF SETTLEMENT

Artist unknown, *Sowing*, National Archives of Canada, C-126252

To the great French philosopher Voltaire, cited frequently in the late 18th century as the wisest man in Europe, Canada was "a few acres of snow." To the British government of Voltaire's era, it was of so little value there was serious talk of trading it for the Caribbean island of Guadeloupe.

Today this "few acres of snow" ranks among the most prosperous nations on earth. It has the world's seventh largest economy among western industrialized nations and occupies almost 10 million square kilometres.

Yet when Voltaire dismissed it, it consisted of just a few fishing settlements on the Atlantic coast, a necklace of towns strung along the St. Lawrence River, and trading posts inland, where fur trappers and traders retreated from their incursions into the vast silences of forest and rock.

Already resident in this land were some half a million Aboriginal peoples, who lived either by hunting and fishing, or by farming. For both Aboriginal peoples and early European settlers, Canada's cold climate and its expanses of rock and thin soil limited large-scale settlement to a few parts of the country.

In fact, many Canadians now live on the sites of former Aboriginal settlements, in a narrow band of land largely hugging the American border. This narrow band contains

Forging Smiths

From Cougar Smith Creek in British Columbia to Hick Smith Stillwater in Newfoundland, Canada's place names are favoured with Smiths—439 to be exact. We have mountains called Smith, and creeks called Smith, and points and capes and rivers called Smith. Smith is the most common family name among Canada's place names.

Ontario has the largest number of geographical features and places named Smith (90), followed by Newfoundland (71), British Columbia (58) and Saskatchewan (52).

In the English-speaking world, Smith is the most common family name. The most recent statistics tell us there were about 2.8 million Smiths in the world, with about 75,000 of them living in Canada. In the 1950s and 1960s, Canada used Smith to name about 40 rivers, lakes and other geographical features to commemorate those Smiths killed during the Second World War.

The name Smith dates back to pre-Roman days in Europe when those who worked in metal were call "smiths." Smiths forged horseshoes, ploughshares, swords and armour. In fact, the importance of this job meant the widespread use of Smith as an occupational surname throughout Europe, and eventually throughout the world.

three-quarters of the country's population and all of its largest metropolitan areas. With their skyscrapers, shopping malls and hectares of concrete, the latter have much in common with urban areas throughout the industrialized world.

Yet, from their names, we can remember their history. Saskatoon is derived from the Cree name for a prairie berry. Quebec is Algonquian for "narrowing of the river." Winnipeg, also a Cree word, means "murky water." Miramichi is the "land of the Micmacs," as the Montagnais Indians told Jacques Cartier.

An Urban Nation

Sometime around 1921, Canada crossed a watershed: for the first time, more people were living in urban areas than in rural areas. In the decades since, Canadians have gravitated to

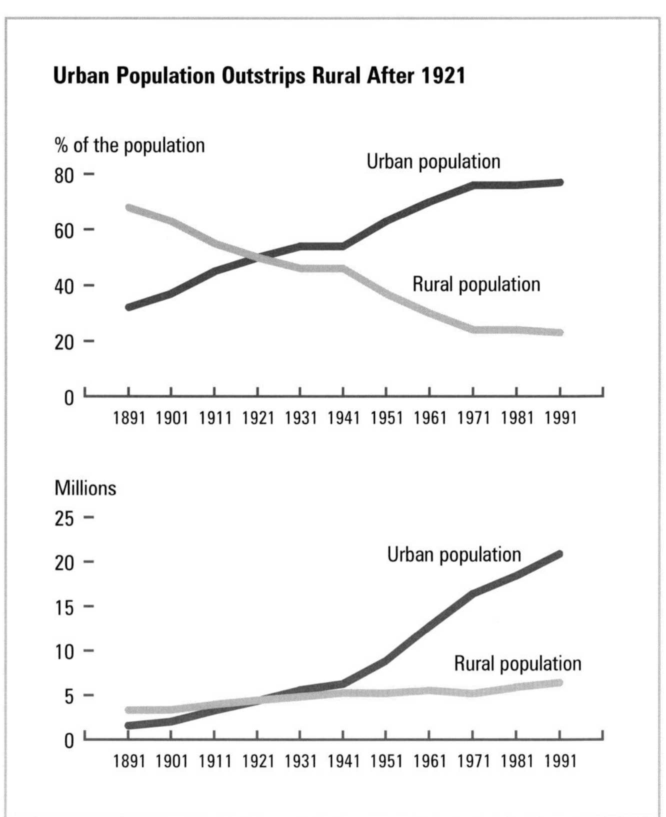

Canada's metropolitan areas—particularly the three largest, Toronto, Montreal and Vancouver. In 1971, 24% of Canadians lived in these three urban areas; by 1994, 32% did. In the early 1980s, Canada's smallest urban places—those with populations of 30,000 or less—actually shrank.

Why are Canada's biggest metropolises getting bigger? The most important factor is the powerful economic pull of these urban centres.

Canadians are particularly drawn to urban centres that specialize in high-tech, service-based industries. These "smart" centres are continually creating new kinds of resources: pools of knowledge, the capacity for innovation, venture capital, universities and research facilities. In the past two decades, metropolitan areas with knowledge-based industry, like Ottawa–Hull, Saskatoon, Toronto, London and Kitchener–Waterloo, have had populations growing more quickly than resource-based urban centres like Winnipeg, Saint John, Windsor, Hamilton and Thunder Bay.

Canada's "Main Street"

In the south of Ontario and Quebec, Canada's so-called Main Street is a string of urban areas from Quebec City on the St. Lawrence River to Sault Ste. Marie on the shores of Lake Superior. About 60% of Canadians live here, although this belt occupies only 2.2% of Canada's land. Canada's two largest metropolitan areas, Toronto and Montreal, are here, as is Canada's capital, Ottawa.

Outside of this "Main Street," Canadian urban-dwellers are also crowded into the coastal plains and mountain valleys of southwestern British Columbia. This area takes up less than 5% of Canada's land, but 13% of Canadians and 80% of British Columbians live there. It is dominated by Vancouver, Canada's third largest metropolitan area.

Only 3% of Canadians lived and worked on farms in 1991, compared with 27% in 1941. Many live outside cities but not on farms, often within easy commuting of downtown. In fact, even Canada's farmers are closely linked to urban life; in 1990, about a third had jobs off the farm, often in the city.

Frontier Canada

Outside Canada's "Main Street" and southern British Columbia, Canadians live in thousands of small communities. Some are mining and forestry towns scattered across Canada's North, others are towns and small urban areas that act as the service centres of agricultural areas. Along the coasts of the Atlantic, Pacific and Arctic oceans, thousands of Canadians live in fishing communities.

Most of these communities are small and relatively isolated. Most are too small to be classed as urban; for example, Newfoundland's hundreds of outport fishing villages, Manitoba's farm towns, British Columbia's coastal logging communities, and the hundreds of Aboriginal settlements and reserves across the country. In some, many people work in government administration, as in Yellowknife in the Northwest Territories, or at national defence bases, as in Happy Valley–Goose Bay, Labrador.

Settlement Costs

Canada's highly productive, urban-based economy has given Canadians an enviable standard of living—but at an increasingly high environmental cost.

Canada's resource industries—agriculture, forestry, fishing and mining—have been the inspiration for our settlement patterns. But often they have severely damaged the resources they depend on, as with parts of the Northern cod fishery in Atlantic Canada.

Thousands of chemicals from vehicles, factories and industrial plants pollute our land, air and water. Near industrial areas, these chemicals can concentrate to dangerous levels. In the St. Lawrence River, for example, beluga whales that wash ashore are so contaminated they are treated as toxic waste.

City Air

The air quality in our urban areas is one example of the costs of settlement. As in other industrialized countries, our air is under constant attack from cars, factories and incinerators, all releasing chemicals and particles that can damage our health.

The major urban culprit is the car. For example, in most large Canadian metropolitan areas, car exhaust produces pollutants that under certain conditions cause unacceptably high concentrations of ground-level ozone, which can damage our lungs and slow the growth of crops.

In the 1990s, though, urban Canadians have been breathing a little easier. We know this through the Air Quality Index (AQI), which measures the air quality in Canada's cities. Even in industrial urban centres like Hamilton, residents breathe what the AQI terms poor air only 6% of the time. In urban areas with little heavy industry, such as Quebec City or Halifax, residents rarely breathe poor air.

Canada's urban air quality is improving partly because today's cars release fewer pollutants.

Climate Warming

As well as airborne pollutants, industrialized economies release large quantities of "greenhouse" gases. When produced naturally, these regulate the earth's temperature, keeping it within a range suitable for life. But by burning coal, oil and natural gas, and by stripping trees from vast areas of the planet, we are dramatically increasing the amounts of carbon dioxide and other heat-trapping greenhouse gases in the atmosphere. Scientists believe this may warm the planet by between 1°C and 3.5°C by 2100.

Such a change could have serious consequences in many parts of Canada. Sea levels could rise enough to cause problems for coastal cities and low-lying agricultural regions, such as the lower Fraser Valley, in British Columbia. Heat waves, droughts and other climatic extremes could become more common, threatening crops in many regions. In the Arctic, permafrost could melt, damaging the roads, bridges and pipelines built on it. Local climate changes might be so rapid that many plant and animal species would not adjust quickly enough to survive.

Canada and the other industrialized nations produce two-thirds of worldwide greenhouse gas emissions. However, many developing nations are just beginning to industrialize, and are expected to increase their greenhouse gas emissions significantly in the next century.

As one of the world's highest per capita producers of greenhouse gases, Canada is committed to stabilizing its emissions at 1990 levels by 2000. Yet Canada's emissions have continued to increase since 1990.

Most greenhouse gases in Canada are produced by transportation. In 1990, the largest producer was the transport sector, followed by the electric power and utilities industries. Together, these three industries accounted for 68% of total emissions. Not surprisingly, all of these industries were Canada's biggest users of fossil fuels—the major source of greenhouse gases.

Ozone Erosion

In the past decade, the ozone layer that protects the earth from the sun's harmful ultraviolet (UV) rays has been rapidly eroding. The loss of this protective layer increases the incidence of sunburns, skin cancer and cataracts, and may damage the body's immune system. It also damages crops and marine food chains.

The chief contributors to ozone depletion include chlorofluorocarbons (CFCs), commonly used in car air conditioners, refrigerators, insulating foams, solvents, and other products. Canada has agreed to phase out CFC production altogether by 1996.

Even so, ozone depletion will likely be with us for many years to come: CFCs released before 1997 will continue to destroy atmospheric ozone for up to 100 years.

Waste Not

Canadians have the dubious distinction of ranking among the world's leading garbage generators. Every year, Canadian households and industry produce more than 32 million

Today, more than a million Canadians claim Aboriginal ancestry. Of these, 626,000 identify themselves as members of the three Aboriginal groups recognized by Canada's Constitution Act, 1982, namely: North American Indian (461,000), Inuit (36,000) and Métis (135,000). Métis are of mixed European and North American Indian ancestry.

Compared to the Canadian population in general, Canada's Aboriginal population is much younger and faster-growing, with higher fertility and mortality levels. In 1991, the median age among Aboriginal peoples was around 23, compared with about 34 for Canadians overall.

The fertility level among registered North American Indians in 1991, for example, was estimated to be about 2.7 children per woman, compared with 1.7 children per woman for Canadians in general. In the same year, life expectancy for registered Indians was about 67 years for men, and 74 years for women, compared with 75 for men and 81 for women in Canada in general.

Canada's Aboriginal population is projected to increase by about 50% between 1991 and 2016 (given current trends). This means the Aboriginal population is growing more rapidly than the overall Canadian population. As a consequence, Aboriginal peoples are steadily becoming a larger, though still small, proportion of Canada's population.

Declining trends in Aboriginal fertility and mortality levels mean that the Aboriginal population is aging, but from a much younger starting point, compared to the Canadian population. By the year 2016, given current trends, the median age of the population with Aboriginal ancestry is projected to reach about 30, compared to a median of about 40 years for Canadians in general.

The Department of Indian Affairs and Northern Development reports that there are 607 Indian bands in Canada, and 2,370 Indian reserves. These reserves cover 27,509 square kilometres—roughly a third the area of New Brunswick. Fewer than 900 reserves are inhabited. Some are only a fraction of a hectare in size, while others are as large as 120,000 hectares. Many are in remote areas with no year-round road to the nearest town. About 59% of the registered Indian population lived on a reserve in 1994.

Besides reserves, Native peoples are claiming lands that they have traditionally used or occupied, or that they feel are theirs according to the terms of historical treaties. The first claim was settled in 1974, for land in James Bay, Northern Quebec. The largest of these claims so far resolved is the Nunavut Final Agreement.

The Agreement came into effect in 1993. It gives the Inuit of the eastern Arctic ownership of more than 350,000 square kilometres of land in what is now the District of Keewatin in the Northwest Territories. As a result of the land claim agreement, the government also negotiated the Nunavut Political Accord, also in 1993. This sets out the legal framework for setting up a new territory—Nunavut—by 1999. Nunavut (which means "Our Land" in the Inuktitut language) will have its own legislative assembly and public service. It will encompass an area of some two million square kilometres.

tonnes of solid waste, including 3.2 million tonnes of hazardous waste. This mountain of refuse is rapidly filling our landfill sites; in 1989, the Ontario Ministry of Environment estimated that it takes only three years to lose 40% of the province's landfill capacity.

There is good news, however. Over the past several years, Canadians have actually been producing less of many wastes. In 1994, close to 70% of Canadian households had access to curbside recycling programs or recycling depots for paper, and more than 80% of these households used them. On the other hand, in 1990, recycling accounted for only 9% of the waste collected by Canada's large municipalities.

Canadian industries are investing heavily in reducing wastes, particularly toxic wastes. In 1989, they spent $1.2 billion on pollution abatement and control. Paper and allied industries spent almost a third of this, but the primary metals industry invested the highest proportion of capital expenditures: 12.3%.

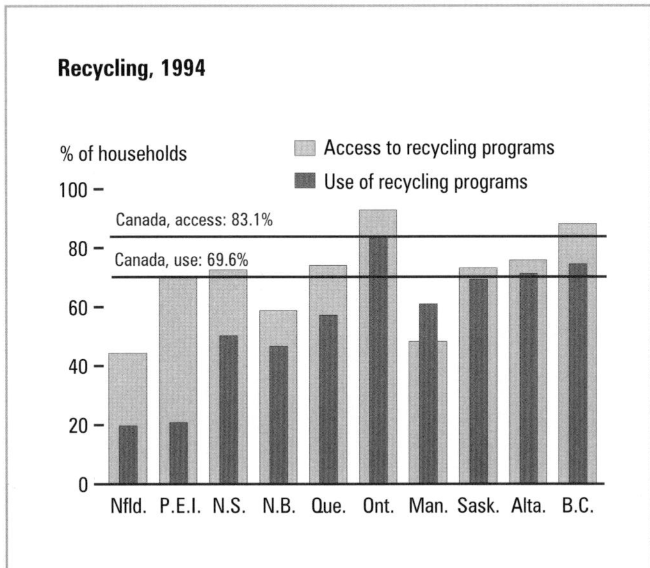

Decline of the Groundfish

Until cod and other groundfish stocks dropped to dangerously low levels in the early 1990s, cod fishing was part of the very fabric of life on Canada's Atlantic coast. Indeed, the coast was first settled by Europeans who crossed the Atlantic to fish in the waters off the Grand Banks of Newfoundland.

Consequently, almost half of Newfoundland's half million people now live in rural areas, many in small "outport" fishing villages with colourful names like Joe Batt's Arm and Seldom Come By. Few Newfoundlanders are farmers; only 0.1% of the land is farmed, the lowest proportion of any province. About 0.5% of Newfoundlanders work in forestry. But by and large, what Newfoundlanders do, and have done traditionally, is fish.

Five hundred years ago, in 1497, explorer John Cabot described the waters off Newfoundland as so "swarming with fish [that they] could be taken not only with a net but in baskets." Cabot and his crew claimed that at times the cod were so thick around their ship, it could not move.

Stories like these attracted fishermen from Europe's North Atlantic ports. By 1500, French and Portuguese ships were fishing in Newfoundland waters, and soon hundreds of ships and thousands of men were crossing the Atlantic each spring to fish Canadian waters.

For more than a century, the crews caught and dried their cod, then returned in the fall to Europe. But by the mid-1600s a few French and English traders and fishermen were willing to brave Newfoundland's stormy, cold winters to be able to protect trading locations and shore constructions.

As a result, fishing settlements began to dot the coast. Settlement grew steadily through the 18th century and even quickened during the Napoleonic wars. The British found it difficult, expensive, and dangerous to operate a migratory fishery during wartime. The resident fishery thus grew as it replaced the migratory fishery, and settlement flourished as a result.

While the fish were abundant, crops refused to grow in the poor soils of what one English settler, George Calvert, called "this wofull country," where "from the middest of October to the middest of May there is a sadd face of wynter upon all this land."

"Wynter" notwithstanding, the fishery endured. In the hundred years before 1950, the annual Northern cod catch taken by small boats and other traditional means annually averaged about 250,000 tonnes. However, beginning in the 1960s, the domestic and international fishing industry began to expand as fishermen bought bigger boats with longer ranges and bigger nets. In 1968, the catch peaked at 800,000 tonnes, most of it taken by large ocean-going vessels rather than small boats fishing close to shore.

Foreign ships—mostly from Spain and Portugal—were catching a large part of that. Fishing just outside Canada's 200-mile (370-kilometre) zone, by 1991 these ships were taking one-quarter of the total catch, contrary to quotas established by the Northwest Atlantic Fisheries Organization.

The waters that had once literally choked the passage of ships, so full were they of cod, began to empty. In 1992, the Canadian government imposed a domestic two-year ban on the commercial Northern cod fishery that was later extended indefinitely. After generations of overfishing, the cod and other groundfish stocks were so depleted that, in 1994, scientists estimated their numbers at 1% of what they would have been in the late 1980s.

The results of all this change have been nothing short of catastrophic for Atlantic Canadians. Many now depend on a $1.9 billion federal government assistance program, and many Newfoundlanders have been leaving the outports to look for work in St. John's or on the mainland. Some 40,000 people who were forced out of work have applied for benefits under the program.

Also in 1995, Canada signed a global agreement that, for the first time, allows countries to enforce fishery conservation measures outside their coastal boundaries. To become international law, however, the agreement must be ratified by 30 countries.

Wildlife Threats

It has been argued that Canada exists today because 16th century Europeans were eager to buy hats made from beaver pelts. In search of beavers for hats, traders from the St. Lawrence River valley had explored much of present-day Canada by 1800. Travelling by canoe along river routes used for centuries by Aboriginal peoples, the traders built posts that eventually became major cities, such as Quebec, Winnipeg and Edmonton.

Yet the first Europeans to explore Canada were searching not for furs but for the Northwest Passage, a short sea route from Europe to the Orient—the source of silks, spices and other highly profitable luxury goods. In the late 1500s and early 1600s, this search took English sailors such as Henry Hudson and Martin Frobisher northwards up the Atlantic coast into the frozen seas of the eastern Arctic, where many of them died. At the same time, it lured sailors all the way from France to the innermost reaches of the St. Lawrence River.

The first French sailor to explore the St. Lawrence, in 1534, was Jacques Cartier, who was certain that the river led to the Orient. But Cartier thought that the Gulf of St. Lawrence was a land of "horrible rugged rocks," and on his third voyage in 1541, made it to the Lachine rapids, above Montreal, but never found the Northwest Passage.

Eventually, the dream of a Northwest Passage gave way to the practicalities of Canada. And what was practical and lucrative were its fur-bearing creatures. These became the focus of a fur trade that lasted several centuries, until changing fashions in Europe caused the trade to dwindle to insignificance.

The beaver population was hunted heavily and eventually recovered, but other overhunted animals have not been as fortunate. By the turn of this century, Canadians and

Lawrence Paul Yuxweluptun, National Gallery of Canada, Ottawa

Scorched Earth, Clear-cut Logging on Native Sovereign Land, Shaman Coming to Fix.

Europeans had hunted great auks, sea minks, passenger pigeons and several species of fish into extinction. Other animals, including the black-footed ferret and the greater Prairie chicken, have lost their grassland habitat to farmers. Altogether, 20 Canadian species or populations have disappeared forever.

Today, very few Canadians make their living from wildlife, yet it continues to be important to us. In 1991, we spent about $8.4 billion on wildlife-related activities; 5.5 million of us fished recreationally and 1.5 million hunted recreationally, while almost four million enjoyed less "consumptive" activities such as bird-watching or wildlife photography.

In many parts of the country, however, Canada's wildlife is still at risk. It is threatened by continuing loss of habitat, contamination of ecosystems by toxic substances, and competition from such foreign intruders as the zebra mussel in the Great Lakes. Across Canada, 275 species of native wild animals, fish and plants are extinct, extirpated, endangered, threatened or vulnerable. These include the polar bear, the sea otter and the whooping crane.

To help protect Canada's wildlife, the federal government is considering a new law that would make it illegal to kill, disturb, injure or sell endangered plants, birds, fish, mammals and their embryos.

Already, Canada's federal and provincial governments have agreed to protect 12% of Canada's land and water areas as national and provincial parks, wildlife reserves or ecological reserves. These protected areas will preserve representative portions of Canada's biological diversity. By 1993, close to 9.7% of Canada's land area was protected to some degree.

Troubled Waters

Canada has one-fifth of the world's supply of freshwater, most of it in the Great Lakes. Twenty million people draw their drinking water from the lakes into which waste is poured—20% of it from U.S. industry and 50% from Canadian industry.

There are about 360 identified chemical pollutants in the Great Lakes, by-products of the chemical revolution that began in the 1950s. Many of these pollutants contribute to the destruction of aquatic ecosystems and have adverse effects on wildlife and human health. Chemicals such as polychlorinated biphenyls (PCBs) accumulate in large fish and birds: PCBs have been found in the eggs of herring gulls in concentrations of over 100,000 times the level found in lake water.

Some of these toxic chemicals—particularly DDT—can cause birth defects and reduced ability to reproduce in fish-eating birds. As well, tumours and cancers occur in some Great Lake fish populations.

Fare-thee-well, fare-thee-well

Tradition has it that the gray jay, ***Perisoreus canadensis****, makes but one cry as it flies overhead: "Poor Canada, poor Canada." The voice of the prophet is still heard in the land, though not so insistently. The number of songbirds in eastern Canada is on the decline.*

Canada's songbirds face enemies both domestic and foreign. They are losing their breeding habitat in eastern Canada's urban areas as more trees come down and more houses go up. Since the end of the Second World War, many species of thrushes, warblers and tanagers have disappeared from urban cores. Those songbirds may have an even harder time after flying south to winter. In the tropical regions where they winter, forests are also coming down, in some cases at alarming rates.

As if this weren't difficult enough, our songbirds face another foe in their own ranks. Bluebirds often find their food and nesting sites a target of the birds we know best: starlings and house sparrows. In addition, there is the problem of urbanization. If cities continue to grow as quickly as they do now, ornithologists predict that unless greater efforts are made to protect habitat, some songbird species may eventually disappear.

Like his golden-winged ancestor, Pegasus, a 12-year-old Newfoundland pony named Trigger once again proved that horses can fly—and do it in style.

On a warm July day in 1995, the roan-coloured pony boarded a Vancouver-bound jumbo jet at Toronto's Pearson International Airport, making him the first known member of his breed to cross the Rockies.

Trigger's journey was to publicize the plight of his disappearing breed. While uniquely adapted to its craggy Newfoundland home, the pony finds its future threatened. In 1976, Newfoundland ponies numbered around 13,500. In 1992, there were less than 1,000. Today, it's estimated fewer than 135 ponies are still in existence.

The pony's decline began in the mid-1900s, an inevitable by-product of the modern machinery that gradually supplanted four-legged horsepower. During the 1980s, some Newfoundland municipalities passed bylaws to fence in traditionally free-roaming ponies. Because this was expensive, the slaughterhouse frequently became the solution.

Trigger's heavy coat, dark legs and furry ears make him a worthy representative of his breed. Newfoundland ponies stand an average of 12 hands high—about 125 centimetres—and they have traditionally spent their lives hauling boats, pulling logs and tugging sleighs, the classic life of winter workhorses. During the summer, they have generally been allowed to roam free.

Trigger's ancestors—believed to be Dartmoor, Exmoor and other British moorland ponies—arrived with fishing immigrants during the seventeenth century. They adapted well to the harsh Newfoundland climate, their thick coats withstanding the cold and their sure-footedness an advantage in the rugged landscape.

The federal Livestock Pedigree Act does not presently recognize the Newfoundland pony as a registered breed. But some Newfoundlanders see the pony as an irreplaceable part of Newfoundland's heritage. Working to save the breed from extinction, these Newfoundlanders hope to protect the pony with provincial legislation.

An important step in that direction took place in June 1994, when the Newfoundland House of Assembly voted unanimously to accept a resolution to recognize the pony as a heritage animal, calling it "the virtual engine of outport and rural life."

Trigger represents a small part of Canada's endangered species. As of late 1995, some 255 species were listed as being at risk, including the piping plover, the peregrine falcon and the beluga whales of Ungava Bay, the St. Lawrence River and Cumberland Sound. Some species, like the swift fox, disappeared altogether from Canadian soil and have since been reintroduced. Fortunately, there are success stories. The once-threatened white pelican has increased its total numbers, removing it from the list of species at risk.

Canada is working to develop new legal means of protecting endangered species as part of its commitment to the international Convention on Biological Diversity.

Clifford George

Newfoundland ponies.

Patterns in Canadian history offer some insight into the decline of the Great Lakes. Until the 1880s, the settled land surrounding the Lakes was largely farmland. With the construction of the Canadian Pacific Railway (CPR), the Prairies opened to immigrant homesteaders who created a huge market for farm machinery. At the same time, the federal government's National Policy protected Canadian farm machinery manufacturers with high tariffs on imported goods.

The policy paid off: money and workers poured into Montreal, Toronto and other Central Canadian urban areas, and industrial productivity increased rapidly. When electricity replaced steam power around the turn of the century, mining companies began to use electrical processes to refine minerals other than iron and steel. Soon industry was drawing on the vast reserves of minerals that had been discovered in the Precambrian Shield.

The manufacturing boom drew hundreds of thousands of people into urban areas. In 1871, 18% of Canadians lived in urban areas; 40 years later, this had jumped to 42%.

Today, close to two in three Canadians live in Canada's industrial heartland: the central St. Lawrence River valley in Quebec and the lowlands between the Great Lakes in southern Ontario. Throughout this area, industry, urban areas and farming have torn at the water, land and air. And nowhere have these effects been more extreme than in the Great Lakes.

Human health may well be affected by long-term exposure to Great Lakes contaminants. A study of Michigan women who regularly ate Great Lakes fish during their pregnancies found that their newborns had neurobehavioural and physical defects and, as 4-year-olds, suffered learning deficits.

In response to these problems, Canada and the United States signed the Great Lakes Water Quality Agreement in 1978. The Agreement aims to restore and maintain the chemical, physical and biological integrity of the Great Lakes basin ecosystem.

By 1995, reports on the health of the Great Lakes were mixed. Some indicators have generally improved, including the condition of some aquatic communities. But other indicators have worsened, including habitat loss, encroachment and development in wetlands, and the imbalance of some aquatic communities in Lake Michigan, Lake Ontario and the eastern basin of Lake Erie.

Risks to human health seem to be gradually lessening, as concentrations of persistent toxic chemicals decline throughout the Great Lakes. However, many contaminants must be further reduced to reach acceptable levels of risk.

As well, aquatic habitat and wetlands are rapidly declining in quality as well as quantity. Habitats for some species, however, remain in relatively good condition—stream habitat for brook trout in the upper lakes, for example.

Prairie Farms

The construction of the Canadian Pacific Railway contributed not only to the "citification" of Central Canada, it also led to the settling of Canada's Prairie provinces.

Between 1900 and 1910 alone, hundreds of thousands of people came from many parts of Europe to settle 180 million hectares of Prairie farmland—an area the size of Italy. The Prairie population grew from 420,000 in 1901 to more than 2.3 million by 1931. Together, these new settlers produced an ocean of wheat; by 1928, wheat accounted for 40% of Canada's exports.

Today, Prairie farmers grow more than 90% of Canada's grain and oilseed crops, and in 1995, farming was worth $5.25 billion in Saskatchewan and $5.85 billion in Alberta.

To fuel their farm machinery, however, Prairie farmers burn large amounts of gas and oil. They use chemical fertilizers to feed hybrid crop varieties that need more nutrients than the soil can give. Often, they use chemical pesticides to protect their crops from insects and disease.

From Yukon to Quebec, fires raged across the country, consuming an area the size of New Brunswick. The summer of 1995 was the second-worst forest fire season in Canada's recorded history. Nearly seven million hectares went up in flames. The worst forest fire season was just six years earlier in 1989, when 7.55 million hectares were lost.

Forest fire activity in Canada appears to be on the rise. Before 1980, forest fires burned an average of one million hectares a year. Since 1980, that has doubled to 2.2 million hectares a year. In fact, five of the seven worst forest fire years recorded have happened in the last 15 years.

In 1995, Ontario alone spent $100 million fighting its forest fires, after budgeting only $18 million. The largest fire in the country, in northern Saskatchewan, destroyed 100,000 hectares of forest, an area equivalent to one-sixth of Prince Edward Island.

Forest fires are typically caused by lightning, careless people and spark-driven machinery. Another key cause appears to be climate, since the hotter the weather, the drier the wood. The summer of 1995 was one of the hottest on record, while 1989 ***was*** *the hottest. In fact, eight of the earth's warmest years on record have occurred in the past 15 years. Globally, 1995 was possibly the earth's warmest year to date.*

Such temperature records are persuasive evidence of global warming. Known as the "enhanced greenhouse effect," this phenomenon occurs when gases, such as carbon dioxide, build up in the atmosphere and trap the sun's heat, warming the earth. These carbon dioxide emissions have been linked to human activity such as burning fossil fuels. Unfortunately, forest fires also contribute to this effect. As more trees burn, the amount of carbon dioxide released into the atmosphere increases, speeding up global warming.

Climatologists warn that global warming may make forest fires more frequent and more destructive because of drier wood and more dead wood. Although the recent heat waves and forest fires can't be attributed solely to global warming—chaotic and extreme weather occurs for other reasons as well—they may reveal something of what will come. Future heat waves and droughts may be more frequent, more intense and less forgiving.

Canada's economy has always depended on its trees and other natural resources. In 1993, forestry generated $49 billion a year in economic activity, and 254,000 jobs. In 1995, the cost of fighting Canada's forest fires came to a scorching quarter of a billion dollars.

S.A. Chandler, National Archives of Canada, C-063256

This girl represented Canada at the England Carnival in Exeter, England in 1907. (She took first prize.)

In fact, in 1990, Prairie farmers used five times more chemical fertilizer than in 1970. But these fertilizers were used to partly compensate for decreased organic matter in soils; when this happens, soil holds less water, and erosion from rainfall increases. Soil erosion removes from one to four tonnes of topsoil every year from an average hectare of cropland in Canada. It was estimated in 1982 that Prairie soils had lost as much as 50% of their organic nutrients over a 44-year period.

Erosion is costly for farmers. Natural nutrients must be replaced with other fertilizers and the soil may need more tillage and irrigation, which can lead to still further erosion. Every year, erosion costs farmers about $1 billion. Prairie farmers have begun to fight this problem. In 1991, more than 70% reported using at least one kind of soil conservation practice.

The increased dependence on chemical pesticides has also affected Prairie farm land. In 1990, Prairie farmers applied 10 times as much pesticide as they had used in 1970. This is partly because one-crop farmlands lack the resilience of complex natural ecosystems, and are more likely to have serious outbreaks of weeds, insects and disease. In 1991, more than 75% of Canada's crops were grown on one-crop farms.

But farm pests can build their own defences and many pesticides are no longer effective; by 1991, more than 500 insects had developed resistance to one or more pesticides. To eliminate pests like these, farmers require increasingly toxic pesticides.

Today, some Prairie farmers are beginning to explore natural pest controls. They alternate crops annually or grow several kinds in the same year; they have even introduced "friendly" insects that eat pests.

All Canadians have a stake in the health of Prairie farms. Soil erosion and agricultural chemicals can damage areas far from farmers' fields. Washed into rivers and lakes, eroded soil can destroy fish habitats and choke reservoirs and harbours. Pesticides can poison streams and ground water, while excess fertilizers flushed into a lake can cause algae and other weeds to grow so excessively that they choke off the lake's oxygen, killing fish and other organisms.

Forest Fights

In the 1980s and early 1990s, the pristine beauty of areas like Clayoquot Sound and the Carmanah Valley became rallying points over the fate of old-growth forests on British Columbia's Pacific coast. Clearly, many Canadians now strongly believe that the value of forests extends far beyond economics.

The old growth forests of the Pacific coast are dominated by immense trees such as the Douglas Fir, which can reach heights of 100 metres. Large trees make British Columbia forests highly productive; the province has only 21% of Canada's commercial forest, yet produces almost half of all wood cut and more than 44% of Canada's forest product exports. In 1993, these exports were worth $11.8 billion.

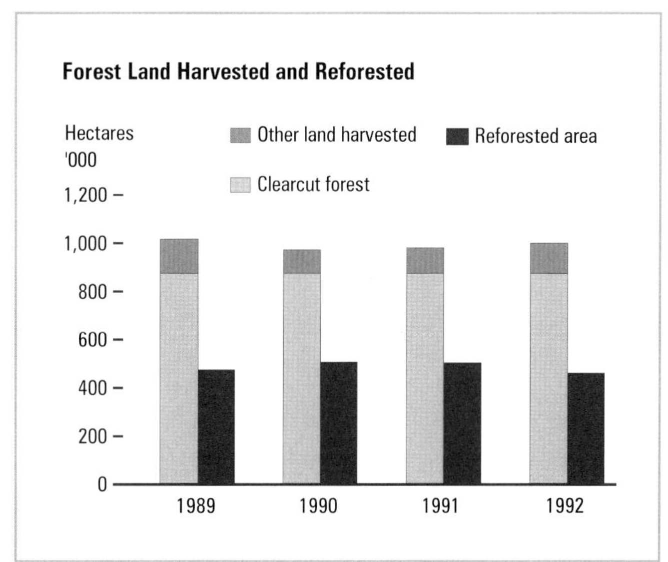

Old growth forests survive in British Columbia partly because, compared with Central and Atlantic Canada, the province is young; Europeans did not reach Canada's Pacific coast until 1774. A hundred years later, British Columbia had only 12,000 settlers—about 12% of the population of Montreal, Canada's largest urban area at the time. Blessed with vast forests, huge stocks of salmon and a wide range of minerals, British Columbia had immense economic potential; however, to sell its products, it needed to be linked with the rest of Canada.

In 1871, British Columbia agreed to become a province of Canada on one condition: the federal government must build a railway through the Rocky Mountains to the Pacific coast. The government agreed, and in 1886, the Canadian Pacific Railway reached Vancouver.

The CPR triggered an economic boom. Vancouver was virtually uninhabited before the railway came through: by 1901, it had 30,000 people, as entrepreneurs and workers poured in from every region of Canada.

The Klondike Gold Rush also helped Vancouver grow. In 1896, three prospectors found gold in Bonanza Creek, a tributary of the Klondike River in present-day Yukon Territory. Within two years, 100,000 people had made their way to the Yukon gold fields, stopping in Vancouver or Victoria to purchase the supplies they would need.

While Klondikers rushed to Yukon, other prospectors found gold, lead and zinc in southeastern British Columbia, which become Canada's most important mining region.

By this time, entrepreneurs had built lumber mills near Vancouver and on Vancouver Island. But the forest industry had to wait until the 1920s. Logging companies cut into forests near their existing mills, and built new mills along the coast and into the interior.

Today, the issue, in its simplest terms, is that 70 years of intensive cutting have left their mark on the province. Once the remaining old growth forests are cut, the province's long-term sustainable yearly harvest will be an estimated 57 million cubic metres, compared with a harvest of 71 million cubic metres in 1993.

Some of the old growth forests will be spared the axe. In 1992, the provincial government announced its intention to double the total areas of British Columbia's parks and wilderness reserves. Since 1992, the government has created 125 new parks and other protected areas, increasing the total to more than 9% of the province—an area larger than New Brunswick. These protected areas included one-third of Clayoquot Sound and half of the Carmanah Valley.

British Columbia is also changing how it manages commercial forests. From 1994 to 1999, a forest renewal plan will raise a projected $2 billion from higher fees for logging companies using provincially owned forest lands. Part of this money will pay for forest thinning, fertilization and other techniques that increase harvest yields.

In 1994, the province's Forest Practices Code became law. The Code established strict sustainable forestry standards and heavy penalties—up to $2 million a day for repeat offenders—and reduces the average size of clearcuts.

Environmentalists, however, argue that the Code fails to address clearcutting, which took 86% of the province's total forest harvest in 1992. Clearcutting, as the name indicates, refers to the wholesale cutting of wooded areas, leaving no timber standing.

Clearcutting can destroy wildlife habitats and cause severe soil erosion that degrades forest ecosystems permanently. Critics advocate selective cutting; in other words, removing only a portion of a forest's harvestable timber in a given year. The forestry industry counters that selective logging is prohibitively expensive, and that most clearcut areas regenerate naturally. Future forestry conflicts in British Columbia will likely focus as much on clearcutting as on further protecting old growth forests.

Other provinces do not have British Columbia's extensive old growth forests, but how forests are managed is an issue across

Northwest Passage

Westward from the Davis Strait, 'tis
there 'twas said to lie
The sea-route to the Orient for
which so many died
Seeking gold and glory, leaving weathered,
broken bones
And a long-forgotten lonely cairn of stones.

Ah, for just one time I would take the Northwest
Passage
To find the hand of Franklin reaching for the
Beaufort Sea
Tracing one warm line through a land so wide
and savage
And make a Northwest Passage to the sea.

Northwest Passage *by Stan Rogers*

Canada. In 1994, for example, Ontario completed a 4-year environmental assessment of timber management on Crown lands in the province. The result was 115 legally binding requirements, including local committees of citizens to advise on forest management, and a conservation strategy for old growth forests. Quebec and some other provinces have recently introduced similar changes in management plans for new, multi-use forests.

Pollutants in the North

Canada's North is sparsely settled and remote, yet even here the history of Canada can be recalled through the state of the land today.

Particularly in recent decades, air-borne pollutants such as chlorinated organic compounds and heavy metals have begun to appear here, thousands of kilometres from their sources in the urban areas of the world. As well, mining, exploration for oil and gas, and community activities have contaminated some parts of the Arctic.

Travel by land in the North was difficult and time-consuming until the early 1940s, when American and Canadian troops built the 2,451 kilometre-long Alaska Highway in just eight months. Along with other roads linking Yukon with towns in the Mackenzie River delta, the Alaska Highway made it possible to begin developing the North's mineral and oil reserves. In the 1950s, Inuvik in the Mackenzie River delta became the western Arctic's major centre for services and transportation, and the base for oil exploration.

There has been a cost, however. Canada's Arctic ecosystems are particularly vulnerable to contaminants: organic chemical contaminants degrade more slowly in the Arctic's cold temperatures and reduced sunlight. For example, oil degrades 10 to 20 times more slowly at 5°C than at 25°C. These contaminants tend to persist in the Arctic longer than they would at southern latitudes, and of course, they threaten Arctic wildlife and human health. The Inuit, who account for most of the Arctic's population, eat large amounts of wild game. As a result, many may be accumulating unsafe levels of toxic substances.

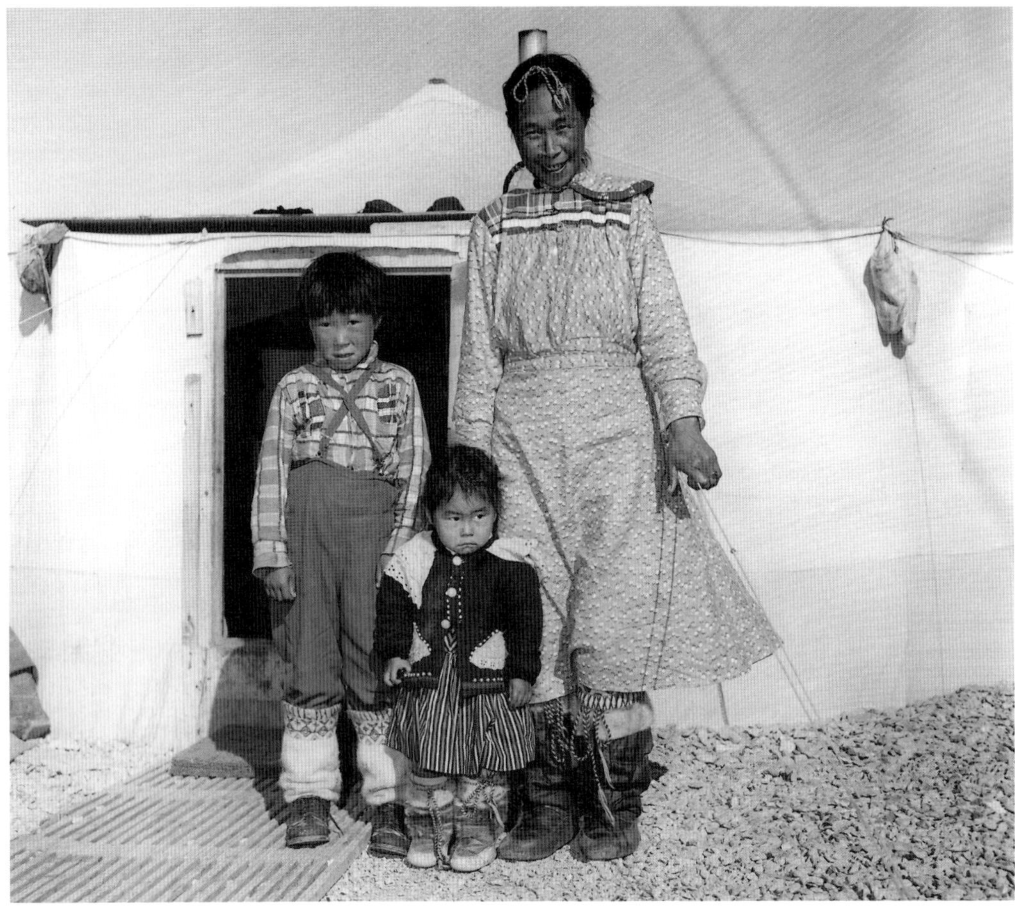

James Scrimger, courtesy of Gerard I. Kenney

Inuit family, Resolute Bay, N.W.T., 1958.

The event that first interrupted this once pristine land was the Klondike Gold Rush of the 1890s. So many gold rushers poured into the Yukon Territory that Dawson City, located where the Klondike River meets the Yukon River, was for a time the largest community west of Winnipeg and north of Seattle.

When the gold rush ended, Dawson's population collapsed and today, Whitehorse, also on the Yukon River, is Yukon's largest town, with a population in 1991 of 18,000. About two in three Yukoners live in or near Whitehorse.

The eastern Arctic is in many ways still a frontier. No road reaches beyond 55° north, and most communities can be reached only by air. Zinc and lead mined on Baffin Island and on Little Cornwallis Island must be transported by sea. The region's largest town, Iqaluit, has a population of about 3,500.

The global circulation of air masses has also caused ozone-depleting pollutants to appear in the Arctic. In 1992, Canada's largest depletions in stratospheric ozone occurred in early spring over Western Canada and the Arctic.

SOURCES

Environment Canada
Natural Resources Canada
Statistics Canada

FOR FURTHER READING

Selected publications from Statistics Canada

- **Human Activity and the Environment**. Occasional. 11-509E

Selected publications from other sources

- **The Canadian Encyclopedia Plus (CD-ROM)**. McClelland & Stewart. 1995.
- **Historical Atlas of Canada**, Volume 1. University of Toronto Press. 1987.
- **The State of Canada's Environment**. Environment Canada. 1991.
- **The State of Canada's Forests**. Natural Resources Canada. 1994.

Legend

–	nil or zero	..	not available	x	confidential
--	too small to be expressed	...	not applicable or not appropriate		*(Certain tables may not add due to rounding)*

2.1 FEDERAL GOVERNMENT SPENDING ON POLLUTION

	1986	1987	1988	1989	1990	1991	1992	1993	1994
					$ '000				
Pollution abatement and control expenditures[1]	445,727	498,091	530,011	610,270	690,326	703,176	714,158	751,185	935,259
Sewage collection and disposal	–	–	–	–	–	–	150	275	–
Pollution control	61,983	67,297	87,142	113,085	118,855	20,221	4,329	1,004	5,870
Other environmental services	383,744	430,794	442,869	497,185	571,471	682,955	709,679	749,906	929,389

1. There are no federal government expenditures on waste collection and disposal.

Source: Statistics Canada, Catalogue no. 11-528.

2.2 NEW SUPPLIES[1] OF OZONE-DEPLETING SUBSTANCES

	Total	Chlorofluorocarbons (CFCs)	Other ozone-depleting substances	Gross Domestic Product
		Kilotonnes		$ Constant 1986 (billions)
1979	20.7	17.3	3.4	418.33
1980	16.8	14.0	2.8	424.54
1981	18.0	15.2	2.8	440.13
1982	17.4	14.2	3.2	425.97
1983	19.3	15.6	3.7	439.45
1984	21.6	16.9	4.7	467.17
1985	23.1	18.5	4.6	489.44
1986	24.9	19.9	5.0	505.67
1987[2]	27.8	21.2	6.6	526.73
1988	27.6	21.0	6.6	552.96
1989	23.9	18.8	5.1	566.49
1990	17.0	13.1	3.9	565.00
1991	11.9	8.8	3.1	555.05
1992	12.5	10.7	1.8	559.30
1993	5.8	4.5	1.3	571.72
1994	5.7	4.8	0.9	597.94

1. New supplies are production of ozone-depleting substances in Canada, plus importation minus exportation.
2. Signing of the Montreal Protocol. This Protocol calls for the phase-out of production of major ozone-depleting substances.

Source: Environment Canada, *Stratospheric Ozone Depletion*, National Environmental Indicator Series.

2.3 PROVINCIAL, TERRITORIAL AND MUNICIPAL GOVERNMENT SPENDING[1] ON POLLUTION

		Canada	Nfld.	P.E.I.	N.S.	N.B.	Que.	Ont.	Man.	Sask.	Alta.	B.C.	Y.T.	N.W.T.
								$ '000						
Provincial and Territorial Governments														
Pollution abatement and control expenditures	1989	669,496	5,367	4,848	29,861	29,776	94,745	229,416	14,410	75,814	79,815	101,527	3,143	774
	1990	867,469	2,871	5,561	36,014	35,096	147,799	266,040	15,165	104,023	88,679	162,642	2,790	789
	1991	1,050,062	3,239	6,530	37,304	50,145	157,476	325,708	17,339	151,500	94,234	202,597	3,168	821
	1992	936,508	5,174	7,206	30,893	44,264	170,805	315,255	21,255	48,486	94,639	194,604	3,212	715
Sewage collection and disposal[2]	1989	72,412	–	–	720	9,554	–	–	–	–	–	59,729	2,409	–
	1990	75,327	–	–	127	9,367	–	–	–	95	–	63,557	2,181	–
	1991	100,597	–	–	92	8,191	–	–	–	64	–	89,873	2,377	–
	1992	97,741	–	933	47	6,730	–	–	–	49	–	87,715	2,268	–
Waste collection and disposal	1989	114,495	163	2,150	8,817	4,579	–	36,648	5,481	–	31,029	25,425	202	–
	1990	121,947	296	2,268	12,546	5,850	–	50,234	5,415	–	38,515	6,667	158	–
	1991	156,545	261	3,170	12,672	5,907	–	73,066	6,493	8	40,108	14,657	202	–
	1992	161,330	361	3,710	7,483	8,483	–	80,391	6,659	–	42,575	11,446	223	–
Pollution control	1989	280,066	3,679	113	4,601	13,802	19,820	188,239	393	4,314	40,973	3,437	32	662
	1990	296,300	2,559	176	5,312	13,834	–	202,993	399	29,465	40,754	11	8	789
	1991	341,901	2,956	348	6,103	18,420	–	240,212	746	29,730	42,626	–	–	759
	1992	295,129	3,014	286	2,248	16,910	–	220,643	393	4,579	44,667	1,684	–	705
Other environmental services	1989	202,524	1,525	2,585	15,722	1,840	74,925	4,530	8,537	71,500	7,813	12,936	500	111
	1990	373,895	16	3,117	18,029	6,045	147,799	12,813	9,351	74,464	9,410	92,408	444	–
	1991	451,019	22	3,012	18,437	17,627	157,476	12,430	10,100	121,699	11,500	98,067	589	62
	1992	382,309	1,799	2,277	21,115	12,142	170,805	14,221	14,203	43,859	7,397	93,758	722	10
Local Governments														
Pollution abatement and control expenditures	1988	2,305,888	30,016	2,444	60,989	40,968	589,183	1,027,278	65,274	54,335	172,454	247,984	2,108	12,855
	1989	2,753,189	30,954	2,686	55,460	42,873	759,031	1,232,339	75,854	58,349	197,358	280,920	1,641	15,724
	1990	3,210,233	37,001	2,953	70,495	55,399	915,031	1,405,400	78,470	60,327	228,555	335,496	2,714	18,392
	1991	3,263,443	33,607	3,430	105,622	59,567	823,321	1,500,246	82,422	55,560	219,391	357,103	4,901	18,273
	1992	3,258,664	31,859	3,633	82,440	58,102	778,120	1,494,662	121,135	58,223	220,652	384,044	6,936	18,858
	1993	3,183,478	32,300	3,141	113,955	63,574	759,279	1,350,010	92,168	63,418	269,523	404,564	6,432	25,114
Sewage collection and disposal	1988	1,413,609	19,426	1,796	38,941	30,740	377,887	597,643	40,072	36,301	118,368	142,171	1,483	8,781
	1989	1,734,756	19,028	1,945	31,176	30,702	531,371	723,837	49,106	41,358	138,229	154,934	1,061	12,009
	1990	2,001,997	24,951	2,165	38,281	40,240	659,991	778,073	52,055	42,458	161,963	185,334	2,074	14,412
	1991	1,954,272	19,420	2,580	63,118	42,898	537,628	838,006	55,495	37,362	146,430	192,799	4,216	14,320
	1992	1,899,753	18,450	2,558	40,592	40,963	471,149	826,209	89,248	37,129	139,037	213,709	6,105	14,604
	1993	1,869,010	19,996	2,127	72,645	45,536	433,920	750,029	61,193	43,356	188,897	227,954	5,549	17,808
Waste collection and disposal	1988	817,079	10,576	497	21,941	9,824	178,308	391,866	24,526	17,841	53,813	103,199	625	4,063
	1989	935,818	11,915	581	24,059	12,156	195,986	462,601	26,080	16,766	58,925	122,472	580	3,697
	1990	1,125,905	12,044	612	31,928	13,305	223,016	584,145	25,682	17,595	66,592	146,467	640	3,879
	1991	1,228,222	14,183	667	41,172	14,825	267,306	607,933	26,043	17,993	72,961	160,562	684	3,893
	1992	1,274,745	13,405	882	41,401	15,258	292,196	606,829	31,123	20,787	81,615	166,224	831	4,194
	1993	1,228,072	12,300	825	40,843	16,066	300,507	546,422	30,220	19,761	80,626	172,373	883	7,246
Other environmental services[3]	1988	75,200	14	151	107	404	32,988	37,769	676	193	273	2,614	–	11
	1989	82,615	11	160	225	15	31,674	45,901	668	225	204	3,514	–	18
	1990	82,331	6	176	286	1,854	32,024	43,182	733	274	–	3,695	–	101
	1991	80,949	4	183	1,332	1,844	18,387	54,307	884	205	–	3,742	1	60
	1992	84,166	4	193	447	1,881	14,775	61,624	764	307	–	4,111	–	60
	1993	86,396	4	189	467	1,972	24,852	53,559	755	301	–	4,237	–	60

1. Local government expenditures exclude transfers between municipalities. Provincial/territorial government expenditures include intergovernmental transfer payments.
2. Some provinces and territories report their sewage expenditures under water supply expenditures, which are not considered as environmental protection expenditures.
3. Local government expenditures on other environmental services may include expenditures specific to pollution control.

Source: Statistics Canada, Catalogue no. 11-528.

2.4 INTERNATIONAL EMISSIONS OF CO_2 AND CONSUMPTION OF CFCS AND HALONS

	1960[1]	1970[2]	1980[3]	1991[4]	1985	1990				
	CO_2 emissions					Consumption of CFCs and halons[5]				
	From fossil fuel combustion and cement manufacturing				Net from deforestation	Total	CFCs	Halons	% of world consumption	Per capita
	Kilotonnes					Tonnes			%	Kilograms
World	2,498,367	3,854,546	5,079,161	5,858,953	855,938	1,027,748	..	..	100.0	0.7
Canada	52,700	90,610	117,399	112,071	-79,050	15,302	13,174	2,128	1.5	0.6
Australia	24,060	38,884	55,348	71,457	-2,576	7,222	7,204	18	0.7	–
Austria	8,394	13,729	14,247	16,466	-2,671	1,858	1,802	57	–	–
Belgium	25,033	34,396	34,860	27,860	125	..	..	..	..	..
Denmark	8,141	16,920	17,254	17,209	-627	3,276	2,473	803	–	0.6
Finland	4,132	10,997	15,036	14,205	-8,274	2,375	1,859	516	–	–
France[6]	74,791	116,176	132,129	102,105	-7,741	62,765	38,989	23,776	6.1	1.1
Germany	..	..	..	264,637	..	94,380	78,470	15,910	9.2	1.2
Federal Republic of Germany	148,614	200,840	207,885	..	-6,833	..	..	..	..	..
Former German Democratic Republic	71,940	73,845	83,678	..	..	..	..	..	..	..
Greece	2,545	6,559	14,031	19,887	-381	..	..	..	..	..
Iceland	331	379	509	492	..	166	133	33	–	0.7
Ireland	3,039	4,915	6,845	8,798	-2,110	..	..	..	..	..
Italy[7]	301,434	779,554	1,015,644	1,098,574	-67	..	..	..	..	..
Japan	63,997	202,973	254,881	297,802	4,391	120,074	97,723	22,351	11.7	1.0
Luxembourg	3,175	3,755	2,902	2,814	..	136	..	..	–	–
Netherlands	20,173	34,813	41,704	37,934	516	17,609	249	1,360	1.7	1.2
New Zealand	3,167	3,884	4,802	6,507	-826	1,195	558	637	–	–
Norway	3,582	6,846	10,919	16,013	-2,476	2,054	722	1,332	–	–
Portugal	2,248	3,716	7,396	11,406	-1,945	..	..	..	..	..
Spain	13,423	30,194	54,596	60,010	-6,214	23,596	23,596	..	2.3	0.6
Sweden	13,454	25,179	19,494	14,601	-8,315	2,214	1,818	396	0.2	–
Switzerland	53,465	107,805	111,695	114,205	-305	3,394	2,920	473	0.3	–
Turkey	4,587	11,504	20,741	38,907	-2,079	..	..	..	..	–
United Kingdom	160,770	175,397	160,551	157,521	419	73,117	58,081	15,036	7.1	1.3
United States	799,544	1,165,477	1,261,778	1,345,969	-60,306	145,593	111,039	34,554	14.2	0.9

1. Emissions include a contribution from gas flaring activities for Canada and the United States.
2. Emissions include a contribution from gas flaring activities for Canada, Japan, the Netherlands, New Zealand, the United Kingdom and the United States.
3. Emissions include a contribution from gas flaring activities for Canada, France, Japan, the Netherlands, New Zealand, Norway, the United Kingdom and the United States.
4. Emissions include a contribution from gas flaring activities for Canada, Denmark, Germany, Greece, the Netherlands, Norway, Spain, the United Kingdom and the United States.
5. The European Union member states (Belgium, Denmark, France, Germany, Greece, Ireland, Italy, Luxembourg, Netherlands, Portugal, Spain and the United Kingdom) report CFC/halon consumption data collectively. The data for member countries are included where available.
6. Includes Monaco for CO_2 emissions.
7. Includes San Marino for CO_2 emissions.

Source: United Nations, *Statistical Yearbook*, New York, 1994.

2.5 AIR QUALITY INDEX[1] [2]

	1988		1989		1990		1991		1992	
	Hours	%	Hours	%	Hours	%	Hours	%	Hours	%
St. John's (Nfld.)	8,663	100.0	8,760	100.0	8,749	100.0	8,760	100.0	8,783	100.0
Good	8,655	99.9	8,547	97.6	8,710	99.6	8,685	99.1	8,740	99.5
Fair	8	0.1	184	2.1	39	0.4	75	0.9	43	0.5
Poor	–	–	29	0.3	–	–	–	–	–	–
Halifax (N.S.)[3]	8,676	100.0	8,760	100.0	4,040	100.0	8,084	100.0	8,781	100.0
Good	8,552	98.6	8,719	99.5	4,018	99.5	8,059	99.7	8,728	99.4
Fair	124	1.4	41	0.5	22	0.5	25	0.3	53	0.6
Poor	–	–	–	–	–	–	–	–	–	–
Montreal (Que.)	8,153	100.0	8,395	100.0	8,003	100.0	7,962	100.0	8,751	100.0
Good	5,370	65.9	5,433	64.7	6,527	81.6	5,438	68.3	6,577	75.2
Fair	2,299	28.2	2,366	28.2	1,416	17.7	2,039	25.6	1,992	22.8
Poor	484	5.9	596	7.1	60	0.7	485	6.1	182	2.1
Quebec (Que.)	8,743	100.0	8,517	100.0	8,560	100.0	8,650	100.0	8,624	100.0
Good	8,632	98.7	8,408	98.7	8,431	98.5	8,538	98.7	8,594	99.7
Fair	111	1.3	109	1.3	129	1.5	112	1.3	30	0.3
Poor	–	–	–	–	–	–	–	–	–	–
Ottawa (Ont.)	8,767	100.0	8,717	100.0	8,744	100.0	8,679	100.0	8,784	100.0
Good	7,566	86.3	6,440	73.9	7,223	82.6	7,678	88.5	7,604	86.6
Fair	1,108	12.6	2,107	24.2	1,362	15.6	967	11.1	1,156	13.2
Poor	93	1.1	170	2.0	159	1.8	34	0.3	24	0.3
Toronto (Ont.)	8,777	100.0	8,760	100.0	8,746	100.0	8,740	100.0	8,781	100.0
Good	6,524	74.3	6,054	69.1	6,712	76.7	6,789	77.7	7,697	87.7
Fair	2,090	23.8	2,429	27.7	1,994	22.8	1,862	21.3	1,081	12.3
Poor	163	1.9	277	3.2	40	0.5	89	1.0	3	–
Hamilton (Ont.)	8,776	100.0	8,746	100.0	8,760	100.0	8,737	100.0	8,264	100.0
Good	5,000	57.0	5,576	63.8	5,740	65.5	4,905	56.1	5,417	65.5
Fair	3,299	37.6	2,903	33.2	2,798	31.9	3,306	37.8	2,404	29.1
Poor	477	5.4	267	3.1	222	2.5	526	6.0	443	5.4
Winnipeg (Man.)	8,767	100.0	8,754	100.0	8,744	100.0	8,760	100.0	8,783	100.0
Good	8,076	92.1	7,924	90.5	8,705	99.6	8,500	97.0	8,466	96.4
Fair	687	7.8	823	9.4	39	0.4	260	3.0	262	3.0
Poor	4	–	7	0.1	–	–	–	–	55	0.6
Regina (Sask.)	8,784	100.0	8,758	100.0	8,675	100.0	8,724	100.0	8,778	100.0
Good	8,579	97.7	8,601	98.2	8,669	99.9	8,701	99.7	8,771	99.9
Fair	204	2.3	152	1.7	6	0.1	23	0.3	6	0.1
Poor	1	–	5	0.1	–	–	–	–	1	–
Edmonton (Alta.)	8,718	100.0	8,760	100.0	8,760	100.0	8,760	100.0	8,784	100.0
Good	7,553	86.6	7,908	90.3	7,934	90.6	7,042	80.4	7,405	84.3
Fair	1,091	12.5	803	9.2	799	9.1	1,650	18.8	1,260	14.3
Poor	74	0.8	49	0.6	27	0.3	68	0.8	119	1.4
Calgary (Alta.)	8,784	100.0	8,760	100.0	8,760	100.0	8,760	100.0	8,784	100.0
Good	7,742	88.1	8,130	92.8	8,484	96.8	8,314	94.9	8,533	97.1
Fair	969	11.0	623	7.1	267	3.0	401	4.6	251	2.9
Poor	73	0.8	7	0.1	9	0.2	45	0.5	–	–
Vancouver (B.C.)	8,784	100.0	8,759	100.0	8,646	100.0	8,760	100.0	8,784	100.0
Good	7,979	90.8	7,452	85.1	4,779	55.3	6,110	69.7	6,656	75.8
Fair	783	8.9	1,173	13.4	3,552	41.1	2,305	26.3	1,845	21.0
Poor	22	–	134	1.5	315	3.6	345	3.9	283	3.2

1. Air quality index numbers were taken from one representative Class 1 National Air Pollution Surveillance Network monitoring station.
2. Air quality index derived using 24-hour running average for coefficient of haze.
3. National Air Pollution Surveillance Network station closed for half the year in 1990.

Source: Environment Canada, *Air Quality Indicators Database*, 1993.

2.6 HOUSEHOLD ENVIRONMENTAL PRACTICES, 1994

	Canada	Nfld.	P.E.I.	N.S.	N.B.	Que.	Ont.	Man.	Sask.	Alta.	B.C.
						% of households					
Access to recycling programs											
Paper	69.6	19.7	20.8	50.3	46.7	57.2	83.5	61.0	69.3	71.2	74.5
Metal cans	67.2	21.3	16.7	47.6	69.8	48.9	82.3	61.0	77.3	72.2	69.6
Glass bottles	67.4	12.0	18.8	47.3	72.9	50.1	82.0	58.9	74.8	72.6	70.7
Plastics	62.8	18.6	16.7	42.5	61.2	49.5	77.7	61.0	73.7	66.2	55.7
Special disposal	40.2	3.3	10.4	12.0	12.2	41.8	45.9	29.0	34.9	56.9	32.2
Use of recycling programs[1]											
Paper	83.1	44.4	70.0	72.5	58.8	74.0	92.9	48.3	73.2	75.8	88.2
Metal cans	83.5	48.7	62.5	69.6	81.5	70.7	93.3	51.2	81.0	78.7	86.0
Glass bottles	83.5	40.9	66.7	68.8	82.8	70.9	93.3	46.2	81.1	78.8	86.1
Plastics	81.7	47.1	62.5	67.4	77.6	71.4	92.2	51.2	80.8	70.8	82.4
Special disposal	57.1	66.7	80.0	65.0	64.5	54.5	60.1	48.7	46.8	53.8	59.1
Use of disposable diapers[2]											
All of the time	76.9	92.3	100.0	68.2	82.4	81.9	79.0	70.4	62.5	67.1	73.2
Most of the time	9.5	7.7	--	13.6	5.9	10.2	7.6	7.4	12.5	11.8	13.4
Sometimes	11.1	--	--	--	--	--	11.3	--	25.0	19.7	12.2
Never	2.0	--	--	4.5	5.9	1.7	2.1	--	--	--	--
Children not in diapers	--	--	--	--	--	--	--	--	--	--	--
Regularly purchase paper towels or toilet paper made from recycled paper	58.3	68.3	56.3	65.7	66.3	60.7	59.9	48.6	49.3	51.5	53.9
Regularly take their own bag when shopping	24.4	4.4	12.5	14.8	22.7	17.6	25.4	35.0	32.7	31.3	31.1
Use a compost heap, compost container or composting service	22.7	9.3	16.7	19.0	16.1	7.9	30.3	18.1	21.6	21.2	37.9
Use chemical pesticides[3]	31.1	9.4	11.6	18.7	19.7	29.8	34.3	30.1	37.2	36.1	29.6
Use chemical fertilizer[3]	46.8	26.4	23.3	35.3	35.8	41.4	50.7	38.5	57.0	58.1	47.2
Have programmable thermostat[4]	16.0	5.6	6.7	9.4	9.1	9.7	23.6	14.9	10.2	15.1	15.3
Regularly lower temperature[5]	71.1	82.1	87.8	82.4	75.3	70.5	64.4	65.9	77.0	72.0	81.0
Use energy efficient compact fluorescent light bulbs	18.9	8.2	20.8	13.3	17.6	14.2	24.6	13.1	14.1	15.9	20.0
Have water-saving, low-flow or modified shower head	42.3	27.9	33.3	40.7	42.4	46.0	44.9	34.0	26.6	32.2	43.4
Have water-saving, low-volume toilet	14.8	6.0	6.3	12.7	11.4	8.7	18.0	19.4	12.5	20.6	15.9
Have water filter or purifier for drinking water	19.5	9.8	2.1	16.3	14.1	9.7	24.9	18.4	22.7	16.4	29.1
Purchase bottled water	21.9	8.7	6.3	18.1	16.9	33.4	19.6	13.4	8.9	15.3	19.9
Principal method of travel to work[6]											
Public transit	13.7	–	–	6.7	2.7	14.9	16.3	10.1	3.7	11.2	14.4
Motor vehicle as driver	78.8	79.3	85.7	80.0	82.7	76.6	79.7	78.5	80.4	80.3	77.8
Motor vehicle as passenger	10.6	18.5	17.9	16.9	17.3	9.6	10.0	13.4	11.0	9.5	10.7
Bicycle	2.3	--	--	--	--	2.0	1.9	5.3	4.1	2.4	3.7
Walk only	7.8	12.0	–	8.7	6.7	8.5	6.3	11.3	11.4	7.4	8.7
Other	0.3	--	--	--	--	--	--	--	--	--	--
Not ascertained	5.8	5.4	--	6.7	6.7	6.2	5.5	5.3	7.3	6.3	5.2

1. Percentage calculated among households with access to each type of program.
2. Percentage calculated among households with children under 2 years old.
3. Percentage calculated among households with a lawn, yard or garden.
4. Percentage calculated among households with thermostats.
5. Percentage calculated among households with thermostats, excluding households with programmable thermostats.
6. Percentage calculated among households where at least one member worked outside the home.

Source: Statistics Canada, *Household Environment Survey*, Catalogue no. 11-526.

2.7 WATER USE

		Water withdrawals						
		Total water withdrawals	Agriculture	Mining	Manufacturing	Thermal power	Municipal	Water consumption
		Cubic metres (millions)						
Canada	1981	37,254	3,125	648	9,937	19,281	4,263	3,892
	1986	42,217	3,559	593	7,984	25,364	4,717	4,279
	1991	45,095	3,991	363	7,282	28,357	5,102	5,367
Atlantic Provinces	1981	2,882	12	86	640	1,837	307	127
	1986	4,012	13	212	958	2,490	339	193
	1991	3,175	15	77	601	2,126	356	118
Quebec	1981	4,185	82	107	2,319	308	1,369	416
	1986	4,132	89	52	1,521	986	1,484	387
	1991	4,498	100	74	1,616	1,005	1,703	383
Ontario	1981	21,066	148	124	4,414	14,930	1,450	715
	1986	25,598	166	100	3,763	19,967	1,602	794
	1991	28,485	186	87	3,457	23,095	1,660	512
Prairie Provinces	1981	5,342	2,338	197	382	1,846	579	1,981
	1986	5,729	2,688	142	357	1,867	675	2,254
	1991	6,221	3,014	50	447	2,025	685	3,630
British Columbia[1]	1981	3,779	545	134	2,182	360	558	653
	1986	2,746	603	87	1,385	54	617	651
	1991	2,716	676	75	1,161	106	698	724

1. Includes the Yukon and Northwest Territories.

Source: Environment Canada, Water and Habitat Conservation Branch.

2.8 REFORESTATION

	1990		1991		1992		1993	
	Seeded	Seedlings	Seeded	Seedlings	Seeded	Seedlings	Seeded	Seedlings
	Hectares							
Canada	36,838	473,990	43,086	470,698	31,462	435,452	34,296	417,669
Newfoundland	–	3,548	–	2,891	120	3,411	–	2,790
Prince Edward Island	–	833	–	1,032	–	1,161	–	1,227
Nova Scotia	–	11,255	–	8,198	–	7,502	–	5,213
New Brunswick	69	22,079	32	19,497	–	16,526	–	13,089
Quebec	96	108,292	44	108,051	120	98,772	65	85,983
Ontario	27,021	80,840	36,710	83,917	24,466	71,792	28,000	73,684
Manitoba	5	6,277	2	8,039	–	7,142	13	5,646
Saskatchewan	645	5,367	–	6,545	–	6,403	60	6,619
Alberta	9,002	26,251	6,298	33,065	6,754	37,766	6,158	33,008
British Columbia	–	209,168	–	199,422	–	184,922	–	190,176
Yukon	–	–	–	–	–	–	–	174
Northwest Territories	–	80	–	41	2	55	–	60

Source: Statistics Canada, CANSIM, matrix 6089.

2.9 FOREST AREA, 1991

	Total inventoried forest land[1]	Timber productive forest land	Timber productive forest land[2]				Unclassified
			Provincial	Territorial	Private	Federal	
	km² ('000)						
Canada	4,175.8	2,445.7	1,944.3	193.5	242.5	62.4	3.0
Newfoundland	225.2	112.7	110.2	–	1.9	0.6	–
Prince Edward Island	3.0	2.8	0.2	–	2.6	–	–
Nova Scotia	39.2	37.7	10.3	–	26.2	1.1	–
New Brunswick	61.1	59.5	28.9	–	30.0	0.7	–
Quebec	839.0	539.9	459.1	–	77.7	3.1	–
Ontario	580.0	422.0	363.5	–	55.4	2.7	0.5
Manitoba	262.8	152.4	138.2	–	10.8	3.4	–
Saskatchewan	288.1	126.3	117.8	–	3.9	4.6	–
Alberta	382.1	257.1	224.6	–	12.8	17.0	2.5
British Columbia	605.6	517.4	491.5	–	21.2	4.7	X
Yukon	275.5	74.7	–	74.0	–	0.7	–
Northwest Territories	614.4	143.2	–	119.5	–	23.7	–

1. Land primarily intended for growing, or currently supporting forest. Includes productive forest land and reserved forest land not available by law for production.
2. Productive forest land available for growing and harvesting forest crops.

Source: Statistics Canada, CANSIM, matrix 6076.

2.10 FOREST FIRES, 1993

	Forest fires				Forest land burned			
	Total forest fires	Due to human activities	Due to lightning	Due to unknown cause	Total forest land burned	Due to human activities	Due to lightning	Due to unknown cause
	Number				Hectares			
Canada	5,848	3,470	2,229	149	1,967,388	168,319	1,797,730	1,339
Newfoundland	83	58	25	–	26,998	82	26,916	–
Prince Edward Island	29	23	–	6	87	78	–	9
Nova Scotia	317	303	3	11	368	363	3	2
New Brunswick	234	181	31	22	668	324	324	20
Quebec	543	429	111	3	128,234	1,047	127,172	15
Ontario	743	563	163	17	104,705	9,056	95,609	40
Manitoba	239	154	68	17	67,275	2,195	64,158	922
Saskatchewan	646	463	183	–	660,565	149,063	511,502	–
Alberta	848	309	517	22	25,633	1,143	24,461	29
British Columbia	1,497	842	609	46	5,183	3,103	1,783	297
Yukon	137	62	75	x	86,116	57	86,059	x
Northwest Territories	469	63	402	4	858,557	87	858,465	5
National parks	63	20	42	1	2,999	1,721	1,278	–

Source: Statistics Canada, CANSIM, matrix 6081.

2.11 SPECIES EXTINCT OR AT RISK, 1995

	Mammals	Birds	Fish and marine mammals	Reptiles and amphibians	Plants
Extinct[1]	Caribou, Woodland (Queen Charlotte Islands population) Mink, Sea	Auk, Great Duck, Labrador Pigeon, Passenger	Cisco, Deepwater Cisco, Longjaw Dace, Banff Longnose Walleye, Blue		
Extirpated[2]	Bear, Grizzly (Prairie population) Ferret, Black-footed Fox, Swift	Prairie-Chicken, Greater	Chub, Gravel Paddlefish Walrus, Atlantic (Northwest Atlantic population) Whale, Gray (Atlantic population)	Lizard, Pygmy Short-horned	Blue-eyed Mary Trefoil, Illinois Tick
Endangered[3]	Caribou, Peary (Banks Island and High Arctic populations) Cougar (Eastern population) Marmot, Vancouver Island Wolverine (Eastern population)	Bobwhite, Northern Crane, Whooping Curlew, Eskimo Duck, Harlequin (Eastern population) Falcon, *Anatum* Peregrine Flycatcher, Acadian Owl, Burrowing Owl, Spotted Plover, Mountain Plover, Piping Rail, King Shrike, Loggerhead (Eastern population) Sparrow, Henslow's Thrasher, Sage Warbler, Kirtland's	Otter, Sea Sucker, Salish Whale, Beluga (St. Lawrence River, Ungava Bay and Southeast Baffin Island – Cumberland Sound populations) Trout, Aurora Whale, Bowhead (Eastern and Western Arctic populations) Whale, Right Whitefish, Acadian	Frog, Blanchard's Cricket Snake, Blue Racer Snake, Lake Erie Water Turtle, Leatherback	Agalinis, Gattinger's Agalinis, Skinner's Cactus, Eastern Prickly Pear Clover, Slender Bush Coreopsis, Pink Fern, Southern Maidenhair Gentian, White Prairie Lady's-slipper, Small White Lousewort, Furbish's Milkwort, Pink Mint, Hoary Mountain Mountain Avens, Eastern Mouse-ear-cress, Slender Orchid, Western Prairie White Fringed Plantain, Heart-leaved Pogonia, Large Whorled Pogonia, Small Whorled Poppy, Wood Quillwort, Engelmann's Sundew, Thread-leaved Tree, Cucumber Water-pennywort Wintergreen, Spotted
Threatened[4]	Bison, Wood Caribou, Peary (Low Arctic population) Caribou, Woodland (Gaspé population) Marten (Newfoundland population) Shrew, Pacific Water	Chat, Yellow-breasted (B.C. population) Murrelet, Marbled Shrike, Loggerhead (Prairie population) Sparrow, Baird's Tern, Roseate Warbler, Hooded Woodpecker, White-headed	Beluga (Eastern Hudson Bay population) Cisco, Blackfin Cisco, Shortjaw Cisco, Shortnose Darter, Channel Darter, Eastern Sand Madtom, Margined Porpoise, Harbour (Northwest Atlantic population) Redhorse, Black Redhorse, Copper Sculpin, Great Lakes Deepwater Sculpin, Shorthead Stickleback, Enos Lake Whale, Humpback (North Pacific population) Whitefish, Lake Simcoe	Rattlesnake, Eastern Massasauga Turtle, Blanding's (Nova Scotia population) Turtle, Spiny Softshell	Ash, Blue Aster, Anticosti Aster, White Wood Bluehearts Chestnut, American Colicroot Deerberry Fern, Mosquito Flag, Western Blue Gentian, Plymouth Ginseng, American Golden Crest Golden Seal Greenbrier, Carolinean Helleborine, Giant Jacob's Ladder, van Brunt's Lipocarpha, Small-flowered Mulberry, Red Paintbrush, Golden Pepperbush, Sweet Pogonia, Nodding Redroot Spiderwort, Western Thistle, Pitcher's Thrift, Athabasca Coffee-tree, Kentucky Coffee Twayblade, Purple Verbena, Sand Violet, Bird's-foot Violet, Yellow Montane Water-willow, American Willow, Tyrrell's Woodsia, Blunt-lobed

1. Any species that no longer exists.
2. Any species no longer existing in the wild in Canada, but occurring elsewhere.
3. Any species facing imminent extirpation or extinction.
4. Any species likely to become endangered if limiting factors are not reversed.

Source: Environment Canada, Canadian Wildlife Service.

SECTION 2

THE PEOPLE

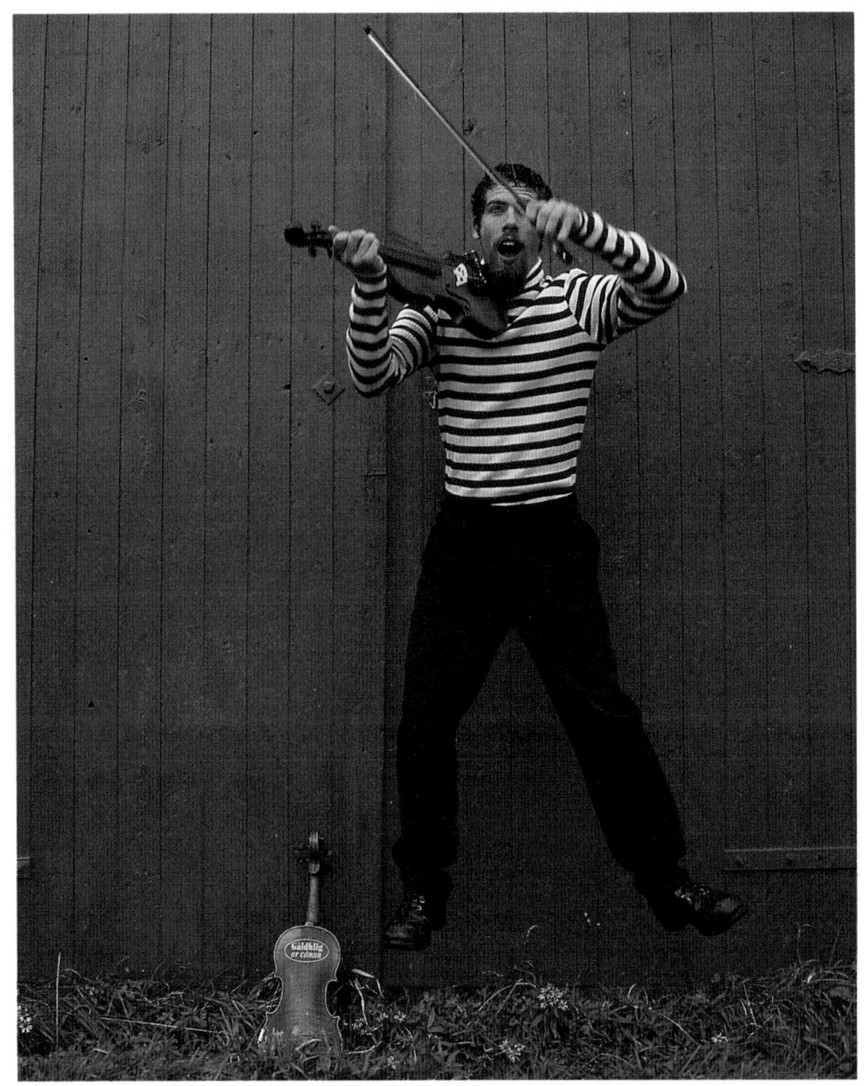

PHOTO BY **DAVID TRATTLES**

Chapter 3

THE POPULATION

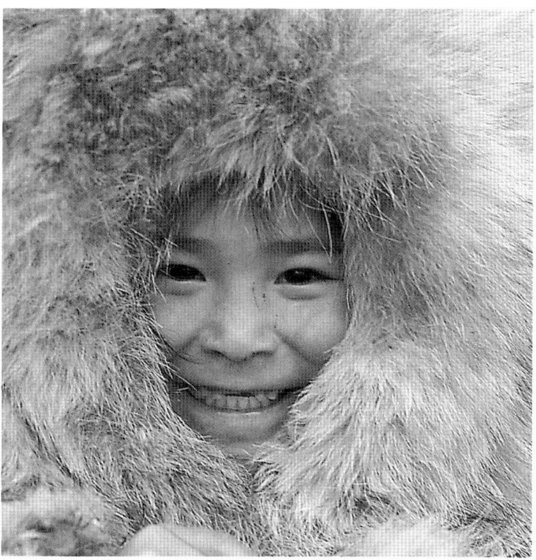
Photo by Mike Beedell

In a 1906 speech to Toronto's Empire Club, famous author and humorist Stephen Leacock predicted that the "little people" of Canada would grow to "...10 millions tomorrow, twenty millions in our children's time and a hundred millions yet ere the century runs out."

While his numbers were ambitious—the hundred million haven't materialized—Leacock would nonetheless have been pleased at his own prescience: today, we rank in the top one-fifth of the world in terms of population size. The United Nations lists more than 200 countries in the world with fewer people than Canada.

We share the top quintile, however, with some of the most populated countries on earth. This makes for some humbling comparisons: with its 1.2 billion citizens in 1993, China's population—the largest on earth—is about 41 times larger than ours. India's population also dwarfs ours: with about 900 million people, its population is 31 times larger than Canada's.

Still, Leacock would be proud. When Queen Victoria signed the British North America Act on March 29, 1867—clearing the way for the July 1 proclamation that brought Canada into being that same year—Canada's entire population numbered only 3.4 million souls, about the count in Montreal today. One hundred and twenty-eight years later, we'd grown to almost nine times that size: on July 1, 1995, Canada's population reached 29,606,100, nearly 30 million people.

Breathing Space

While this does not make us a population giant, we do have plenty of breathing room: we are one of the most spacious nations in the world. If we were to spread out evenly across the ten million square kilometres of Canadian soil, every three of us would share a square kilometre of land. That's a lot of breathing space, compared with some of the most densely populated places in the world. In Hong Kong, the most crowded spot on the planet, there are 5,506 people per square kilometre and in Singapore, 4,650 people per square kilometre.

Far from being spread out evenly across this vast space, as Russian poet Andrei Vosnesensky once observed, we have settled along the southern border with the United States "like a layer of cream on a jug of milk." In this layer, the vast majority of Canadians live, concentrated heavily in the urban areas.

Indeed in 1995, three-fifths of us (more than 18 million people) inhabited the 25 largest census-metropolitan regions in the country. Here, populations can be very dense, especially in the neighbourhoods of the biggest cities: in Montreal, the Montreal North area contained more than 7,753 people per square kilometre in 1991. Outside Toronto, the Markham region housed 727 people in a square kilometre.

Yet, in some parts of the country, the population spreads out in a thin layer. In Canada's North, neither Yukon nor the Northwest Territories has a population larger than a small city. In 1995, Yukon had just over 30,000 people; the Northwest Territories had almost 66,000, and this is in an area that covers more than 40% of the land mass of Canada.

Historical Perspectives

Since before Confederation, Canada's population has been moving from the high birth and death rates of the past towards the low birth and death rates of the present. As breakthroughs in medicine, improvements in sanitation and public health, and better living conditions have arrived, there have been fewer infant deaths and because of that, life expectancy has increased. In 1921, life expectancy at birth was only 59 years of age for men and 61 years for women. Today, most Canadians can expect to live to a ripe old age: life expectancy at birth is about 73 years of age for infant boys, and 80 years for baby girls.

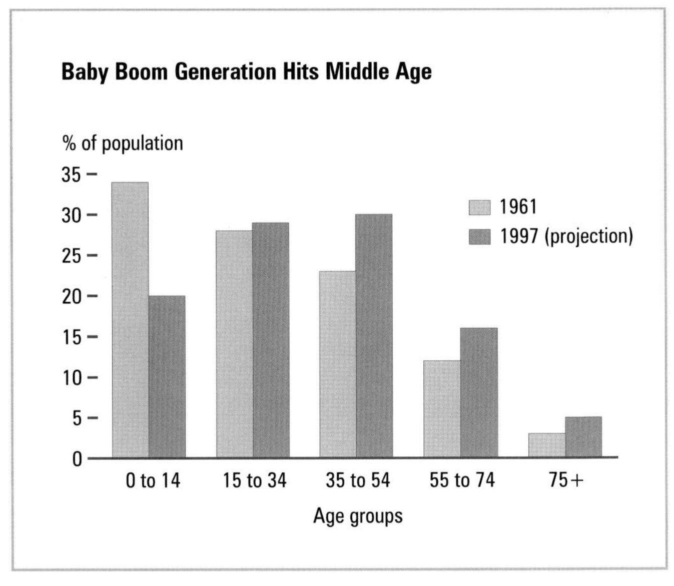

Large families were common in Canada's early history—in 1851, a woman could be expected to have an average of seven children in her lifetime. But by Confederation in 1867, with an increasingly urban and industrialized society, the total fertility rate (the average number of children born to each woman of childbearing age) began to drop. This decline continued into the 20th century, with a particularly significant dip during the Great Depression of the 1930s.

When the economy revived in the 1940s, this trend was suddenly reversed by the huge "baby boom." As a result, more than 8 million children were born in Canada in 20 years (1946 to 1966), compared with only five million in the two decades between 1926 and 1946. By 1959, the fertility rate had reached the all-time high of 4.0 children per woman.

Afterwards, the decline in fertility resumed. Since the mid-1970s, however, our total fertility rates have been low but stable, with an average of less than two children per woman.

First World Problems

Today, we belong to the group of more slowly-growing countries in the world, lagging far behind most of the developing populations. Compared with the growth rate of other industrialized nations, however, we are the front-runner. Canada's average annual growth rate between 1991 and 1994 was 1.3%. Meanwhile, Australia grew about 1%, and Europe and Japan increased their populations by less than 0.5% in the same period.

Our low fertility rate indicates that we aren't giving birth to enough children to replace our population. To do so would require that Canadian women have an average of 2.1 children each in their lifetimes, the so-called replacement level. Since 1981, however, the total fertility rate has been below 2.0, a rate that is lower than that of the United States, but slightly higher than those of Japan and most European countries.

A New Stage

Canada is aging. Every year, the ranks of older Canadians become a bigger and bigger percentage of our population as the pool of young people shrinks. Decades of low fertility and our increased life expectancy have tilted the Canadian population in a direction that will continue until well into the next century. By 1993, there were already 3.4 million seniors in Canada, a number that is projected to reach up to 6.3 million by 2016, and triple to between nine and 11 million by 2041.

Some parts of Canada are further along this road than others. In 1994, half the population of Quebec had passed the age of 35, making Quebec the oldest provincial population in Canada. Meanwhile, the tiny population of the Northwest Territories is the youngest in the country: half its population was only 25 years of age and younger in 1994.

In the first few decades of the 21st century, there will be a seniors' boom. One-third of our current population—of which there are 8 million baby boomers—are entering middle age, and the oldest will start turning 65 shortly after the year 2010.

Population Profile

Canada's population clock ticks slowly but constantly. We're a population in perpetual motion. On a typical day in 1995, an average of 1,050 babies were born, 573 immigrants arrived from other lands and 61 Canadians returned home from overseas.

On the same typical day, an average 583 people died, and 127 Canadians emigrated to another country. Altogether, when the dust had settled—including the departure of non-permanent residents—the population had grown by 1,089 individuals, in just one day.

By the middle of 1996, Canada's population was projected to have reached 30 million people. To put that into perspective, the capital of Mexico, a country the size of the three Prairie provinces, will likely have a population of 25.6 million people by the year 2000. In recent years, other countries to reach the 30 million mark have been Argentina (34.1 million) and Colombia (34.5 million).

Canada's population continues to age. Between 1996 and 2000, some 1.3 million Canadians will turn 60 years of age, another 1.2 million will turn 65, and 350,000 will celebrate an 85th birthday.

Photo by Susie King

Saukrates, Hip Hop artist/musician, Toronto, 1995.

Canadian demographers tell us that the aging of the population will have inevitable impacts on governments, markets and services. In 1996, for example, the first wave of boomers started turning 50. While nobody knows for certain, the economist David Foot has predicted that the passage of this generation will drive up the value of stocks, cause a drop in housing prices, escalate the value of summer cottages and cause an increase in such pursuits as golfing, bird watching, gardening, curling, darts, walking and hiking.

"Grey Power"

In late 1995, an eager crowd of Ottawa business people, managers and planners flocked to a conference—billed as "Your road map to the future"—to listen to Canadian demographers outline their projections for the region's economy.

As our population ages, some Canadians see the future as an irresistible, and potentially profitable, gamble. Anticipating changes in demands for products and services, forecasters and financial advisers are placing their bets on industries such as eyeware companies, investment firms and pharmaceutical companies that will cater to the needs of an aging population.

Television executives, famous for keeping a close eye on the "demographics," have now been joined by business owners and managers, government officials and urban planners who are scrambling to consult the demographic crystal ball, looking for information to prepare themselves for the opportunities and challenges of a new age and stage of Canada's population.

How Canada Grows

As our population becomes bigger and proportionately older, the number of deaths each year has been rising. In 1995, more than 212,000 people died, the highest number of deaths ever recorded in a single year in Canada. With the age shift that is now under way, a mere 35 years from now there will probably be more deaths than there are births each year, if the fertility rate stays at its current level.

SENIOR STATS

Share of men in 1991 aged 75 and older who were married: two-thirds.

Share of women the same age who were widowed: two-thirds.

Likelihood that a woman aged 75 or older was living alone in 1991, compared with a man of the same age: four times greater.

Percentage of women aged 75 and over who were living alone in 1971: 26%.

Percentage of all women who were living alone in 1991: 39%.

Percentage of all women who will likely be living alone in 2011: 42%.

Percentage of seniors aged 75 and over in 1991 who lived in a dwelling they owned: 56%.

Percentage of these seniors who still owed money on their mortgage: 4%.

Share of older seniors in 1991 receiving benefits from government pensions, including Old Age Security: 92%.

Percentage of seniors aged 75 and older in 1990 who said their incomes and investments satisfied their current needs adequately or very well: 85%.

Percentage of seniors aged 75 and older with incomes under $10,000 who said in 1990 that they were very satisfied with their lives as a whole: 45%.

Percentage with incomes of $40,000 and over who said the same thing: 45%.

"Goodbye God, I'm going to Canada."

These rather poignant words of farewell came from a little girl who crossed the border from the United States into Canada in the 1930s. Altogether, from 1851 to 1991, some 12.5 million immigrants came to Canada. Annual numbers of new arrivals have fluctuated dramatically over the years—down to barely a trickle during the Depression and the Second World War—but the stream of people has never stopped. Historically, immigrants' children, and not the waves of immigrants themselves, have populated Canada.

But this is changing. In 1993-94, natural increase (births minus deaths) contributed to the lowest level population growth in two decades. The number of immigrants who arrive each year now plays a much more important role in our population growth.

Border Crossings

Throughout Canada's history, the flow of human traffic has moved ceaselessly back and forth across our borders. Indeed, as John Porter pointed out in *The Vertical Mosaic*, "It is unlikely that any other society has resembled a huge demographic railway station as much as has the non-French part of Canada."

In the 19th and early 20th centuries in particular, many new arrivals used Canada as a stopover, usually on their way to the United States. Indeed, in the decades between 1860 and 1900, emigrants—many heading for the United States—outnumbered immigrants by 100,000 or more.

Until 1965, when the United States first imposed immigration quotas on Canada, as it already had on other nations, the flow of people over the border from Canada into the United States was relatively unimpeded. Since then, the numbers who head for the United States or elsewhere have fluctuated, but have never again matched the 2.8 million residents who left Canada between 1901 and 1931. Altogether, in the 140 years between 1851 and 1991, almost eight million people, including many who had immigrated here, left Canada.

While it's difficult to know the exact numbers, some have estimated that, in 1980, one million Canadian-born people were living outside Canada. Most were concentrated in the United States (84%); some settled in the United Kingdom (6%) and others were scattered all over the world (10%).

Certainly, Canada is a study in famous expatriates. Many high-profile Canadians, such as singers Robbie Robertson and Joni Mitchell and hockey player Wayne Gretzky, have left, heading mostly to the United States. Writer Anne Hébert now makes her home in France.

Fortunately, not everyone who leaves stays away. Many emigrants eventually make their way back to Canada. Between 1992 and 1993, 22,728 Canadians returned home.

Taking Stock

Canadians seem to like a change of scenery. We have always been unapologetic movers: for example, almost half of all Canadians changed their addresses in the five years between 1986 and 1991. After slowing the pace somewhat in the early 1990s, Canadians resumed moving when 341,863 of us picked up stakes and moved to another province or territory, the highest number in more than a decade.

This revolving door of movement tends to be tied to economic realities. When jobs and opportunities are hard to come by in one region, Canadians often hit the road in search of better luck elsewhere. From the late 1970s to the early 1980s, Alberta's buoyant oil boom economy drew thousands of Canadians to the province. A few years later, oil prices nose-dived and unemployment rose, and a wave of migrants began to leave the province.

Generally speaking, when Canadians change provinces or territories, they head west. As a result, Ontario, British Columbia and Alberta have steadily increased their population share, while the share of Canada's eastern provinces has declined, decade after decade.

British Columbia has become a magnet for Canadian migrants. Between 1993 and 1994, once the arrivals and departures had been tallied, the province had won the interprovincial migration stakes with 37,871 new residents.

Rural Nirvanas

Despite the call of the big city, more than six million Canadians were living in rural areas in 1991. Some lived on the edge of the urban frontier, nestled next to or inside a city boundary. Others made their homes in the areas that have been dubbed "rural nirvanas," sections of countryside within easy reach of the large towns and cities, where droves of young city dwellers have sought refuge in recent years.

In those rural communities that still rely primarily on agriculture, however, populations have usually either stopped growing or are declining. In resource-rich regions, people live in towns that rely on mining, oil exploration and drilling, or forestry for survival. In Atlantic Canada, where the main source of income is the fishery, rural dwellers face low incomes and high unemployment.

Open Doors

Today more than ever, Canadians weigh the pros and cons of immigration: it's clear that newcomers have helped build this country—and their numbers help keep the population growing—but there are ongoing debates about the economic and social impact of immigration, and about how wide open our doors should be.

For many reasons (humanitarian, economic, political) immigration into Canada has always been a series of ups and downs, with fluctuating, "tap open, tap closed" cycles. We reached a low in the mid-1980s—about 84,000 immigrants came to Canada in 1985—and an important high in the early 1990s, when Canada was welcoming about 220,000 new arrivals a year. At the same time, opinion polls were showing that Canadians seemed less and less enthusiastic about the high immigration levels, partly due to concerns about unemployment.

Recently, we've started to make major changes to our immigration policy. For 1995, the federal government dropped its annual target to between 190,000 and 215,000 immigrants.

Downtown Canada

Since the end of the Second World War, Canada's big urban centres have acted as magnets, drawing people into their networks of streets and highways, traffic lights and construction zones.

Urban centres beckon the Canadian-born and immigrants alike. In fact, the growth in Canada's urban areas outpaces that of the country as a whole. In the Toronto area, the population doubled in the thirty years between 1961 and 1991. In 1995, its population reached 4,338,374. In the same year, three other Canadian metropolitan centres also passed the one million mark: Montreal, Vancouver and Ottawa–Hull.

Part of this growth has been due to immigration. In 1992-93, some 97,000 immigrants settled in Toronto, 34,000 in Vancouver, and 17,000 in Ottawa–Hull (all figures that have doubled since 1988-89). In the same year, 38,300 newcomers arrived in Montreal.

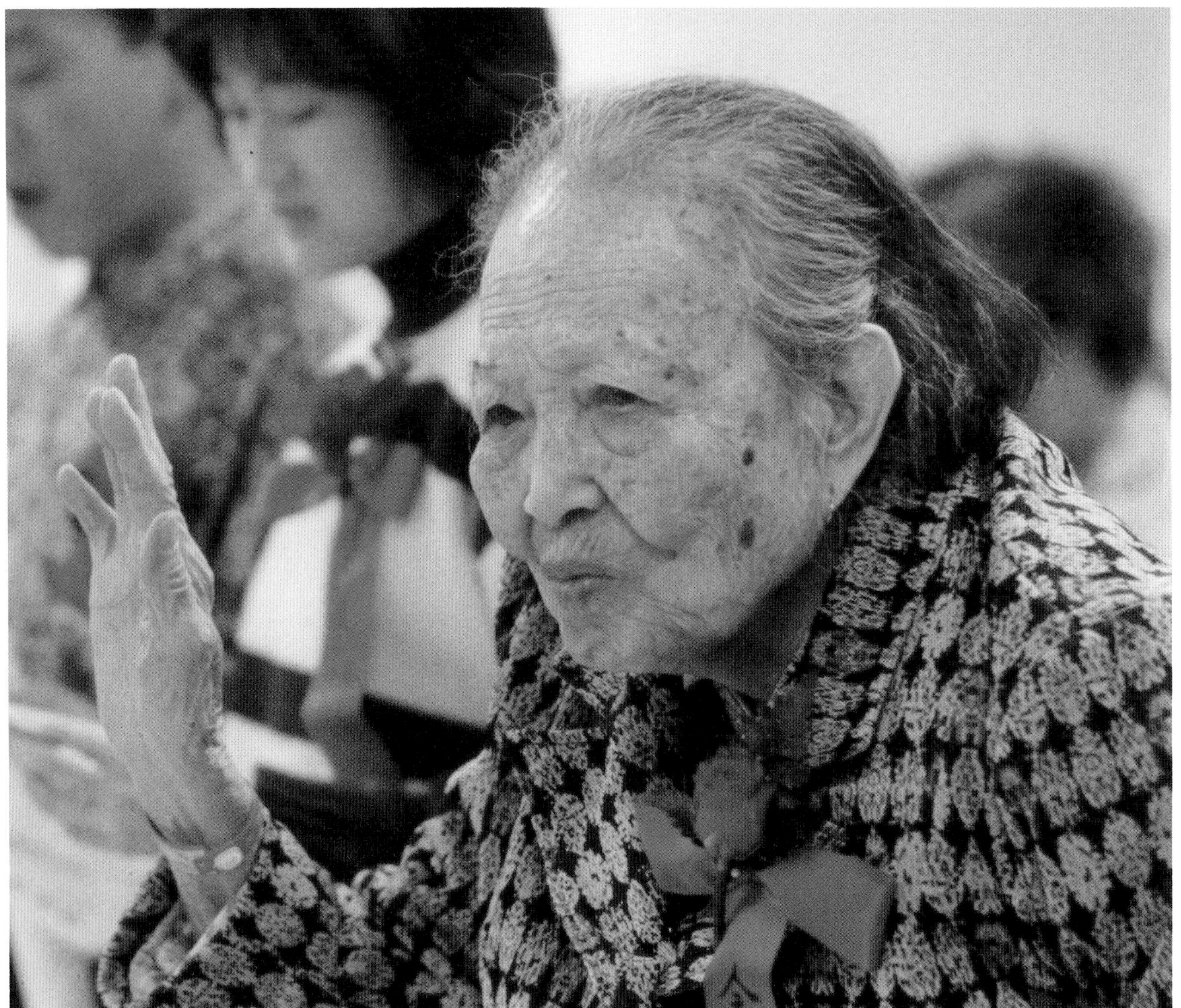

Pierre Obendrauf, CANAPRESS Photo Service

A new citizen sings O Canada.

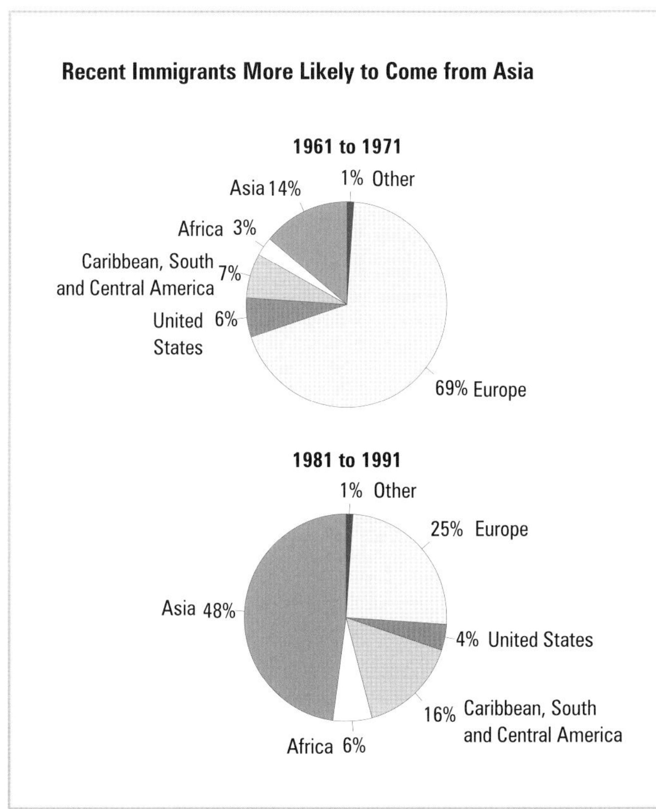

Then, for 1996, planned levels of immigration were increased slightly to between 195,000 and 225,000. By 1994, the total number of new arrivals had already gone down: just over 217,000 new arrivals came to Canada in 1994, down 37,000 from the previous year. This was the first such drop since 1985.

There are also new rules. Everyone who becomes a permanent resident of Canada must now pay a $975 Right-of-Landing Fee (some immigrants will be eligible for a loan to cover the cost). The long-term strategy is to try to attract more "economic" immigrants, including skilled workers and business immigrants, to Canada.

In its Immigration Plan 1994, the government described new selection criteria that will focus on applicants' language, education, work experience and their "adaptability to a changing labour market." According to Citizenship and Immigration Canada, by the year 2000 more than half of all immigrants to Canada may be economic immigrants.

There is no such thing as a "typical" immigrant. Canada welcomes three diverse categories of people. "Family class" immigrants includes spouses, dependent children, parents and grandparents who join relatives already settled in Canada. "Refugees" includes those who come into Canada and apply for safe haven, as well as people brought to Canada by the federal government and/or private sponsors, such as churches. "Economic" immigrants includes independents: that is, skilled workers and assisted relatives (and their dependents), live-in care-givers and retirees. This category also includes business immigrants (entrepreneurs, investors and others) and their families.

Today, Canada welcomes newcomers from a wider spectrum of countries than ever before. In 1994, people arrived from some 200 different countries, including countries that did not exist in past decades.

Today, only about one-fifth of all newcomers come from Europe and the United States, and about half come from Asia. The largest groups—almost half (42.6%) of all immigrants in 1994—came from Hong Kong (44,089), the Philippines (18,910), India (17,137) and China (12,427). Mid-sized groups of between 1,000 and 8,000 arrived from more than 30 different nations. From some places, however, the flow was barely a trickle: in 1994, we welcomed only one person each from countries such as Bhutan, Mongolia, Tibet and Reunion.

Between 1961 and 1971, 75% of Canada's immigrants came from Europe and the United States. In the 1960s, the immigration laws were changed. As a result, Canada welcomes people from all over the world, and more and more newcomers have arrived from Asia, the Middle East, the Caribbean, and Central and South America.

Canada is proud of its humanitarian reputation. Since the Second World War, we have welcomed more than 700,000 refugees to this country. We continue to be one of the more welcoming countries in the world. In 1994, more than 15,000 people who applied for refugee status were accepted.

Sicilian or Italian?

Today, Canadian ancestral roots reach around the globe. The 1991 Census identified more than 100 ethnic groups in Canada, defining ethnic origin as one's "roots," or the ethnic background of one's ancestors. This should not be confused with citizenship, nationality or language.

But ethnicity is still an elusive concept; it can depend on how long one has lived in this country, how many ancestries crop up in one's background, how much one knows about family history, and how one feels about policies such as multiculturalism, official bilingualism, or problems of racism and discrimination.

Certainly, many of us have more than one ethnic identity: in 1991, over one-quarter (29%) of all Canadians (almost eight million people) reported more than one ethnic origin.

One thing is certain: the ethnic make-up of Canada's population is changing. Although British and French ancestors are still the most common—more than half of all Canadians reported either British or French ancestry or a combination of the two in 1991—almost one-third of the population reported origins other than British or French, up from only one-quarter of the population in 1986.

In 1991, the "top ten" single ethnic backgrounds reported in Canada included French, British, German, Canadian, Italian, Chinese, Aboriginal, Ukrainian, Dutch and East Indian. More recent groups included Somali, Ethiopian, Guyanese, Guatemalan, Nicaraguan, Uruguayan, Hispanic, Salvadorean, Colombian, Kurdish and Ghanaian.

Canada's ethnic map still reflects some of the immigration and settlement patterns of earlier eras. In 1991, the Atlantic provinces had the highest proportion of British-only origins (62%). Not surprisingly, Quebec had the highest percentage of French-only ancestry (75%). Apart from the Northwest Territories, the Prairie provinces were home to the highest proportion of persons with neither British nor French origins: almost half (44%) of the population.

More recent immigration patterns show up, too. Ontario now includes some of the largest ethnic communities in Canada. More than half of all those who reported single West Asian, South Asian, African or Caribbean origins live in the province.

The largest Arab and Haitian communities in Canada live in Quebec, while British Columbia now includes the highest proportion of people with Asian origins (although Ontario's Asian population is still larger in terms of sheer numbers with 723,395 people in Ontario reporting single Asian origins in 1991). Of course, not all members of these groups are recent arrivals: many of Canada's ethnic communities trace their roots back many generations in Canada.

Languages of Choice

For a former Canadian Prime Minister, Louis St. Laurent, bilingualism was something he just took for granted, especially as a youngster: "I didn't know at first that there were two languages in Canada. I just thought that there was one way to speak to my father and another to speak to my mother." For most members of the two largest ethnic groups in Canada, English and French are not just languages, they are a powerful blend of identity and history.

Canada recognizes two official languages. However, the debate about this policy continues. Some Canadians worry about the costs (the Official Languages Program in federal institutions cost $584.8 million in 1993–94). Many francophones worry about the survival of their language. Many Canadians believe having two official languages in Canada is essential.

Meanwhile, the number of bilingual Canadians has risen in every province. By 1991, more than four million Canadians (16% of the population) could conduct a conversation in both French and English, an increase of 1.5 million in 20 years. This is a 52% growth rate for bilingual Canadians, almost double the growth rate for the Canadian population (28%). The ranks of bilingual Canadians included about 2.6 million francophones (58%), 1.4 million anglophones (31%) and 466,580 allophones (11% of those whose first language is

*The familiar flip through Canada's Yellow Pages now takes place with a difference in Toronto. The Yellow Pages there are available in Chinese. Released in 1995, **Wong Yip**, as Toronto's Chinese version is called, targets the city's growing Chinese population, and recognizes a group among the large number of Canadians whose mother tongue is neither English nor French.*

Chinese is growing rapidly in Canada. Between 1971 and 1991, the number of Canadians who reported Chinese as their mother tongue doubled, then tripled, and finally quintupled. At the time of the 1991 Census, 586,000 people who reported Chinese as their mother tongue were living in Canada. Between 1989 and 1992, more than 150,000 Chinese—about 411 a day—arrived in Canada from mainland China and Hong Kong.

*The Chinese Yellow Pages is a project shared by **Ming Pao News**, a Chinese daily newspaper published in Canada, and Tele-Direct, the publisher of the Yellow Pages.*

*Altogether, **Wong Yip** runs to about 370 pages, and is distributed to Chinese-speaking households and businesses in the greater Metro Toronto area—about 75,000 in all.*

***Wong Yip** is simply one example of the growing Chinese presence in Canada. **Maclean's**, a national news magazine, launched a Chinese edition in Vancouver in 1995. Other publishers have launched Chinese-language magazines in recent years. **Ming Pao**, **Sing Tao** and **The World Journal** are all Chinese-language newspapers published in Canada. In addition, if you live in Vancouver or Toronto, you can tune into Chinese television programs, both news and entertainment.*

This commercial awareness of Chinese reflects a basic fact about the changing mosaic we call Canada. A growing proportion of the Canadian population—8.4% in 1991—speaks a primary language other than English or French. There is also a proportion of the population (about 308,500 Canadians in 1991) that speaks neither language. In this group, the number of people with Chinese, Spanish and Punjabi mother tongue languages has increased.

neither English nor French). There are signs that Canadians value the richness of both languages.

In a 1994 poll, 64% of Canadians made it clear that they supported Canada's two official languages, and 57% said Canada's official languages policy was worth preserving. On the eve of the Quebec referendum, an opinion poll suggested that 40% of Canadians outside Quebec wanted to keep Canada bilingual, regardless of the outcome of the vote.

For French-speaking Canadians, as well as others, support for bilingualism is based on concern for the survival of the French language in Canada. In 1991, about 85% of all francophones in Canada (some 5.6 million people) lived in Quebec, the historic centre of French Canada. Here, francophones have consistently dominated in terms of population (about 79%) for the past 40 years, while the number of anglophones has dropped.

Although the majority of Quebec's allophone population has, until recently, tended to adopt English as its home language, there are signs of a change: two-thirds of those who have arrived since the mid-1970s now speak French at home rather than English. The shift may be due to Quebec's French language law, Bill 101, its education requirements for immigrant children, and the province's control over immigration.

In 1991, there were almost one million francophones living outside Quebec. Of these, almost one-third (about 300,000 Canadians) lived in the Atlantic provinces, with the majority concentrated in New Brunswick. Another half a million francophones make their homes in Ontario, mostly in the eastern and northern areas of the province. Manitoba and the other provinces also have vibrant francophone communities within their borders.

For these Canadians, however, it's an ongoing challenge to keep their language alive: in 1991, 35% of francophones living outside Quebec reported that they spoke English at home more often than they did French.

Even though federal government services are supposed to be available in French wherever numbers warrant, a 1994 study by Canada's Commissioner of Official Languages suggests francophones living outside Quebec can't always get government services in French. According to the report, "It is time for federal institutions once and for all to clean up their act."

Languages of the World

Canadians can speak over 100 of the world's estimated more than 5,000 living languages. Our diversity isn't surprising considering more than four million Canadians reported a mother tongue other than English or French in 1991. The largest groups included those whose first language was Italian, Chinese, German, Portuguese, Ukrainian, Polish, Spanish, Punjabi, Dutch or Greek.

Changing immigration patterns—seven out of every 10 immigrants to Canada in the decade between 1981 and 1991 had a first language other than English or French—have boosted some language groups. The population of Chinese-speaking Canadians, for example, mushroomed from less than 100,000 in 1971 to more than half a million by 1991. After Italian, Chinese is now the second largest non-official language group in Canada, and since it's growing at a much faster rate than Italian, Chinese could conceivably become Canada's third language.

Canada has also gained a growing pool of people who are unable to speak English or French. By 1991, more than 300,000 people in Canada could not speak either official language. In Vancouver, the number of people without English or French language skills almost doubled in the decade between 1981 and 1991. Many of those without English or French were women (partly because they are less likely than men to be in the workplace). A startling 18,000 of these women lived alone.

To help newcomers learn the language skills they needed, in 1994-95, the federal government spent $93.2 million on basic-level language training programs, and another $20.7 million on language training for those heading for the labour market. The total bill for all federal settlement programs for immigrants, including language training, was $159.2 million in 1992-93.

Sometimes, the language is almost Dickensian. The "Nominal Return of the Living" and the "Nominal Return of the Deaths" are just two expressions found in the first census of the Dominion of Canada, conducted shortly after Confederation in 1867. As might be expected, they refer to the arrival of new inhabitants, and the departure of others.

In Canada, a Census of Population occurs every five years, and is a key measure of social and economic change. Census data are used in a wide variety of ways, from determining federal-provincial transfer payments, as well as other federal acts that legally require census data, from the Official Languages Act and the Canada Health Act to the Railway Relocation and Crossing Act.

The introduction of the modern census actually dates to the 17th century , and indeed, the first efforts to count people in areas larger than cities took place in French Canada in 1665, under the Great Intendant, Jean Talon.

With the establishment of the Dominion of Canada in 1867, came this country's first national census, and a thorough accounting of the country's social and economic life. Since 1956, there has been a separate national Census of Agriculture, which gives us information on Canada's agricultural operations.

The Census has served as a kind of mute historian of life in Canada, in addition to its great utility in providing information. The clues to our changes as a nation have come, above all, in the language the Census has used.

For example, until 1971, the Census usually defined the "family head" as the husband. In 1976, "head of the household" referred to either a husband or a wife. In 1981, this term was changed: the person who filled out the household questionnaire became "person one," a testament to changing values.

In 1891, a question asked whether the home of the respondent was made of sod. But, as Canadians moved out of sod, the Census moved on to new questions. By 1921 and 1931, it was asking whether respondents rented or owned, and how many rooms they had.

In 1971, as baby boomers geared up to buy real estate, new interest prompted questions about everything from running water and sewage to heat, freezers, washers, dryers, and black-and-white and colour televisions. A new growth in vacation homes inspired the Census to ask about cottage ownership. In 1981, questions were included on condominium ownership and dwelling repairs.

Other questions have traced developments in technology and the economy. In 1931, families were asked if they owned a radio. At the time, this "newfangled" invention was becoming very popular.

The Census continues to evolve. In 1991, for the first time, there was a question on common-law relationships and in 1996, an unprecedented question about unpaid work in the household.

While legislation relies on census data, these data have many uses outside government. Researchers in universities use the Census to look for patterns and trends in Canadians' lives. Retail companies use it to find the best locations for new stores, or to discover untapped markets for products and services. Teachers and students also use the Census in the classroom. Whether the subject is economics, history, geography or culture, the Census provides both historical perspective and up-to-date information on Canada.

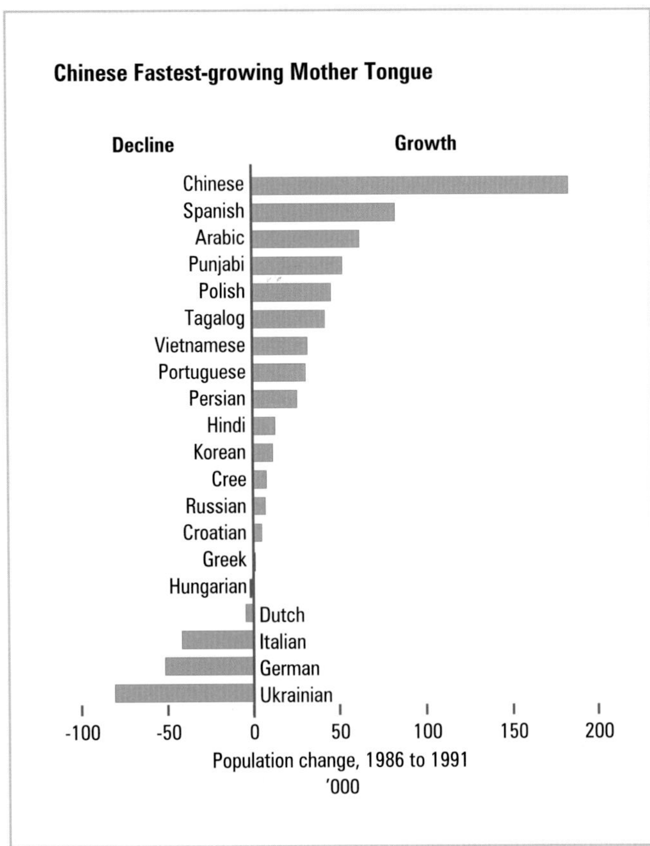

Religion

Not long ago, religion in school was thoroughly commonplace; for example, Ontario school children routinely recited the Lord's Prayer in the classroom, a practice that has now been banned. Today, the extent of religion in the schools is the subject of intense debate in many parts of Canada.

In 1995, Newfoundland held a referendum on religion in the schools, and controversy erupted in Quebec when the province's largest teachers' union called for a ban on the wearing of "ostentatious religious symbols" such as skullcaps, hijabs and turbans in Quebec's public schools. In many ways, the passions aroused by these events reflect a larger issue about the role of religion in our lives.

Although Canada is still a predominantly Christian country—more than 80% of us identified ourselves as either Roman Catholic or Protestant in the 1991 Census—Sunday doesn't find the majority of us in church. In 1991, 3.3 million Canadians described themselves as having "no religion," a 90% increase in only one decade.

On the other hand, some of the smaller groups—Spiritualist, Evangelical, Christian and Missionary Alliance, Wesleyan, Missionary Church, Moravian, New Apostolic and Hutterite—have surged ahead, and the numbers among the largest Protestant denominations have been declining since the 1960s. The number of Canadians practising eastern non-Christian religions such as Buddhism, Islam, Hinduism and Sikhism has increased the most dramatically. And small but increasing numbers of Canadians are exploring New Age spirituality and other alternatives such as paganism.

Meanwhile, at least one prominent opinion poll has suggested that, even if Canadians are not involved in organized religion, many still value spirituality or have their own personal sense of religion. While traditional religious practice is less important, it seems Canadians may still be relying on the moral tenets of religious practice to guide their sense of what's right and wrong.

On-line religion is another new force. Canadians can now connect to one another through religious forums, such as Ecunet, now available on the Internet. On air, the well-respected, interdenominational Vision TV—the world's only multifaith network—continues to garner praise. The Canadian Radio-television and Telecommunications Commission (CRTC) has put in place a rigorous code of ethics requiring that religious programming in Canada be balanced and provide diverse points of view. This has already had an impact.

In late 1995, seven applications for new, single-faith religious television stations in Winnipeg, Edmonton, Saskatoon and Steinbach, Manitoba, were denied because the CRTC was not convinced the stations would meet the code's requirements.

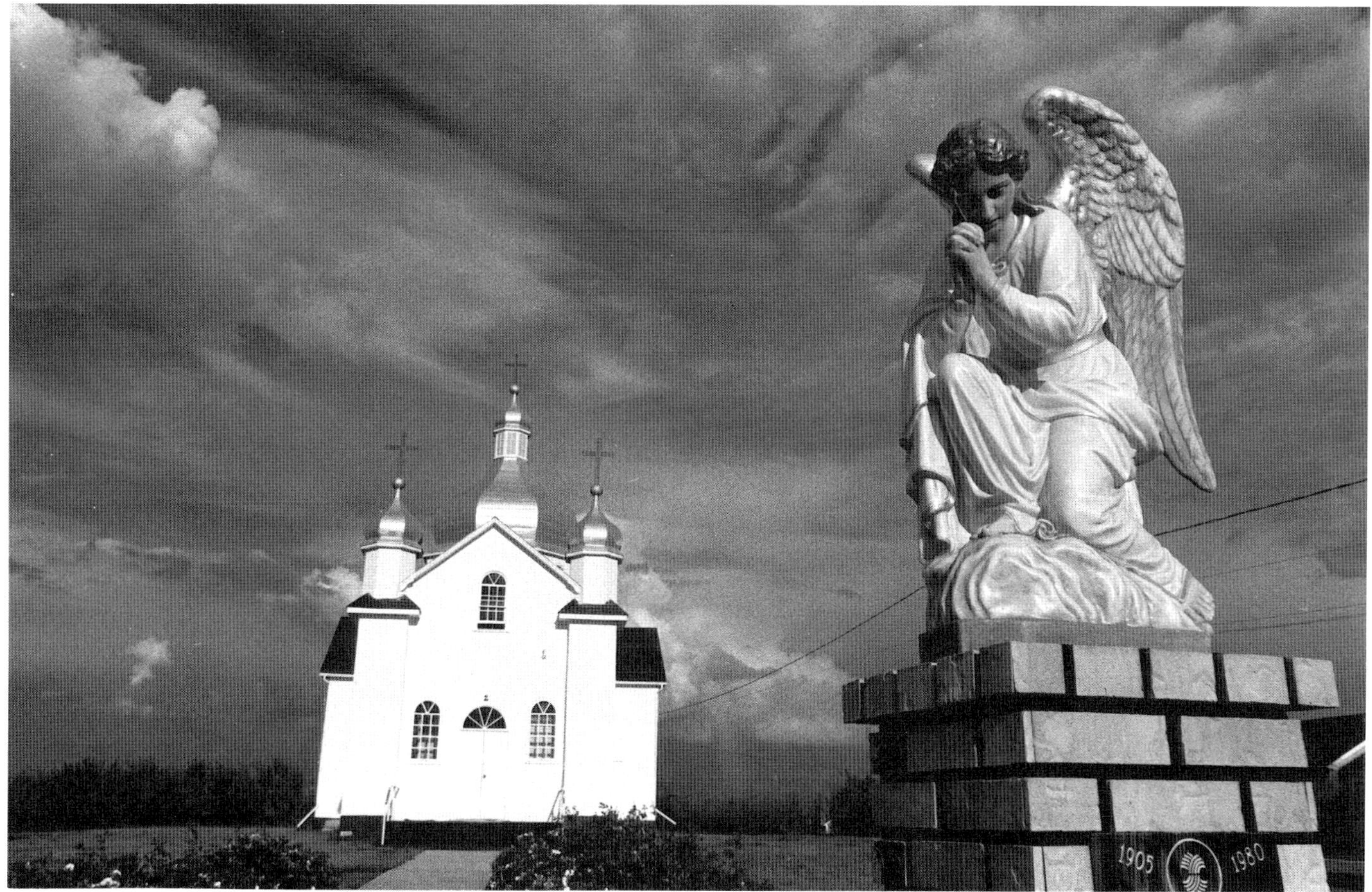

Photo by Ursula Heller

Ukrainian church and statue, Hafford, Saskatchewan.

Canada's First Peoples

Slowly but surely, Canada's Aboriginal peoples are taking steps toward forms of self-government. In 1995, the federal government signed a historic agreement with the First Nations people in Manitoba, as part of the dismantling of the Department of Indian and Northern Affairs' regional operations in Manitoba. With self-government comes the need for qualified people to make the dream become reality. To meet the need, more and more Aboriginal young adults are obtaining post-secondary degrees, diplomas or certificates in relevant fields such as commerce, management and business administration (over 25%), social sciences (12%), as well as education-related (9%) and health-related professions (8%).

As well, Aboriginal communities now have a growing pool of people with the skills to contribute to self-governance: the proportion of Aboriginal workers who have experience in government service occupations rose almost 33% between 1981 and 1991.

Photo by Ursula Heller

Ukrainian immigrants, Hafford, Saskatchewan.

At the same time, there's evidence of growing entrepreneurship. Native innovators such as successful fashion designer D'Arcy Moses combine business savvy with traditional Aboriginal materials and designs to create new products and new markets. In 1991, more than 18,000 Aboriginal people reported that they owned a business. The number of Aboriginal people who reported being self-employed rose significantly between 1981 and 1991.

Despite these signs of progress, each of the three Aboriginal groups in Canada—the Indian, Métis and Inuit peoples—continue their long struggle against poverty, unemployment, violence and substance abuse. The 1991 Aboriginal Peoples Survey confirmed what had long been suspected: Aboriginal people have a much higher level of disability than the rest of the Canadian population. In fact, 31% of Aboriginal adults over the age of 15 have disabilities, more than twice the national rate.

Even more disturbing is adolescent suicide, especially among young men. Nationally, Canada has one of the worst adolescent suicide problems in the world: the suicide rate for Canadian teens aged 15 to 19 has risen 70% since the 1960s. But the risk of suicide appears to be far higher among "registered" or "status" Indian children and youth. Between 1987 and 1991, Indian teens between the ages of 10 and 19 were more than five times more likely to die from suicide than non-Indian adolescents.

In *Choosing Life*, a special 1995 report on suicide among Aboriginal peoples, the Royal Commission on Aboriginal Peoples warned that the problem may get worse. With more than one-third (38%) of the Aboriginal population below the age of 15 in 1991, many young Aboriginals will pass through the highest-risk period for suicide—the ages of 15 to 29—in the next 15 years.

SOURCES

Canadian Heritage
Canadian Radio-television and Telecommunications Commission
Citizenship and Immigration Canada
Statistics Canada

FOR FURTHER READING

Selected publications from Statistics Canada

- **Canadian Social Trends**. Quarterly. 11-008E
- **Schooling, Work and Related Activities, Income, Expenses and Mobility**. Occasional. 89-534
- **Report on the Demographic Situation in Canada**. Annual. 91-209E
- **Annual Demographic Statistics**. Annual. 91-213
- **Population Projection for Canada, Provinces and Territories 1991 Census, 1993-2016**. Occasional. 91-520
- **Urban Areas**. Census. 93-305
- **Ethnic Origin**. Census. 93-315
- **Knowledge of Languages**. Census. 93-318
- **Religions in Canada**. Census. 93-319
- **Language Retention and Transfer**. Census. 94-319
- **Canadian Agriculture at a Glance 1994**. Census. 96-301
- **Canada's Changing Immigrant Population. Focus on Canada**. Census. 96-311E
- **Languages in Canada**. Census. 96-313E

Selected publications from other sources

- **Choosing Life: Special Report on Suicide Among Aboriginal People**. Royal Commission on Aboriginal Peoples. 1995.
- **Commissioner of Official Languages, Annual Report**. 1995.
- **Perspectives on Canada's Population: An Introduction to Concepts and Issues**. Carl F. Grindstaff and Frank Trovato. 1994.
- **United Nations Demographic Yearbook**. 1993.

Legend

–	nil or zero	..	not available	x	confidential
--	too small to be expressed	...	not applicable or not appropriate		*(Certain tables may not add due to rounding)*

3.1 INTERNATIONAL POPULATION COMPARISONS, 1993

	Area	Population		Total increase	Births	Deaths	Natural increase	Net migration	Population distribution by age		
									0-14	15-64	65+
	Km² '000	'000	Residents per km²	Rate per 1,000					%		
Canada	9,970.6	28,753	2.9	13.9	13.5	7.2	6.3	7.6	20.7	67.5	11.8
Australia	7,686.8	17,657	2.3	8.8	14.7	6.9	7.8	1.0	21.7	66.7	11.7
Austria[1]	83.9	7,884	94.0	6.2	12.0	10.5	1.5	4.7	17.5	67.3	15.2
Belgium[1]	30.5	10,045	329.3	4.6	12.5	10.6	2.0	2.6	18.2	66.5	15.3
Denmark	43.1	5,189	120.4	2.9	12.9	12.1	0.8	2.1	17.1	67.5	15.5
Finland	338.0	5,066	15.0	4.5	12.8	10.1	2.8	1.8	19.1	67.0	13.8
France[2]	549.0	57,667	105.0	5.4	13.0	9.1	3.9	1.6	19.8	65.5	14.6
Germany[3]	356.9	81,190	227.5	8.7	10.0	11.0	-0.9	9.6	16.3	68.6	15.0
Greece	132.0	10,368	78.5	4.2	9.8	9.4	0.5	3.8	17.4	67.8	14.8
Iceland[4]	103.0	258	2.5	14.7	17.5	7.0	10.5	4.3	24.8	64.5	10.7
Ireland[4]	70.3	3,524	50.1	6.5	15.0	8.8	6.2	0.3	26.8	61.8	11.4
Italy[2]	301.2	56,120	186.3	3.6	10.1	9.6	0.5	3.0	16.5	68.9	14.6
Japan	377.8	124,670	330.0	2.2	9.5	7.0	2.5	-0.2	16.8	69.8	13.4
Luxembourg[4]	2.6	387	148.9	19.4	13.0	9.6	3.4	16.1	17.8	69.3	13.6
Netherlands	40.8	15,300	375.0	7.2	12.8	9.0	3.8	3.4	18.3	68.7	13.0
New Zealand	268.7	3,480	13.0	11.4	16.8	7.7	9.1	2.3	23.2	65.3	11.6
Norway	324.2	4,312	13.3	6.0	13.9	10.9	3.0	3.0	19.2	64.6	16.1
Portugal	92.4	9,888	107.0	2.8	11.5	10.7	0.8	2.0	18.4	67.3	14.2
Spain[2]	504.8	39,083	77.4	2.2	10.0	8.5	1.5	0.6	17.7	67.9	14.4
Sweden	450.0	8,745	19.4	6.1	13.5	11.1	2.4	3.7	18.7	63.7	17.6
Switzerland	41.3	6,938	168.0	8.8	12.1	9.1	3.0	5.8	17.0	68.0	15.0
Turkey	780.6	59,490	76.2	17.7	23.3	6.7	16.6	1.1	33.7	62.0	4.3
United Kingdom[2]	244.8	58,191	237.7	3.3	13.5	10.9	2.5	0.8	19.4	64.8	15.8
United States	9,372.6	257,908	27.5	10.7	15.7	8.8	7.0	3.7	22.0	65.3	12.7

1. All data are for 1992.
2. Population data and age distribution are for 1993. Rates are for 1992.
3. Population data are for 1993. Rates and age distribution are for 1992.
4. All data are for 1991.

Source: Organisation for Economic Co-operation and Development. *Labour Force Statistics, 1973-1993,* Paris, 1995.

3.2 POPULATION[1] OF CANADA, THE PROVINCES AND TERRITORIES

	Canada	Nfld.	P.E.I.	N.S.	N.B.	Que.	Ont.	Man.	Sask.	Alta.	B.C.	Y.T.	N.W.T.
							'000						
1971	22,026.4	532.9	112.8	799.3	644.4	6,155.6	7,868.4	1,000.8	934.4	1,671.9	2,250.2	19.1	36.7
1972	22,284.5	541.2	113.7	804.1	650.7	6,194.4	7,982.3	1,003.6	923.1	1,700.0	2,312.1	20.3	39.1
1973	22,559.5	547.8	114.8	814.1	658.7	6,235.2	8,094.4	1,009.3	914.2	1,731.0	2,377.6	21.3	41.1
1974	22,874.7	551.2	116.1	820.4	666.7	6,290.6	8,222.9	1,020.2	910.7	1,760.0	2,453.2	21.2	41.4
1975	23,209.2	557.6	117.9	828.1	679.0	6,352.4	8,338.1	1,026.9	919.6	1,813.9	2,510.5	22.0	43.2
1976	23,517.5	563.9	118.8	836.6	691.5	6,420.5	8,432.1	1,033.7	933.8	1,874.3	2,545.0	22.6	44.6
1977	23,796.4	566.6	120.2	841.2	697.8	6,455.1	8,525.6	1,040.0	947.0	1,953.6	2,581.2	23.0	45.0
1978	24,036.3	568.6	121.9	846.1	701.6	6,463.4	8,613.3	1,043.3	954.2	2,028.7	2,625.8	23.9	45.6
1979	24,276.9	571.0	123.2	850.9	705.2	6,488.8	8,685.9	1,039.4	961.8	2,105.4	2,675.0	24.1	46.1
1980	24,593.3	574.2	124.0	854.6	708.1	6,528.2	8,770.1	1,036.7	969.7	2,201.2	2,755.5	24.5	46.7
1981	24,900.0	576.5	124.0	856.4	708.4	6,568.0	8,837.8	1,038.5	978.2	2,303.8	2,836.5	24.1	47.9
1982	25,201.9	576.3	124.2	862.0	710.4	6,600.6	8,951.4	1,048.9	989.9	2,377.5	2,886.3	24.7	50.0
1983	25,456.3	581.2	125.8	871.4	717.6	6,624.7	9,073.4	1,063.2	1,004.7	2,399.3	2,919.6	23.8	51.5
1984	25,701.8	581.8	127.0	879.6	723.4	6,654.7	9,206.2	1,074.1	1,018.6	2,398.6	2,960.6	24.1	53.1
1985	25,941.6	580.9	128.1	887.7	726.1	6,690.3	9,334.4	1,084.6	1,028.8	2,411.1	2,990.0	24.6	55.0
1986	26,203.8	578.1	128.8	892.1	727.7	6,733.8	9,477.2	1,094.0	1,032.9	2,438.7	3,020.4	24.8	55.4
1987	26,549.7	576.5	129.0	896.3	730.5	6,805.9	9,684.9	1,100.5	1,036.4	2,443.5	3,064.6	26.0	55.7
1988	26,894.8	576.2	129.7	900.2	733.1	6,860.4	9,884.4	1,104.7	1,031.7	2,463.0	3,128.2	26.9	56.3
1989	27,379.3	577.4	130.6	906.7	738.0	6,948.0	10,151.0	1,106.2	1,023.0	2,504.3	3,209.2	27.4	57.5
1990	27,790.6	578.9	131.0	912.5	743.0	7,020.7	10,341.4	1,108.4	1,010.8	2,556.4	3,300.1	28.0	59.4
1991	28,120.1	580.3	130.8	917.9	748.5	7,080.6	10,471.5	1,112.5	1,006.3	2,601.3	3,379.8	29.1	61.3
1992	28,542.2	583.4	131.6	924.6	753.0	7,161.2	10,646.4	1,117.6	1,008.0	2,646.8	3,476.9	30.3	62.6
1993	28,947.0	584.2	133.2	930.4	755.5	7,238.6	10,815.5	1,124.1	1,010.8	2,686.0	3,574.6	30.4	63.7
1994	29,251.3	581.2	134.6	933.9	757.7	7,287.1	10,936.4	1,129.6	1,012.1	2,714.8	3,669.5	29.7	64.7
1995	29,606.1	575.4	136.1	937.8	760.1	7,334.2	11,100.3	1,137.5	1,015.6	2,747.0	3,766.0	30.1	65.8
							Average annual growth rate (%)						
1971-1995	1.24	0.32	0.79	0.67	0.69	0.73	1.44	0.54	0.35	2.09	2.17	1.92	2.46
1981-1995	1.24	-0.01	0.67	0.65	0.50	0.79	1.64	0.65	0.27	1.26	2.05	1.60	2.30
1991-1995	1.30	-0.21	1.00	0.54	0.38	0.88	1.47	0.56	0.23	1.37	2.74	0.82	1.80

1. On July 1 of each year.

Source: Statistics Canada, CANSIM, matrices 6367–6379.

3.3 POPULATION GROWTH COMPONENTS, CANADA, THE PROVINCES AND TERRITORIES

	July 1, 1991–June 30, 1992						July 1, 1992	
	Births	Deaths	Immigration	Emigration	Net inter-provincial migration	Returning Canadian	Non-permanent residents	Population
1991-92								
Canada	403,107	196,968	241,810	45,633	–	22,562	378,287	28,542,213
Newfoundland	6,929	3,791	710	296	-1,838	142	3,185	583,382
Prince Edward Island	1,866	1,167	164	89	-54	36	256	131,631
Nova Scotia	12,028	7,486	1,923	946	192	342	4,899	924,623
New Brunswick	9,429	5,499	800	915	-426	445	2,726	752,962
Quebec	97,704	49,191	51,057	6,211	-11,870	3,138	64,889	7,161,244
Ontario	152,065	73,611	128,282	19,462	-11,487	9,758	211,008	10,646,359
Manitoba	17,018	8,999	4,781	1,873	-7,374	1,092	6,527	1,117,563
Saskatchewan	15,177	8,061	2,518	906	-8,219	461	4,959	1,008,004
Alberta	42,737	14,501	16,907	7,888	2,370	3,763	27,238	2,646,752
British Columbia	46,055	24,281	34,439	6,927	38,262	3,317	52,138	3,476,868
Yukon	576	121	114	74	551	32	211	30,268
Northwest Territories	1,523	260	115	46	-107	36	251	62,557
	July 1, 1992–June 30, 1993						July 1, 1993	
1992-93								
Canada	392,399	201,808	265,405	43,993	–	22,268	348,790	28,946,987
Newfoundland	6,689	3,815	802	258	-3,156	139	3,605	584,203
Prince Edward Island	1,820	1,122	163	67	707	36	261	133,173
Nova Scotia	11,635	7,560	2,602	784	-326	356	4,715	930,362
New Brunswick	9,334	5,802	742	914	-1,262	442	2,735	755,511
Quebec	93,798	50,648	48,261	5,930	-8,801	3,080	62,484	7,238,599
Ontario	148,880	74,638	144,962	18,635	-12,426	9,597	182,444	10,815,535
Manitoba	16,531	9,247	5,405	2,195	-5,424	1,042	6,957	1,124,105
Saskatchewan	14,642	8,013	2,561	947	-5,969	461	5,038	1,010,818
Alberta	40,992	14,938	18,920	7,379	-1,491	3,723	26,631	2,685,972
British Columbia	45,961	25,629	40,706	6,740	38,823	3,324	53,428	3,574,603
Yukon	546	125	127	64	-370	32	239	30,442
Northwest Territories	1,571	271	154	80	-305	36	253	63,664
	July 1, 1993–June 30, 1994						July 1, 1994	
1993-94								
Canada	389,286	207,528	227,860	44,807	–	22,448	265,829	29,251,285
Newfoundland	6,360	3,963	670	260	-5,217	140	2,856	581,184
Prince Edward Island	1,728	1,174	141	74	711	39	268	134,551
Nova Scotia	11,536	7,611	3,043	804	-2,228	392	3,892	933,867
New Brunswick	8,848	5,780	573	936	-534	444	2,345	757,736
Quebec	92,600	52,419	34,577	6,036	-8,931	3,088	48,121	7,287,115
Ontario	148,303	76,631	116,270	18,972	-9,534	9,624	134,215	10,936,366
Manitoba	16,737	9,254	4,418	2,238	-3,975	1,055	5,669	1,129,560
Saskatchewan	14,139	8,224	2,244	969	-5,348	460	4,052	1,012,134
Alberta	40,274	15,501	17,614	7,506	-2,937	3,781	19,774	2,714,840
British Columbia	46,725	26,643	48,072	6,864	39,377	3,358	44,336	3,669,536
Yukon	491	108	103	65	-1,109	33	153	29,701
Northwest Territories	1,545	220	135	83	-275	34	148	64,695

3.3 POPULATION GROWTH COMPONENTS, CANADA, THE PROVINCES AND TERRITORIES (concluded)

	July 1, 1994–June 30, 1995						July 1, 1995	
	Births	Deaths	Immigration	Emigration	Net inter-provincial migration	Returning Canadian	Non-permanent residents	Population
1994-95								
Canada	382,870	212,830	215,652	45,949	–	22,387	258,511	29,606,097
Newfoundland	6,295	4,110	607	260	-8,410	139	2,860	575,449
Prince Edward Island	1,685	1,175	184	73	875	37	304	136,120
Nova Scotia	11,205	7,885	3,513	819	-2,817	380	4,200	937,752
New Brunswick	8,960	6,010	660	964	-833	453	2,401	760,058
Quebec	89,525	53,190	26,943	6,193	-15,284	3,064	50,348	7,334,207
Ontario	146,230	79,215	116,761	19,451	4,602	9,557	119,684	11,100,319
Manitoba	16,395	9,450	3,723	2,306	-2,162	1,067	6,370	1,137,528
Saskatchewan	13,935	8,290	2,107	1,002	-4,167	474	4,497	1,015,636
Alberta	39,435	16,170	16,361	7,698	-4,078	3,738	20,387	2,747,041
British Columbia	47,160	26,935	44,570	7,036	32,412	3,409	47,265	3,766,045
Yukon	465	140	88	64	94	32	93	30,116
Northwest Territories	1,580	260	135	83	-232	37	102	65,826

Source: Statistics Canada, CANSIM, matrices 5772 to 5778 and 6367 to 6379.

3.4 POPULATION GROWTH COMPONENTS, FROM 1851 TO 1991[1]

Period	Total population growth	Births	Deaths	Natural increase	Ratio of natural increase to total growth	Immigration[2]	Emigration[3]	Net migration	Ratio of net migration to total growth	Census population at the end of period
	'000				%	'000			%	'000
1851-1861	793	1,281	670	611	77.0	352	170	182	23.0	3,230
1861-1871	459	1,370	760	610	132.9	260	411	-151	-32.9	3,689
1871-1881	636	1,480	790	690	108.5	350	404	-54	-8.5	4,325
1881-1891	508	1,524	870	654	128.7	680	826	-146	-28.7	4,833
1891-1901	538	1,548	880	668	124.2	250	380	-130	-24.2	5,371
1901-1911	1,836	1,925	900	1,025	55.8	1,550	739	811	44.2	7,207
1911-1921	1,581	2,340	1,070	1,270	80.3	1,400	1,089	311	19.7	8,788
1921-1931	1,589	2,415	1,055	1,360	85.6	1,200	971	229	14.4	10,377
1931-1941	1,130	2,294	1,072	1,222	108.1	149	241	-92	-8.1	11,507
1941-1951[4]	2,141	3,186	1,214	1,972	92.1	548	379	169	7.9	13,648
1951-1956	2,072	2,106	633	1,473	71.1	783	184	599	28.9	16,081
1956-1961	2,157	2,362	687	1,675	77.7	760	278	482	22.3	18,238
1961-1966	1,777	2,249	731	1,518	85.4	539	280	259	14.6	20,015
1966-1971[5]	1,553	1,856	766	1,090	70.2	890	427	463	29.8	21,568
1971-1976[6]	1,492	1,755	824	931	62.4	1,053	492	561	37.6	23,518
1976-1981	1,382	1,820	843	977	70.7	771	366	405	29.3	24,900
1981-1986	1,304	1,872	885	987	75.7	677	360	317	24.3	26,204
1986-1991	1,916	1,933	946	987	51.5	1,198	269	929	48.5	28,120

1. Includes Newfoundland since 1951.
2. Starting with July 1, 1971, immigration figures include landed immigrants, returning Canadians plus net change in the numbers of non-permanent residents.
3. Emigration figures are estimated by the residual method.
4. Data on components of growth shown for 1941-1951 were obtained by excluding data for Newfoundland.
5. The June 1, 1971 figure is the Census count without adjustment for net Census undercount. The July 1, 1971 population adjusted for net Census undercount is 22,026,000.
6. Starting with 1971, the reference date is July 1 instead of June 1 and population estimates are based on Census counts adjusted for net undercount.

Source: Statistics Canada, Demography Division.

3.5 BIRTHS[1]

	Canada	Nfld.	P.E.I.	N.S.	N.B.	Que.	Ont.	Man.	Sask.	Alta.	B.C.	Y.T.	N.W.T.
							Number of births						
1972-73	345,815	12,624	1,897	13,414	11,625	83,801	124,353	16,990	15,280	29,596	34,598	461	1,176
1973-74	339,888	11,294	1,932	12,839	11,218	83,569	122,122	17,080	14,680	29,146	34,462	439	1,107
1974-75	353,513	10,830	1,944	13,093	11,787	87,675	127,258	17,330	15,217	30,582	36,241	468	1,088
1975-76	364,278	11,030	1,939	13,137	11,847	99,695	123,664	16,984	15,809	32,491	36,077	395	1,210
1976-77	358,261	10,633	1,958	12,597	11,675	94,362	122,300	16,653	16,328	33,882	36,239	449	1,185
1977-78	359,954	10,071	1,915	12,345	11,082	96,476	121,839	16,708	16,463	34,728	36,679	446	1,202
1978-79	362,226	9,653	2,053	12,608	10,733	96,126	121,719	16,332	16,813	36,422	38,045	490	1,232
1979-80	367,286	10,291	1,935	12,420	10,806	98,355	121,954	15,967	16,906	37,917	38,918	487	1,330
1980-81	372,139	10,325	1,903	12,118	10,603	96,725	123,213	16,058	17,201	41,343	40,882	487	1,281
1981-82	372,472	9,593	1,924	12,173	10,400	93,340	123,120	16,030	17,359	44,016	42,664	547	1,306
1982-83	373,594	9,142	1,910	12,317	10,620	88,580	126,841	16,461	17,856	45,470	42,398	540	1,459
1983-84	374,533	8,724	1,895	12,397	10,424	88,172	127,980	16,558	17,912	44,845	43,657	526	1,443
1984-85	376,265	8,323	1,977	12,579	10,162	86,919	131,884	16,901	18,137	43,868	43,549	501	1,465
1985-86	375,381	8,346	2,055	12,316	10,104	85,584	133,481	17,091	17,916	44,166	42,401	462	1,459
1986-87	373,021	7,899	1,916	12,321	9,623	84,539	134,909	17,178	17,461	42,966	42,196	503	1,510
1987-88	370,033	7,656	1,883	12,068	9,493	84,468	135,656	16,860	16,604	41,437	41,876	481	1,551
1988-89	384,035	7,396	1,984	12,263	9,600	89,408	140,808	17,149	16,772	43,106	43,563	490	1,496
1989-90	403,280	7,996	2,028	12,856	9,908	95,673	150,087	17,376	16,499	43,564	45,212	509	1,572
1990-91	402,924	7,354	1,940	12,438	9,654	98,189	150,627	17,287	15,655	42,544	45,056	554	1,626
1991-92	403,107	6,929	1,866	12,028	9,429	97,704	152,065	17,018	15,177	42,737	46,055	576	1,523
1992-93	392,399	6,689	1,820	11,635	9,334	93,798	148,880	16,531	14,642	40,992	45,961	546	1,571
1993-94	389,286	6,360	1,728	11,536	8,848	92,600	148,303	16,737	14,139	40,274	46,725	491	1,545
1994-95	382,870	6,295	1,685	11,205	8,960	89,525	146,230	16,395	13,935	39,435	47,160	465	1,580
							Birth rate per 1,000						
1975-76	15.3	23.0	16.5	16.5	17.6	13.4	15.4	16.8	16.7	17.1	14.6	21.6	28.6
1980-81	15.5	19.6	16.3	15.7	17.1	15.5	14.7	16.4	16.9	17.3	14.2	17.5	27.1
1985-86	14.9	17.9	15.3	14.1	15.0	14.7	13.9	15.5	17.6	17.9	14.4	20.2	26.7
1990-91	14.3	14.4	16.0	13.8	13.9	12.7	14.1	15.6	17.3	18.1	14.0	18.6	26.3
1991-92	14.1	11.9	14.2	13.0	12.5	13.7	14.3	15.2	15.0	16.1	13.2	19.0	24.3
1992-93	13.6	11.4	13.7	12.5	12.3	13.0	13.8	14.7	14.5	15.2	12.9	18.0	24.7
1993-94	13.3	10.9	12.8	12.3	11.7	12.7	13.6	14.8	13.9	14.8	12.7	16.6	23.9
1994-95	12.9	10.9	12.4	11.9	11.8	12.2	13.2	14.4	13.7	14.3	12.5	15.4	24.0

1. From July 1 of one year to June 30 of the next year.

Source: Statistics Canada, CANSIM, matrix 5772.

3.6 DEATHS[1]

	Canada	Nfld.	P.E.I.	N.S.	N.B.	Que.	Ont.	Man.	Sask.	Alta.	B.C.	Y.T.	N.W.T.
							Number of deaths						
1972-73	162,618	3,400	1,013	6,897	5,023	42,401	59,033	8,236	7,591	10,750	17,921	93	260
1973-74	166,284	3,362	1,073	7,022	5,145	42,946	60,376	8,411	7,806	10,945	18,830	130	238
1974-75	168,751	3,237	1,100	6,776	5,166	44,116	61,232	8,394	7,681	11,312	19,421	105	211
1975-76	166,428	3,260	1,062	6,892	5,223	42,469	60,582	8,251	7,765	11,499	19,080	114	231
1976-77	165,747	3,192	1,077	7,075	5,160	43,015	60,226	8,205	7,830	11,461	18,207	110	189
1977-78	169,030	3,139	1,019	6,765	5,189	43,782	62,128	8,233	7,657	11,907	18,917	97	197
1978-79	165,805	3,144	966	6,868	5,117	42,519	60,248	8,261	7,318	11,938	19,101	119	206
1979-80	171,460	3,285	1,065	6,937	5,279	44,139	62,837	8,388	7,642	12,309	19,237	128	214
1980-81	170,535	3,232	1,002	7,006	5,141	42,768	62,694	8,362	7,514	12,751	19,729	117	219
1981-82	172,352	3,322	1,007	6,923	5,151	42,864	62,947	8,779	7,822	13,002	20,165	141	229
1982-83	176,522	3,465	1,011	7,085	5,356	44,943	64,895	8,436	7,969	12,746	20,277	117	222
1983-84	174,159	3,548	1,106	7,055	5,169	43,630	64,058	8,442	7,675	12,738	20,392	105	241
1984-85	179,085	3,478	1,090	6,988	5,288	45,362	66,436	8,471	7,872	12,942	20,804	124	230
1985-86	183,353	3,575	1,091	7,270	5,394	46,554	67,149	8,907	8,128	13,494	21,444	109	238
1986-87	182,599	3,578	1,129	7,218	5,342	46,389	67,390	8,754	7,862	13,338	21,287	108	204
1987-88	189,917	3,612	1,112	7,190	5,472	48,405	70,232	9,066	8,079	13,739	22,665	135	210
1988-89	188,408	3,611	1,085	7,456	5,466	47,889	69,657	8,779	7,875	13,687	22,559	108	236
1989-90	192,608	3,894	1,103	7,562	5,553	48,695	71,274	8,887	8,059	13,979	23,267	100	235
1990-91	192,437	3,816	1,199	7,248	5,354	48,241	71,506	8,770	7,921	14,335	23,726	116	205
1991-92	196,968	3,791	1,167	7,486	5,499	49,191	73,611	8,999	8,061	14,501	24,281	121	260
1992-93	201,808	3,815	1,122	7,560	5,802	50,648	74,638	9,247	8,013	14,938	25,629	125	271
1993-94	207,528	3,963	1,174	7,611	5,780	52,419	76,631	9,254	8,224	15,501	26,643	108	220
1994-95	212,830	4,110	1,175	7,885	6,010	53,190	79,215	9,450	8,290	16,170	26,935	140	260
							Death rate per 1,000						
1972-73	7.0	5.6	9.0	8.4	7.4	6.7	7.1	7.9	8.3	5.9	7.1	4.8	4.2
1975-76	7.0	5.5	8.4	8.0	7.4	6.8	7.2	7.9	8.0	5.9	7.2	4.1	4.3
1980-81	6.8	5.5	7.8	8.1	7.3	6.6	6.9	7.9	7.6	5.7	7.1	4.9	4.5
1985-86	7.0	5.7	8.6	8.1	7.5	6.8	7.2	8.1	7.9	5.6	7.0	5.2	4.6
1991-92	6.8	5.6	8.1	8.2	7.3	6.5	7.1	8.1	7.7	5.5	7.0	4.9	4.6
1992-93	6.8	5.8	8.1	8.0	7.3	6.5	7.0	8.4	7.9	5.5	7.0	5.7	4.6
1993-94	6.9	6.0	8.0	8.1	7.5	6.8	7.2	7.9	7.9	5.3	6.9	4.9	4.3
1994-95	6.8	6.1	8.7	8.0	7.1	6.6	7.0	7.9	7.5	5.3	6.9	4.4	4.5

1. From July 1 of one year to June 30 of the next.

Source: Statistics Canada, CANSIM, matrix 5773.

3.7 NON-IMMIGRANT[1] POPULATION BY PLACE OF BIRTH AND PLACE OF RESIDENCE, 1991[2]

	Canada	Nfld.	P.E.I.	N.S.	N.B.	Que.	Ont.	Man.	Sask.	Alta.	B.C.	Y.T.	N.W.T.
						Province or territory of residence							
							'000						
Total non-immigrants	22,427.7	554.6	123.9	850.1	691.2	6,175.1	7,481.7	936.8	915.4	2,123.6	2,496.3	24.6	54.5
Born in Canada	22,343.3	554.1	123.5	847.3	688.9	6,162.8	7,445.2	933.0	913.2	2,113.5	2,482.9	24.5	54.4
Place of birth													
Newfoundland	709.6	525.8	1.4	25.5	7.0	13.8	94.6	4.6	1.9	19.7	13.7	0.3	1.2
Prince Edward Island	150.4	0.6	102.0	9.0	6.0	2.6	19.6	0.8	0.8	4.9	3.9	0.1	0.2
Nova Scotia	950.4	5.7	6.0	709.7	26.5	12.0	125.4	5.7	2.9	25.2	29.9	0.4	1.0
New Brunswick	802.6	2.4	3.9	27.6	591.8	48.8	86.2	4.0	2.2	17.6	17.4	0.2	0.6
Quebec	6,424.0	3.1	2.0	15.0	22.6	5,908.7	348.9	8.9	4.7	45.6	61.9	0.9	1.6
Ontario	7,115.3	12.4	5.8	41.6	25.8	146.3	6,454.6	45.2	23.8	152.4	200.7	2.9	3.8
Manitoba	1,159.5	1.0	0.5	4.2	2.0	8.6	95.5	786.2	38.2	88.0	130.3	1.2	3.9
Saskatchewan	1,343.2	0.5	0.4	2.8	1.4	5.4	74.4	48.2	790.9	210.6	204.3	1.9	2.5
Alberta	1,836.6	1.7	1.0	6.4	3.3	7.7	75.3	17.2	33.0	1,443.8	239.8	3.0	4.5
British Columbia	1,783.3	0.9	0.5	5.1	2.3	7.1	64.3	11.4	13.8	98.9	1,572.9	4.0	2.0
Yukon	19.9	–	–	0.2	0.1	1.0	1.4	0.3	0.3	2.0	5.1	9.3	0.2
Northwest Territories	48.6	0.1	–	0.3	0.1	0.8	5.0	0.7	0.7	4.9	2.8	0.4	32.8
Born outside Canada	84.4	0.6	0.4	2.8	2.3	12.3	36.5	3.7	2.1	10.1	13.4	0.1	0.1

1. Persons who are Canadian citizens by birth.
2. Based on a 20% sample of the population.

Source: Statistics Canada, Catalogue no. 93-316.

3.8 POPULATION BY SEX AND AGE

	1971			1995			1971			1995		
	Both sexes	Male	Female	Both sexes	Male	Female	Both sexes	Male	Female	Both sexes	Male	Female
	'000						% of total population					
All ages	22,026.4	11,065.0	10,961.4	29,606.1	14,664.3	14,941.8	100.0	100.0	100.0	100.0	100.0	100.0
0-4	1,840.3	940.7	899.6	1,987.5	1,019.2	968.3	8.4	8.5	8.2	6.7	7.0	6.5
5-9	2,271.9	1,161.6	1,110.3	1,998.5	1,021.3	977.3	10.3	10.5	10.1	6.8	7.0	6.5
10-14	2,332.0	1,191.5	1,140.5	2,003.3	1,023.9	979.4	10.6	10.8	10.4	6.8	7.0	6.6
15-19	2,171.9	1,104.0	1,067.9	1,979.9	1,014.8	965.1	9.9	10.0	9.7	6.7	6.9	6.5
20-24	1,991.4	999.5	991.9	2,044.0	1,036.4	1,007.6	9.0	9.0	9.0	6.9	7.1	6.7
25-29	1,651.2	844.0	807.2	2,245.1	1,133.2	1,111.9	7.5	7.6	7.4	7.6	7.7	7.4
30-34	1,348.0	689.5	658.5	2,675.8	1,355.9	1,319.9	6.1	6.2	6.0	9.0	9.2	8.8
35-39	1,290.2	664.3	625.9	2,602.2	1,309.7	1,292.5	5.9	6.0	5.7	8.8	8.9	8.7
40-44	1,288.2	658.2	630.0	2,322.8	1,159.6	1,163.2	5.8	5.9	5.7	7.8	7.9	7.8
45-49	1,255.0	625.2	629.8	2,083.2	1,047.3	1,035.9	5.7	5.7	5.7	7.0	7.1	6.9
50-54	1,067.4	527.6	539.7	1,595.4	799.6	795.8	4.8	4.8	4.9	5.4	5.5	5.3
55-59	966.8	480.1	486.6	1,295.2	643.2	651.9	4.4	4.3	4.4	4.4	4.4	4.4
60-64	786.7	386.9	399.9	1,214.5	596.8	617.7	3.6	3.5	3.6	4.1	4.1	4.1
65-69	627.5	299.8	327.7	1,119.0	527.6	591.4	2.8	2.7	3.0	3.8	3.6	4.0
70-74	462.7	208.3	254.4	968.4	425.8	542.7	2.1	1.9	2.3	3.3	2.9	3.6
75-79	329.1	141.6	187.6	671.0	274.9	396.1	1.5	1.3	1.7	2.3	1.9	2.7
80-84	206.5	86.7	119.8	456.0	170.4	285.6	0.9	0.8	1.1	1.5	1.2	1.9
85-89	101.3	41.2	60.2	228.9	73.8	155.1	0.5	0.4	0.5	0.8	0.5	1.0
90 and over	38.2	14.2	23.9	115.2	30.8	84.4	0.2	0.1	0.2	0.4	0.2	0.6

Source: Statistics Canada, CANSIM, matrix 6367.

3.9 POPULATION BY AGE, CANADA, THE PROVINCES AND TERRITORIES

		All ages	Age group					
			0-14		15-64		65 and over	
		'000	'000	%	'000	%	'000	%
Canada	1971	22,026.4	6,444.2	29.3	13,816.8	62.7	1,765.4	8.0
	1986	26,203.8	5,496.6	21.0	17,964.9	68.6	2,742.3	10.5
	1995	29,606.1	5,989.3	20.2	20,058.3	67.8	3,558.5	12.0
	Male	14,664.3	3,064.4	20.9	10,096.6	68.9	1,503.3	10.3
	Female	14,941.8	2,925.0	19.6	9,961.6	66.7	2,055.2	13.8
Newfoundland	1971	532.9	196.3	36.8	304.0	57.0	32.5	6.1
	1986	578.1	147.6	25.5	380.1	65.7	50.4	8.7
	1995	575.4	115.3	20.0	400.7	69.6	59.5	10.3
	Male	288.5	58.7	20.3	203.3	70.5	26.5	9.2
	Female	286.9	56.5	19.7	197.4	68.8	33.0	11.5
Prince Edward Island	1971	112.8	35.6	31.6	64.9	57.5	12.4	11.0
	1986	128.8	29.5	22.9	83.0	64.4	16.3	12.7
	1995	136.1	29.3	21.5	89.2	65.5	17.6	12.9
	Male	67.2	15.0	22.3	44.7	66.5	7.5	11.2
	Female	68.9	14.2	20.6	44.5	64.6	10.1	14.7
Nova Scotia	1971	799.3	242.1	30.3	484.3	60.6	72.9	9.1
	1986	892.1	189.5	21.2	597.8	67.0	104.8	11.7
	1995	937.8	184.1	19.6	634.4	67.6	119.3	12.7
	Male	462.6	94.0	20.3	318.9	68.9	49.8	10.8
	Female	475.1	90.1	19.0	315.5	66.4	69.5	14.6
New Brunswick	1971	644.4	204.5	31.7	384.7	59.7	55.1	8.6
	1986	727.7	162.8	22.4	485.1	66.7	79.8	11.0
	1995	760.1	148.5	19.5	516.9	68.0	94.7	12.5
	Male	376.6	75.9	20.2	260.7	69.2	40.0	10.6
	Female	383.5	72.6	18.9	256.2	66.8	54.6	14.2
Quebec	1971	6,155.6	1,802.8	29.3	3,933.3	63.9	419.4	6.8
	1986	6,733.8	1,360.4	20.2	4,714.6	70.0	658.8	9.8
	1995	7,334.2	1,401.9	19.1	5,060.3	69.0	872.0	11.9
	Male	3,614.1	717.0	19.8	2,542.6	70.4	354.5	9.8
	Female	3,720.2	684.9	18.4	2,517.7	67.7	517.6	13.9
Ontario	1971	7,868.4	2,229.9	28.3	4,987.3	63.4	651.3	8.3
	1986	9,477.2	1,917.1	20.2	6,549.1	69.1	1,011.0	10.7
	1995	11,100.3	2,239.6	20.2	7,514.9	67.7	1,345.9	12.1
	Male	5,481.3	1,146.2	20.9	3,766.6	68.7	568.5	10.4
	Female	5,619.0	1,093.4	19.5	3,748.3	66.7	777.4	13.8
Manitoba	1971	1,000.8	288.4	28.8	616.3	61.6	96.1	9.6
	1986	1,094.0	239.5	21.9	718.8	65.7	135.7	12.4
	1995	1,137.5	246.5	21.7	736.6	64.8	154.4	13.6
	Male	564.1	126.6	22.4	372.6	66.1	64.8	11.5
	Female	573.4	119.9	20.9	364.0	63.5	89.6	15.6
Saskatchewan	1971	934.4	281.3	30.1	557.8	59.7	95.2	10.2
	1986	1,032.9	249.0	24.1	654.1	63.3	129.8	12.6
	1995	1,015.6	235.2	23.2	633.2	62.3	147.3	14.5
	Male	504.8	120.2	23.8	320.3	63.5	64.3	12.7
	Female	510.9	115.1	22.5	312.8	61.2	83.0	16.2

3.9 POPULATION BY AGE, CANADA, THE PROVINCES AND TERRITORIES (concluded)

		All ages	Age group					
			0-14		15-64		65 and over	
		'000	'000	%	'000	%	'000	%
Alberta	1971	1,671.9	521.2	31.2	1,029.9	61.6	120.8	7.2
	1986	2,438.7	570.9	23.4	1,674.0	68.6	193.8	7.9
	1995	2,747.0	623.8	22.7	1,856.5	67.6	266.8	9.7
	Male	1,383.5	319.8	23.1	946.8	68.4	117.0	8.5
	Female	1,363.5	304.1	22.3	909.7	66.7	149.8	11.0
British Columbia	1971	2,250.2	620.3	27.6	1,421.7	63.2	208.1	9.2
	1986	3,020.4	606.7	20.1	2,054.3	68.0	359.4	11.9
	1995	3,766.0	736.7	19.6	2,551.5	67.8	477.8	12.7
	Male	1,872.2	376.4	20.1	1,287.2	68.8	208.7	11.1
	Female	1,893.8	360.4	19.0	1,264.4	66.8	269.1	14.2
Yukon	1971	19.1	6.5	34.0	12.1	63.4	0.5	2.6
	1986	24.8	6.1	24.6	17.7	71.4	0.9	3.6
	1995	30.1	7.2	23.9	21.5	71.4	1.4	4.7
	Male	15.3	3.7	24.2	10.8	70.6	0.7	4.6
	Female	14.8	3.5	23.6	10.7	72.3	0.6	4.1
Northwest Territories	1971	36.7	15.3	41.7	20.6	56.1	0.8	2.2
	1986	55.4	17.6	31.8	36.2	65.3	1.6	2.9
	1995	65.8	21.2	32.2	42.7	64.9	1.9	2.9
	Male	34.1	10.9	32.0	22.2	65.1	1.0	2.9
	Female	31.7	10.3	32.5	20.5	64.7	0.9	2.8

Source: Statistics Canada, CANSIM, matrices 6367–6379.

3.10 POPULATION[1] OF CENSUS METROPOLITAN AREAS

	1987	1988	1989	1990	1991	1992	1993	1994	1995	Average annual growth rate 1987-1995
					'000					%
Toronto (Ontario)	3,722.5	3,813.2	3,937.8	4,000.4	4,036.3	4,116.8	4,198.3	4,254.5	4,338.4	1.9
Montreal (Quebec)	3,081.7	3,112.3	3,167.3	3,195.1	3,213.2	3,251.5	3,288.7	3,307.5	3,328.3	1.0
Vancouver (British Columbia)	1,484.4	1,524.9	1,573.9	1,613.2	1,648.7	1,690.9	1,734.4	1,778.5	1,826.8	2.6
Ottawa–Hull (Ontario–Quebec)	866.5	884.0	907.5	932.0	952.2	974.6	997.4	1,010.2	1,026.9	2.1
Edmonton (Alberta)	804.0	808.7	823.5	841.7	856.3	870.5	880.3	881.6	882.9	1.2
Calgary (Alberta)	698.1	711.4	729.8	752.3	768.7	785.2	798.0	812.5	828.5	2.2
Quebec (Quebec)	627.0	633.6	643.0	653.3	663.1	672.4	682.5	689.3	695.2	1.3
Winnipeg (Manitoba)	647.3	651.9	654.7	659.6	664.2	668.0	671.9	673.5	676.5	0.6
Hamilton (Ontario)	589.3	597.3	610.3	17.6	621.8	626.8	631.0	635.7	641.5	1.1
London (Ontario)	362.0	369.7	380.4	390.9	395.6	400.5	404.3	408.2	412.6	1.6
Kitchener (Ontario)	331.8	341.4	353.8	364.1	369.5	376.3	382.3	388.4	395.5	2.2
St. Catharines–Niagara (Ontario)	357.5	361.3	367.3	373.7	378.0	381.8	383.6	384.4	385.4	0.9
Halifax (Nova Scotia)	307.9	312.1	317.7	322.8	326.9	331.3	335.0	338.8	342.8	1.4
Victoria (British Columbia)	272.2	277.5	284.6	290.8	296.4	300.9	304.8	308.2	311.2	1.7
Windsor (Ontario)	265.0	266.1	268.4	270.6	271.7	274.4	277.7	281.4	286.2	1.0
Oshawa (Ontario)	218.1	228.6	239.5	244.6	248.9	256.7	263.4	269.6	276.2	3.0
Saskatoon (Saskatchewan)	210.2	212.0	212.7	212.5	213.6	215.7	217.0	218.1	219.9	0.6
Regina (Saskatchewan)	194.0	195.2	194.8	194.6	195.0	196.1	197.5	197.9	198.7	0.3
St. John's (Newfoundland)	166.1	167.8	170.4	173.1	175.4	177.4	178.6	178.4	177.3	0.8
Chicoutimi–Jonquière (Quebec)	162.0	161.9	162.4	163.6	165.0	165.7	166.9	167.2	167.2	0.4
Sudbury (Ontario)	153.6	154.4	157.2	160.3	163.4	166.0	166.9	166.6	166.3	1.0
Sherbrooke (Quebec)	136.0	137.7	139.9	141.2	142.7	144.1	145.4	146.8	148.0	1.1
Trois-Rivières (Quebec)	133.7	135.0	136.3	138.0	139.8	141.4	141.8	142.5	143.0	0.8
Saint John (New Brunswick)	124.7	125.6	127.0	128.3	128.9	129.4	129.6	129.4	129.1	0.4
Thunder Bay (Ontario)	126.3	127.1	127.5	128.2	129.0	130.2	130.6	130.7	130.9	0.4

1. On July 1 of each year.

Source: Statistics Canada, CANSIM, matrix 6231.

3.11 POPULATION PROJECTIONS[1]

	1996			2001			2006			2011			2016		
	Both sexes	Male	Female	Both sexes	Male	Female	Both sexes	Male	Female	Both sexes	Male	Female	Both sexes	Male	Female
	'000														
All ages	29,963.7	14,836.8	15,126.9	31,877.3	15,781.2	16,096.1	33,677.5	16,674.3	17,003.2	35,420.3	17,541.8	17,878.5	37,119.8	18,387.5	18,732.2
0-4	1,991.5	1021.8	969.7	1,924.4	988.2	936.2	1,924.6	988.4	936.2	1,980.1	1,017.0	963.1	2,052.8	1,054.4	998.4
5-9	2,036.9	1,043.3	993.5	2,082.2	1,069.0	1,013.1	2,016.0	1,035.9	980.1	2,016.6	1,036.4	980.3	2,072.2	1,065.0	1,007.2
10-14	2,035.2	1,041.4	993.8	2,124.8	1,089.2	1,035.6	2,170.1	1,115.0	1,055.2	2,104.8	1,082.3	1,022.5	2,105.7	1,082.9	1,022.8
15-19	1,996.3	1,023.8	972.5	2,124.5	1,088.0	1,036.4	2,213.7	1,135.8	1,078.0	2,259.2	1,161.6	1,097.6	2,194.8	1,129.5	1,065.4
20-24	2,027.0	1,031.8	995.2	2,115.2	1,080.1	1,035.0	2,242.9	1,144.3	1,098.6	2,332.3	1,192.2	1,140.1	2,378.2	1,218.3	1,159.9
25-29	2,217.5	1,119.4	1,098.1	2,177.7	1,103.0	1,074.7	2,265.9	1,151.5	1,114.5	2,392.8	1,215.3	1,177.5	2,482.2	1,263.3	1,218.9
30-34	2,615.4	1,324.2	1,291.2	2,366.4	1,192.9	1,173.4	2,328.3	1,177.5	1,150.8	2,416.1	1,225.8	1,190.3	2,541.4	1,288.9	1,252.5
35-39	2,657.3	1,337.4	1,319.9	2,723.4	1,376.1	1,347.3	2,479.5	1,248.0	1,231.5	2,443.0	1,233.4	1,209.6	2,530.4	1,281.5	1,248.9
40-44	2,377.8	1,185.3	1,192.5	2,716.3	1,363.9	1,352.3	2,782.9	1,403.0	1,379.8	2,544.5	1,278.2	1,266.2	2,509.9	1,264.8	1,245.1
45-49	2,146.6	1,077.5	1,069.1	2,399.6	1,193.9	1,205.7	2,734.2	1,370.2	1,363.9	2,801.9	1,410.1	1,391.8	2,569.5	1,289.1	1,280.4
50-54	1,667.4	835.7	831.7	2,140.1	1,069.8	1,070.3	2,391.1	1,185.4	1,205.7	2,722.0	1,359.6	1,362.4	2,791.4	1,400.6	1,390.8
55-59	1,327.3	659.5	667.8	1,651.4	820.1	831.3	2,113.8	1,048.2	1,065.7	2,362.2	1,162.6	1,199.6	2,688.7	1,334.1	1,354.5
60-64	1,209.4	593.8	615.6	1,300.9	636.8	664.0	1,615.3	791.5	823.7	2,063.6	1,011.0	1,052.6	2,308.2	1,123.7	1,184.5
65-69	1,129.7	535.9	593.9	1,154.0	554.2	599.7	1,244.6	597.0	647.6	1,544.5	742.8	801.7	1,971.6	949.4	1,022.2
70-74	980.4	432.7	547.7	1,027.1	470.6	556.6	1,054.0	490.0	564.1	1,142.5	531.6	610.8	1,420.6	664.2	756.4
75-79	704.9	288.9	416.0	831.9	345.9	486.1	877.1	380.4	496.7	906.1	400.1	506.0	989.8	439.0	550.7
80-84	471.7	174.8	296.9	541.8	201.3	340.5	644.0	244.1	399.9	685.0	272.9	412.1	714.1	291.2	422.9
85-89	246.8	78.7	167.2	308.5	98.3	210.2	361.0	116.4	244.6	433.2	143.7	289.5	466.5	164.4	302.0
90 and over	125.4	30.9	94.5	167.4	39.8	127.6	218.5	51.9	166.6	269.9	65.1	204.8	331.7	83.0	248.7

1. Figures represent a medium-growth projection.

Source: Statistics Canada, CANSIM, matrix 6900.

3.12 IMMIGRANTS BY PLACE OF BIRTH,[1] 1991

	Immigrant population	Period of immigration									
		Before 1961		1961-1970		1971-1980		1981-1987		1988-1991[2]	
	'000	'000	%	'000	%	'000	%	'000	%	'000	%
All places of birth	4,342.9	1,239.0	100.0	828.0	100.0	1,037.4	100.0	645.0	100.0	593.5	100.0
United Kingdom	717.7	328.2	26.5	178.6	21.6	139.6	13.5	48.6	7.5	22.7	3.8
Southern Europe	711.6	256.0	20.7	257.7	31.1	136.1	13.1	32.5	5.0	29.4	5.0
Western Europe	431.5	264.9	21.4	75.4	9.1	48.9	4.7	27.8	4.3	14.5	2.4
Eastern Europe	420.5	219.0	17.7	44.5	5.4	34.8	3.4	58.9	9.1	63.3	10.7
Eastern Asia	377.2	22.2	1.8	39.2	4.7	108.8	10.5	88.0	13.6	118.9	20.0
South East Asia	312.0	2.9	0.2	14.7	1.8	116.5	11.2	99.4	15.4	78.5	13.2
United States	249.1	61.8	5.0	55.5	6.7	76.4	7.4	37.1	5.8	18.3	3.1
Caribbean and Bermuda	232.5	8.2	0.7	46.3	5.6	100.2	9.7	46.0	7.1	31.9	5.4
Southern Asia	228.8	5.1	0.4	30.0	3.6	85.3	8.2	56.1	8.7	52.3	8.8
Africa	166.2	5.6	0.5	27.1	3.3	59.8	5.8	32.9	5.1	40.7	6.9
South America	150.6	5.1	0.4	16.5	2.0	62.8	6.1	38.8	6.0	27.4	4.6
Western Asia and Middle East	146.8	5.4	0.4	13.8	1.7	30.2	2.9	37.8	5.9	59.6	10.0
Other Northern Europe	83.4	47.0	3.8	15.6	1.9	11.5	1.1	5.0	0.8	4.3	0.7
Central America	68.8	1.9	0.2	2.8	0.3	9.3	0.9	28.1	4.4	26.7	4.5
Oceania and other countries	46.3	5.8	0.5	10.2	1.2	17.4	1.7	8.0	1.2	5.0	0.8

1. Based on data from a 20% sample of the population. Non-permanent residents are not included in this table.
2. Includes the first five months only of 1991.

Source: Statistics Canada, Catalogue no. 93-316.

3.13 INTERPROVINCIAL MIGRANTS, 1994-95[1]

	Total out-migrants	Province of destination											
		Nfld.	P.E.I.	N.S.	N.B.	Que.	Ont.	Man.	Sask.	Alta.	B.C.	Y.T.	N.W.T.
Province of origin													
Newfoundland	18,867	...	208	2,710	815	382	9,140	314	116	2,447	2,204	61	470
Prince Edward Island	2,623	157	...	624	435	65	757	43	33	207	298	4	–
Nova Scotia	22,700	1,804	955	...	3,441	1,105	8,208	555	396	2,295	3,688	56	197
New Brunswick	16,130	545	719	3,191	...	2,618	5,580	396	157	1,546	1,306	–	72
Quebec	43,042	351	92	1,098	3,035	...	28,143	719	346	1,954	7,101	28	175
Ontario	85,609	5,379	986	7,404	4,891	18,107	...	7,204	2,490	12,113	26,425	194	506
Manitoba	25,448	197	45	510	429	699	7,180	...	4,020	5,112	6,871	46	339
Saskatchewan	27,689	87	64	270	215	279	3,219	4,249	...	12,971	5,923	86	326
Alberta	66,727	1,027	163	1,910	1,065	1,655	11,412	5,025	10,793	...	31,649	633	395
British Columbia	55,130	750	262	1,973	861	2,745	15,846	4,368	4,874	21,828	...	1,124	499
Yukon	2,289	–	4	9	16	39	133	17	41	560	1,308	...	162
Northwest Territories	4,373	160	–	184	94	154	593	396	256	1,616	769	151	...
Total in-migrants	370,627	10,457	3,498	19,883	15,297	27,758	90,211	23,286	23,522	62,649	87,542	2,383	4,141
Net interprovincial migration		-8,410	875	-2,817	-833	-15,284	4,602	-2,162	-4,167	-4,078	32,412	94	-232

1. From July 1 of one year to June 30 of next year.

Source: Statistics Canada, CANSIM, matrix 6365.

3.14 OFFICIAL LANGUAGE KNOWLEDGE

	Total	English only		French only		Both English and French		Neither English nor French	
	'000	'000	%	'000	%	'000	%	'000	%
1931[1]	10,376.8	6,999.9	67.5	1,779.3	17.1	1,322.4	12.7	275.2	2.7
1941[1]	11,506.7	7,735.5	67.2	2,181.7	19.0	1,474.0	12.8	115.4	1.0
1951[1]	13,648.0	9,031.0	66.2	2,741.7	20.1	1,723.5	12.6	151.9	1.1
1951	14,009.4	9,387.4	67.0	2,741.8	19.6	1,727.4	12.3	152.8	1.1
1961	18,238.2	12,284.8	67.4	3,489.9	19.1	2,231.2	12.2	232.4	1.3
1971	21,568.3	14,469.5	67.1	3,879.3	18.0	2,900.2	13.4	319.4	1.5
1981	24,083.5	16,122.9	66.9	3,987.2	16.6	3,682.0	15.3	291.4	1.2
1991	26,994.0	18,106.8	67.1	4,110.3	15.2	4,398.7	16.3	378.3	1.4
1991									
Newfoundland	563.9	544.4	96.5	0.2	–	18.5	3.3	0.8	0.1
Prince Edward Island	128.1	114.8	89.6	0.3	0.2	13.0	10.1	0.1	0.1
Nova Scotia	891.0	811.9	91.1	1.6	0.2	76.5	8.6	1.0	0.1
New Brunswick	716.5	415.0	57.9	89.5	12.5	211.5	29.5	0.5	0.1
Quebec	6,810.3	373.8	5.5	3,958.9	58.1	2,413.0	35.4	64.6	0.9
Ontario	9,977.1	8,593.6	86.1	54.2	0.5	1,136.2	11.4	192.9	1.9
Manitoba	1,079.4	965.1	89.4	1.9	0.2	98.8	9.2	13.6	1.3
Saskatchewan	976.0	919.1	94.2	0.5	0.1	50.8	5.2	5.7	0.6
Alberta	2,519.2	2,318.9	92.0	1.9	0.1	167.2	6.6	31.2	1.2
British Columbia	3,247.5	2,976.3	91.6	1.1	–	207.2	6.4	62.9	1.9
Yukon	27.7	25.0	90.3	--	--	2.6	9.4	--	--
Northwest Territories	57.4	48.9	85.2	0.1	0.2	3.5	6.1	5.0	8.7

1. Excluding Newfoundland.

Sources: Statistic Canada, Catalogue nos. 11-402 and 93-318.

3.15 SELECTED ETHNIC ORIGIN, 1991

	Canada	Nfld.	P.E.I.	N.S.	N.B.	Que.	Ont.	Man.	Sask.	Alta.	B.C.	Y.T.	N.W.T.
Total Population	26,994,045	563,935	128,100	890,950	716,495	6,810,300	9,977,050	1,079,390	976,040	2,519,180	3,247,505	27,655	57,430
Single origins	19,199,790	465,650	72,930	532,845	503,820	6,237,905	6,698,995	669,405	558,675	1,451,000	1,952,855	14,160	41,540
French	6,129,680	9,690	11,680	54,775	228,990	5,068,450	527,005	53,565	30,045	74,560	68,665	870	1,375
English	3,958,405	378,685	29,465	256,265	167,940	159,260	1,813,105	121,960	106,130	337,330	581,185	3,220	3,855
German	911,560	1,320	645	24,830	4,480	31,345	289,420	93,995	121,310	185,630	156,635	1,060	885
Scottish	893,125	7,735	16,660	98,550	33,080	42,910	390,285	38,290	30,595	88,120	144,710	1,075	1,110
Canadian	765,095	1,230	795	9,675	9,325	20,025	525,240	15,375	28,855	92,490	60,320	735	1,035
Italian	750,055	295	40	2,715	1,320	174,530	486,765	8,120	1,975	24,745	49,265	135	160
Irish	725,660	56,070	10,155	35,850	34,740	82,790	318,700	21,915	22,675	62,360	78,645	920	835
Chinese	586,645	740	90	1,965	1,255	36,820	273,870	11,145	7,550	71,635	181,185	100	275
Ukrainian	406,645	120	65	1,365	470	11,450	104,995	74,280	55,955	104,350	52,760	385	445
North American Indian	365,375	2,350	370	7,185	4,030	49,880	65,710	55,125	52,050	47,400	69,060	3,550	8,665
Dutch	358,180	445	1,250	8,960	3,045	7,100	179,760	24,465	11,285	54,750	66,525	295	305
East Indian, not included elsewhere	324,840	710	95	1,945	755	17,460	172,960	6,850	2,380	32,240	89,265	50	135
Polish	272,810	175	145	2,365	580	23,695	154,155	21,600	11,770	32,840	25,225	110	150
Portuguese	246,890	190	40	510	260	37,165	176,300	8,220	475	6,830	16,860	15	15
Jewish	245,840	65	50	1,515	620	77,600	132,110	12,265	1,060	7,870	12,625	30	35
Black	214,265	85	20	10,705	1,015	39,065	144,720	4,330	1,045	7,995	5,200	20	60
Filipino	157,250	185	10	275	150	9,920	78,550	22,045	1,635	16,310	27,925	35	210
Greek	151,150	155	–	1,280	325	49,890	83,780	2,075	1,255	3,830	8,465	40	30
Hungarian	100,725	50	55	495	260	8,990	53,055	3,215	7,920	12,100	14,345	140	90
Vietnamese	84,005	65	–	540	175	19,980	34,335	3,005	1,335	13,280	11,175	30	90
Métis	75,150	320	25	250	170	8,670	4,680	18,850	14,145	20,485	5,065	165	2,320
Inuit	30,085	2,670	10	95	70	6,850	620	365	75	560	290	60	18,430
Other single origins	1,446,355	2,300	1,265	10,735	10,765	254,060	688,875	48,350	47,155	153,290	227,460	1,120	1,030
Multiple origins	7,794,250	98,290	55,165	358,105	212,675	572,395	3,278,055	409,985	417,360	1,068,180	1,294,650	13,495	15,890

Source: Statistics Canada, Catalogue no. 93-315.

3.16 MOTHER TONGUE, 1991

	Canada	Nfld.	P.E.I.	N.S.	N.B.	Que.	Ont.	Man.	Sask.	Alta.	B.C.	Y.T.	N.W.T.
Total population	26,994,040	563,940	128,100	890,950	716,495	6,810,300	9,977,050	1,079,395	976,035	2,519,180	3,247,505	27,660	57,435
Single response	26,663,790	563,345	127,740	887,810	711,745	6,735,260	9,835,180	1,059,390	964,180	2,486,375	3,209,160	27,340	56,255
English	16,169,875	555,645	120,590	830,120	460,540	599,145	7,380,370	784,210	807,115	2,031,115	2,545,495	24,410	31,135
French	6,502,865	2,770	5,590	36,635	241,565	5,556,105	485,395	49,130	20,885	53,715	48,835	865	1,375
Italian	510,990	35	–	945	555	133,210	326,035	5,220	965	14,465	29,405	45	110
Chinese	498,845	560	60	1,535	1,020	30,755	234,175	9,825	6,510	60,265	153,850	80	205
German	466,245	415	165	2,170	1,315	19,795	162,675	67,975	42,260	80,030	88,595	525	330
Portuguese	212,090	125	20	365	180	33,890	150,630	7,245	400	5,545	13,685	–	15
Polish	189,810	90	60	1,130	240	19,105	118,845	11,985	4,295	19,950	14,025	20	60
Ukrainian	187,010	40	5	310	115	6,460	54,890	36,915	27,615	43,195	17,250	95	115
Spanish	177,425	140	85	720	255	51,735	85,850	4,325	1,800	15,580	16,890	10	40
Dutch	139,035	115	570	1,980	875	3,840	76,185	4,915	2,505	20,635	27,230	80	105
Punjabi	136,460	145	55	405	25	3,475	48,580	3,265	370	12,425	67,620	30	55
Greek	126,205	90	–	930	235	46,105	66,670	1,675	895	2,925	6,630	20	25
Arabic	107,750	40	115	1,560	345	46,165	46,565	570	380	9,315	2,670	–	25
Tagalog (Filipino)	99,715	105	–	200	80	5,475	50,980	13,865	960	10,055	17,825	30	140
Hungarian	79,770	65	50	270	265	9,330	45,585	2,260	3,515	7,955	10,335	90	50
Vietnamese	78,565	50	–	490	205	17,790	31,735	2,855	1,315	12,770	11,235	30	95
Cree	73,780	–	–	40	–	11,510	4,400	21,420	21,020	13,800	1,375	25	200
Inuktitut	24,100	490	–	15	5	6,535	240	130	15	115	35	5	16,520
Other non-official language	1,213,505	3,020	735	11,130	8,675	209,875	607,245	51,610	33,215	105,325	174,520	1,300	6,835
Multiple response	330,250	585	360	3,140	4,750	75,040	141,875	20,000	11,855	32,810	38,345	315	1,175
English and non-official language	186,820	380	40	1,230	480	12,235	93,935	15,200	9,375	24,050	28,690	220	990
English and French	91,895	180	315	1,665	4,185	39,485	31,395	2,950	1,545	5,350	4,625	65	130
French and non-official language	22,550	–	–	105	40	17,210	3,485	260	215	510	685	15	20
English, French and non-official language	5,925	5	–	20	25	3,590	1,520	125	80	265	290	–	10
Non-official languages	23,060	15	–	120	20	2,520	11,540	1,470	640	2,630	4,060	20	30

Source: Statistics Canada, Catalogue no. 93-333.

3.17 HOME LANGUAGE, 1991

	Canada	Nfld.	P.E.I.	N.S.	N.B.	Que.	Ont.	Man.	Sask.	Alta.	B.C.	Y.T.	N.W.T.
Total population	26,994,045	563,940	128,100	890,950	716,495	6,810,300	9,977,050	1,079,390	976,040	2,519,180	3,247,505	27,655	57,430
Single response	26,506,310	563,100	127,735	887,705	710,475	6,683,135	9,764,695	1,055,195	964,140	2,478,530	3,189,090	27,400	55,095
English	18,220,175	559,095	124,435	856,585	485,580	716,150	8,397,000	935,225	915,210	2,285,525	2,881,565	26,615	37,185
French	6,211,240	1,235	2,935	21,590	220,590	5,604,020	300,085	23,545	6,350	17,805	12,120	360	610
Chinese	389,235	285	50	880	685	25,270	187,680	7,380	4,485	45,185	117,150	55	130
Italian	241,420	–	–	250	130	70,480	152,830	1,960	280	5,205	10,245	–	35
Portuguese	133,815	55	0	205	125	21,300	98,735	4,025	180	3,135	6,060	–	–
Spanish	123,130	80	35	510	145	37,070	61,710	3,150	1,155	9,765	9,500	–	–
German	114,270	30	10	535	280	5,130	40,960	22,790	6,915	22,950	14,545	110	25
Polish	103,905	40	30	540	140	10,960	68,870	5,045	1,140	10,565	6,570	–	20
Punjabi	101,260	105	10	165	–	2,295	36,875	2,430	170	8,950	50,190	20	30
Greek	79,340	55	0	600	135	33,440	39,695	825	390	1,175	3,000	15	–
Vietnamese	71,550	20	–	475	165	17,120	29,355	2,365	1,160	11,310	9,495	–	80
Arabic	64,935	–	90	790	155	28,520	28,720	115	115	5,130	1,280	–	15
Cree	50,770	–	–	–	–	10,840	3,100	16,385	13,315	6,895	215	–	20
Tagalog (Filipino)	48,135	20	–	65	15	2,790	24,725	8,510	515	4,060	7,385	–	35
Ukrainian	39,530	–	–	–	–	2,700	19,185	6,895	4,010	5,500	1,230	–	–
Hungarian	26,240	60	–	60	60	3,965	16,040	610	335	2,190	2,865	45	15
Inuktitut	20,075	165	–	–	–	6,280	10	50	–	30	–	–	13,535
Dutch	14,550	10	110	210	140	665	7,695	680	230	2,375	2,435	–	10
Other non-official language	452,735	1,845	30	4,245	2,130	84,140	251,425	13,210	8,185	30,780	53,240	180	3,350
Multiple response	487,730	840	360	3,245	6,020	127,160	212,355	24,195	11,895	40,650	58,420	260	2,330
English and non-official language	320,055	605	130	1,835	640	27,420	169,400	20,755	10,155	34,740	51,995	185	2,190
English and French	113,185	195	230	1,255	5,325	58,285	34,275	2,900	1,550	4,445	4,520	65	135
French and non-official language	33,710	–	–	80	20	31,650	1,610	30	25	145	140	–	–
English, French and non-official language	11,220	25	–	–	–	8,415	2,030	85	75	245	315	–	10
Non-official languages	9,560	15	–	60	20	1,390	5,040	415	95	1,075	1,445	–	–

Source: Statistics Canada, Catalogue no. 93-317.

3.18 RELIGION, CANADA, THE PROVINCES AND TERRITORIES, 1991

	Canada	Nfld.	P.E.I.	N.S.	N.B.	Que.	Ont.	Man.	Sask.	Alta.	B.C.	Y.T.	N.W.T.
							'000						
Total population[1]	26,994.0	563.9	128.1	891.0	716.5	6,810.3	9,977.1	1,079.4	976.0	2,519.2	3,247.5	27.7	57.4
Catholic	12,335.3	208.9	60.6	331.3	386.6	5,861.2	3,554.5	327.8	316.9	666.8	603.1	5.6	21.9
Roman Catholic	12,203.6	208.9	60.6	331.0	386.5	5,856.0	3,506.8	294.0	296.7	640.5	595.3	5.5	21.8
Ukrainian Catholic	128.4	--	--	0.3	0.1	4.0	36.5	33.4	20.2	26.2	7.5	--	0.1
Other Catholic	3.2	–	–	–	–	1.2	1.2	0.4	0.1	0.1	0.2	–	–
Protestant	9,780.7	344.0	62.0	482.2	287.4	398.7	4,428.3	550.1	521.7	1,219.2	1,446.5	11.9	28.7
United Church	3,093.1	97.4	26.0	153.0	75.6	62.0	1,410.5	200.4	222.1	419.6	420.8	2.4	3.3
Anglican	2,188.1	147.5	6.7	128.4	61.2	96.1	1,059.9	94.2	69.9	173.2	328.6	4.1	18.4
Baptist	663.4	1.4	5.3	98.5	80.9	27.5	264.6	20.2	15.4	63.7	84.1	1.0	0.7
Presbyterian	636.3	2.2	11.0	31.2	10.1	18.9	422.2	16.1	11.6	48.4	64.0	0.4	0.4
Lutheran	636.2	0.4	0.1	11.5	1.6	10.7	227.9	55.1	82.2	137.1	108.2	0.7	0.7
Pentecostal	436.4	40.1	1.3	10.7	22.8	29.0	167.2	21.2	17.7	53.0	70.6	0.6	2.2
Other Protestant	2,127.2	55.0	11.6	48.9	35.2	154.5	876.0	142.9	102.8	324.2	370.2	2.7	3.0
Eastern non-Christian	747.5	1.2	0.3	4.7	1.7	97.6	379.6	16.6	6.5	78.5	160.0	0.3	0.5
Islam	253.3	0.3	0.1	1.4	0.3	44.9	145.6	3.5	1.2	31.0	24.9	--	0.1
Buddhist	163.4	0.1	0.1	1.5	0.4	31.6	65.3	5.3	1.9	20.7	36.4	--	0.1
Hindu	157.0	0.4	--	1.0	0.6	14.1	106.7	3.5	1.7	10.8	18.1	--	0.1
Sikh	147.4	0.1	0.1	0.3	--	4.5	50.1	3.5	0.6	13.6	74.6	--	0.1
Other Eastern non-Christian	26.4	0.3	0.1	0.5	0.4	2.5	11.9	0.8	1.1	2.4	6.0	0.3	0.1
Eastern Orthodox	387.4	0.4	0.1	2.3	0.8	89.3	187.9	20.7	19.5	42.7	23.5	0.1	0.2
Jewish	318.1	0.1	0.1	2.0	0.9	97.7	175.6	13.7	1.4	9.9	16.6	--	0.1
Para-religious groups	28.2	0.1	--	0.3	0.3	1.9	9.5	1.8	2.3	4.0	7.6	0.2	0.1
No religious affiliation	3,386.4	9.3	4.9	68.0	38.7	262.8	1,247.6	148.2	107.2	496.2	988.0	9.5	6.0
Other religions	10.6	--	--	0.1	0.2	1.1	3.9	0.6	0.5	1.8	2.3	0.1	--

1. Based on sample data, which exclude institutional residents.

Source: Statistics Canada, Catalogue no. 93-319.

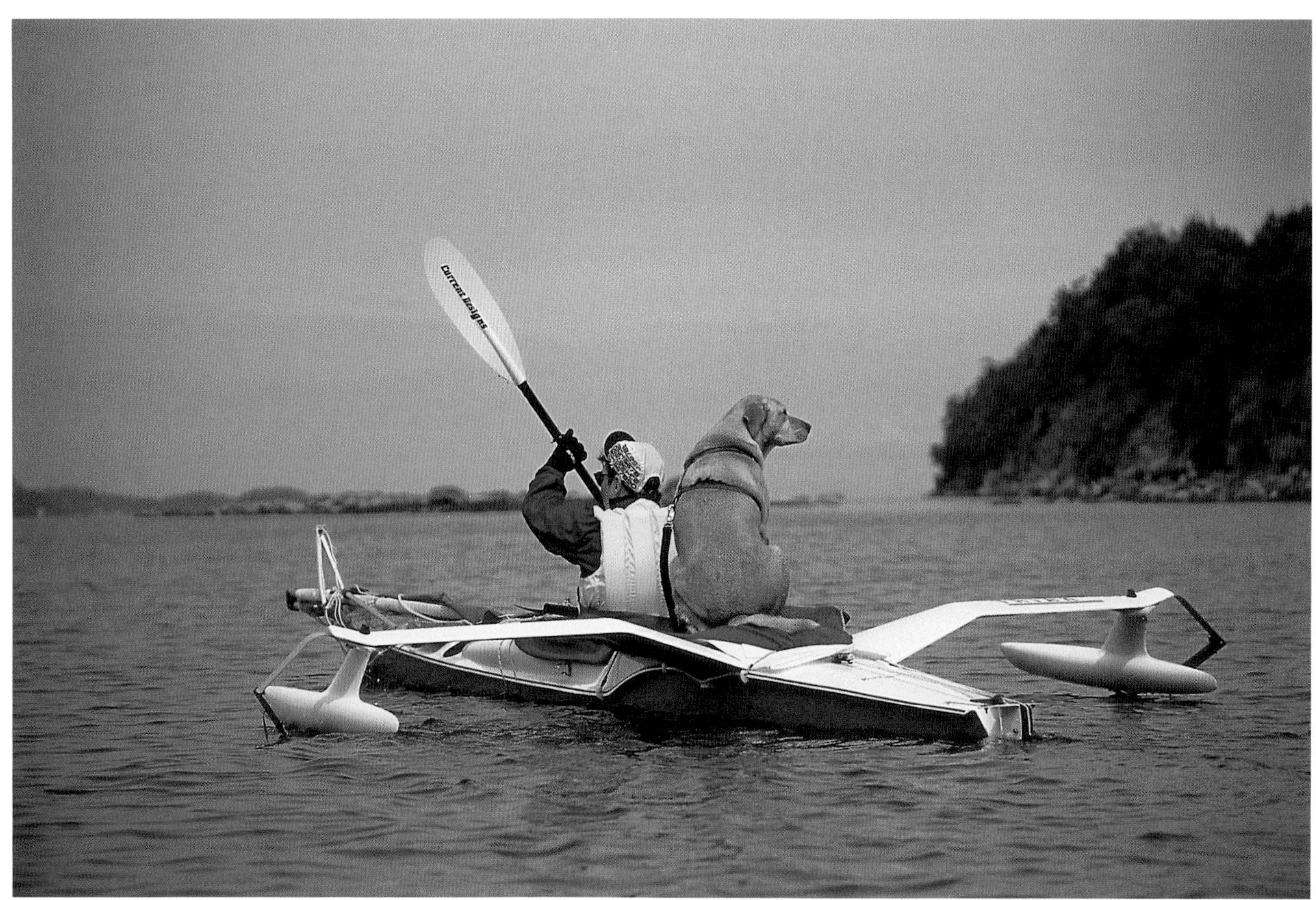

PHOTO BY **MIKE BEEDELL**

Chapter 4

HEALTH

Denis Boissavy, Masterfile

Few parents smiling into the faces of their newborn babies today in Canada are shadowed by the fears that haunted our grandparents, or even parents today in many other countries.

Our infant mortality rate is among the lowest in the world (six deaths per 1,000 children under one year of age in 1993), and our life expectancy rates among the highest: a baby girl born today can expect to live until she is 81 and a baby boy until he is 75.

In 1994, 62% of adults (over 15 years of age) rated their health as excellent or very good, and only 11% reported fair or poor health. Much of our good health we owe to our systems of public sanitation, housing, health care, prenatal and postnatal care, nutrition and disease prevention. Together this matrix of care has substantially increased our life and health expectancy from that of our grandparents.

But just as the passage of years has seen an improvement in our health and life expectancy, other challenges remain: disadvantaged groups have significantly lower life expectancy, poorer health and a higher prevalence of disability than most Canadians; preventable diseases and injuries continue to harm health and quality of life; and many Canadians suffer from chronic disease, disability, or stress, and lack adequate community support to help them cope and live meaningful, productive and dignified lives.

Health Care System

Throughout our lives our health care system forms a web of care around us that promotes health, prevents illness and disability, provides us with medical care and treatment when we need it, and comfort—or palliative care—when we are dying. Universal health care is an idea that has been around for decades; William Lyon Mackenzie King, Canada's tenth prime minister, first proposed universal health insurance in 1919. Over the years momentum grew to create a taxpayer-financed, comprehensive health care system that covers all medically necessary hospital and doctors' services regardless of ability to pay.

In most provinces, when Canadians need medical care they go to the doctor of their choice, who in turn bills the provincial government according to a fee schedule negotiated between the provincial medical association and the provincial government.

Our health care system, popularly called medicare, is made up of 12 interlocking provincial and territorial plans. Saskatchewan was the first province to establish public universal hospital insurance in 1947. By 1949, British Columbia had followed suit with a similar program and Alberta and Newfoundland had hospital plans that provided partial coverage. The Parliament of Canada passed legislation in 1957 that allowed the federal government to share in the cost of provincial hospital insurance plans that met certain eligibility and coverage standards. By 1961, every province and territory had public insurance plans to provide in-hospital care coverage.

This coverage expanded to include physicians' services outside hospitals (beginning once again in Saskatchewan, in 1962). In 1968, the federal government enacted medical care legislation and by 1972, all of the provincial and territorial health insurance plans included doctors' services. Today health services remain under provincial jurisdiction. The two territorial governments and the federal government provide health care for special groups such as Aboriginal people, immigrants, federal employees and the military.

Federal contributions toward each provincial plan are governed by the principles of the Canada Health Act: accessibility, comprehensiveness, public administration, portability and universality. If provinces allow extra billing by doctors or hospital user fees for insured health services, the Canada Health Act provides for an automatic dollar-for-dollar penalty. Statutory transfer payments to the provinces of $6.9 billion constitute 81% of Health Canada's 1995-96 total estimated annual expenditures of $8.5 billion.

The role of Health Canada is to help Canadians maintain and improve their health by taking into account the factors that determine health: genetics, behaviour, society, biology, economics and the environment. The emphasis is on fostering healthy individuals and families, and ultimately, a healthy society through disease prevention and health promotion initiatives.

Health Care Costs

Although we don't pay for services directly, Canadians spend a lot of money on health care. In 1991, Canada spent $66.8 billion on health care—$2,474 per Canadian. One out of every ten dollars in the Canadian economy pays for health care costs. One-third of provincial budgets and an increasing share of employer expenses go to pay for health care.

Over 70% of health care in Canada is financed through public expenditures. The remaining 30% comes from private insurance premiums and private sources. This ratio of

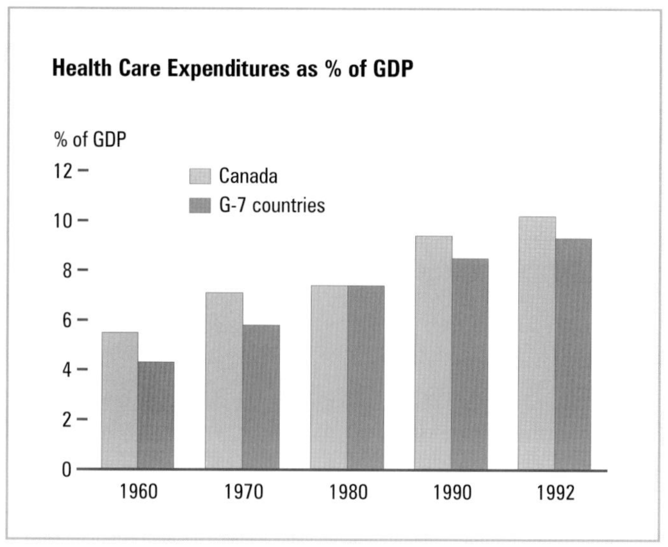

public-to-private health expenditures in Canada is similar to that of other industrialized countries.

Countries that spend the most on health do not always have the best health records. The United States, for example, spent 13.2% of its Gross Domestic Product (GDP) in 1991 on health care, yet its infant mortality rate (8.3 deaths per 1,000 births in 1993) was higher than that of Canada and several other Organisation for Economic Co-operation and Development (OECD) countries: Australia, France, New Zealand and the United Kingdom. Japan, on the other hand, has some of the best health indicators in the world, yet according to the United Nations (UN), in 1991, it spent only 6.8% of its GDP on health care; Canada spends about 10%.

As Canadians, we consider health care to be a basic right and we value our health system highly. But Canada's health care system is under pressure from rapidly escalating costs, due to an aging population, expensive new technology and rising consumer expectations. Recent estimates predicted that national health expenditures will drop to below 10% of the Gross Domestic Product. Provinces also spent a smaller percentage of their budgets on health care in 1994: 32.0% compared with 34.5% in 1990.

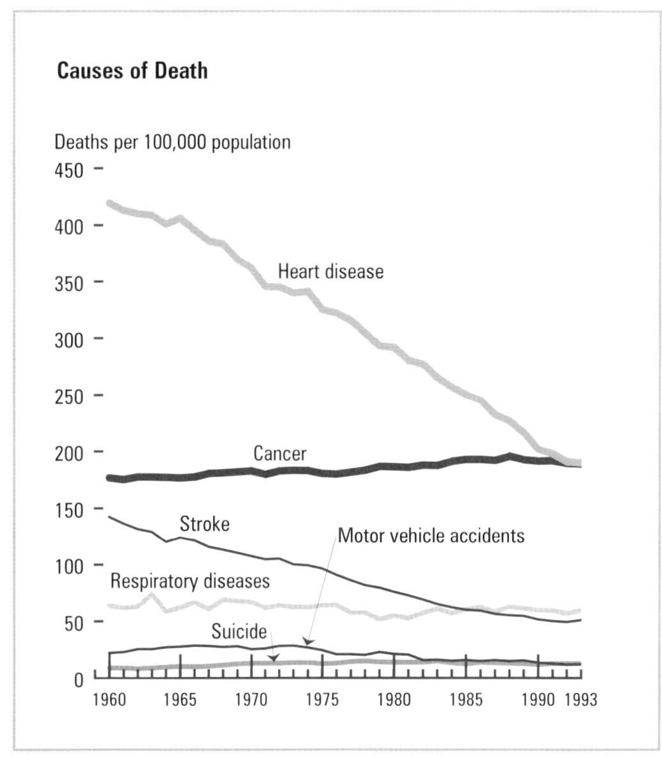

Causes of Death

In 1993, heart diseases were the leading cause of death in Canada: 190 deaths per 100,000 people. Cancer followed closely as the second killer, with 189 deaths per 100,000. Cardiovascular diseases followed with 51 deaths, and accidents claimed 31 per 100,000 Canadians.

In Childhood

Childhood mortality rates in Canada have fallen dramatically in this century thanks to better maternal and child health care, public hygiene and immunization programs. Between 1961 and 1990, prenatal programs, better management of pregnancies, and fewer teens giving birth all led to a decline in low birth weight, a factor related to mental and physical disabilities and many infant deaths.

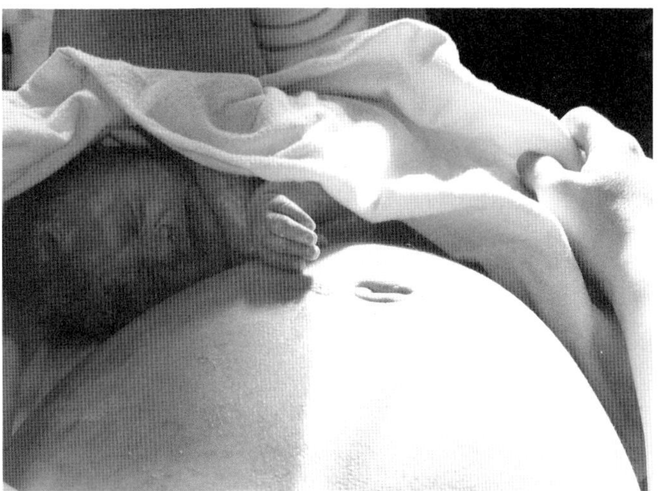

Photo by Gordon Laird

Cézanne, first portrait, 1 minute old.

Cigarette in hand, drink on the bar before him, Bogart says: "Of all the gin joints in all the towns in all the world, she walks into mine!" The movie? ***Casablanca***. *The message? Glamour and romance both drink and smoke.*

But, these days, with smoking and excessive drinking identified as two leading causes of premature death among Canadians, the message is changing. Bogey, after all, died in Hollywood in 1957, after a long battle with throat cancer.

In 1994, close to one-third of all Canadians smoked and more than half of all adults, or about 13 million, drank.

Smoking is the leading cause of preventable illness, disability and premature death in Canada. Tobacco kills three times more Canadians than alcohol, illegal drugs, car accidents, suicides and murder combined. Every year, two in every 10 Canadian deaths are caused by smoking.

During the 1930s and '40s—when Humphrey Bogart, Lauren Bacall and other film stars glamourized smoking—lung cancer death rates in men increased rapidly, from about three per 100,000 in 1932 to 15 per 100,000 in 1950. In recent years, they have increased more slowly, to about 70 deaths per 100,000 in 1991.

Up to 1960, lung cancer death rates for women rose slowly and unevenly, but have actually increased steeply since. During the 1970s and 1980s, lung cancer death rates for women almost doubled, but the rate was still less than half that for men in 1991.

Although smoking rates dropped during the two decades from 1970 to 1990, they have been fairly stable since then. In 1994, close to one-third of all Canadians over the age of 15—about seven million people—were smokers. Some 25% smoked daily, while 5% smoked occasionally.

Men were slightly more likely than women to smoke (33% vs. 29%). Among young people aged 15 to 19, however, about 30% of women smoked, compared with 28% of men.

When asked to describe their health, smokers were slightly more likely than non-smokers to describe it as fair or poor (12% versus 10%).

There are also links between smoking and stress. For example, 46% of men who had high levels of chronic stress were also smokers, close to double the rate of men with low levels of chronic stress (27%). The link was even more noticeable among women. Some 45% of women with high levels of chronic stress smoked, compared with only 21% among those with low stress levels.

In Bogart's day, the leading man and woman in popular movies invariably smoked as well as drank. Today, Canadian adults are more likely to drink than to smoke— almost twice as likely, in fact. In 1994, only one in ten Canadian adults said they had never drunk alcohol.

Drinking habits are related to both sex and age. Overall, men were more likely than women to be current drinkers, and for both sexes drinking is most common at younger ages, peaking in the 20s. Nevertheless, Canadians are drinking less alcohol than they used to. In 1993, the proportion of Canadians aged 15 and older who reported drinking in the previous year was 74.4%, compared with 79.0% in 1991.

Midwifery

The earliest mention of a non-Aboriginal midwife in Canada dates back to February 12, 1713, when the women of Ville-Marie (part of present-day Montreal) elected Catherine Guertin as their midwife. Today, almost 300 years later, the midwifery movement remains consumer-driven as women choose who will attend them in pregnancy, labour, and the early weeks of motherhood.

The word midwife means "with woman." Although midwives attend 80% of all births throughout the world, Canada remains one of only eight countries in the World Health Organization that has not officially recognized midwives. Ontario legislated midwifery in 1994. Alberta, British Columbia and Manitoba are expected to follow suit. Quebec and the Northwest Territories are conducting midwifery pilot projects and New Brunswick is studying the issue.

Results from a 1995 survey show that almost all of Canada's children (94.1%) are vaccinated against the childhood diseases that our grandparents feared: diphtheria, pertussis (whooping cough), and tetanus. Similarly high immunization rates (87.4%) protect children against polio. While 96.2% of children receive a one-time immunization against measles, there has been an increase in the number of measles outbreaks in Canada. As a result, the National Advisory Committee on Immunization now advocates a routine two-dose vaccination and Health Canada is encouraging a massive vaccination campaign against measles.

Despite prenatal and health care, the first year of life remains the most dangerous one of childhood. During these fragile months, about three-quarters (72%) of infant deaths are due to prematurity or congenital anomalies, such as structural defects of the heart.

A high proportion of Aboriginal infants are included in infant mortality statistics. The death rates for Status Indian and Inuit babies are twice as high as the rate for the total Canadian population. The death rate from sudden infant death syndrome (SIDS) is three times higher for the Indian population, and four times higher for the Inuit, than for the total Canadian population.

In Adulthood

Once the candle on the first birthday cake has been blown out, the automobile emerges as a major threat to the health and lives of Canadian children. Car crashes are the leading cause of death of boys and girls from ages one through 19. Cancer is the second leading cause of death up to age 14, when it is replaced by suicide.

During the teen years (10 to 19) car crashes remain the leading killer, followed by suicide. The spectre of suicide hangs over young male adults (20 to 44) who are more likely to die at their own hand than by any other cause. For women aged 20 to 44, car crashes, breast cancer and suicide are the three leading causes of death.

In middle age (45 to 64), cancer is the leading cause of death for men and women, followed by diseases of the circulatory system. Diseases of the circulatory system are the leading causes of death for seniors over 65, claiming 42% of men and 46% of women. Cancer follows as the second leading cause of death.

Illness and Disability

It is generally agreed that many factors determine our health, including genetics, the physical environment, social and economic circumstances, and our psychological state. At a global level, we know that countries with a more equal distribution of income and opportunity have better health outcomes. At the individual level, we know that those at the greatest risk of ill health are people without work, single parents, the working poor, and children in poverty.

Social Status and Health

A growing body of evidence links higher socio-economic status with better health. In fact, the World Bank states that "Economic policies conducive to sustained growth are among the most important measures governments can take to improve their citizens' health." The emphasis, however, should be on a more equitable distribution of wealth as evidenced by Japan which has some of the best health status indicators in the world, and the smallest relative difference in income between the top and bottom 20% of all member countries of the OECD.

In 1994, almost three-quarters (72%) of Canadians with a post-secondary degree or diploma surveyed reported excellent or very good health, compared with less than half (49%) of those people with less than secondary school completion.

In 1986, infants from lower-income neighbourhoods were 30% to 50% more likely to have a low birth weight, a factor linked to mental and physical disabilities and many early infant deaths.

Evidence also suggests that chronic diseases, such as cancer and heart disease, affect more people with lower socio-economic status. In 1990, adults living in households with lower incomes were more likely to smoke daily, and to use tranquilizers or sleeping pills. They were also less likely to know some of the causes of heart disease and methods to prevent the spread of sexually transmitted diseases.

Infectious Diseases

History tells the tragedy of infectious disease: raging smallpox epidemics, communities decimated by tuberculosis, cholera pandemics during the 19th century, immigrant workers on the Rideau Canal being stricken by malaria, the global influenza epidemic of 1917 to 1918, polio epidemics leading to school closures, and the spread of typhoid fever in urban centres until clean water could be supplied in cities. Today public health measures, immunizations and antibiotics often hold most of these diseases at bay.

One infectious disease, however, acquired immune deficiency syndrome (AIDS), still has no cure. As of December 1995, a total of 12,552 adult cases of AIDS had been reported in Canada: 11,819 of these were men, 733 were women. Another 118 cases were children. AIDS is now the third leading cause of death among Canadian men aged 20 to 44 following suicide and car crashes.

Men who have sex with men continue to be a high risk group for infection, as are injection drug users. According to one study, every year in Canada since 1990, 2,500 to 3,000 people have been infected with the human immunodeficiency virus (HIV) that causes AIDS. People are also becoming infected at a younger age: in 1983-84, the median age of infection was 27; now it is down to 23.

As the disease affects a broader population at a younger age, prevention, and care and treatment of those infected with HIV or AIDS, continues to pose special challenges to epidemiologists, public health authorities, and front-line health workers.

Tuberculosis, a major killer of Canadians until the 1950s, is on the wane. In 1993, the rate of tuberculosis in Canada fell to an all-time low of 6.9 cases per 100,000 people compared with 9.8 cases per 100,000 people in the United States. More than half (53%) of the 2,011 cases diagnosed in 1993 were among foreign-born individuals. Potential immigrants to Canada are examined to ensure they do not import active tuberculosis, but it is possible for some to arrive in Canada with a latent form of tuberculosis.

One-fifth of all tuberculosis cases are among Aboriginal people. Factors that contribute to the high rate of tuberculosis among Aboriginal people include a high rate of existing infection, crowded living conditions, poor nutrition and poverty.

Heart Disease

Cardiovascular disease is the leading cause of death worldwide, although rates have been declining steadily since the mid-1960s. Fewer people smoking, reduced consumption of dietary fat, improved identification and control of high blood pressure, and better medical and surgical care of people with heart disease are factors that may have contributed to this decline.

In 1991, death rates from cardiovascular disease were 423 per 100,000 for men and 261 per 100,000 for women. Within Canada, rates were highest in Newfoundland for both men (363 per 100,000) and women (244 per 100,000); they were lowest in British Columbia for men (288 per 100,000) and in Saskatchewan for women (166 per 100,000).

Cardiovascular diseases accounted for 20% of disability pensions paid by the Canada Pension Plan in 1992 to people over 65, second only to musculoskeletal disabilities. Cardiovascular diseases were also responsible for 12% of hospital admissions, more than 19% of all patient days in hospital, and almost 10% of visits to physicians in 1994.

Cancer

In 1995, an estimated 125,400 new cases of cancer were diagnosed and 61,500 people died of cancer. The most frequently diagnosed cancers were breast cancer for women and prostate cancer for men, but lung cancer was the leading cause of cancer death for women and men in 1995.

While the rate of breast cancer has risen in the past decade, mortality rates have remained stable. Lung cancer rates among women have more than tripled between 1969 and 1995, a sharp increase that surpasses the 58% growth in lung cancer among men over the same period. One explanation for this increase is that after the Second World War women began smoking in greater numbers and are now suffering the consequences.

Chronic Conditions

As Canadians live longer, the percentage of elderly Canadians has been increasing. Between 1990 and 2013, the percentage of Canadians aged 55 and over will increase by 80% to a total of 9.9 million people, representing almost one-third (28%) of the projected population. The aging of our population means we can expect in the coming years to see increases in chronic disease and disabilities.

Disability is defined by the World Health Organization (WHO) as any restriction or lack of ability to perform an activity in the manner or within the range considered normal for a human being.

In 1991, 4.2 million Canadians, 15.4% of the population, reported some kind of disability. Two out of five Canadian seniors (43%) reported having a disability or health condition that limited their activities. Approximately 250,000 Canadian children (5%) have a disability. Very few of these children live in institutions, and a relatively small minority have serious disabilities.

Over half (55%) of adults responding to the 1994-95 National Population Health Survey reported that they had at least one chronic condition. The most common problem was allergies (20% of all adults), followed by back problems (15%), arthritis and rheumatism (13%), and high blood pressure (9%).

Chronic health problems increase with age. Neck and hip fractures, in particular, are an important cause of mortality and disability among the elderly. In 1990, 974 elderly people died after having fractured their hips. Women 75 and over made up 63% of all hospital days for hip fractures.

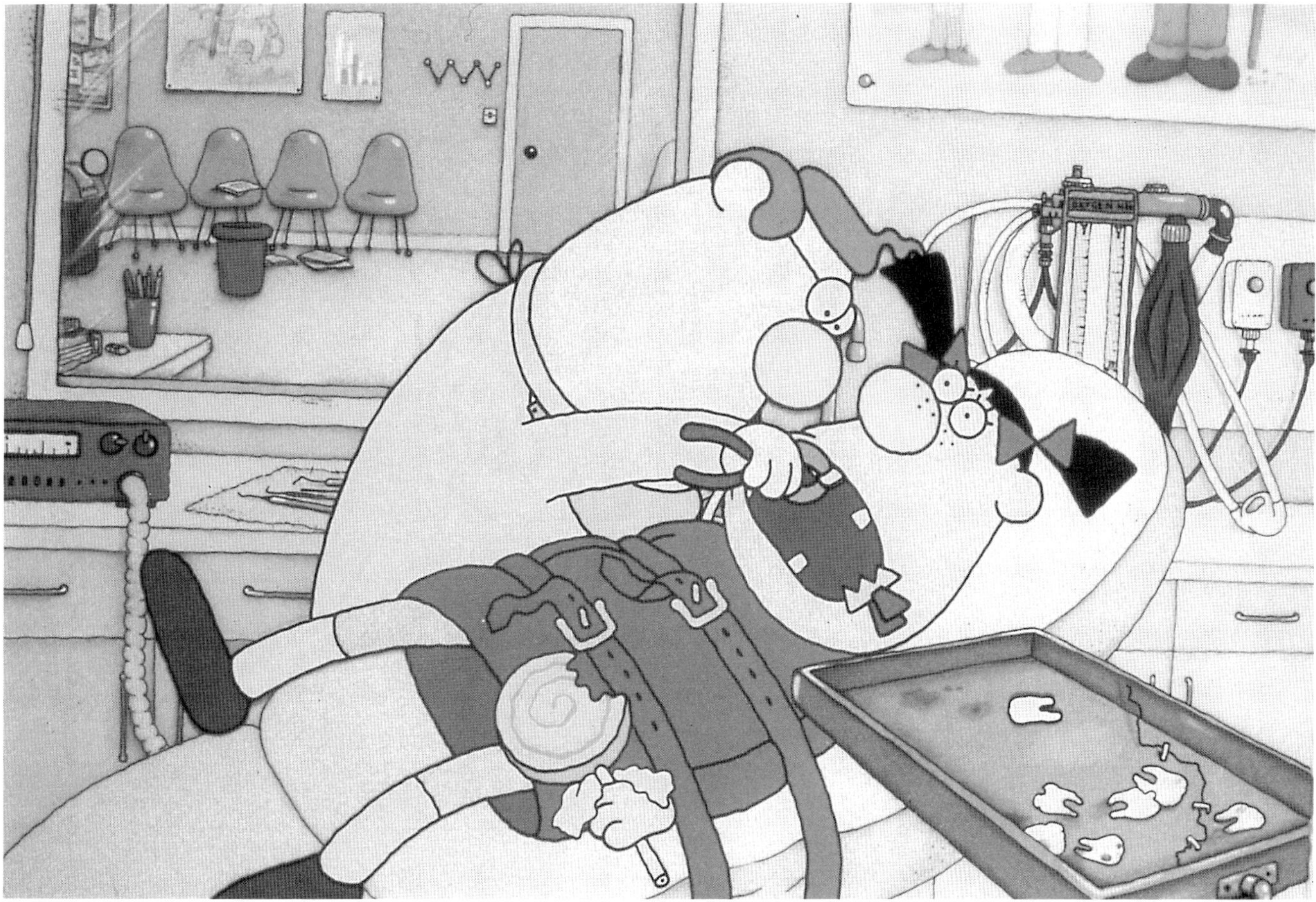

Courtesy of the National Film Board of Canada

A still from the animated film *Bob's Birthday*. (A Snowden Fine Animation for Channel 4, co-produced in association with the National Film Board of Canada.)

Care-Givers

In 1994, Canadians made an estimated 264 million visits to physicians. There were more doctors than 15 years earlier: one doctor per 534 Canadians, an increase from 1980, when there was one doctor per 664 people. The average net professional earnings for Canadian doctors in 1992 was $129,036, up from $60,830 in 1980. Women, who in 1980 represented only 12% of all physicians, in 1994 made up a quarter of all physicians.

On the front line in health care, there was one nurse for every 125 Canadians in 1994. In 1982, three out of four nurses (74%) worked in hospitals; this dropped to 66% in 1994. Only 3% of

It's been almost 75 years since Canada was first vaulted onto the world medical research scene with the discovery of insulin by Sir Frederick Banting and Charles Best. In many ways, their achievement, which has saved millions of lives, was to be a harbinger of the work of future Canadian medical researchers.

The range of accomplishments has been impressive. In the 1940s, Wilder Penfield pioneered the way in neurology with discoveries leading to the development of brain-mapping, bringing international acclaim to Canada. More recently, scientists have made major advances in the surgical treatment of life-threatening brain artery weaknesses. Dr. Albert Aguayo, for example, of the Neuro-Science Network in Montreal, has discovered that the regrowth and restoration of neural connections are possible in the central nervous system.

At the University of Toronto, Dr. Peter St. George Hyslop and colleagues have identified genes linked to two forms of Alzheimer's disease. More than 300,000 Canadians suffer from this disease. Elsewhere in Canada, neuroscientists are advancing knowledge about other brain disorders such as Huntington's and Parkinson's diseases, and schizophrenia, using sophisticated scanning machines.

Canadian scientists are also leading the way in the discovery of defective genes responsible for diseases like cystic fibrosis, several forms of muscular dystrophy, heart and blood vessel disease and cancer, including breast cancer. In 1994 and 1995, Dr. Leigh Field of the University of Calgary discovered three genes linked to juvenile diabetes which strikes one in 300 children.

In 1993, Dr. Michael Smith, of the University of British Columbia, won a Nobel Prize in Chemistry for a technique that makes it possible to change the structure of a gene and to obtain new insights into diseases like cancer, and bacterial and viral infection.

Canadians are also among world authorities in the field of virology and immunology. Dr. Tak Mak of the Ontario Cancer Institute has been heading research that has resulted in the cloning and sequencing of the T-cell receptor, a critical component of the body's defense system against disease. At McGill University, Dr. Philippe Gros has now cloned two genes, one responsible for resistance to multiple cancer drugs and the other which appears to control natural resistance to infections responsible for diseases like tuberculosis, salmonella poisoning and leprosy.

Since Dr. Wilfred Bigelow's development of the hypothermia "cold heart" method of open heart surgery in the 1950s, others have made major contributions in the development of heart pacemakers, heart-lung machines, improved heart surgery techniques and the first coronary care units.

Although by no means a comprehensive account of Canada's accomplishments, the work of these scientists is part of a growing body of medical research which is attracting worldwide attention.

One of the largest federal contributors to this activity is the Medical Research Council of Canada (MRC). MRC funds the health research efforts of about 10,000 scientists, technicians and their research support staff at Canada's 16 medical schools, as well as at more than 65 research institutes and teaching hospitals across the country.

nurses were men, a rate that has remained stable since 1990. In 1994, the salary for most registered nurses providing direct care ranged from $29,700 to $59,300 per year.

Hospitals

The hospital, along with the post office, the school, and the public library, is an object of civic pride in Canadian communities, a symbol of caring no population centre wants to be without. In 1993, there were 1,200 hospitals across Canada with a total bed capacity of 163,399 and an occupancy rate of 79%. They employed the equivalent of almost 400,000 full-time workers. The average cost per patient-day in public hospitals in 1992-93 increased to $553, up 6.8% from $516 in 1991-92.

Among the member countries of the OECD, Canada spends the largest proportion of its health care budget on hospital care (48.9%) and only 21.9% of its health care budget on "ambulatory care", that is, doctors' and health professionals' services.

In 1993-94, there were 3.5 million hospital admissions in Canada for a total of 39 million patient-days. Women and men were likely to stay in hospital an average of 11 days per visit. Women tend to go to hospital more often than men. Children under one year of age are more likely to be hospitalized than children at any other age.

Medicines

Just over three out of four adult Canadians in 1994 (77%) had used at least one prescription or over-the-counter medication in the month before they were surveyed about drug use. Pain relievers were the most commonly used drugs (62%), followed by cough or cold remedies (15%) and allergy medications (10%).

More than 220 million prescriptions were dispensed in Canada in 1994. The most common category of prescription drugs was for cardiovascular disease (13%), followed by anti-infectives (12%), and psychotherapeutics (10%).

In 1994, 3.3 million Canadians (15%) said they had used some form of alternative health care in the past year. These are services offered outside the traditional health care system. The most common form of alternative health care used by Canadians was chiropractic services (11%), followed by homeopathy (2%) and massage therapy (2%).

Lifestyle Trends

It is a well-accepted notion that health is more than the absence of disease. The state of well-being associated with good health is determined to a large extent by how we live our lives and cope with life's challenges.

On Smoking

Fewer than one-third of Canadian adults have smoked since the late 1980s. The proportion fell fairly steadily from almost half of all adults in 1965 to only 33% in 1986, then levelled off. In 1994, only 31% of all adults smoked. Long-term declines in smoking rates point to the success of anti-smoking campaigns, taxes on tobacco, higher insurance premiums for smokers, and restrictions on smoking in the workplace and other public places.

Overall, men were more likely to smoke than women (33% versus 29%). This trend held true at all ages except for 15 to

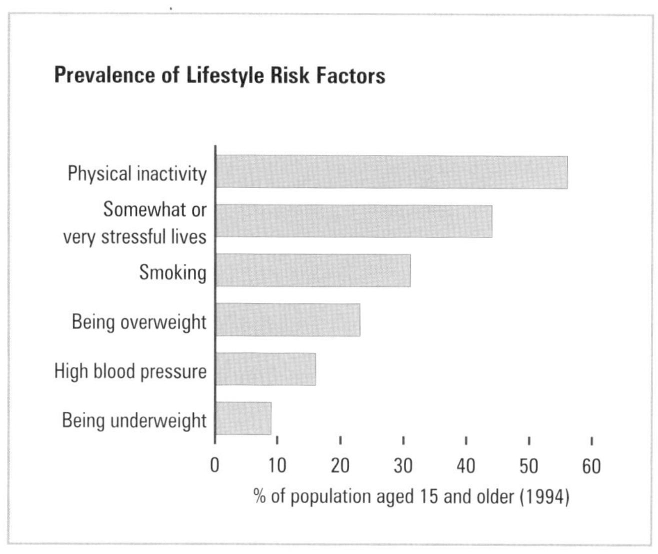

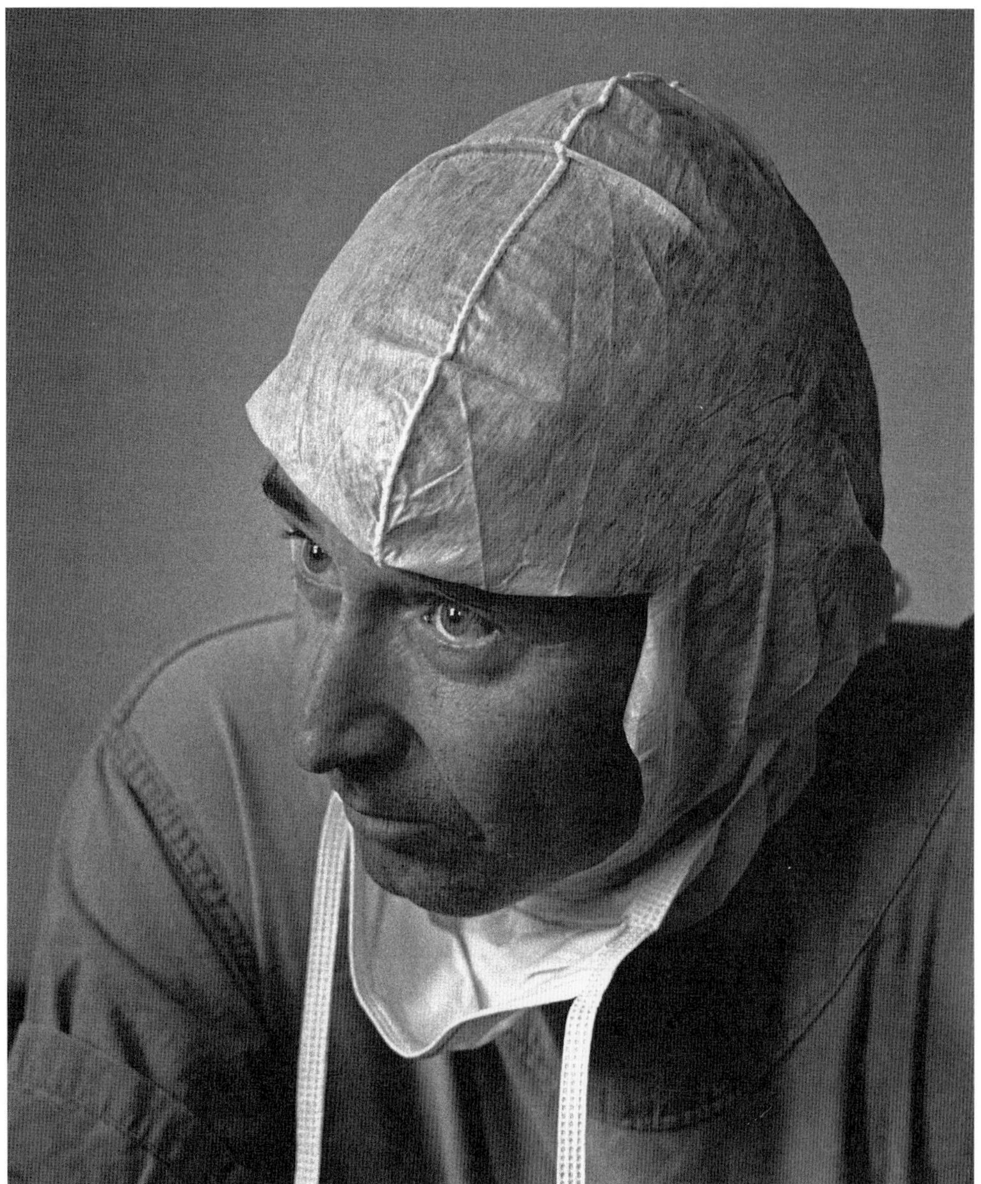

Ted Grant, Ted Grant Photography Ltd.

Portrait of a doctor. (From the book : *This is Our Work* ***The Legacy of Sir William Osler***, by Ted Grant.)

19-year-olds, where more women smoked than men. Close to half (44%) of the total Aboriginal population smokes daily.

On Drinking

Despite the fact that in 1994, almost three-quarters of adult Canadians (15.7 million) reported drinking in the previous year, Canada is far behind European countries as far as alcohol consumption is concerned. In 1991, the total per capita absolute alcohol consumption in Canada was 7.1 litres, compared with 11.9 in France.

Of Canadians who reported drinking in 1994, 26% drank less than once a month, 5% drank every day and the rest fell somewhere in between. Average consumption by current drinkers was four drinks per week. The highest rates of current drinkers were in Alberta and British Columbia (each 76%) and Quebec (74%). The lowest rates of current drinking were from the Maritimes: Prince Edward Island and New Brunswick, both at 68%.

Also in 1994, approximately one in five current drinkers stated that they drove after consuming two or more drinks in the previous hour—a drop from 23% in 1989. Men were three times as likely as women to drive after drinking: 28% compared with 11%.

On Nutrition

Canadians are now eating differently than we did 20 years ago. We have cut down on red meat, eggs, and butter and are eating more poultry, fish, low-fat milk, cheese, yogurt, and fresh vegetables.

A 1988 survey of young people 10 to 14 years of age showed that four in five eat in accordance with *Canada's Food Guide to Healthy Eating.* Sixty per cent said they limit the amount of fat in their diet; girls are more likely than boys to do so.

Based on the body mass index, which looks at both height and weight, results from the 1994-95 National Population Health Survey showed that almost a quarter (23%) of Canadians aged 20 to 64 were overweight. Another quarter (23%) had some excess weight; 43% were in the acceptable range, and 9% were underweight.

The Silent Thief

In coming years, more than two million Canadians will likely develop osteoporosis, or "porous bones," which causes bones to thin and weaken. In Canada, one in four women and one in eight men over the age of 50 have osteoporosis. For them, simply bending to pick up a heavy bag or even sneezing could cause a bone to fracture. The cost of treating hip fractures alone is more than $600 million a year. These costs will likely increase as the baby boom generation ages. In 1993, the overall cost of treating these fractures in Canadians was estimated to be $1.3 billion.

Research has proven that weight-bearing exercises, such as walking, tennis, stair climbing, and low-impact aerobics can prevent loss of bone mass. One study has revealed that a group of women aged 50-70 increased their resistance to risk of fractures by lifting weights two days a week. As an added bonus, the women increased muscle strength and improved balance, thereby lessening the risk of falls and fractures.

An estimated 1.4 million Canadians currently suffer from osteoporosis, sometimes called the "silent thief," as it robs bones of their density.

Chinese folklore has it that the more a ginseng root resembles the human form, the more potent its medicinal value. While Canada's medical establishment does not formally recognize ginseng's curative benefits, this has not damaged its business case. Ginseng production in Canada is a thriving concern with farm cash receipts for some $60 million in 1994 alone.

Ginseng comes in every form from teas and tablets to capsules and jellies. Historically, the emperors of China's Forbidden City dined on ginseng every day to improve their intellectual capacities, while the peasants used the root to cure disease and boost their energy levels in the fields. Today, some say ginseng can remedy everything from acne to ulcers, including leprosy, smallpox, breast cancer, diabetes and the common cold.

In the early 18th century, a Jesuit priest discovered ginseng near Montreal, and soon merchants began exporting it to China. But over-harvesting caused this native ginseng to become endangered by the mid-19th century. In fact, its survival was ensured only when domestic cultivation was developed around the turn of the century.

Since 1980, production of ginseng in Canada has tripled to 900,000 kilograms in 1994. In all, about 500 growers concentrated in Ontario and British Columbia cultivate ginseng with 90% of their harvest exported to China and Hong Kong.

The unlikely-looking root is a precious investment. Typically, a ginseng producer can gross some $44,000 per hectare.

On the other hand, from planting to harvest, ginseng takes about three to four years to fully mature. By the time the crop reaches market, a grower will have spent considerable amounts planting, tending and harvesting.

Ginseng comes in two forms, depending on where it's grown. The variety grown in North America is called American ginseng, and it grows wild in parts of Quebec, Ontario and Manitoba in Canada and south of the border in Wisconsin. American ginseng is chemically different from its Asian cousin. While Asian ginseng is said to invigorate, the American variety is said to be more cooling—that is, more calming. Canada produces about 45% of the world's American ginseng and by the late 1990s, production could rise to 75% of world supplies.

Researchers in Russia and Japan have spent decades trying to isolate the active ingredients of ginseng. Canadians are also researching its medicinal benefits with independent studies to explore the way it may affect hypertension, Alzheimer's disease and athletic endurance.

Keeping Fit

The 1994-95 National Population Health Survey of Canadians reported that more than half (56%) of respondents said they spent their leisure time in some kind of sedentary activity. Women were more likely than men to pursue an inactive leisure activity (61% compared with 51%). Physical activity peaks between 15 to 19 when three-quarters of young men and two-thirds of women have high levels of vigorous leisure-time physical activity.

Health Issues

Many health issues in Canada have stirred great debate and controversy. For example, ethical and political debates rage around abortion, considered by many Canadians to be much more than a health issue. In 1993, Canadian women obtained 104,400 abortions, an increase of 2.3% from the previous year.

More women are having abortions earlier in their pregnancies (before 13 weeks), which may account for a substantial decrease in abortion-related complications. In 1992, women between 18 and 24 were more likely than those in other age groups to have abortions, and more than half (63.7%) were single. Fewer women now travel to the United States to obtain abortions: 1,551 women went south of the border in 1989, compared with 526 women in 1992.

Sexual Health

In 1992, more than 38,000 women under 20 became pregnant. Teenage pregnancy varies across the country: Quebec has the lowest rate at 30 per 1,000 women aged 15 to 19. The highest rates are in the Northwest Territories (125 per 1,000) and Yukon (74 per 1,000). Teenage pregnancy rates have dropped from 49 per 1,000 in 1975 to 40 per 1,000 in 1993.

In 1990, only half of the 15- to-19-year-olds surveyed believed they were at risk of acquiring a sexually transmitted disease (STD). Young women have the highest incidence of sexually transmitted diseases. In 1993, young women aged 15 to 19 were six times more likely to be diagnosed with chlamydia than their male counterparts.

Depression

Depression is one of the most common psychiatric disorders and affects Canadians of every age. Depressed Canadians are not alone, however. Research shows an increasing prevalence of depression in industrialized countries for generations born after 1940. Symptoms include feelings of sadness or hopelessness, low self-esteem, guilt, increased or decreased sleep and/or appetite, and destructive behaviour.

Women are twice as likely as men to report feeling depressed. Younger women living in urban areas are especially at risk. Income is also associated with depression: the prevalence of depression among people with lower incomes in 1994 was 8% compared with 5% for other income groups.

Suicide

Young Canadian men (aged 20 to 29) and senior men (over 75) are at high risk with suicide rates of 30 per 100,000. Between 1989 and 1992, the Northwest Territories recorded the highest suicide rates for men and women. Men are more likely to use firearms to commit suicide, while women are more likely to use poison.

Aboriginal people are two to three times more likely to commit suicide than non-Aboriginal people. Aboriginal youth (aged 15 to 24) are five times more likely to take their own lives than their non-Aboriginal counterparts. Studies have suggested that in Aboriginal society the home situation and child-rearing practices have deteriorated under "westernizing" influences. Alcohol abuse, rapid cultural changes, frequent bereavement, and exposure to pain through neglect, hunger, physical abuse and disease lead to feelings of depression and alienation. Suicide may often be viewed as a brave and heroic act.

Dementia

As we age, our physical health may outlast our mental health. Slightly more than 2% of Canadians 65 and over experience some kind of dementia. Women are more likely than men to be hospitalized because of mental disorders. In 1993-94, more than one-third of women over age 75 who were

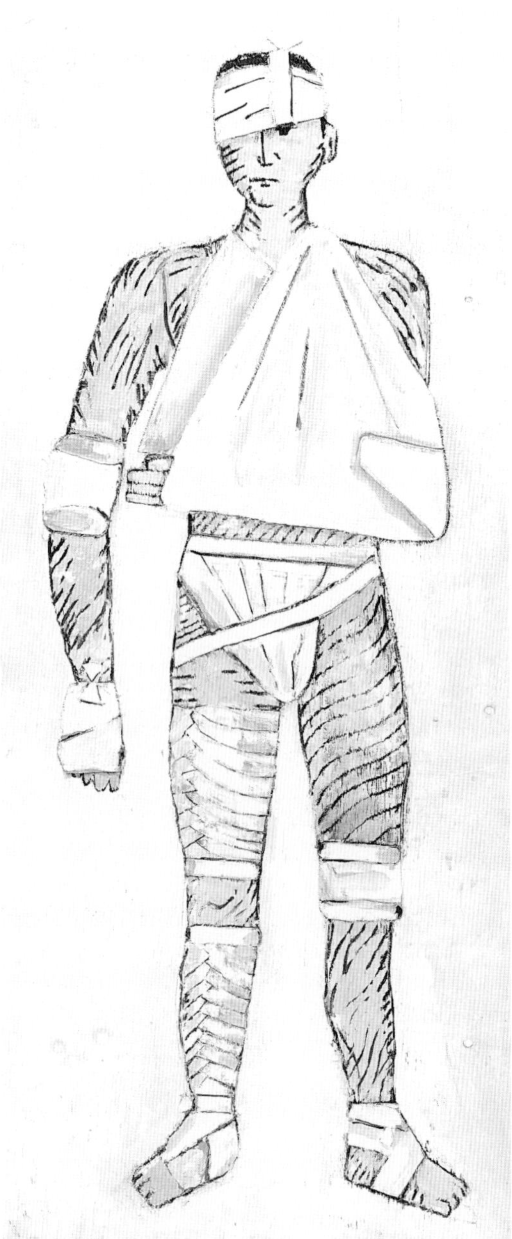

Paterson Ewen. National Gallery of Canada, Ottawa

***The Bandaged Man,* 1973.**

hospitalized were suffering from mental disorders related to senile and pre-senile conditions. If current trends continue, more than half a million Canadians (592,000) will have dementia in 2021.

Death

Canadians are asking themselves whether preserving life at all costs is the best course of action in the case of some illnesses. Christian Barnard, the South African surgeon who performed the first heart transplant, cautioned, "if your treatment does not alleviate suffering, but only prolongs life, that treatment should be stopped."

Headlines from British Columbia told the anguishing story of Sue Rodriguez, a British Columbia woman with amyotrophic lateral sclerosis (ALS). Rodriguez spent two years challenging the law that makes doctor-assisted suicide illegal. Her case went to the Supreme Court, which in 1993 ruled five to four to uphold the 1892 law prohibiting doctor-assisted suicide.

SOURCES

Canadian Institute of Child Health
Health Canada
Heart and Stroke Foundation
Osteoporosis Society of Canada
Statistics Canada

FOR FURTHER READING

Selected publications from Statistics Canada

- **Canadian Social Trends**. Quarterly. 11-008
- **Health Reports**. Quarterly. 82-003
- **National Population Health Survey Overview**. Occasional. 82-567
- **Canadian Cancer Statistics**. Annual. 82F0008E
- **Women in Canada**. Occasional. 89-503
- **A Portrait of Children in Canada**. Occasional. 89-520
- **Language, Tradition, Health, Lifestyle and Social Issues**. Occasional. 89-533

Selected publications from other sources

- **Canada's Health Care System: its funding and organization**. Anne Critchon, David Hsu, Stella Tsang. 1990.
- **The Health of Canada's Children**. Canadian Institute of Child Health. 1994.
- **Health Care in Canada**. Health Canada. 1993.

Legend

–	nil or zero	..	not available	x	confidential
--	too small to be expressed	...	not applicable or not appropriate		*(Certain tables may not add due to rounding)*

4.1 HEALTH EXPENDITURES[1]

	1975	1980	1990	1991	1992	1993	1994
				$ Millions			
Health expenditure	12,254.8	22,398.4	61,041.6	66,290.3	70,032.1	71,775.3	72,462.6
Hospitals	5,512.0	9,395.2	23,870.5	25,725.1	26,778.0	27,138.8	26,999.1
Other institutions	1,124.3	2,536.6	5,720.3	6,315.9	6,834.1	7,007.9	7,090.3
Physicians	1,839.9	3,287.5	9,258.3	10,219.6	10,463.9	10,362.6	10,322.6
Other professionals	901.7	1,906.6	5,179.5	5,636.8	5,912.9	6,056.1	6,192.9
Drugs, prescribed and non-prescribed	1,073.5	1,877.5	6,903.1	7,670.6	8,451.6	8,841.7	9,179.3
Other expenditures	1,803.5	3,391.1	10,109.9	10,722.3	11,591.4	12,368.4	12,678.5
				%			
Expenditures as a percentage of GDP							
Health expenditures[1]	7.1	7.2	9.1	9.8	10.1	10.1	9.7
Hospitals	3.2	3.0	3.6	3.8	3.9	3.8	3.6
Other institutions	0.7	0.8	0.9	0.9	1.0	1.0	0.9
Physicians	1.1	1.1	1.4	1.5	1.5	1.5	1.4
Other professionals	0.5	0.6	0.8	0.8	0.9	0.8	0.8
Drugs, prescribed and non-prescribed	0.6	0.6	1.0	1.1	1.2	1.2	1.2
Other expenditures	1.1	1.1	1.5	1.6	1.7	1.7	1.7

1. Health expenditures include spending by federal, provincial and local governments, workers compensation boards and the private sector.

Source: Health Canada, *National Health Expenditures in Canada, 1975-1994*.

4.2 PER CAPITA HEALTH EXPENDITURES[1]

	1975	1980	1990	1991	1992	1993	1994
				$			
Canada	529	911	2,196	2,358	2,463	2,496	2,478
Newfoundland	474	920	1,918	2,033	2,097	2,185	2,259
Prince Edward Island	502	987	1,980	2,119	2,263	2,308	2,299
Nova Scotia	465	772	2,061	2,166	2,248	2,278	2,231
New Brunswick	409	794	2,060	2,123	2,223	2,341	2,389
Quebec	532	901	1,999	2,161	2,243	2,252	2,263
Ontario	534	873	2,296	2,499	2,602	2,638	2,614
Manitoba	532	937	2,279	2,374	2,509	2,567	2,546
Saskatchewan	487	857	2,264	2,349	2,362	2,357	2,352
Alberta	560	984	2,327	2,401	2,556	2,555	2,400
British Columbia	552	1,067	2,231	2,407	2,560	2,629	2,631
Yukon and Northwest Territories	676	1,051	3,582	4,007	3,977	4,088	4,418

1. Health expenditures include spending by federal, provincial and local governments, workers compensation boards and the private sector.

Source: Health Canada, *National Health Expenditures in Canada, 1975-1994*.

4.3 EMPLOYMENT IN HEALTH AND SOCIAL SERVICES

	1985	1986	1987	1988	1989	1990	1991	1992	1993	1994	1995	Average annual growth rate 1985-1995
	Employees[1] '000											%
Health and social services	933.5	970.0	1,010.6	1,064.3	1,092.5	1,128.0	1,135.8	1,135.3	1,138.9	1,145.3	1,187.1	2.4
Institutional health and social services, non-institutional social services	755.1	782.7	797.2	830.4	845.4	864.7	869.2	861.9	867.5	870.6	891.6	1.7
Hospitals	505.6	513.5	525.9	545.5	554.1	568.3	574.2	571.6	564.2	553.9	542.4	0.7
Other institutional health and social services	172.2	186.7	187.9	196.6	201.7	202.9	195.3	190.0	194.6	202.0	224.7	2.7
Non-institutional social services	77.3	82.5	83.3	88.3	89.6	93.4	99.8	100.3	108.7	114.7	124.5	4.9
Other health and social services	178.4	187.4	213.4	233.9	247.1	263.4	266.5	273.4	271.4	274.7	295.5	5.2
Non-institutional health services	12.5	13.7	19.8	21.8	25.7	31.8	31.5	28.6	31.9	44.0	51.5	15.2
Offices of physicians, surgeons and dentists	91.6	94.8	109.4	115.3	119.5	127.2	128.0	134.8	130.6	123.8	129.7	3.5
Offices of other health practitioners	13.9	16.0	16.1	19.8	21.6	23.8	26.7	27.4	25.1	27.2	35.1	9.7
Offices of social services practitioners	0.6	0.7	0.6	0.6	0.7	0.8	1.1	1.4	1.6	2.5	2.5	15.3
Medical and other health laboratories	15.0	16.2	19.0	22.5	23.2	22.5	23.5	23.4	25.6	24.0	21.8	3.8
Health and social services associations and agencies	44.9	46.1	48.5	53.9	56.4	57.3	55.7	57.7	56.6	53.2	54.8	2.0
All industries[2]	9,651.1	9,927.2	10,329.1	10,659.0	11,054.7	11,146.1	10,549.5	10,246.9	10,271.4	10,447.1	10,447.1	1.0
	% of total employment											
Health and social services	9.7	9.8	9.8	10.0	9.9	10.1	10.8	11.1	11.1	11.0	11.1	

1. Excludes owners or partners of unincorporated businesses and professional practices, the self-employed, unpaid family workers, persons working outside Canada, military personnel and casual workers for whom a T4 is not required.
2. Excludes agriculture, fishing and trapping, private household services, religious organizations and the military.

Source: Statistics Canada, Catalogue no. 72F0002.

4.4 EARNINGS IN HEALTH AND SOCIAL SERVICES, BY INDUSTRY GROUP

	1985	1986	1987	1988	1989	1990	1991	1992	1993	1994	1995	Earnings in 1995 as a % of all industry earnings
	Average weekly earnings[1] $											
Health and social services	346.82	359.19	375.44	392.39	411.97	435.37	466.91	485.06	498.45	504.63	503.44	88.8
Institutional health and social services, non-institutional social services	354.53	364.71	383.75	399.47	416.44	444.28	478.60	499.44	512.41	515.40	515.01	90.8
Hospitals	386.99	396.65	420.84	439.74	458.00	488.91	529.66	553.03	571.30	575.43	580.29	102.3
Other institutional health and social services	290.53	304.60	313.91	323.00	338.72	360.80	380.40	408.81	416.83	423.46	425.69	75.1
Non-institutional social services	284.79	301.96	307.12	320.84	334.38	354.13	377.04	365.71	377.84	387.37	391.83	69.1
Other health and social services	314.19	336.12	344.43	367.28	396.70	406.14	428.79	439.75	453.84	470.51	468.54	82.6
Non-institutional health services	396.21	428.94	469.37	490.09	522.84	455.44	492.63	502.09	503.00	506.72	507.18	89.4
Offices of physicians, surgeons and dentists	275.10	299.62	297.48	328.17	363.25	370.98	391.80	404.06	423.84	448.52	443.81	78.3
Offices of other health practitioners	220.16	235.04	249.59	255.93	247.69	328.66	353.88	341.83	364.65	365.91	372.17	65.6
Offices of social services practitioners	322.91	347.51	363.88	361.09	374.55	448.68	472.44	546.58	607.39	520.33	524.39	92.5
Medical and other health laboratories	387.27	397.36	414.20	434.10	472.34	485.79	504.30	516.75	510.13	521.68	536.86	94.7
Health and social services associations and agencies	375.64	397.07	403.08	414.38	436.26	457.19	480.95	504.94	505.01	519.83	522.59	92.1
All industries[2]	412.02	424.25	440.26	459.75	483.31	505.14	528.60	547.01	556.76	567.11	572.49	100.9

1. Excludes owners or partners of unincorporated businesses and professional practices, the self-employed, unpaid family workers, persons working outside Canada, military personnel and casual workers for whom a T4 is not required.
2. Excludes agriculture, fishing and trapping, private household services, religious organizations and the military.

Source: Statistics Canada, Catalogue no. 72F0002.

4.5 HEALTH CARE BEDS,[1] 1991-1992

	Approved beds[2]	Short-term	Rehabilitation	Extended care	Other long-term	Minimal care	Self-sufficient
	Number of approved beds per 1,000 population[3]						
Canada	15.0	4.1	0.2	2.4	3.8	1.6	1.5
Newfoundland	12.8	4.5	0.1	3.9	1.3	2.2	0.9
Prince Edward Island	22.3	5.1	0.3	5.6	5.3	4.5	1.6
Nova Scotia	16.2	5.5	0.2	1.6	5.1	2.6	1.3
New Brunswick	17.8	5.2	0.1	3.4	4.2	2.7	2.2
Quebec[4]	13.7	4.0	0.2	2.0	1.7	0.0	0.0
Ontario	14.9	3.7	0.2	2.1	4.9	2.2	1.7
Manitoba	17.5	4.8	0.1	8.0	2.3	0.9	1.3
Saskatchewan	19.6	6.9	0.1	3.2	6.4	1.5	1.6
Alberta	16.2	4.6	0.1	0.3	5.2	1.6	4.3
British Columbia	14.3	3.2	0.2	3.5	3.5	2.2	1.7
Yukon	10.6	4.4	0.0	0.1	0.4	1.8	3.8
Northwest Territories	11.1	4.6	0.0	1.2	0.3	1.5	3.4

1. Beds are beds approved for the facility by the provincial authorities at the end of the reporting year. Includes only the facilities that were in operation for the entire fiscal year and reported beds in the Annual Hospital Survey.
2. Only facilities with four or more beds are included.
3. Population is based on October 1 estimated populations of each fiscal year.
4. Quebec residential care facilities are not classified by type of care so beds appear only in the approved beds column. As a result, total beds for Canada will not equal the sum of beds by type of care.

Source: Statistics Canada, Catalogue no. 82-221-XDE.

4.6 FERTILITY RATE[1]

	15-19 years[2]	20-24 years	25-29 years	30-34 years	35-39 years	40-44 years	45-49 years[3]
	Rate per 1,000						
1961	56	227	214	142	79	28	2
1966	47	165	160	101	56	19	2
1971	39	131	139	76	33	9	1
1976	33	104	126	64	21	4	–
1981	26	91	123	67	19	3	–
1986	23	79	119	73	22	3	–
1991	26	78	120	84	28	4	–
1992	26	75	119	85	29	4	–
1993	25	73	115	85	30	4	–

1. Age-specific fertility rates are calculated by dividing the number of live births in each age group by the total female populaton (in thousands) in each age group
2. Births to women aged 14 and under are included in the 15-19 age group.
3. Births to women aged 50 and over are included in the 45-49 age group.

Source: Statistics Canada, Catalogue no. 82-221-XDE.

4.7 SUICIDES

	1991	1993	1961	1971	1981	1991	1993
	Number of suicides		Suicide rate per 100,000 population				
All ages	3,593	3,803	7.49	11.86	13.98	13.31	13.14
Males	2,875	3,014	11.91	17.29	21.30	21.61	21.01
Females	718	789	2.97	6.43	6.79	5.25	5.41
1-14 years	29	45	0.14	0.30	0.68	0.55	0.81
Males	20	27	0.27	0.45	0.99	0.74	0.95
Females	9	18	–	0.14	0.36	0.35	0.67
15-19 years	253	237	2.30	7.95	12.66	13.75	12.19
Males	217	193	3.70	12.66	21.15	23.00	19.39
Females	36	44	0.85	3.08	3.80	4.02	4.63
20-24 years	362	344	5.75	14.40	19.59	18.17	16.47
Males	322	295	9.03	23.15	33.21	31.73	27.87
Females	40	49	2.51	5.70	5.90	4.09	4.76
25-44 years	1,643	1,723	9.61	16.99	17.39	18.11	17.64
Males	1,298	1,391	15.06	24.24	26.18	28.75	28.25
Females	345	332	4.09	9.52	8.55	7.57	6.85
45-64 years	859	990	17.36	22.79	20.10	16.22	17.02
Males	674	760	27.15	32.12	28.60	25.70	26.17
Females	185	230	7.20	13.70	11.89	6.92	7.89
65 years and over	447	464	17.18	15.08	18.26	14.24	13.69
Males	344	348	30.11	24.68	30.37	26.28	24.40
Females	103	116	5.02	7.27	9.19	5.63	5.91
Not stated	...	...	...	...	...	...	...
Males	...	...	...	0.01	...	...	...
Females	...	...	...	...	...	...	...

Source: Statistics Canada, Catalogue no. 82 221-XDE.

4.8 PERSONS WITH AT LEAST ONE DISABILITY,[1] 1991

	All ages	15-24 years	25-44 years	45-64 years	65 years and over
Persons with at least one disability	3,795,330	266,135	917,172	1,163,149	1,448,874
Household	3,533,089	263,601	895,345	1,138,187	1,235,955
Institution	262,241	2,533	21,827	24,962	212,919
Men	1,734,051	133,034	449,054	582,221	569,742
Household	1,644,955	131,168	436,155	569,001	508,631
Institution	89,097	1,866	12,899	13,221	61,111
Women	2,061,279	133,101	468,118	580,928	879,132
Household	1,888,135	132,433	459,191	569,187	727,324
Institution	173,145	668	8,928	11,741	151,808

1. Any restriction or lack of ability to perform an activity in the manner or within the range considered normal for a human being not fully corrected by a technical aid and lasting or expected to last six months.

Source: Statistics Canada, *Health and Activity Limitation Survey, 1991*, Catalogue no. 82-602.

4.9 NATURE OF DISABILITY,[1] 1991

	Any disability	Mobility	Agility	Seeing	Hearing	Speaking	Other	Unknown
	% of population							
Canada	17.0	10.4	9.6	2.7	5.3	1.5	5.6	1.0
Newfoundland	10.9	7.4	6.4	1.9	3.4	1.1	3.2	0.3
Prince Edward Island	19.3	12.1	11.1	3.0	6.3	1.7	6.4	0.7
Nova Scotia	23.8	14.9	14.3	3.2	7.3	1.7	6.7	1.2
New Brunswick	19.6	11.8	10.4	3.2	7.1	2.1	7.2	0.5
Quebec	13.7	8.4	7.8	2.4	3.4	1.4	4.7	0.8
Ontario	17.6	11.2	10.1	2.9	5.4	1.5	5.9	1.0
Manitoba	19.4	11.7	11.2	3.5	7.2	1.5	5.3	0.7
Saskatchewan	20.0	11.4	10.7	3.6	7.0	1.9	6.7	1.4
Alberta	18.7	10.6	9.3	2.6	6.2	1.3	6.0	1.5
British Columbia	18.0	9.8	9.9	2.5	6.7	1.6	5.6	1.5
Yukon	12.1	5.3	5.4	0.9	4.4	0.8	3.8	1.2
Northwest Territories	14.0	6.2	5.5	1.6	5.3	0.9	4.5	0.9

1. Any restriction or lack of ability to perform an activity in the manner or within the range considered normal for a human being not fully corrected by a technical aid and lasting or expected to last six months.

Source: Statistics Canada, *Health and Activity Limitation Survey, 1991*, Catalogue no. 82-602.

4.10 MORTALITY RATES[1] BY CAUSES

	1970			1980			1990			1992		
	Both sexes	Male	Female	Both sexes	Male	Female	Both sexes	Male	Female	Both sexes	Male	Female
	Rate per 100,000 population											
All causes	956.8	1,215.8	750.4	822.7	1,077.7	626.2	703.1	914.1	543.3	678.3	882.1	525.5
Malignant neoplasms	182.9	227.6	151.6	186.6	240.3	148.3	191.6	246.6	153.2	189.7	244.0	152.8
Intestine, except rectum	31.3	34.5	29.1	25.4	29.4	22.6	21.5	26.2	17.9	20.8	26.3	16.9
Lung	29.3	55.2	8.4	42.0	73.9	17.1	50.0	79.6	27.6	50.0	77.4	29.6
Breast	..	0.0	30.7	..	0.0	29.6	..	0.0	31.3	..	0.0	30.4
All other malignant neoplasms	122.3	137.9	83.4	119.2	137.0	79.0	120.1	140.8	76.4	118.9	140.3	75.9
Diabetes	19.9	19.0	20.4	14.2	14.6	13.8	15.2	17.6	13.4	15.4	17.9	13.6
Diseases of the heart	359.1	471.2	267.4	292.0	392.1	213.5	201.8	267.5	150.6	191.0	255.8	141.4
Ischaemic heart diseases	317.3	425.5	228.7	242.3	333.0	170.6	160.9	219.1	115.7	150.1	207.3	106.3
All other heart diseases	41.8	45.7	38.7	49.7	59.1	42.9	40.9	48.4	34.9	40.9	48.5	35.1
Cerebrovascular diseases	106.7	115.4	100.0	75.9	83.7	70.1	51.6	57.7	47.0	49.7	54.0	46.3
Atherosclerosis	21.3	23.9	19.6	18.1	19.9	16.8	8.1	8.5	7.6	6.7	7.3	6.1
Respiratory diseases	66.0	96.8	44.3	55.3	86.8	34.6	59.9	89.9	41.3	57.3	84.9	40.3
Pneumonia and influenza	37.9	49.3	30.3	24.7	33.8	19.3	24.7	32.8	19.7	22.8	30.2	18.4
Bronchitis, emphysema and asthma	20.5	37.2	8.4	12.1	21.6	5.8	8.1	12.1	5.6	7.0	10.7	4.7
All other respiratory diseases	7.6	10.3	5.6	18.5	31.4	9.5	27.1	45.0	16.0	27.5	44.0	17.2
Chronic liver diseases and cirrhosis	10.1	14.2	6.6	12.1	17.6	7.2	7.9	11.7	4.5	7.4	10.7	4.5
Congenital anomalies	7.8	7.9	7.7	6.3	6.6	6.0	4.9	5.3	4.5	4.3	4.7	3.8
Perinatal mortality excluding stillbirths	14.0	16.2	11.6	6.4	7.2	5.5	4.2	4.7	3.7	3.4	3.8	3.1
Accidents and adverse effects	74.6	106.0	43.8	65.7	95.4	37.6	47.2	68.9	26.6	45.7	66.8	25.8
Motor vehicle accidents	25.6	38.1	13.6	21.5	31.2	12.0	13.7	19.6	8.0	12.1	17.1	7.3
Suicide	13.1	19.1	7.4	14.1	21.6	7.0	12.2	19.6	5.0	13.0	20.8	5.4
Homicide	2.2	2.8	1.6	2.1	2.9	1.3	2.0	2.6	1.4	2.1	2.8	1.4
Other accidents and adverse effects	33.7	46.0	21.2	28.0	39.7	17.3	19.3	27.1	12.2	18.5	26.1	11.7
Other causes	94.4	117.6	77.4	90.1	113.5	72.8	110.7	135.7	90.9	107.7	132.2	87.8

1. Rates are age-standardized using the 1991 population for Canada.

Source: Statistics Canada, Catalogue no. 82-221-XDE.

4.11 INFANT MORTALITY RATES[1]

	Canada	Nfld.[2]	P.E.I.	N.S.	N.B.	Que.	Ont.	Man.	Sask.	Alta.	B.C.	Y.T.	N.W.T.
	Infant mortality rate												
1976	13.03	15.61	14.42	13.81	14.16	11.69	12.35	15.60	14.34	14.25	13.81	22.32	34.66
1989	7.13	9.11	6.20	5.82	7.14	6.84	6.78	6.64	8.05	7.50	8.22	4.17	16.23
1990	6.84	10.31	5.96	6.29	7.23	6.24	6.27	7.95	7.64	8.05	7.54	7.19	11.99
1991	6.39	7.81	6.90	5.74	6.11	5.94	6.29	6.42	8.23	6.66	6.53	10.56	12.24
1992	6.10	7.08	1.62	5.98	6.28	5.43	5.88	6.81	7.33	7.23	6.20	3.78	16.73
1993	6.30	7.79	9.12	7.09	7.18	5.73	6.24	7.06	8.06	6.65	5.74	7.87	9.62

1. The infant mortality rate is calculated as the number of deaths of children less than one year of age per 1,000 live births.
2. The totals for Newfoundland are estimated for 1976, 1989, and 1990.

Source: Statistics Canada, Catalogue no. 82-221-XDE.

4.12 CHANCES OF DYING, INTERNATIONAL COMPARISONS, 1991

	Age	Life expectancy at age x	Survivors to age x out of 100,000 at birth	Infectious and parasitic diseases	Malignant neoplasms	Diseases of the circulatory system	Heart diseases	Cerebro-vascular diseases	Diseases of the respiratory system	Injury and poisoning	Motor vehicle traffic accidents
	Years		Number	Chances per 1,000							
Canada	0	74.4	100,000	7.1	272.0	400.8	298.7	66.0	107.3	57.3	13.4
	15	60.2	98,925	7.0	274.4	404.9	301.8	66.7	108.1	56.0	12.8
	65	15.7	79,705	7.0	262.6	433.2	316.2	75.7	125.3	25.5	3.7
Sweden[1]	0	74.9	100,000	6.4	213.5	511.5	374.1	89.4	81.1	59.1	8.9
	15	60.6	99,027	6.3	215.0	516.3	377.6	90.2	81.8	58.6	8.6
	65	15.4	81,599	6.2	205.8	550.7	397.1	99.7	91.7	29.5	2.8
Australia[2]	0	74.8	100,000	7.0	260.5	440.5	317.8	85.1	101.4	47.5	11.2
	15	60.6	98,874	6.9	263.0	445.4	321.4	86.0	102.2	46.2	10.6
	65	15.6	81,071	6.7	248.8	477.1	337.9	97.2	114.6	20.5	3.3
Greece	0	74.7	100,000	6.4	231.6	490.3	305.0	165.3	60.0	46.9	25.2
	15	60.6	98,757	6.4	234.1	496.5	308.8	167.4	60.6	45.5	24.5
	65	15.9	80,517	6.5	214.6	527.0	315.9	189.2	66.8	16.7	7.4
Italy[1]	0	73.7	100,000	3.7	282.8	411.1	236.0	119.5	85.0	53.5	18.4
	15	59.6	98,772	3.7	285.6	416.0	238.7	120.9	85.6	52.9	18.0
	65	15.1	78,999	3.3	261.0	455.5	251.9	138.5	99.0	31.3	7.1
United Kingdom[2]	0	73.7	100,000	4.6	269.8	457.2	321.1	96.8	117.4	34.1	8.5
	15	59.4	98,934	4.4	272.2	461.9	324.4	97.8	118.2	33.1	8.1
	65	14.4	79,461	3.6	261.2	476.8	323.5	109.8	134.6	12.5	2.4
France	0	73.5	100,000	12.9	302.5	315.9	195.8	80.1	78.4	86.3	17.9
	15	59.4	98,773	12.8	305.7	319.6	198.1	81.1	79.0	85.1	17.5
	65	16.2	76,156	13.7	287.0	362.0	220.9	95.0	93.6	51.8	4.7
New Zealand	0	72.9	100,000	5.3	249.7	456.0	330.6	85.2	116.4	58.1	18.7
	15	59.0	98,497	5.0	252.8	462.8	335.5	86.4	117.3	55.8	17.6
	65	14.9	77,805	4.4	237.4	492.1	38.4	98.2	137.6	20.0	3.3
United States[1]	0	71.9	100,000	13.1	240.7	433.3	339.6	57.5	100.5	67.8	18.8
	15	58.0	98,479	13.0	243.9	439.6	344.5	58.3	101.5	65.9	18.1
	65	15.2	74,060	12.6	238.7	480.8	372.2	67.9	119.7	26.0	5.1
Mexico	0	69.3	100,000	50.9	113.8	276.3	177.7	65.1	112.2	112.6	25.9
	15	56.7	96,496	46.6	117.2	285.6	183.7	67.3	110.9	112.0	25.6
	65	15.0	70,055	46.0	125.2	329.9	209.8	79.5	136.0	51.9	11.9

1. 1990.
2. 1992.

Source: World Health Organization, *1993 World Health Statistics,* Geneva, 1994.

4.13 POTENTIAL YEARS OF LIFE LOST,[1] BY CAUSE OF DEATH, 1993

	Total all causes	Neoplasms	Accidental deaths	Diseases of the heart	Suicides	Respiratory diseases	Cerebrovascular diseases	Congenital anomalies	Other causes
					Years				
All ages	1,076,842	302,585	228,106	145,394	108,488	33,023	29,554	14,402	447,979
1-4 years	33,969	3,685	11,993	1,139	..	2,948	201	5,494	4,824
5-9 years	19,813	4,125	9,625	563	63	438	250	1,000	4,688
10-14 years	21,045	3,508	8,108	748	2,530	633	403	863	4,256
15-19 years	62,318	4,883	34,755	1,155	12,443	998	315	1,103	6,038
20-24 years	69,588	4,988	33,915	1,520	16,340	1,235	380	1,235	6,508
25-29 years	78,158	8,160	31,748	2,210	16,575	1,275	723	1,148	10,370
30-34 years	96,938	13,800	30,900	4,838	17,888	1,500	1,763	675	18,638
35-39 years	105,885	21,710	24,863	9,328	14,723	1,918	2,828	943	31,038
40-44 years	105,765	32,395	16,088	13,613	11,083	2,420	3,493	688	46,008
45-49 years	112,140	41,940	11,318	20,138	8,325	2,700	4,028	518	62,078
50-54 years	107,748	47,093	6,755	23,695	4,305	3,290	3,693	280	70,788
55-59 years	109,425	49,725	4,200	25,688	2,575	4,313	4,588	250	75,413
60-64 years	103,875	45,983	2,768	27,113	1,260	5,940	4,320	150	73,096
65-69 years	50,178	20,593	1,073	13,650	380	3,418	2,573	58	34,243

1. Potential years of life lost are calculated by taking the median age in each age group, subtracting from 70, and multiplying by the number of deaths in that age group disaggregated by sex and cause of death.

Source: Statistics Canada, Catalogue no. 82-221-XDE.

4.14 LIFE EXPECTANCY AT BIRTH

	Both sexes	Males	Females	Difference
		Years		
Canada				
1920-22	59.37	58.84	60.60	1.76
1930-32	61.00	60.00	62.06	2.06
1940-42	64.58	63.04	66.31	3.27
1950-52	68.51	66.40	70.90	4.50
1960-62	71.14	68.44	74.26	5.82
1970-72	72.74	69.40	76.45	7.05
1980-82	75.39	71.88	79.06	7.18
1990-92	77.80	74.61	80.97	6.36
1990-92				
Newfoundland	76.51	73.72	79.54	5.82
Prince Edward Island	76.86	73.22	80.79	7.57
Nova Scotia	77.00	73.74	80.33	6.59
New Brunswick	77.55	74.26	80.90	6.64
Quebec	77.40	73.77	80.93	7.16
Ontario	78.03	75.01	80.96	5.95
Manitoba	77.68	74.61	80.75	6.14
Saskatchewan	78.33	75.26	81.55	6.29
Alberta	78.08	75.08	81.20	6.12
British Columbia	78.29	75.25	81.38	6.13

Source: Statistics Canada, Catalogue no. 82-221-XDE.

4.15 CASES OF NOTIFIABLE DISEASES[1]

	1987	1988	1989	1990	1991	1992	1993	1994
	Number of cases							
AIDS	634	801	1,118	1,050	1,014	1,286	1,161	462
Male	597	749	1,043	1,004	952	1,215	1,091	429
Female	37	52	75	46	62	71	70	33
Gonococcal infections	27,918	20,736	19,110	13,822	12,457	9,159	6,769	4,443
Male	14,755	10,682	10,278	7,681	3,986	5,088	3,703	2,314
Female	12,923	9,834	8,778	6,024	3,078	4,059	3,062	1,918
Gonococcal ophthalmia	4	2	1	4	4	–	4	–
Male	1	1	–	2	3	–	2	–
Female	2	1	1	2	1	–	2	–
Syphilis	2,376	1,583	1,497	1,444	1,429	919	648	194
Male	1,483	991	862	840	236	540	340	112
Female	869	588	627	586	144	375	276	78
Campylo-bacteriosis	10,415	11,098	11,602	11,817	12,741	8,607	9,277	8,771
Male	2,049	2,834	2,759	6,048	3,504	4,511	4,734	4,507
Female	1,720	2,579	2,496	5,712	3,123	4,057	4,534	4,205
Chicken pox	52,957	42,312	41,560	20,254	13,687	4,514	3,509	2,282
Male	11,496	6,948	7,912	9,611	6,437	1,163	1,310	666
Female	11,195	6,728	7,728	9,037	6,191	1,176	1,313	661
Giardiasis	9,109	9,075	9,543	8,786	9,168	4,242	4,164	3,138
Male	2,579	2,648	2,617	4,493	2,761	2,246	2,336	1,629
Female	2,216	2,290	2,426	4,229	2,619	1,979	1,820	1,483
Hepatitis A	1,130	1,533	1,854	1,939	3,020	2,100	1,256	966
Male	381	622	757	1,157	1,308	1,427	746	592
Female	313	450	557	770	691	660	504	356
Hepatitis B	3,005	3,132	3,456	3,001	2,683	2,639	2,551	2,580
Male	1,396	1,461	1,748	1,899	1,430	1,701	1,582	1,510
Female	739	852	965	1,052	742	916	957	1,050
Measles	2,385	609	11,145	1,033	6,178	1,710	58	157
Male	1,235	291	5,646	522	481	892	29	83
Female	1,098	280	5,417	504	414	816	28	74
Pertussis	1,292	1,106	2,440	8,030	2,724	644	1,564	1,731
Male	266	366	1,051	3,782	1,037	256	621	655
Female	285	455	1,235	4,229	1,148	386	939	1,060
Rubella	1,260	559	1,384	402	704	1,989	829	45
Male	637	274	771	207	486	1,578	631	16
Female	539	260	573	191	122	410	198	28
Salmonella	11,712	11,626	10,673	8,947	9,055	3,900	4,182	2,970
Male	2,564	2,654	2,624	4,281	2,583	1,845	2,065	1,480
Female	2,682	2,813	2,740	4,596	2,644	2,039	2,104	1,467
Tuberculosis	1,972	2,031	1,902	1,964	1,942	2,065	2,010	..
Male	1,134	1,173	1,140	1,083	697	1,146	1,134	..
Female	838	858	834	879	498	916	876	..

1. Components may not add to total as sex was not stated for some respondents.

Source: Statistics Canada, Catalogue no. 82-221-XDE.

4.16 CANCER PROBABILITIES[1]

	Probability of developing cancer by age							Lifetime probability of:	
	30	40	50	60	70	80	90	developing	dying
	%								
Male									
All cancers	0.7	1.3	2.9	8.1	19.8	33.4	40.3	41.6	26.7
Prostate	--	--	--	0.7	3.6	8.4	11.1	11.6	3.7
Lung	--	--	0.3	1.5	4.5	7.8	9.3	9.5	8.5
Colorectal	--	0.1	0.3	1.0	2.8	4.9	6.2	6.5	2.8
Bladder	--	--	0.1	0.4	1.1	2.1	2.8	2.9	0.9
Lymphoma	0.2	0.3	0.5	0.8	1.4	2.1	2.4	2.5	1.3
Oral	--	--	0.2	0.5	1.0	1.4	1.7	1.8	0.6
Stomach	--	--	0.1	0.3	0.7	1.2	1.6	1.7	1.1
Kidney	--	0.1	0.2	0.4	0.8	1.2	1.5	1.5	0.6
Leukemia	0.1	0.2	0.2	0.4	0.7	1.0	1.4	1.5	0.9
Pancreas	--	--	0.1	0.2	0.5	0.9	1.2	1.2	1.2
Melanoma	--	0.1	0.2	0.4	0.5	0.7	0.8	0.8	0.2
Female									
All cancers	0.7	1.8	4.6	10.2	18.8	28.5	35.0	37.1	22.4
Breast	--	0.4	1.7	3.8	6.5	9.2	10.8	11.2	4.0
Colorectal	--	0.1	0.3	0.9	2.1	3.9	5.7	6.2	2.7
Lung	--	--	0.3	1.0	2.4	3.9	4.5	4.7	4.2
Lymphoma	0.1	0.2	0.3	0.6	1.1	1.7	2.2	2.3	1.3
Body of uterus	--	--	0.2	0.6	1.3	1.9	2.2	2.3	0.5
Ovary	--	0.1	0.3	0.5	0.9	1.3	1.5	1.6	1.1
Pancreas	--	--	--	0.1	0.4	0.7	1.1	1.3	1.3
Leukemia	0.1	0.1	0.2	0.3	0.4	0.7	1.0	1.1	0.8
Stomach	--	--	--	0.1	0.3	0.6	0.9	1.0	0.7
Bladder	--	--	0.1	0.2	0.3	0.6	0.9	1.1	0.4
Kidney	--	--	0.1	0.2	0.5	0.8	0.9	1.0	0.4
Cervix	0.1	0.2	0.3	0.5	0.6	0.8	0.9	0.9	0.3
Melanoma	0.1	0.1	0.3	0.4	0.6	0.7	0.8	0.9	0.2

1. The probability of developing cancer is based on data from 1990-1992 while the probability of dying is based on 1993 data.

Source: National Cancer Institute of Canada, *Canadian Cancer Statistics 1996*, Toronto, 1996.

4.17 TIME-LOSS WORK INJURIES[1]

	1983	1985	1987	1989	1990	1991	1992	1993
15 years and over, both sexes	471,929	555,991	602,531	620,979	586,770	520,547	455,659	423,184
15-29 years	195,119	229,712	248,090	242,411	213,330	177,556	146,835	131,181
30-49 years	196,430	238,270	262,042	281,974	279,606	263,730	240,043	229,088
50 years and over	71,174	78,603	79,173	78,347	77,487	72,465	66,412	61,352
Unknown age	9,206	9,406	13,226	18,247	16,347	6,796	2,369	1,563
Men, 15 years and over	368,626	446,636	473,741	478,408	442,005	387,403	335,546	311,854
15-29 years	155,257	189,392	201,455	194,616	168,869	137,473	112,941	101,326
30-49 years	152,419	189,397	202,549	215,162	210,285	193,826	174,806	167,062
50 years and over	53,701	60,524	59,542	57,894	56,535	51,495	46,225	42,434
Unknown age	7,249	7,323	10,195	10,736	6,316	4,609	1,574	1,032
Women, 15 years and over	83,747	108,839	127,733	137,439	135,604	130,744	118,762	110,693
15-29 years	31,189	40,153	46,307	47,411	44,045	39,344	33,495	29,645
30-49 years	36,324	48,696	59,137	66,317	68,755	68,723	64,557	61,737
50 years and over	14,404	17,991	19,510	20,297	20,796	20,637	19,974	18,830
Unknown age	1,830	1,999	2,779	3,414	2,008	2,040	736	481
Sex unknown, 15 years and over	19,556	516	1,057	5,132	9,161	2,400	1,351	637
15-29 years	8,673	167	328	384	416	739	399	210
30-49 years	7,687	177	356	495	566	1,181	680	289
50 years and over	3,069	88	121	156	156	333	213	88
Unknown age and sex	127	84	252	4,097	8,023	147	59	50

1. A time-loss work injury is where an employee is compensated for a loss of wages following an accident, or where a worker is compensated for a permanent disability with or without any time lost in employment.

Source: Statistics Canada, Catalogue no. 82-221-XDE.

4.18 HOSPITAL SEPARATIONS,[1] 1992-93

	All ages	Less than 15 years	15-24 years	25-44 years	45-64 years	65 years and over
	Number of separations per 100,000 population					
All diagnostic groups	12,462	6,393	8,924	10,298	12,520	33,668
Complications of pregnancy and childbirth	1,836	8	3,680	3,876	4	–
Diseases of the circulatory system	1,617	38	78	355	2,398	8,617
Diseases of the digestive system	1,458	702	794	1,067	1,984	3,838
Diseases of the respiratory system	1,209	2,222	698	411	772	3,108
Injury and poisoning	1,009	722	1,004	767	887	2,434
Neoplasms	885	89	107	387	1,474	3,676
Diseases of the genito-urinary system	873	227	537	866	1,094	2,064
Symptoms, signs and ill-defined conditions	654	513	334	374	795	1,868
Mental disorders	595	81	522	737	645	1,089
Diseases of the musculoskeletal system	594	113	307	479	858	1,676
Diseases of the nervous system and sense organs	452	301	153	231	454	1,725
Endocrine, nutritional, metabolic and immunity diseases	237	104	112	132	307	813
Infectious and parasitic diseases	187	327	150	117	116	308
Diseases of the skin and subcutaneous tissue	151	104	124	119	169	336
Diseases of blood and blood-forming organs	93	93	45	30	71	368
Congenital anomalies	87	292	55	33	27	20
Conditions originating in the perinatal period	51	247	–	–	–	–
Other	473	209	222	313	464	1,727

1. Discharges or deaths.

Source: Statistics Canada, Catalogue no. 82-221-XDE.

4.19 HEALTH IMPROVEMENT MEASURES

	1985						1990					
	Both sexes		Male		Female		Both sexes		Male		Female	
	Number	%	Number	%	Number	%	Number	%	Number	%	Number	%
Total[1]	19,611,090	100.0	9,622,569	100.0	9,988,521	100.0	20,643,380	100.0	10,097,210	100.0	10,546,170	100.0
Nothing	7,279,057	37.1	3,770,325	39.2	3,508,732	35.1	10,281,920	49.8	5,335,934	52.8	4,945,988	46.9
Increase exercise	5,703,226	29.1	3,028,424	31.5	2,674,801	26.8	3,677,456	17.8	1,907,437	18.9	1,770,019	16.8
Improve eating habits	2,269,250	11.6	771,755	8.0	1,497,495	15.0	2,760,942	13.4	1,027,367	10.2	1,733,574	16.4
Quit smoking/reduce amount smoked	766,516	3.9	466,818	4.9	299,698	3.0	841,994	4.1	451,172	4.5	390,822	3.7
Lose weight	783,324	4.0	220,957	2.3	562,368	5.6	712,924	3.5	260,123	2.6	452,801	4.3
Learn to manage stress and reduce stress level	250,065	1.3	100,347	1.0	149,718	1.5	309,870	1.5	153,988	1.5	155,882	1.5
Receive medical treatment	698,147	3.6	287,652	3.0	410,494	4.1	308,535	1.5	117,358	1.2	191,177	1.8
Drink less alcohol	204,916	1.0	157,091	1.6	47,826	--	164,755	0.8	121,332	1.2	43,423	--
Reduce drug/medication use	56,337	--	30,503	--	25,834	--	45,237	--	--	--	33,994	--
Control blood pressure and have blood pressure checked	209,560	1.1	109,560	1.1	100,000	1.0	--	--	--	--	--	--
Other	1,155,566	5.9	561,995	5.8	593,571	5.9	989,513	4.8	434,372	4.3	555,141	5.3
Not stated	235,127	1.2	117,142	1.2	117,985	1.2	530,978	2.6	264,778	2.6	266,200	2.5

1. Population 15 years and older.

Source: Statistics Canada, Catalogue no. 82-221-XDE.

4.20 EXERCISE[1] FREQUENCY, 1995

	Total[2]	Three or more times weekly	1 or 2 times weekly	Less than once weekly or never
	Number of people			
15 years and over	23,948,603	12,534,045	4,706,700	5,280,753
15-19 years	3,372,401	2,195,234	530,250	285,788
20-24 years	1,739,548	993,307	325,269	303,066
25-34 years	4,755,494	2,468,685	1,065,008	1,019,873
35-44 years	4,864,333	2,366,455	1,122,598	1,159,277
45-54 years	3,504,060	1,666,861	790,673	875,296
55-64 years	2,461,801	1,321,822	428,853	588,683
65 years and over	3,250,967	1,521,681	444,049	1,048,770
Men	11,780,335	6,191,179	2,292,534	2,336,516
15-19 years	1,763,015	1,204,599	219,250	121,939
20-24 years	837,416	479,909	154,602	136,882
25-34 years	2,337,762	1,244,492	518,996	426,439
35-44 years	2,474,090	1,176,697	587,317	547,856
45-54 years	1,817,047	825,620	400,988	454,529
55-64 years	1,152,384	561,630	239,905	271,232
65 years and over	1,398,620	698,233	171,475	377,640
Women	12,168,269	6,342,865	2,414,166	2,944,237
15-19 years	1,609,386	990,635	311,000	163,849
20-24 years	902,131	513,398	170,667	166,184
25-34 years	2,417,731	1,224,194	546,012	593,434
35-44 years	2,390,243	1,189,758	535,281	611,421
45-54 years	1,687,013	841,242	389,685	420,768
55-64 years	1,309,417	760,192	188,948	317,452
65 years and over	1,852,347	823,448	272,574	671,130

1. Exercise includes vigorous activities such as calisthenics, jogging or racquet sports, team sports, dance classes or brisk walking for a period of at least 15 minutes.
2. Components may not add to total as frequency was not stated for up to 1% of respondents.

Source: Health Canada, Catalogue no. 82-221-XDE.

4.21 HIGH BLOOD PRESSURE, 1995

	Both sexes	Men	Women
	% of age group with high blood pressure		
15 years and over	9	7	10
15-19 years	–	–	–
20-44 years	3	3	2
45-64 years	14	13	16
65 years and over	29	23	33

Source: Statistics Canada, Catalogue no. 82-221-XDE.

4.22 SMOKERS[1]

	1989			1995		
	Both sexes	Men	Women	Both sexes	Men	Women
	% of age group who are smokers					
15 years and over	30	31	29	25	27	23
15-19 years	22	21	23	23	21	25
20-44 years	34	34	33	29	31	28
45-64 years	32	33	30	25	27	22
65 years and over	17	20	15	11	14	10

1. Those reporting smoking daily.

Source: Statistics Canada, Catalogue no. 82-221-XDE.

4.23 DRINKERS[1]

	1989			1995		
	Both sexes	Men	Women	Both sexes	Men	Women
	% of age group who are drinkers					
15 years and over	61	71	51	78	82	73
15-19 years	49	54	43	93	91	95
20-44 years	69	78	58	81	84	78
45-64 years	60	68	52	78	83	73
65 years and over	39	54	28	57	68	49

1. Drinkers are those who reported drinking an alcoholic beverage at least once a month.

Source: Statistics Canada, Catalogue no. 82-221-XDE.

KENNON COOKE, VALAN PHOTOS

Chapter 5

EDUCATION

Photo by Mike Pinder

The advancement of education in Canada has been motivated by varying philosophies in the 12 or so decades since the country first came into being. Toward the turn of the last century, a Quebec educator, Charles Baillargé, cautioned that too much university education might be "ill adapted to the farmer's son, if he is to follow in the footsteps of his sire." Nearly a century later, Canadian Senator Grattan O'Leary noted, "The true education is not to give a man a standard of living, but a standard of life."

Lofty values continue in Canada, with high expectations for the education system. In 1994, Canada spent about $56 billion on education, in relative terms more than most members of the Organisation for Economic Co-operation and Development (OECD). In 1995, almost one in every two Canadians had attended a post-secondary institution, compared with one in 10 adults for their parents' generation. In 1995, more than one in every eight adults held a university degree and seven in 10 had graduated from high school. By way of comparison, in most OECD countries in 1992, just over half of 25- to 64-year-olds had completed a high school equivalent.

In 1992, the percentage of Canadians holding a university graduate degree topped that of all OECD nations except the United States and the Netherlands, ranked at 24% and 21% respectively. Canada also leads the way in non-university (such as community college) attainment levels—26% of the adult population. That's twice the rate of its nearest rivals—New Zealand, Norway and Switzerland, which puts Canada first among the G-7 countries. In 1992, four in every 10 of those aged 25 to 64 had completed some form of postsecondary education.

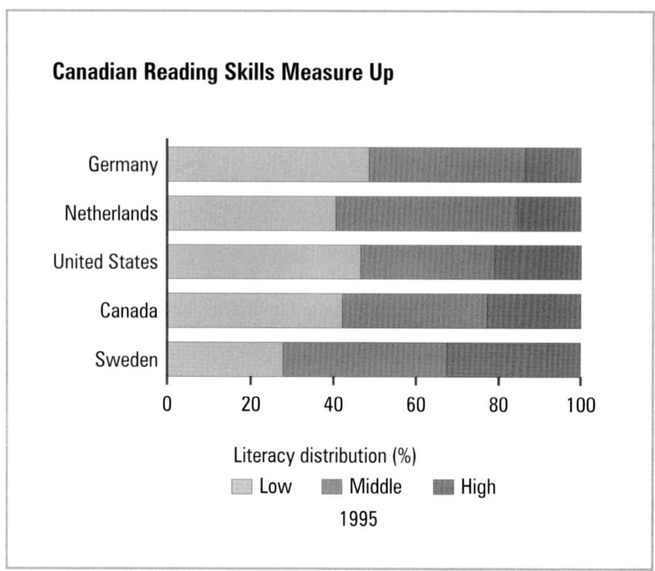

In terms of gender equity, women now outnumber men on university campuses, but not yet at the postgraduate level.

There's been a recent explosion in distance learning and continuing education, with more than 700,000 people 25 years and older enrolled in some kind of program. The percentage of adults from the overall population who take part has more than doubled in the past two decades. Even preschool attendance is rising. In 1993-94, almost half a million children attended pre-school, up 22% from 1983-84.

Tests at the national and international levels show Canadian students can hold their own in reading, writing and mathematics. On the down side, while Canada compares well with several other industrialized countries in adult literacy tests, four in every 10 adults are so limited in reading skills they can't deal with much of the written material they encounter daily.

How It Works

At the time of Confederation, the nation's builders recognized the value of educated citizens, but they also understood that regional differences would require different school systems. Therefore, control over education was given to the provinces in the British North American Act of 1867. The cost would be shared, however, through "statutory subsidies" paid to the provinces by the federal government.

Special protection was built into the Act to preserve denominational schools—those run according to the doctrines and beliefs of a particular church or sect. Thus, certains rights and privileges of denominational schools were protected from legislative change.

The result has been education systems that vary from one province or territory to another.

This historical framework has also ensured that the church-run schools in five provinces continue to operate alongside those which are non-denominational, specifically Alberta, Newfoundland, Ontario, Quebec and Saskatchewan. In all but Newfoundland, this protection exists specifically for Catholics and Protestants; eight different religious denominations are recognized in Newfoundland. However, in a 1995 referendum, Newfoundlanders narrowly approved a provincial government proposal to strip away the right of churches to run schools. The province has consulted federal authorities to determine the legalities of the situation.

In the other provinces, public education is non-sectarian and non-denominational. In some provinces, religious schools exist as private schools. However, some provinces don't allow funding for private schools.

Since education falls under provincial jurisdiction in Canada, it falls to the provinces and territories to set policy and curriculum. This is done through a provincial (or territorial) minister and department or ministry of education, with local school districts and elected school board trustees managing schools and staff within a given area.

The federal government directly funds schooling for First Nations students, for those living in the territories, for students at National Defence bases overseas and military colleges, and for those in prisons and reform schools. Federal money also finances postsecondary school loans, research done at postsecondary institutions, and minority official language training.

Public education in Canada is free to all children in the elementary and secondary grades, and Canadian children are required by law to attend school between the ages of six or seven and 15 or 16. Alternatively, they may study at home under local supervision. Schooling levels are: elementary and secondary (including pre-elementary) for children to their mid-teens, trade and vocational for various ages, and postsecondary for adults who attend community colleges and universities.

Other forms of schooling—such as religious training, special language instruction, and education for those with disabilities—meet diverse needs and interests. For the most part, these are provided through private or independent schools with varying degrees of public funding.

Although the road to "free" public education ends after high school, the process can continue, for a fee, in the universities, colleges and trade or specialty schools of the land. The exception is Quebec, where college training is free to full-time students.

Financing

In 1994, Canadians spent an estimated $56 billion on education, almost four times the amount spent two decades earlier. There are many reasons the cost keeps rising, including inflation, higher salaries and more expensive equipment, such as classroom computers. Students are also staying in school longer.

Education accounts for a significant chunk of the country's gross domestic product (GDP)—8.1% in 1992. That's less than 1% more than the share of GDP committed in 1982. According to the Council of Ministers of Education, Canada (CMEC), spending on education and training is second to that on health care in our economy.

In 1992, Canada was first among OECD nations in per capita spending on public education. Since 1982, spending on education has climbed about 91%, similar to the rate of increase for personal incomes in Canada.

In 1993, provincial governments footed more than half the bill, topping up federal contributions through higher local education taxes. The local share continued to increase, providing some 21% of the $55.8 billion spent in 1992-93.

About one-fifth of the money came from taxpayers through direct taxes at the local level. In 1992-93, provincial grants covered about 58%, and tuition fees, direct federal contributions, and other private funding made up the rest.

Most of the money went to the elementary and secondary school system, some 62%. Another 10% went to postsecondary programs, and 9% to trade and vocational programs.

Federal government funding comes in direct payments and as contributions through the Federal-Provincial Fiscal Arrangements and Federal Postsecondary Education and Health Contributions Act of 1977, and the Official Languages in Education Program.

Enrolments

Almost all Canadians attend school at some point in their lives—especially in the early grades—and the number enrolled has grown for each age group in recent years. While only 18% of 18- to 24-year-olds attended university either full or part time in 1976, for example, that figure had increased to almost 31% by 1993.

You can stand up to anyone, says Canadian CEO Trevor Eyton, armed with nothing but an education. So it's no surprise teachers are troubled by violent students who prefer concealed weapons to revealing insight and a cutting wit.

The double-digit growth rates of violent youth crime in the 1980s has passed and there has now been the first slight decline—in 1994. That was also the year a Ministry of the Solicitor General study spotlighted educators and police who believe weapons use in schools is a growing problem.

What teachers and police said was that knives were confiscated daily in some big city schools and firearms were discovered monthly in Montreal and Toronto. They expressed concerns that more young children have weapons than a few years ago, although they said gang violence rarely happens on school property.

The media was also criticized as some thought sensational media accounts of violence created fear among students who are then motivated to turn to weapons for protection. This unbalanced reporting was said to desensitize Canadians to violence, which was glorified, while remorse and consequences were rarely depicted.

Similarly, criticism was aimed at some schools which refused to report weapons use in an effort to protect their image and future enrolments, or to remove the threat of media scrutiny.

In the face of this fear over violent youth crime, the Canadian Center for Justice Statistics reports that in 1994, youths aged 12 to 17 represented about two in 10 persons charged with violent crimes. Although the youth violent crime rate has more than doubled since 1986, compared with the 40% rate increase for adults, violent crime represented 18% of all charges against youth, compared to 30% for adults.

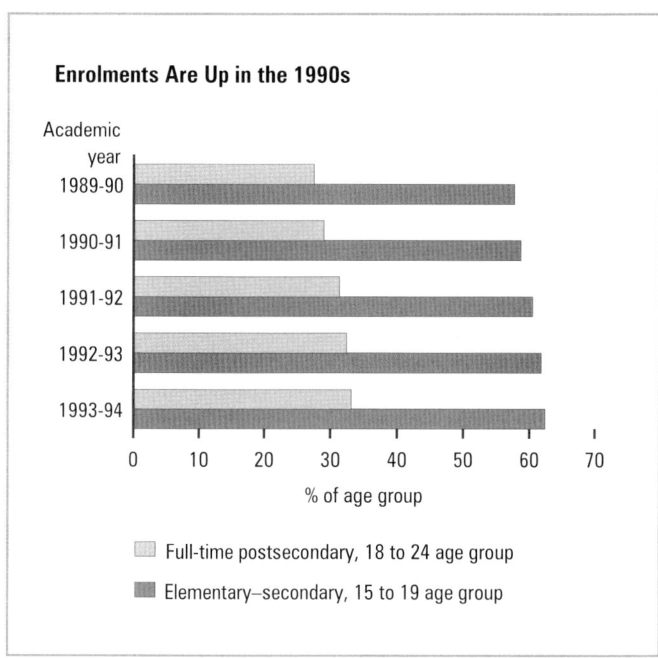

In 1994-95, there were 5.4 million young people in elementary or secondary schools, compared with about 1.7 million in postsecondary institutions or technical institutes. Some 536 new elementary or secondary schools have opened since 1992-93 to handle the growth, bringing the facilities total to 16,288.

Preschool

Many parents send their kids to school before age six, even though it is not legally required. Pre-elementary programs are most plentiful in Ontario, our most populous province, with 241,652 children enrolled. In 1993-94, there were 490,820 children attending kindergarten or pre-kindergarten programs in most provinces and territories, and overseas. Demand for schooling before Grade 1 has climbed steadily since 1978-79. Over the past 20 years, participation in public preschool programs has grown from 39% to 72% of the population of four- and five-year-olds.

Elementary-Secondary

The infamous baby boomers are once again flexing their collective muscle—in the schoolyard. This time, however, it is their children who are filling classrooms. In 1993-94, 5.3 million young people were enrolled in elementary or secondary classes—an increase of 1.3% over the previous year. But this new group is more of a "boomlet"—the pinnacle of 5.8 million in 1970-71 remains untouched.

At the secondary level, in 1993-94 more than six in 10 of all 15- to 19-year old Canadians were still in school. That's slightly more than the 57.7% of these students in 1989-90. Ontario ends Grade 13 in its secondary education program in 2000. Quebec's secondary school program ends after Grade 11.

Keeping kids in school long enough to get essential training seems obvious, but participation drops off noticeably after age 16. While more than nine in 10 of all 16-year-olds attend school, only four in five young people are doing so a year later. Only about half are in full-time classes by age 19.

The urge to leave school seems stronger east of Manitoba than elsewhere in the country; in 1991, 25% of 20-year-old Prince Edward Islanders and 24% of Newfoundlanders the same age had left school, compared with the lowest rate—14% in Alberta.

Private and Specialty Schools

In 1993-94, private schools continued to attract a significant minority, accounting for 5% of full elementary-secondary enrolment, a slight increase since 1989-90. Private schools can operate anywhere in Canada, providing they follow the general educational standards set for that jurisdiction. Some financial assistance is given by provincial governments in Alberta, British Columbia, Manitoba, Quebec and Saskatchewan, but fees are charged to raise the bulk of operating funds.

Photo by Daryl Kahn Cline

"Call on me. Please call on me. I'll die if you don't call on me."

Private school attendance is rising slightly everywhere except New Brunswick, Newfoundland and the Yukon—it's negligible in the Northwest Territories—but growing fastest in P.E.I. and Manitoba. In 1993-94, those private schools that registered with provincial or federal authorities had enrolments of 265,321 children.

There are 19 schools for blind and deaf children, but the trend is to integrate special-needs children into regular classrooms where some extra help is provided. In 1993-94, there were 2,339 blind and deaf children enrolled in special schools across the country.

Trade School

Students who choose what they consider a shorter route to the workplace via trade or vocational training are growing in number. An estimated 269,000 Canadians are taking trade or vocational training. Consequently, this form of schooling is commanding more education dollars than ever before.

While postsecondary received almost half of 1994-95 federal funds allocated to education—the lowest level in a decade—vocational training received its highest share over the same period: 42.5%. Provinces spent $1.9 billion in that year.

Unlike community colleges, which provide mainly technological training, trade and vocational schools offer fewer courses of shorter duration that emphasize manipulative skills in various occupations. In 1992-93, engineering and applied science courses—including computer science—attracted the greatest numbers of students.

Private vocational schools may welcome entrants without prior testing or proof of high school graduation, and try to accommodate their personal schedules. There were an estimated 2,440 of these schools in 1992, concentrated mainly in British Columbia, Ontario and Quebec. Tuition fees are generally higher than those in public institutions, and diplomas or credits from vocational schools are rarely recognized by provincial education ministries. The labour market recognizes their worth, however; these schools respond to market needs and can often guarantee jobs to graduates of their courses.

Schooling in the 1930s

Scarcely a half-century ago, in most of the country's rural areas and pioneer settlements, education was not available to everyone. To get to school, the children of the day had to overcome many obstacles, including long distances, inclement weather, a lack of shoes in some cases, or warm clothing, as well as work obligations. For many, it meant they had to remain at home. The 1901 census tells us that only 48% of all Canadian children over 10 were actually in school.

*In this excerpt from **Where Nests the Water Hen**, Gabrielle Roy paints this picture of the situation in Manitoba in the 1930s for those who were.*

"True enough, his own little school had been all by itself on a lonely rise, flanked by its supply of firewood and two cabins at a slight distance, one marked BOYS and the other GIRLS. Yet what was the reason for this remoteness? It was merely because each family on the Prairies fought to have a school at its front door. On this point no one would yield. So it had been necessary, to satisfy everyone, to locate the school as much as possible at the same distance from all the farms."

Most private vocational schools are businesses that specialize in training—such as computer and personnel firms—but some are operated by professional associations, volunteer organizations or correspondence schools. A professional association of property appraisers, for example, may provide special courses to raise the standards and abilities of its members.

There are about 53,600 teachers in private vocational schools. More than 75% of them are part-time teachers, and more men than women teach in these private settings, most often in the fields traditionally associated with their gender.

Campus Life

With job prospects dim in many areas, Canada's postsecondary institutions are crowded—and with good reason. The Canadian government estimates almost half of the jobs created in the 1990s will require more than 16 years of education or training.

In 1994-95, nearly a million students attended community colleges and universities full time. Campus life is where it's at for six in every 10 young people immediately after high school graduation. In 1994-95, almost 40% were enrolled in community colleges; the rest attended university.

Canada's community colleges—now numbering 289—were established in the 1960s, and bestow diplomas or certificates upon completion of their programs. They offer trade and vocational, continuing education and academic upgrading courses with specialized training in the arts, agriculture, fisheries, teaching, paramedical technology and more. The CEGEPs of Quebec, which provide the two-year preparation mandatory for admission to a Quebec university, are also in this category. College fees are generally lower than those for university programs.

There are 78 universities in Canada; they provide advanced study in disciplines as diverse as agriculture, engineering, fine arts and social sciences. Undergraduate programs last from three to five years and are a prerequisite for postgraduate programs. Some professions, such as law, may also require a bachelor's degree or the completion of some of its course requirements. A master's degree is generally required for entry to certain doctoral programs.

Considerable resources are spent on postsecondary training. In 1992, we spent more than any other OECD country, as far as the OECD estimates show, on post-secondary institutions–slightly more than 37.1%.

Full-time postsecondary enrolment has increased by almost 24% since 1983-84. Enrolment at community colleges has expanded considerably since 1990-91, serving some 388,610 students in 1994-95. In that same year, universities claimed an estimated 581,070 students.

On the other hand, news headlines suggest university enrolment is dropping and some preliminary estimates have revealed declines between 1994 and 1995 for both full- and part-time programs. That contrasts with almost two decades of steady growth.

The distinction between college and university is blurring in many areas, with some colleges offering courses and credits that will count towards university training. In 1993-94, an estimated 108,610 full-time college students were enrolled in university transfer programs, in addition to 39,786 part-time transfer students.

Community colleges in Canada registered 178,000 part-timers in 1992-93, a decline from the previous year that is mainly attributed to courses reclassified from part- to full-time. Part-time enrolment in universities also dropped by about 15,000 in both 1993 and 1994, so in 1994, total part-time enrolment came to only 285,000 students. Despite the recent drop for both graduate and undergraduate programs, university part-time enrolments have grown 40% between 1974 and 1994.

College course selections continue to follow gender stereotypes, with women choosing secretarial science or health sciences programs like nursing. Men overwhelmingly pick engineering and applied sciences, especially engineering technologies. Men and women are almost equally represented in management and administration. Between 1970 and 1994, social sciences was the fastest growing of all

CLASS FACTS

Percentage increase in university tuition between 1985 and 1995: 134%.

Age of Canada's oldest university (Laval University), in years: 334.

Age of Canada's youngest (University of Northern British Columbia): 3.

Number of students at Canada's largest university (University of Toronto): 53,759.

At Canada's smallest (King's University College, Alberta): 504.

1994 rank of University of Toronto among North American universities, in size: 5th.

First university in the British Empire to award a bachelor's degree to a woman (1875): Mount Allison University, New Brunswick.

Number of women enrolled in full-time graduate programs in engineering and applied sciences in 1989-90: 936.

Number in 1994-95: 1,729.

Number of men enrolled in full-time undergraduate engineering programs in 1994-95: 33,970.

Number of women: 8,028.

university selections, with general arts and sciences coming second for women and engineering and applied sciences next for men.

Ever since they began pouring into the workplace in ever larger numbers, especially during the 1970s, women have sought higher education to help them qualify for higher-paying jobs. It follows, then, that women account for more than half of all full-time college enrolments, and outpace men in full-time university enrolments.

The number of students in university graduate programs has burgeoned more quickly than that of undergrads, both full- and part-time, but women remain in the minority at this level.

Women are entering some professional programs in increasing numbers, but their participation remains low in fields traditionally chosen by men: engineering, mathematics and sciences. Women select careers mainly in education, health and social sciences. In 1990, they accounted for 47.7% of new lawyers and 40.3% of dentists, for example, but only 19.6% of computer science and 14.6% of engineering graduates. The mix has been almost half-and-half in such fields as medicine and optometry.

Older faces are becoming more visible on campus, as mature students may be taking advantage of more leisure time, and reduced or waived fees. In 1993-94, adults aged 25 and more made up about 67% of all college students and one-quarter of all full-time university students, and in 1993 they dominated the part-time student body. Since 1972, their presence at universities has increased at more than twice the rate for those under 25.

Canada's reputation as an educator attracts thousands of foreign students annually. In 1994, an estimated 36,000 foreign nationals studied in Canadian universities, matching a peak reached in 1983. Another 25,447 attended community colleges and trade schools, up almost 150% from 1982-83, and 27,308 were enrolled in elementary or secondary schools. Most of these students come from countries in Asia and Europe.

Tuition fees

Access to good, fully rounded education is a growing concern in Canada, because the cost of postsecondary study keeps rising. Between 1988 and 1992, tuition fees jumped an average of 15% per year. Undergraduate students paid an extra 7.1% between 1994 and 1995.

Only Quebec has been spared in recent years, with fees remaining at about $1,700 between 1994 and 1996. In 1995, fees were highest in Nova Scotia ($3,172), but they have been going up at a faster rate in Alberta and Ontario than in the rest of the country. Late in the year, Ontario announced its intention to review tuition fees, given severe budget cuts.

In 1994, the federal government introduced legislation to provide larger loans for students in need, establish a national grant program, and improve assistance to part-time students. There's no doubt the need is there: about half of all college and university students take out student loans to further their education. In 1992-93, the full tally was $1.45 billion, including scholarships and all postsecondary aid to students. Of that, $918 million was for student loans alone.

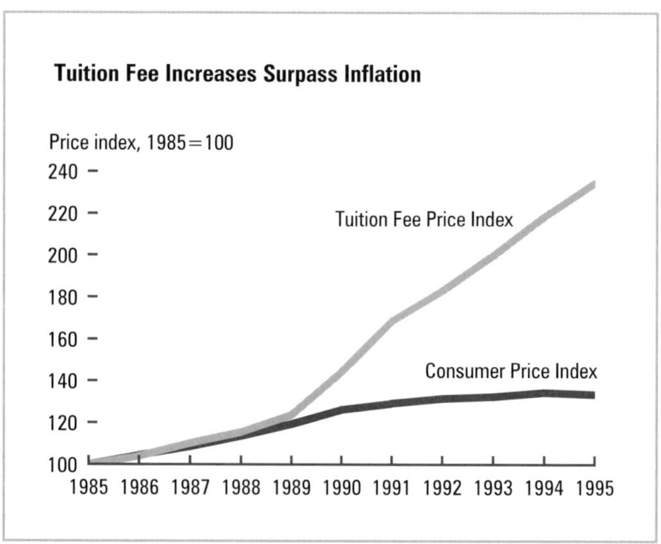

A year's tuition for basic undergraduate study at a university costs almost three times as much as college tuition: about $2,179. Tuition fees account for about 12% of community college operating income and for about one-fifth of a university's general operating income.

Most loans from the federal government are granted through the Canada Student Loans Program. The average annual loan is close to $3,000, but a researcher with the Canadian Federation of Students estimated in 1993 that a year of university costs $10,500 when books, accommodation, living and other expenses are included. Student loan systems operate at the provincial, territorial and federal levels; whether students live in Rankin Inlet, Northwest Territories, or Mount Pearl, Newfoundland, they can seek loan assistance.

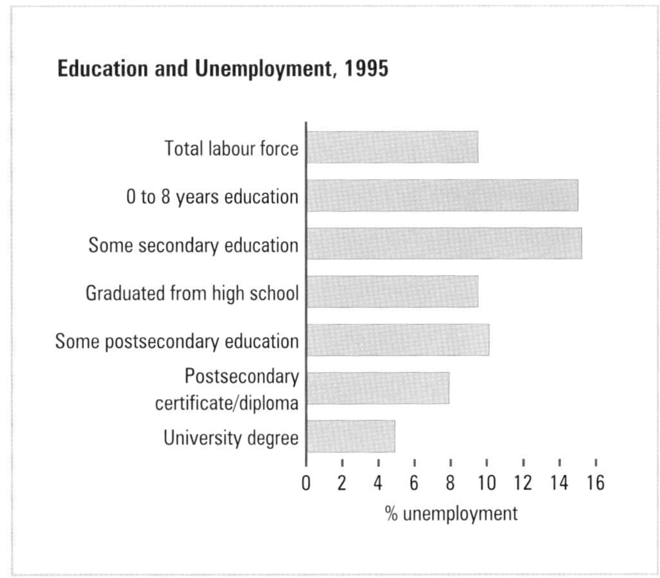

The Dropouts

More than one in eight Canadians held a university degree in 1994. That would bode well for their standard of living: the average income for a university graduate in 1993 was $40,247, compared with $23,644 for a high school graduate.

Having a degree, however, does not guarantee gainful employment. In 1992, 11% of bachelor's graduates from universities and 10% of graduates from career or technical schools could not find work, and almost twice as many 1990 graduates of trade and vocational programs remained unemployed two years after graduating.

The picture is far worse for dropouts—about 17% of high school dropouts in 1993 were unemployed, as were 16.5% of those with only primary school exposure. In 1993, the unemployment rate for the general population was 11.2%.

The recessions of the early 1990s are partly responsible for these high jobless rates. Unable to find work, many young people have remained in school, resulting in an almost 70% increase in the number of community college graduates between 1982 and 1990, and a corresponding 29% leap in university graduates. On the other hand, the number of typically university-aged people has been declining. In 1994, 123,040 students graduated with bachelor's degrees, and an additional 21,330 with master's degrees. An estimated 85,286 college diplomas were awarded in 1992.

Continuing Education

In Canada, the thirst for knowledge shows up in increased vocational training, job retraining and continuing education of every description. Even those who leave school generally say they intend to go back for more at some point in their lives. Eighty-five per cent of respondents to the 1991 School Leavers Survey said they hoped to continue their education at some point in their lives.

Continuing education spokespersons say people enrol to sharpen or upgrade job skills that may help them hang on to jobs in tough economic times.

There has been a flurry of university registrations for non-degree, non-credit courses. In 1993-94, more than 338,000 people enrolled in continuing education courses, a 6.8% hike

Roloff Beny, National Archives of Canada, PA-182745. Courtesy of the Nickle Arts Museum

Many-tiered staircase in the Grand Seminary of Laval University.

over the previous year and a record high. New Brunswickers and Newfoundlanders led the way with increases of more than 60% in that time period.

Courses in business and commerce and liberal arts were most popular everywhere; computer courses accounted for at least 6% of registrations in every province except Saskatchewan. Professional development courses may also figure in this category.

Women's enrolments more or less matched men's in every field except engineering/applied science, where fewer than one in five students was female.

Continuing education courses at university are not prohibitively expensive. Most cost less than $1,000, and the average fee in 1993-94 was $320. Fees are even lower for most continuing education courses offered at community colleges or at public schools through local school boards.

Distance Education

For some Canadians, the desire to keep on learning—whether for personal interest or to upgrade job skills—is challenged by work and family commitments, isolation, or some other impediment. Nevertheless, in 1993, more than 420,000 adult Canadians participated in some form of distance education.

Defined as learning that takes place in the home or workplace without direct supervision, distance education has always been popular in this country. It began with correspondence courses in the latter half of the 1800s, but now encompasses a range of media such as television, video-conferencing and interactive computer learning. Most distance learners are between 25 and 44 years of age, and most hold jobs.

Flexibility is the main attraction, but new technologies like the Information Highway have broadened the application of distance courses.

Distance courses are especially popular for sales and service and blue-collar workers because they can be scheduled around irregular working hours.

Teachers

Ontario's 1994 Royal Commission on Learning declared teachers "our heroes," the vital engines of the process of learning. In 1993-94, there were 377,002 full-time teachers at all levels, including trade schools. The bulk of them—81%—were teaching at the elementary–secondary level. Another 10% were at universities, 7% at colleges, and about 2% in the trade and vocational schools.

Probably most Canadians are involved in some way with someone who works in the education field: education and related services employ more than 900,000 people. That's almost 9% of total employment in most Canadian industries.

Over the last decade, and mostly in the last five years, more than 48,000 teaching positions have been added to the country's education rolls. In the same period there has been a 9% increase in the number of full-time university teachers; they now number 37,300. There has also been expansion in the number of part-time university teachers, up 5,757 since 1989-90. That may be because budget cuts have forced school boards, colleges and universities to cut back on full-time employees drawing full benefits, or it may indicate a growing preference for part-time employment. With an ever-growing workload, burnout may also be a factor.

The surge in enrolments, especially at the elementary–secondary level, has produced larger classes—a concern for parents because big classes mean teachers have fewer opportunities to pay close attention to individual students. In 1992-93, there were 15.8 students per teacher, and that ratio dropped only marginally in 1993-94.

Literacy, Language and Immersion

"Words are as necessary to a people as bread," wrote Quebec writer Alice Parizeau in 1988. In 1994, an estimated 58% of adult Canadians could read well enough to cope with every-day reading requirements, 17% more could not, and the remaining 26%, while not identifying themselves as having language difficulties, did not score well.

In Canada, governments are investing considerable time and money to evaluate literacy levels and develop strategies to improve our literacy levels. One example—a first—is the International Adult Literacy Survey (IALS), conducted in 1994. Under the direction of Statistics Canada, the OECD and the Educational Testing Service in the United States, several thousand people from Canada, Germany, the Netherlands, Poland, Sweden, Switzerland and the United States took part.

Not surprisingly, Canada's showing was respectable—suggesting our education system does produce mainly literate adults who can read and do arithmetic. Fewer than 20% of Canadians ranked in the lowest levels; they find reading a newspaper, completing an application form and calculating a tip for a restaurant meal difficult. Slightly more than 20% of us were in the highest prose literacy category. The United States presented a similar profile, while Sweden came out on top with less than 10% at the bottom and more than 30% at the upper level.

The IALS confirmed the link between literacy and education. Couch potatoes who watch lots of television may get a great deal of information, but their literacy skills do not get exercised and often they don't read as well as those who watch less TV.

Among Canadian schoolchildren, the School Achievement Indicators Program (SAIP) 1993 tests in mathematics and 1994 tests in reading and writing indicated basic skill levels have been reached by most 13- and 16-year-olds.

In the math results, almost half of all 16-year-olds were able to do simple arithmetic, algebra and geometry; they had far more sophisticated skills than those demonstrated by 13-year-olds, but few students could do complex problem-solving.

In 1994, some 58,000 students in all provinces except Saskatchewan were tested for reading and writing ability. About 72% of 16-year-olds and 45% of 13-year-olds could

Distance Learning

Distance education is becoming increasingly popular in Canada. In 1993, it attracted 420,000 adult students, up an impressive 11% over 1991. Most distance students are young adults, under 35 years of age. They account for nearly 58% of all enrolments. (Distance education refers to a method of education whereby the teacher and student are separated by geography or time.)

Distance education first originated in the latter half of the mid-nineteenth century, with courses by correspondence. Since then it has evolved, gradually incorporating new communications techniques as they have come into use. A famous example was the CBC's National Farm Radio Forum, which ran from 1941 to 1953 and provided the Canadian agricultural community with new knowledge of farming. In the 1970s, television came to the forefront, and both provinces and universities established educational channels, including Radio-Québec, ACCESS in Alberta and KNOWLEDGE in British Columbia.

Distance education is, however, used in many places of learning, from schools and colleges to various private sector organizations, as well as universities. New information techniques have truly revolutionized its use. For example, Queen's University now offers an MBA program via a telecommunications network available in 22 regional centres. The University of Waterloo, Memorial University and Athabaska University, to name only a few in the university sector, are making great strides.

"interpret, evaluate and explore complex and sophisticated text." The writing results were even better: 80% of 16-year-olds and 62% of 13-year-olds "demonstrated an effective control of the elements of writing." Provincial variations were small, and girls consistently outperformed boys.

In both tests, performance improved considerably between ages 13 and 16. There is considerable concern about those 16-year-olds who are not performing at a level typically associated with that age. Math skills pose the greatest problem, with 35% of 16-year-old students working below the middle level; reading and writing skills were particularly weak in 24% and 20% of students respectively.

In 1994-95, the National Literacy Secretariat, a federal agency that works with non-government organizations and provincial governments to improve literacy levels, had an annual budget of $24.3 million.

Bilingualism

In 1969, English and French were declared the country's two official languages. In that same year, historian Arnold Toynbee stated: "At present, Canada is not a bilingual country; it is a di-lingual one, for most Canadians speak only one of the two national languages." But almost 30 years later, we are making strides.

Some 16% of Canadians are comfortable in both official languages, compared with 13% in 1971. In 1995, in the aftermath of the Quebec referendum on separation, bilingualism remains important to many Canadians. In 1992-93, some $296.5 million was spent through the federal Official Languages Program.

In 1992-93, more than two million students studied in second language programs outside Quebec while another 652,000 received second language training in *la belle province.* Participation in second language training has increased steadily at the elementary level. English classes are compulsory for all Quebec students in Grades 4 to 6, and have close to 100% participation for Grades 7 to 11. On the other hand,

Walter Curtin, National Archives of Canada, PA-137084

Drama professor Dora Mavor Moore visiting a class.

in high schools participation has dropped. Enrolments are highest in New Brunswick and lowest in the Northwest Territories.

Education in the (official) minority language of a community is provided through federal funding as well, and 160,344 students outside Quebec took advantage of this in 1993-94. Another 95,851 were enrolled in minority language studies in Quebec. New Brunswickers embraced minority language studies enthusiastically, with one in three of the province's public school pupils participating. The comparable rate in Quebec was 9.2%, and 4% for the rest of the country.

Context of the Times

In 1901, the Census of Canada found that 17% of Canadians could not read or write. Not only that, but only 52% of boys aged 10 and older were actually in school.

Today, all Canadian children must be in school, at least until the age of 15. Yet, a 1989 national survey of literacy found that about 16% of Canadians cannot read or write well enough to cope with their daily activities. The proportions appear to be the same, yet nearly a century has gone by.

There's more to the story than the numbers, however. In 1901, Canada was still largely agrarian. People lived and worked on farms all their lives. For some, the idea of an education was an impossible luxury, given the work at hand. After all, there were no income tax forms to fill out: income tax didn't exist. There were no 10-page VCR manuals to be plumbed. Life was, in many ways, harder and simpler.

Today, Canadians must survive in a much more sophisticated world. Farm life for many dwells only in the memories of ancestors. Even the way we measure literacy has changed. In 1901, it was a simple matter of yes or no; people identified themselves as literate or not. Today, literacy is measured in the way we cope with the complexities of an entirely different age, the age of information.

There are also students learning another language through immersion, a program where subjects such as math or history are taught in the second language. At least 25% of each day's learning must take place in the second language for the program to qualify as immersion. In 1992-93 outside Quebec, 263,991 students learned a second official language through immersion. That represents 12.7% of total French second language enrolment. There were also 34,341 students taking second language immersion in Quebec.

SOURCES

The Council of Ministers of Education, Canada
Statistics Canada

FOR FURTHER READING

Selected publications from Statistics Canada

- **Canadian Social Trends**. Quarterly. 11-008
- **Education Quarterly Review**. Quarterly. 81-003
- **Education in Canada**. Annual. 81-229
- **Literacy, Economy and Society: Results of the first International Adult Literacy Survey**, 1995. Occasional. 89-545

Selected publications from other sources

- **Education at a Glance, OECD Indicators**. Organisation for Economic Co-operation and Development. 1995.
- **The Love of Learning (Short Version)**. Queen's Printer for Ontario. 1994.
- **Report on Education in Canada**. Council of Ministers of Education, Canada. 1995.
- **School Achievement Indicators Program, Report on Mathematics Assessment**. Council of Ministers of Education, Canada. 1994.
- **School Achievement Indicators Program, Reading and Writing Assessment**. Council of Ministers of Education, Canada. 1994.

Legend

–	nil or zero	..	not available	x	confidential
--	too small to be expressed	...	not applicable or not appropriate		*(Certain tables may not add due to rounding)*

5.1 EDUCATION FUNDING

	All funds	Government			Fees	Other sources
		Federal[1]	Provincial	Municipal[2]		
	$ Millions					
1970-71	7,674.7	930.1	4,314.6	1,719.4	320.5	390.1
1975-76	12,948.0	1,198.8	8,403.6	2,356.3	529.4	459.9
1980-81	22,201.6	1,891.0	14,717.4	3,850.8	872.7	869.5
1985-86	34,155.7	3,661.5	21,967.4	5,480.5	1,545.2	1,501.1
1991-92	53,075.7	5,438.4	31,371.7	10,835.8	2,796.2	2,633.6
1992-93	55,760.3	6,220.0	32,104.1	11,639.5	3,101.5	2,670.8
1993-94	56,844.4	6,581.1	32,564.3	11,928.4	3,279.7	2,490.9

1. In addition to the direct funding reported here, the federal government also provides indirect support in respect of postsecondary education to provinces and territories under the Federal–Provincial Fiscal Arrangements and Federal Postsecondary Education and Health Contributions Act, 1977 and under the Official Languages in Education Program.
2. Includes local school taxation.

Source: Statistics Canada, CANSIM, Cross-classified tables 00590203, 00590204, 00590206 and 00590306.

5.2 EXPENDITURES ON EDUCATION, CANADA, THE PROVINCES AND TERRITORIES, 1993-94

	Canada	Nfld.	P.E.I.	N.S.	N.B.	Que.	Ont.	Man.	Sask.	Alta.	B.C.	Y.T.	N.W.T.	Overseas and undistributed
	$ Millions													
Education expenditures[1]	56,844.4	1,298.7	223.4	1,593.9	1,376.2	13,963.7	21,679.0	2,103.0	1,816.6	5,218.0	6,474.6	104.4	345.6	647.3
Level														
Elementary and secondary	35,715.0	657.2	132.8	928.1	822.6	7,915.3	15,226.0	1,434.4	1,134.8	3,215.4	3,876.1	77.5	260.7	34.3
Community college	3,877.8	28.7	10.3	41.3	78.5	1,697.9	1,049.5	41.0	43.2	318.8	524.1	5.4	36.1	3.1
University	11,328.9	238.2	46.7	433.1	289.7	3,142.1	3,740.6	443.3	422.9	1,015.6	1,299.8	6.7	25.4	224.8
Vocational training	5,922.7	374.7	33.6	191.4	185.6	1,208.4	1,662.9	184.2	215.7	668.2	774.7	14.9	23.4	385.1
Direct source of funds														
Federal government[2]	6,581.1	363.4	37.7	238.8	217.4	1,328.7	1,781.8	307.6	281.7	538.8	768.3	23.1	91.0	602.9
Provincial governments	32,564.3	846.1	169.1	1,051.9	1,042.0	10,611.6	9,803.5	1,084.6	900.1	2,906.5	3,835.3	79.4	234.2	–
Municipal governments[3]	11,928.4	–	–	136.8	--	680.8	7,910.9	499.1	480.9	1,242.0	969.6	–	8.3	–
Fees and other sources	5,770.6	89.3	16.6	166.4	116.8	1,342.6	2,182.7	211.8	153.9	530.6	901.4	2.0	12.0	44.5

1. Includes operating, capital, student aid and all departmental expenditures.
2. In addition to the direct funding reported here, the federal government also provides indirect support in respect of postsecondary education to provinces and territories under the Federal–Provincial Fiscal Arrangements and Federal Postsecondary Education and Health Contributions Act, 1977 and under the Official Languages in Education Program.
3. Includes local school taxation.

Source: Statistics Canada, CANSIM, Cross-classified tables 00590203, 00590204, 00590206 and 00590306.

5.3 EXPENDITURES ON ELEMENTARY AND SECONDARY EDUCATION, 1992-93

	Canada	Nfld.	P.E.I.	N.S.	N.B.	Que.	Ont.	Man.	Sask.	Alta.	B.C.	Y.T.	N.W.T.	Overseas and undistributed
								$ Millions						
Expenditures	34,710.0	648.9	128.6	890.9	816.7	7,882.3	14,425.9	1,408.4	1,154.0	3,145.8	3,836.0	85.8	245.9	40.9
School boards[1]	30,197.8	634.6	124.3	856.2	800.1	7,207.9	13,702.8	1,283.3	1,075.1	2,955.9	3,497.3	74.5	204.2	0.1
Teachers salaries[2] including fringe benefits	18,458.1	403.1	76.5	524.2	376.6	3,766.2	8,363.0	660.1	556.7	1,701.5	1,916.7	34.2	79.4	–
Other operating expenses	9,295.5	128.6	30.2	196.9	199.5	2,400.4	3,820.3	381.6	302.9	736.0	1,027.5	18.1	53.5	–
Capital and debt charges	2,444.2	48.9	13.5	69.6	1.9	438.2	1,054.0	93.9	73.1	333.4	298.2	14.6	5.0	–
Government expenditures[3]	2,218.4	54.0	4.2	65.5	222.0	603.2	465.4	147.7	142.3	185.0	254.9	7.7	66.3	0.1
Indian and Inuit schools	459.0	0.4	1.7	8.4	7.5	36.4	104.5	56.0	51.0	51.8	50.2	10.0	40.1	40.9
Special education	195.4	x	x	x	3.5	11.2	92.0	11.4	4.9	37.1	16.8	–	0.4	–
Departmental administration	142.9	7.7	0.9	5.9	2.4	44.6	34.7	4.0	8.7	14.6	17.0	1.2	1.2	–
Private schools[4]	1,526.4	x	x	x	3.2	606.2	492.2	53.7	14.9	91.1	254.9	0.1	–	–
All sources of funds	34,710.0	648.9	128.6	890.8	816.7	7,882.3	14,425.9	1,408.4	1,154.0	3,145.8	3,836.0	85.8	245.9	40.9
Federal government	786.5	1.4	2.7	15.0	15.6	78.4	183.4	95.5	85.7	97.2	88.6	16.4	65.7	40.9
Provincial governments	20,348.2	607.3	124.4	717.5	784.2	6,546.0	5,870.0	727.6	576.0	1,651.3	2,506.9	69.1	167.9	–
Municipal governments[5]	11,631.2	18.6	–	134.7	–	691.7	7,562.6	487.1	468.7	1,239.1	1,020.3	–	8.4	–
Fees and other sources	1,944.0	21.6	1.4	23.6	17.0	566.2	809.9	98.2	23.6	158.2	220.2	0.3	3.9	–

1. Expenditures of school boards cover calendar year 1992.
2. Includes principals and vice-principals.
3. Includes departmental services to school boards, contribution to teachers' pension fund, other departmental expenditures and federal departments in foreign countries.
4. Includes transfers to private schools from school boards.
5. Includes local school taxation.

Source: Statistics Canada, CANSIM, Cross-classified tables 00590303, 00590305 and 00590306.

5.4 EXPENDITURES ON VOCATIONAL EDUCATION, 1993-94

	Canada	Nfld.	P.E.I.	N.S.	N.B.	Que.	Ont.	Man.	Sask.	Alta.	B.C.	Y.T.	N.W.T.	Overseas and undistributed
								$ Millions						
Total	5,922.7	374.7	33.6	191.4	185.6	1,208.4	1,662.9	184.2	215.7	668.2	774.7	14.9	23.4	385.1
Human resource training[1]	4,789.8	x	x	x	x	1,166.0	1,150.9	142.1	169.4	592.0	695.0	9.1	2.8	135.6
Federal government	3,469.5	318.7	27.8	143.6	159.8	844.5	932.8	130.1	103.8	261.9	410.7	0.1	--	135.6
Provincial and municipal governments	930.4	7.4	2.8	25.6	1.1	274.9	124.8	6.1	52.5	266.7	158.3	7.8	2.3	–
Fees and other sources	389.9	x	x	x	x	46.7	93.3	5.9	13.1	63.4	126.0	1.1	0.5	–
Other[2]	1,034.1	x	x	x	x	30.5	488.5	39.3	43.0	72.1	76.1	5.8	20.6	205.0
Private	98.8	x	x	x	x	11.9	23.5	2.9	3.4	4.2	3.5	–	–	44.5

1. Includes training courses purchased by the federal government, capital expenditures, grants for training in industry and allowances to trainees.
2. Includes nursing assistants training, trades training in reform schools and penitentiaries and other training programs within federal and provincial departments.

Source: Statistics Canada, CANSIM, Cross-classified table 00590204.

5.5 EXPENDITURES ON POSTSECONDARY EDUCATION, 1993-94

	Canada	Nfld.	P.E.I.	N.S.	N.B.	Que.	Ont.	Man.	Sask.	Alta.	B.C.	Y.T.	N.W.T.	Overseas and undistributed
								$ Millions						
Postsecondary education	15,206.7	266.9	57.0	474.4	368.1	4,839.9	4,790.1	484.4	466.1	1,334.4	1,823.9	12.0	61.5	227.9
Operating	12,682.2	240.3	52.4	442.7	308.0	3,974.4	4,458.9	403.0	356.4	1,087.3	1,324.7	3.8	30.4	–
Community colleges	3,156.3	19.6	9.9	36.8	72.3	1,358.2	970.6	30.6	32.7	215.8	375.6	3.8	30.4	–
Universities	9,526.0	220.7	42.5	405.8	235.7	2,616.2	3,488.3	372.4	323.7	871.5	949.1	–	–	–
Capital	850.9	x	x	x	19.8	392.5	21.1	5.8	19.2	85.9	287.9	0.2	1.0	–
Scholarships, awards and cost of loans[1]	1,173.9	28.1	5.0	23.8	22.6	426.0	249.5	30.4	54.9	133.0	108.4	2.0	9.1	81.2
Other direct departmental expenditures	499.6	x	x	x	17.7	47.0	60.6	45.2	35.6	28.2	102.9	6.1	21.1	146.8
All sources of funds	15,206.7	266.9	57.0	474.4	368.1	4,839.9	4,790.1	484.4	466.1	1,334.4	1,823.9	12.0	61.5	227.9
Federal government[2]	1,890.8	26.6	5.8	74.5	36.6	390.2	572.4	72.8	68.5	147.5	241.5	5.4	21.2	227.9
Provincial governments	9,969.5	189.8	37.5	265.0	244.9	3,731.9	2,928.8	297.3	282.2	891.1	1,060.7	6.0	34.5	–
Municipal governments	8.1	–	–	0.2	–	0.6	5.2	0.1	0.2	1.2	0.6	–	--	–
Fees and other sources	3,338.2	50.6	13.8	134.8	86.6	717.2	1,283.7	114.1	115.2	294.6	521.1	0.6	5.8	–

1. Excluding the value (principal) of loans.
2. In addition to the direct funding reported here, the federal government also provides indirect support in respect of postsecondary education to provinces and territories under the Federal–Provincial Fiscal Arrangements and Federal Post-Secondary Education and Health Contributions Act, 1977 and under the Official Languages in Education Program.

Source: Statistics Canada, CANSIM, Cross-classified tables 00590203 and 00590206.

5.6 UNDERGRADUATE ARTS TUITION

	1994-95	1995-96	1994-95 to 1995-96 % change
	Average tuition fees[1]		
	$		%
Canada	2,179	2,333	7
Newfoundland	2,150	2,312	8
Prince Edward Island	2,620	2,820	8
Nova Scotia	2,946	3,172	8
New Brunswick	2,353	2,496	6
Quebec	1,694	1,694	–
Ontario	2,252	2,458	9
Manitoba	2,227	2,338	5
Saskatchewan	2,458	2,591	5
Alberta	2,450	2,708	11
British Columbia	2,249	2,366	5

1. Using the most current enrolment data available, average tuition fees have been weighted by the number of students.

Source: Statistics Canada, Education, Culture and Tourism Division.

5.7 CANADA STUDENT LOANS PROGRAM[1] LOAN CERTIFICATES FOR FULL-TIME STUDIES

	1989-90[2]		1990-91[2]		1991-92[2]		1992-93[2]		1993-94[2]		1994-95[2]	
	Loan	Students	Loan	Students	Loan	Students	Loan	Students	Loan	Students	Loan	Students
	$'000	Number	$'000	Number	$'000	Number	$'000	Number	$'000	Number	$'000	Number
All loans	703,625	236,772	712,171	272,225	854,156	295,013	924,365	298,299	1,101,484	322,102	1,367,203	342,236
Full-time studies												
Canada	701,467	235,468	709,727	270,792	851,619	293,552	919,802	296,031	1,096,593	319,710	1,358,665	339,171
Newfoundland	35,698	11,617	39,933	14,837	37,494	13,545	36,613	11,886	42,277	12,855	61,197	14,011
Prince Edward Island	7,487	2,640	6,288	2,618	6,275	2,578	6,628	2,296	6,820	2,288	8,394	2,310
Nova Scotia	44,722	14,353	44,954	16,414	46,492	15,931	44,664	14,518	47,417	14,959	56,923	14,948
New Brunswick	41,662	12,978	41,667	14,535	45,106	14,954	49,534	14,604	49,066	14,201	38,277	12,004
Ontario	218,543	95,050	250,390	112,596	370,147	138,723	413,300	145,374	568,688	165,895	759,962	189,902
Manitoba	39,783	11,463	39,880	12,706	40,206	12,355	42,181	12,324	39,448	11,449	37,438	10,101
Saskatchewan	54,446	16,568	51,504	17,396	54,245	16,888	59,369	17,084	56,317	16,130	62,620	15,546
Alberta	132,413	41,195	125,352	42,394	124,239	39,669	132,813	39,887	141,277	41,543	128,915	36,428
British Columbia	125,798	29,381	108,847	36,933	126,240	38,454	133,403	37,658	144,031	40,011	203,820	43,602
Yukon	915	223	912	363	1,175	455	1,297	400	1,252	379	1,119	319
Part-time studies	2,158	1,304	2,444	1,433	2,537	1,461	4,563	2,268	4,891	2,392	8,538	3,065

1. The province of Quebec and the Northwest Territories do not participate in the Canada Student Loans Program.
2. From August 1 of one year to July 31 of the next.

Sources: Human Resources Development Canada, *1996-97 Estimates, Part III; 1995-96 Estimates, Part III* and *1994-95 Estimates, Part III.*

5.8 ENROLMENT IN ELEMENTARY AND SECONDARY SCHOOLS

	Canada[1]	Public	Private	Federal	Schools for the blind and the deaf
1960-61	4,204,520	3,989,257	168,381	44,187	2,695
1965-66	5,163,192	4,909,788	203,681	46,067	3,656
1970-71	5,836,193	5,655,431	142,601	34,290	3,871
1975-76	5,594,684	5,372,014	182,001	37,087	3,582
1980-81	5,106,288	4,855,766	209,399	37,973	3,150
1985-86	4,927,806	4,646,398	234,188	44,408	2,812
1990-91	5,141,003	4,845,308	240,968	52,285	2,442
1991-92	5,218,237	4,915,630	245,255	55,221	2,131
1992-93	5,284,146	4,967,849	257,605	56,416	2,276
1993-94	5,347,389	5,022,351	265,321	57,378	2,339

1. Canada total also includes Department of National Defence schools overseas.

Sources: Statistics Canada, CANSIM, Cross-classified table 00570202; Catalogue no. 81-229.

5.9 ENROLMENT IN ELEMENTARY AND SECONDARY SCHOOLS, CANADA, THE PROVINCES AND TERRITORIES, 1993-94

	Elementary and secondary schools	Public	Private	Federal	Schools for the blind and the deaf
Canada	5,347,389	5,022,351	265,321	57,378	2,339
Newfoundland	118,659	118,273	274	–	112
Prince Edward Island	24,490	24,242	196	48	4
Nova Scotia	168,637	164,722	2,100	1,137	678
New Brunswick	140,378	138,686	797	895	–
Quebec	1,149,555	1,039,690	103,520	5,742	603
Ontario	2,125,543	2,039,709	74,850	10,275	709
Manitoba	221,610	195,761	11,826	13,895	128
Saskatchewan	212,677	198,331	3,200	11,146	–
Alberta	540,501	512,255	19,209	8,932	105
British Columbia	622,697	568,668	49,334	4,695	–
Yukon	5,777	5,762	15	–	–
Northwest Territories	16,252	16,252	–	–	–
DND Overseas[1]	613	–	–	613	–

1. Department of National Defence schools overseas.

Sources: Statistics Canada, CANSIM, Cross-classified table 00570202; Catalogue no. 81-229.

5.10 SECONDARY SCHOOL GRADUATES

	1981	1986	1991	1992	1993
Canada	305,142	275,708	260,668	272,918	281,350
Newfoundland	6,580	6,840	7,327	7,592	7,539
Prince Edward Island	1,727	1,483	1,502	1,469	1,565
Nova Scotia	9,190	8,666	9,333	9,341	9,378
New Brunswick	9,898	8,835	9,588	9,650	9,631
Quebec[1]	83,775	76,192	59,124	64,671	66,914
Ontario	113,939	100,826	101,328	104,616	107,972
Manitoba	12,618	11,160	11,906	12,581	12,833
Saskatchewan	12,149	10,848	10,740	10,729	11,163
Alberta	24,000	23,048	22,452	23,093	24,378
British Columbia	30,918	27,458	26,990	28,794	29,528
Yukon	144	148	174	161	194
Northwest Territories	204	204	204	221	255

1. Excludes adults for Quebec.

Source: Statistics Canada, Catalogue no. 81-229.

5.11 POSTSECONDARY ENROLMENT[1] IN COMMUNITY COLLEGES[2]

	Both sexes				Male				Female			
	1986-87	1991-92	1992-93	1993-94	1986-87	1991-92	1992-93	1993-94	1986-87	1991-92	1992-93	1993-94
Full-time enrolment												
Canada	321,495	349,098	361,511	376,840	153,323	162,168	169,600	176,950	168,172	186,930	191,911	199,890
Newfoundland	2,945	4,361	4,758	5,124	1,445	2,210	2,475	2,665	1,500	2,151	2,283	2,459
Prince Edward Island	1,016	1,225	926	985	475	577	416	443	541	648	510	542
Nova Scotia	2,360	2,653	3,375	3,787	888	1,075	1,372	1,539	1,472	1,578	2,003	2,248
New Brunswick	2,334	2,988	3,194	3,415	1,194	1,558	1,613	1,725	1,140	1,430	1,581	1,690
Quebec	163,190	163,768	169,583	176,928	76,059	73,497	76,693	80,520	87,131	90,271	92,890	96,408
Ontario	95,231	111,362	117,113	121,330	46,228	54,055	57,787	59,452	49,003	57,307	59,326	61,878
Manitoba	3,709	3,936	3,850	3,900	1,656	1,700	1,710	1,732	2,053	2,236	2,140	2,168
Saskatchewan	2,972	3,509	3,541	3,325	1,218	1,463	1,528	1,435	1,754	2,046	2,013	1,890
Alberta	24,571	25,464	25,323	25,183	12,136	11,779	11,775	10,325	12,435	13,685	13,548	14,858
British Columbia	22,973	29,288	29,304	32,270	11,945	14,004	13,981	16,842	11,028	15,284	15,323	15,428
Yukon	63	262	262	277	24	126	126	133	39	136	136	144
Northwest Territories	131	282	282	316	55	124	124	139	76	158	158	177
Part-time enrolment												
Canada	166,332	216,748	177,640	181,040	70,619	82,839	69,015	72,172	95,713	133,909	108,625	108,868
Newfoundland	72	180	233	167	64	86	124	65	8	94	109	102
Prince Edward Island	–	–	–	–	–	–	–	–	–	–	–	–
Nova Scotia	521	215	179	252	92	15	12	113	429	200	167	139
New Brunswick	51	48	42	64	18	19	13	26	33	29	29	38
Quebec[3]	55,410	60,954	22,060	22,060	22,822	23,193	9,175	8,824	32,588	37,761	12,885	13,236
Ontario	73,061	88,630	88,735	93,290	32,683	33,604	33,663	37,316	40,378	55,026	55,072	55,974
Manitoba	110	1,697	1,646	1,646	44	646	634	658	66	1,051	1,012	988
Saskatchewan	103	1,027	710	581	39	99	80	227	64	928	630	354
Alberta	7,547	16,768	16,764	16,764	2,695	6,863	6,862	6,873	4,852	9,905	9,902	9,891
British Columbia	29,218	46,667	46,709	45,709	12,089	18,071	18,209	17,827	17,129	28,596	28,500	27,882
Yukon	137	206	206	257	53	84	84	116	84	122	122	141
Northwest Territories	102	356	356	250	20	159	159	127	82	197	197	123

1. Includes both full-time and part-time.
2. Includes related institutions such as hospital schools and agricultural, arts, and other specialized colleges.
3. Decrease between 1991-92 and 1992-93 is due to the reclassification of some part-time enrolment to continuing education.

Sources: Statistics Canada, CANSIM, matrix 8008; Catalogue no. 81-229.

5.12 COMMUNITY COLLEGE[1] DIPLOMAS IN CAREER PROGRAMS

	1981	1986	1990	1991
Canada	48,694	58,654	58,818	59,772
Male	20,373	26,306	24,131	24,565
Female	28,321	32,348	34,687	35,207
Business and commerce	12,869	15,371	15,799	15,847
Male	4,239	5,016	5,141	5,111
Female	8,630	10,355	10,658	10,736
Engineering and applied sciences	11,031	15,843	12,280	12,547
Male	9,315	13,054	10,143	10,370
Female	1,716	2,789	2,137	2,177
Social sciences and services	6,931	8,021	10,214	11,002
Male	1,740	2,206	2,721	2,884
Female	5,191	5,815	7,493	8,118
Health sciences	9,721	10,590	11,229	10,908
Male	1,032	1,522	1,867	1,826
Female	8,689	9,068	9,362	9,082
Arts	4,105	4,284	5,003	5,084
Male	1,616	1,832	1,946	2,003
Female	2,489	2,452	3,057	3,081
Natural sciences and primary industries	3,192	3,365	2,823	2,845
Male	2,218	2,311	1,873	1,915
Female	974	1,054	950	930
Humanities	616	847	986	1,144
Male	123	230	250	297
Female	493	617	736	847
Arts and sciences	146	245	324	343
Male	38	66	105	122
Female	108	179	219	221
Not reported	83	88	160	52
Male	52	69	85	37
Female	31	19	75	15

1. Includes related institutions such as hospital schools and agricultural, arts and other specialized colleges.

Source: Statistics Canada, Catalogue no. 81-229.

5.13 ENROLMENT IN UNIVERSITIES[1]

	Both sexes					Male					Female				
	1981-82	1986-87	1991-92	1992-93	1993-94	1981-82	1986-87	1991-92	1992-93	1993-94	1981-82	1986-87	1991-92	1992-93	1993-94
Full-time enrolment															
Canada	401,911	475,428	553,954	569,480	574,314	218,794	245,178	267,646	273,024	272,644	183,117	230,250	286,308	296,456	301,670
Newfoundland	7,631	10,828	12,912	13,213	13,029	4,015	5,201	5,901	5,902	5,853	3,616	5,627	7,011	7,311	7,176
Prince Edward Island	1,390	1,837	2,609	2,724	2,691	677	849	1,174	1,230	1,161	713	988	1,435	1,494	1,530
Nova Scotia	19,458	23,667	28,601	29,427	29,996	10,220	11,764	13,264	13,718	13,812	9,238	11,903	15,337	15,709	16,184
New Brunswick	12,041	14,940	18,096	19,110	19,493	6,554	7,642	8,544	9,029	9,099	5,487	7,298	9,552	10,081	10,394
Quebec	93,562	116,391	129,993	135,020	137,750	51,651	59,799	62,359	64,374	65,053	41,911	56,592	67,634	70,646	72,697
Ontario	167,874	187,153	225,525	230,570	231,156	92,039	96,380	109,594	111,405	110,724	75,835	90,773	115,931	119,165	120,432
Manitoba	17,716	19,905	20,572	20,576	20,296	9,786	10,578	10,201	10,127	9,920	7,930	9,327	10,371	10,449	10,376
Saskatchewan	15,820	20,535	22,392	22,847	23,018	8,426	10,791	10,878	10,961	10,924	7,394	9,744	11,514	11,886	12,094
Alberta	33,745	44,050	48,791	50,344	51,083	17,735	22,921	23,625	24,060	24,073	16,010	21,129	25,166	26,284	27,010
British Columbia	32,674	36,122	44,463	45,649	45,802	17,691	19,253	22,106	22,218	22,025	14,983	16,869	22,357	23,431	23,777
Part-time enrolment															
Canada	300,290	287,458	313,327	316,165	300,290	107,176	113,793	118,699	121,287	117,003	144,699	173,665	194,628	194,878	183,287
Newfoundland	4,368	4,690	4,753	4,642	4,368	1,710	1,850	1,888	1,908	1,783	2,226	2,840	2,865	2,734	2,585
Prince Edward Island	776	685	951	914	776	337	234	293	292	274	444	451	658	622	502
Nova Scotia	7,989	6,921	8,694	8,453	7,989	2,779	2,484	3,097	3,052	2,867	4,106	4,437	5,597	5,401	5,122
New Brunswick	5,566	4,936	5,702	5,712	5,566	1,798	1,789	1,860	1,909	1,886	2,823	3,147	3,842	3,803	3,680
Quebec	117,804	117,799	119,722	122,451	117,804	41,584	48,555	46,135	47,524	46,443	53,582	69,244	73,587	74,927	71,361
Ontario	99,567	95,714	109,050	108,478	99,567	38,880	36,817	40,463	40,832	38,680	52,303	58,897	68,587	67,646	60,887
Manitoba	16,758	14,556	16,611	17,012	16,758	4,839	5,843	6,900	7,223	7,196	7,894	8,713	9,711	9,789	9,562
Saskatchewan	8,689	9,250	9,435	10,050	8,689	3,155	3,360	3,634	3,895	3,237	5,264	5,890	5,801	6,155	5,452
Alberta	17,605	17,299	17,155	17,929	17,685	5,370	6,375	6,036	6,362	6,346	6,958	10,924	11,119	11,567	11,339
British Columbia	21,088	15,608	21,254	20,524	21,088	6,724	6,486	8,393	8,290	8,291	9,099	9,122	12,861	12,234	12,797

1. Both full-time and part-time.

Source: Statistics Canada, CANSIM, Cross-classified tables 00580701 and 00580702.

5.14 UNIVERSITY DEGREES GRANTED

	1981	1986	1991	1992	1993	1994
Canada	115,581	139,768	159,806	168,872	173,928	178,074
Male	58,664	66,857	70,347	73,671	75,443	76,470
Female	56,917	72,911	89,459	95,201	98,485	101,604
Social sciences	38,137	51,502	63,027	66,248	68,050	69,586
Male	21,785	25,453	28,529	30,053	30,542	30,701
Female	16,352	26,049	34,498	36,195	37,508	38,885
Education	26,372	23,158	28,074	30,033	30,438	30,383
Male	8,883	7,315	8,614	9,030	8,954	9,140
Female	17,489	15,843	19,460	21,003	21,484	21,279
Humanities	11,586	15,147	20,489	22,098	23,038	23,057
Male	4,780	5,839	7,497	8,005	8,561	8,416
Female	6,806	9,308	12,992	14,093	14,477	14,641
Health professions and occupations	7,403	9,832	10,769	11,262	11,832	12,183
Male	2,892	2,911	3,125	3,206	3,412	3,475
Female	4,511	6,921	7,644	8,056	8,420	8,708
Engineering and applied sciences	9,184	11,194	10,895	11,505	11,795	12,597
Male	8,421	9,915	9,269	9,687	9,887	10,285
Female	763	1,279	1,626	1,818	1,908	2,312
Agriculture and biological sciences	6,237	7,561	8,975	9,224	9,687	10,087
Male	3,328	3,558	4,064	4,037	4,268	4,309
Female	2,909	4,003	4,911	5,187	5,419	5,778
Mathematics and physical sciences	5,540	10,384	8,859	9,163	9,325	9,551
Male	4,049	7,477	6,329	6,458	6,572	6,697
Female	1,491	2,907	2,530	2,705	2,753	2,854
Fine and applied arts	3,202	4,026	4,445	4,993	5,126	5,308
Male	1,187	1,418	1,426	1,703	1,686	1,773
Female	2,015	2,608	3,019	3,290	3,440	3,535
Arts and sciences	7,920	6,964	4,273	4,346	4,637	5,322
Male	3,339	2,971	1,494	1,492	1,561	1,710
Female	4,581	3,993	2,779	2,854	3,076	3,612

Source: Statistics Canada, CANSIM, Cross-classified table 00580602.

5.15 UNIVERSITY DEGREES GRANTED, CANADA AND THE PROVINCES

	1981	1986	1991	1992	1993	1994
Canada	115,581	139,768	159,806	168,872	173,928	178,074
Undergraduate[1]	99,445	119,958	136,611	144,061	147,324	150,879
Graduate[2]	16,136	19,810	23,195	24,811	26,604	27,195
Newfoundland	1,578	2,346	2,557	2,445	2,649	2,718
Undergraduate	1,460	2,163	2,328	2,212	2,359	2,465
Graduate	118	183	229	233	290	253
Prince Edward Island	289	358	462	498	499	573
Undergraduate	289	358	457	489	485	562
Graduate	–	–	5	9	14	11
Nova Scotia	4,898	6,065	6,947	7,591	7,808	8,103
Undergraduate	4,297	5,327	5,958	6,475	6,709	6,978
Graduate	601	738	989	1,116	1,099	1,125
New Brunswick	2,680	3,157	3,559	3,748	3,944	4,005
Undergraduate	2,407	2,838	3,214	3,351	3,527	3,607
Graduate	273	319	345	397	417	398
Quebec	36,065	43,205	51,805	54,587	56,413	57,853
Undergraduate	31,680	37,137	44,111	46,391	47,686	48,626
Graduate	4,385	6,068	7,694	8,196	8,727	9,227
Ontario	46,412	54,262	60,473	63,547	64,804	66,189
Undergraduate	38,911	46,095	51,267	53,740	54,415	55,766
Graduate	7,501	8,167	9,206	9,807	10,389	10,423
Manitoba	4,661	5,735	5,788	5,830	5,957	6,285
Undergraduate	4,138	5,121	5,249	5,206	5,300	5,641
Graduate	523	614	539	624	657	644
Saskatchewan	3,876	4,926	5,567	6,007	6,216	5,416
Undergraduate	3,524	4,503	5,042	5,390	5,627	4,866
Graduate	352	423	525	617	589	550
Alberta	7,647	9,798	11,301	11,477	11,638	12,280
Undergraduate	6,449	8,220	9,457	9,627	9,625	10,194
Graduate	1,198	1,578	1,844	1,850	2,013	2,086
British Columbia	7,475	9,916	11,347	13,142	14,000	14,652
Undergraduate	6,290	8,196	9,528	11,180	11,591	12,174
Graduate	1,185	1,720	1,819	1,962	2,409	2,478

1. Includes bachelor's and first professional degree, undergraduate diploma and certificate and other undergraduate qualifications.
2. Includes master's degree, doctoral degree and graduate diploma and certificate.

Source: Statistics Canada, CANSIM, Cross-classified table 00580602.

5.16 LABOUR FORCE BY EDUCATIONAL ATTAINMENT

	Population 15 years and over	0-Grade 8		Some secondary education[1]		Graduated from high school		Some postsecondary		Postsecondary certificate or diploma		University degree	
	'000	'000	%	'000	%	'000	%	'000	%	'000	%	'000	%
Both sexes													
1976	17,124	4,334	25.31	8,236	48.10	..	..	1,578	9.22	1,746	10.20	1,229	7.18
1981	18,883	4,167	22.07	9,683	51.28	..	..	1,510	7.99	1,905	10.09	1,618	8.57
1986	20,182	3,695	18.31	10,008	49.59	..	..	1,905	9.44	2,445	12.12	2,130	10.55
1991	21,613	3,062	14.17	4,944	22.87	4,523	20.93	1,919	8.88	4,742	21.94	2,423	11.21
1992	21,986	3,002	13.65	4,836	22.00	4,676	21.27	1,954	8.89	4,904	22.31	2,615	11.89
1993	22,371	2,879	12.87	4,722	21.11	4,791	21.42	1,998	8.93	5,152	23.03	2,830	12.65
1994	22,717	2,958	13.02	4,678	20.59	4,513	19.87	1,975	8.69	5,586	24.59	3,007	13.23
1995	23,027	2,914	12.66	4,645	20.17	4,519	19.63	2,043	8.87	5,843	25.38	3,063	13.30
Men													
1976	8,471	2,199	25.95	3,865	45.62	..	..	860	10.15	756	8.92	792	9.35
1981	9,308	2,099	22.55	4,595	49.36	..	..	784	8.42	842	9.05	988	10.62
1986	9,929	1,829	18.43	4,794	48.29	..	..	973	9.80	1,115	11.23	1,217	12.26
1991	10,615	1,483	13.97	2,447	23.05	2,042	19.24	943	8.88	2,338	22.03	1,362	12.83
1992	10,801	1,442	13.35	2,408	22.30	2,116	19.59	955	8.84	2,432	22.51	1,449	13.41
1993	10,989	1,387	12.62	2,358	21.45	2,170	19.75	983	8.95	2,523	22.96	1,568	14.27
1994	11,153	1,415	12.69	2,343	21.01	2,062	18.49	958	8.59	2,734	24.51	1,641	14.71
1995	11,303	1,378	12.19	2,319	20.52	2,082	18.42	996	8.81	2,878	25.47	1,650	14.60
Women													
1976	8,652	2,136	24.69	4,371	50.52	..	..	718	8.30	990	11.45	437	5.05
1981	9,575	2,068	21.60	5,088	53.14	..	..	726	7.58	1,063	11.10	630	6.58
1986	10,253	1,865	18.19	5,214	50.85	..	..	932	9.09	1,330	12.98	913	8.90
1991	10,998	1,580	14.36	2,497	22.70	2,481	22.56	976	8.87	2,404	21.86	1,061	9.64
1992	11,185	1,559	13.94	2,428	21.70	2,561	22.89	999	8.93	2,473	22.11	1,166	10.42
1993	11,383	1,492	13.11	2,364	20.77	2,621	23.03	1,014	8.91	2,629	23.10	1,262	11.08
1994	11,564	1,543	13.34	2,335	20.19	2,451	21.19	1,017	8.80	2,852	24.66	1,366	11.81
1995	11,724	1,537	13.11	2,326	19.84	2,437	20.79	1,047	8.93	2,965	25.29	1,413	12.05

1. In 1976, 1981 and 1986, includes persons who had either completed their secondary education or had at least some secondary education, but who had not had any postsecondary education.

Source: Statistics Canada, Catalogue no. 71F0004-XCB.

5.17 LABOUR FORCE BY EDUCATIONAL ATTAINMENT, CANADA AND THE PROVINCES, 1995

	Population 15 years and over	0-Grade 8		Some secondary education		Graduated from high school		Some postsecondary		Postsecondary		University degree	
	'000	'000	%	'000	%	'000	%	'000	%	'000	%	'000	%
Canada	23,027	2,914	12.7	4,645	20.2	4,519	19.6	2,043	8.9	5,843	25.4	3,063	13.3
Newfoundland	455	91	20.0	104	22.9	68	14.9	35	7.7	120	26.4	36	7.9
Prince Edward Island	105	13	12.4	29	27.6	16	15.2	7	6.7	28	26.7	12	11.4
Nova Scotia	731	90	12.3	186	25.4	98	13.4	62	8.5	208	28.5	87	11.9
New Brunswick	598	104	17.4	121	20.2	117	19.6	48	8.0	150	25.1	59	9.9
Quebec	5,805	1,147	19.8	1,068	18.4	914	15.7	385	6.6	1,570	27.0	721	12.4
Ontario	8,720	891	10.2	1,782	20.4	1,865	21.4	852	9.8	2,027	23.2	1,303	14.9
Manitoba	850	112	13.2	200	23.5	169	19.9	79	9.3	194	22.8	97	11.4
Saskatchewan	749	99	13.2	179	23.9	151	20.2	64	8.5	184	24.6	72	9.6
Alberta	2,067	157	7.6	424	20.5	430	20.8	202	9.8	574	27.8	281	13.6
British Columbia	2,947	210	7.1	552	18.7	690	23.4	309	10.5	790	26.8	396	13.4

Source: Statistics Canada, Catalogue no. 71F0004-XCB.

5.18 FULL-TIME TEACHERS

	1981-82	1986-87	1991-92	1992-93	1993-94	1994-95
	Elementary and secondary schools[1]					
Canada	277,566	269,899	303,055	303,272	306,227	308,914
Newfoundland	7,830	8,118	7,978	7,925	7,760	7,703
Prince Edward Island	1,361	1,299	1,370	1,381	1,372	1,363
Nova Scotia	10,949	10,320	10,148	9,878	9,991	9,757
New Brunswick	7,736	7,630	8,269	8,143	7,983	7,780
Quebec	76,068	64,971	64,921	65,027	65,225	64,679
Ontario	95,440	100,925	125,350	126,158	127,541	130,503
Manitoba	12,236	12,545	12,739	12,752	12,675	12,593
Saskatchewan	11,381	11,429	11,310	10,797	10,851	10,549
Alberta	24,525	25,097	27,354	27,251	28,098	28,445
British Columbia	28,839	26,314	31,907	32,138	33,012	33,697
Yukon	279	292	381	421	411	432
Northwest Territories	680	706	1,091	1,171	1,253	1,392
Overseas	242	253	237	230	55	21
	1981-82	1986-87	1991-92	1992-93	1993-94	1994-95
	Community colleges[2]					
Canada	4,494	24,144	25,092	25,972	27,113	28,014
Newfoundland	112	216	370	404	474	507
Prince Edward Island	49	65	81	60	64	69
Nova Scotia	61	290	310	395	442	501
New Brunswick	221	251	317	339	362	387
Quebec	–	11,780	11,672	12,087	12,610	13,165
Ontario	2,109	6,773	7,009	7,371	7,636	7,611
Manitoba	392	360	391	382	387	392
Saskatchewan	224	414	382	386	362	342
Alberta	633	2,148	2,198	2,186	2,174	2,175
British Columbia	693	1,801	2,226	2,227	2,453	2,702
Yukon	–	10	73	73	78	83
Northwest Territories	–	36	63	63	71	80
Overseas	–	–	–	–	–	–
	1981-82	1986-87	1991-92	1992-93	1993-94	1994-95
	Universities					
Canada	33,647	35,453	36,845	37,266	36,957	36,361
Newfoundland	866	956	1,023	1,049	959	943
Prince Edward Island	124	132	171	178	199	196
Nova Scotia	1,727	1,977	2,081	2,062	2,067	1,998
New Brunswick	1,058	1,137	1,242	1,208	1,189	1,181
Quebec	7,645	7,926	8,590	8,924	9,013	9,019
Ontario	12,973	13,725	14,115	14,050	13,854	13,456
Manitoba	1,677	1,708	1,720	1,784	1,740	1,717
Saskatchewan	1,457	1,584	1,483	1,509	1,480	1,422
Alberta	2,944	3,260	3,248	3,233	3,198	3,080
British Columbia	3,176	3,048	3,172	3,269	3,258	3,349
Yukon	–	–	–	–	–	–
Northwest Territories	–	–	–	–	–	–
Overseas	–	–	–	–	–	–

1. Teachers at the elementary–secondary level include all teaching and non-teaching academic staff (principals, vice-principals, department heads and subject supervisors). Those on leave are excluded.
2. Excludes trade level (community colleges) and public trade schools.

Sources: Statistics Canada, Catalogue nos. 81-229 and 81-003.

5.19 EMPLOYMENT, EDUCATION AND RELATED SERVICES

	1984	1985	1986	1987	1988	1989	1990	1991	1992	1993	1994	1995	Average annual growth rate 1984-1995
							Employees[1] '000						%
All industries[2]	9,311.9	9,651.1	9,927.2	10,329.1	10,659.0	11,054.7	11,146.1	10,549.5	10,246.9	10,271.4	10,447.1	10,673.6	1.2
Educational and related services	753.7	765.4	779.7	812.2	838.4	863.8	888.1	905.7	916.3	932.2	933.3	933.6	2.0
Educational services	718.7	731.2	744.4	773.9	798.5	824.1	845.1	865.7	877.3	893.2	890.9	888.2	1.9
Elementary and secondary education	475.5	479.3	488.4	499.1	517.7	537.8	551.1	564.1	571.9	584.8	587.0	585.2	1.9
Postsecondary non-university education	82.6	88.4	91.8	99.8	101.3	104.2	107.7	111.8	112.8	115.0	112.1	112.6	2.9
University education	160.6	163.5	164.2	175.0	179.5	182.1	186.3	189.8	192.6	193.5	191.8	190.4	1.6
Libraries, museums and other educational services	34.9	34.1	35.3	38.3	39.8	39.7	43.0	40.0	38.9	39.0	42.4	45.3	2.4
Library services	19.4	18.9	20.0	21.0	21.3	21.6	23.3	22.5	21.0	20.6	20.6	20.1	0.3
Museums and archives	8.2	7.8	8.1	8.7	8.9	8.8	9.8	9.9	8.4	8.6	9.9	10.4	2.2
Other educational services	7.3	7.5	7.2	8.6	9.6	9.3	9.9	7.5	9.6	9.9	11.9	14.8	6.6
							% of total employment						
Educational and related services	8.1	7.9	7.9	7.9	7.9	7.8	8.0	8.6	8.9	9.1	8.9	8.7	
Educational services	7.7	7.6	7.5	7.5	7.5	7.5	7.6	8.2	8.6	8.7	8.5	8.3	
Libraries, museums and other educational services	0.4	0.4	0.4	0.4	0.4	0.4	0.4	0.4	0.4	0.4	0.4	0.4	

1. Excludes owners or partners of unincorporated business and professional practices, the self-employed, unpaid family workers, persons working outside Canada, military personnel and casual workers for whom a T4 is not required.
2. Excludes agriculture, fishing and trapping, private household services, religious organizations and the military.

Source: Statistics Canada, Catalogue no. 72F0002.

5.20 EARNINGS, EDUCATION AND RELATED SERVICES

	1984	1985	1986	1987	1988	1989	1990	1991	1992	1993	1994	1995	Earnings in 1995 as a % of all industry earnings
							Average weekly earnings[1] $						%
Educational and related services	486.33	499.38	513.02	532.05	557.98	576.76	605.91	640.33	667.74	674.05	671.41	669.37	116.92
Educational services	495.53	508.39	522.09	541.25	568.05	586.74	617.45	652.23	679.36	685.03	681.92	680.62	118.89
Elementary and secondary education	523.42	539.46	554.91	575.28	601.80	619.33	650.81	688.28	719.06	719.57	717.42	715.05	124.90
Post secondary non-university education	449.75	452.72	460.51	475.45	504.91	512.81	542.02	578.91	600.08	622.71	611.30	613.57	107.18
University education	436.50	447.38	458.87	481.70	506.36	532.78	562.33	588.30	607.90	617.67	614.54	614.46	107.33
Libraries, museums and other educational services	297.05	306.49	321.66	346.28	355.98	369.65	378.98	382.61	405.96	422.68	450.63	448.97	78.42
Library services	277.97	288.62	301.27	318.12	325.10	344.71	357.14	359.58	390.04	394.21	419.17	422.76	73.85
Museums and archives	351.51	370.59	386.04	406.29	413.99	443.26	467.36	445.20	477.37	510.85	525.13	533.06	93.11
Other educational services	286.21	285.21	305.94	354.53	370.78	358.27	342.52	368.83	378.31	405.64	443.38	425.75	74.37
All industries[2]	398.10	412.02	424.25	440.26	459.75	483.31	505.14	528.60	547.01	556.76	567.11	572.49	100.00

1. Excludes owners or partners of unincorporated business and professional practices, the self-employed, unpaid family workers, persons working outside Canada, military personnel and casual workers for whom a T4 is not required.
2. Excludes agriculture, fishing and trapping, private household services, religious organizations and the military.

Source: Statistics Canada, Catalogue no. 72F0002.

5.21 ENROLMENT IN SECOND LANGUAGE IMMERSION PROGRAMS

	1980-81		1985-86		1990-91		1991-92		1992-93		1993-94	
	Elementary	Secondary	Elementary	Secondary	Elementary	Secondary	Elementary	Secondary	Elementary	Secondary	Elementary	Secondary
Canada	53,250	11,511	120,622	41,717	170,766	78,757	197,497	102,906	225,218	72,114	223,362	80,068
Newfoundland	333	59	1,669	346	3,003	1,266	3,108	1,891	2,967	1,829	2,844	1,695
Prince Edward Island	1,072	208	1,584	908	1,678	1,693	1,679	1,832	1,705	1,563	1,678	1,798
Nova Scotia	526	64	1,375	484	2,648	2,638	2,779	4,769	2,684	5,367	2,721	6,254
New Brunswick	4,271	1,261	7,253	7,277	6,534	10,159	6,537	8,450	6,534	9,934	6,562	9,642
Quebec	..	..	..	..	..	..	22,959	9,958	23,264	10,077	23,824	10,389
Ontario	38,065	8,573	64,121	23,698	94,004	39,902	98,584	51,439	124,907	19,112	123,699	24,992
Manitoba	3,612	674	10,230	2,351	14,166	5,438	13,885	5,784	13,489	6,123	13,082	6,116
Saskatchewan	1,453	150	5,340	625	8,507	2,206	8,240	2,611	7,794	3,166	7,308	3,348
Alberta	..	..	15,588	3,429	20,246	6,678	20,033	7,011	19,867	7,882	19,505	8,079
British Columbia	3,846	522	13,026	2,564	19,403	8,581	19,135	8,905	21,688	6,818	21,527	7,490
Yukon	35	-	247	-	294	75	288	103	31	93	339	116
Northwest Territories	37	-	189	35	283	121	270	153	288	150	273	149
Total outside Quebec	53,250	11,511	120,622	41,717	170,766	78,757	174,538	92,948	201,954	62,037	199,538	69,679

Sources: Statistics Canada, CANSIM, Cross-classified table 00570304; Catalogue no. 81-257.

5.22 EDUCATION INDICATORS, INTERNATIONAL COMPARISONS, 1991-92

	Canada	Australia	France	Germany	Italy	Japan	Netherlands	Spain	Sweden	Switzerland	United Kingdom	United States
						%						
Social and economic context												
Educational attainment												
Lower secondary or less[1]	29	47	48	18	72	..	42	77	30	19	32	16
Tertiary	41	23	16	22	6	..	21	13	24	21	19	31
Labour force participation												
Upper secondary education	89.4	89.2	90.6	85.6	89.6	..	88.5	92.2	94.8	95.5	91.1	89.4
University education	93.8	94.8	91.2	93.8	93.9	..	91.3	90.5	96.1	97.6	94.2	93.8
Costs and school processes												
Education expenditure as a percentage of total public expenditures[2]	14.0	14.0	10.6	8.5	9.5	11.3	9.5	10.4	11.7	16.5	11.9	14.2
Participation rate in formal education	58.0	..	58.4	49.8	50.0	55.7	54.4	56.9	50.2	49.1	51.9	54.2
Net university enrolment rate[2]	23.9	18.8	20.2	7.4	..	..	20.1	22.5	4.3	4.8	14.2	25.0
Educational outcomes												
Secondary school graduation rate[2 3]	68.4	87.8	78.2	109.6	58.9	92.2	95.6	74.8	83.0	82.6	80.1	75.7
University, first degree graduation rate	32.2	26.3	..	..	0.7	23.4	17.8	8.0	11.4	..	20.4	27.4
University, second degree graduation rate[2]	4.8	..	14.5	13.0	9.8	1.6	8.6	12.1	..	8.0	7.2	9.1
Unemployment rate by level of educational attainment												
Upper secondary education	9.7	8.9	7.4	6.4	8.2	..	4.7	14.1	4.3	2.2	8.3	7.2
University education	5.2	4.4	4.4	3.7	6.0	..	3.9	9.9	2.0	3.0	3.6	2.9

1. 1993 data for Australia.
2. Germany (former territory of the Federal Republic).
3. It is likely that many of the graduates may be older than the reference age for Germany.

Source: Organisation for Economic Co-operation and Development, *Education at a Glance: OECD Indicators*, Paris, 1995.

JIM LOGAN, *NATIONAL PASTIMES,* DEPARTMENT OF INDIAN AND NORTHERN AFFAIRS

Chapter 6

HOUSEHOLD AND FAMILY LIFE

Photo by David Trattles

Behind the doors of Canada's almost 11 million dwellings, amid a growing clutter of consumer goods, our private lives unfold: a patchwork quilt of living arrangements, lifestyles and possessions.

Virtually every Canadian neighbourhood displays the heterogeneity of home life in the nineties. Side by side, we find single people living with other, non-family members, in couples, as families, as roommates. We find part-time parents with joint custody arrangements or visitation rights. We find married couples, we find others living common law. And in almost 60% of households, we find either a dog, a cat, or both.

Living Together

In the end, much of this diversity still adds up to togetherness, in one form or another. Although most Canadians live in families of one kind or another, the language of newspaper ads—"spacious, semi-detached, share with two others, working or students, microwave, cable, dishwasher, laundry, quiet area. Leave message."—offers a glimpse into the world of non-family living options.

Still, live-in relationships with spouses and/or children remain our most popular choice, especially at mid-life. Certainly, for the majority of Canadians in their middle years (aged 30 to 54), domestic life has a remarkably similar look and feel: about three-quarters of Canadians of this age live with their spouse or their children or both. Most are married, working parents living in a two-generation family.

But not everyone follows the same pattern. The proportion of Canadians who live with a spouse has been dropping over the past 50 years. In 1921, 80% of women and 71% of men aged 30 to 34 were married, compared with 69% of women and 62% of men who were

Furry Friends

Canadians love to keep pets. Between 1969 and 1992, we literally doubled our spending on pets. In 1990, 41% of households surveyed in 17 selected metropolitan areas owned pets, a percentage that has remained about the same since 1982. Animal companions cost an average $462 a year. Of this amount, $139 generally went to the veterinarian and other services, $127 on canned food, and $107 on other food.

Households with pet expenses tended to have more people, more children, and more money than the typical Canadian household. Pet owners were likely to be homeowners with single detached homes. However, married couples without children spent the most ($545) on their pets, while lone-parent families spent the least ($313).

A dog was generally costlier than a cat: dog owners spent $416 in 1990, while cat owners spent $304. Perhaps for this reason, 38% of households with pet expenses had cats but no dogs, while just 28% had dogs but no cats.

either married or living common law in 1991. Similarly, in 1991, an increasing proportion (35%) of Canadians between the ages of 30 to 54 did not have children; almost one-quarter (23%) were not married or living common law.

Living Alone

In 1991, more than 2.3 million Canadians lived alone, due in part to population aging and increases in divorce and separation. The most dramatic increase in the likelihood of living alone has occurred among Canadians 55 years of age and older. In the past sixty years, the proportion of older Canadians who live alone has doubled. Living alone is especially common among older women. At age 55 and over, almost one-third (30%) of women live alone; at the age of 75, almost half live alone.

For older Canadians, marital status largely determines whether or not they live alone. But the presence or absence of children also plays an important part: the more surviving children a woman has, the less likely she is to live alone. Individual income is also an important factor, particularly for older women. The higher an older woman's income is, the more likely she is to live alone, possibly because she has the resources to support this independence.

This does not mean that older Canadians are socially isolated—many live in at least two-generation households, and even when family members live in separate households, older Canadians, especially women, tend to be in frequent touch with their children and siblings.

For young adults, moving out into a space of one's own has become a luxury few can afford. At the same time, many young Canadians have been delaying marriage—traditionally, one of the most common means of becoming an adult. Young unmarried women aged 24 to 26, for example, have become much more likely to stay home with mom and dad: 46% lived with their parents in 1991, compared with 38% in 1981.

Young adults whose parents are still together are much more likely to remain in the so-called "cluttered nest." In 1990, more than two-thirds of young adults between the ages of 18

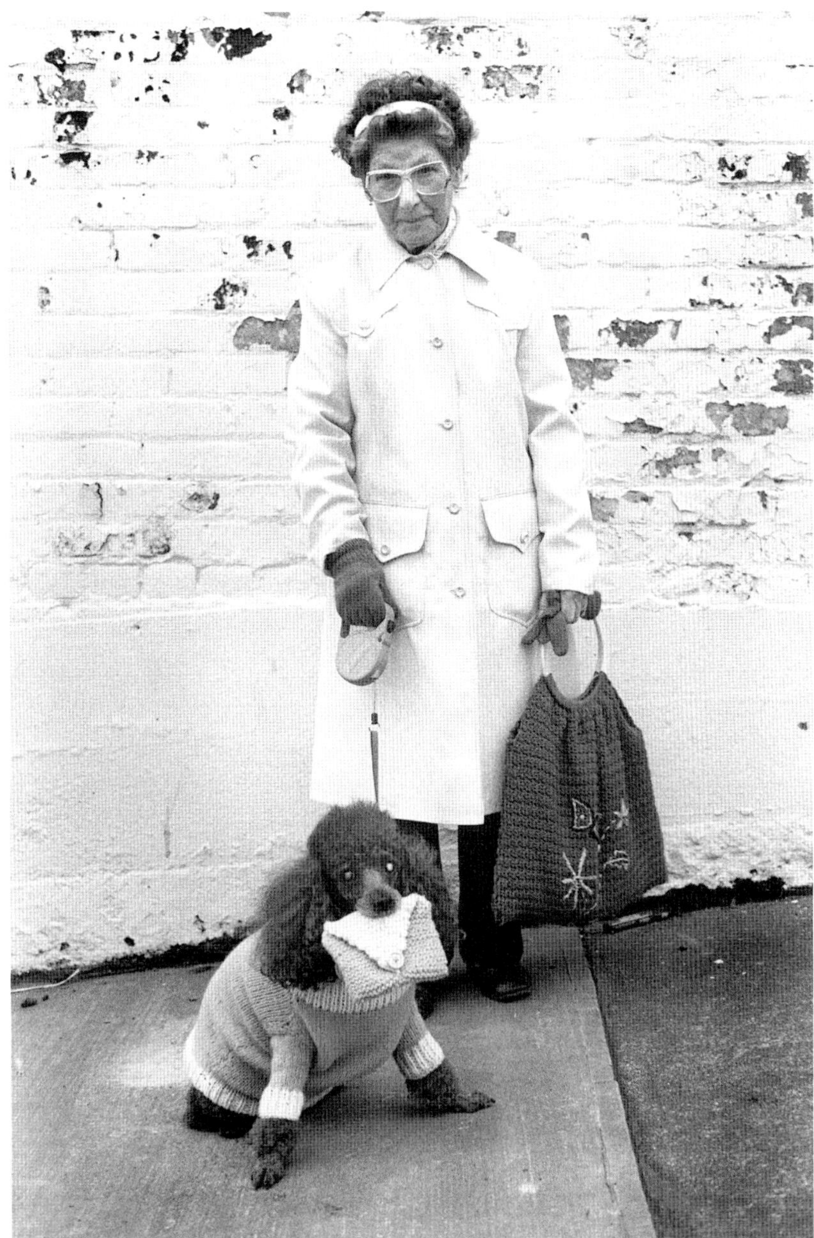

Photo by Brett Lowther

Woman and poodle.

Gadgets Galore

If Canadians today spend less time reading books, it could be because we're busy reading myriad operating manuals for our many electronic gadgets.

Between 1985 and 1995, the number of video cassette recorders, televisions, compact disc players and computers in our homes climbed steadily. For example, the percentage of homes with CD players soared from 8% in 1986 to 47% in 1995. More than three times as many of us (82%) had VCRs in 1995 than in 1986, and almost the same increase has been true for home computers (up from 10% to 29%). In 1995, half of homes had two or more colour televisions.

Canadians have also acquired more houseware items. In 1995, 83% of homes had microwave ovens, 54% had gas barbecues, and 47% automatic dishwashers.

and 29 whose parents were together lived at home, compared with only about half of those with separated or divorced parents. The narrowing of the generation gap may play a role here. Some experts have suggested that today's young people have more in common with their parents, in terms of values, than they used to.

Collectives

Sharing living quarters doesn't necessarily mean one family living in a private household. In 1991, almost half a million Canadians (446,885) lived with others in "collective dwellings." More than 280,000 people lived in hospitals or institutions, including about 224,000 elderly or chronically ill residents of special care homes. Still others lived in children's group homes, orphanages, correctional institutions, religious institutions, hotels, motels, tourist homes, lodging and rooming houses, work camps, military camps and Hutterite colonies.

Shelters

The four walls around us are equally varied. In 1994, more than half of Canadian households lived in single detached homes. Another one-third were in apartments. A much smaller group (less than 10% of all households) were in "single-attached homes," such as rowhouses. In recent years, condominiums have become an increasingly popular choice, especially for childless couples, empty-nesters, and those who live alone. In 1991, there were 367,360 owner-occupied condos, about 60% more than in 1986. In 1994, two-thirds of Canadian householders actually owned their homes.

Home Toys

There's little doubt that Canadian householders are good consumers, given the profusion of gadgets and equipment in our homes. In 1994, more than 75% of all Canadian households owned at least one automobile. Almost 80% owned a VCR, and one in four had a computer. Virtually all Canadian households (99%) were equipped with telephones, and three-quarters, particularly urbanites, were hooked up to cable television. Time-saving devices were ubiquitous, especially in the kitchen: eight out of 10 Canadian homes were outfitted with microwave ovens, almost half relied on dishwashers, and more than half could fire up a gas barbecue.

On the other hand, only seven out of every 100 elderly households (where the head of the household was 65 years of age or older) had a computer, and single-occupant households had even fewer gadgets.

Relationships

In February 1995, *Maclean's* magazine posed the question, "Is Dating Dead?", and answered, "No, but it sure has changed." Such a question seems to beg the answer, but the new uncertainty about romance and courtship comes as no surprise given the shifting territory of our relationships, and the new rules these changes engender. Divorce, common-law relationships, remarriage and single parenthood have become significant signposts of social change in Canada since the Second World War.

Marriage Patterns

Yes, there are still thousands of marriages celebrated in Canada each year—159,623 couples married in 1993—and married life is common. In fact, for the majority of Canadians now in their mid-forties to mid-fifties, the most common life path has been to be in a union at age 30, and to stay that way until at least age 54.

Still, marriage patterns have definitely changed. Among Canadians between the ages of 30 and 34, the proportion of married people hit its highest peak in 1971, and it's been declining ever since. For Canadians in their early thirties, for example, 62% of men and 69% of women were married in 1991, compared with 85% of men and 88% of women of the same age in 1971.

Meanwhile, those who decide to marry are waiting longer before taking the plunge. In 1980, for people marrying for the first time, the average age was 26 for grooms and 23 for brides. By 1994, it had risen to 29 years for grooms and 27 for brides.

The likelihood of being married depends on our age, sex and social standing. Up to the age of 40, women are more likely to be married than men, and then things reverse; by age 50 to 54, men are more likely to be married. Intriguingly, social status may affect men and women differently in the marriage market. American research has found that high-powered men are more likely to be married than are successful women.

Certainly, marital status seems to matter more—in terms of our well-being—as we get older. Among older Canadians, those who are married tend to be healthier—and wealthier.

For women, getting married and having children tends to have a major impact on labour force participation. Over age 55, for example, men have twice as much paid work experience as women. Having a family tends to reduce women's income and increase a man's and helps explain the income differences between men and women in mid-life.

Common Law

Living together has soared in popularity in the last 25 years. Since the 1960s, more and more Canadian adults, at all levels of society, are moving in together without getting married first. In 1991, almost 1.5 million Canadians (1,452,000) were living common law.

Young people are especially keen: about one-quarter of Canadians aged 25 to 29 who were in a union in 1991 were living common law, double the 1981 figure. A recent survey found that, while only one-quarter of married couples were under the age of 35, almost two-thirds of those living common law were younger than 35. Some of this reluctance to wed may be economic; perhaps it's a response to uncertain employment and lower incomes.

Living common law tends to be a shorter-term, less permanent arrangement than marriage. In fact, some have estimated that about three-quarters of all common-law relationships end within five years. Couples who live together before marriage have a greater chance of divorce. In general, women who live common law have fewer children than married women.

"I would like to marry you . . . say 'yes,' say 'yes'," sang well-known Quebec songwriter Jean-Pierre Ferland in 1995. However, as Quebec's marital landscape changes, the more likely musical lyric might be "I'd like to live with you . . . say 'yes', say 'yes'."

Common-law relationships have become increasingly popular in Canada, particularly in Quebec. Quebec has the highest rate of common-law couples among the provinces and the fastest increase in this rate. In fact, 42% of all common-law couples in Canada live in Quebec, and in the last 15 years, the numbers in Quebec have increased a dramatic 154%.

But Quebec appears to be leading a national trend. Across the country, common-law relationships are on the rise—in the 1991 Census, some 1.4 million people reported that they lived common law, an increase of almost 50% since the previous census in 1986. That means one in every nine couples who shared a residence in Canada was living common law.

However, when it comes to setting related trends in common-law relationships, we're back to Quebec. Common-law couples in Quebec are more than twice as likely as other Canadians to have children: 14% of such couples have children compared with 6% in the other provinces.

Across the country as a whole, common-law relationships are especially popular among younger people. In 1991, some 57% of people in common-law unions were between 20 and 35 years old. In Quebec, the percentage of young childless couples who were living common law was almost double that of the other provinces combined: 61% compared with 32%.

Quebec's empty-nesters are also more likely than those in other provinces to have common-law relationships. In 1991, couples who no longer had children at home and who lived common law made up 9% of the total in Quebec compared with 6% in the rest of the provinces.

There appears to be, within Quebec, a correlation between language and common-law relationships. Quebec couples in which both partners reported French as their mother tongue and their home language were more than twice as likely to be living common law as those who reported English. Common-law relationships were also much more prevalent among non-immigrant than among immigrant couples.

While Quebec has the highest proportion of couples living common law, with 19%, British Columbia has the second-highest with 11%, followed by Nova Scotia and Alberta, each with 10%. The lowest proportion is 2% in Newfoundland. In Canada, Aboriginal peoples have long been practising unions much older than those supported by marriage legislation. However, common-law relationships in the North are growing at a rapid pace, with the percentage of couples living common law at 27% in the Northwest Territories and 23% in Yukon.

Divorce

When critic and author Nathalie Petrowski wrote ruefully that the future tense of the verb to marry is to divorce, she was commenting on another of the social changes which occurred in Canada's post-war era: the risky nature of marriage. Canadian *chanteur* Félix Leclerc put it this way: "Marriage is two one-way plane tickets for an unknown island. You either come back swimming, or not at all."

By 1987, the total divorce rate had hit an all-time high: 4.8 divorces for every 10 marriages— almost one in two. Two rounds of legal changes preceded this peak in divorce. In 1968, Canada's newly liberalized Divorce Act made it much easier to dissolve a marriage (and the total divorce rate each year subsequently rose from 1.4 for every 10 marriages in 1968 to 3.9 in 1986).

In 1986, a new Divorce Act loosened the strings even further, reducing the length of time two people had to be separated before they could obtain a divorce. Since 1987, the total divorce rate had declined each year. In 1993, there were only 3,812 divorces for every 10,000 marriages.

Remarriage

Since every divorce creates two new candidates for remarriage, it comes as no surprise that remarriage has become more common than it was a few decades ago. From the mid-fifties to the mid-sixties, less than 13% of Canadian marriages involved a partner who had previously been married. But, by the early nineties, this had changed dramatically: almost one in three marriages involved a bride or groom who'd been married before.

In 1993, of all the Canadians who have ever been married, close to one out of every 10 (9%) had been married more than once. Men are twice as likely as women to remarry, and older men are even more likely to remarry. At age 60 and over, men are four times more likely to remarry than women.

Widowhood

Although the proportion of Canadians who are widowed in mid-life is much lower than it used to be, women are still much more likely to be widowed; in fact, a recent survey found that 84% of the widowed are women. Women have a longer life expectancy than men, and many women are younger than their husbands. Also, men who lose their wives are more likely to remarry.

Widowhood can be devastating, especially for those older women who are left economically vulnerable once they've lost their husbands. Still, there is evidence that, among older women, those who are widowed tend to have higher incomes, better health and more social support than those older women who are divorced or separated.

Singlehood

Among Canadians who choose not to marry or move in with a partner, those still single at the age of 30 tend to remain so. But their numbers are relatively small. Estimates suggest that fewer than one in 10 Canadians now in their mid-forties and fifties would not have experienced a live-in partnership during their middle years.

For some women, remaining solo can make a certain amount of economic sense. A 1995 Statistics Canada report on Canadian family life commented wryly that "the easiest route to equality is to be single and childless." This is because single, childless women are more likely to work full time, to remain in the work force, and to earn more, than women who are married with children.

Family Ties

Many Canadians dream of having children one day, and young people have the highest parenting expectations of all. In 1990, fewer than 10% of Canadians aged 15 to 29 said they did not want to have any children. About half wanted at least two, and more than a quarter said they would be happy to have three. Most people between 30 and 44, regardless of marital status, age or sex, expected to have two or more children, and women expected fewer children than men. But dreams are not necessarily realistic expectations, and young people may set their sights somewhat lower as they get older.

Harlan Smith, Canadian Museum of Civilization, #64379

Mr. and Mrs. Frank Benson, Gitksan Indians, after their wedding ceremony, August 24, 1925.

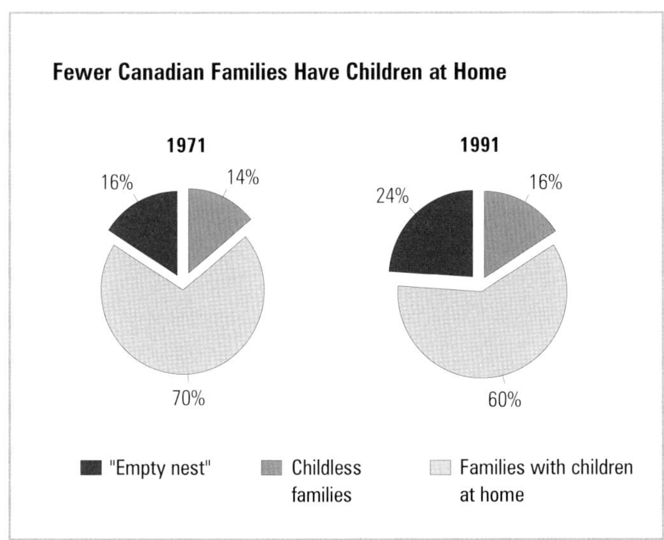

In 1993, about 70% of Canadian women over the age of 18 had at least one child. Of those, 5% had either adopted a child or were raising someone else's offspring. Indeed, most Canadian women (82%) who became mothers did so between the ages of 20 and 29. Only 9% gave birth to their first child in their teens, while another 9% waited until they were 30 years of age or older.

Young women of the 1990s, however, are more reluctant than those of the 1980s to have children. Largely, this is because having children competes with work, education and the achievement of a higher standard of economic well-being.

Despite this, parenthood—and the parenting industry—is going strong in Canada. Parenting television programs, books, magazines and trade shows all target millions of baby-boomer parents in Canada.

Family Portraits

As difficult as it may be to define, it's clear that family—of one type or another—is a central unit of social life in Canada. As of July 1, 1994, there were an estimated 7,797,200 families in Canada. The average Canadian family had approximately three members. Altogether, 84% of us were living in families as either husbands, wives, common-law spouses, lone parents or children.

In 1991, for every 100 families in Canada, 48 were married parents with children, 29 were married couples without children (including empty-nesters), 13 were single-parent families, six were common-law couples without children, and four were common-law couples with children.

Remarkably, in a single decade (from 1981 to 1991), the proportion of common-law families (with or without children) has almost doubled. In 1991, one in 10 Canadian families was a couple living together common-law. With the acceptance of couples who choose to live common law, the social stigma of "illegitimacy" for children born out of wedlock has faded.

In 1991, there were almost one million lone-parent families—about 13% of all Canadian families. This is actually about the same percentage as in 1931. Back then, however, most lone parents were widowed, whereas most of today's lone parents are divorced, separated or unmarried. The percentage of lone-parent families declined into the 1960s—only 8% of families were headed by lone parents in 1966—and then began to rise again, a trend that continues to this day.

Lone-parenthood is still primarily the realm of women: they were at the helm of more than eight out of 10 such families in 1991. Significant, too, is that 40% of Canadian couples did not have children at home (either because they were childless or their children had left home).

More than half of all Canadians who remarried in the early nineties were aged 45 or younger. And, not surprisingly, many of these "newly reweds" were also parents. About one in 10 families with children younger than 19 years of age were step or "blended" families.

Families with one or two children have become more common, while large families—those with three or more children—have become much rarer.

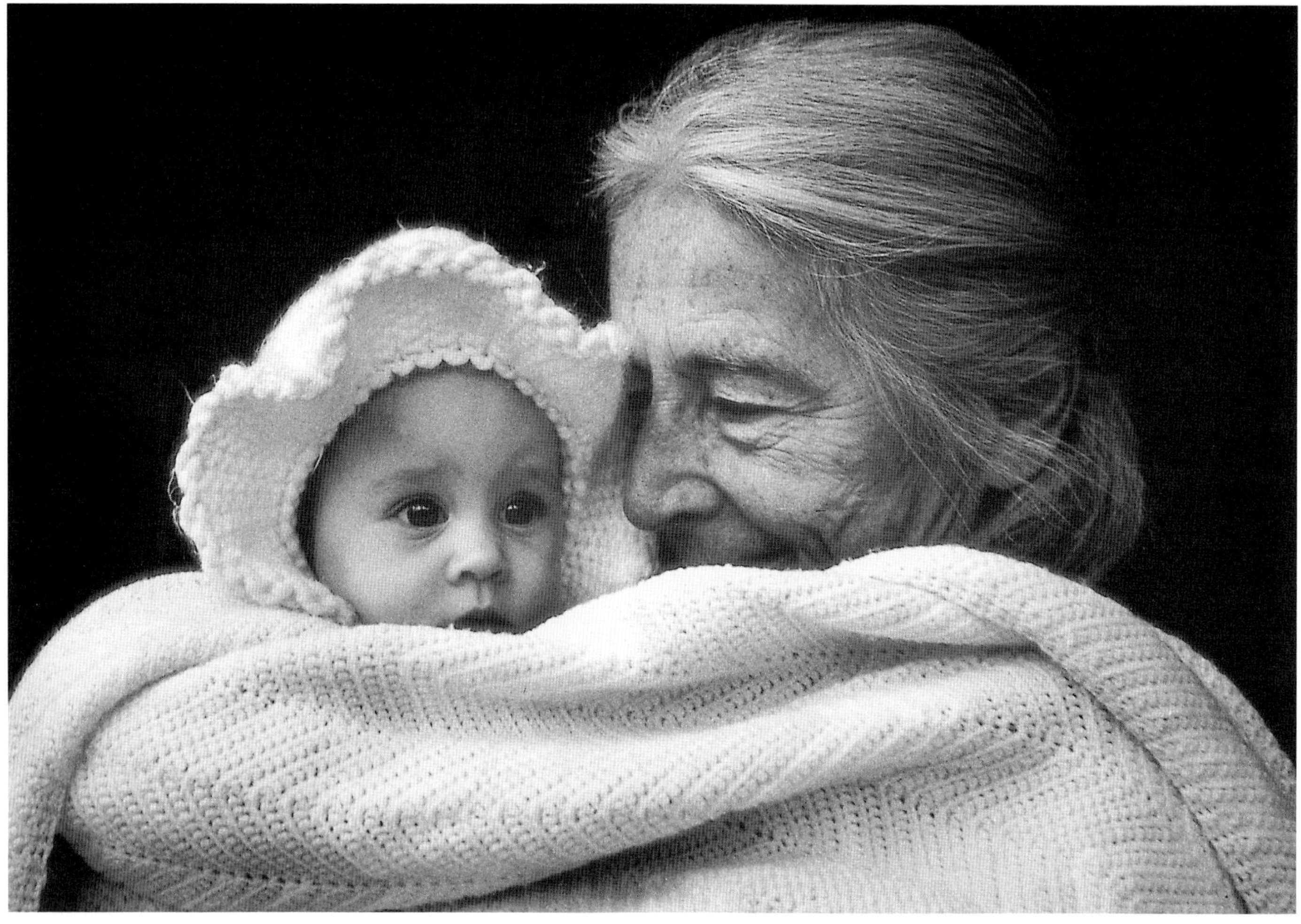

Photo by Pamela Harris

My Mother/My Daughter, (Toronto 1976, Family Series).

Family Incomes

Although the average family income in Canada was a healthy $54,153 in 1994, this is not quite as comforting as it sounds. There were significant differences between two-parent families with children and lone-parent families.

In 1994, families with children and two sources of income averaged $63,112, while lone-parent families earned an average of only $25,585. Two-parent families with children, living on one income, averaged $45,572.

Since most lone-parent families are headed by women—and women have yet to catch up to the earnings of men—it's families led by women that fare worst of all. In 1991, single mothers were raising their children on about two-thirds of the income of single fathers. In 1994, more than half of all female lone parents (56.4%) were making ends meet on low incomes.

Lone-parent families rely more heavily on government assistance—including Unemployment Insurance, social assistance, GST rebates and Worker's Compensation—than do husband–wife families, thus they may be more vulnerable to changes to our social "safety net." And changes at all levels have already begun.

The new Canada Health and Social Transfer (CHST) reduces the federal government's contribution for health care, social assistance and post-secondary education by $7 billion. At the provincial level, in 1995, Ontario cut its welfare rates by 21.6%.

A single parent with one child who received about $1,221 per month now receives $957 per month to pay for housing, food, utilities, transportation and other expenses. British Columbia changed its welfare eligibility requirement in 1995, and Manitoba cut its welfare rates in 1996.

At the same time, the federal government has focused its attention on Canada's most needy families. For many years, Canadian parents with children under 18 received a monthly cheque in the mail—a family allowance also known as the "baby bonus." Each year at tax time, Canadian families claimed child tax deductions on their income tax forms. In 1993, these programs were replaced by the Child Tax Benefit, a monthly payment that is sent only to the 3.2 million Canadian families who live on low and modest incomes.

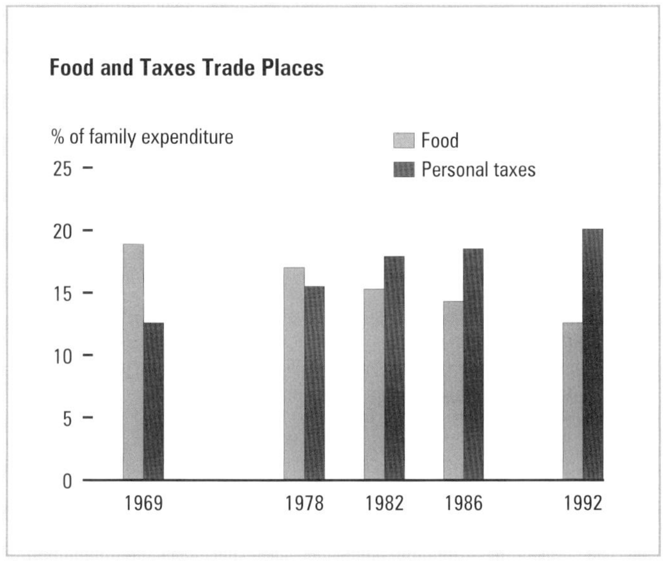

Shelter Costs

Even rock bands have made the cost of running a household the subject of a song. "If I had a million dollars (If I had a million dollars) I'd buy you a house (I would buy you a house)" run the lyrics from Canada's Barenaked Ladies. Although a million dollars is high for the average Canadian home, to say the least, our homes are certainly the biggest big-ticket item after taxes.

In 1992, Canadians found themselves paying the highest proportion of their incomes on shelter since 1969. Those who have paid off their mortgages fared best, spending an average of $5,535 a year on shelter. Those with mortgage payments spent an average of $11,692, while apartment dwellers spent about $6,978.

Food takes the third biggest bite (22%) out of household income, but the proportion has been dropping as real household incomes have increased. Food prices rose 21% between 1986 and 1992. As a result, households spent an average of $110 on food each week in 1992.

The more people, the cheaper per person it is to eat; for example, one-person households spent about $60 a week, while households of five or more spent about $30 a person. Each week, almost one-third of the average household food budget was spent in restaurants.

City dwellers tend to eat out more than those who live in the country—urbanites spent about $3.75 a person more each week on restaurant meals in 1992 than did their country neighbours.

The cost of getting around shot up 21% between 1986 and 1992, though the cost of public transit increased by only 5%. Also, the way we get around is changing; for example, Canadians have doubled their spending on trucks and minivans

Canadians today are spending proportionately less of their after-tax money on clothing, health care and food, and more on household operation and shelter and recreation than they did a quarter-century ago.

In fact, the biggest leap in household spending has been on recreation. Spending on recreational equipment and services increased from 4.7 cents on the dollar in 1969 to 6.4 cents in 1992. Personal computers, unknown in 1969, now claim a large share of spending on recreation, equipment and supplies.

Food and shelter have traded places as the number one item in household expenditures. In 1969, putting food on the table was the single biggest item on the list at 22%, while keeping a roof over one's head accounted for 18%. In 1992, food took just 16% of household spending, and shelter took the biggest chunk at 22%.

Today's households have fewer mouths to feed, however. Spending on food is therefore taking up less of the household budget. From 1969 to 1992, household size has declined from 3.3 people to 2.6.

On the other hand, there has been an increase in spending on housing. More Canadians own their homes than rent them, and homeowners tend to spend more on their homes than do renters. In 1969, 59% of Canadians owned their homes; in 1992, 63% did.

Although Canadians are spending more on recreation equipment and services (such as spectator sports, recreation facilities and packaged travel tours), they are paying out proportionately less of their household dollar on home entertainment items while buying more of them. Prices for these items have not kept pace with overall price increases. In 1992, prices for home entertainment equipment were about 150% what they were in 1969, whereas overall prices were more than four times higher.

On the costlier side was the cost of running a household, where spending on long-distance calls, child care services and pets doubled between 1969 and 1992.

On the other hand, clothing and health care, like food, is consuming proportionately less of the household budget. Clothing costs are down: the result of both smaller households and the cost of clothing, which has not increased as much as the cost of other commodities. Health care expenses have dropped largely because of the introduction of provincial health care plans, which are paid for through taxes.

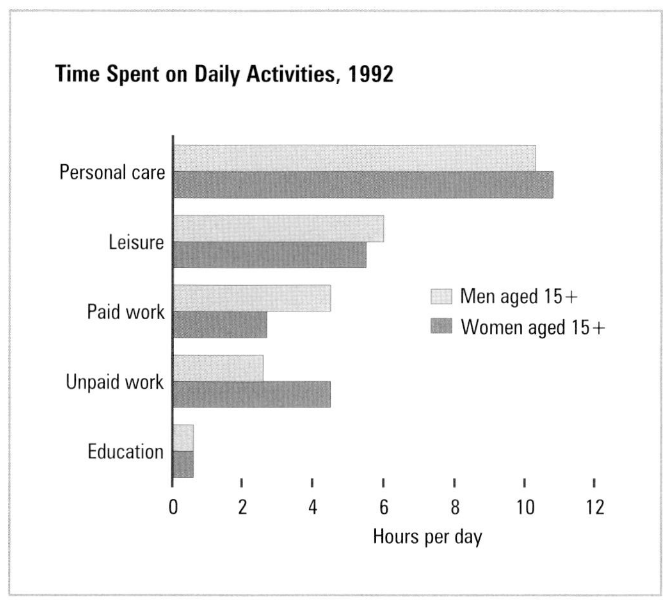

since 1986. Maintenance and repair expenses grabbed an additional 30% of average household expenditure in the same period.

For households paying for child care, expenditures jumped 51% between 1986 and 1992. Spending more than doubled for the most expensive options: day-care centres and nurseries.

Buying clothes accounted for 6% less of the household budget in 1992. Average spending on women's clothing dropped 4% between 1986 and 1992 (the first such decline since 1969), although women still spent 40% more than men on clothes.

Family Issues

As women have flooded into the workplace in the past few decades, the question of how to raise children while holding down a job has become a central issue for Canadian parents. Many parents decide to adjust their work lives when children arrive, often splitting the paid work and family responsibilities rather unequally.

Among the baby boomer generation of parents, more fathers work full time, while mothers often cut back or withdraw from paid employment. In 1992, the proportion of women working full time dropped from 71% for those without children to 45% for mothers.

While rearranging work schedules gives families the flexibility to care for their young and still earn a living, women often pay a steep economic price for the rewards of family life. Since they tend to be the ones whose work lives are interrupted, they may pay a penalty in lost wages, lost opportunities, and lower earnings.

If work interruptions make women economically vulnerable in general, women whose marriages end are more so. Even for those women who remain at work full time, motherhood makes a difference. Regardless of their marital or parental status, men who work full time consistently spend almost seven hours a day at their jobs, averaged over a seven-day week.

Women's roles, on the other hand, tend to multiply and start to collide as their lives unfold. One way of coping is to spend fewer hours on the job. Married moms who work full time spend about 5.3 hours a day at work, while unmarried younger women (18 to 24 years of age) with no children put in the most time on the job (7.3 hours each day).

Home Work

Throughout their lives, women spend more time than men (an extra hour a day) on unpaid work, a category that includes household chores (cooking, cleaning, laundry, shovelling snow, cutting the lawn, painting), caring for others (children, spouse and elders), shopping and volunteer work.

Having children means doing a lot more household work. In 1992, boomer women with full-time jobs who decided to have children doubled their unpaid workload to 4.8 hours a day, even though they stayed in the labour force full time. Their new tasks included child care, as well as more time spent cooking, cleaning and shopping. Men's unpaid work also increased, but consisted primarily of more time spent on child care.

Violence in the Home

Family and friends don't always offer safe haven. Crime statistics tell a chilling story. In a startling 40% of all solved murders in 1994, the victims were killed by their partner or another family member.

In almost half (48%) of the cases of spousal homicide, there was a history of domestic violence to which police had been called. Between 1974 and 1992, married women were nine times more likely to be killed by their husband than by a stranger. And there is a greater rate of spousal homicide in common-law unions compared with marriages. More than one-third of women who were stalked in 1994 were being criminally harassed by their current (8%) or former (27%) partner.

Children are at the greatest risk in their first year of life. In 1994, 27 children aged one and younger were murdered; 20 were killed by a parent, two by a grandfather, one by a sibling, and one by a family acquaintance (the accused was unknown in the remaining cases). In almost half of all homicides, the victims were killed in their own homes.

The biggest gender gap in unpaid work existed between boomer-aged mothers and fathers—men in this age group spent 1.7 hours less than their partners on unpaid work. Nevertheless, boomer fathers did spend an hour a day more on unpaid labour than did full-time employed married men in other age groups.

The Struggle to Juggle

People in their middle years often juggle with what Faith Popcorn calls "99 lives," as they try to be good parents, workers, householders, citizens and dutiful grown children. The result, for many of Canada's 10 million baby boomers, is an all-too-familiar time squeeze, the so-called "struggle to juggle." But men and women don't experience the time crunch the same way.

Even at a younger age, women tend to be more time-stressed than men their age, and their stress levels soar as they get older and become workers, wives and mothers. For many of the working mothers in the baby boom generation, life is a pressure cooker.

In 1992, almost one-third (32%) of those who were working full time reported that they were highly time-stressed. Meanwhile, for men, getting married and having children doesn't seem to have much impact on stress: a consistent 17% reported being highly stressed throughout their working lives, primarily because of their jobs.

Leisure

When it comes to time off, Canadian men enjoy more leisure time than women: in fact, they reported having an average of an hour more per day. But marriage and childrearing cut into the free time of both sexes. Being married costs us an hour of rest and recreation each day, often because we spend more time on cooking, cleaning and other domestic activities, and raising children requires another half hour. Not surprisingly, seniors have twice as much leisure time as full-time employed parents (although senior men still enjoy an hour a day more than their wives).

Ken Ginn, GeoStock

For many boomer parents, one of the sacrifices is fun. More than half (53%) of boomer mothers who work full time say they just don't have any time to kick back and have fun any more. More than one-third (36%) of boomer fathers agree.

The luxury of solitude is something many women, especially boomer mothers employed full time, can only dream about. Almost 50% of these mothers reported that they would like to have time to themselves more often, while only about a quarter of men expressed the same desire.

Sometimes giving up on sleep is the answer. Almost 60% of parents cut back on sleep when they're short of time.

In general, people who work full time get the least amount of sleep, while students, those not employed and older Canadians get the most.

Precious Moments

Despite the hectic pace, and the sacrifices, there are signs that Canadians are increasingly making their families their priority. Between 1986 and 1991, young parents between the ages of 20 and 34—mothers and fathers alike—began to find more time to spend with their children, doing basic child care tasks or pursuing recreational activities.

Although women still spend more time on basic child care than men, fathers are becoming more involved. In 1992, fathers aged 20 to 44 had made small but significant increases in the time they spent on basic child care; for example, helping, teaching, reprimanding, or providing medical care for kids. Younger dads (20 to 34) also spent a little more time on recreational activities, such as going to hockey games, reading, and watching TV, with their children.

Family Matters

Canadians have consistently declared family to be one of the most important aspects of their lives. Canadian novelist Adele Wiseman expressed this poignantly when she wrote: "There is only one thing that is worse than to be left without your parents. And that is to be left without your children."

A telling illustration of the generosity and durability of family feelings are the close cross-generational ties within Canadian families. The amount of contact between the generations suggests that, despite their own traditional family lives, the older generation of Canadians have been remarkably accepting of the very different choices many of their children have made.

Certainly, that long-distance feeling seems to be real. Women tend to be better at keeping in touch with family and friends. Within families, older women in particular are usually the "kin keepers." They tend to see their children and siblings more often than men do, especially women who lose their spouses.

Questions about the meaning of family in our lives—and our responsibilities to one another—will take on new urgency as the number and proportion of older Canadians increases. For today's older Canadians, having the help of their children is a key source of support. But although many of today's seniors had large numbers of children, given the decrease in family size, this will not be the case for tomorrow's elderly.

SOURCES

Statistics Canada

FOR FURTHER READING

Selected publications from Statistics Canada

- **Canadian Social Trends**. Quarterly. 11-008E
- **Income Distribution by Size in Canada**. Annual. 13-207
- **Family Expenditure in Canada**. Occasional. 62-555
- **Household Facilities and Equipment**. Annual. 64-202
- **Dynamics of Labour and Income**. Annual. 75-201E
- **As Time Goes By: time use of Canadians**. Occasional. 89-544E
- **Report on the Demographic Situation in Canada**. Annual. 91-209E
- **Annual Demographic Statistics**. Annual. 91-213
- **Dwellings and Households**. 1991 Census. 93-311
- **Families in Canada**. **Focus on Canada**. 1991 Census. 96-307E

Selected publications from other sources

- **Profiling Canada's Families**. The Vanier Institute of the Family. 1994.

Legend

– nil or zero	.. not available	x confidential
-- too small to be expressed	... not applicable or not appropriate	*(Certain tables may not add due to rounding)*

6.1 DIVORCES

	Canada	Nfld.	P.E.I.	N.S.	N.B.	Que.	Ont.	Man.	Sask.	Alta.	B.C.	Y.T.	N.W.T.
						Number of divorces							
1978	57,155	427	135	1,960	1,153	14,865	20,534	2,187	1,428	6,059	8,265	65	77
1979	59,474	483	144	2,275	1,223	14,379	21,793	2,152	1,528	6,531	8,826	62	78
1980	62,019	555	163	2,314	1,326	13,899	22,442	2,282	1,836	7,580	9,464	82	76
1981	67,671	569	187	2,285	1,334	19,193	21,680	2,399	1,932	8,418	9,533	75	66
1982	70,436	625	206	2,281	1,663	18,579	23,644	2,392	1,815	8,882	10,165	117	67
1983	68,567	711	215	2,340	1,942	17,365	23,073	2,642	2,000	8,758	9,348	88	85
1984	65,172	590	195	2,264	1,427	16,845	21,636	2,611	1,988	8,454	8,988	100	74
1985	61,976	561	213	2,337	1,360	15,814	20,851	2,313	1,927	8,102	8,330	96	72
1986	78,304	687	199	2,609	1,729	19,026	27,549	2,982	2,479	9,556	11,299	94	95
1987	96,200	1,117	275	2,759	1,995	22,098	39,095	3,923	2,968	9,535	12,184	142	109
1988	83,507	906	269	2,494	1,673	20,340	32,524	3,102	2,501	8,744	10,760	82	112
1989	80,998	1,005	248	2,527	1,649	19,829	31,298	2,912	2,460	8,237	10,658	82	93
1990	78,463	1,016	281	2,419	1,699	20,474	28,977	2,798	2,364	8,489	9,773	81	92
1991	77,020	912	269	2,280	1,652	20,274	27,694	2,790	2,240	8,388	10,368	67	86
1992	79,034	867	227	2,304	1,633	19,695	30,463	2,657	2,325	8,217	10,431	117	98
1993	78,226	930	227	2,376	1,606	19,662	28,903	2,586	2,239	8,612	10,889	94	102
1994	78,880	933	249	2,286	1,570	18,224	30,718	2,746	2,354	8,174	11,437	97	92

Source: Statistics Canada, CANSIM, matrix 7.

6.2 COMMON-LAW UNIONS

	1981	1986	1991	1991 Share of all common-law unions	Average annual growth rate 1986-1991	1981-1991
		'000			%	
Canada	713.2	973.9	1,451.9	100.0	8.3	7.4
Newfoundland	5.6	10.1	19.9	1.4	14.5	13.5
Prince Edward Island	1.6	2.6	4.1	0.3	9.5	9.9
Nova Scotia	18.4	26.4	40.3	2.8	8.8	8.2
New Brunswick	12.7	19.2	31.8	2.2	10.6	9.6
Quebec	241.8	377.3	613.8	42.3	10.2	9.8
Ontario	203.7	269.4	364.3	25.1	6.2	6.0
Manitoba	23.8	30.6	42.6	2.9	6.8	6.0
Saskatchewan	19.3	27.5	35.5	2.4	5.2	6.3
Alberta	80.5	90.3	119.9	8.3	5.8	4.1
British Columbia	102.1	115.3	171.3	11.8	8.2	5.3
Yukon	1.7	2.0	2.8	0.2	7.0	5.1
Northwest Territories	2.1	3.2	5.7	0.4	12.2	10.5

Source: Statistics Canada, Demography Division.

6.3 POPULATION BY MARITAL STATUS

	Total			Single			Married[1]			Widowed			Divorced		
	Both sexes	Male	Female	Both sexes	Male	Female	Both sexes	Male	Female	Both sexes	Male	Female	Both sexes	Male	Female
	'000														
Canada															
1971	22,026.4	11,065.0	10,961.4	10,940.7	5,804.7	5,136.0	9,943.7	4,986.7	4,957.0	957.2	194.3	762.9	184.8	79.3	105.5
1976	23,517.5	11,764.9	11,752.6	10,974.3	5,857.6	5,116.6	11,143.5	5,569.4	5,574.1	1,069.4	200.0	869.4	330.3	137.9	192.4
1981	24,900.0	12,399.0	12,501.0	11,067.8	5,911.5	5,156.4	12,138.7	6,065.6	6,073.1	1,168.3	201.8	966.5	525.2	220.1	305.1
1986	26,203.8	13,012.9	13,190.9	11,359.4	6,084.8	5,274.6	12,828.4	6,411.2	6,417.3	1,279.1	214.7	1,064.4	736.9	302.2	434.7
1991	28,120.1	13,939.4	14,180.7	11,894.4	6,349.5	5,545.0	13,892.5	6,952.1	6,940.4	1,377.3	234.6	1,142.8	955.8	403.2	552.5
1992	28,542.2	14,149.7	14,392.5	12,118.2	6,467.7	5,650.5	13,985.3	6,998.6	6,986.7	1,400.2	240.9	1,159.2	1,038.5	442.4	596.1
1993	28,947.0	14,349.6	14,597.4	12,344.2	6,587.4	5,756.7	14,058.6	7,032.7	7,025.9	1,421.9	247.3	1,174.6	1,122.3	482.1	640.2
1994	29,251.3	14,494.1	14,757.2	12,517.1	6,676.4	5,840.7	14,085.1	7,042.4	7,042.7	1,443.6	253.8	1,189.7	1,205.5	521.5	684.1
1995	29,606.1	14,664.3	14,941.8	12,718.0	6,780.8	5,937.1	14,129.2	7,060.2	7,069.0	1,466.6	260.8	1,205.8	1,292.3	562.5	729.8
1995															
Newfoundland	575.4	288.5	286.9	254.9	136.3	118.6	279.6	141.1	138.5	27.4	5.1	22.3	13.5	6.1	7.5
Prince Edward Island	136.1	67.2	68.9	59.5	31.6	27.9	65.7	33.0	32.7	7.4	1.2	6.2	3.5	1.5	2.0
Nova Scotia	937.8	462.6	475.1	394.5	210.1	184.4	454.5	227.6	226.9	51.5	8.9	42.6	37.2	16.1	21.1
New Brunswick	760.1	376.6	383.5	322.7	172.0	150.6	371.3	185.9	185.4	40.3	7.1	33.3	25.7	11.6	14.2
Quebec	7,334.2	3,614.1	3,720.2	3,208.3	1,697.2	1,511.1	3,362.0	1,680.0	1,682.0	383.2	70.9	312.4	380.7	166.0	214.7
Ontario	11,100.3	5,481.3	5,619.0	4,713.9	2,505.6	2,208.4	5,387.0	2,688.5	2,698.4	552.2	96.2	456.0	447.2	191.0	256.2
Manitoba	1,137.5	564.1	573.4	498.5	267.1	231.4	534.0	268.2	265.8	62.7	10.6	52.1	42.2	18.1	24.1
Saskatchewan	1,015.6	504.8	510.9	448.1	240.7	207.3	476.1	238.6	237.5	56.8	9.4	47.4	34.7	16.1	18.6
Alberta	2,747.0	1,383.5	1,363.5	1,209.4	654.8	554.6	1,303.5	652.1	651.4	106.2	18.6	87.6	128.0	58.0	70.0
British Columbia	3,766.0	1,872.2	1,893.8	1,554.7	836.7	718.0	1,857.8	926.8	931.0	176.9	32.3	144.7	176.6	76.5	100.1
Yukon	30.1	15.3	14.8	14.2	7.7	6.6	13.9	6.7	7.2	0.6	0.2	0.4	1.4	0.8	0.7
Northwest Territories	65.8	34.1	31.7	39.2	21.1	18.1	23.9	11.9	12.0	1.3	0.4	0.9	1.4	0.8	0.7

1. Includes persons legally married, legally married and separated, and persons living in common-law unions.

Source: Statistics Canada, CANSIM, matrix 6213.

6.4 MARRIAGES

	Canada	Nfld.	P.E.I.	N.S.	N.B.	Que.	Ont.	Man.	Sask.	Alta.	B.C.	Y.T.	N.W.T.
1980	191,069	3,783	939	6,791	5,321	44,848	68,840	7,869	7,561	20,818	23,830	200	269
1981	190,082	3,758	849	6,632	5,108	41,005	70,281	8,123	7,329	21,781	24,699	235	282
1982	188,119	3,727	855	6,486	4,923	38,152	71,595	8,264	7,491	22,312	23,831	225	258
1983	184,675	3,778	937	6,505	5,260	36,144	70,893	8,261	7,504	21,172	23,692	243	286
1984	185,597	3,567	1,057	6,798	5,294	37,433	71,922	8,393	7,213	20,052	23,397	212	259
1985	184,096	3,220	956	6,807	5,312	37,026	72,891	8,296	7,132	19,750	22,292	185	229
1986	175,518	3,421	970	6,445	4,962	33,083	70,839	7,816	6,820	18,896	21,826	183	257
1987	182,151	3,481	924	6,697	4,924	32,616	76,201	7,994	6,853	18,640	23,395	189	237
1988	187,728	3,686	965	6,894	5,292	33,519	78,533	7,908	6,767	19,272	24,461	209	222
1989	190,640	3,905	1,019	6,828	5,254	33,325	80,377	7,800	6,637	19,888	25,170	214	223
1990	187,737	3,791	996	6,386	5,044	32,060	80,097	7,666	6,229	19,806	25,216	218	228
1991	172,251	3,480	876	5,845	4,521	28,922	72,938	7,032	5,923	18,612	23,691	196	215
1992	164,573	3,254	850	5,623	4,313	25,841	70,079	6,899	5,664	17,871	23,749	221	209
1993	159,316	3,163	885	5,403	4,177	25,021	66,575	6,752	5,638	17,860	23,446	180	216
1994	159,959	3,318	850	5,374	4,219	24,985	66,694	6,585	5,689	18,096	23,739	169	241
1995	160,616	3,250	871	5,418	4,187	24,832	67,032	6,590	5,651	18,158	24,211	170	246

Source: Statistics Canada, CANSIM, matrix 6.

6.5 CENSUS FAMILIES

	All families[1]		Husband-wife families		Lone-parent families	
	Number	Average size	Number	Average size	Number	Average size
	'000		'000		'000	
1971[2]	5042.6	3.7	4566.3	3.8	476.3	3.1
1976[2]	5714.5	3.5	5156.7	3.5	557.9	2.9
1981[2]	6309.2	3.3	5597.2	3.3	712.0	2.7
1986[2]	6726.7	3.1	5874.7	3.2	852.1	2.6
1991[3]	7497.4	3.1	6524.9	3.1	972.5	2.6
1993[3]	7722.3	3.0	6711.0	3.1	1011.3	2.5
1994[3]	7794.4	3.0	6768.6	3.1	1025.8	2.5
1995[3]	7879.7	3.0	6837.5	3.1	1042.2	2.5

1. Excluding Yukon and Northwest Territories.
2. At June 1 and unadjusted for net census undercoverage.
3. At July 1 and adjusted for net census undercoverage.

Source: Statistics Canada, Catalogue no. 91-213.

6.6 CENSUS FAMILIES BY SIZE

	All families[1]	Family size 2	3	4	5	6 or more	Persons in families	Average family size
				'000				Number
1947[2]	3,030.0	948.0	741.0	582.0	327.0	432.0	11,362.0	3.7
1951[2]	3,282.4	1,024.5	785.9	656.6	361.8	453.6	12,196.9	3.7
1956[2]	3,705.6	1,123.9	815.3	757.9	455.0	553.6	14,053.2	3.8
1961[2]	4,140.4	1,198.0	855.5	853.7	554.1	679.2	16,065.5	3.9
1966[2]	4,518.4	1,308.7	893.2	921.9	622.5	772.1	17,646.2	3.9
1971[2 3]	5,042.6	1,589.2	1,044.4	1,054.8	661.4	710.4	18,806.1	3.7
1976[2 3]	5,714.5	2,008.0	1,217.8	1,284.8	683.9	520.0	19,729.5	3.5
1981[2 3]	6,309.2	2,395.5	1,394.9	1,516.8	675.9	326.2	20,543.9	3.3
1986[2 3]	6,726.7	2,689.0	1,535.0	1,642.2	639.2	221.3	21,160.7	3.1
1991[3 4]	7,497.4	3,202.3	1,704.0	1,755.7	638.5	196.9	22,991.3	3.1
1992[3 4]	7,625.3	3,298.4	1,731.4	1,770.5	634.6	190.5	23,265.9	3.1
1993[3 4]	7,722.3	3,382.2	1,751.7	1,777.4	627.8	183.2	23,447.8	3.0
1994[3 4]	7,794.4	3,455.6	1,765.8	1,778.1	619.0	175.9	23,554.5	3.0
1995[3 4]	7,879.7	3,534.7	1,782.8	1,781.3	611.3	169.6	23,703.3	3.0

1. Excluding Yukon and Northwest Territories.
2. At June 1st and unadjusted for net census undercoverage up to 1991.
3. Starting with the 1971 Census, the number of families excludes the families in collective households and in households outside Canada.
4. At July 1st and adjusted for net census undercoverage.

Source: Statistics Canada, Catalogue no. 91-213.

6.7 CENSUS FAMILIES BY SIZE, CANADA AND THE PROVINCES, 1995

	All families	Family size					Persons in families	Average family size
		2	3	4	5	6 or more		
	'000						Number	
Canada	7,879.7	3,534.7	1,782.8	1,781.3	611.3	169.6	23,703.3	3.01
Husband-wife families	6,837.5	2,913.6	1,469.9	1,696.3	593.3	164.3	21,058.5	3.08
Lone-parent families	1,042.2	621.1	312.9	85.0	18.0	5.2	2,644.8	2.54
Newfoundland	159.5	55.7	42.3	44.5	14.7	2.2	505.2	3.17
Husband-wife families	139.3	44.1	36.1	42.6	14.4	2.1	453.5	3.26
Lone-parent families	20.1	11.6	6.3	1.9	0.3	0.1	51.7	2.57
Prince Edward Island	36.1	14.4	8.4	8.2	3.7	1.3	113.8	3.15
Husband-wife families	31.3	11.6	7.1	7.8	3.6	1.3	101.4	3.24
Lone-parent families	4.8	2.8	1.3	0.5	0.1	–	12.4	2.58
Nova Scotia	254.1	113.2	61.9	56.8	18.2	4.1	757.2	2.98
Husband-wife families	218.8	91.9	51.5	54.0	17.6	3.9	667.9	3.05
Lone-parent families	35.3	21.3	10.4	2.8	0.6	0.2	89.3	2.53
New Brunswick	210.1	90.3	52.0	50.2	14.9	2.6	629.3	2.99
Husband-wife families	181.6	72.8	43.4	48.1	14.6	2.6	558.5	3.08
Lone-parent families	28.5	17.4	8.6	2.1	0.3	–	70.8	2.49
Quebec	2,000.1	917.4	490.5	440.0	127.0	25.2	5,865.0	2.93
Husband-wife families	1,716.5	735.5	408.7	423.0	124.7	24.7	5,172.9	3.01
Lone-parent families	283.5	181.9	81.8	17.0	2.3	0.5	692.1	2.44
Ontario	2,929.5	1,285.7	659.9	681.8	235.9	66.1	8,892.4	3.04
Husband-wife families	2,545.1	1,062.3	542.5	648.1	228.3	63.9	7,905.7	3.11
Lone-parent families	384.4	223.4	117.4	33.7	7.6	2.2	986.8	2.57
Manitoba	298.1	133.4	63.0	66.0	26.4	9.2	911.6	3.06
Husband-wife families	257.1	109.9	50.8	62.2	25.3	8.8	804.5	3.13
Lone-parent families	41.0	23.5	12.2	3.8	1.1	0.4	107.1	2.61
Saskatchewan	262.8	118.7	50.5	55.0	27.4	11.1	818.0	3.11
Husband-wife families	230.6	101.1	41.1	51.4	26.4	10.7	731.8	3.17
Lone-parent families	32.2	17.6	9.4	3.6	1.1	0.5	86.2	2.68
Alberta	717.3	308.4	151.4	168.1	65.6	23.9	2,225.7	3.10
Husband-wife families	624.7	257.4	122.4	158.5	63.2	23.2	1,981.8	3.17
Lone-parent families	92.7	51.0	29.0	9.6	2.4	0.7	243.9	2.63
British Columbia	1,012.3	497.6	202.9	210.7	77.5	23.7	2,985.1	2.95
Husband-wife families	892.6	427.1	166.3	200.7	75.3	23.2	2,680.6	3.00
Lone-parent families	119.7	70.5	36.6	9.9	2.2	0.5	304.5	2.54

Source: Statistics Canada, Demography Division.

6.8 HOUSEHOLDS

	All households	Household size					Average household size
		1	2	3	4	5 or more	
	'000						Number
Canada							
1980	7,787	1,442	2,266	1,394	1,483	1,202	2.93
1981	8,200	1,664	2,325	1,422	1,582	1,207	2.88
1982	8,336	1,712	2,369	1,506	1,595	1,154	2.85
1983	8,474	1,761	2,433	1,520	1,615	1,145	2.83
1984	8,618	1,812	2,487	1,555	1,664	1,100	2.80
1985	8,762	1,864	2,571	1,591	1,665	1,071	2.78
1986	8,909	1,918	2,610	1,636	1,703	1,042	2.73
1987	9,082	2,014	2,693	1,635	1,703	1,037	2.73
1988	9,244	2,089	2,790	1,601	1,717	1,047	2.71
1989	9,477	2,173	2,864	1,708	1,753	979	2.67
1990	9,624	2,224	2,966	1,701	1,727	1,006	2.66
1991	9,873	2,361	2,999	1,752	1,758	1,003	2.64
1992	10,056	2,445	3,077	1,735	1,766	1,033	2.63
1993	10,247	2,466	3,163	1,856	1,753	1,009	2.62
1994	10,387	2,535	3,145	1,832	1,903	972	2.62
1995	11,243	2,801	3,700	1,854	1,885	1,003	2.56
1995							
Newfoundland	194	26	58	43	44	23	2.95
Prince Edward Island	50	12	15	8	9	6	2.69
Nova Scotia	357	79	124	63	65	26	2.58
New Brunswick	286	64	93	55	50	24	2.60
Quebec	2,937	823	939	513	464	198	2.44
Ontario	4,143	954	1,370	686	725	408	2.63
Manitoba	419	108	137	67	68	39	2.55
Saskatchewan	385	102	135	54	56	38	2.51
Alberta	1,009	244	321	167	166	111	2.64
British Columbia	1,463	390	509	198	239	127	2.49

Source: Statistics Canada, Catalogue no. 64-202.

6.9 LOW INCOME[1]

	1980	1989	1993	1994	1980	1989	1993	1994	1980	1989	1993	1994
	Incidence of low income				Estimated number				Percent distribution			
	%				'000				%			
All people	16.0	14.1	18.0	17.1	3,871	3,770	5,143	4,941	100.0	100.0	100.0	100.0
Children under 18 years	15.8	15.3	21.3	19.5	1,061	1,016	1,484	1,362	27.4	27.0	28.9	27.6
Elderly, 65 years and older	34.0	22.4	22.8	19.3	742	640	732	635	19.2	17.0	14.2	12.8
All others	13.6	12.3	15.9	15.9	2,068	2,114	2,927	2,944	53.4	56.1	56.9	59.6
Persons in families	12.7	10.8	14.6	13.5	2,718	2,527	3,599	3,381	70.2	67.0	70.0	68.4
Children under 18 years	15.8	15.3	21.3	19.5	1,061	1,016	1,484	1,362	27.4	27.0	28.9	27.6
Elderly, 65 years and older	17.8	8.9	8.7	6.1	263	174	187	137	6.8	4.6	3.6	2.8
All others	10.5	9.0	12.4	11.9	1,394	1,337	1,928	1,882	36.0	35.5	37.5	38.1
Unattached individuals	43.5	37.1	40.5	40.6	1,153	1,243	1,544	1,559	29.8	33.0	30.0	31.6
Elderly, 65 years and older	68.6	51.5	51.9	47.6	479	466	545	497	12.4	12.4	10.6	10.1
Non-elderly, less than 65	34.5	31.7	36.2	38.0	674	777	999	1,062	17.4	20.6	19.4	21.5

1. Estimates based on Low Income Cut-offs, 1992 base.

Source: Statistics Canada, Catalogue no. 13-207.

6.10 BIRTHS BY MOTHER'S LEGAL MARITAL STATUS, 1993[1]

	All births	Single	Married	Widowed	Divorced	Separated	Not stated
Canada	388,394	98,761	259,059	573	5,600	1,904	22,497
Newfoundland	6,421	1,687	4,124	4	67	538	1
Prince Edward Island	1,754	430	1,290	2	30	2	–
Nova Scotia	11,568	3,509	7,999	6	49	2	3
New Brunswick	9,049	2,836	6,071	7	133	–	2
Quebec	92,391	40,210	48,608	226	2,134	403	810
Ontario	147,848	23,189	106,017	184	769	6	17,683
Manitoba	16,709	4,918	11,320	26	272	167	6
Saskatchewan	14,269	4,515	9,501	22	226	3	2
Alberta	40,292	9,273	29,866	42	1,071	2	38
British Columbia	46,026	7,008	33,420	53	828	778	3,939
Yukon	508	211	282	–	13	–	2
Northwest Territories	1,559	975	561	1	8	3	11

1. Calendar year.

Source: Statistics Canada, Catalogue no. 91-213.

6.11 FAMILIES BY INCOME, 1994

	Canada	Nfld.	P.E.I.	N.S.	N.B.	Que.	Ont.	Man.	Sask.	Alta.	B.C.
						%					
All incomes	100.0	100.0	100.0	100.0	100.0	100.0	100.0	100.0	100.0	100.0	100.0
Under $10,000	2.2	3.9	0.9	2.8	2.5	2.2	1.9	2.2	3.2	2.5	2.4
$10,000 to $14,999	4.0	8.5	2.4	6.1	7.1	5.6	2.8	3.5	4.4	3.4	3.4
$15,000 to $19,999	5.9	9.0	6.2	7.4	6.9	7.1	5.0	5.9	7.7	4.6	5.3
$20,000 to $24,999	7.2	8.9	8.5	8.6	7.6	8.3	6.2	8.3	9.3	7.3	6.1
$25,000 to $29,999	6.6	8.2	10.5	7.6	8.7	7.4	6.0	7.9	7.7	5.3	5.8
$30,000 to $34,999	6.7	9.0	9.5	9.4	9.0	7.5	6.1	7.9	7.6	6.1	5.3
$35,000 to $39,999	6.9	7.4	7.6	7.3	8.3	7.5	6.2	6.7	8.2	6.7	6.9
$40,000 to $44,999	6.4	5.9	8.2	7.7	6.9	6.7	6.0	7.4	6.3	7.1	6.2
$45,000 to $49,999	6.6	5.5	8.3	6.4	7.2	7.0	6.2	7.0	6.9	7.2	6.5
$50,000 to $54,999	6.3	5.6	8.2	5.9	6.4	6.1	6.3	6.5	6.8	6.4	6.7
$55,000 to $59,999	6.1	4.8	6.4	5.0	6.0	5.7	6.2	5.8	5.0	7.0	6.7
$60,000 to $64,999	5.4	4.6	3.6	5.1	4.0	4.9	5.6	6.0	5.0	5.8	6.0
$65,000 to $69,999	4.6	4.3	4.8	4.7	3.4	4.5	4.9	4.4	4.9	4.3	4.6
$70,000 to $74,999	4.0	3.2	3.0	2.7	3.3	3.5	4.6	3.9	3.3	3.8	3.9
$75,000 to $79,999	3.4	1.9	3.1	2.7	2.5	2.6	4.0	3.4	2.9	3.2	3.9
$80,000 to $89,999	5.3	4.0	2.8	3.0	3.7	4.8	5.7	4.9	4.1	6.3	6.1
$90,000 to $99,999	3.8	2.5	2.2	2.7	2.8	2.7	4.6	3.3	2.4	4.6	4.1
$100,000 and over	8.7	2.9	3.8	4.8	3.7	5.8	11.9	5.1	4.5	8.6	10.3
						$					
Average annual income	54,153	42,678	46,742	46,524	45,398	49,130	59,324	49,749	47,207	55,355	57,046
Median annual income	48,091	36,670	42,675	40,522	39,953	43,350	52,922	45,118	41,507	49,870	51,704
						Number					
Number of families	8,102,000	165,000	36,000	268,000	216,000	2,050,000	3,064,000	299,000	275,000	724,000	1,005,000

Source: Statistics Canada, Catalogue no. 13-207.

6.12 FAMILY AND UNATTACHED INDIVIDUAL INCOME

	1981	1982	1983	1984	1985	1986	1987	1988	1989	1990	1991	1992	1993	1994
	Average annual income													
	$ Constant 1994													
Economic families[1]	53,049	51,733	51,180	51,014	52,323	53,292	53,970	55,154	56,777	55,905	54,572	54,273	53,157	54,153
Elderly families[2]	35,877	37,748	35,345	37,762	38,148	38,192	36,891	37,898	42,597	41,943	41,162	39,812	40,559	40,183
Married couples only	31,649	34,803	32,343	34,016	33,565	35,023	33,427	33,965	38,886	38,269	36,940	36,331	37,460	37,369
All other elderly families	44,305	44,332	42,167	45,328	47,338	45,927	45,218	47,450	51,375	51,234	51,279	48,361	47,746	47,426
Non-elderly families[3]	55,531	53,796	53,481	53,056	54,567	55,714	56,713	57,996	59,129	58,238	56,880	56,827	55,365	56,629
Married couples only	53,144	51,129	51,763	51,087	52,130	52,117	54,068	55,860	55,031	55,273	54,926	56,958	54,090	54,142
One earner	41,972	42,023	43,136	40,442	43,427	42,847	43,638	48,031	46,672	46,075	42,220	43,260	44,105	43,678
Two earners	59,733	57,391	57,419	57,990	58,256	58,484	60,502	61,333	60,762	61,671	62,251	64,611	61,259	61,489
Two parent families with children[4]	57,723	56,372	56,173	56,432	58,084	59,250	60,633	61,767	63,599	62,302	60,836	61,260	59,800	61,105
One earner	45,016	44,566	45,188	41,800	44,248	45,250	43,731	44,932	48,331	44,780	44,362	44,412	43,415	45,572
Two earners	58,455	57,049	58,173	59,243	59,355	60,541	61,322	62,278	62,534	62,337	61,709	62,992	61,241	63,112
Three or more earners	75,193	74,554	71,898	72,868	74,576	75,830	77,560	78,227	81,595	79,529	77,416	76,379	77,287	77,406
Married couples with other relatives[5]	76,290	74,271	70,929	69,177	72,505	76,290	75,055	77,080	78,938	79,944	75,867	75,345	75,345	76,570
Lone-parent families[4]	27,242	24,891	23,904	25,018	24,759	25,155	26,334	26,035	28,142	26,173	24,867	26,171	24,799	25,585
Male lone-parent families	44,048	40,265	36,509	38,760	37,523	38,386	46,850	41,165	48,219	39,207	38,236	40,389	34,813	34,869
Female lone-parent families	24,343	22,365	22,176	22,998	23,026	22,801	23,419	23,661	25,470	23,877	22,901	24,234	23,145	24,057
No earner	10,920	11,895	11,781	12,094	12,183	13,139	12,614	13,005	13,392	13,006	13,643	13,933	14,614	14,246
One earner	25,260	24,020	25,267	24,825	23,736	24,834	24,373	25,047	26,415	25,436	25,051	27,124	25,561	26,761
All other non-elderly families	44,497	44,001	39,852	41,977	41,735	44,511	43,883	45,141	46,724	46,633	45,253	41,255	43,247	44,890
Unattached individuals	23,725	23,539	22,478	22,581	23,139	23,164	23,602	23,900	24,651	24,909	23,634	23,970	23,544	23,746
Elderly	16,546	17,075	15,678	16,873	17,327	16,915	17,865	17,526	18,970	19,049	18,863	18,978	17,916	18,780
Male	19,172	21,627	18,541	20,033	20,394	18,217	20,125	20,476	22,485	21,749	21,194	22,433	20,873	23,782
Female	15,587	15,589	14,743	15,891	16,394	16,513	17,149	16,627	17,856	18,175	18,091	17,838	16,888	17,106
Non-elderly	26,405	24,749	25,020	24,557	25,142	25,343	25,627	26,252	26,750	27,132	25,387	25,764	25,680	25,604
Male	29,964	28,173	27,501	27,158	27,556	27,600	27,353	29,032	28,867	29,437	27,246	27,483	27,195	27,867
Female	22,158	22,723	21,779	21,200	21,844	22,371	23,334	22,598	23,990	23,941	22,903	23,264	23,436	22,304

1. An economic family is a group of individuals sharing a common dwelling unit who are related by blood, marriage (including common-law relationships) or adoption.
2. Head 65 years of age and over.
3. Head less than 65 years of age.
4. With single children less than 18 years of age. Children 18 years of age and over and/or other relatives may also be present.
5. Children less than 18 years of age are not present, but children 18 years of age and over may be present.

Source: Statistics Canada, Catalogue no. 13-207.

6.13 FAMILY AND UNATTACHED INDIVIDUAL INCOME, TRANSFER PAYMENTS AND TAXES, 1994

	Average income before transfers	Average transfer payments	Average total money income	Average income tax	Average income after tax	Effective average rate	
						Transfer payments[1]	Income tax[2]
			$			%	
Economic families[3]	47,380	6,774	54,153	10,668	43,486	12.5	19.7
Elderly families[4]	22,697	17,486	40,183	5,335	34,849	43.5	13.3
Married couples only	19,867	17,502	37,369	4,916	32,453	46.8	13.2
All other elderly families	29,980	17,446	47,426	6,412	41,014	36.8	13.5
Non-elderly families[5]	51,754	4,875	56,629	11,613	45,016	8.6	20.5
Married couples only	50,735	3,407	54,142	11,572	42,570	6.3	21.4
One earner	38,887	4,791	43,678	8,834	34,844	11.0	20.2
Two earners	59,508	1,981	61,489	13,642	47,847	3.2	22.2
Two parent families with children[6]	56,362	4,742	61,104	12,911	48,193	7.8	21.1
One earner	39,337	6,248	45,585	9,415	36,170	13.7	20.7
Two earners	59,291	3,820	63,112	13,727	49,385	6.1	21.8
Three or more earners	73,185	4,221	77,406	15,956	61,450	5.5	20.6
Married couples with other relatives[7]	71,464	5,107	76,570	15,690	60,881	6.7	20.5
Lone-parent families[6]	17,773	7,813	25,585	3,078	22,507	30.5	12.0
Male lone-parent families	29,141	5,728	34,869	6,562	28,307	16.4	18.8
Female lone-parent families	15,901	8,156	24,057	2,505	21,553	33.9	10.4
No earner	1,575	12,672	14,246	192	14,054	89.0	1.3
One earner	21,048	5,712	26,761	3,287	23,474	21.3	12.3
All other non-elderly families	37,577	7,294	44,871	7,757	37,114	16.3	17.3
Unattached individuals	18,600	5,146	23,746	4,332	19,414	21.7	18.2
Elderly	7,178	11,602	18,780	1,915	16,865	61.8	10.2
Male	11,834	11,947	23,782	3,624	20,157	50.2	15.2
Female	5,619	11,486	17,106	1,343	15,762	67.1	7.9
Non-elderly	22,872	2,732	25,604	5,236	20,368	10.7	20.4
Male	25,225	2,642	27,867	6,020	21,847	9.5	21.6
Female	19,442	2,862	22,304	4,093	18,210	12.8	18.4

1. Transfer payments as a percentage of total money income (before tax).
2. Percentage of total money income payable in income tax.
3. An economic family is a group of individuals sharing a common dwelling unit who are related by blood, marriage (including common-law relationships) or adoption.
4. Head 65 years of age and over.
5. Head less than 65 years of age.
6. With single children less than 18 years of age. Children 18 years of age and over and/or other relatives may also be present.
7. Children less than 18 years of age are not present, but children 18 years of age and over may be present.

Source: Statistics Canada, Catalogue no. 13-210.

6.14 UNATTACHED INDIVIDUALS BY INCOME, 1994

	Canada	Nfld.	P.E.I.	N.S.	N.B.	Que.	Ont.	Man.	Sask.	Alta.	B.C.
						%					
All incomes	100.0	100.0	100.0	100.0	100.0	100.0	100.0	100.0	100.0	100.0	100.0
Under $2,500	2.0	2.7	0.3	4.2	2.5	1.6	2.0	2.5	2.5	1.7	2.0
$2,500-$4,999	2.5	4.3	2.8	3.5	3.2	2.7	1.9	5.3	3.5	3.2	1.5
$5,000-$7,499	6.3	7.3	5.9	8.1	9.0	9.3	3.5	4.9	5.6	5.8	7.9
$7,500-$9,999	7.9	9.8	6.9	9.5	8.2	11.6	7.0	6.0	6.6	4.8	5.8
$10,000-$12,499	11.5	20.6	18.9	16.6	17.5	12.4	9.3	15.7	14.2	9.6	11.9
$12,500-$14,999	12.3	13.6	17.5	10.6	11.2	10.8	14.0	14.3	15.0	11.1	10.8
$15,000-$17,499	8.6	5.4	9.3	11.3	8.7	8.9	8.1	8.1	10.4	9.4	8.0
$17,500-$19,999	4.8	3.5	6.4	6.8	4.8	4.2	4.8	3.6	5.0	6.9	4.1
$20,000-$22,499	4.8	3.1	4.9	3.8	5.4	4.3	4.8	4.9	4.9	4.8	5.7
$22,500-$24,999	3.6	3.9	9.0	3.0	3.4	3.4	3.8	4.6	2.7	3.1	3.5
$25,000-$29,999	7.6	6.6	6.6	5.7	6.2	7.4	7.8	6.8	6.4	8.7	7.7
$30,000-$39,999	12.1	8.6	6.0	8.0	9.2	9.7	14.2	11.4	11.1	11.7	13.6
$40,000-$49,999	7.8	3.8	0.9	4.7	5.3	7.6	8.5	6.5	6.8	6.6	8.9
$50,000 and over	8.4	6.7	4.7	4.4	5.3	5.9	10.4	5.4	5.6	12.5	8.5
						$					
Average annual income	23,746	20,501	19,824	18,410	19,706	21,067	26,319	21,044	21,651	25,224	24,625
Median annual income	17,196	13,473	14,681	14,424	14,645	15,448	19,711	15,403	15,656	19,047	18,753
						Number					
Number of individuals	3,836,000	35,000	16,000	108,000	87,000	1,019,000	1,332,000	146,000	128,000	372,000	594,000

Source: Statistics Canada, Catalogue no. 13-207.

6.15 PERCEPTIONS OF TIME BY FULL-TIME, EMPLOYED, AGED 25-44, 1992

	Men			Women		
	Unmarried[1]	Married no children	Married[2] with children	Unmarried[1]	Married no children	Married[2] with children
	% Affirmative responses					
Do you plan to slow down in the coming year?	19	20	20	19	30	29
Do you consider yourself a workaholic?	35	29	32	28	32	33
When you need more time, do you tend to cut back on your sleep?	56	45	57	48	48	55
At the end of the day, do you often feel that you have not accomplished what you had set out to do?	47	44	49	49	55	58
Do you worry that you don't spend enough time with your family or friends?	45	43	51	45	48	51
Do you feel that you're constantly under stress trying to accomplish more than you can handle?	35	35	39	40	38	52
Do you feel trapped in a daily routine?	44	30	34	35	43	48
Do you feel that you just don't have time for fun anymore?	28	26	36	34	41	52
Do you often feel under stress when you don't have enough time?	50	49	51	58	60	69
Would you like to spend more time alone?	23	25	26	20	31	46

1. Includes never married, divorced and widowed.
2. Includes legally married and common-law.

Source: Statistics Canada, *General Social Survey*, 1992.

6.16 HOUSEHOLD SPENDING, 1992

	Household annual income												
	All households	Under $10,000	$10,000-$14,999	$15,000-$19,999	$20,000-$24,999	$25,000-$29,999	$30,000-$34,999	$35,000-$39,999	$40,000-$49,999	$50,000-$49,999	$60,000-$69,999	$70,000-$89,999	$90,000 and over
						$							
Average income before tax	46,076	6,358	12,392	17,535	22,456	27,450	32,304	37,348	44,748	54,548	64,605	78,748	119,563
Average expenditure per household	45,548	13,116	14,427	20,082	24,965	29,870	34,583	38,563	45,721	54,350	61,689	73,558	106,005
Total current consumption	32,416	12,186	13,347	18,009	21,311	24,382	27,154	29,183	34,204	38,498	41,559	48,220	63,046
Food	5,686	2,379	2,810	3,635	4,111	4,618	4,906	5,321	6,102	6,585	6,862	8,207	9,864
Shelter	8,102	4,281	4,640	5,583	6,056	6,710	6,668	7,347	8,410	8,912	10,027	10,613	14,641
Principal accommodation	7,624	4,236	4,513	5,427	5,909	6,465	6,431	7,021	8,006	8,301	9,457	9,814	13,015
Rented living quarters	2,279	2,547	2,814	2,916	3,017	2,920	2,795	2,632	2,472	1,797	1,594	1,511	884
Owned living quarters	3,912	985	856	1,467	1,702	2,321	2,325	2,994	4,047	4,871	6,145	6,422	9,907
Water, fuel and electricity	1,433	704	843	1,045	1,190	1,225	1,311	1,395	1,487	1,632	1,718	1,881	2,224
Other accommodation	478	45	128	155	147	245	237	326	404	611	570	799	1,626
Household operation	1,974	767	931	1,175	1,394	1,474	1,619	1,804	2,018	2,236	2,535	2,882	3,850
Household furnishings and equipment	1,372	297	439	688	736	938	1,103	1,223	1,387	1,672	1,788	2,169	3,107
Household furnishings	699	119	211	313	351	435	549	617	661	875	861	1,176	1,719
Household equipment	593	159	199	335	345	443	501	546	646	719	822	860	1,183
Services related to furnishings and equipment	80	19	29	40	40	59	53	60	80	78	105	132	206
Clothing	2,222	530	642	915	1,179	1,463	1,723	1,755	2,266	2,595	3,065	3,708	5,281
Transportation	5,640	1,611	1,528	2,445	3,339	3,959	4,710	5,266	6,269	7,255	7,409	8,831	11,319
Private transportation	5,198	1,374	1,302	2,126	3,005	3,616	4,398	4,870	5,861	6,843	6,900	8,213	10,308
Public transportation	442	237	225	320	334	343	312	397	408	412	509	618	1,011
Health care	867	347	359	514	718	727	852	868	930	1,072	1,029	1,166	1,421
Personal care	844	268	372	497	600	678	757	755	872	1,014	1,047	1,253	1,552
Recreation	2,300	496	511	856	1,075	1,271	1,628	1,877	2,352	2,902	3,437	4,026	5,461
Reading materials and other printed matter	248	117	96	134	160	196	194	212	249	283	333	357	526
Education	430	156	96	140	245	169	318	274	390	565	671	740	1,110
Tobacco products and alcoholic beverages	1,410	570	626	901	1,033	1,174	1,446	1,367	1,597	1,686	1,665	2,056	2,114
Miscellaneous	1,322	368	298	525	666	1,007	1,230	1,113	1,361	1,719	1,692	2,212	2,800
Personal taxes	9,378	404	393	991	1,988	3,291	4,596	6,109	7,904	11,202	14,568	18,715	33,409
Pensions, life and unemployment insurance	2,289	57	129	299	627	1,017	1,387	1,822	2,318	3,090	3,882	4,662	6,047
Gifts and contributions	1,464	469	558	783	1,039	1,180	1,445	1,449	1,294	1,560	1,680	1,960	3,503

Source: Statistics Canada, *Family Expenditure Survey*, Catalogue no. 62-555.

6.17 HOUSEHOLD SPENDING, CANADA AND THE PROVINCES, 1992

	Canada	Nfld.	P.E.I.	N.S.	N.B.	Que.	Ont.	Man.	Sask.	Alta.	B.C.
					$						
Average income before tax	46,076	40,411	37,476	39,957	39,160	41,784	50,986	41,298	38,866	48,596	46,603
Average expenditure per household	45,548	39,285	36,881	38,389	37,722	41,362	50,161	40,370	38,480	46,834	48,256
Total current consumption	32,416	29,321	27,637	27,463	27,623	29,152	35,592	28,311	27,429	33,346	34,941
Food	5,686	6,029	5,488	4,981	5,116	5,626	5,877	5,092	4,791	5,763	5,898
Shelter	8,102	5,356	6,202	6,459	5,294	6,876	9,900	6,410	5,964	7,190	8,679
Principal accommodation	7,624	4,945	5,753	6,063	4,930	6,480	9,306	5,997	5,495	6,796	8,230
Rented living quarters	2,279	877	962	1,638	1,058	2,210	2,652	1,527	1,569	2,177	2,500
Owned living quarters	3,912	2,054	2,772	2,716	2,254	2,940	5,100	3,089	2,416	3,268	4,594
Water, fuel and electricity	1,433	2,014	2,019	1,709	1,618	1,330	1,554	1,381	1,509	1,351	1,137
Other accommodation	478	410	449	396	364	396	594	412	469	395	449
Household operation	1,974	1,933	2,015	1,999	1,956	1,635	2,186	1,846	1,909	2,203	1,967
Household furnishings and equipment	1,372	1,411	1,227	1,142	1,312	1,174	1,526	1,081	1,098	1,426	1,545
Household furnishings	699	708	579	513	524	588	786	515	526	764	829
Household equipment	593	664	592	559	716	521	643	498	496	567	650
Services related to furnishings and equipment	80	40	56	70	73	65	96	68	77	96	66
Clothing	2,222	2,445	1,906	1,868	1,979	2,127	2,365	1,966	1,993	2,459	2,095
Transportation	5,640	4,968	4,589	4,409	5,230	5,115	5,967	5,226	5,161	5,670	6,579
Private transportation	5,198	4,526	4,401	4,145	5,016	4,822	5,409	4,791	4,948	5,257	5,973
Public transportation	442	442	189	264	214	293	558	435	213	414	606
Health care	867	768	992	803	793	818	726	811	864	1,198	1,206
Personal care	844	865	814	778	779	791	919	755	749	899	778
Recreation	2,300	2,013	1,840	1,875	2,110	1,926	2,414	1,909	1,969	3,058	2,635
Reading materials and other printed matter	248	199	244	233	221	235	266	240	186	266	247
Education	430	570	305	301	403	322	519	408	419	450	419
Tobacco products and alcoholic beverages	1,410	1,601	884	1,472	1,143	1,365	1,469	1,403	1,198	1,374	1,454
Miscellaneous	1,322	1,163	1,129	1,144	1,287	1,141	1,459	1,164	1,126	1,389	1,439
Personal taxes	9,378	6,832	5,777	7,364	6,796	9,242	10,486	8,028	7,392	9,241	9,033
Pensions, life and unemployment insurance	2,289	1,949	2,060	2,379	2,046	2,155	2,498	2,096	1,982	2,418	2,094
Gifts and contributions	1,464	1,183	1,407	1,182	1,256	814	1,585	1,934	1,677	1,829	2,188

Source: Statistics Canada, *Family Expenditure Survey*, Catalogue no. 62-555.

6.18 HOUSEHOLD DWELLING FEATURES, CANADA AND THE PROVINCES, 1995

	Canada	Nfld.	P.E.I.	N.S.	N.B.	Que.	Ont.	Man.	Sask.	Alta.	B.C.
Total households ('000)	11,243	194	50	357	286	2,937	4,143	419	385	1,009	1,463
Average number of:											
Persons per household	2.56	2.95	2.69	2.58	2.60	2.44	2.63	2.55	2.51	2.64	2.49
Rooms per dwelling	5.89	6.40	5.92	6.00	5.89	5.41	6.07	5.79	5.98	6.31	5.96
						% of households					
Dwelling type											
Single detached	56.2	73.7	72.0	67.8	67.5	44.9	57.0	69.9	72.5	63.3	55.2
Single attached	10.5	12.9	6.0	7.0	6.6	7.8	13.1	7.4	6.8	13.0	10.4
Apartment or flat	31.3	12.4	14.0	21.3	20.3	46.0	29.3	20.0	18.2	18.8	30.7
Mobile home	2.0	1.0	6.0	4.2	5.2	1.3	0.7	2.6	2.6	4.9	3.8
Tenure											
Owned	63.7	78.9	72.0	69.7	73.4	56.7	64.3	71.8	69.4	69.2	63.0
With mortgage	32.9	26.8	36.0	32.8	33.6	30.3	34.5	34.6	27.3	36.4	33.1
Without mortgage	30.8	52.1	38.0	37.0	39.5	26.4	29.9	37.0	42.1	32.8	29.8
Rented	36.3	21.1	26.0	30.5	26.6	43.3	35.7	28.2	30.6	30.8	37.1
Dwelling repairs											
Repairs needed	23.8	25.3	28.0	33.3	30.0	22.8	22.9	31.5	28.9	22.5	21.2
Major	7.9	8.8	10.0	13.7	11.5	8.5	7.0	11.5	8.1	6.1	6.6
Minor	15.9	16.5	18.0	19.6	18.5	14.3	15.9	20.0	20.8	16.4	14.6
No repairs needed	76.3	74.7	70.0	66.9	69.6	77.2	77.1	68.3	71.2	77.5	78.9
Principal heating equipment											
Steam or hot water furnace	14.3	9.3	54.0	28.3	10.1	12.5	15.1	8.1	15.6	13.5	14.6
Hot air furnace	52.8	34.5	34.0	40.3	29.0	19.2	67.7	68.7	80.7	85.6	53.9
Forced	51.6	34.0	34.0	39.5	27.3	17.8	66.5	67.5	79.7	84.4	53.0
Other	1.2	0.5	--	0.8	1.7	1.4	1.2	1.2	1.0	1.2	0.9
Heating stoves	2.9	8.8	6.0	7.0	7.0	3.5	2.1	1.9	1.3	0.7	3.2
Electric heating	29.8	46.9	2.0	24.1	53.5	64.5	14.9	21.5	2.3	0.2	28.0
Principal heating fuel											
Oil or other liquid fuel	14.4	35.1	84.0	62.5	26.6	19.0	12.0	3.6	6.5	0.7	7.2
Piped gas	46.9	--	--	--	--	5.8	66.0	59.2	85.7	96.1	56.0
Electricity	33.9	48.5	2.0	24.6	58.4	70.8	18.4	33.2	4.2	0.6	31.9
Wood	3.8	16.0	10.0	10.9	14.7	4.3	2.6	2.9	2.1	0.4	3.4
Air conditioners	27.6	1.0	2.0	3.4	8.0	15.9	50.1	48.9	33.2	6.6	8.5
Window	10.4	--	--	2.2	5.2	8.5	16.7	16.0	14.0	1.9	4.5
Central	17.2	0.5	--	1.1	2.8	7.5	33.4	32.9	19.2	4.8	4.0
Fuel for cooking											
Electricity	94.4	97.4	88.0	91.3	97.9	98.4	92.3	98.6	97.1	90.7	92.7
Piped gas	4.5	--	--	--	--	1.1	7.0	1.4	2.3	8.2	5.9
Smoke detectors	95.0	95.4	96.0	94.1	94.1	95.8	96.0	94.5	94.0	93.3	92.4
Owner-occupied dwellings	96.5	94.8	97.2	94.4	94.8	97.8	97.4	94.4	94.8	94.8	94.8
Tenant-occupied dwellings	92.4	95.1	100.0	93.6	92.1	93.3	93.5	94.9	92.4	89.7	88.0
Portable fire extinguishers	50.8	59.3	60.0	55.5	50.3	51.5	50.0	50.1	50.1	53.3	48.0
Owner-occupied buildings	64.5	63.4	69.4	65.1	56.7	69.4	63.6	62.1	61.4	64.8	61.7
Tenant-occupied dwellings	26.7	43.9	38.5	33.9	31.6	28.0	25.6	19.5	25.4	27.7	24.7

Source: Statistics Canada, *Household Facilities and Equipment Survey*, Catalogue no. 64-202.

6.19 HOUSEHOLD FACILITIES AND EQUIPMENT

	1985	1990	1993	1994	1995
			% of households		
Refrigerators	99.2	99.4	99.8	99.3	99.7
One	84.2	81.1	80.4	80.4	80.4
Two or more	14.9	18.3	19.4	18.9	19.3
Radios	98.7	99.1	98.9	98.9	98.9
One	23.2	18.9	21.8	22.2	17.9
Two	31.3	27.8	28.3	29.2	25.6
Three or more	44.2	52.4	48.9	47.5	55.4
Colour televisions	91.2	96.9	97.6	98.2	98.5
One	69.6	58.0	52.2	50.3	48.8
Two or more	21.5	38.9	45.4	47.9	49.7
Telephones	98.2	98.5	98.9	99.0	98.5
One	48.1	31.5	27.4	25.6	24.2
Two	33.7	36.8	36.9	37.5	36.9
Three or more	16.3	30.2	34.6	35.8	37.5
Owned vehicles	81.8	83.1	84.1	83.1	83.9
Automobiles	77.1	77.7	77.2	74.9	74.5
One	54.5	53.3	53.9	53.4	52.9
Two or more	22.6	24.3	23.3	21.5	21.7
Vans and trucks	21.6	23.1	28.0	29.4	30.8
Microwave ovens	22.7	68.2	78.8	81.1	83.4
Video cassette recorders	23.4	66.2	73.3	79.2	82.1
One	..	60.6	64.7	65.3	66.0
Two or more	..	5.5	12.6	13.9	16.1
Electric washing machines	76.2	78.1	78.4	78.3	79.2
Automatic	68.8	74.7	76.2	76.2	77.6
Other	7.4	3.4	2.3	2.1	1.6
Cassette or tape recorders	61.0	67.5	74.1	76.6	78.8
Clothes dryers	67.5	72.9	74.4	74.5	76.0
Cable television	62.9	71.4	72.6	74.3	73.4
Freezers	55.9	56.8	57.5	57.7	57.1
Gas barbecues	32.0	45.7	51.4	52.4	53.5
Compact disc players	8.0	15.5	33.6	40.9	47.4
Automatic dishwashers	36.6	41.6	44.6	45.8	47.1
Built in	24.5	31.5	36.5	38.0	39.9
Portable	12.2	10.2	8.1	7.8	7.2
Home computers	10.3	16.2	23.2	25.0	28.8
Modem	..	..	..	8.4	12.1
Camcorders	2.7	5.6	12.2	14.2	14.9

Source: Statistics Canada, *Household Facilities and Equipment Survey*, Catalogue no. 64-202.

6.20 HOUSEHOLD FACILITIES AND EQUIPMENT, CANADA AND THE PROVINCES, 1995

	Canada	Nfld.	P.E.I.	N.S.	N.B.	Que.	Ont.	Man.	Sask.	Alta.	B.C.
						% of households					
Refrigerators	99.7	100.0	98.0	100.0	99.3	99.7	99.5	99.8	100.0	99.6	100.0
One	80.4	92.3	94.0	88.2	92.7	83.8	77.2	73.3	75.8	75.7	82.5
Two or more	19.3	7.7	4.0	12.0	7.0	15.9	22.3	26.5	24.2	23.9	17.6
Radios	98.9	99.0	98.0	98.9	98.6	99.3	98.7	98.8	99.0	98.3	99.1
One	17.9	18.6	14.0	16.2	19.6	22.6	17.0	16.2	16.9	13.7	14.6
Two	25.6	25.3	24.0	25.2	25.9	28.5	24.6	23.9	24.4	21.9	26.0
Three or more	55.4	55.7	60.0	57.4	53.1	48.1	57.1	58.7	57.9	62.7	58.6
Colour televisions	98.5	99.0	98.0	98.6	98.3	98.8	98.6	97.1	98.2	98.8	98.1
One	48.8	42.3	50.0	51.3	51.7	47.6	48.8	45.8	48.8	47.1	52.5
Two or more	49.7	56.7	48.0	47.3	46.2	51.2	49.7	51.1	49.4	51.7	45.6
Telephones	98.5	96.9	96.0	97.5	97.6	98.9	98.7	98.1	97.9	98.5	98.1
One	24.2	22.2	22.0	24.9	28.7	28.6	21.2	26.0	29.6	17.6	25.7
Two	36.9	36.1	44.0	38.1	41.6	38.0	35.2	35.6	41.6	36.2	37.5
Three or more	37.5	38.7	30.0	34.5	27.6	32.3	42.4	36.5	26.8	44.7	34.9
Owned vehicles	83.9	81.4	86.0	82.6	84.6	80.2	83.5	85.4	88.1	90.8	86.3
Automobiles	74.5	67.0	80.0	73.4	75.2	73.1	75.4	76.1	76.6	77.0	73.3
One	52.9	53.1	58.0	57.1	57.7	54.0	51.5	53.0	57.7	52.2	51.5
Two or more	21.7	13.4	22.0	16.2	17.8	19.2	23.8	22.9	19.0	24.8	21.8
Vans and trucks	30.8	37.6	36.0	31.4	37.8	20.6	28.0	37.5	47.3	47.2	39.6
Microwave ovens	83.4	80.4	84.0	84.0	83.2	81.9	83.5	82.6	86.5	88.6	82.3
Video cassette recorders	82.1	83.5	80.0	81.2	81.1	77.7	84.3	79.7	77.9	86.1	84.3
One	66.0	68.6	70.0	66.7	67.8	64.2	67.0	60.6	64.9	66.2	67.5
Two or more	16.1	14.9	8.0	14.6	13.3	13.4	17.3	18.9	13.0	19.9	16.7
Electric washing machines	79.2	90.2	84.0	81.2	84.6	85.6	74.6	80.9	83.9	82.6	72.2
Automatic	77.6	78.4	78.0	76.2	80.8	85.0	73.1	77.6	80.5	81.6	71.8
Other	1.6	11.9	6.0	5.0	3.8	0.6	1.4	3.3	3.4	1.0	0.5
Cassette or tape recorders	78.8	86.1	80.0	81.5	83.2	70.1	79.8	81.1	81.8	85.7	84.6
Clothes dryers	76.0	80.9	74.0	73.7	80.4	81.0	71.7	78.3	82.6	81.9	70.8
Cable television	73.4	82.0	68.0	75.6	69.2	64.2	78.2	66.8	59.0	70.7	85.4
Freezers	57.1	78.4	68.0	61.9	66.8	45.8	57.2	71.8	76.9	67.0	56.9
Gas barbecues	53.5	55.2	58.0	54.9	53.1	45.6	54.9	59.7	63.1	65.7	52.4
Compact disc players	47.4	41.2	38.0	41.2	38.1	44.3	49.0	44.4	39.7	52.4	52.8
Automatic dishwashers	47.1	27.8	34.0	32.8	35.0	48.5	44.6	48.2	48.6	56.8	52.5
Built in	39.9	23.7	30.0	25.5	29.4	42.2	37.6	36.8	38.7	47.4	45.8
Portable	7.2	4.1	4.0	7.3	5.6	6.3	7.0	11.2	9.9	9.4	6.7
Home computers	28.8	19.6	16.0	22.4	19.9	23.5	32.5	24.8	23.4	34.2	32.7
Modem	12.1	7.2	8.0	9.2	8.7	8.4	14.5	8.8	7.8	15.7	14.0
Camcorders	14.9	14.4	8.0	12.3	13.6	11.6	16.8	13.1	14.3	18.0	16.1

Source: Statistics Canada, *Household Facilities and Equipment Survey*, Catalogue no. 64-202.

MILLER BRITTAIN, *LONGSHOREMEN*, NATIONAL GALLERY OF CANADA, OTTAWA

Chapter 7

THE LABOUR FORCE

Laurence Hyde, *Factory*, Glenbow Collection, Calgary

A few decades ago, the last rite of passage for many Canadian men leaving the work force was the company retirement party, complete with the gift of a gold watch or a set of golf clubs.

The party jokes were about the retirees driving their wives crazy hanging around the house. More and more women were entering the paid work force, but many were still full-time homemakers. If employees had any preparation for retirement, it emphasized getting their finances in order and finding a useful hobby.

When those men began work, they may have had some high school education. As expected, they joined firms producing consumer products like cars or refrigerators—places where jobs were plentiful, unions were winning wage increases, and employee benefits were growing. With skill, the workers could climb the company ladder and spend their entire careers with the same employer. Canada's social security net was expanding, and they could depend on financial help during occasional layoffs. They looked ahead to a reasonably secure future when they retired at age 65.

Call our retiree John Doe. Today, John Doe's firm has likely closed, a victim of the recession of the early 1990s. His sons and daughters are mid-career, and his grandchildren are trying to find their first permanent jobs. Both generations face a radically different world: a world where work is often part-time and young people without postsecondary education have trouble getting full-time jobs, middle-aged people leave the work force early, and almost no one expects to have one job for life anymore.

Labour Trends

"There's many more fellows been leaving their homes/ Where the whales make free in the harbour," sang the Canadian singer–songwriter Stan Rogers, lamenting the loss of Newfoundlanders to the West in search of jobs as the fisheries collapsed.

At the end of 1995, Newfoundland was experiencing the nation's highest unemployment rate, at 16.9%. In fact, like an invisible line dissecting the country along the Quebec–Ontario border, all the provinces east of the Ottawa River had unemployment rates above the national figure of 9.4%, and all those to the west were lower. Unemployment was lowest in Saskatchewan at 7.1%.

Overall, Canada has been successful in creating jobs for its people. Most of these jobs are full-time. In late 1995, over 13.5 million Canadians were working—more than 11 million of them full time. Employees earned an average $574.49 a week. In 1994, wages and salaries totalled over $358 billion, up nearly 3% from 1993.

But today, in more than a million Canadian families, at least one person is unemployed. Hundreds of thousands of jobs have vanished. Job growth rebounded in 1994, totalling 382,000 job gains, but slowed in 1995, when only 88,000 jobs were created, almost all of them part-time.

Where we work and how we work is changing dramatically. For one thing, jobs can quickly move elsewhere these days due to the increasing globalization of the economy, deregulated trading, lower tariff barriers, and the greater mobility of capital. Some labour market experts talk about our "structural unemployment": a long term level of joblessness that can't be explained simply by the ups and downs of business cycles.

Manufacturing, which has traditionally supplied many well-paid Canadian jobs, has lost ground to the growing service sector. Restructuring and downsizing are affecting the public sector as well as private business, and technological changes are requiring new and updated skills from those who remain.

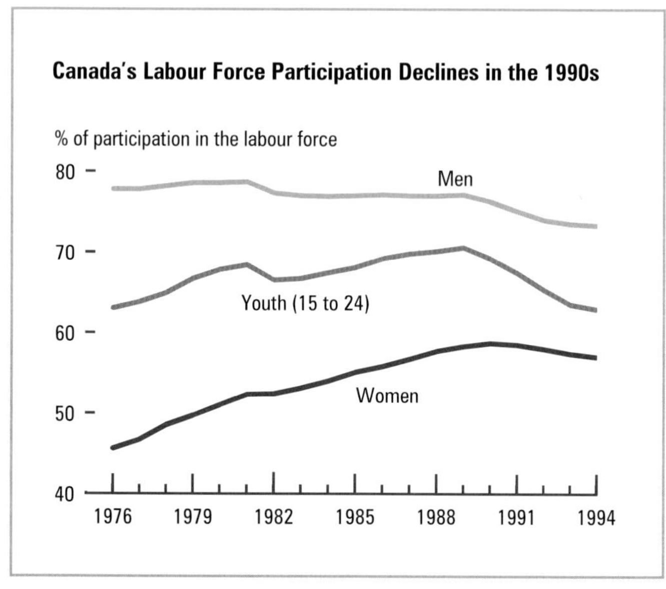

Few Canadians are sheltered from the winds of job loss and job change, but the current trends in the labour market have markedly different effects on Canadians: the young, the middle-aged, older workers, men and women, and different sectors of the work force. Doors close for some, doors open for others. And many enterprising Canadians are forging solutions to their employment problems by creating their own opportunities.

A contemporary wisdom has it that, in predictable times, it's useful to be smart, but when times are unpredictable, it's best to be adaptive. In this era of massive job change, Canadians are profoundly affected, and their creative adaptations are helping reshape the nature of work and the work force.

The Growth of Services

In 1994, there were 3.5 million more jobs in Canada than in 1976. This growth was overwhelmingly dominated by services, where the number of jobs skyrocketed 55%, compared with a mere 2% growth in the goods-producing sector. That meant that, by 1994, 73% (9.7 million) of all jobs in the Canadian economy were in the service industries, compared with 64% in 1976.

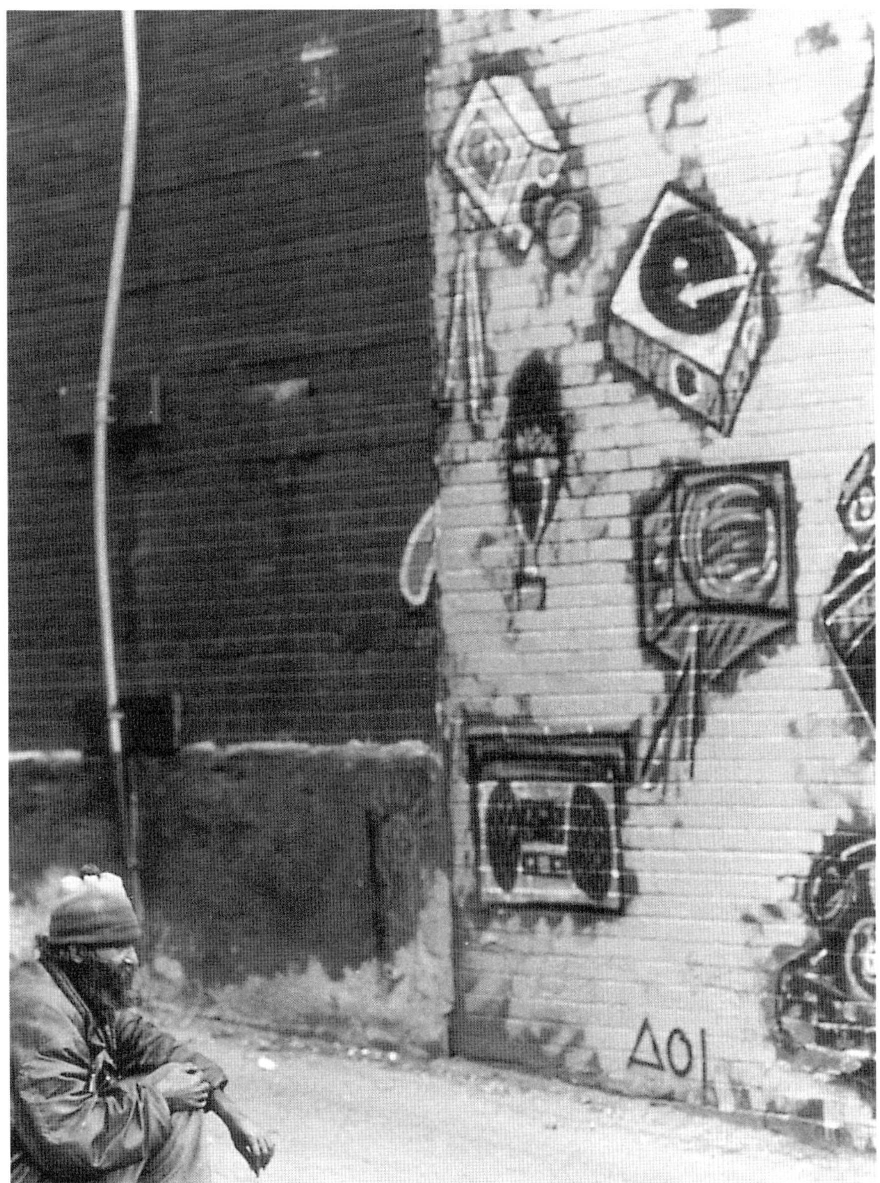

Photo by Jeffrey M. Thomas

Kensington Market, Toronto, Ontario. From the series ***Exploring Metropolis***.

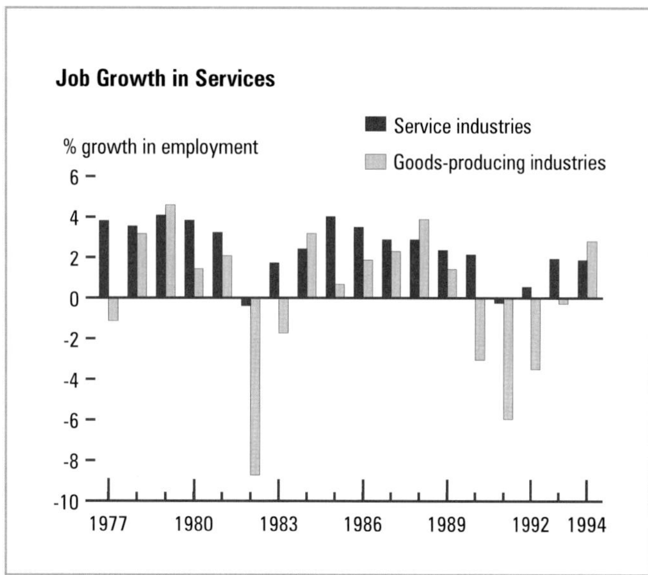

Service areas that experienced especially strong growth between 1984 and 1994 included computer and related services, employment and personnel, architecture, engineering and other technical services. In recent years, other services have expanded including travel, vehicle rental leasing and funeral services. Consultants, personnel agencies, and computer experts have been contracting out parts of their business. The growth in travel and vehicle rental leasing services demonstrates the interest in tourism shown by Canadians and out-of-country visitors.

Goods producers include agriculture, fishing and hunting, forestry, mining, manufacturing, construction, and utilities. In 1995, they collectively employed 3.7 million Canadians in an average week. The traditional source of many full-time, well-paying jobs, this sector suffered strong, sustained declines in the recessions of the 1980s and 1990s and has only partially recovered since then.

Today's Occupations

From the 1950s on, white-collar and professional job growth intensified, as governments, health care institutions, social services, and the education system expanded. John Doe's children found work in these organizations, which employed 3.1 million Canadians in 1995. Since 1976, managerial and administrative positions have had the fastest rate of growth. But total public sector employment peaked in 1992 and, since then, has declined at increasing rates each year.

Average earnings vary greatly from occupation to occupation. One of the goods-producing industries, crude petroleum and natural gas, provided the highest average weekly pay in Canada in late 1995—$1,200. At the opposite end of the wage spectrum, workers in food and beverage services earned just $216 a week.

Today, young people prepare for jobs as high-tech suppliers and computer analysts, technicians in cable TV and satellite broadcasting, personal trainers at fitness clubs, all jobs which barely existed 30 years ago.

In recent years, Canadians losing their jobs have found it more difficult to locate other work. Of every 100 unemployed people in 1994, 15 had been without jobs more than a year. Only four years earlier, the average length of unemployment was 17 weeks; by 1994, it had jumped to almost 26 weeks.

The Part-Timers

For most part-timers, it's still a matter of choice: they're taking care of children or are enrolled in school or just don't want full-time jobs. But an increasing number of Canadians are working part time and they're doing so because they can't find full-time employment. Almost half of the 3.5 million jobs created in Canada between 1976 and 1993 were part-time. By 1994, part-time work made up 17% of all Canadian jobs, compared with under 11% in 1976.

The best place to look for a part-time job is the service sector, which accounted for fully 87% of part-time work in 1993. In fact, the industries with the highest proportion of part-time jobs are all in services: accommodation, food and beverages; amusement, recreational, personal and household services; and retail trade. Many of these jobs are low-paying and non-unionized and offer few benefits and little job security.

Your Own Boss

In the 1930s, when agriculture made up a much bigger share of the labour market, one in four Canadian workers was self-employed. With the growth of manufacturing, a decline in self-employment set in. By the 1970s, the trend was clear: only 7% of the labour force was self-employed.

Today, whether by choice or necessity, Canadians are increasingly working for themselves. They're a varied lot—restaurant owners, artists, child-care givers, dentists, trappers. In 1994, the self-employed surpassed 2 million. Again, the growth was almost entirely in the service sector.

Self-employed workers go without many benefits other Canadians take for granted. They don't have access to private pension plans offered by employers. They often can't rely on a dependable paycheque. Running a small business requires a wide range of business skills like financial planning, accounting, marketing, and production inventory.

Despite these challenges, more and more Canadians are taking the risk. The climate of an expanding service sector and the scarcity of other jobs encourage this. In addition, Canada now has a work force that is older and more skilled and therefore ready to take the leap into self-employment. Last, but not least, there is the growing tendency to contract out services.

Men are more likely than women to be self-employed. In 1993, some 18% of male taxfilers reported self-employed income compared with just under 11% of females. But women's self-employment is rising, and there's been a sharp increase in the number of women running small businesses.

The Moonlighters

In the England and Ireland of the 1800s, a moonlighter was someone who perpetrated outrages against people or property as part of a marauding gang late at night. The term took on a more benign cast in the mid-20th century, referring to people with full-time day jobs who held down a second job in the evening. In Canada, moonlighting has skyrocketed in recent years: from 1 in 40 workers in 1977 to 1 in 20 by 1993. Modern moonlighters tend to be highly educated but in financial need: 43% of them earned less than $20,000 in 1992. Young people are most likely to moonlight. It's often the solution for students who need the flexibility of several part-time jobs or for young workers who find it tough to get full-time work. Some 78% of moonlighters have their main jobs in a service industry, most in farming, the arts, recreation, and teaching.

Working "9 to 5"?

At the turn of this century, Canadians typically worked a 60-hour week, and it was spread over six days. By 1960, the week was reduced to 37 to 40 hours over five days, and Canadians got used to having "the weekend" free, while Mondays through Fridays were devoted to the "9-to-5" routine. This reliable pattern of work and rest has had a profound influence on Canadian life. It has helped determine the hours shops are open, the scheduling of TV shows, football games, even bus routes.

Today, fewer Canadians work the traditional week. While the 9-to-5 routine is still the most common, part-time work, multiple job-holding, and longer hours are all changing our work

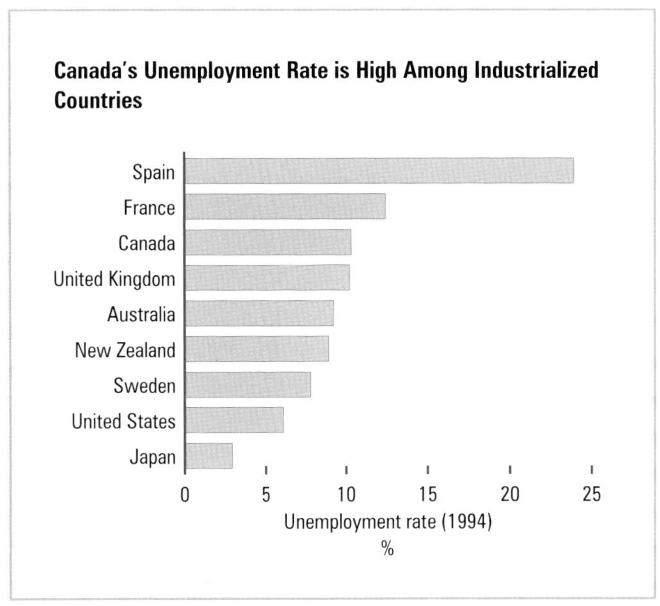

The past 100 years have given the Canadian workplace several new phrases: "part-time worker," "nine-to-five," "forty-hour week" and "workaholic." Another expression, "non-standard work week," has also taken its place among this lexicon of work terms. Today's work week is less standard than any other in our history.

At the turn of the century, Canadian workers generally toiled 10 hours a day, six days a week, and rested from their labours on the Sabbath, usually Sunday. Not until 1960 did the average work week reach 40 hours. This change in work hours was brought about by increased productivity and higher wages. Some predicted that technological improvements would reduce the standard work week even further—but it has remained unchanged for more than 20 years.

Underlying the apparent stability in work hours, however, is a new trend. In 1993, only 61% of all paid workers were working the traditional 35- to 40- hour week. Canada's work force is polarizing: since 1981, a growing proportion of young people and those with less education have shorter work weeks, while older workers and those with higher education are working more than 40 hours a week.

Many people are also choosing to work part time, particularly those with school or family responsibilities. In 1993, 28% of part-timers working chose to do so because of school. Even more, 36%, did not want to work full time or worked part time for reasons related to personal and family responsibilities. However, there has also been growth in the proportion of part-timers who want full-time work but can't find it. In 1993, they accounted for just over a third (35%) of all part-time workers.

Although young people are working fewer hours while they stay in school, many older workers are working longer hours because they stayed in school. Most of these workers are in management or technical fields where workers are highly educated.

Some analysts have argued that firms are reluctant to hire new workers who require disproportionate employer contributions. Once an employee's earnings rise above a certain level, Canada and Quebec Pension Plans, Unemployment Insurance and fringe benefits typically stop increasing. This may encourage firms to use highly-paid employees for longer hours rather than to hire more workers.

Also, some firms may find it cheaper to encourage employees to work longer hours than to hire and train new workers. For some workers, putting in longer hours with paid overtime may be the only way to increase an income. For others, long hours may simply be the requirement that goes with the job.

schedules. By 1993, only 61% of paid workers put in 35- to 40- hour weeks, down from 71% in 1976.

Most of this shift is due to shorter hours, related to the increase in part-time jobs. On the other hand, in 1993, 13% of men and 4% of women worked 50 or more hours per week. The increased disparity in work hours may be due to employers counteracting declining revenues and stiffer competition by restricting hiring, requiring full-time employees to work longer hours, and relying more on seasonal and part-time staff.

The growing number of self-employed Canadians is also a factor: they work much longer hours than employees. In 1991, employees averaged just over 37 hours of work a week, but independent self-employed workers put in nearly 40 hours.

"Last In, First Out"

Young people usually have to line up for their chances in the job market. As the "last in, first out," they are also vulnerable to losing their jobs during an economic downturn. But Canadians aged 15 to 24 face particularly tough challenges today. In late 1995, the unemployment rate for young men who didn't intend to go to school was 18.4%. For young women in the same age group planning not to go to school, it was 24.5%. The rate at which young Canadians participate in the labour force—by either working or looking for work—reached its lowest level in 20 years.

If young people have jobs, they may well be part-time, a fact consistent with the steady rise of youths who are full-time students. In 1995, over 55% of all 15- to 24-year-olds were enrolled in school.

Job prospects for people with only high school education have rarely been poorer. In 1993, a high school-educated man aged 25 to 29 was considerably less likely to be employed and, if employed, to have a year-round, full-time job, than a man with the same qualifications in 1979. If he was employed, he earned 27% less than he would have in 1979.

Wages for Men and Women

In 1994, men were earning more than women. That year, men's average full-year, full-time earnings grew after years of stagnation to $40,717, up 2.9% from 1993. Those for women remained unchanged from 1993 at $28,423. The increase for men was due in part to employment growth in the higher-waged goods-producing industries where men hold most of the jobs. The growth in men's earnings caused women's earnings to drop to 70% of what men earn, down from 72% in 1993.

However, women are having a degree of success. Throughout the 1980s and 1990s, they earned more than half the university degrees: 64% by 1993. Once in the work world, female graduates tend to earn less than their counterparts, but the gap has slowly been diminishing. In 1994, for those with university degrees, female earnings were 72% those of males. For university-educated women who remained single, the gap narrowed to 95%. Women with PhDs earned as much as men with similar qualifications.

Find every family in Canada that has an income of at least $185,000 per year, gather them in one place, and you would have a population the size of Victoria, British Columbia. You would also have the top percentile of Canada's families when ranked by income—73,600 families in 1990.

In Canada, families "at the top" have an average income of $295,000, and together collect nearly 6% of all family income in the country. The average Canadian family, on the other hand, has an income of $51,300. (Statistics Canada defines a "census family" as a married couple or a couple living common law, with or without never-married children, or a lone parent with at least one never-married child living at home.)

Even at the top, however, there are great differences in income levels. Some high-income families in 1990, for example, had incomes several times more than their peers. About 19% of these families had incomes less than $200,000, while some 7% earned $500,000 or more.

"We're not rich. We are merely guardians of wealth," said Eric Molson in 1986, referring to the Molson family fortune. An above-average income is not the only thing that distinguishes families in the top percentile. These families truly do guard their wealth, as Molson pointed out.

The 1991 Census shows that families in the top percentile are twice as likely as all Canadian families to make money through investments. In 1990, high-income families received about $68,000 from investments—close to 10 times the national average of $7,100.

The Canadian financial writer Gordon Pape has defined wealth as "the ability to do whatever I want in life without compromising my standard of living. In other words, comfortable independence." While earning a high income does not necessarily indicate that one is wealthy, it usually indicates that one is independent. Families in the top percentile are four times more likely than average Canadian families to be self-employed.

High-income family members stand out in two other ways. They stay in school longer and they stay at work longer. Among 63% of high-income families, at least one spouse had a university degree. Among all families, less than 19% had a spouse with a degree. Parents in high income families also tend to retire later in life than in other families. Among high-income earners 70 years and older, 59% of the male parents and 24% of the female parents still worked.

Although these Canadian families form a small group, their impact on society is larger than their numbers suggest. A study based on the 1981 Census found that high-income families' savings are frequently an important source of investment and economic activity in the country. Many of the heads of these families are in the legal and medical professions. Indeed, more than a quarter of all earners who were physicians, surgeons and dentists were also in the top percentile of earners.

In 1993, even full-time male workers with university degrees earned little more in real terms than high school graduates did in the late 1970s. Human Resources Development Canada estimates that nearly half (45%) of the new jobs being created in this decade require more than 16 years of education and training.

Working Men

Over the past two decades, unemployment has generally been more severe for women than for men. But Canadian men were hit very hard by the recessions in the 1980s and 1990s largely because of their impact on the goods-producing sector. Men make up three-quarters of all workers in goods industries.

Particularly striking was the loss of full-time, year-round jobs. Between 1989 and 1993, men accounted for over 84% of the decrease in these jobs. Once they lost their jobs, they were also unemployed for longer periods than women: in 1993, men were out of work an average of 27 weeks as opposed to women's 23. In 1994, full-time, year-round jobs increased by 228,000; this was still below 1989 levels. Men accounted for most of the growth.

Even men's earnings have taken a beating: they've been virtually stagnant since 1977, while the earnings of women have climbed steadily since 1986, though suffering a slight decline in 1993.

Working Women

One of the most widely known trends in the labour force over the last several decades has been the increased participation of women. Currently women represent almost half of the work force. Between 1975 and 1993, women were responsible for almost three-quarters of all growth in employment.

Between 1990 and 1995, women's participation in the labour force—which had been rising since the 1950s—levelled off. On the other hand, the participation of men in the labour force levelled off many years ago and then began a long-term decline.

The work women do is changing. They've made inroads into occupations that were once almost the exclusive preserves of men: they're now 26% of all doctors and dentists, and the number of females employed in management is growing. Yet, women remain overwhelmingly concentrated in one-quarter of all occupations; that is, jobs traditionally associated with females like teaching, nursing, clerical work, sales and service.

Slowly, but so far surely, women are also narrowing the gender wage gap, but they have yet to reach parity with men. In 1994, women who were employed full time and all year round earned 70% of what their male counterparts earned, up from 58% in 1967. Earnings for men employed in full-time, year-round jobs averaged $40,717 in 1994, and those of women $28,423.

Single women are leading the way to full pay equality. They now earn almost as much as single men. Those with university educations are virtually on a par with university-educated men.

Retirement

Whether they are pushed out of work by permanent layoffs or enticed into retirement by buyouts and incentive packages, the most striking aspect of the older work force is the rate at which men 55 years and up are leaving it. Middle-aged and older workers have not fared well in recent years. They are more likely to be laid off and tend to have longer periods of unemployment than Canadians under 45. They also have lower earnings and lower levels of formal education than younger workers and are concentrated in the industries hardest hit by restructuring.

The transition from work to retirement is no longer a function of age. Mandatory retirement has been eliminated in many Canadian jurisdictions, making it possible for workers to remain on the job past age 65. At the same time, many

Photo by David Trattles

Carl Rumbolt, Newfoundland fisherman.

Canadians are retiring well before 65, some because of personal choice, others because of changes in the labour market. In 1994, the average retirement age was 61.

People leave the work force early for many reasons, including illness or disability, the need to care for a family member or friend, or simply to stop work and enjoy other pursuits. But in the 1990 to 1992 period, the number of those leaving earlier than they planned, because of layoffs and plant closures, was more than double the figure for 1987 to 1989.

An increased number retired early due to layoffs and plant closures, as well as offers of retirement packages. In both the public and private sectors, enriched severance packages and other retirement incentives have been used to downsize the work force.

Early retirement is more common in households with higher incomes; in fact, the higher the income, the earlier people retire. The availability of an employee pension or retirement benefits also encourages early departures.

In 1994, nearly half of all Canadians who had retired early reported being happy with that choice: they found they were getting more out of life after retirement than they did on the job. Many Canadian workers are preparing themselves for their retirement years by avoiding debts, building up savings and developing hobbies and other interests.

Organized Labour

In 1992, the last year for which comprehensive information is available, labour union membership in Canada fell to under 3.9 million, down slightly from the preceding year and representing just under 35% of Canadian workers. The major cause was a decrease in male union members, triggered by the loss of men's jobs in manufacturing.

But Canada's labour movement is in relatively good health compared with its counterparts in many other countries. The likelihood of any particular type of worker being represented by a union in Canada is about twice that of the United States.

Unions are making some inroads in the parts of the work force experiencing the greatest growth. Female membership has increased in recent years, and in 1992, women made up over 41% of all union members. The service sector accounted for over 37% of unionized employees in 1992, more than four times its share in 1966.

The four unions with the largest memberships in 1992 were the Canadian Union of Public Employees, the Canadian Auto Workers, the United Food and Commercial Workers International Union and the Public Service Alliance of Canada.

Wage settlements have been very restrained in recent years, a result of the continuing high level of unemployment and a relatively low rate of inflation. In 1995, for all collective agreements covering 500 or more employees, wage adjustments averaged just under 1%. Over the past few years, public sector settlements have been primarily responsible for the downward pressure on wage settlements.

Canada's Safety Net

Canada's famed social security system is a hallmark of our nation. It embodies "the values of justice, tolerance and compassion that mark our country," as the federal government pointed out in its 1994 discussion paper on improving social security in Canada.

But our social security arrangements were set up for a very different era. Today, part-time employment, two parents at work, and joblessness of long duration are all more common. We have more self-employed people, more single parents, and a growing proportion of seniors. Populations are aging in most of the industrialized world, but nowhere is the projected increase in the proportion of the population 45 years and older as great as in Canada.

The changes and concerns about government deficits are prompting unprecedented scrutiny of social programs. Canadians debate whether we can afford to maintain our safety net and are concerned about what weakening it will mean to individuals and our deeply held common values. Canadians have already seen a series of erosions in Unemployment

Photo by Lorraine Gilbert

Lucie and Joanne, cooks for a tree-planting camp, Maniwaki, Quebec, 1987.

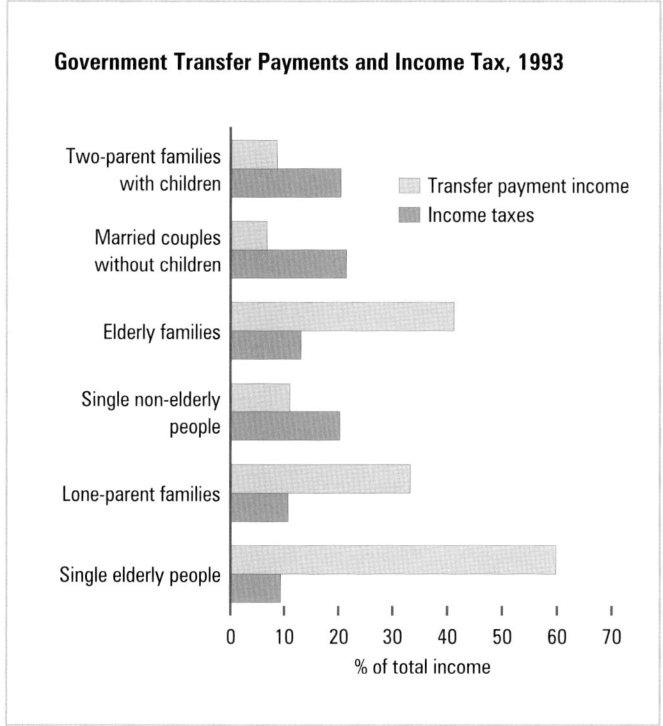

Insurance (UI) benefits. Looking ahead to their retirement years, three-quarters of respondents in a 1995 survey said they lacked confidence that the Canada/Quebec Pension Plans (C/QPP) would provide them with a retirement income.

Worker Rights

Under the Canadian Constitution, labour legislation is primarily a provincial responsibility. The federal government administers labour legislation for canals, railways, telephone and cable systems, air transport, banks, and broadcasting. Provincial or territorial legislation protects most other workers.

Canadian employers are legally required to pay adult workers at least the minimum wage. The federal government sets the minimum for employees in industries under federal jurisdiction. Provincial and territorial wages apply to most other workers. These wages vary widely by province or territory

The New "EI"

Unemployment insurance, the federal government program that Canadians have known for decades as "UI," has now been renamed "Employment Insurance." A number of changes have come with the new name.

The new system has two main parts: it will continue to provide income support but will strengthen the value of work. It will be based on hours worked instead of weeks—a more realistic measurement of the way people work. This will mean that all part-time work will become insurable. Another main feature involves active employment benefits which will help the unemployed get back to work more quickly and will be tailored to meet the needs of individuals and local circumstances.

Other changes will take into account different job market realities across the country such as seasonal work and high unemployment areas. EI will include a new formula for calculating and qualifying for benefits and the Family Income Supplement will provide income protection for claimants with low incomes who are raising families. Repeat claimants could be subject to a 1% to 5% point reduction in benefits and there will be tougher sanctions against fraud to the system.

Young Canadians used to be told to head for the big city if they wanted good jobs. The information revolution has reversed that advice: now the really good high-technology jobs are heading for the smart young people. And increasingly, these highly qualified employees live in Canada's smart cities.

"Smart cities," says the business consultant Nuala Beck, "are cities where an uplink to a satellite matters ten times more than having a divided highway running through town."

According to a 1995 national study by The Globe and Mail ***Report on Business Magazine****, indicators of a smart city include the number of university degrees per person, the degree of corporate research and development spending, the participation rate in continuing education, an advanced telecommunications infrastructure, and the presence of university research parks populated with high-tech spin-off companies.*

High-tech companies in the burgeoning knowledge industries will locate where their best workers prefer to live, and the study indicated that the five urban centres with a clear edge in brainpower were Saskatoon, Halifax, Edmonton, Toronto and Ottawa–Carleton. Runners-up were Calgary, Kitchener–Waterloo, Montreal, Victoria and Fredericton.

Perhaps we should consider UDP (university degrees per person) rather than GDP (gross domestic product) as a measurement of prosperity. In 1994, 13.2% of Canadians had a university degree, but four of the five top cities did better: Ottawa (22.6%), Halifax (16.8%), Toronto (16.6%) and Saskatoon (14.2%).

Although Montreal's UDP of 13.3% was only slightly above the national average, nearly a quarter of all Canadian high-tech research and development spending takes place in the city. Quebecers buy the largest number of books per capita in Canada, and 31.6% are enrolled in continuing education courses.

Industry analysts have noted that apart from the Silicon Valley area of California, very few North American cities are challengers for the kind of infrastructure being developed in Ottawa. In 1995, Ottawa had about 700 high-tech companies employing 36,000, and business leaders were complaining that between 2,000 and 5,000 skilled jobs (mainly in software development and customer support) were difficult to fill.

Saskatoon has attracted more than 700 scientists working in agricultural biotechnology; for example, genetic engineering of crops to increase their resistance to insects and herbicides. At the research park at the University of Saskatchewan, the number of companies working in this area increased from four in 1992 to 25 in 1995.

Nova Scotia's 4,000 researchers are mainly located in Halifax, which has seven degree-granting institutions: more per capita than anywhere else in Canada. With strengths in health care, engineering and oceanography, in 1993, Nova Scotia had three times as many knowledge workers as it had production employees.

and are frequently reviewed and revised. Many workers, especially those who do not work for an hourly wage, earn less than minimum wage. Students, casual workers, fishermen, farmers and babysitters are a few examples.

Canadians are also protected by human rights codes with employment provisions prohibiting discrimination on the basis of various grounds. The federal government's Employment Equity Act, passed in 1986, designated people with disabilities, women, visible minorities and Aboriginal peoples as groups that had been disadvantaged in the labour market. The Act requires employers under federal jurisdiction to file annual reports on the representation, hiring, promotion, and termination of designated group members.

In 1995, new employment equity legislation received royal assent; it extended coverage to the public sector, clarified existing employer obligations and gave the Canadian Human Rights Commission the authority to enforce employer obligations.

Industrial relations legislation in the provinces and territories governs the certification of trade unions and matters related to collective bargaining and labour disputes. Some recent laws have responded to technological changes that affect workers.

In the early 1960s, the first technological change laws dealt with railway "run throughs," so named because of the diesels that replaced steam-driven locomotives and threatened job losses. Today, laws governing technology deal with the effects of computer and information technologies. New Brunswick introduced a measure in 1989, and British Columbia updated its legislation in 1993, following provisions in place since the 1970s in Manitoba and Saskatchewan and in the Canada Labour Code.

The Canada Labour Code deals with industrial relations, occupational safety and health, and labour standards. Along with provincial and territorial regulations, these workplace regulations set minimum health and safety standards for virtually all aspects of the workplace. Under the laws, employers must submit to regular safety inspections and face stiff penalties for breaking the rules. Workers have the right to refuse to work when their health or safety could be endangered.

Minimum employment standards for holidays and overtime pay are established by the Canada Labour Code. Under the Code, the maximum work week is 48 hours, and employees working beyond 40 hours must be paid a minimum of one and one-half times their regular hourly wage. Employers must offer their workers a minimum of two to three weeks of paid vacation each year, based on tenure. Provincial and territorial governments also impose their own employment standards, including compensation for general holidays.

The first workers' compensation program was introduced in Canada just before the First World War to protect workers against wage loss due to injuries in the course of their employment. Today, each province and territory has such a program, administered by a compensation board or commission.

In 1994, the boards and commissions accepted 429,034 claims for injuries and illnesses for compensation, the second lowest level since Statistics Canada began recording such data in 1982. In addition, a total of 724 fatalities were accepted for work-related deaths in 1994.

Legislation also determines how employees must be treated if they are terminated. Employers must give notice of termination, and various federal and provincial laws prohibit termination under certain circumstances and specify severance payments.

Unemployment Insurance

Introduced in 1940, Unemployment Insurance was greatly expanded in 1971, but it has been cut back significantly since then. It provides income insurance in the event of job loss to many Canadians who receive a salary or an hourly wage. Among Canadian income support programs, UI is one of the largest. In 1994, it paid almost $16 billion to some 3.1 million individuals who experienced an interruption in employment income. The program is financed by employees, employers and the federal government.

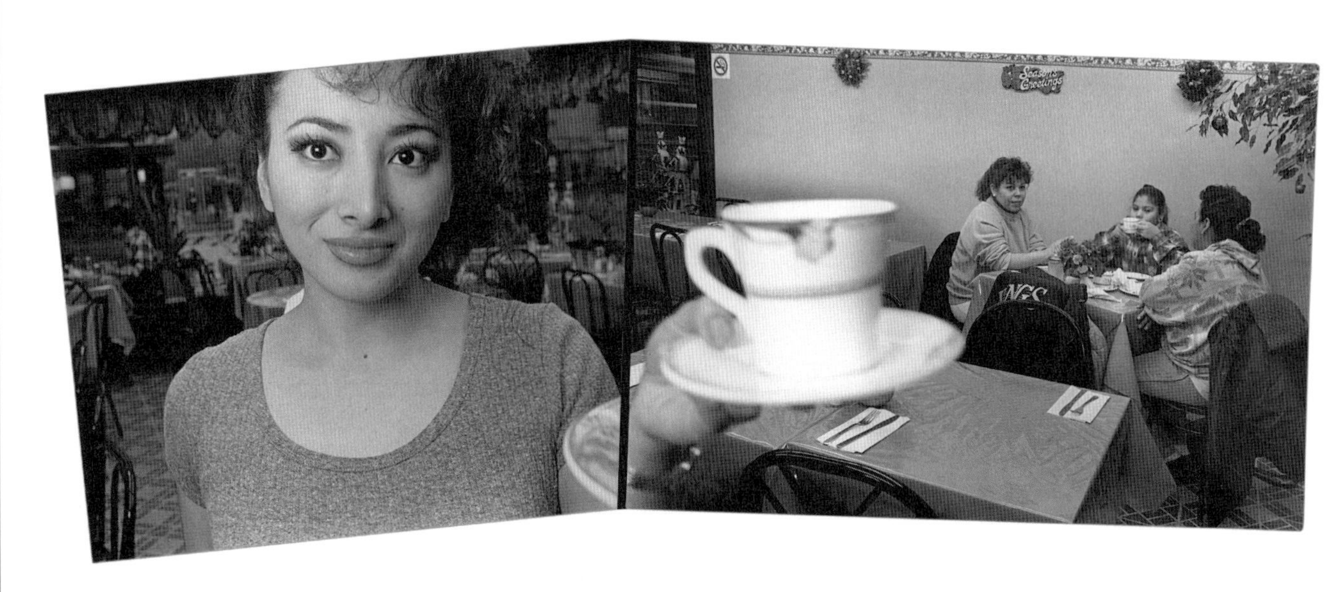

Photo by Susie King

Joanne Kamuza, El Bodegon Restaurant, Toronto.

But the number of people who receive UI has dropped dramatically. Between 1993 and 1994, it fell 14%. In the first half of 1995, UI payments were down 15% from the same time a year earlier, to the lowest amount paid since 1990.

One of the key reasons for the decline is that an increasing number of Canadians have simply exhausted their benefits. They've been unemployed longer than 12 months. In addition, the government has added new restrictions. In 1993, people who quit their jobs without just cause or lost them because of misconduct became ineligible for UI.

In 1994, the minimum number of weeks of work required to obtain insurance benefits rose from 10 to 12. At the same time, the number of weeks a person could receive benefits was reduced, and the benefit rate dropped, except for those with dependents and very low earnings.

Generally, UI benefits are concentrated among the workers of a small number of firms. Some 12% of firms, with only 14% of all jobs, have netted over 38% of all benefits.

In addition to regular benefits, UI claimants may qualify for training, maternity, sickness or fishing benefits.

Protecting Retirees

To support ourselves in old age, Canadians depend on a variable mix of public pensions through the Canada Pension Plan or the Quebec Pension Plan and affiliated benefits, pensions provided by our employers, and such personal savings, investment income and other resources like registered retirement savings plans (RRSPs) as we've been able to accumulate.

There was a time in Canada when post-retirement old age was fraught with much more financial anxiety. Becoming old all too frequently meant becoming poor. One of Canada's major achievements has been the rising income level of its seniors.

Between 1971 and 1985, the incomes of the elderly grew more than did those of the rest of the population. Canada/Quebec Pension Plan benefits, registered retirement plans (RRPs), and investment income were all more widely distributed among the elderly and constituted a larger share of total income.

From the early 1980s to the early 1990s, the portion of the elderly with incomes below Statistics Canada's low income cut-offs declined steadily, though more dramatically and successfully for couples than for unattached individuals, most of whom are women.

The amount any one of us will have available in our retirement years depends on our personal circumstances, including the savings, RRSPs and other assets we've acquired and the benefits to which we are entitled from public pensions and employer plans.

In 1992, the average benefit paid out under C/QPP was $4,360. Payments from the federal Old Age Security (OAS) and Guaranteed Income Supplement (GIS) averaged $5,632. Employer pension plans provided an average $10,494 to those Canadians covered by such plans.

Canada/Quebec Pension Plans

The Canada/Quebec Pension Plans are earnings-related retirement programs. They supply minimum levels of retirement, disability and survivors' benefits for Canada's work force. CPP covers workers outside Quebec and is administered by the federal government. QPP covers Quebec workers and is administered by the Government of Quebec.

In addition to these earnings-related benefits, the federal government provides Old Age Security, a universal benefit for Canadians aged 65 and over meeting minimum residency standards, and Guaranteed Income Supplement and Spouse's Allowance payments to recipients with little or no other income.

In 1993-94, CPP paid out $14.4 billion in total benefits. QPP benefit expenditures totalled $4.2 billion. In March 1994, the two programs provided retirement pensions (by far the largest category of spending in the plans) to some three million Canadians.

CPP and QPP offer virtually full coverage of the working population because the plans are compulsory for most employed and self-employed Canadians between the ages of 18 and 70. The plans are funded through employer, employee and self-employed contributions, plus interest earned on the investment of funds.

To meet the demands of increasing benefit payments, the federal and provincial governments agreed to raise worker and employer contribution rates on a graduated scale starting in 1987. The rate schedule is reviewed every five years. A review was under way in 1996.

Given the aging Canadian population, ensuring that future retirees will have adequate income has become an important concern, particularly when there is growing pressure to reduce government expenditures.

In 1991, government pensions were the main source of income for 66% of Canadians age 65 and older. Even with the recent growth of RRPs and RRSPs, public pensions remain the most universally available source of retirement income. Canadians are asking themselves whether their future public pensions will be eroded as UI benefits have been. Taking no chances, they are putting an increasing amount of money away in RRSPs.

Private Pension Plans

Many Canadians—just under half of the paid work force in January 1993—belong to RRPs. These are employee retirement benefit programs provided by employers or unions in the public and private sectors. The 5.2 million workers participating in these plans in 1993 represented a 12% increase from 1986. In 1991, RRPs were the main source of income for only 18% of Canadians 65 years and older, but they were clearly a growing income source for some.

Unlike C/QPP, however, these plans are not universally available. They are restricted to paid workers having an employer–employee relationship, and as a result are not available to the self-employed in unincorporated businesses, unpaid family workers or the unemployed. Also, because employers are not obliged to provide a pension plan for their employees, not all paid workers are covered. At the beginning of 1994, just under 45% belonged to RRPs.

There are profound disparities in RRP coverage between different income groups. In 1991, only 24% of workers with incomes under $20,000 participated in RRPs, compared with over 80% of those with personal incomes between $40,000 and $59,999. RRPs are also disproportionately concentrated in the public sector. The public sector had only 7% of all RRPs in 1993, but those plans represented almost half of all the covered employees.

Registered Retirement Savings Plans

RRSPs are a growing phenomenon in Canada. The number of contributors and the amount invested are both growing annually at substantial rates. In 1994, Canadians made a record $20.9 billion in contributions to RRSPs, a 9% jump from the preceding year.

SOURCES

Human Resources Development Canada
Statistics Canada

FOR FURTHER READING

Selected publications from Statistics Canada

- **Earnings of Men and Women**. Annual. 13-217
- **Labour Force Information**. Monthly. 71-001
- **Historical Labour Force Statistics**. Annual. 71-201
- **CALURA Labour Unions, Part II: Labour Unions**. Annual. 71-202
- **Labour Force Annual Averages**. Annual. 71-220
- **Employment, Earnings and Hours**. Monthly. 72-002
- **Annual Estimates of Employment, Earnings and Hours**. Annual. 72F0002
- **Unemployment Insurance Statistics**. Monthly. 73-001
- **Unemployment Insurance Statistics**. Annual Supplement. 73-202S
- **Perspective on Labour and Income**. Quarterly. 75-001E
- **Women in the Labour Force**. Occasional. 75-507E
- **The Self Employed. Focus on Canada**. Occasional. 96-316E

Selected publications from other sources

- **Agenda: Jobs and Growth: Improving Social Security in Canada**. Discussion Paper, Human Resources Development Canada. 1994.
- **Basic Facts on Social Security Programs**. Human Resources Development Canada. 1994.
- **Canada Pension Plan; Old Age Security**. Statistical Bulletin. Human Resources Development Canada. 1995.
- **Major Wage Settlements**. Human Resources Development Canada. 1995.

Legend

–	nil or zero	..	not available	x	confidential
--	too small to be expressed	...	not applicable or not appropriate		*(Certain tables may not add due to rounding)*

7.1 LABOUR FORCE, CANADA AND THE PROVINCES, 1995

	Canada	Nfld.	P.E.I.	N.S.	N.B.	Que.	Ont.	Man.	Sask.	Alta.	B.C.
						'000					
Population, 15 years and over											
Both sexes	23,027	455	105	731	598	5,805	8,720	850	749	2,068	2,947
Men	11,303	228	51	354	293	2,839	4,268	417	370	1,032	1,452
Women	11,724	227	54	377	305	2,966	4,453	433	379	1,036	1,495
Labour force											
Both sexes	14,928	242	69	437	354	3,612	5,732	563	494	1,489	1,935
Men	8,198	136	37	241	193	2,009	3,118	309	275	819	1,061
Women	6,730	106	32	196	161	1,603	2,614	255	219	670	874
Employed											
Both sexes	13,506	197	59	384	314	3,204	5,231	521	460	1,373	1,762
Men	7,397	109	31	210	170	1,775	2,844	285	255	755	963
Women	6,109	88	27	174	144	1,430	2,388	236	205	619	799
Unemployed											
Both sexes	1,422	44	10	53	41	408	501	42	34	116	173
Men	801	27	6	30	24	234	274	24	20	65	98
Women	621	17	4	23	17	174	226	18	15	52	76
Not in the labour force											
Both sexes	8,100	214	36	294	244	2,193	2,988	287	255	578	1,012
Men	3,106	92	14	113	99	830	1,149	108	96	213	391
Women	4,994	122	22	181	144	1,363	1,839	179	160	365	621
						%					
Participation rate											
Both sexes	64.8	53.1	65.6	59.8	59.3	62.2	65.7	66.3	66.0	72.0	65.7
Men	72.5	59.7	72.4	68.0	66.0	70.8	73.1	74.1	74.2	79.4	73.0
Women	57.4	46.4	59.1	52.1	52.8	54.1	58.7	58.7	57.9	64.7	58.5
Unemployment rate											
Both sexes	9.5	18.3	14.7	12.1	11.5	11.3	8.7	7.5	6.9	7.8	9.0
Men	9.8	19.8	15.9	12.6	12.3	11.7	8.8	7.6	7.1	7.9	9.2
Women	9.2	16.3	13.3	11.5	10.5	10.8	8.7	7.2	6.7	7.7	8.6
Employment/population ratio											
Both sexes	58.6	43.4	56.0	52.6	52.5	55.2	60.0	61.4	61.4	66.4	59.8
Men	65.4	47.8	60.9	59.4	57.9	62.5	66.6	68.5	68.9	73.1	66.3
Women	52.1	38.9	51.2	46.1	47.2	48.2	53.6	54.5	54.1	59.7	53.4

Source: Statistics Canada, Catalogue no. 71F0004-XCB.

7.2 LABOUR FORCE AND PARTICIPATION RATES

	Labour Force			Participation rates by age group									
				15 years and over		15-24 years		25-44 years		45-64 years		65 years and over	
	Both sexes	Men	Women	Men	Women	Men	Women	Men	Women	Men	Women	Men	Women
	'000			%									
1976	10,530	6,588	3,942	77.8	45.6	68.4	57.5	95.5	54.0	85.6	40.9	16.0	4.2
1977	10,860	6,732	4,128	77.8	46.7	69.3	58.3	95.4	56.3	85.3	41.4	15.6	4.4
1978	11,265	6,891	4,374	78.2	48.5	70.1	59.7	95.6	59.4	85.6	42.5	15.2	4.5
1979	11,630	7,058	4,572	78.6	49.7	71.7	61.7	95.8	60.9	85.4	43.5	15.4	4.2
1980	11,983	7,192	4,790	78.6	51.0	72.3	63.3	95.5	62.9	85.2	44.4	14.8	4.3
1981	12,332	7,322	5,010	78.7	52.3	72.8	64.0	95.5	65.7	84.8	45.2	14.1	4.5
1982	12,398	7,302	5,096	77.3	52.4	69.9	63.1	94.5	66.5	83.6	45.4	14.0	4.3
1983	12,610	7,370	5,240	77.0	53.1	69.8	63.6	94.2	68.0	83.0	46.1	13.1	4.0
1984	12,853	7,453	5,400	76.9	54.0	70.4	64.3	94.2	69.8	81.9	46.5	12.8	4.2
1985	13,123	7,551	5,572	77.0	55.1	70.6	65.5	94.5	71.1	81.4	47.9	12.4	4.3
1986	13,378	7,656	5,721	77.1	55.8	71.9	66.5	94.5	73.3	80.9	47.4	11.8	3.7
1987	13,631	7,737	5,893	77.0	56.7	72.4	67.0	94.4	74.3	80.3	50.0	11.9	3.5
1988	13,900	7,826	6,075	77.0	57.7	72.7	67.3	94.4	75.8	80.0	51.6	11.4	3.8
1989	14,151	7,934	6,217	77.1	58.3	73.4	67.8	94.4	76.8	80.1	52.0	11.0	4.1
1990	14,329	7,970	6,359	76.3	58.7	71.4	67.0	94.0	77.9	79.3	53.4	11.4	3.8
1991	14,408	7,970	6,438	75.1	58.5	69.1	65.5	93.1	77.9	78.3	54.5	11.3	3.5
1992	14,482	7,997	6,485	74.0	58.0	67.0	63.6	92.2	77.0	78.0	55.9	10.9	3.6
1993	14,663	8,078	6,585	73.5	57.9	65.5	61.5	92.2	77.4	77.7	56.8	10.2	3.7
1994	14,832	8,174	6,658	73.3	57.6	65.2	60.6	91.9	77.2	77.7	57.3	11.0	3.5
1995	14,928	8,198	6,730	72.5	57.4	63.9	60.4	91.7	77.3	77.1	57.4	10.1	3.3

Source: Statistics Canada, Catalogue no. 71F0004-XCB.

7.3 WORKERS BY EARNINGS CLASS, 1994

	Canada	Nfld.	P.E.I.	N.S.	N.B.	Que.	Ont.	Man.	Sask.	Alta.	B.C.
	%										
Total	100.0	100.0	100.0	100.0	100.0	100.0	100.0	100.0	100.0	100.0	100.0
Under $5,000	16.2	25.2	22.1	22.4	22.1	15.8	14.8	18.6	20.9	16.5	15.2
$5,000-$9,999	11.8	16.5	18.5	14.3	15.5	12.2	10.8	12.3	13.0	12.0	11.1
$10,000-$14,999	10.0	11.9	13.2	11.7	10.8	10.7	8.7	11.4	11.4	11.8	9.3
$15,000-$19,999	8.6	8.1	10.6	9.6	9.5	9.5	7.7	9.6	10.2	8.4	8.8
$20,000-$24,999	8.8	8.7	8.1	8.1	9.7	9.8	8.7	9.5	9.3	7.8	8.2
$25,000-$29,999	8.3	6.4	9.1	7.3	7.3	9.6	7.8	8.0	7.5	8.3	7.9
$30,000-$34,999	8.2	4.8	4.2	6.4	5.4	7.7	9.2	8.7	6.5	7.2	8.5
$35,000-$39,999	6.4	4.2	4.0	5.7	5.5	6.1	7.2	5.4	5.6	6.5	6.1
$40,000-$44,999	5.3	3.7	3.3	4.0	4.7	4.6	6.0	4.6	4.2	5.6	5.8
$45,000-$49,999	3.7	2.9	1.6	3.4	2.4	3.6	4.1	2.8	3.3	3.2	4.2
$50,000-$59,999	6.0	4.1	2.7	3.5	3.8	5.3	6.8	5.0	3.8	5.7	7.2
$60,000 and over	6.6	3.3	2.3	3.7	3.5	5.1	8.3	3.9	4.3	6.9	7.7
Average earnings ($)	25,750	19,283	17,985	20,782	20,364	24,274	28,240	22,415	21,680	25,092	27,208
Median earnings ($)	21,879	13,490	13,537	15,863	15,861	20,906	24,631	18,984	17,284	20,793	23,460
Number ('000)	15,648	285	76	477	402	3,752	5,910	597	529	1,584	2,037

Source: Statistics Canada, Catalogue no. 13-217.

7.4 LABOUR FORCE CHARACTERISTICS, 1995

	Population	Labour Force[1]	Employment	Unemployment	Not in Labour Force	Participation rate[2]	Unemployment rate[3]	Employment/ population ratio
			'000				%	
Both sexes	23,027	14,928	13,506	1,422	8,100	64.8	9.5	58.6
15-24 years	3,945	2,454	2,072	382	1,491	62.2	15.6	52.5
15-19 years	1,943	947	772	175	996	48.8	18.5	39.7
20-24 years	2,002	1,507	1,300	207	495	75.3	13.7	64.9
25 years and over	19,082	12,473	11,433	1,040	6,609	65.4	8.3	59.9
25-44 years	9,663	8,165	7,438	728	1,498	84.5	8.9	77.0
25-34 years	4,821	4,041	3,647	394	781	83.8	9.7	75.6
35-44 years	4,842	4,124	3,791	334	718	85.2	8.1	78.3
45-64 years	6,103	4,100	3,796	304	2,003	67.2	7.4	62.2
45-54 years	3,628	2,926	2,718	208	702	80.6	7.1	74.9
55-64 years	2,476	1,175	1,078	96	1,301	47.4	8.2	43.6
55-59 years	1,280	772	705	67	507	60.4	8.7	55.1
60-64 years	1,196	402	373	29	794	33.6	7.3	31.2
65 years and over	3,316	208	200	9	3,108	6.3	4.1	6.0
65-69 years	1,098	131	124	7	967	11.9	5.6	11.3
70 years and over	2,218	77	76	1	2,140	3.5	1.5	3.4
55 years and over	5,791	1,383	1,278	105	4,409	23.9	7.6	22.1
Men	11,303	8,198	7,397	801	3,106	72.5	9.8	65.4
15-24 years	2,005	1,282	1,064	218	723	63.9	17.0	53.1
15-19 years	995	490	393	97	505	49.3	19.8	39.5
20-24 years	1,010	792	671	121	218	78.4	15.2	66.5
25 years and over	9,298	6,916	6,332	584	2,383	74.4	8.4	68.1
25-44 years	4,832	4,429	4,025	404	403	91.7	9.1	83.3
25-34 years	2,418	2,202	1,980	222	215	91.1	10.1	81.9
35-44 years	2,414	2,227	2,045	182	188	92.2	8.2	84.7
45-64 years	3,038	2,342	2,168	174	696	77.1	7.4	71.4
45-54 years	1,815	1,622	1,508	114	193	89.4	7.0	83.1
55-64 years	1,222	720	660	60	503	58.9	8.3	54.0
55-59 years	635	461	421	40	174	72.6	8.6	66.3
60-64 years	587	259	239	20	329	44.1	7.7	40.7
65 years and over	1,429	145	140	5	1,284	10.1	3.7	9.8
65-69 years	518	88	84	5	430	17.1	5.1	16.2
70 years and over	911	56	56	1	854	6.2	1.5	6.1
55 years and over	2,651	864	799	65	1,787	32.6	7.5	30.1
Women	11,724	6,730	6,109	621	4,994	57.4	9.2	52.1
15-24 years	1,940	1,173	1,008	165	768	60.4	14.0	51.9
15-19 years	948	457	379	78	491	48.2	17.0	40.0
20-24 years	992	716	629	87	277	72.1	12.1	63.4
25 years and over	9,784	5,558	5,101	457	4,226	56.8	8.2	52.1
25-44 years	4,831	3,736	3,412	324	1,095	77.3	8.7	70.6
25-34 years	2,404	1,838	1,667	172	565	76.5	9.3	69.3
35-44 years	2,428	1,898	1,746	152	530	78.2	8.0	71.9
45-64 years	3,066	1,758	1,629	130	1,307	57.4	7.4	53.1
45-54 years	1,812	1,303	1,210	94	509	71.9	7.2	66.8
55-64 years	1,254	455	419	36	798	36.3	8.0	33.4
55-59 years	645	312	285	27	333	48.3	8.7	44.1
60-64 years	609	144	134	9	465	23.6	6.5	22.0
65 years and over	1,887	63	60	3	1,824	3.3	5.0	3.2
65-69 years	580	43	40	3	538	7.3	6.7	6.8
70 years and over	1,307	21	20	0	1,286	1.6	1.4	1.6
55 years and over	3,140	518	479	40	2,622	16.5	7.6	15.2

1. The labour force is composed of those members of the civilian non-institutional population 15 years of age and over who, during the reference week, were employed or unemployed.
2. The participation rate represents the labour force expressed as a percentage of the population 15 years of age and over. The participation rate for a particular group (age, sex, marital status, etc.) is the labour force in that group expressed as a percentage of the population for that group.
3. The unemployment rate represents the number of unemployed persons expressed as a percentage of the labour force. The unemployment rate for a particular group (age, sex, marital status, etc.) is the number unemployed in that group expressed as a percentage of the labour force for that group.

Source: Statistics Canada, Catalogue no. 71F0004-XCB.

7.5 PARTICIPATION AND UNEMPLOYMENT RATES, INTERNATIONAL COMPARISONS, 1994

	Canada	United States[1]	Japan	Australia	New Zealand	France	Spain[1]	Sweden[1]	United Kingdom[1 2]
					%				
Participation rate[3]									
Both sexes	76.1	79.0	76.4	73.3	68.9	67.0	61.8	79.3	62.4
15-24	62.9	66.4	47.6	68.4	66.0	30.7	49.1	49.6	71.1
25 and over	79.5	82.1	84.4	74.8	69.9	76.8	65.7	86.0	31.2
Men	83.7	87.0	90.6	84.1	84.6	74.5	78.0	82.2	72.7
15-24	65.2	70.3	48.0	70.7	69.7	33.5	54.7	49.4	76.0
25-54	91.4	91.7	97.5	91.4	92.3	95.1	92.9	89.8	93.4
55-64	60.3	65.5	85.0	60.7	63.0	42.1	56.1	74.7	64.3
65 and over	11.0	16.8	37.6	9.0	9.5	2.8	2.9	14.1	7.4
Women	68.5	71.4	62.1	62.4	53.5	59.6	45.8	76.4	52.8
15-24	60.6	62.5	47.1	65.9	62.2	27.8	43.1	49.9	66.0
25-54	75.7	75.3	65.3	67.4	52.6	76.7	54.3	86.0	73.8
55-64	37.4	48.9	48.1	26.5	36.7	30.1	19.3	62.5	39.7
65 and over	3.5	9.2	15.9	2.3	3.4	1.4	1.4	4.3	3.5
Unemployment rate									
Both sexes	10.3	6.1	2.9	9.2	8.9	12.4	23.9	7.8	10.2
15-24	16.5	12.5	5.5	16.2	15.0	27.5	42.8	16.6	17.3
25 and over	9.1	4.8	2.5	7.3	7.1	10.8	19.6	6.7	8.5
Men	10.7	6.2	2.8	9.4	8.5	10.8	19.5	8.9	12.4
15-24	18.5	13.2	5.6	16.7	15.6	24.2	37.4	18.9	20.8
25-54	9.5	4.9	2.0	7.5	7.0	9.7	16.4	7.9	10.4
55-64	9.5	4.4	4.5	8.8	5.5	7.3	13.3	7.9	13.0
65 and over	--	4.0	1.9	..	2.5	--	1.3	..	4.6
Women	9.8	6.0	3.0	8.8	9.4	14.3	31.4	6.7	7.5
15-24	14.3	11.6	5.3	15.7	14.3	31.6	50.1	14.3	13.2
25-54	9.0	5.0	2.8	6.9	8.2	13.1	28.4	5.8	6.3
55-64	8.4	3.9	1.9	4.3	3.7	6.7	9.8	5.0	6.0
65 and over	--	4.0	0.6	..	1.4	0.7	3.5	..	3.9

1. Estimates are for people aged 16 and older.
2. Data are for 1993.
3. The participation rate for all ages is defined as the total (or civilian) labour force for all ages divided by the total population for ages 15 to 64.

Source: Organisation for Economic Co-operation and Development, *Labour Force Statistics 1973-1993,* Paris, 1995.

7.6 EMPLOYMENT, BY INDUSTRY

	1982	1983	1984	1985	1986	1987	1988	1989	1990	1991	1992	1993	1994	1995
							'000							
All industries	11,035	11,106	11,402	11,742	12,095	12,422	12,819	13,086	13,165	12,916	12,842	13,015	13,292	13,506
Agriculture	479	492	491	481	476	474	451	438	441	457	437	450	425	431
Other primary industries	274	282	298	296	293	296	307	304	298	295	267	260	277	296
Manufacturing	2,010	1,961	2,046	2,064	2,098	2,127	2,214	2,235	2,105	1,956	1,879	1,893	1,949	2,061
Construction	616	585	592	608	652	708	765	809	824	732	717	694	750	724
Transportation, communications and other utilities	916	901	888	918	937	943	951	1,008	995	961	971	961	978	1,033
Trade	1,918	1,920	2,003	2,088	2,176	2,205	2,272	2,293	2,356	2,276	2,267	2,253	2,314	2,307
Finance, insurance and real estate	632	632	662	660	690	732	763	769	790	794	804	810	788	809
Service	3,397	3,525	3,601	3,795	3,943	4,090	4,244	4,351	4,487	4,572	4,621	4,790	4,932	5,036
Public administration	793	807	822	830	829	848	850	879	869	873	879	903	877	810
Goods-producing industries	3,503	3,443	3,553	3,577	3,644	3,728	3,873	3,928	3,809	3,582	3,457	3,448	3,545	3,653
Service-producing industries	7,532	7,662	7,849	8,165	8,451	8,695	8,946	9,158	9,356	9,334	9,385	9,567	9,746	9,852
							% of total employment							
Goods-producing industries	31.7	31.0	31.2	30.5	30.1	30.0	30.2	30.0	28.9	27.7	26.9	26.5	26.7	27
Service-producing industries	68.3	69.0	68.8	69.5	69.9	70.0	69.8	70.0	71.1	72.3	73.1	73.5	73.3	73

Source: Statistics Canada, Catalogue no. 71F0004-XCB.

7.7 DISTRIBUTION OF EMPLOYED PEOPLE BY INDUSTRY AND PROVINCE, 1995

	Nfld.	P.E.I.	N.S.	N.B.	Que.	Ont.	Man.	Sask.	Alta.	B.C.
						%				
All Industries	100.0	100.0	100.0	100.0	100.0	100.0	100.0	100.0	100.0	100.0
Goods-producing industries	22.6	28.1	23.0	25.8	27.7	27.7	26.7	31.2	28.4	23.5
Service-producing industries	77.4	71.9	77.0	74.2	72.3	72.3	73.3	68.8	71.6	76.5
Agriculture	0.6	7.0	2.0	1.9	2.1	2.1	7.5	15.6	7.0	1.6
Other primary industries	8.8	4.9	3.9	4.3	1.4	0.9	1.4	3.1	5.8	3.1
Fishing and trapping	4.9	4.3	1.9	1.5	0.1	–	0.1	–	–	0.3
Logging and forestry	1.1	0.5	0.9	1.7	0.7	0.2	0.2	0.4	0.4	2.1
Mining, quarrying and oil wells	2.9	0.2	–	1.1	0.6	0.6	1.2	2.7	5.4	0.8
Manufacturing	6.6	8.5	11.3	12.7	18.5	18.6	11.9	6.8	8.0	10.9
Construction	5.4	7.0	5.0	5.5	4.5	5.0	4.5	4.6	6.8	7.2
Transportation, communications and other utilities	9.1	6.3	7.8	8.5	7.5	7.3	9.6	8.0	7.7	7.9
Transportation	4.9	3.9	4.3	4.6	4.2	3.5	5.6	4.5	4.6	4.7
Communications	3.0	1.7	2.7	2.5	2.1	2.6	2.8	2.3	2.3	2.4
Trade	17.9	16.7	18.3	18.3	17.3	16.5	16.4	16.9	17.0	18.0
Wholesale trade	4.0	3.1	3.4	4.2	4.5	4.4	4.7	4.7	4.8	5.0
Retail trade	13.9	13.8	14.9	14.1	12.9	12.1	11.7	12.2	12.2	13.0
Finance, insurance and real estate	3.7	3.9	5.3	4.2	5.8	6.7	5.3	5.3	4.7	6.3
Finance and insurance	2.2	2.4	3.3	2.7	4.0	4.7	3.8	3.6	2.8	3.7
Real estate and insurance agencies	1.5	1.5	2.0	1.6	1.8	2.1	1.5	1.7	1.9	2.6
Service	38.9	35.9	37.7	37.2	36.5	37.2	36.5	33.4	38.0	39.4
Business services	3.4	3.4	4.3	3.7	5.8	7.5	4.4	3.5	6.5	7.1
Educational services	9.2	7.2	7.1	7.6	7.0	6.8	6.9	6.9	7.3	6.9
Health and social services	13.5	9.9	11.6	11.7	10.7	9.4	11.0	9.7	8.9	9.3
Accommodation, food and beverage	5.4	7.3	6.3	6.7	5.8	6.0	7.0	6.0	7.1	7.8
Other service industries	7.3	8.0	8.4	7.5	7.2	7.5	7.1	7.3	8.1	8.4
Public administration	9.1	9.9	8.8	7.3	6.3	5.6	6.7	6.3	5.1	5.6

Source: Statistics Canada, Catalogue no. 71F0004-XCB.

7.8 EMPLOYMENT BY DETAILED INDUSTRY AND SEX, 1995

	Number employed			Percentage of total employed		
	Both sexes	Men	Women	Both sexes	Men	Women
	'000			%		
All industries	13,506	7,397	6,109	100.0	100.0	100.0
Goods-producing industries	3,653	2,774	879	27.0	37.5	14.4
Service-producing industries	9,852	4,622	5,230	73.0	62.5	85.6
Agriculture	431	292	138	3.2	4.0	2.3
Other primary industries	296	255	41	2.2	3.4	0.7
Fishing and trapping	33	29	4	0.2	0.4	0.1
Logging and forestry	91	81	10	0.7	1.1	0.2
Mining, quarrying and oil wells	172	145	27	1.3	2.0	0.4
Manufacturing	2,061	1,477	584	15.3	20.0	9.6
Construction	724	642	82	5.4	8.7	1.3
Transportation, communications and other utilities	1,033	765	268	7.6	10.3	4.4
Transportation and storage	561	455	107	4.2	6.1	1.7
Communications	329	202	127	2.4	2.7	2.1
Other utilities	142	108	34	1.1	1.5	0.6
Trade	2,307	1,271	1,036	17.1	17.2	17.0
Wholesale trade	608	434	174	4.5	5.9	2.9
Retail trade	1,699	837	862	12.6	11.3	14.1
Finance, insurance and real estate	809	330	479	6.0	4.5	7.8
Finance and insurance	541	182	359	4.0	2.5	5.9
Real estate and insurance agencies	268	148	120	2.0	2.0	2.0
Services	5,036	1,911	3,126	37.3	25.8	51.2
Business services	867	479	388	6.4	6.5	6.4
Educational services	944	358	585	7.0	4.8	9.6
Health and social services	1,340	275	1,065	9.9	3.7	17.4
Accommodation, food and beverage industries	861	370	491	6.4	5.0	8.0
Other service industries	1,025	429	596	7.6	5.8	9.8
Public administration	810	453	357	6.0	6.1	5.8

Source: Statistics Canada, Catalogue no. 71F0004-XCB.

7.9 FULL-TIME AND PART-TIME EMPLOYMENT

	Both sexes			Men		Women	
	Total	Full-time	Part-time	Full-time	Part-time	Full-time	Part-time
	'000						
1989	13,086	10,918	2,169	6,718	638	4,199	1,530
1990	13,165	10,929	2,236	6,652	668	4,277	1,568
1991	12,916	10,574	2,343	6,389	715	4,185	1,627
1992	12,842	10,467	2,375	6,294	737	4,173	1,638
1993	13,015	10,534	2,480	6,341	786	4,194	1,695
1994	13,292	10,798	2,493	6,511	779	4,287	1,715
1995	13,506	10,997	2,509	6,613	783	4,384	1,725
15-24 years	2,072	1,140	932	646	419	494	514
25-44 years	7,438	6,478	959	3,836	189	2,642	770
45 years and over	3,996	3,378	617	2,131	176	1,247	441

Source: Statistics Canada, Catalogue no. 71F0004-XCB.

7.10 EMPLOYMENT BY OCCUPATION AND SEX, 1995

	Number employed			Percentage of total employed		
	Both sexes	Men	Women	Both sexes	Men	Women
		'000			%	
All occupations	13,506	7,397	6,109	100.0	100.0	100.0
Managerial and other professional occupations	4,449	2,190	2,258	32.9	29.6	37.0
Managerial and administrative	1,901	1,067	834	14.1	14.4	13.7
Other professional	2,548	1,123	1,425	18.9	15.2	23.3
Natural sciences, engineering and mathematics	547	435	112	4.0	5.9	1.8
Social sciences	297	115	182	2.2	1.6	3.0
Religion	33	26	7	0.2	0.4	0.1
Teaching	647	230	417	4.8	3.1	6.8
Medicine and health	730	153	578	5.4	2.1	9.5
Artistic, literary and recreational	294	165	129	2.2	2.2	2.1
Clerical occupations	1,969	392	1,578	14.6	5.3	25.8
Sales occupations	1,339	721	618	9.9	9.7	10.1
Service occupations	1,846	797	1,048	13.7	10.8	17.2
Primary occupations	606	478	128	4.5	6.5	2.1
Farming, horticultural and animal husbandry	452	333	120	3.3	4.5	2.0
Fishing and trapping	30	27	3	0.2	0.4	0.0
Forestry and logging	65	61	4	0.5	0.8	0.1
Mining and quarrying	59	58	1	0.4	0.8	--
Processing, machining and fabricating, etc.	1,619	1,310	308	12.0	17.7	5.0
Processing	356	275	82	2.6	3.7	1.3
Machining	219	205	14	1.6	2.8	0.2
Fabricating, assembling and repairing	1,043	830	213	7.7	11.2	3.5
Construction trades	689	670	19	5.1	9.1	0.3
Transport equipment operating	520	469	51	3.8	6.3	0.8
Material handling and other crafts	470	369	101	3.5	5.0	1.6
Material handling	308	240	68	2.3	3.2	1.1
Other crafts	162	129	33	1.2	1.7	0.5

Source: Statistics Canada, Catalogue no. 71F0004-XCB.

7.11 LABOUR FORCE BY CLASS OF WORKER AND INDUSTRY, 1995

	All workers	Paid workers total	Private sector			Government	Self-employed unincorporated	Unpaid family workers
			Total	Employees	Self-employed			
					'000			
All industries	13,506	12,067	9,959	9,263	697	2,107	1,382	57
Agriculture	431	184	184	143	41	--	219	28
Non-agriculture	13,075	11,883	9,775	9,120	655	2,107	1,163	29
Other primary industries	296	262	251	236	15	10	33	1
Manufacturing	2,061	2,021	2,014	1,952	62	7	39	2
Construction	724	573	573	475	98	--	147	4
Transportation, communications and other utilities	1,033	964	665	633	32	299	68	1
Trade	2,307	2,089	2,072	1,886	186	17	207	11
Finance, insurance and real estate	809	742	686	651	35	56	67	1
Service	5,036	4,424	3,512	3,284	228	912	604	9
Public administration	810	810	4	4	–	806	–	–

Source: Statistics Canada, Catalogue no. 71F0004-XCB.

7.12 EARNINGS FOR ALL EMPLOYEES[1] BY INDUSTRY

	1984	1985	1986	1987	1988	1989	1990	1991	1992	1993	1994	1995
						Average weekly earnings $						
All industries[2]	398.10	412.02	424.25	440.26	459.75	483.31	505.14	528.60	547.01	556.76	567.11	572.49
Goods-producing industries	490.86	511.29	523.49	544.65	569.01	597.41	629.44	657.60	680.70	693.99	709.87	720.62
Logging and forestry	515.93	519.84	539.60	568.45	584.13	626.06	643.46	679.83	697.27	709.99	730.83	732.50
Mining	634.11	661.68	687.38	703.16	762.60	806.66	849.63	893.99	934.52	946.41	972.67	1,013.75
Crude petroleum and natural gas	775.38	834.10	847.98	873.20	919.80	986.20	1,043.34	1,110.13	1,098.68	1,148.77	1,165.58	1,202.52
Quarries and sand pits	544.51	538.86	519.85	548.85	579.58	601.68	621.74	650.78	672.02	640.86	669.64	724.13
Manufacturing	466.37	486.65	500.09	521.31	543.69	570.18	598.97	624.39	652.54	668.95	685.07	693.91
Non-durable goods	444.67	463.92	479.12	495.29	517.89	545.30	571.27	597.31	619.47	631.49	640.36	650.08
Durable goods	486.10	506.91	518.87	544.37	565.80	591.11	623.23	649.04	681.62	702.83	723.38	730.08
Food	403.29	414.12	435.04	450.29	468.93	487.80	512.51	533.62	542.05	560.48	568.74	575.58
Beverages	543.29	555.33	576.62	610.28	633.96	653.48	670.64	690.01	711.56	755.62	769.65	755.81
Tobacco products	593.50	653.09	683.41	735.03	790.48	844.04	891.97	958.03	996.97	1,027.06	1,141.55	1,153.45
Rubber products	451.74	462.40	479.90	506.74	517.28	545.17	581.24	634.12	679.70	689.96	713.30	703.55
Plastic products	410.05	436.94	446.13	454.46	490.04	502.66	528.69	554.61	561.74	562.31	573.53	576.39
Leather and allied products	327.87	342.92	363.31	375.81	386.74	402.87	423.50	403.11	396.01	410.33	420.15	435.75
Primary textiles	397.59	415.55	432.98	452.60	476.76	498.69	522.56	562.08	608.83	631.48	655.56	681.59
Textile products	371.06	384.76	386.93	405.57	413.23	442.63	461.84	466.10	493.30	492.06	462.14	495.66
Clothing	289.29	311.17	318.54	313.16	319.05	342.51	361.44	374.63	378.24	375.24	382.74	397.82
Wood	450.58	468.24	467.44	492.21	502.82	529.03	560.10	577.95	594.90	608.52	619.01	633.74
Furniture and fixtures	374.53	377.32	390.79	408.74	411.26	449.19	463.01	471.71	498.27	509.30	529.47	529.13
Paper and allied products	573.71	604.00	630.06	654.46	683.72	718.20	745.89	795.13	828.16	846.78	871.60	900.98
Printing	426.75	452.48	463.14	481.29	506.20	534.40	555.14	576.52	605.39	618.51	612.83	625.28
Primary metals	589.94	616.18	630.30	665.05	692.51	726.64	758.81	786.82	831.75	864.33	876.10	896.15
Fabricated metal products	453.39	465.87	481.50	516.53	532.76	561.78	589.01	612.09	634.24	632.58	648.22	666.67
Machinery	473.32	498.77	510.08	553.79	574.35	591.90	629.14	647.02	689.32	695.84	721.22	737.18
Transportation equipment	539.04	572.90	592.26	608.04	641.10	656.66	687.60	722.56	760.62	803.52	845.04	849.45
Electrical and electronic products	483.95	505.00	525.75	547.46	570.60	593.68	645.29	675.68	728.80	744.12	753.40	736.66
Non-metallic mineral products	498.12	515.59	541.20	561.39	585.08	611.75	630.53	660.78	695.08	698.31	702.76	719.06
Refined petroleum and coal products	787.87	806.20	805.14	860.90	907.47	957.99	991.00	916.66	877.55	1,055.05	1,090.97	1,108.76
Chemical and chemical products	530.37	559.71	582.99	611.27	639.18	667.49	703.67	728.62	768.49	790.88	810.18	803.28
Construction	486.91	502.33	512.23	535.64	559.42	591.52	622.96	635.38	637.40	639.74	657.87	675.50
Service-producing industries	364.48	375.98	388.23	402.17	419.96	441.98	463.24	488.22	506.92	516.34	524.39	528.31
Transportation and storage	503.91	516.57	530.03	544.53	574.51	590.61	605.48	639.40	652.99	664.25	675.48	689.24
Communications	514.26	530.51	548.71	562.49	566.30	603.00	621.81	654.21	679.60	678.49	683.53	697.42
Utilities	630.93	661.12	684.13	715.43	745.63	769.93	816.94	873.54	905.55	921.10	923.54	937.94
Trade	297.19	307.77	321.58	329.23	342.20	360.42	375.48	391.08	401.16	409.38	422.14	431.66
Wholesale trade	413.67	433.19	456.95	470.13	487.41	516.81	538.75	557.57	579.21	590.93	605.56	622.11
Retail trade	246.01	253.71	264.93	270.26	280.83	292.87	306.86	317.77	320.80	329.65	339.51	342.48
Finance and insurance	424.62	444.96	467.96	500.54	516.21	544.26	566.55	599.19	626.86	668.49	670.14	687.33
Real estate operators and insurance agencies	346.48	362.01	392.06	424.98	488.70	536.55	488.01	483.25	520.44	521.78	556.88	558.97
Business services	361.73	381.50	390.32	412.89	449.24	490.61	533.59	557.60	583.53	586.14	607.24	623.29
Public administration	504.06	524.02	543.20	571.84	592.97	636.52	689.12	701.92	727.64	746.59	752.88	749.83
Educational services	495.53	508.39	522.09	541.25	568.05	586.74	617.45	652.23	679.36	685.03	681.92	680.62
Libraries	297.05	306.49	321.66	346.28	355.98	369.65	378.98	382.61	405.96	422.68	450.63	448.97
Health and social services	334.44	346.82	359.19	375.44	392.39	411.97	435.37	466.91	485.06	498.45	504.63	503.44
Accommodation, food and beverage	172.99	181.67	178.38	188.71	191.89	195.96	206.38	209.49	215.84	217.77	227.19	231.80
Amusement and recreation	249.24	258.03	264.18	276.15	283.18	310.77	336.78	347.77	354.03	357.52	367.26	369.95
Personal services (excluding private households)	208.97	222.43	231.34	240.27	240.78	265.82	287.97	292.68	305.58	309.44	312.53	322.22

1. Excludes owners or partners of unincorporated business, the self-employed, unpaid family workers, persons working outside Canada, military personnel and casual workers for whom a T4 is not required.
2. Excludes agriculture, fishing and trapping, private household services, religious organizations and the military.

Source: Statistics Canada, Catalogue no. 72F002.

7.13 FULL-TIME, FULL-YEAR WORKERS BY EARNINGS CLASS, 1994

	Canada	Nfld.	P.E.I.	N.S.	N.B.	Que.	Ont.	Man.	Sask.	Alta.	B.C.
						%					
Total	100.0	100.0	100.0	100.0	100.0	100.0	100.0	100.0	100.0	100.0	100.0
Under $5,000	2.1	1.9	3.4	2.2	2.5	1.8	1.7	4.0	4.6	3.4	1.3
$5,000-$9,999	3.9	6.3	5.4	5.5	5.1	4.2	3.1	5.3	7.4	4.7	3.4
$10,000-$14,999	7.1	8.7	9.9	8.8	9.1	8.1	5.6	9.2	8.9	9.7	6.0
$15,000-$19,999	8.4	9.9	13.9	11.8	11.8	9.4	7.0	10.6	12.0	7.9	8.5
$20,000-$24,999	10.7	13.9	13.6	12.0	13.0	11.8	10.2	12.1	12.3	9.1	9.6
$25,000-$29,999	11.5	12.1	18.1	12.0	11.9	13.8	10.4	11.5	10.7	11.1	10.4
$30,000-$34,999	12.0	9.0	7.7	10.6	9.5	11.4	13.2	13.2	9.4	10.2	11.9
$35,000-$39,999	9.9	8.8	8.7	10.0	9.8	9.4	10.6	8.3	8.7	9.8	9.4
$40,000-$44,999	8.3	7.7	6.9	7.4	8.7	7.3	8.9	7.1	6.7	8.8	8.9
$45,000-$49,999	6.0	5.8	2.7	6.4	4.5	5.8	6.2	4.5	5.5	5.2	6.9
$50,000-$59,999	9.5	8.9	5.4	6.5	7.4	8.6	10.4	8.0	6.4	9.0	11.3
$60,000 and over	10.6	7.0	4.2	6.7	6.8	8.4	12.7	6.2	7.3	11.2	12.4
Average earnings ($)	35,861	32,377	28,214	32,124	31,551	33,735	38,446	30,850	30,735	34,612	37,680
Median earnings ($)	32,621	28,829	26,067	29,021	28,593	30,415	34,535	28,853	27,233	32,058	34,517
Number ('000)	9,291	126	35	240	201	2,210	3,685	356	304	941	1,193

Source: Statistics Canada, Catalogue no. 13-217.

7.14 PART-TIME AND PART-YEAR WORKERS BY EARNINGS CLASS, 1994

	Canada	Nfld.	P.E.I.	N.S.	N.B.	Que.	Ont.	Man.	Sask.	Alta.	B.C.
						%					
Total	100.0	100.0	100.0	100.0	100.0	100.0	100.0	100.0	100.0	100.0	100.0
Under $2,000	17.7	22.1	15.0	21.5	17.9	16.1	17.4	19.6	22.9	18.8	17.2
$2,000-$2,999	7.4	7.7	7.2	8.6	7.8	7.6	7.7	6.9	8.6	6.4	6.4
$3,000-$3,999	5.9	6.8	9.5	6.7	7.8	5.9	5.5	7.6	6.6	5.4	5.9
$4,000-$4,999	5.9	7.2	6.7	6.0	8.1	6.2	5.8	5.9	5.0	5.1	5.2
$5,000-$6,999	11.4	10.9	15.8	12.0	13.7	11.5	11.7	11.9	9.3	10.8	10.2
$7,000-$9,999	11.9	13.7	14.0	11.2	12.1	12.2	11.8	10.9	11.3	12.0	11.8
$10,000-$11,999	6.5	6.7	8.3	6.2	5.9	6.8	6.2	6.4	6.6	6.9	6.3
$12,000-$14,999	7.7	7.8	7.8	8.4	6.6	7.6	7.7	8.4	8.1	8.0	7.6
$15,000-$19,999	8.9	6.7	7.8	7.3	7.2	9.7	8.9	8.1	7.8	9.2	9.2
$20,000-$24,999	6.1	4.6	3.4	4.1	6.4	7.0	6.1	5.8	5.3	5.9	6.1
$25,000-$29,999	3.5	1.9	1.3	2.5	2.7	3.5	3.4	3.0	3.1	4.3	4.4
$30,000 and over	6.9	3.9	3.1	5.5	3.8	5.8	7.7	5.4	5.5	7.0	9.6
Average earnings ($)	10,970	8,850	9,129	9,304	9,214	10,709	11,335	9,939	9,444	11,158	12,411
Median earnings ($)	7,425	6,148	6,465	6,197	6,217	7,648	7,494	6,664	6,499	7,867	8,280
Number ('000)	6,357	158	41	237	202	1,541	2,225	241	225	643	844

Source: Statistics Canada, Catalogue no. 13-217.

7.15 EARNINGS BY SEX

	All workers			Full-year full-time workers[1]			Other workers		
	Men	Women	Earnings ratio	Men	Women	Earnings ratio	Men	Women	Earnings ratio
	$ Constant 1994		%	$ Constant 1994		%	$ Constant 1994		%
1967	25,230	11,631	46.1	30,405	17,760	58.4	12,617	6,380	50.6
1969	26,948	12,315	45.7	33,166	19,457	58.7	16,485	7,578	46.0
1971	28,926	13,557	46.9	35,953	21,449	59.7	14,197	7,158	50.4
1972	29,989	13,828	46.1	37,222	22,267	59.8	14,224	7,351	51.7
1973	30,537	14,127	46.3	37,922	22,475	59.3	14,389	7,512	52.2
1974	31,242	14,813	47.4	39,430	23,486	59.6	15,387	8,211	53.4
1975	31,983	15,378	48.1	40,438	24,341	60.2	16,061	8,130	50.6
1976	34,077	15,911	46.7	43,294	25,603	59.1	17,039	8,936	52.4
1977	32,332	16,413	50.8	40,198	24,944	62.1	14,951	9,086	60.8
1978	32,196	16,357	50.8	40,900	25,765	63.0	14,772	8,666	58.7
1979	32,053	16,528	51.6	39,683	25,187	63.5	15,549	9,010	57.9
1980[2]	32,094	16,584	51.7	40,391	25,993	64.4	14,455	8,876	61.4
1981	31,323	16,800	53.6	39,639	25,265	63.7	14,842	9,245	62.3
1982	29,847	16,433	55.1	39,198	25,087	64.0	13,682	8,623	63.0
1983	30,031	16,584	55.2	40,050	25,956	64.8	13,031	8,117	62.3
1984	29,474	16,959	57.5	39,032	25,601	65.6	12,946	9,070	70.1
1985	30,177	16,998	56.3	39,132	25,464	65.1	12,510	8,764	70.1
1986	30,597	17,587	57.5	39,329	25,879	65.8	12,922	9,568	74.0
1987	30,877	17,852	57.8	39,808	26,331	66.1	12,816	9,772	76.2
1988	31,653	18,200	57.5	40,394	26,432	65.4	13,009	9,646	74.2
1989	31,721	18,741	59.1	40,146	26,488	66.0	13,697	10,095	73.7
1990	31,339	18,754	59.8	40,297	27,285	67.7	13,795	9,757	70.7
1991	30,474	18,754	61.5	39,992	27,847	69.6	13,129	9,220	70.2
1992	30,375	19,404	63.9	40,383	29,032	71.9	12,506	9,493	75.9
1993	29,754	19,145	64.3	39,572	28,580	72.2	12,424	9,266	74.6
1994	31,087	19,359	62.3	40,717	28,423	69.8	12,449	9,725	78.1

1. "Full-year" is defined as 50 to 52 weeks for data prior to 1981 and 49 to 52 weeks for more recent data.
2. Revised 1991 weights are only present for the years of 1980 to 1994.

Source: Statistics Canada, Catalogue no. 13-217.

7.16 WEEKLY HOURS FOR EMPLOYEES PAID BY THE HOUR, 1995

	Canada	Nfld.	P.E.I.	N.S.	N.B.	Que.	Ont.	Man.	Sask.	Alta.	B.C.	Y.T.	N.W.T.
	Hours												
All industries[1]	30.7	33.4	32.0	31.8	33.3	31.5	31.0	29.9	28.3	30.1	28.9	32.2	31.5
Goods-producing industries	38.4	41.0	41.6	39.3	40.2	38.0	39.5	38.0	36.3	37.8	35.1	38.1	37.4
Logging and forestry	39.6	...	...	...	43.0	41.0	41.1	...	...	36.9	38.1	...	...
Mining, quarrying and oil wells	39.9	39.8	...	44.0	37.4	40.1	42.1	41.7	39.1	37.7	40.7	...	...
Manufacturing	38.5	37.4	37.7	38.1	39.7	38.1	39.6	36.9	36.3	37.9	35.4	...	...
Non-durable goods	37.1	37.2	37.1	37.1	39.3	37.1	37.7	36.1	35.8	36.8	34.6	...	...
Durable goods	39.5	38.0	40.3	39.7	40.3	39.1	40.6	37.6	36.8	38.7	35.9	...	...
Construction	37.2	45.8	45.5	40.9	41.6	36.7	37.9	40.8	35.0	37.8	32.4	38.5	...
Service-producing industries	27.6	30.5	28.8	29.1	30.5	28.6	27.0	27.2	26.4	27.6	26.8	30.1	30.1
Transportation, communications and other utilities	36.8	37.7	38.2	39.2	38.4	36.7	37.8	38.4	34.5	36.1	34.4	36.9	36.6
Trade	27.9	29.1	30.1	28.6	29.4	29.7	26.6	27.1	27.4	27.8	28.1	27.4	29.1
Wholesale trade	35.3	40.5	...	35.2	37.3	36.5	35.2	33.7	34.7	34.7	33.6	...	...
Retail trade	26.0	27.6	28.2	27.4	27.7	27.6	24.4	25.3	25.4	26.0	27.0	...	...
Finance, insurance and real estate	25.8	25.8	...	26.9	26.7	27.2	25.7	20.7	23.6	25.5	24.4	34.2	...
Community, business and personal services	26.4	30.6	26.4	28.5	30.5	27.1	26.2	25.9	25.0	26.7	24.9	29.3	27.1
Business services	29.9	36.8	...	32.8	31.5	31.0	29.4	28.2	27.1	29.1	30.2	...	...
Educational services	34.1	34.8	38.5	30.6	35.8	33.6	34.5	34.0	34.8	35.2	33.5	32.7	...
Health and social services	27.8	31.5	28.2	29.2	33.4	27.4	28.2	28.3	26.4	28.5	25.3	31.9	...
Accommodation, food and beverage services	24.2	28.9	...	27.5	26.5	24.6	23.9	22.2	23.4	24.6	23.4	26.8	...
Miscellaneous services	25.3	29.2	...	27.8	28.0	28.2	23.4	24.2	24.4	26.1	24.2	...	...

1. Excludes agriculture, fishing and trapping, private household services, religious organizations and the military.

Source: Statistics Canada, Catalogue no. 72F0002.

7.17 EFFECTIVE WAGE INCREASES IN NEW COLLECTIVE AGREEMENTS

	1982	1983	1984	1985	1986	1987	1988	1989	1990	1991	1992	1993	1994	1995
	%													
All industries	10.4	4.9	3.6	3.7	3.4	4.0	4.4	5.2	5.8	3.7	2.4	0.7	0.4	0.9
Primary industries	9.3	5.1	3.6	3.2	1.5	3.6	5.8	5.1	5.4	4.6	2.8	1.0	1.1	2.5
Manufacturing	9.5	5.3	3.9	4.3	3.5	4.0	4.9	5.5	5.1	3.7	2.3	1.9	1.9	2.4
Construction	..	8.2	2.1	1.6	2.7	2.5	5.5	7.8	5.7	5.1	3.4	1.5	1.4	1.0
Transportation, communications and utilities	10.5	5.3	4.4	4.2	3.6	4.4	4.3	5.0	5.8	3.5	2.4	0.7	0.2	0.7
Trade, finance, insurance and real estate	11.0	5.6	3.3	3.2	2.6	2.5	3.5	4.4	6.4	3.9	2.5	0.6	0.2	0.7
Service	11.3	3.9	3.2	3.5	3.9	4.1	3.8	5.4	5.8	4.4	2.5	0.8	--	0.5
Public administration	10.5	5.3	4.4	4.2	3.6	4.4	4.3	5.0	5.8	3.5	2.4	0.7	0.2	0.7
Commercial sector	10.2	5.7	3.5	3.6	3.1	3.8	4.7	4.9	5.7	3.9	2.5	0.8	1.2	1.3
Non-commercial sector	10.7	4.5	3.7	3.9	3.6	4.2	4.0	5.3	5.9	3.7	2.4	0.7	-0.2	0.4
Private sector	10.0	5.7	3.3	3.4	3.1	3.8	5.0	5.1	5.6	4.1	2.5	0.9	1.1	1.5
Public sector	10.7	4.7	3.8	3.8	3.7	4.1	3.9	5.2	5.9	3.7	2.4	0.7	0.1	0.6
Federal Public Service Staff Relations Act	9.1	5.6	4.8	3.3	3.6	3.4	3.5	4.2	5.2	3.4	..	–	–	..
Federal Crown corporations	10.4	5.5	4.2	3.8	3.5	3.2	3.0	3.9	4.6	3.6	3.0	2.3	1.8	0.9
Provincial administration	12.0	5.4	4.0	4.1	3.9	4.5	4.2	5.7	6.4	3.2	2.2	0.3	-0.0	0.9
Local administration	11.6	5.6	2.6	4.7	3.4	4.5	4.7	5.3	4.9	4.9	3.2	0.8	0.8	0.6
Education, health and welfare	11.5	3.9	3.1	3.6	3.7	4.1	3.8	5.6	5.8	4.5	2.4	0.8	-0.3	0.4
Telephone, electricity and water	11.6	6.7	3.2	4.0	2.0	2.9	3.5	5.2	5.3	3.1	3.2	1.7	0.7	0.6

Source: Statistics Canada, CANSIM, matrix 4049.

7.18 DAYS OF WORK LOST PER WORKER

	1980	1984	1988	1990	1991	1992	1993	1994	1995
					Days				
Both sexes	8.2	8.7	9.0	9.3	9.3	9.1	9.2	9.1	9.1
15-24 years	7.0	6.9	6.8	7.5	7.5	7.3	7.1	6.7	6.9
25-44 years	8.0	8.6	9.2	9.4	9.4	9.5	9.9	9.5	9.7
45 years and over	9.8	10.6	10.4	10.2	10.0	9.2	8.6	9.3	8.9
Men	7.3	7.3	7.2	7.3	7.0	6.7	6.5	6.3	6.3
Women	9.8	11.2	11.9	12.4	12.7	12.7	13.1	13.2	13.3
All industries	8.2	8.7	9.0	9.3	9.3	9.1	9.2	9.1	9.1
Agriculture	4.3	4.1	5.9	5.8	5.3	5.7	5.1	5.3	6.3
Other primary industries	8.7	9.1	7.9	9.1	9.1	8.7	7.4	6.6	7.5
Manufacturing	9.5	9.9	10.2	10.5	10.5	9.7	9.5	9.6	9.1
Construction	7.4	6.8	8.6	8.4	7.8	6.8	6.6	7.0	7.5
Transportation, communications and other utilities	9.1	9.0	10.5	9.0	9.7	9.1	9.8	9.1	9.4
Trade	6.7	6.4	6.8	7.4	7.4	7.8	7.3	6.8	8.4
Finance, insurance and real estate	7.2	8.0	8.3	9.3	8.4	8.2	8.8	9.7	9.2
Service	7.8	9.2	9.2	9.6	9.8	9.9	10.3	10.2	9.7
Public administration	9.0	10.3	9.5	10.7	10.4	9.9	10.2	10.1	9.9
All occupations	8.2	8.7	9.0	9.3	9.3	9.1	9.2	9.1	9.1
Managerial and administrative	6.3	7.5	7.6	7.9	8.0	7.7	8.4	8.1	8.3
Clerical	8.5	9.6	9.6	10.4	10.7	11.4	11.4	11.4	11.2
Sales	5.6	5.9	6.4	6.8	6.7	7.1	6.2	7.4	7.2
Service	8.5	9.4	9.3	9.8	9.4	9.8	10.2	10.5	9.8
Primary occupations	7.4	7.6	8.0	7.7	7.5	8.3	6.5	6.5	7.6
Processing, machining and fabrication	10.7	10.7	10.9	11.6	11.4	10.6	10.4	10.1	9.8
Construction	8.2	8.8	9.5	9.3	9.1	7.7	7.5	7.9	7.3
Transport equipment operating	10.1	9.5	11.7	9.7	10.3	10.5	10.3	9.0	10.2
Material handling and other crafts	9.6	9.2	11.9	11.1	11.6	9.8	9.3	9.0	10.7

Source: Statistics Canada, Catalogue no. 71F0004XCB.

7.19 TIME LOST IN WORK STOPPAGES

	1982	1983	1984	1985	1986	1987	1988	1989	1990	1991	1992	1993	1994	1995
							'000 person-days							
All industies	5,795.4	4,444.0	3,871.6	3,180.7	7,133.8	3,983.8	5,045.7	3,723.6	5,153.7	2,582.0	2,201.5	1,602.5	1,618.0	1,607.4
Logging and forestry	7.8	13.7	9.6	8.0	2,024.8	2.5	19.5	53.2	0.8	44.4	4.1	1.4	2.3	3.8
Fishing and trapping	–	3.0	–	–	–	–	–	35.6	–	2.0	1.0	–	–	–
Mining, quarrying and oil wells	257.1	178.4	37.2	90.3	351.9	228.7	161.6	186.8	411.2	153.0	275.7	114.5	71.7	24.4
Manufacturing	1,690.5	1,385.4	2,356.0	1,578.0	1,387.0	1,757.8	1,394.9	1,211.3	2,474.2	788.0	910.4	501.2	657.3	722.1
Construction	2,199.6	243.6	212.7	11.2	1,963.4	53.7	632.5	133.9	1,149.9	35.2	151.4	156.7	21.2	202.2
Transportation, communications and other utilities	565.7	275.0	550.1	478.8	305.2	698.7	2,012.2	472.9	399.5	109.6	120.9	65.4	233.8	277.3
Wholesale trade	49.6	24.9	24.4	74.0	28.9	39.7	42.6	43.4	36.0	54.3	10.2	31.6	14.7	11.8
Retail trade	121.7	227.0	163.6	393.8	209.7	286.4	147.1	159.8	134.0	89.8	104.0	208.3	204.5	61.5
Public administration and service	903.4	2,093.0	518.0	546.6	862.9	916.3	636.1	1,427.1	549.0	1,305.9	624.5	524.0	412.9	281.4

Source: Statistics Canada, CANSIM, matrix 28.

7.20 UNIONIZATION RATE,[1] 1992

	Membership			Paid workers			Unionization Rate		
	Both sexes	Men	Women	Both sexes	Men	Women	Both sexes	Men	Women
	'000						%		
All industries	3,802.8	2,216.3	1,586.5	10,889.1	5,803.1	5,085.9	34.9	38.2	31.2
Agriculture	2.4	1.4	1.0	143.1	90.9	52.2	1.6	1.5	1.9
Forestry	28.5	26.8	1.7	53.6	48.7	4.9	53.1	54.9	34.4
Fishing and trapping	7.0	6.1	1.0	13.1	11.2	2.0	53.5	54.4	48.4
Mining, quarrying and oil wells	40.9	39.0	1.9	139.3	119.9	19.4	29.4	32.5	9.9
Metal mines	21.5	20.6	0.9	41.4	39.6	1.8	52.0	52.1	49.8
Mineral fuels	8.2	7.6	0.7	72.9	62.6	10.3	11.3	12.1	6.3
Other mines	11.1	10.8	0.4	25.0	17.7	7.3	44.4	60.7	5.1
Manufacturing	608.1	491.1	117.0	1,727.8	1,235.6	492.2	35.2	39.7	23.8
Food and beverage	101.4	75.4	26.0	230.0	152.8	77.2	44.1	49.3	33.6
Tobacco	2.6	1.6	1.0	7.7	4.8	2.9	34.5	34.1	35.1
Rubber	18.3	14.2	4.1	76.3	52.6	23.7	24.0	27.0	17.2
Leather	3.4	1.4	1.9	14.5	7.2	7.2	23.2	19.9	26.5
Textiles, knitting and clothing	38.8	13.2	25.7	140.4	48.5	91.9	27.7	27.1	27.9
Wood	34.5	31.6	2.9	106.2	92.6	13.6	32.5	34.2	21.2
Furniture	7.4	5.6	1.8	45.8	36.7	9.2	16.2	15.4	19.4
Paper	73.9	66.8	7.0	107.6	93.4	14.2	68.7	71.5	49.6
Printing	29.3	22.0	7.4	151.8	88.3	63.5	19.3	24.9	11.6
Primary metal	54.2	51.8	2.5	89.7	81.5	8.3	60.4	63.5	29.7
Metal fabrication	44.3	41.0	3.3	113.0	99.1	13.9	39.2	41.4	23.6
Machinery	16.8	15.0	1.8	58.2	44.5	13.7	28.9	33.6	13.5
Transportation equipment	97.2	83.9	13.3	240.1	196.7	43.4	40.5	42.7	30.7
Electrical products	32.7	22.2	10.5	135.3	92.3	43.0	24.2	24.0	24.5
Non-metallic mineral products	19.9	17.9	2.0	37.9	31.7	6.2	52.6	56.5	32.8
Petroleum and coal products	5.9	5.6	0.3	14.2	11.8	2.4	41.5	47.4	13.3
Chemicals	16.5	13.7	2.8	92.9	63.9	29.0	17.8	21.5	9.6
Miscellaneous	10.9	8.2	2.7	66.2	37.3	28.9	16.5	21.9	9.5
Construction	336.5	328.1	8.4	516.1	445.5	70.6	65.2	73.6	11.9
Transportation, communications and other utilities	462.2	344.4	117.9	865.1	638.8	226.3	53.4	53.9	52.1
Transportation	222.3	188.7	33.7	444.6	364.3	80.3	50.0	51.8	41.9
Communications	168.9	98.3	70.6	279.0	164.9	114.1	60.5	59.6	61.9
Other utilities	71.0	57.4	13.6	141.4	109.5	31.9	50.2	52.4	42.7
Trade	231.5	141.1	90.4	1,941.6	1,054.2	887.4	11.9	13.4	10.2
Wholesale trade	55.0	45.5	9.5	515.7	365.1	150.5	10.7	12.5	6.3
Retail trade	176.6	95.6	81.0	1,425.9	689.1	736.9	12.4	13.9	11.0
Finance	22.8	5.8	17.1	484.7	154.0	330.7	4.7	3.8	5.2
Real estate operators and insurance agencies	5.6	3.6	1.9	236.3	129.9	106.4	2.4	2.8	1.8
Service industries	1,413.5	465.0	948.5	3,954.9	1,411.1	2,543.8	35.7	33.0	37.3
Business services	24.4	18.9	5.5	581.1	314.4	266.7	4.2	6.0	2.1
Educational services	662.4	262.5	400.0	904.6	345.1	559.5	73.2	76.0	71.5
Health and social services	585.8	108.5	477.3	1,149.8	200.6	949.2	50.9	54.1	50.3
Accommodation, food and beverage	60.8	28.7	32.1	700.1	282.9	417.1	8.7	10.2	7.7
Other services	80.1	46.4	33.7	619.3	268.1	351.2	12.9	17.3	9.6
Public administration	643.8	364.0	279.8	813.2	463.3	349.9	79.2	78.6	80.0

1. Excludes pensioners, unemployed and members in the Territories.

Source: Statistics Canada, Catalogue no. 71-202.

7.21 LABOUR ORGANIZATIONS IN CANADA, BALANCE SHEET, 1992

	Total	International unions	National unions	Government unions
		$ '000		
Assets	4,674,289	3,705,425	762,494	206,370
Cash on hand and in banks	286,583	187,204	76,702	22,677
Accounts receivable and accrued income	189,473	88,680	77,922	22,871
Prepaid expenses and supplies inventory	59,510	51,336	6,423	1,751
Loans and advances	84,021	66,221	7,979	9,821
Investments in Canada	693,942	173,260	416,699	103,983
Foreign investments	2,801,716	2,788,765	12,951	–
Land, buildings and equipment	520,108	312,970	162,433	44,705
Other assets	38,936	36,989	1,385	562
Liabilities	526,746	286,272	175,705	64,769
Accounts payable and accrued liabilities	203,505	113,017	62,800	27,688
Loans payable	76,086	56,547	12,695	6,844
Provision for future liabilities	116,057	25,951	70,832	19,274
Mortgages and other debt	37,761	14,141	14,865	8,755
Other liabilities	93,337	76,616	14,513	2,208
Fund reserves	4,147,543	3,419,153	586,789	141,601
Strike and defence	1,657,152	1,394,746	179,978	82,428
Pension, health and welfare	525,098	516,471	7,518	1,109
Convention	14,711	14,359	202	150
Other	346,944	121,969	221,454	3,521
Unappropriated	1,603,638	1,371,608	177,637	54,393
Total liabilities and fund balances	8,821,832	7,124,578	1,349,283	347,971

Source: Statistics Canada, Catalogue no. 71-202.

7.22 UNEMPLOYMENT INSURANCE AVERAGE MONTHLY BENEFICIARIES

	1985	1986	1987	1988	1989	1990	1991	1992	1993	1994	1995
All benefits	1,145,209.2	1,095,470.8	1,032,967.5	1,014,652.5	1,029,686.7	1,120,811.7	1,365,327.5	1,388,278.3	1,291,914.2	1,114,303.3	956,960.0
Regular	1,019,001.7	972,139.2	909,045.8	883,919.2	888,624.2	962,734.2	1,156,006.7	1,148,107.5	1,073,182.5	895,643.3	736,584.2
Sickness	24,896.7	25,801.7	28,430.0	31,092.5	32,370.8	32,728.3	31,266.7	32,115.8	32,445.0	34,390.8	35,720.0
Maternity	43,370.0	44,294.2	46,029.2	49,399.2	52,504.2	55,820.0	55,528.3	57,917.5	55,708.3	54,236.7	53,535.0
Retirement	2,190.8	1,983.3	1,960.8	1,714.2	1,685.8	1,277.5	–	–	–	–	-
Fishing	15,568.3	15,803.3	14,573.3	14,997.5	17,837.5	16,795.0	17,074.2	15,066.7	12,675.0	11,959.2	10,362.5
Training	24,800.0	23,306.7	22,933.3	22,629.2	24,721.7	27,668.3	34,588.3	71,875.8	64,206.7	68,007.5	68,740.8
Work sharing	7,501.7	5,990.0	4,264.2	4,631.7	5,955.8	17,236.7	36,640.0	23,395.8	11,430.8	4,994.2	3,370.0
Job creation	7,885.8	6,155.8	5,734.2	6,276.7	5,745.8	5,826.7	5,651.7	5,307.5	4,767.5	5,380.0	6,697.5
Adoption	..	..	..	..	332.2	368.3	432.5	312.5	304.2	293.3	342.5
Parental	..	..	..	..	..	2,080.0	28,141.7	33,513.3	32,810.8	32,560.0	32,401.7
Self-employment assistance	..	..	..	..	..	..	..	1,608.0	4,386.7	6,838.3	9,214.2

Source: Statistics Canada, CANSIM, matrix 5705.

7.23 UNEMPLOYMENT INSURANCE AVERAGE WEEKLY PAYMENTS

	1982	1983	1984	1985	1986	1987	1988	1989	1990	1991	1992	1993	1994	1995
								$						
All benefits	141.88	152.72	161.42	171.05	181.07	190.28	202.75	215.88	231.18	243.91	254.72	260.20	258.07	260.14
Regular	143.94	153.91	160.08	169.15	178.81	187.37	199.36	212.78	230.25	244.71	253.20	256.83	252.94	253.86
Sickness	149.24	160.64	171.51	184.12	195.99	207.11	217.01	228.02	239.32	248.46	255.12	255.26	245.49	245.20
Maternity	154.73	169.26	178.53	187.88	197.22	207.59	218.80	232.34	246.21	260.85	272.72	275.58	273.69	274.97
Retirement	173.62	190.00	205.22	219.31	233.94	247.92	261.40	276.24	291.00	...	...	...	...	...
Fishing	162.56	182.11	204.72	224.75	247.85	272.93	298.76	313.28	329.55	346.53	366.88	383.25	375.89	391.81
Training	139.97	152.75	159.31	165.99	177.80	188.40	199.21	211.89	227.87	266.77	275.31	283.00	279.57	274.09
Work sharing	46.84	48.40	54.44	57.35	66.84	68.21	69.72	69.94	74.35	81.55	88.92	89.17	86.27	83.26
Job creation	237.64	244.20	290.49	293.18	302.86	309.52	329.52	347.52	364.96	387.18	396.24	402.15	402.07	406.17
Adoption	...	...	200.26	213.39	230.57	243.83	259.65	275.59	293.77	322.61	330.74	342.12	341.12	348.05
Parental	...	...	...	...	...	...	...	...	269.95	272.43	275.73	282.35	279.20	279.38
Self-employment assistance	...	...	...	...	...	...	...	...	...	...	331.14	338.84	345.45	349.60

Source: Statistics Canada, Catalogue no. 73F0003-XDB.

7.24 LABOUR FORCE[1] AND PAID WORKERS COVERED BY A REGISTERED PENSION PLAN (RPP)[2]

	1983	1985	1987	1989	1991	1993
Both sexes						
Number of RPP members	4,564,623	4,668,381	4,845,107	5,109,363	5,318,090	5,214,647
Percentage of labour force (%)	36.0	35.3	35.3	35.9	36.7	35.4
Percentage of paid workers (%)	45.4	43.9	42.9	42.7	45.4	44.6
Men						
Number of RPP members	3,039,449	3,047,160	3,082,391	3,128,225	3,129,263	2,966,086
Percentage of labour force (%)	40.8	39.9	39.4	39.0	38.9	36.4
Percentage of paid workers (%)	52.4	50.1	48.4	47.0	49.2	46.8
Women						
Number of RPP members	1,525,174	1,621,221	1,762,716	1,981,138	2,188,827	2,248,561
Percentage of labour force (%)	29.1	29.1	29.9	31.8	34.0	34.1
Percentage of paid workers (%)	35.9	35.6	35.8	37.4	40.8	41.9

1. The data used from the Labour Force Survey are annual averages, to which the number of Canadian Forces members was added. The difference between the labour force and paid workers is equal to the sum of unpaid family workers, the self-employed (in unincorporated companies) and the unemployed.
2. Registered pension plans are as of January 1. They are plans established by either employers or unions to provide retirement income to employees.

Source: Statistics Canada, Catalogue no. 74-401.

7.25 CANADA PENSION PLAN AVERAGE MONTHLY BENEFIT PAYMENTS,[1] 1996

	Combined	Retirement	Disability	Child's	Survivor's	Orphan's	Death
				$			
Canada[2]	532	393	657	164	244	164	2,568
Newfoundland	472	337	648	164	242	164	2,331
Prince Edward Island	450	319	612	164	219	164	2,081
Nova Scotia	510	379	638	164	246	164	2,488
New Brunswick	477	350	635	164	238	164	2,365
Quebec	530	356	670	164	261	164	2,516
Ontario	549	412	657	164	248	164	2,648
Manitoba	508	370	654	164	237	164	2,540
Saskatchewan	488	367	660	164	227	164	2,354
Alberta	522	383	665	164	240	164	2,517
British Columbia	531	391	676	164	246	164	2,560
Yukon	560	401	658	164	241	164	1,793
Northwest Territories	527	321	668	164	243	164	2,184
Outside Canada	460	226	620	164	234	164	2,424

1. Does not include benefits paid by the supplementary cheques system or under international agreements on social security.
2. Includes benefits paid outside Canada.

Source: Human Resources Development Canada, *Canada Pension Plan & Old Age Security Statistical Bulletin,* March 1996.

LAWREN S. HARRIS, *ALGOMA HILL*, THE TORONTO HOSPITAL COLLECTION

Chapter 8

ARTS AND LEISURE

Percy J. Robinson, Untitled pen drawing, c. 1919-21

In a 1922 art exhibition, Canada's Group of Seven challenged Canadians to accept a new art and journey away from the conventions of European predecessors. "It is as impossible," they stated, "to depict the autumn pageantry of our northern woods with a lead pencil as it is to bind our young art with the conventions and methods of other climates and other ages."

But the new art created quite a stir in Canadian artistic circles. The Group was accused of having "wasted considerable good pigment" on "rough, splashy, meaningless ... weird landscapes." They were decried for their focus on the rocks, ice and snow of Canada.

Seventy-five years later, however, their paintings illuminate the land and even its soul, reminding us of the wildness and beauty of Canada. In 1995, their vision drew some 70,000 visitors to the National Gallery of Canada's *Group of Seven: Art for a Nation* exhibition.

In Canada, the wish to push beyond the boundaries of the conventional and launch into new, unexplored areas seems to find its analogy in the youngness of the country. In other words, Canadian artists continue to explore and to change, furthering the potential and challenging the confines of history and tradition, just as the Group of Seven did.

Writers like Margaret Atwood, Mordecai Richler, Michel Tremblay and Carol Shields have given Canada a literary geography. Tenors Ben Heppner, Richard Margison and Michael

Schade have added to the voices of Canada. Movie-makers like Denys Arcand, Atom Egoyan and Patricia Rozema have proclaimed a cinema of Canada. Sport has produced its own artists: world champion runners Bruny Surin and Donovan Bailey, figure skaters Elvis Stojko and Jennifer Robinson.

The vitality and vigour of these artists are reflected in many Canadian cultural enterprises. In 1993-94, the Canadian recording industry realized revenues of almost $1 billion. Exports of Canadian television productions and books are strong. Canadian artists are sought after and appreciated. Artists such as Bryan Adams and Celine Dion are household names in many other countries.

Nonetheless, the picture is attenuated by the reality of tough economic times. A long Canadian tradition of public investment in culture appears to be on the wane. Governments have cut funding for cultural activities. The Canadian Broadcasting Corporation (CBC), Canada's national public broadcaster, is in trouble, as it attempts to continue its mandate with less money. The number of national sports organizations eligible for federal support is down. Private radio stations are collectively in the red as are performing arts companies in the not-for-profit sector.

While federal support for culture peaked in 1990, it has been falling ever since. In 1997-98, it will be $2.2 billion, down more than half a billion from 1994-95. As Canada's cultural managers find they can no longer rely on governments for stable support, they are looking more and more to other sectors for survival.

One key target, of course, is the Canadian consumer. Despite the fact that Canadians report having less free time—it's dropped almost an hour a day since 1986 and stands at under five hours per day—we devote much of that time to the arts and to leisure activities. The latest data tell us that, in 1992, in our free time, 81% of us aged 15 and older listened to recorded music, 80% read a magazine, and 71% watched a video. Outside the home, more than half of us visited a heritage institution, 49% went to the movies, and 31% attended a professional sports event.

We appear to be full of energy. Almost one of every two Canadian adults regularly plays hockey, skis or swims. In this country, whose landscape has so moved its artists, it is not surprising that Canadians are inspired by its geography and climate, even in the way we spend our spare time.

Arts Infrastructure

With Canadian involvement in leisure activities so high, culture and sports are significant economic forces. In fact, more than just ways for Canadians to have fun, or to become fit, or to experience artistic pursuits, the arts, culture and sports involve an infrastructure of industry that is far-reaching and highly effective.

For example, printing and publishing are mainstays of our cultural identity. To support these industries, there is a strong production network in place. In 1993-94, we printed almost 10,000 new books and we reprinted a further 7,822 titles, on a wide variety of subjects. In 1991, the publishing and printing industries, including their distribution networks, employed some 73,000 people. These publishers, along with the exclusive agents who control the book publishing industry, together generated total revenues of $1.7 billion in 1993-94.

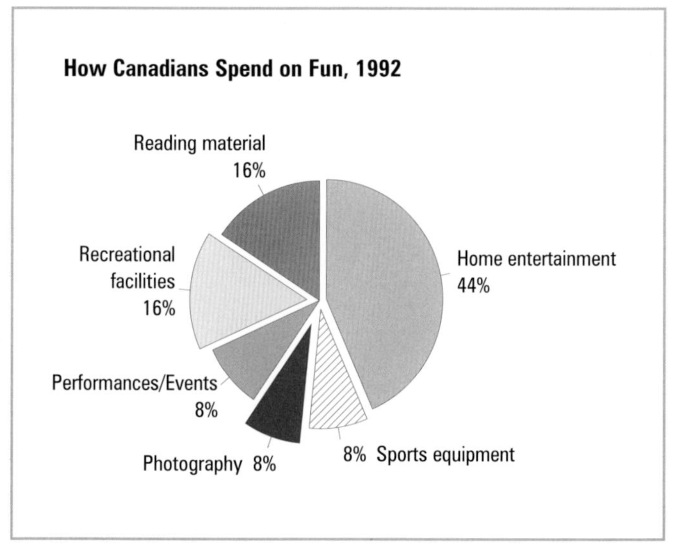

Canada has a very active film production industry. In 1993-94, there were almost 17,000 works produced in Canada—ranging from feature films and television productions to advertisements and educational products. Thanks to a sturdy distribution system, these films are finding their ways into more Canadian homes and theatres. Consequently, in 1993-94, film and video distribution and videocassette wholesaling revenues rose by 9% over the previous year. Television revenues also increased: conventional TV revenues jumped 36% and pay TV revenues soared by 56%. The theatrical market also grew for the first time in four years, with a 15% increase in revenues.

The total activity of all arts and cultural activities is substantial. In 1992-93, they generated revenues in the neighbourhood of $16 billion, or about 2.7% of Gross Domestic Product (GDP). About 670,000 Canadians reported culture-related work (in 1991) as their chief employment; this includes everyone from artists, publishers, and telecommunications carriers, to advertising agencies, museums, and film distributors.

For Canadian families, cultural and recreational activities are a part of the cost of running a household. In 1992, they spent an average $1,600 on culture and recreation, or 4% of average household expenditures. Collectively, Canadians spent about $12.2 billion on cultural pursuits, and another $3.8 billion on recreational goods and services, including sports.

The breakdown can also give a sense of priorities. For example, in 1992, families spent an average of $677 on home entertainment, $248 on newspapers, magazines and books, $386 on sporting activities, including children's camp fees, and $51 on live stage performances.

Public Sector Support

In Canada, there has been a long tradition of public sector support for both cultural and sporting industries. For example, in 1936, the federal government created the Canadian Broadcasting Corporation, in 1939, the National Film Board of Canada (NFB), in 1953, the National Library of Canada, and four years later, the Canada Council, which provides grants to many Canadian artists and artistic organizations.

Aboriginal Achievement

According to Canada's government, "only Canadian culture can express the uniqueness of our country, which is bilingual, multicultural, and deeply influenced by its Aboriginal roots, the North, the oceans, and its own vastness."

Aboriginal Canadians have a long, majestic history of achievement in the arts in Canada. To acknowledge this, the Canadian Native Arts Foundation provides scholarships for training and education in the performing and visual arts to students. Since 1988, over $4 million has been awarded to young people of the highest academic standards across the country.

In addition, the foundation's National Aboriginal Achievement Awards honour Aboriginal Canadians for career achievements and contributions in the areas of sports, business, law, medicine, public service, education and the arts.

Those who have won achievement awards for their artistic contributions include some of Canada's finest artists: Inuit singer-songwriter Susan Aglukark; Haida carver Bill Reid; filmmaker Alanis Obomsawin; award-winning writer Maria Campbell; North of Sixty television star Tom Jackson, inventor Albert Rock (whose creations are used by NASA), and many more.

The first Canadian laugh occurred in 1821. We know this most certainly, for in this year was published Thomas McCulloch's **Letters of Mephibosheth Stepsure**, *the first major work of Canadian humour. McCulloch was a clergyman. Presbyterian. Scottish-born. His other books included* **Popery Condemned by Scripture** *and* **Calvinism**. *McCulloch's humour consisted chiefly in wagging a bony finger at the locals, thereby establishing what Northrop Frye later called "the prevailing tone of Canadian humour."*

Canadians laugh in more than 100 languages, including Canada's two official ones—English and French. Is there a humour that is peculiar to Canada, a truly "Canadian Humour"? John Candy thought so. The Toronto-born comedian once observed: "Wherever you go in the world, you just have to say you're Canadian and people laugh."

But seriously. A trend in Canadian humour did begin in 1912, with the publication of Stephen Leacock's **Sunshine Sketches of a Little Town**. *His style was sardonic, vivid, human. His subject was the foibles of small-town Canada. Today, the Stephen Leacock Medal for Humour, an annual award for the best humorous book published in Canada the previous year, gives Canadian humorists the publicity they need to make a fortune in the U.S.A.*

Francophone Canada does not have a counterpart to the Stephen Leacock Medal for Humour, partly because humour in French Canada is largely an oral tradition. Today's francophone humour also has its roots in a kind of European absurdist streak.

Consider **La Petite Vie** *(meaning a banal or suburban life), the TV series created by Claude Meunier. Pôpa is a nerd in brown polyester slacks whose beard is as fake as Môman's gender. Môman, after all, is an obviously male actor in a shapeless granny dress. Môman simply lives for Pôpa, and in their weird comic world, both sleep standing up in a bed propped against the wall. Their home is decorated in Early Canadian Garage Sale.*

La Petite vie, *says its creator, is really a spoof of an American mentality that has permeated much of Canadian experience. Clearly, this spoof resonates with many Quebecers—a recent episode drew 3,933,000 viewers. And a stage comedy,* **Broue**, *which Meunier co-wrote with several colleagues, is still filling houses 16 years after its first performance.*

Canadian humour is so popular that some of the country's best comics are in the export business. Impersonator André-Philippe Gagnon, for example, who has a repertoire of 300 impressions—from Brian Mulroney to Mick Jagger—produces one show for Quebec, one for North America, and another for Europe.

Canadians have found success in television comedy in the United States for decades. Take Wayne and Shuster (please!). They starred on the **Ed Sullivan Show** *more times than any other act. And they created a taste among Canadians for radio and television sketch comedy that persists today: intellectual, yet often sophomoric, silly yet well-crafted.*

Two of the most popular programs to air on U.S. television in the last 20 years were **Saturday Night Live** *and* **SCTV**—*both comedy shows created by Canadians* *and made popular with Canadian talent. The superb comic and satiric material that became **SCTV**'s trademark was almost entirely written by Canadians who also performed on the show: Eugene Levy, John Candy, Catherine O'Hara, Dave Thomas and Rick Moranis.*

*Next to Stephen Leacock, the Canadian comics best known around the world during the early 1980s were **SCTV**'s McKenzie brothers, two Canadian hicks created by Dave Thomas, Martin Short and Rick Moranis. "Take off, eh, ya hoser?" is still heard at many a late-night boardroom meeting.*

*When Canadians aren't laughing at the McKenzie brothers they are laughing at **Les midis fous**, a francophone radio program that draws more listeners each show than does any other comedy show in Canada. Or they are laughing at **The Royal Canadian Air Farce** or **Double Exposure**, two popular comedy/political satire shows produced by CBC radio, or chuckling through **This Hour has 22 Minutes**, a CBC-TV production.*

*Another laughable radio group is **Les bleu poudre**, a Quebecois comedy team whose members like to phone world leaders and pretend to be Prime Minister Jean Chrétien. Pope John Paul, Queen Elizabeth II and Yasser Arafat have all been hoodwinked by **Les bleu poudre** in recent years.*

But Canada has its fair share of standing jokers, too. Jim Carrey, Yvon Deschamps, Mike MacDonald and Howie Mandel, for example. Howie Mandel: "I ordered a chicken and an egg, 'cause I just wanted to see what would come first."

*All in all, Canada may be the laughing centre of the world. Every year, Montreal hosts the world's largest and most renowned showcase for world-class comedy. Entitled **Juste pour rire** (Just for Laughs), this international bilingual festival features stand-up comics, clowns, novelty acts and others.*

*Quebec comics Daniel Lemire and Michel Courtemanche launched their careers partly because of **Juste pour rire**. Every year, the festival attracts half a million spectators, plus bookers, producers and talent scouts from Europe and across North America. Its international reputation for producing superb humour proves one thing about Canada: our comedians come from good laughing stock.*

Every year, about 900 international-calibre Canadian athletes receive stipends from Sports Canada. Supported as they are, they are free to pursue the highest standards of athletic excellence in an international environment. They compete successfully in international games and earn Canada great distinction in many sporting events.

Today, however, government support both for the arts and for sports has fallen. Grants to artists and cultural organizations have declined, and far fewer sports organizations now receive government funding.

In 1993-94, all three levels of government in Canada spent a combined $5.8 billion on culture. That, however, marked a decline from the previous year, and the first in nine years. Grants to artists and cultural organizations dropped 7%. In 1995-96, only 37 single-sport and multi-sport organizations were eligible for federal contributions. Three years earlier, 88 organizations had received support.

The lion's share of the cultural dollar in Canada is directed to libraries: in 1993-94, they received close to $1.9 billion from the three levels of government. Close behind them was broadcasting, which received over $1.7 billion. Museums, art galleries, and other heritage institutions ranked third at a little more than $850 million. The CBC accounted for over half of all federal cultural spending.

But the story is not simply one of government cutbacks. Neither the arts nor the sports industry has been immune to other larger forces that are affecting many areas of Canadian life. For example, they must also deal with issues such as globalization, increased competition from larger players, and the pace of technological change. Cutbacks and sharply felt market forces have forced organizations to become more streamlined and cost-effective.

Artistic Careers

In Canada, young visual artists, just graduated from art college and starting professional careers, might be surprised to learn that they resemble the emerging work force. Self-employed, running their own small businesses, these people are often well educated and highly motivated, despite meagre financial rewards from their artistic pursuits.

The determination to make a career in the arts is shared by a surprising number of Canadians: since 1981, the cultural labour force has grown 32%, while the total labour force has increased only 15%. In 1991, more than 670,000 Canadians worked in the arts and culture sector. They were far more likely than other Canadians to be self-employed and to hold two or more jobs.

Of the 157,000 artists and cultural workers surveyed by Statistics Canada about their working lives in 1993, nearly 59,000 said they worked primarily as artists. Another 83,000 were administrators, curators, librarians, teachers, or technicians. Almost 30% were self-employed, and an additional 24% were both self-employed and employees. Fully 45% had university degrees, compared with 15% of the Canadian labour force as a whole.

Artists frequently supplement their cultural income with other jobs; in 1993, 40% of cultural workers held two or more distinct jobs. Earnings varied greatly depending on occupation. In 1993, while the mean income for the entire Canadian work force was $30,200, the only artists with higher incomes were directors, producers, choreographers and actors.

Incomes of all other artists ranked below the Canadian average, with visual artists, craftspeople and dancers at the bottom. Painters and sculptors brought in an average of $7,800 from their art. When their other earnings were added, incomes rose, but only to an average of $14,100. At the opposite end of the spectrum, cultural teachers and managers had incomes well above the national average.

Athletic Careers

In 1991, nearly 53,000 Canadians worked in the sports and recreation sector, a 14% increase since 1986. Besides those who play and compete in games, these Canadians select and train athletes, direct athletic programs, officiate at games and competitions, and provide related services. Coaches, trainers and instructors make up the largest number of these workers,

Photo by Paul Martens

***Angels in Architecture*, Royal Winnipeg Ballet.**

at close to 26,000. In 1994, the membership of national sports organizations included about 188,000 coaches and 140,000 officials.

But paid professionals are just part of the team. It has been estimated that 1.5 million Canadians work without pay in sports and recreation, including a vast community of Little League coaches and umpires, Tai Chi instructors, soccer and hockey managers.

Sound Recordings

When Canada's well-known rock group "The Tragically Hip" sings about "the brand new renaissance," it could be describing the Canadian sound recording industry, with its nearly $1 billion in revenues.

In this industry, there are 196 Canadian-owned and 14 foreign-controlled companies, and they are riding an all-time high in sales and profits. Their fastest-growing products are recordings with Canadian content.

In 1993-94, revenues directly related to sound recording earned the industry $861 million, a 41% increase from 1989-90. In the same year, over 6,300 new releases were issued, 719 of them Canadian. Sales of Canadian recordings almost tripled from five years earlier, reaching a record $92.7 million in 1993-94 and making up 13% of all sales.

In recent years, Canadian artists have become international presences in popular music. Canadian mega-stars include k.d. lang, Alanis Morissette, Roch Voisine and Celine Dion. In fact, Dion was recently honoured as the world's top-selling female francophone recording artist. Country singer Michelle Wright has won over 25 major awards for her talent, and new country music sensation Shania Twain has a huge following. Cape Breton Island alone has produced international recording artists Rita MacNeil, the Rankin Family, and the charismatic fiddler Ashley MacIsaac, among others. Canadian rock musicians include the Crash Test Dummies, Barenaked Ladies and Éric Lapointe.

The dominant format for sales is now the compact disc. In 1993-94, Canadians bought over 56 million CDs, four times the number they purchased five years earlier. By 1995, over 47% of Canadian homes had a CD player. Sales of cassette tapes remain high, but they are losing their share to CDs.

In terms of content, it's the rockers who are leading this vigorous industry trend: with a strong youth market, rock music accounted for the largest number of new releases with Canadian content in 1993-94. In fact, in that year, sales of rock eclipsed all other categories, bringing in nearly $402 million.

While the majority of companies in this industry are Canadian-owned, the 14 that are foreign-controlled account for much of the business. In 1993-94, 66% of the new releases came from these companies, and they had 84% of total sales.

The number of full-time jobs in the industry rose 18% from 1989-90 to reach nearly 2,500 in 1993-94. But this counts only regular employment; record contracts are frequently signed with self-employed musicians and musical groups. Close to 12,000 Canadians work as musicians and singers.

Radio Waves

Every day, nearly 123,000 Canadians start their day by listening to local morning programs on Radio-Canada, the French voice of the CBC. The average quarter-hour audience for CBC's "Double Exposure," with its satirical take on Canadian political life, is 401,000 people, aged 12 and up. Whether it's for a quick update on local weather conditions, to hear new music or the latest sports results, or simply to enjoy comforting background sound, the radio is often on in Canadian homes and cars.

Some 55% of Canadian households have three or more radios. From 1982 to 1992, when our spending on other kinds of home entertainment rose dramatically, radio sales actually fell, undoubtedly because most of us already owned one, if not more.

We average about 21 hours of radio listening a week, a figure that closely rivals that top-draw for our attention, the "tube,"

ORCHESTRE SYMPHONIQUE DE MONTRÉAL
Charles Dutoit
directeur artistique

Vittorio Fiorucci, National Archives of Canada, C-116663

Montreal Symphony Orchestra poster.

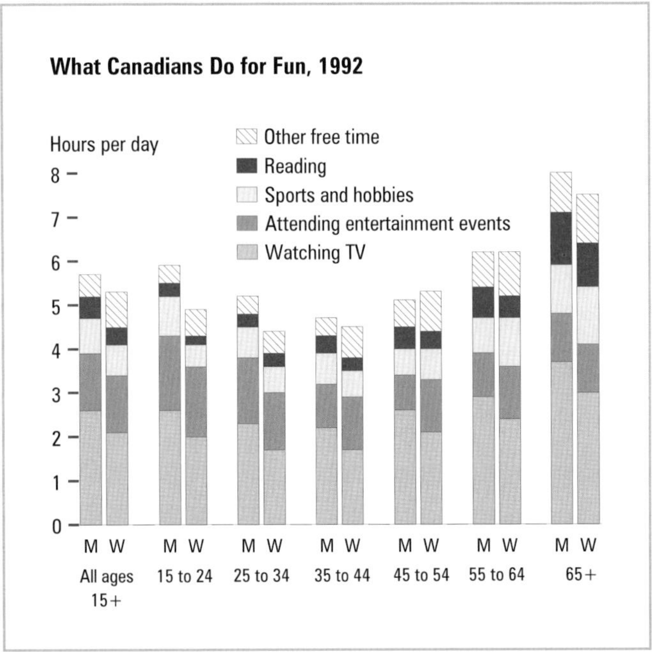

where we clock nearly 23 hours. But while radio was once the focal point for family get-togethers, it has long since shared our attention with a growing number of other home entertainment options.

For radio broadcasters, the results have been dramatic. Private stations (some 484 in 1994) are in financial trouble. In 1994, they lost $28 million collectively, their fifth straight year of losses, though a great improvement over the $50 million shortfall in 1993. Operating expenses were the lowest since 1989, but costs still outran revenues.

A key issue is sales of air time, which account for almost 97% of station revenues. With all the competition from television ads and ad displays like those on buses and hot-air balloons, radio has had to work hard to keep its advertising dollars. Sales of air time amounted to some $740 million in 1994, up somewhat from the previous year, but still below the $764 million of 1990. The number of employees in private radio has dropped steadily, from a high of nearly 11,000 in 1989 to just over 9,000 in 1994.

Another development is the approach of digital radio. Some industry experts think it may give radio a firmer lease on life. The advantage of this new digital technology is that it produces a sound quality rivalling that of the CD.

Rabbit Ears

In September 1952, when the CBC broadcast the first television shows in Canada, there were 146,000 TV sets in the country. By Christmas, 78,000 more had been purchased, despite the extremely high price at the time: $377 for the set plus $100 for the antenna, known as "rabbit ears." Four years later, 27 private and CBC-owned stations had sprung up across the country, all carrying CBC-affiliated programming. Some 50 hours of programming were available every week, almost half Canadian.

Today, there are two or more colour televisions in close to half of all households. As a result of the mushrooming of TV stations after the 1950s, the extensive "cabling" of Canada beginning in the 1960s, and the recent arrival of pay TV and specialty services, we now have a huge number of television choices. Though viewing has been dropping, especially among young people, it still commands our attention 23 hours a week, making it our dominant leisure activity.

The pace of change is relentless in this medium. In 1994, some 7.8 million Canadians subscribed to cable television and more than two-thirds also bought services beyond the basic package; for example, pay TV or specialty channels. Almost 11% of our viewing was devoted to pay TV and specialty services, and another 5% went to playbacks on our VCRs.

In 1994, Canada's 101 private television stations had total operating revenues of nearly $1.5 billion, of which $1.4 billion came from sales of air time. Television stations have not experienced the long decline afflicting radio, but a slow drop in profits over the 1980s culminated in a substantial $70 million loss in 1991. Since then, the industry has pulled itself up by restructuring, and it reported pre-tax profits of $82 million in 1994. In that year, TV stations employed over 8,000 Canadians.

The cable industry has performed well over the past decade. It reported pre-tax profits of $385 million in 1994, compared with only $65 million in 1983. Subscription revenues more than doubled between 1987 and 1994. Over the same period, the number of cable employees rose more than 8% to 9,300.

Remote Control

When Canadians pick up the remote, it's often to watch a foreign program, usually American: "Oprah," "Seinfeld," "Friends" and "America's Funniest Home Videos" have all become household names. Anglophone Canadians watch many more foreign shows than other Canadians, devoting nearly three-quarters of their viewing time in 1994 to foreign fare. Francophones, on the other hand, spent only 36% of viewing time watching non-Canadian programs.

For both anglophones and francophones, news and public affairs rank highest among the Canadian programs watched. In 1994, Canadian comedy and drama took up only 13% of francophone viewing time, and a mere 4% of anglophone viewing.

Our predilection for foreign programs is at the heart of vigorous debate in Canada. To ensure that the broadcasting system provides space for the communication of Canadian stories and values, Canada has regulatory and licensing requirements and supports the CBC as the national public broadcaster.

The role of the federal regulator, the Canadian Radio-television and Telecommunications Commission (CRTC), is to "encourage the development of Canadian expression by providing a wide range of programming that reflects Canadian attitudes, opinions, ideas, values and artistic creativity." Licensed broadcasters must offer a minimum level of Canadian programming.

The CBC

Journalist Jean-V. Dufresne once commented in the *Journal de Montréal*, that "After hockey, CBC-bashing is our most popular national sport." The President of the CBC has noted wryly that all Canadians have two jobs: their own and running the CBC. Certainly Canadians like to debate the issues; for example, the amount of public money the CBC receives, its professional sports telecasts, its American afternoon television shows, and even the hour at which it broadcasts its late-night news.

The CBC lives with uncertainty about its future. Once the dominant force in broadcasting in this country, it has lost some of its audience to the proliferation of other media outlets. Heavily dependent on government support ($951.3 million in 1994-95), it anticipates that it may have $350 million fewer federal dollars by the end of 1997-98. In 1994-95, the CBC's total operating expenses after tax were just over $1.5 billion. Advertising revenues netted nearly $308 million.

For many Canadians, the CBC is the forum for information on national issues and a way of keeping in touch with the farthest reaches of the country. CBC radio is entirely Canadian, and CBC television broadcasts over 83% Canadian content during prime time.

First Nations artist Jane Ash Poitras sums up the views of many Canadians when she says: "I travel in both Canada and the United States, and when I hang out in the States the thing I miss most—the reason I couldn't move there—is that I get homesick for the CBC."

Film and Video

Before the era of television, Canadians thronged in great numbers to their movie theatres—small local cinemas in towns across the country and sumptuous movie palaces in the major cities. But with the advent of TV, attendance plummeted at theatres and drive-ins. Many great urban palaces were turned into multi-screen houses offering more choices, each for a smaller number of viewers.

Between 1988 and 1993, the number of movie theatres dropped from 657 to 581, but the number of screens grew from 1,490 to 1,555. Unprofitable theatres in small towns closed, leaving many with no movie theatre at all. The industry cut full-time staff 36% to 1,305 by 1993-94, and hired more part-time help.

But, in 1993-94, we once again stepped up our movie-going. While we may never match the massive attendance of the 1950s and 1960s (when theatres and drive-ins welcomed 250 million patrons a year), total attendance hit a four-year high of 76.5 million, a 7% increase from the previous year.

Export Boom

In 1993-94, Canadian producers made more than 16,000 films and videos. The film and video industry has experienced unparalleled growth in recent years, and the growth is led by exports. After fluctuating around the $80-million mark in the early 1990s, export revenues rose to $149 million in 1993-94. Made-for-TV productions accounted for over 80% of these revenues.

Canadians are now regarded as leading television animators through the work of firms like Cinar Films Inc. of Montreal, Nelvana Ltd. of Toronto, and Lacewood Studios Ltd. of Ottawa. The "Road to Avonlea" TV series, produced by Sullivan Entertainment, has been sold to more than 120 countries. Films like *The Boys of St. Vincent*, *Louis 19* and *32 Short Films about Glenn Gould* have been international hits.

Several factors help explain the export boom. Canada has signed many co-production agreements with other countries. Canadians and people from other countries are increasingly investing in Canadian productions. Our dollar has been in a relatively favourable position, and the high-quality work of Canadian producers, actors and crews is recognized internationally.

The 16,000 films and videos made in 1993-94 generated almost $734 million in revenue, up 47% from four years earlier. For many years, the most lucrative production area was the non-theatrical sector, which includes advertising and work for educational markets. But this sector's share of revenues has fallen in recent years, while revenues for television and pay TV productions have risen. In 1993-94, productions for television garnered 35% of all revenues.

Canadian films have traditionally had difficulty reaching Canadian movie screens, which are heavily dominated by Hollywood products. In 1993-94, Canadian movies registered a small improvement. Their share of the theatrical market increased from 5% in 1992-93 to 10% in 1993-94, when they brought in $20 million, still a very small part of all revenues.

In 1993-94, full-time employment in production, distribution, and motion picture theatres totalled 6,520. When part-time workers, freelancers, and working proprietors are included, total employment in film production was nearly 15,000 in 1993-94.

On the Net

More Canadians than ever are buying computers and becoming computer-literate. By 1995, almost three in 10 households had computers, and four of every 10 home computers had modems, part of the necessary equipment to plug into the information highway. Canadians use their computers for work and school-related activities, and as another form of entertainment.

Culture organizations are also on "the Net." With CultureNet, a new electronic information network, museums and galleries can download facility floor plans to assist curators planning an exhibit, and music directors can listen to musicians' audio samples. Pioneered by the Faculty of Fine Arts at the University of Calgary, the Canadian Institute for Theatre Technology, and the Canadian Conference of the Arts, CultureNet intends to be an electronic home for Canada's cultural community.

Because the new technologies conquer space, they are particularly useful in a country as vast as Canada. A new virtual art gallery on the Internet, the Arts Alliance of British Columbia, is an example. From Gabriola Island and Nanaimo in British Columbia, it markets the work of accomplished British Columbian artists to the world of Net surfers through the World Wide Web. Interested buyers can view images of works, learn about their creators, and arrange sales. The Canadian Museum of Civilization in Hull is in the process of planning a virtual museum of New France. This world-class project is intended to expand knowledge about New France while making use of the information highway and digital technologies.

Performing Arts

In 1993-94, attendance at performances by Canada's not-for-profit performing arts companies fell, as did the number of performances they gave. Government funding declined, and the organizations reported a collective operating deficit of $3.1 million. These professional companies had greatly increased their fundraising and donation revenues from the previous year. But that gain was not sufficient to stop a deficit of $1.1 million in 1992-93 from growing almost threefold.

The 471 dance, music, theatre and opera companies surveyed in 1993-94 had a total of 13.3 million spectators—the equivalent of six of every 10 Canadians. Collectively, the companies had income of over $383 million. Earned revenue made up 47% of that amount, while government grants provided just over 35%, and fundraising and donations 18%.

Performing arts organizations employ a wide range of talented people. They include directors, choreographers, actors, musicians, dancers, set and costume designers, lighting and sound engineers, and a host of others. Many are hired on a per-production basis. Over 4,000 Canadians are actors, more than 15,000 are producers and directors, and nearly 7,000 are technicians and other skilled workers. Many work freelance for not-for-profit companies and also take gigs on TV and radio, make commercials, work on films, and do stints in commercial theatre.

Festival country

In all the arts, Canada is "festival country." In 1993, the federal government provided financial support to 162 arts festivals in music, dance, theatre, visual arts, film, video, comedy and literature. These festivals had total revenues of nearly $73 million, of which slightly more than a third came from box-office and other sales, a third from the private sector and a third from all three levels of government. One of Canada's largest celebrations is the Festival international de jazz de Montréal, which attracted 1.5 million spectators to 360 shows in 1994. The same year, the Edmonton Fringe Festival drew more than half a million people. British Columbia and the Yukon alone regularly host some 40 festivals.

Our festivals showcase world-class talent. From the Canada Dance Festival to the Festival international de jazz de Montréal, audiences thrill to the exquisite movements of Deepti Gupta, La la la Human Steps, the National Ballet of Canada and more, while other music festivals offer opportunities to hear the Tafelmusik Baroque Orchestra, Nexus, Susan Aglukark, Amici and Quartette and many others.

Publishing

In an article in a British newspaper, Canadian writer Robertson Davies once said, "The acceptance Canadian literature now enjoys all over the world rests simply on the quality of the work—quality and individuality." Works by Canadian writers like Arlette Cousture, Anne Hébert, Alice Munro, Michael Ondaatje, and Robertson Davies have large and enthusiastic followings in Canada and abroad.

Exports of Canadian books have been booming in recent years. This boom has benefited publishers in all regions of

"Theatre is the most human of the arts," wrote British director Mike Alfreds in 1988. "It consists of people watching people becoming other people. This art of transformation is the essence of theatre, what is known as its magic." The magic, with its painted faces and dancing images, is both an enduring part of Canada's artistic landscape and a successful formula for two of its leading theatre festivals—the Stratford and the Shaw.

In 1995, box office sales, for both the Stratford and Shaw festivals, were record-breakers. The Stratford reached almost $19 million and the Shaw topped $9 million, up from $17 million and $8 million the previous year.

Stratford

The Stratford Festival, located in the small Ontario city of Stratford, ranks itself among the three great classical theatres of the English-speaking world (the other two are the Royal Shakespeare Company and the National Theatre of Great Britain). It is the largest classical repertory company in North America, and audience and cast alike come from around the world.

The festival began in 1953, when hometown journalist Tom Patterson decided to open a Shakespearean theatre in a Canadian town named after the playwright's birthplace. From these Shakespearean roots, the Stratford Festival evolved to offer classical and modern plays, everything from **Macbeth** to **Shirley Valentine**.

On-stage, the Stratford Festival has nurtured much Canadian theatrical talent. In recent productions, noted young Canadian actresses Megan Follows (**Anne of Green Gables**) and Sarah Polley (**Road to Avonlea**) have performed, as have theatre veterans such as Christopher Plummer and Albert Millaire. The Stratford has also commissioned or premiered works by well-known Canadian writers, among them Michael Ondaatje, Jean Marc Dalpé and Sharon Pollock.

The Stratford Festival had humble beginnings; the first performance was staged in a large, circus-sized tent. Today the Festival comprises three permanent theatres on the banks of the Avon River. In 1995, during the six-month season, more than 460,000 people visited Stratford. The festival generates an estimated $100 million in spinoffs in the town of Stratford and its surroundings.

Shaw

While Stratford began with Shakespeare, the Shaw Festival has dedicated its existence to playwright George Bernard Shaw. The only theatre company in the world exclusively devoted to the Irish playwright and his contemporaries, it also was one of just two theatres anywhere to receive a Coat of Arms from the College of Heralds in recognition of its work—the other one is the National Theatre of Great Britain.

The Shaw was founded in 1962 when a local lawyer, Brian Doherty, converted part of an old Niagara-on-the-Lake courthouse into a theatre. The festival has since expanded to three theatres within this historic community, not far from Niagara Falls.

The Shaw's theatrical company prides itself on producing plays that explore "the beginning of the modern world"—drama that reflects the speed of change in the world during Shaw's lifetime (1856 to 1950). Its repertoire includes Victorian dramas, mystery and suspense plays, European plays, classic American drama, and, of course, the works of Shaw.

In recent seasons, Canadian actress Jackie Burroughs (**Road to Avonlea**), Tony van Bridge (star of CBC's **The Judge**) and Canadian theatre great William Hutt have all graced the Shaw Festival stages. The 1996 lunchtime theatre series included a work by well-known national broadcaster and producer Patrick Watson.

The Shaw's theatre season lasts seven months—in 1996, that meant 11 productions and 733 performances, and audiences of some 280,000.

the country but is especially strong in Quebec. Foreign sales by Quebec-controlled firms rose from about $9 million in 1989-90 to $76 million in 1993-94.

Despite competition from television and computer media, book publishing is a relatively strong cultural industry. In 1993-94, 316 publishers and 42 exclusive agents reported total revenues of $1.7 billion. The number of books released has increased steadily in recent years; in 1993-94, nearly 9,800 new titles and some 7,800 reprints were issued. As usual, trade books—books for the general public such as mass-market paperbacks, history, biography, fiction, poetry and drama—accounted for most of the new titles.

In 1993-94, foreign-controlled companies made up 11% of the firms in the industry, but they took in 36% of the revenues. Many foreign companies are active in the relatively lucrative educational trade, producing textbooks for school use.

There are other difficulties on the horizon for Canadian publishers. After rising sharply in the early 1990s, government support for book publishing levelled off in 1993-94 . In 1995-96, federal support dropped steeply. The customer base for Canadian publishers has also changed dramatically: public libraries are buying fewer books, while sales to bookstore chains and book clubs are growing. Bookstore mergers and the arrival of mega-book chains have raised concerns about the future of independent bookstores and publisher revenues.

Canadian publishers are entering the multi-media trade. The *Canadian Encyclopedia*, published by McClelland and Stewart, has been transferred to CD-ROM as *The 1996 Canadian Encyclopedia Plus* and now can be much more quickly updated. As any visit to a public library reveals, the book world is embracing the new technologies. In your local library, you're likely to find CD-ROMs containing hundreds of general interest magazines, FreeNet terminals, and computers where you can search for jobs or register a small business.

Full-time employment in book publishing has fallen; in 1993-94, there were about 6,800 employees, down more than 8% from 1989-90. But employees represent only a

The Roaring Girl

*An excerpt from the 1995 Governor General's Literary Award winner, **The Roaring Girl**, by Greg Hollingshead.*

*"IN THE AUTUMN Alex moved to Vancouver and got a job driving a cab, because a woman he had fallen in love with was taking classes at Simon Fraser, but in the spring she grew tired of him and asked him to move out. One day, weeping over some little thing, he answered in his neat hand an ad in the **Province** and ten days later was offered, for a small rent, a home on Vancouver Island.*

Rose Cottage was a single-storey frame building with a concrete floor and white plaster walls and ceilings. Seventy years earlier it had been built against the east wall of Rose House for the use of the groundskeeper and his daughter, a servant in the main residence. Rose House was a stone mansion with a view of the ocean. It was now owned by a trust company in the name of a beautiful raw-faced widow of seventy-two named Lady Beatrice Cooper, who at some time before a succession of small strokes had damaged her brain specified that Rose Cottage should always be rented to a Canadian writer. Alex became the latest in a shabby line. He was not a writer but said he was when he answered the ad because he had always enjoyed the confidence that he could be. Who was to gainsay him?"

portion of the jobs in the industry. Books are written under contracts between writers and publishers, and the industry hires designers, illustrators, and editors on a freelance basis. In 1991, some 41,550 Canadians reported that they worked as writers and editors.

Magazines

In the fall of 1995, two of Canada's biggest magazines, *Maclean's* and *Toronto Life*, launched Chinese-language editions, distributing them through Chinese-language newspapers and on the newsstands. Canada's magazine industry is moving quickly to serve a country of many cultures. The industry includes consumer magazines like *L'actualité* and *Canadian Living*, business and trade periodicals such as *Canadian Business* and *L'Automobile*, religious, farm and scholarly publications, and special interest magazines.

Canada's periodicals are weathering tough times. Circulation and revenues have declined steeply, and some magazines have folded. In 1993-94, revenues were just over $795 million, down more than 10% from 1989-90, and the number of magazines reporting had dropped by 160 to 1,331. Advertising revenues plunged more than 14% in that period.

But special interest publications have escaped the downward spiral. These are magazines dedicated to a particular subject, like computers, sports, parenting, or popular music. They accounted for over 30% of total circulation in 1993-94, compared with only 18% four years earlier.

Periodicals have managed to earn profits only by keeping tight control of costs. The number of full- and part-time employees has fallen, and the use of contract workers has increased. In 1993-94, there were just over 5,500 full- and part-time jobs in periodicals. Nearly 4,000 more people worked as volunteers. As do book publishers, magazines usually hire freelance writers, illustrators, and designers, and often they provide the first opportunities for emerging Canadian writers to bring their work to Canadian readers.

Heritage Preserves

Canadians love going to heritage institutions: in 1993-94, we logged about 55 million visits, nearly twice the number of our population. In that year, 2,123 heritage institutions with operating revenues totalling $869 million were surveyed. Governments provided 70% of the revenues, a drop of more than 2% from four years earlier. Earned revenues contributed 23%, over half from boutique and concession sales.

Volunteers play an essential role in Canada's heritage institutions. They run gift shops, give guided tours, serve on boards, and belong to organizations which support the institutions. In 1993-94, volunteers numbered 55,000, a 42% increase from four years earlier. The paid work force included more than 24,000 full- and part-time employees.

The wilderness is never far away in Canada. Vast forests, mountains, prairies or seas seem to begin just where the last city lights fade into dark. The wintry climate that prevails in most of the country may keep us indoors more than we like, but we frequently enjoy getting away to the wilderness. In 1994-95, over 25 million person-visits were logged at our national parks and historic sites and canals, a significant increase of almost four million from two years earlier.

In a recent Environics poll that asked Canadians to name the most important symbols of their national identity, our national parks finished a close third, just behind the Canadian flag and the national anthem.

On Your Mark

Some 9.6 million people, 15 years and older, regularly participate in amateur sports. Popular activities include baseball and softball, hockey, downhill skiing, swimming, golf and bowling. About one-quarter of regular sports participants also jog, cycle, do aerobics or other exercises.

Canadian couch potatoes may be out for a jog. Twenty-five years ago, only 5% of Canadian adults were active enough to derive desirable health benefits from their exercise. By 1995, however, 37% of Canadian adults were this active—a 740% improvement.

Much of the impetus to exercise in Canada comes from ParticipACTION, an independent, non-profit organization created by the Canadian government. It is now celebrating its 25th anniversary.

Back in 1973, ParticipACTION ran a 15-second TV commercial contrasting a 30-year-old Canadian with a 60-year-old Swede, who could run circles around the 30-year-old. In a way, the commercial hit a collective Canadian nerve and many of us decamped from our couches to meet the "Swedish" challenge.

Today, Canadians streak through streets on roller skates, attack mountain trails on exotic bicycles, schuss down slopes on neon snow boards, and fling Frisbees in a co-operative team game that players call simply "Ultimate."

But although we are more active than we used to be, we are not as active as we ideally should be. Activity surveys over the years have arrived at different numbers. The latest, in 1995, from the Canadian Fitness and Lifestyle Research Institute, shows that 12% of Canadians are inactive during their leisure time and another 23% are only somewhat active. Some 65% of adults—18.2 million people—are moderately or very physically active in their leisure time.

Women are slightly less active than their male counterparts, and we all tend to be less active as we get older. Also, Canadians are more physically active the farther west we live. In Prince Edward Island, the very physically active proportion of the population is about 12%, in Quebec, it's about 13%, and in British Columbia, it is roughly 26%.

ParticipACTION is not the only organization which helps Canadians get active. Health Canada has invested slightly more than $16 million in ParticipACTION to change attitudes about fitness and activity in Canada, while private sector supporters throughout the country have invested another $30 million. This money has been used to develop and manage mass media campaigns and distribute targeted educational resources that encourage positive attitudes about physical fitness and health.

While the effects of all this are hard to measure, independent research in 1995 showed that close to 90% of Canadians are familiar with ParticipACTION and its program, and, of these, 64% say they have been positively influenced by the ParticipACTION message. In social marketing terms, these statistics would suggest success.

W. Brook, Canadian Pacific Limited, A-6120

Almost one out of every two Canadian adults regularly plays hockey, skis or swims.

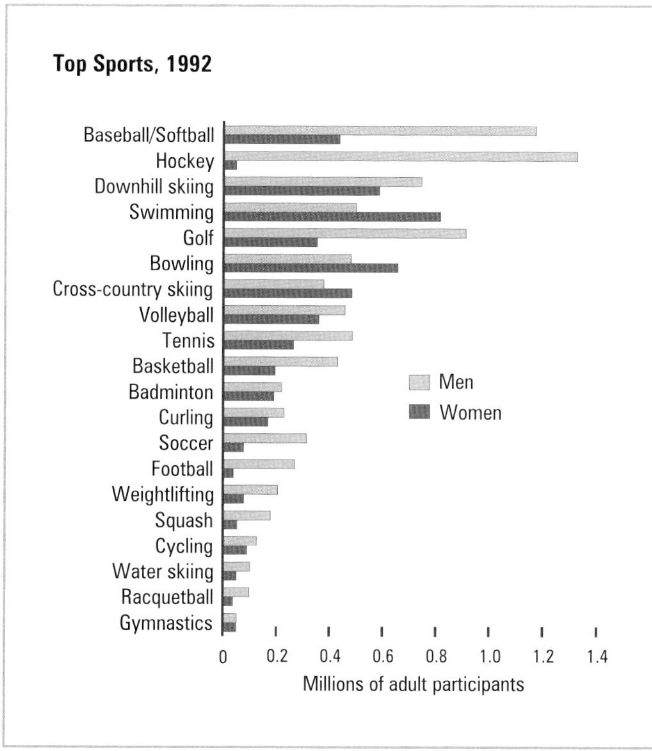

Naturally, sports are most popular among young people: 77% of Canadians 15 to 18 years of age regularly play. That compares with about half of the people aged 25 to 34, and only a quarter of those who are 55 years and older. More men than women play sports.

Children six to 10 years of age are most active in swimming, followed by baseball, soccer and hockey. The preferred sports among 11- to 14-year-olds are baseball, swimming, hockey and basketball. But sports like bowling, cross-country skiing, golf, tennis and curling appeal to people of many ages. Indeed, two-thirds of cross-country skiers, golfers and curlers are 35 or older.

Several factors predispose us to take up sports. Participating in organized sport while in school is particularly important. Another factor is gender: men are considerably more likely to play sports. Because of the costs involved in many sports, people with higher incomes are more likely to participate. The region of the country is another factor: British Columbians are the most active, followed by residents of Quebec and Nova Scotia; the lowest participation rate is in Newfoundland.

World-Class Athletes

In 1995, Montrealer Bruny Surin became the world's fastest indoor sprinter, winning the gold medal in the 60-metre race at the World Indoor Track and Field Championships in Barcelona, Spain. Joining him on the podium was Robert Esmie of Sudbury, Ontario, winner of the bronze medal.

Canadian runners had multiple successes in 1995. At the World Track and Field Championships in Goteborg, Sweden, Canada had a stunning one–two finish with Donovan Bailey of Oakville, Ontario, winning first place and Bruny Surin taking the silver in the 100-metre race. Michael Smith of Kenora, Ontario, won the bronze medal in the decathlon. These wins gave Canada its best-ever showing in this world championship. As if this weren't enough, the quartet of Bailey, Surin, Esmie and Glenroy Gilbert of Ottawa won the men's sprint relay.

Canada regularly places teams at major international sporting competitions like the Olympic, Pan-American, Commonwealth, Paralympic and World University Games. Canada also sends outstanding athletes like Bailey and Surin to world athletic championships. Sport Canada estimates that some 10,000 to 15,000 Canadian athletes are at the highest performance levels.

Canadian women rowers are another success story. In 1995, at the World Rowing Championships in Tampere, Finland, Canada collected four medals—two golds and two silvers. Marnie McBean of Toronto and Kathleen Heddle of Vancouver won the 2,000-metre race in women's double sculls. Silken Laumann of Victoria took the silver medal in single sculls. McBean, Heddle, Diane O'Grady of North Bay and Laryssa Biesenthal of Walkerton, Ontario, earned the

Photo by Roger Charbonneau

The goalie, Hochelaga district, Montreal.

silver in quadruple sculls, and Wendy Wiebe of St. Catharines, Ontario, and Winnipeg's Colleen Miller won gold in the lightweight double sculls for the third year in a row.

Pro Leagues

Professional sports leagues are now big business in Canada and the United States. Teams can make or lose a great deal of money, and franchises can be bought, sold and moved, even across national borders.

Canadians have a long history of trading sports with our southern neighbour. We first shared hockey, our unofficial national sport, through the U.S.-based National Hockey League (NHL) franchises. The Americans responded by exporting their defining game, baseball, to Canada when the Montreal Expos and later the Toronto Blue Jays arrived. The next volley was the south-bound expansion of the Canadian Football League into the United States. Finally in 1995, the National Basketball Association (NBA) expanded north of the 49th parallel, bringing Canada its first two NBA teams.

The NHL

"Hockey captures the essence of the Canadian experience in the New World," wrote Bruce Kidd. "Hockey is the dance of life, an affirmation that despite the deadly chill of winter we are alive." Canada's greatest contribution to world sport, hockey as we know it today was first played in Montreal in 1875, with a set of rules formalized by a McGill student. By 1917, the National Hockey League had begun. In 1926, the Stanley Cup came under the control of the NHL and has been the climax of the season ever since.

In 1995-96, Canadian NHL teams included the Montréal Canadiens, the Toronto Maple Leafs, the Edmonton Oilers, the Winnipeg Jets, the Ottawa Senators, the Vancouver Canucks and the Calgary Flames. There were also 20 NHL teams in the United States, including the former Quebec Nordiques, who had moved to Colorado. The Winnipeg Jets finalized arrangements to move to Phoenix for the 1996-97 season.

"The coolest game on earth," as the NHL calls it, hockey is very popular at the amateur level. In 1994-95, there were over 513,000 registered players in Canada, more than 19,000 of them girls and women. Since 1990, female registrations have more than doubled.

Baseball

The first organized baseball team in Canada formed in Hamilton in 1854. Soon the sport spread across the country. In 1904, a Canadian team in Whitehorse won an international competition against a team from the Alaskan town of Skagway.

The first major league franchise to be awarded outside the United States went to Montreal in 1969, when the Montreal Expos joined the National League. Toronto followed in 1977, with the creation of the Toronto Blue Jays in the American League. In 1992, the Blue Jays became the first professional team outside the United States to win the coveted World Series, a coup they repeated in 1993.

Over 450,000 Canadians were registered as amateur baseball participants in 1994. They included more than 36,000 girls and women. These players belonged to some 13,500 teams across Canada.

The CFL

Canadian football is similar to the American game, but it is played on a larger field with more players and different rules. From 1958, when the Canadian Football League (CFL) was formally established, to 1993, all the CFL teams were in this country. Americans watched their own brand of the game, played professionally by the National Football League (NFL). In 1993, however, the CFL began expanding into the States, hopeful that American interest and TV contracts would revive the flagging economic fortunes of the league.

In 1995-96, the CFL teams in Canada were the Calgary Stampeders, the Ottawa Rough Riders, the Edmonton Eskimos, the Winnipeg Blue Bombers, the Hamilton Tiger-Cats, the B.C. Lions, the Toronto Argonauts and the Saskatchewan Roughriders. Five teams operated in the United States. The crowning achievement of the CFL season is the Grey Cup, which was won for the first time by an American-based team, the Baltimore Stallions, at the 1995 Grey Cup game in Regina.

But regardless of who wins the next competition, the Cup will have returned to Canada in 1997, since all American teams have folded and the Baltimore Stallions are returning as the Montreal Alouettes.

Close to 90,000 Canadians are registered players in amateur football, and about 10,000 more are coaches, officials and administrators. Between 1990 and 1995, participation in this sport increased almost 13%.

The NBA

In 1891, when Canadian James Naismith invented the game of basketball, he nailed a peach basket to a gym wall, and the janitor climbed a ladder to retrieve successful shots.

That humble beginning is a far cry from the jazzy, high-tech glamour and speed of modern professional basketball. In 1995, Canada welcomed its first National Basketball Association teams, the Toronto Raptors and the Vancouver Grizzlies. Just before the season opened, the two teams met for the first annual Naismith Cup exhibition game in Winnipeg.

In 1994, nearly 337,000 Canadians took part in organized amateur basketball, with the largest concentration among 10- to 14-year-olds, who numbered almost 197,000.

SOURCES

Canadian Broadcasting Corporation
Canadian Conference of the Arts
Canadian Heritage
Health Canada
Statistics Canada

FOR FURTHER READING

Selected publications from Statistics Canada

- **Canadian Social Trends**. Quarterly. 11-008E
- **Services Indicators**. Quarterly. 63-016
- **Focus on Culture**. Quarterly. 87-004
- **Canada's Culture, Heritage and Identity: A Statistical Perspective**. Annual. 87-211

Legend

–	nil or zero	..	not available	x	confidential
--	too small to be expressed	...	not applicable or not appropriate		*(Certain tables may not add due to rounding)*

8.1 CULTURAL SECTOR LABOUR FORCE, 1991

	Total cultural occupations	Cultural occupations in cultural industries[1]	Cultural occupations in other industries
Total cultural occupations	670,290	441,355	228,940
Cultural occupations	348,160	119,225	228,940
Architects	11,815	95	11,715
Painters, sculptors and related artists	11,450	470	10,975
Product and interior designers	29,970	2,140	27,835
Advertising and illustrating artists	28,715	9,165	19,555
Photographers and camera operators	12,330	9,785	2,550
Other occupations in fine and commercial art	1,080	330	745
Producers and directors, performing and audio-visual arts	15,165	13,205	1,960
Conductors, composers and arrangers	1,635	990	645
Musicians and singers	11,650	8,735	2,910
Other occupations related to music and musical entertainment	1,240	500	735
Dancers and choreographers	1,445	910	540
Actors/actresses	4,125	3,680	450
Radio and television announcers	7,825	7,685	135
Other occupations in performing and audio-visual arts	6,990	4,025	2,965
Writers and editors	41,550	22,155	19,395
Translators and interpreters	9,615	410	9,205
Other occupations in writing	300	125	175
Library, museum and archival supervisors	2,030	1,110	920
Librarians, archivists and conservators	20,875	6,400	14,475
Library, museum and archival technicians	3,410	890	2,520
Other occupations in library, museum and archival sciences	2,625	1,085	1,540
Fine arts teachers	26,670	2,120	24,545
Printing forepersons	5,575	905	4,670
Typesetting and composing occupations	8,045	3,050	4,995
Printing press occupations	24,425	3,630	20,795
Printing engraving except photoengraving.	3,355	310	3,045
Photoengraving occupations	2,065	470	1,595
Bookbinding occupations	9,130	835	8,295
Occupations in labouring and other elemental work: printing	4,025	1,280	2,750
Other printing and related occupations	13,950	2,030	11,920
Electronic and related forepersons	1,395	880	505
Radio and TV broadcast equipment operators	5,525	3,715	1,810
Sound and video equipment operators	2,755	1,920	840
Motion picture projectionists	1,025	840	185
Other electronic and related occupations	590	140	445
Other crafts forepersons	1,055	265	795
Photographic processing occupations	12,320	2,790	9,530
Other crafts and equipment operating occupations	425	140	290
Other occupations in cultural industries	322,130	322,130	...
Administrators, managers, supervisors	77,360	77,360	...
Professionals and semi-professionals	30,770	30,770	...
Skilled and semi-skilled craft and trade workers	44,195	44,195	...
Clerical, sales, service, manual work	165,760	165,760	...
Not stated	4,050	4,050	...

1. Cultural industries include publishing, printing, telecommunications, broadcasting, advertising services, photography, motion picture production, distribution and exhibition, theatre and other staged performances, museums and archives, library services and book and stationery stores.

Source: Statistics Canada, Catalogue no. 87-211.

8.2 RECORDING INDUSTRY

	1989-90	1990-91	1991-92	1992-93	1993-94
Reporting companies	187	181	215	187	210
Canadian	173	167	201	172	196
Foreign	14	14	14	15	14
Atlantic	3	5	6	3	7
Quebec	42	47	61	52	76
Ontario	104	91	97	81	76
Prairies	16	18	29	32	29
British Columbia	22	20	22	19	22
Yukon and Northwest Territories	–	–	–	–	–
New releases[1]	4,439	4,665	7,490	6,271	6,367
With Canadian content	615	618	1,083	669	719
English lyrics	261	340	614	323	376
French lyrics	237	196	327	185	190
Other[3]	117	82	142	161	153
Unspecified	–	–	–	–	–
Without Canadian content	3,824	4,047	6,407	5,602	5,648
English lyrics	2,959	3,442	4,379	3,853	4,199
French lyrics	98	79	173	161	150
Other[2]	767	526	1,487	1,588	1,299
Unspecified	–	–	368	–	–
Musical category					
Adult-oriented popular music	923	740	865	751	798
Top 40/rock/disco	1,890	2,334	3,041	2,153	2,403
Classical and related	683	399	1,440	1,405	1,209
Jazz	244	256	505	352	387
Country and folk	257	371	416	591	491
Children's	30	70	313	151	196
Other[3]	412	495	910	868	883
			%		
Canadian content as % of sales	8.0	10.5	10.0	11.3	12.6
			$ Millions		
Revenue from the sale of recordings	454.3	508.7	579.7	633.5	738.0
Singles	9.5	13.1	5.3	5.6	4.8
Albums	28.9	8.9	5.0	2.1	1.2
Compact discs	148.7	204.3	325.5	394.2	507.3
Tapes (analog)	267.2	280.9	243.4	231.4	224.7
Tapes (digital)	–	–	--	x	--
Unspecified	0.1	1.7	0.5	x	–

1. Excludes singles. A recording released in more than one format (album, tape, CD etc.) is only counted once.
2. Includes instrumental music.
3. Includes unspecified.

Source: Statistics Canada, *Sound Recording Survey*.

8.3 PRIVATE RADIO

	1990	1991	1992	1993	1994
Number of employees	10,417	10,213	9,801	9,591	9,251
			$ Millions		
Revenues	780	756	768	741	766
Sales of air time	764	741	749	721	741
Expenses	811	816	813	785	776
Salaries and other staff benefits	375	387	391	383	386
Net profits before taxes	-20	-34	-32	-50	-28

Source: Statistics Canada, Catalogue no. 56-204.

8.4 RADIO LISTENING TIME, FALL 1994

	All ages	12-17 years	18 years and over	
			Men	Women
		% of listening time		
All stations	100.0	100.0	100.0	100.0
Adult-contemporary/gold/oldies/rock	34.4	31.2	34.6	34.6
Middle-of-the-road	6.9	2.6	6.0	8.3
Country	13.7	8.9	13.6	14.3
Canadian Broadcasting Corporation	9.2	1.5	9.0	10.1
Album-oriented rock	5.6	8.8	7.1	3.9
Contemporary	4.9	21.7	4.3	3.9
Easy listening	1.1	0.2	0.9	1.3
Talk	12.1	1.7	12.0	13.2
Sports	0.5	0.4	0.9	0.1
Dance	4.7	13.6	4.8	3.6
U.S. stations	3.2	6.6	3.1	3.0
Other	3.7	2.8	3.9	3.6

Source: Statistics Canada, Catalogue no. 87-211.

8.5 CANADIAN BROADCASTING CORPORATION

	1990	1991	1992	1993	1994
Number of employees[1]	10,733	9,814	9,294	9,208	12,298
			$ Millions		
Operating revenues	318.0	321.9	346.3	332.2	350.3
Sales of air time	291.0	282.9	308.8	281.9	291.6
Operating expenses	1,338.5	1,345.4	1,375.5	1,423.2	1,490.6
Salaries and other staff benefits	683.2	719.8	711.3	713.3	783.2
Net cost of CBC Operations	988.9	1,007.5	1,004.1	1,069.1	1,121.8

1. 1994 data on employees include part-time positions.

Source: Statistics Canada, *Radio and Television Broadcasting Survey*, Catalogue no. 56-204.

8.6 TELEVISION VIEWING TIME, FALL 1994

	Canada	Nfld.	P.E.I.	N.S.	N.B.	Que.			Ont.	Man.	Sask.	Alta.	B.C.
						Total[1]	English[2]	French[2]					
							Hours per week						
Total population	22.7	24.1	22.3	24.1	23.7	25.7	22.8	26.3	21.8	22.1	21.9	20.5	20.6
2-11 years	17.7	23.8	19.8	19.9	18.3	19.9	17.1	20.1	17.0	17.3	17.2	16.8	15.2
12-17 years	17.1	18.9	16.6	19.9	15.5	18.8	17.3	19.0	16.8	15.8	17.1	17.6	13.9
Men													
18 years and over	21.5	21.8	22.5	22.5	22.6	24.0	22.3	24.3	20.6	21.4	21.4	19.3	20.3
18-24 years	14.8	14.4	12.6	15.4	13.6	15.4	15.0	15.1	14.5	14.7	17.5	14.4	14.4
25-34 years	18.7	22.9	26.8	19.5	20.7	20.2	18.3	20.6	18.2	19.6	18.7	16.9	16.8
35-49 years	19.1	18.6	22.0	20.3	19.8	21.5	18.7	22.1	18.2	18.4	17.9	18.1	17.8
50-59 years	22.9	24.1	21.7	28.8	28.1	25.6	22.3	26.2	21.5	23.6	21.5	20.2	21.1
60 years and over	32.4	32.4	26.3	30.8	32.8	38.2	34.4	39.8	30.7	30.9	30.1	28.5	30.7
Women													
18 years and over	26.8	27.8	24.5	27.9	28.2	30.8	25.8	31.8	25.7	25.9	25.5	23.9	24.2
18-24 years	18.8	22.7	21.6	18.1	21.3	19.7	17.7	19.9	18.9	17.9	20.9	17.1	16.6
25-34 years	24.2	28.8	25.0	28.4	25.8	26.4	23.2	27.0	23.3	22.3	21.7	24.0	21.3
35-49 years	23.0	26.5	21.4	25.3	25.6	26.9	20.1	28.1	21.4	23.1	20.4	21.8	20.4
50-59 years	30.1	29.8	27.3	31.2	37.2	35.6	27.9	37.1	28.0	27.4	26.1	24.8	28.1
60 years and over	36.4	31.1	28.0	33.7	33.7	42.4	35.7	44.8	35.6	34.9	35.0	31.3	33.2

1. Includes respondents who did not indicate a language spoken at home or who indicated a language other than English or French.
2. Language spoken at home.

Source: Statistics Canada, Catalogue no. 87-211.

8.7 FILM AND VIDEO DISTRIBUTION AND WHOLESALING[1]

	1989-90	1990-91	1991-92	1992-93	1993-94
Number of firms	181	172	165	154	156
Canadian control	154	147	142	133	135
Foreign control	27	25	23	21	21
Employment	2,013	2,023	1,973	1,862	1,923
Full-time	1,649	1,751	1,689	1,663	1,682
Part-time	358	269	280	195.0	238
Working proprietors	6	3	4	4	3
Salaries and benefits (%)	21.4	18.1	17.1	17.7	19.7
			$ Millions		
Revenues	1,106.7	1,183.8	1,230.7	1,229.1	1,336.1
Distribution	649.4	655.5	643.3	650.0	784.0
Theatrical	225.5	193.4	184.6	170.8	196.4
Home entertainment	398.2	437.8	435.9	443.7	551.9
Pay TV	33.7	33.5	34.3	35.1	54.8
Conventional TV	309.2	329.5	308.9	275.9	375.5
Home video	55.3	74.9	92.7	132.8	121.5
Non-theatrical	25.7	24.3	22.7	21.9	22.2
Unspecified	--	--	--	13.6	13.6
Wholesaling videocassettes	426.4	495.4	547.3	542.7	514.1
Other revenue	30.8	32.9	40.1	36.4	38.0
Expenses	974.3	1,065.1	1,084.3	1,091.4	1,126.4
Salaries and benefits	55.9	60.9	64.7	64.4	65.6
Licensing costs (rights, royalties and other fees)	409.0	401.0	350.0	284.1	337.3
Depreciation and amortization	16.0	8.8	17.4	13.5	13.9
Interest expenses	2.7	5.5	6.0	9.5	5.7
Other costs	490.7	589.0	646.2	720.3	703.8
			% of revenues		
Profit margin[2]	12.0	10.0	11.9	11.2	15.7

1. From April 1 of one year to March 31 of the next year.
2. Profit margin is defined as total revenue less total expenses (profit or loss) shown as a percentage of total revenues.

Source: Statistics Canada, Catalogue no. 87-204.

8.8 FILM LABORATORIES AND POST-PRODUCTION[1]

	1989-90	1990-91	1991-92	1992-93	1993-94
Number of firms	153	173	162	161	164
Quebec	28	41	50	53	55
Ontario	101	107	89	85	84
Other provinces and territories	24	25	23	23	25
Employment	2,142	2,719	3,173	3,095	3,127
Full-time	1,861	1,908	2,063	1,912	2,042
Part-time	266	272	341	363	271
Freelancers	..	520	753	802	795
Working proprietors	15	19	16	18	19
			$ Millions		
Operating revenues	262.5	264.6	286.9	309.8	323.7
Quebec	52.3	77.3	87.6	96.4	89.9
Ontario	194.9	170.5	184.9	197.5	212.1
Other provinces and territories	15.2	16.8	14.4	15.9	21.7
Operating expenses	216.2	237.7	266.3	294.8	299.5
Quebec	45.1	70.1	86.8	93.1	83.2
Ontario	158.7	153.0	165.3	186.4	195.4
Other provinces and territories	12.4	14.7	14.2	15.3	20.8
Salaries and wages	66.3	75.8	81.6	82.2	82.6
Salaries and wages	61.8	66.3	70.3	70.9	70.4
Benefits	4.6	6.0	7.1	7.4	7.3
Freelancers' fees	..	3.5	4.3	3.9	5.0
			% of operating revenue		
Operating margin	17.6	10.2	7.2	4.8	7.5
Quebec	13.7	9.4	0.9	3.5	7.4
Ontario	18.6	10.3	10.6	5.6	7.9
Other provinces and territories	18.7	12.7	1.1	3.5	4.0

1. From April 1 of one year to March 31 of the next year.

Source: Statistics Canada, Catalogue no. 87-204.

8.9 PERFORMING ARTS ATTENDANCE, 1992

	Total	Sex		Age					
		Male	Female	Under 20 years	20-24 years	25-34 years	35-44 years	45-59 years	60 years and over
	%								
People who attended[1]:									
Music									
Pop/rock	16.3	18.1	14.6	35.0	38.2	21.9	13.9	7.4	3.0
Jazz/blues	6.3	7.0	5.6	8.5	10.4	8.9	7.6	4.3	1.1
Folk music	3.5	3.8	3.3	x	4.2	3.5	4.2	4.4	2.3
Country and western	4.5	4.8	4.3	2.5	4.8	4.7	5.2	6.0	2.8
Pops	2.4	2.2	2.6	x	x	1.4	2.6	3.8	2.8
Contemporary classical	2.9	2.8	2.9	2.6	3.0	1.8	2.8	4.1	2.7
Symphonic music	4.8	4.4	5.2	x	4.1	2.6	6.3	7.0	5.4
Chamber music and soloists	1.8	1.6	1.9	x	x	1.3	1.6	3.1	2.1
Opera	4.4	3.8	4.9	4.1	3.4	3.5	4.3	6.2	4.1
Choral	3.1	2.5	3.6	x	2.3	2.3	3.5	4.1	3.5
Theatre									
Drama	8.6	7.8	9.4	11.6	8.0	7.6	10.1	9.1	6.6
Comedy	10.3	9.6	10.9	8.4	7.9	9.7	11.4	13.2	8.7
Musical comedy	11.2	9.7	12.6	9.3	10.6	9.8	12.7	14.2	9.2
Stand-up comedy	5.7	6.1	5.3	6.1	8.2	6.5	6.1	5.9	2.6
Dance									
Ballet	2.9	2.0	3.7	2.7	4.5	2.7	2.9	3.1	2.1
Contemporary dance	2.5	1.9	3.0	4.0	3.5	2.5	3.1	2.4	x

1. Persons frequently attended more than one type of event.

Source: Statistics Canada, *General Social Survey, 1992.*

8.10 BOOK SALES[1]

	1989-90	1990-91	1991-92	1992-93	1993-94
			$ '000		
Total sales[2] by English-language firms	965,511	995,838	981,981	982,149	980,180
Wholesale	99,479	115,016	89,206	85,330	100,154
Retail	320,733	336,888	361,442	373,735	388,029
Accredited bookstores	3,585	1,978	2,236	3,710	2,489
Other independent bookstores	67,783	68,488	76,969	71,418	79,371
Campus bookstores	76,515	80,348	98,131	105,735	96,192
Chain bookstores	107,970	108,631	102,352	113,943	129,874
Department stores	13,934	13,514	14,890	14,167	14,854
Mail order houses	1,923	1,686	2,756	1,266	1,524
Other retail stores and unallocated	49,023	62,244	64,108	63,497	63,724
Institutions	248,836	244,047	250,195	241,432	233,499
Government and special libraries	19,865	17,422	22,213	24,566	25,242
Public libraries	16,456	13,912	15,570	14,420	12,827
Elementary and secondary institutions	144,927	140,377	135,555	133,132	122,706
Postsecondary institutions	58,766	63,855	64,080	59,227	62,746
Other institutions and unallocated	8,821	8,482	12,776	10,087	9,979
Others	296,463	299,887	281,138	281,652	258,498
Direct to general public	173,502	180,878	135,586	138,120	119,094
Book clubs and unallocated	122,961	119,009	145,552	143,532	139,403
Total sales by French-language firms	238,930	256,950	264,121	304,340	316,765
Wholesale	28,220	37,599	47,346	47,032	45,491
Retail	140,585	149,871	147,282	185,541	172,398
Accredited bookstores	87,280	66,084	74,230	75,915	100,133
Other independent bookstores	10,681	14,358	19,908	22,514	14,258
Campus bookstores	12,235	14,823	15,197	16,063	14,187
Chain bookstores	5,539	34,619	9,292	13,512	11,060
Department stores	8,943	13,023	20,978	27,548	26,396
Mail order houses	222	3,587	745	22,743	859
Other retail stores and unallocated	15,685	3,377	6,931	7,246	5,506
Institutions	46,135	48,637	50,089	52,248	50,145
Government and special libraries	714	907	1,103	388	486
Public libraries	714	706	9,136	742	466
Elementary and secondary institutions	40,278	42,569	33,461	46,676	38,968
Postsecondary institutions	3,318	3,219	4,601	3,236	7,853
Other institutions and unallocated	1,110	1,235	1,789	1,207	2,373
Others	23,991	20,844	19,404	19,519	48,731
Direct to general public	17,298	16,823	17,140	16,120	16,505
Book clubs and unallocated	6,693	4,021	2,264	3,398	32,226

1. Book sales refer to the sales of all titles produced for sale through any of the print, micro format, computer software or audio-visual formats.
2. Includes firms for "other languages".

Source: Statistics Canada, *Survey of Book Publishers and Exclusive Agents*.

8.11 BOOK PUBLISHING AND EXCLUSIVE AGENTS, ENGLISH[1]

	1989-90	1990-91	1991-92	1992-93	1993-94
			Number		
English-language firms	241	241	238	230	225
Publishers	206	210	207	201	197
Exclusive agents	35	31	31	29	28
Full-time employees[2]	6,127	5,964	5,683	5,489	5,369
Titles published	5,941	5,900	6,118	5,901	6,725
Textbooks	1,219	1,266	1,146	947	1,243
Tradebooks	3,492	3,342	3,560	3,661	4,121
Others	1,230	1,292	1,412	1,293	1,361
Titles reprinted	3,791	3,545	3,198	3,532	3,762
Textbooks	2,130	1,747	1,488	1,590	1,743
Tradebooks	1,119	1,174	1,213	1,450	1,610
Others	542	624	497	492	409
Total in print	36,533	39,766	42,081	42,412	46,670
Textbooks	10,502	11,615	13,136	12,983	13,570
Tradebooks	18,465	19,521	20,689	21,732	24,623
Others	7,566	8,630	8,256	7,697	8,477
			$ '000		
Total sales[2]	1,172,695	1,207,407	1,187,914	1,226,601	1,302,495
Sales in Canada	965,511	995,838	981,981	982,149	980,180
Publishers					
Own titles	437,836	466,420	437,655	439,158	443,751
Textbooks	159,127	163,103	156,894	155,726	136,032
Tradebooks	106,691	105,431	99,752	103,053	113,307
Other	172,018	197,886	181,009	180,379	194,411
Exclusive agents	527,675	529,418	544,326	542,991	536,429
Textbooks	143,807	156,024	165,894	152,475	158,999
Tradebooks	296,366	287,933	293,922	332,650	316,864
Other	87,502	85,461	84,510	57,866	60,566
Exports and other foreign sales	207,184	211,569	205,933	244,452	322,315
Revenues[2]	1,202,954	1,238,819	1,225,608	1,275,868	1,341,576
Expenditures[2]	1,129,710	1,161,567	1,185,124	1,222,120	1,279,561
			% of revenues		
Before tax profit margin[2]	6.1	6.2	3.3	4.2	4.6

1. Includes firms for other languages.
2. Includes the activities of both publishers and exclusive agents.

Source: Statistics Canada, *Survey of Book Publishers and Exclusive Agents*.

8.12 BOOK PUBLISHING AND EXCLUSIVE AGENTS, FRENCH

	1989-90	1990-91	1991-92	1992-93	1993-94
			Number		
French-language firms	127	131	132	137	133
Publishers	108	113	115	122	119
Exclusive agents	19	18	17	15	14
Full-time employees[1]	1,364	1,378	1,444	1,498	1,493
Titles published	2,454	2,391	2,604	3,155	3,039
Textbooks	823	804	821	946	1,031
Tradebooks	1,336	1,247	1,427	1,896	1,659
Others	295	340	356	313	349
Titles reprinted	2,035	2,913	2,867	3,887	4,060
Textbooks	1,247	2,025	1,868	2,564	2,641
Tradebooks	652	736	847	1,185	1,290
Others	136	152	152	138	129
Total in print	20,285	19,999	22,578	23,733	27,436
Textbooks	6,881	8,049	9,094	9,346	10,293
Tradebooks	10,689	9,460	11,008	11,782	14,151
Others	2,715	2,490	2,476	2,605	2,992
			$ '000		
Total sales[1]	245,130	264,300	284,343	334,104	338,442
Sales in Canada	238,930	256,950	264,121	304,340	316,765
Publishers					
Own titles	127,692	133,392	144,072	159,192	162,252
Textbooks	75,949	83,302	84,814	94,923	94,198
Tradebooks	39,093	34,991	42,862	47,400	49,757
Other	12,650	15,099	16,395	16,870	18,298
Exclusive agents	111,238	123,558	120,049	145,148	154,513
Textbooks	6,604	8,263	6,542	6,579	5,341
Tradebooks	78,876	94,608	91,878	115,029	124,994
Other	25,759	20,688	21,628	23,540	24,178
Exports and other foreign sales	6,200	7,350	20,222	29,764	21,677
Revenues[1]	261,214	282,871	300,318	352,954	358,007
Expenditures[1]	245,157	265,604	285,489	333,618	336,170
			% of revenues		
Before-tax profit margin[1]	6.1	6.1	4.9	5.4	6.1

1. Includes the activities of both publishers and exclusive agents.

Source: Statistics Canada, Survey of *Book Publishers and Exclusive Agents.*

8.13 PERIODICALS

	1989-90	1990-91	1991-92	1992-93	1993-94
Number of reporting publishers	1,091	1,099	1,055	1,047	1,000
Publishers of one periodical	952	959	915	907	866
Publishers of more than one periodical	139	140	140	140	134
Number of reported periodicals	1,493	1,503	1,440	1,400	1,331
Employment					
Full-Time	4,487	4,651	4,583	4,332	4,106
Part-Time	1,756	1,726	1,690	1,545	1,472
Volunteers	4,528	3,993	4,046	4,112	3,900
Total circulation per issue	39,350	39,457	39,050	37,108	36,396
General consumer periodical	19,175	17,551	14,635	13,211	12,632
Special interest consumer periodical	9,663	10,265	12,498	12,907	13,856
Business or trade periodical	5,380	5,937	5,998	5,673	4,899
Religious periodical	3,139	3,615	3,951	3,597	3,433
Farm periodical	1,298	1,241	1,173	1,080	967
Scholarly periodical	695	848	795	640	609
			%		
Origin of editorial content and artwork of a typical issue					
Text	100.0	100.0	100.0	100.0	100.0
In-house	51.3	50.4	49.3	49.4	48.3
Outside the organization					
Canadian-authored	41.5	42.0	43.0	42.6	43.9
Foreign-authored	7.2	7.6	7.7	8.0	7.8
Illustrations and photography	100.0	100.0	100.0	100.0	100.0
In-house	44.0	44.1	42.2	42.9	40.7
Outside the organization					
Canadian-authored	49.6	49.3	50.5	50.2	52.4
Foreign-authored	6.4	6.6	7.2	6.9	6.9
			$'000		
Revenues	885,635	866,032	838,374	852,041	795,419
Advertising sales	566,495	565,347	536,071	528,954	485,250
Single-copy sales	63,501	61,626	58,880	57,190	55,639
Subscription sales	195,053	181,040	184,508	204,214	199,385
Back issues	2,401	2,538	1,875	2,420	2,083
Other revenues[1]	58,186	55,481	57,039	59,262	53,060
Expenses	851,750	847,645	819,108	806,098	750,237
Salaries, wages, fees	169,149	187,206	185,231	189,069	181,558
Professional fees	20,297	23,715	24,630	27,053	33,585
Non-salaried costs	682,248	660,166	630,224	610,029	568,680
Unspecified	353	273	3,653	7,000	–
Profit before taxes	33,885	18,267	19,266	45,896	45,181
			% of total revenues		
Before-tax profit margin	3.8	2.1	2.3	5.4	5.7

1. "Other revenues" include list sales, grants, transfers, donations, membership fees, and unspecified.

Source: Statistics Canada, *Periodical Publishing Survey.*

8.14 READING HABITS, 1992

	Total	Sex		Education						Age				
		Males	Females	Masters/ doctorate medical/ dental	B.A.	Diploma	Post-secondary/ some post-secondary	Elementary/ secondary	Not stated	Under 20 years	20-34 years	35-44 years	45-59 years	60 years and over
Percentage of Canadians who read:														
A newspaper														
In the last week	82.8	83.9	81.7	94.5	90.4	88.9	85.4	78.3	47.7	73.7	80.9	83.8	87.4	83.8
In the last 12 months	92.1	92.3	91.9	98.1	97.5	96.3	95.3	89.6	50.8	89.4	92.7	93.3	93.1	90.1
A magazine														
In the last week	61.8	58.6	64.8	86.0	77.5	68.5	67.1	52.8	29.9	62.6	61.1	64.0	62.9	59.0
In the last 12 months	79.7	76.0	83.4	94.2	92.7	86.6	85.8	72.4	34.7	86.8	82.0	81.5	78.0	72.9
A book														
In the last week	43.9	34.5	53.0	64.6	59.1	47.2	48.5	36.7	19.3	47.1	41.6	46.7	43.2	44.2
In the last 12 months	66.0	56.8	74.8	90.7	81.9	72.3	73.5	56.5	27.9	72.0	66.8	69.6	63.9	60.3
Type of last book read	100.0	100.0	100.0	100.0	100.0	100.0	100.0	100.0	100.0	100.0	100.0	100.0	100.0	100.0
Fiction	34.9	25.1	44.2	38.3	39.8	39.0	39.8	30.9	13.2	48.1	36.8	36.2	29.2	30.3
Non-fiction	30.4	31.1	29.8	52.1	41.4	32.9	33.3	24.9	12.1	22.6	29.4	32.9	34.2	29.1
Not stated or not applicable	34.7	43.9	25.9	9.5	18.7	28.1	26.9	44.2	74.6	29.3	33.8	30.9	36.6	40.6
Type of fiction or non-fiction:	100.0	100.0	100.0	100.0	100.0	100.0	100.0	100.0	100.0	100.0	100.0	100.0	100.0	100.0
Novel	32.5	22.6	42.1	35.4	37.0	36.7	37.2	28.7	12.3	43.3	34.3	34.0	27.1	29.0
Biography/autobiography	8.9	8.0	9.7	13.0	10.4	9.6	9.0	8.2	1.3	7.9	7.3	8.3	11.5	9.8
History	5.4	6.7	4.1	9.7	5.7	5.0	6.5	4.8	4.2	5.4	4.4	5.3	5.2	7.1
Self-help	7.4	7.5	7.4	7.2	14.6	8.6	8.6	4.9	2.6	3.9	9.0	9.4	7.8	3.9
Other non-fiction	8.7	8.8	8.6	21.5	10.6	9.6	9.1	6.9	4.0	5.3	8.7	9.9	9.4	8.2
Not stated or not applicable	37.1	46.4	28.2	10.2	21.5	30.4	29.7	46.4	74.6	34.2	36.4	33.1	39.0	41.9

Source: Statistics Canada, *General Social Survey, 1992.*

8.15 HERITAGE INSTITUTIONS

	1989-90	1990-91	1991-92	1992-93	1993-94
All heritage institutions (excluding nature parks)					
Institutions	2,125	2,116	2,098	2,120	2,122
Employment[1]	23,474	23,827	23,969	24,229	24,125
Attendance ('000)	57,202	57,120	54,464	54,328	54,929
Revenues[2] ($ '000)	940,924	959,218	1,014,671	991,264	986,051
Expenditures[2] ($ '000)	907,194	953,788	1,004,405	970,408	969,333
All types of museums					
Institutions	1,233	1,228	1,219	1,230	1,236
Employment[1]	11,285	11,489	11,685	12,073	11,890
Attendance ('000)	24,305	24,792	23,319	24,883	25,445
Revenues[2] ($ '000)	558,938	554,123	582,618	576,840	586,772
Expenditures[2] ($ '000)	542,632	556,182	589,914	567,143	588,582
Community museums					
Institutions	702	695	693	700	710
Employment[1]	2,418	2,368	2,470	2,588	2,607
Attendance ('000)	3,294	3,194	3,187	3,285	3,353
Revenues[2] ($ '000)	46,582	41,080	51,231	51,149	53,622
Expenditures[2] ($ '000)	47,601	40,839	52,677	52,530	51,981
Art museums					
Institutions	185	184	185	183	178
Employment[1]	2,860	2,937	2,902	2,952	2,913
Attendance ('000)	5,511	5,891	5,557	5,378	5,589
Revenues[2] ($ '000)	179,044	204,934	190,726	191,963	180,201
Expenditures[2] ($ '000)	177,850	206,914	215,984	196,200	178,055
History museums					
Institutions	256	257	251	253	254
Employment[1]	2,869	2,973	2,915	3,176	3,132
Attendance ('000)	7,267	7,959	7,390	8,958	8,760
Revenues[2] ($ '000)	156,307	138,216	148,365	154,002	170,688
Expenditures[2] ($ '000)	147,693	130,730	147,374	150,722	176,091
Other museums					
Institutions	90	92	90	94	94
Employment[1]	3,138	3,211	3,398	3,357	3,238
Attendance ('000)	8,233	7,748	7,185	7,262	7,742
Revenues[2] ($ '000)	177,004	169,894	192,296	179,726	182,250
Expenditures[2] ($ '000)	169,487	177,699	173,878	167,692	182,455
Historic sites					
Institutions	368	372	369	375	384
Employment[1]	6,314	6,329	6,105	6,010	6,057
Attendance ('000)	16,977	16,940	16,784	16,725	17,020
Revenues[2] ($ '000)	147,093	165,742	174,217	162,409	151,478
Expenditures[2] ($ '000)	139,221	158,581	166,162	153,993	142,698
Archives					
Institutions	355	353	345	343	337
Employment[1]	2,703	2,644	2,685	2,571	2,615
Attendance ('000)	834	722	649	905	933
Revenues[2] ($ '000)	115,117	125,338	126,703	126,086	120,364
Expenditures[2] ($ '000)	113,800	124,258	125,639	128,884	119,337
Other types of institutions					
Institutions	169	163	165	172	165
Employment[1]	3,172	3,365	3,494	3,575	3,563
Attendance ('000)	15,086	14,666	13,712	11,815	11,531
Revenues[2] ($ '000)	119,777	114,015	131,133	125,929	127,446
Expenditures[2] ($ '000)	111,541	114,768	122,689	120,387	118,715
Nature parks					
Institutions	171	169	170	168	169
Employment[1]	8,445	8,057	7,997	8,156	8,005
Attendance ('000)	56,835	54,374	54,372	53,866	56,307
Revenues[2] ($ '000)	316,247	314,084	310,443	311,121	312,911
Expenditures[2] ($ '000)	268,468	267,135	258,392	260,166	262,910

1. Full-time and part-time.
2. Includes operating and capital expenditures and/or revenues.

Source: Statistics Canada, Catalogue no. 87F0002XP.

8.16 CHILDREN'S SPORTS, 1992

	6-10 years	11-14 years
	% of children	
Children who regularly play:		
Baseball	14	16
Basketball	3	11
Gymnastics	3	...
Hockey	12	13
Skiing (cross-country)	3	3
Skiing (downhill)	5	7
Soccer	14	10
Swimming	19	14
Volleyball	...	10

Source: Statistics Canada, Catalogue no. 87-211.

8.17 SPORTS INVOLVEMENT, 1992

	Both sexes	Men	Women
	% of those 15 years and over		
All regular participation in sports	45	52	38
Through a club or organization	21	27	15
Competition and/or tournament	15	21	9
Organized school sport	52	58	44
Member of a sport club or organization	15	20	12
Involved in amateur sport as a:			
Coach	4	6	2
Referee or umpire	3	4	1
Volunteer helper	9	12	7
Spectator	24	27	21
Attendance at professional sporting events	31	41	22

Source: Statistics Canada, Catalogue no. 87-211.

SECTION 3

THE ECONOMY

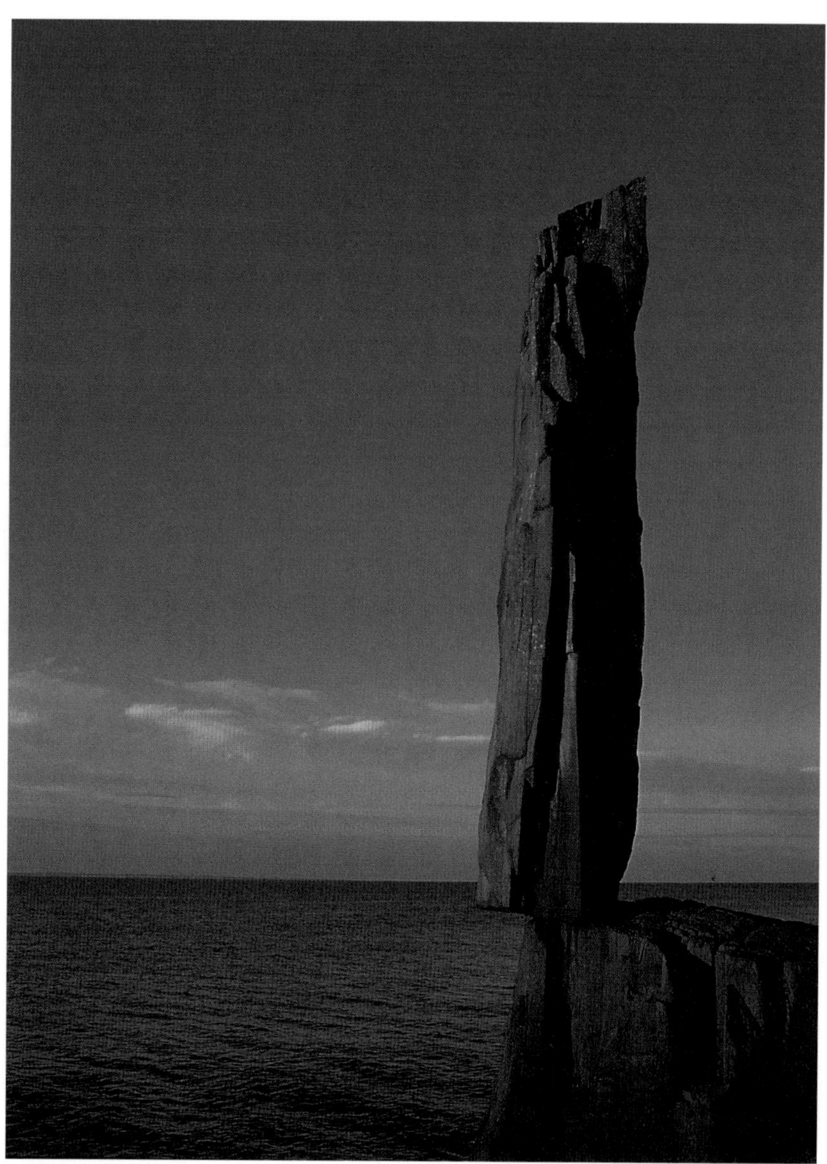

IRWIN BARRETT, FIRST LIGHT

Chapter 9

ECONOMIC CONDITIONS

Photo by Felix H. Man

In 1929, the year before the worst economic depression in Canadian history, the country was in an upbeat and even optimistic mood. "Canadians," wrote author Pierre Berton, "lolled in their summer cottages playing cheerful melodies—'Happy Days Are Here Again,' 'Keep Your Sunny Side Up'—on scratchy gramophones.

They flocked to the new talkies to see *Disraeli* with George Arliss, or the aptly named *Gold Diggers of Broadway.* They listened to 'The Goldbergs' on their Atwater-Kents and gobbled up new murder mysteries by Dashiell Hammett and Ellery Queen."

Sixty years later, on the verge of one of the two worst recessions since the Great Depression, Canadians were still listening to music, only this time on CD players. They were still watching movies, although more often than not at home on VCRs. They were still consuming books, but Hammett and Queen had been replaced by Tom Clancy, Stephen King, and to some extent, Canadians like Robertson Davies and Michel Tremblay. The movie of choice in 1989, at least at the box office, was *Batman.*

For many Canadians, the Depression of the 1930s was more a memory inherited from parents, grandparents and history books. For many, the recession of the 1990s was unrivalled, even unprecedented. Much like the Great Depression of the 1930s, it caught them by surprise.

But perspective is required. Unlike the Depression, the 1990s' recession was not nearly as protracted or miserable. In the 1930s, as many as 20% of working Canadians were jobless. Of those with jobs, half were relief workers. One Canadian in five was a public dependant, and it took 10 years for the economy to recover.

In the 1990-91 recession, Canadians were able to rely on a much stronger social safety net, with Unemployment Insurance (UI), welfare and universal health care. While many Canadians lost their jobs, the unemployment rate was never more than 12%. In fact, after less than three years of recession, there were signs of recovery. Exports began to boom and the Gross Domestic Product (GDP) rose. New jobs were created. By early 1994, the Toronto Stock Exchange was hitting record highs.

But the recession of the early 1990s was still significant, as was its immediate predecessor in 1981. Together these two recessions were the longest and most severe since the Great Depression of the 1930s. Both were part of a worldwide economic downturn. During both, many manufacturing plants closed their doors, in some cases forever, a large number of retail firms went bankrupt, and around half a million Canadians lost their jobs. Those who did continue to work saw their paycheques shrink. Between 1989 and 1993, real average family income in Canada fell more than 6%—the longest and steepest decline since the end of the Second World War.

The 1990 Recession

Throughout 1990 and 1991, most countries in the Organisation for Economic Co-operation and Development (OECD) were in, or moving toward, recession, although Canada's recession was particularly severe, with a steep decline in GDP and unemployment rates well above the OECD average. Recessions occur periodically as part of the business cycle. There have been as many as 13 in Canada since the end of the Second World War. Generally, they are characterized by a drop in output, job loss and weakened consumer confidence.

The last two recessions in Canada, in 1981 and 1990, caused widespread damage to many sectors. During both, Canadians faced higher interest rates designed by monetary authorities to control inflation. As a result, the big-ticket items, like homes, went begging. Residential construction companies suffered. Businesses invested less in plants and equipment.

At the same time, the American economy was also in recession, causing exports of Canadian manufacturing and natural resource-based firms to fall, as well as profits. The high interest rates exacerbated the situation since existing debts were now more expensive, and firms became hesitant to borrow more for investment purposes. Layoffs and lower employment quickly followed. Incomes and personal spending eroded.

Particularly striking about the latest recession is what the popular press has called the "double-dip" in employment. While more people lost their jobs in the 1981 recession than in the early 1990s, in many cases, it took less time for them to resume working. But during the 1990-91 recession, the situation was different. While 1991 was a better year for job prospects in Canada, by mid-1992, the job market was again bleak. As the media relayed this news to Canadians and as more Canadians experienced it first hand, confidence in the economy was shaken.

To add insult to injury, those who lost their jobs were likely to be unemployed for longer periods of time. In 1989, the average hiatus between jobs was about 20 weeks; in 1992, it was nearly 27. For older workers, the prospects were even worse.

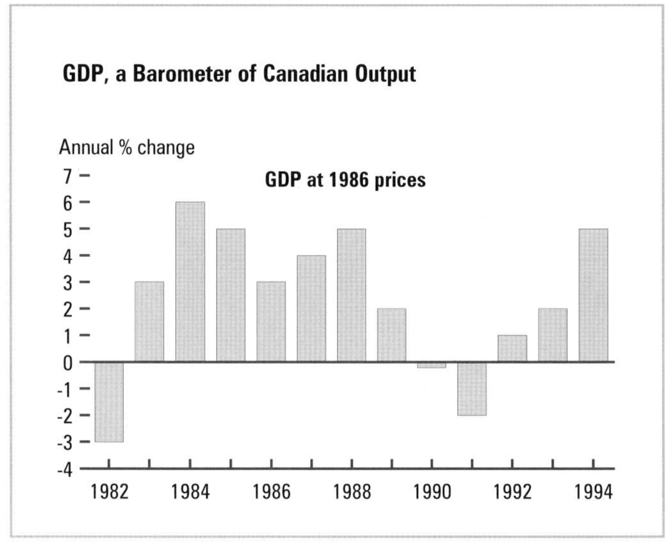

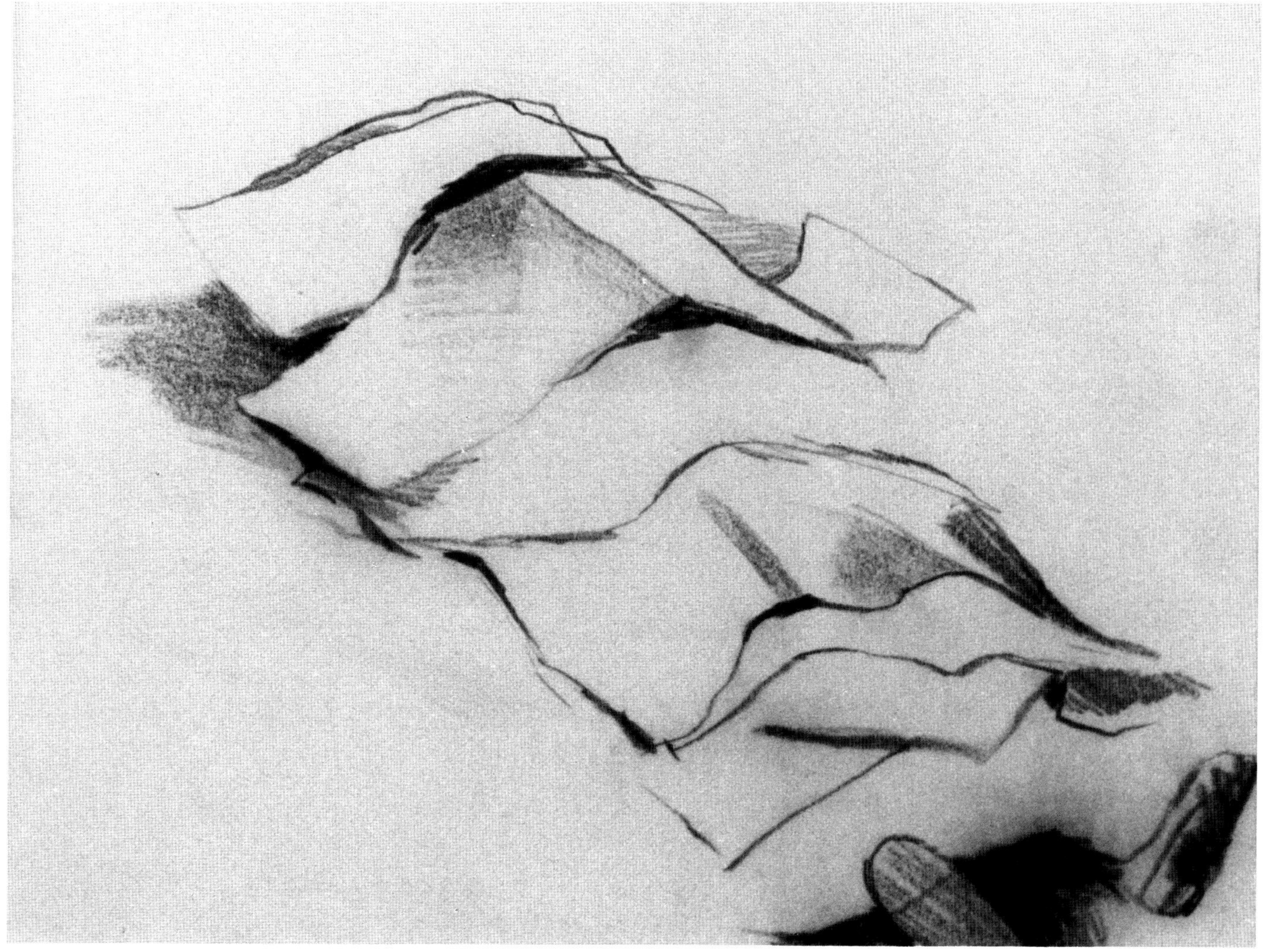

Richard Ciccimarra, courtesy of Murray and Dorothea Adaskin

Untitled.

In the 1990 recession, people were especially vulnerable to job loss and diminishing incomes because their cushions of savings were dramatically low. By 1990, the debt incurred by all Canadians throughout their lifetimes was high at 80% of total incomes. That year, Canadians saved only 10% of their incomes, much less than what they were saving throughout the 1980s. On top of this, over 90% of these savings were "contractual" (such as registered retirement savings plans or RRSPs and trusteed pension funds) and thus, less accessible than the large "piggy bank" of savings Canadians had held a decade earlier.

Civilized countries have always needed a way to measure the economic activity of daily life. In simple agrarian societies, this was fairly easy to do. It generally amounted to placing a value on the size of the annual harvest. In modern, industrialized societies such as Canada, however, with our complex technology, and the enormous variety of products we produce, measuring economic activity is much more difficult.

To address this need, the concept of Gross Domestic Product (GDP) has evolved. In essence, GDP is the total value of goods and services produced by the domestic market economy each year. It includes everything from the cash that Canadians spend on food, clothing, rent, haircuts and movies to the money that governments spend on military hardware or on salaries for public servants. Gross Domestic Product also includes the money companies spend on new factories or shopping malls.

GDP does not include old age pensions, Unemployment Insurance and other transfer payments. Statisticians count these amounts later on, when they are actually spent on food or clothing or rent. Also, GDP does not include the purchase of raw materials needed to create goods and services. The costs of raw materials are counted only once they have been bought by "final" consumers. As a result, GDP represents the value of production without duplication.

Figuring the GDP

Much as a Canadian family counts up its bills and its income to get a good picture of its economic health, statisticians calculate GDP by measuring the country's expenditures and income. Statisticians, in fact, calculate GDP using the same double-entry bookkeeping system that most businesses use.

Using the first, or "primary incomes approach," they count up all wages and salaries paid to workers, plus the profits earned by Canadian stockholders. Using the second, or "final expenditures method," they add up the market value of all commodities produced domestically for final consumption. In this way, items purchased by consumers, governments, businesses and foreigners (who buy Canadian goods) are all added up.

GDP Origins

The notion of national income and ways of measuring it evolved slowly between the two world wars, not just in Canada but elsewhere in the world. Only in the years immediately following the Second World War, when the macroeconomic theories of John Maynard Keynes were attracting widespread interest, did the national accounts blossom.

Keynes' theories, which were primarily designed to avoid the kinds of cataclysmic cycles that lead to depressions, required new statistical measures to monitor what was going on in the economy as a whole.

In Canada, the first national accounts were published by the Dominion Bureau of Statistics in 1946, and covered the period between 1938 and 1945. Later, they were extended back to 1926. Over the last 20 years or so, they have included provincial as well as national GDP, national wealth, and detailed input-output tables that show how much of the output of one industry is needed to fuel the production of another.

In 1986, Canada shifted from GNP to GDP as the primary statistical indicator used to measure output. GDP as a domestic measure tallies all production taking place within Canada's borders. GNP, or the Gross National Product, on the other hand, measures the output of Canadian-owned companies, regardless of whether they are operating in or out of Canada. The United Nations recommends that countries use GDP as their primary economic barometer, since it measures what is actually happening in the country itself.

A Measure of GDP

Gross Domestic Product does not take a philosophical or moral approach to the value of any of the items it tallies. For example, GDP views the output of a highly paid hockey player as equal to his salary. Some Canadians may think his salary is too high. Others, such as loyal sports fans, may think it's not high enough. But those who calculate GDP do not concern themselves with such value judgements. They simply measure the observable market value.

This has led some critics to question if GDP can measure the true value of a country's output. Gross Domestic Product, they argue, does not measure human well-being or the well-being of the country. It does not measure the impact of pollution on the environment. Nor does it measure the value of such ephemeral elements as the quality of air we breathe or the state of peace in which we live.

Gross Domestic Product does not factor in the wide variety of services that households provide for themselves. For example, people wash clothes, prepare meals, repair the toaster, tend the children, weed the garden and feed their pets, yet none of these activities are recorded in the GDP. As the old adage goes: "Whenever a Canadian marries the housekeeper, GDP falls."

In fact, some critics have stated that, since GDP looks only at the market value of goods and services, not the condition of humanity, it may be time to pitch it into the dustbin of history. They believe that a new, broader set of measures is needed that overcomes GDP's limitations.

Defenders of GDP argue that criticizing it in this way is like condemning a thermometer because it doesn't monitor blood pressure or cholesterol levels. They state that while GDP is certainly not a panacea, it nonetheless remains a vital statistical indicator used throughout the world to gauge national income and guide national economic policies.

In 1995, Canada's GDP was $780.03 billion, placing us 7th in the ranks of the G-7, the most industrialized countries in the world.

Services

The teenager who serves up a hamburger at the local fast food outlet and the bank manager who approves our loan applications are but two examples of the many Canadians who work in the services industry. Services are those intangible consumer or producer goods that are usually consumed at the time they are produced and purchased.

In Canada, the services-producing sector is several times larger than the goods-producing sector and accounts for two-thirds of Gross Domestic Product. It also employs almost three-quarters of the Canadian workforce. This is the sector that includes such businesses as restaurants, stores and gas stations as well as health care, government, education and financial institutions.

In Canada, the growth in the services sector has been nothing short of phenomenal. Since the end of the Second World War, it has literally shaped workers' lives.

While the services sector is a source of growing employment, jobs here tend to pay less than jobs in the goods-producing sector, although some jobs in telecommunications and professional services may pay well above the national average. Those employed in retail trade, food and accommodation, and personal service industries (such as hairdressers and drycleaners) tend to earn the least.

As well, Canadians working in the services-producing sector are almost three times more likely to be employed part time than those in the goods-producing sector. Part-time workers tend to earn less and have access to fewer employee benefits.

With little recourse to debt or savings, it was inevitable that the drop in real incomes, due to fewer jobs and higher prices, meant Canadians would slow spending. They did: by almost 2% in 1991.

During the recession of the 1990s, many Canadian business owners found themselves in great difficulty. Throughout the 1950s, 1960s and 1970s, profits had averaged 11% of GDP, and in the 1980s, 10%.

By 1992, profits were down to only 5.1% of GDP. In the last 70 years, only two years have been worse: 1931, when profits were at 5% of GDP and 1932, when they were at 2.8%. In 1992, businesses suffered from slow sales and overwhelming debt, and a record 14,317 declared bankruptcy.

Polls throughout this period registered Canadians' concern. Those working in traditional industries, such as automotive or mining and forestry, worried about job security as these industries seemed to take a back seat to the world of high-tech. It appeared that unemployment would remain chronically high, and that many workers who lost their manufacturing jobs in the early 1990s might never get them back.

A Recovery

Then in mid-1993, the situation began to change. Canada's GDP climbed, as manufacturing began to pick up in Ontario and Quebec and forestry revived in Alberta and British Columbia. The financial services industry prospered, as the globalization of financial markets and low nominal interest rates stimulated record-setting stock market prices and heavy investment in Canadian bonds. By early 1994, the Toronto Stock Exchange had hit record highs.

Canadians began to find work again. Incomes rose and, to some extent, confidence in the economy returned. Consumers loosened their purse strings. Businesses became more efficient and, armed with a new competitive edge, began to increase sales to other countries. A strong U.S. economy and the North American Free Trade Agreement strengthened this effect.

In 1994, production rose 4.5%, the highest rate of growth since the end of the previous expansionary period in the late 1980s. Exporters pulled out all stops to take advantage of a hot American economy hungry for machinery and equipment and automotive products. In 1994, prices for Canadian timber, minerals and other resources recovered and exploded the following year.

Another factor in the extraordinarily high growth in merchandise exports was the lowered value of our dollar, which meant Canadian goods were cheaper for other countries to buy.

Canadian businesses also became more productive. In 1994, productivity increased 2.6%, the strongest growth since 1984. At the same time, unit labour costs fell 0.7%, only the second drop since 1962. This rise in productivity and drop in costs gave our firms a competitive edge and contributed to the export boom.

But despite these encouraging signs, the recovery from Canada's most recent recession has not been unequivocal. While businesses have increased investment to meet foreign demand for their goods, Canadians in general remain cautious, and both federal and provincial governments have embarked on plans to reduce spending and slow the growth of debt loads.

In fact, the Canadian economy has been experiencing something of a roller coaster ride. Indeed, in early 1995, many Canadians had reason to wonder if Canada wasn't once again slipping into a recession. The economic boom in 1994 had raised concerns about a resurgence of inflation, in both Canada and the United States.

Monetary authorities in both countries had hiked interest rates to help "cool off" their respective economies. A resultant slowdown in the United States had dampened export sales; at home, businesses had slowed investment and consumers had cut back on spending. Many companies found their inventories building up because they could not immediately slow production.

By early 1996, however, interest rates had eased and American demand for Canadian goods was once again up. Growth remained slow, however, due to what economists call an "inventory cycle," meaning that, even when domestic demand and exports pick up again, there may be little real production in the economy as businesses continue to try to sell what they already have on their shelves.

In addition, growth prospects in Canada are strongly influenced by the economy of our major trading partner: we export more than 80% of total merchandise to the United States. "When the United States sneezes," goes the expression, "Canada catches cold." The outlook for both countries seems positive as the OECD has predicted that 1996 will be a year of stronger growth.

International Debt

The discussion of debt in Canada may have as many perspectives as it has people debating the issue. Many, for example, view our international debt as an indication that Canadians have been living beyond their means and have supported this by borrowing from other countries. Others argue, however, that Canada's borrowings are part of a long-standing tradition that has been vital to our growth and prosperity. Regardless, it is true that as the Canadian economy has moved from

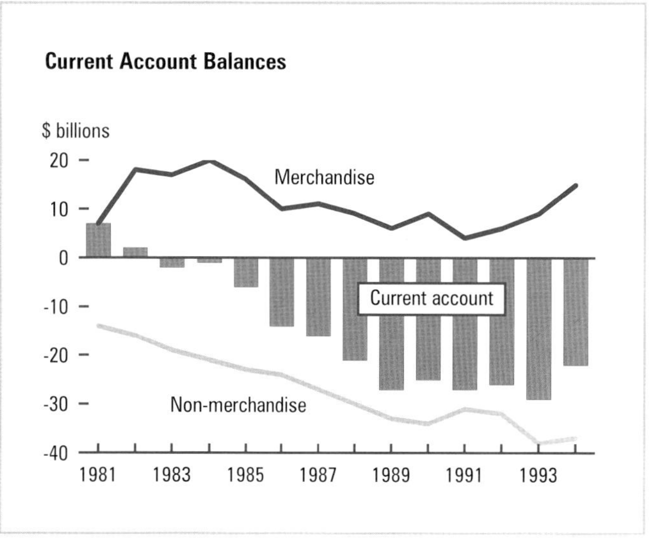

The Consumer Price Index

The Consumer Price Index (CPI) is relevant to all those who earn and spend money. When prices rise, the purchasing power of money drops. When prices drop, a dollar has more purchasing power. The CPI is used to estimate changes in this buying power of money.

Think of the CPI as a measure of the percentage change over time in the average cost of a large basket of goods and services purchased by Canadians. The quantity and quality of the items in the basket are held constant. As a result, changes in the cost of the basket are due to pure price movements and not to changes in the composition of the basket.

If you are concerned with everything in the CPI basket, you would refer to the Canada All-items index. If you are looking for something more specific, you may choose from the many detailed index series available. Examples include the series for food purchased from stores, restaurant meals, rented accommodation, transportation charges, and clothing. CPI information is available at the provincial level and to a lesser extent, for a number of major cities across Canada.

recession to recovery, our high debt level has come to the forefront of both the federal and provincial agendas. It is now a matter of national concern.

To track the size of our international debt, the Canadian government records transactions between all Canadians and the rest of the world in the "balance of payments." The balance of payments, which is actually a record kept by Statistics Canada, is made up of two parts: the current account and the capital account. The current account tracks trade in both goods and services with other countries. It includes interest and dividends as well as profits earned abroad by Canadian firms. It shows the transfers in and out of Canada, such as Canada's official aid to other countries. The capital account measures the international borrowing and lending of all Canadians.

Today, the current account is in deficit even though, over the past 40 years, our exports have grown more rapidly than imports. Any large merchandise trade surplus we have had has been offset by deficits for trade in services and by the interest we must pay to foreigners.

But, like a company's books, the balance of payments must balance. A current account deficit means more money is leaving the country than is returning. This difference needs to be financed, so the current account deficit must be matched by an equivalent amount of foreign borrowing—or, an inflow of capital that is registered in the capital account. In other words, because non-residents invest in Canada, we can spend more than we earn in our dealings with other countries.

In 1995, Canada's current account showed a merchandise trade surplus of $28.3 billion, a services trade deficit of $9 billion and $33 billion more in interest payments than we received. At the end of the day, Canada's external liabilities amounted to $672 billion, while our assets amounted to $333 billion. This left us with a net debt to other countries of $339 billion, or about $12,000 for every Canadian. This figure, often described as Canada's net international investment liability, reflects the extent to which foreign borrowing has financed Canadian consumption and investment through the years.

Percentage increase during last decade in number of families with one or both spouses holding more than one job: 50%.

Average income in 1994 for two-parent families with children: $59,746.

For female lone-parent families: $23,800.

Percentage of dual earner families with low incomes: 5%.

Percentage of families without wives earning: 17%.

Percentage of wives in dual-earner families in 1967 who earned more than their husbands: 11%.

Percentage in 1989: 19%.

Percentage in 1993: 25%.

Percentage of households with video cassette recorders in 1985: 23%.

Percentage in 1995: 82%.

Number of his 16 waking hours that the average Canadian male spends driving a car or earning the money to pay for it: 4.

Number of Canadians working at home for pay in 1991: 1.1 million.

Proportion of these people who were self-employed: one-third.

Percentage of full-time employed fathers belonging to the baby boom generation who said in 1995 that they were too busy to have fun: 36%.

Percentage of full-time employed mothers who said the same: 53%.

Since 1989, Canada's current account deficit has averaged 3.8% of GDP, the highest of the G-7 countries and the third highest in the OECD. In 1995, the current account deficit was the lowest it has been in 10 years, and only 2% of GDP. This tells us that we are spending more money than we earn from abroad, and net investment by other countries makes up the difference.

This has been happening for a long time. In 1950, Canada's net liability was $4 billion, and that figure quadrupled throughout the decade. Then in the 1960s, it doubled and in the 1970s, tripled. In the 1980s, it doubled once again.

There has been a continuous but moderate stream of foreign investment in Canadian bonds since the early 1950s. However, in the mid-1970s, non-residents stepped up their net purchases of Canadian bonds considerably. At the same time, the growth in foreign direct investment, which had been increasing steadily since the early 1950s, subsided. At the end of 1995, foreign investment in Canadian bonds amounted to 47% of Canada's external liabilities, while foreign direct investment was 25%.

Half of what we borrow abroad comes from the United States. At the end of 1995, our debt to the Americans amounted to $166 billion. Throughout the 1980s, our reliance on the United States as a source of foreign capital diminished somewhat, although since 1991, it has again been increasing. The United Kingdom is our second largest creditor: we owe the British $79 billion.

Our heavy reliance on foreign borrowings has caused concern among Canadians, mainly because of what we've done with these borrowings. When we borrow to finance investment, as we did in the 1950s and 1960s—for example, to build new factories or buy new equipment—we expect that there will be returns in the form of employment and incomes. Nonetheless, the promise of future payoffs has not prevented Canadians from worrying about the loss of control over our economy.

With the current shift to a more passive type of foreign investment, particularly in government bonds, the concern has become focused on the use that the governments make of these funds. In fact, these funds have been critical to balancing the books. Government borrowing to finance expenditures is thus a very large part of the discussion. Indeed, federal and provincial governments (along with their enterprises) account for almost half of Canada's gross debt to foreigners. Throughout the last few decades, many Canadians have benefited from the extra cash flow provided by foreigners. But what we have borrowed, we must eventually pay back.

At the same time, Canada also invests in other countries. Although most of the public focus has been on foreign investment here, our assets have grown more rapidly in the last 15 years. Managers of Canadian pension and mutual funds have invested heavily in foreign securities, especially stocks, bringing portfolio investment to 25% of Canada's external assets. However, Canadian corporations also directly invest abroad, and this activity accounts for the lion's share of Canada's external assets, at 43%.

Canadians have some $333 billion invested abroad. In 1995, the United States continued to be the most favoured country, receiving some 54% of our capital invested abroad, although its share has been declining over the past decade. The European Community, on the other hand, has almost doubled its share of Canadian capital invested abroad.

Federal Debt

Whereas Canada's current account tells us what we owe as a people to other countries, our federal and provincial debts tell us what our governments owe, both to Canadians and to foreigners.

In 1995, the federal debt amounted to almost $546 billion—almost $19,000 for every Canadian. Nor does that include provincial and territorial debt, which by early 1995 had reached $181.7 billion.

What is interesting about all this is that the federal government actually runs an operating surplus: almost $5 billion in 1995. But since the federal government has been spending

Photo by Robert Bourdeau

Molsons Bank, Montreal, 1987.

more than it collects in revenues for 25 years, once the public debt is taken into account, the interest payments alone cause this "small surplus" to become a deficit of more than $37 billion dollars. In fact, of every dollar that the federal government collects as revenue (through income taxes, excise taxes and Unemployment Insurance contributions), 34 cents pays interest on the public debt.

These debts mean that Canada's fiscal situation is vulnerable to economic slowdowns. In past recessions, governments could increase their level of spending to boost a slow economy. However, now the public debt and the interest we pay on this debt is too high to do this. In the recession of the early 1990s, Canadian governments chose not to increase spending on goods and services to help boost the ailing economy.

Rather, they chose to offset some of the cyclical increase in the deficit caused by Canadians' increased reliance on welfare and Unemployment Insurance through spending cuts elsewhere.

The Value of Money

The Bank of Canada controls how much money circulates in our economy and how much that money is worth. This job, however, has become more challenging with the globalization of financial markets. Today, potential investors have a considerable influence on the value of the Canadian dollar, and can cause it to fluctuate depending on their decision to invest or not invest in Canada. The impact of these decisions was felt in early 1995 when the exchange rate fell to a nine-year low, and short-term interest rates rose as investors grew a little wary about investing in Canada.

For example, a businessperson from any other country considering investment in Canada in early 1995 would have had to deal with a wide variety of issues, not the least of which was the country's high debt load. Still nervous after Mexico's currency crisis, when investor skittishness over the high debt load and regional riots brought the peso crashing down, that investor may have been unsure of Canada as a good investment.

While tough federal and provincial budgets improved sentiments somewhat, the downgrading of Canada's credit rating and the October 1995 referendum, when Quebecers nearly voted to separate from the rest of the country, contributed to both fluctuations and uncertainty in the worth of Canada's currency.

Inflation

In the early 1990s, Canada was one of a group of countries that announced explicit inflation targets, and the Bank of Canada has been very successful at keeping inflation under control. The targets have been rigorously upheld: inflation levels have remained well within the target range of 1% to 3%. Despite this success (the inflation level of 1994 was the lowest in 40 years), there is a general feeling that a dollar doesn't go as far as it once did. Wages and other forms of personal income have been growing slowly—at times even more slowly than consumer prices. Yearly wage increases in Canada have been the second lowest in the G-7; only the Japanese have experienced lower increases.

The one exception to all this has been the dramatic rise in "producer" prices. Producer prices are distinct from consumer prices because they concern such commodities as metal products, pulp and paper, lumber and timber—commodities used to produce other goods. In 1995, prices for these rose 8%. But consumers are largely sheltered, since half of these commodities go outside the country as exports. As well, they make up less than 2% of the total inputs into the Canadian economy, so any price shock has a small effect on the general level of prices in Canada.

Loonies and Greenbacks

In 1922, Ernest Hemingway, the great American novelist, wrote that "at the present rate of exchange, a Canadian with an income of one thousand dollars a year can live comfortably and enjoyably in Paris. If exchange were normal, the same Canadian would starve to death."

Today, the story might well be the reverse. A Canadian in Paris may be in for an expensive cup of coffee, and even the lightest of snacks can be surprisingly expensive, as the value of our dollar has fallen considerably over the past several years.

Take the price of a Big Mac. In 1994, a Big Mac in Canada cost $2.76. In Australia, it was $2.40; in Russia, $1.56. In France, it was almost $5.00 and in Denmark, close to $6.00.

Although Canadian travellers may wish for a stronger Canadian dollar, it has been a boon for Canadian retailers, as our goods have become relatively cheaper to buy. In 1994, it cost Canadians an average of $1.37 to buy one American dollar. Three years before, it cost $1.15. As a result, in 1994, fewer

James Zagon, National Currency Collection, Bank of Canada, Ottawa

Ten dollar bill, dated May 15, 1929.

Canadians went shopping in the United States. As more Canadians shopped at home, and more visitors from other countries took advantage of our cheap dollar, Canadian retailers have been busier and businesses have been more profitable.

At the same time, the goods we import are relatively more expensive. But again, to some extent, Canadians don't feel these price increases, since our cautious spending habits force many producers, wholesalers and retailers to accept lower profit margins. Canadians are also protected as importers use methods like "currency hedging"; that is, buying foreign currency at a price set out in a contract and in this way avoiding, at least temporarily, some of the risk of a depreciation in the Canadian dollar.

Interest Rates

Since 1981, interest rates in Canada have been generally declining. Early in 1994, they reached their lowest level in 30 years. Now, when Canadians take out a mortgage to purchase a home, they negotiate at rates of between 8% and 10%, as opposed to the early 1980s when rates were as high as 18%. Because inflationary pressures in Canada's economy are down, the need to hike interest rates has diminished.

Nonetheless, both the OECD and the International Monetary Fund (IMF) have suggested that interest rates are still high, as Canada's excellent inflation performance is compromised by high government debt.

Job Trends

In 1994, close to 400,000 new jobs were created in Canada, a stunning record not matched since 1987. Most of them came from the export boom in manufacturing. By the end of the year, 206,000 more Canadians held jobs than five years before.

But slow growth in jobs in 1995 remained a concern, even as the unemployment rate fell to 9.2%, the lowest level since 1990. In addition, although 664,000 more people were employed than in 1992, the unemployment rate for young people remains high.

The old maxim: "last hired, first fired" perfectly describes the early 1990s for Canada's young people. They simply found themselves out of luck as many Canadian businesses shut their doors against new entrants. In 1992, the youth unemployment rate peaked at just under 19%, and many young people gave up looking for work. Young people generally leave the labour force during economic downturns, but a decline of this magnitude was unprecedented. By the end of 1993, only 60% of young people were either working or looking for work, compared with 71% at the end of 1989.

The result has been a growing pool of young people without any work experience to offer employers. In 1994, one in five young Canadians had never held a job, compared with only one in 10 in 1989.

There is one strong message that has come from this: "Stay in school!" In 1993, 56% of Canada's young people were in class as full-time students, compared with 49% four years earlier. Quite likely, their academic travails will earn these young people a job: prospects improve noticeably for those with university degrees.

University degrees notwithstanding, young people won't make as much money as in the past. In 1993, young male university graduates working full time earned little more, in real terms, than did those with only a high school diploma in the late 1970s.

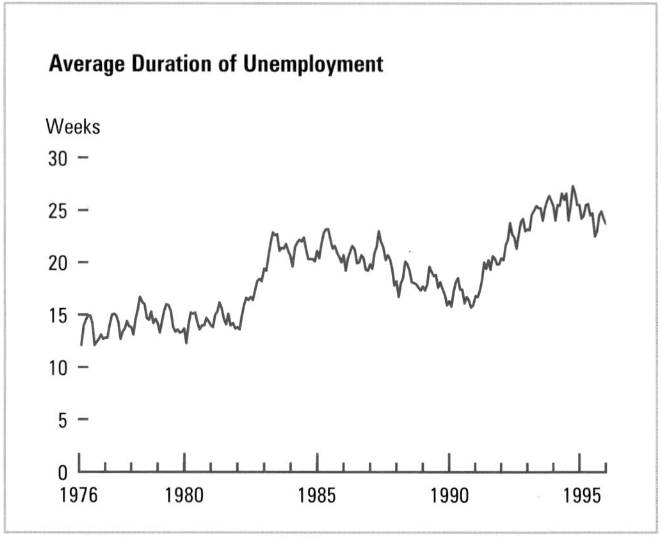

Part Time

More Canadians work part time. Nearly one in five working Canadians have part-time jobs, while 20 years ago, only one out of 10 did.

Although most employed Canadians still have only one full-time permanent job, during the recession, employers in both the private and the public sectors reduced costs by making greater use of part-time, temporary or contract labour.

Many of those in part-time positions hold more than one job. By 1994, close to one million Canadians held two or more jobs. Canadians employed in the services industry are especially likely to work part time.

Small Business

Allan Gould, Canadian journalist and author, once asked, "if the ancestors of Thomas Edison and Walt Disney had not chosen to move down to the United States from Canada, would we not also be claiming the light bulb and Mickey Mouse as our own?" Intelligence, tenacity, creative thinking and entrepreneurial ability have been and continue to be part of the Canadian psyche.

A TAXING REALITY

It has been 80 years since the introduction of personal income tax by the Government of Canada. This would no doubt come as a surprise to Sir Thomas White, Minister of Finance in 1917, who described it as a "temporary" measure and declared that "a year or two after the war is over, the measure should be definitely reviewed."

Although the British North America Act of 1867 had empowered the Canadian government to raise money "by any mode or system of taxation," for the first 50 years, direct taxation was left to the provinces, and federal bills were paid through such indirect taxes as sales taxes, customs duties and excise taxes.

However, the Fathers of Confederation left the most expensive tasks to the federal government: the construction of railways, roads, bridges and harbours. With the additional pressure of financing the First World War, the government began to go directly to Canadians. Eventually, in 1949, the Income War Tax Act was repealed and replaced by the Income Tax Act.

Today, taxes—income-based, consumption-based, taxes on wealth and transfers of wealth, or business taxes—are the primary source of government revenue. Income tax includes personal income tax, corporation income tax and payroll taxes. Today, Canadians remit income tax to both the federal and provincial governments.

Personal income taxes have been climbing steadily in Canada. In 1973, Canadians paid $32 billion in personal income taxes. Twenty years later, in 1993, we paid $86 billion. In 1994, personal income taxes took 19.7% of average total family income.

While personal income tax in Canada has been going up, income taxes paid by corporations have been dwindling. For example, in 1994, personal income tax represented 47% of total federal revenue, up from 40% in 1974. By contrast, corporate tax had dwindled to 10% in 1994, down from 15% in 1974.

For 1996-97, the federal government estimates that the money will go to direct program expenditures (31%, one-fifth of that on defence), public debt charges (30%), payments to persons, such as benefits to the elderly and unemployed (24%), and payments to other levels of government (15%).

As one-time Minister of Trade and Commerce C.D. Howe noted: "There is nothing more permanent than a temporary government building—unless it's a temporary tax."

Ernst Neumann, National Archives of Canada, C-043500

Victims of the Depression in Canada, 1933.

Today, a growing number of Canadians are starting their own businesses. This emergent class of entrepreneurs is fuelling a remarkable surge in small business employment and home-based enterprises. Their strength can be seen in the numbers. Small businesses accounted for 76% of the new jobs created in Canada in the 1980s.

In 1994, there were 2.1 million self-employed Canadians. In the past two decades, self-employment has increased by 92%. It is now just slightly smaller than the public sector. Indeed, a new sector is emerging, and entrepreneurship, whether by choice or necessity, is becoming an increasingly common work style. Young people are especially keen. Of the almost one million small businesses in Canada, 25% of them are owned by people aged 18 to 29.

At least part of this growth in small businesses is an indirect result of the high cost of permanent employees. In Canada today, employers must contribute more to payroll taxes such as Unemployment Insurance and pension plans. This has induced many companies to replace full-time employees with consultants or independent contractors.

Goods and Services

In Canada, as with all major economic powers, the post-war period has been marked by a steady shift away from the production of goods toward more emphasis on services. In 1960, five out of 10 Canadians worked in the services industry. In 1995, some seven out of 10 were employed in this sector. In 1994, the services sector accounted for 66% of GDP.

The star players are the information-based industries such as finance and communications. Also key are transportation and trade services, boosted by the increased volume of international and interprovincial trade. Despite recent cutbacks, government services still account for almost 17% of employment.

The counterpart to this rapid growth in employment in the services industry has been a relative decline in the goods-producing industries. This has been particularly true of manufacturing, where the number of jobs in the economy fell from 25% in 1960 to less than 15% in 1994. The shift can partly be explained by the ability of this industry to produce more with relatively fewer workers. Some suggest that it may also reflect the recent phenomenon of "out-sourcing," when manufacturers contract out for services they once did for themselves.

Canada's manufacturing industry was easily the hardest hit in the early 1990s. But if manufacturing suffered in the recession, the electrical products sector was scarcely touched. Electrical products are immensely popular as businesses invest more and more in information technology. Since 1991, production in this sector has grown almost 40%.

But while electrical products have played a leading role in this recovery, it is still the traditional sectors that have led the pack. In particular, forestry and mining have skyrocketed as a result of soaring world market prices for lumber, aluminum, copper, pulp, oil, natural gas, wheat and other resource products.

Who Owns Canada?

If you shop at a drugstore, purchasing shampoo, toothpaste or soap, you might be interested to note that most of these are produced by a foreign-controlled company. That's because chemicals are used to produce these products and foreign-controlled companies control much of Canada's chemicals industry.

In fact, almost 85% of all revenues earned in this industry go straight to foreign-controlled companies. On the other hand, if you're building a new home or taking a taxi you are generally adding to Canadian business coffers, as the construction and transportation industries are primarily controlled and owned by Canadians.

The extent to which corporate wealth is foreign-controlled is one of the most distinctive features of the Canadian economic landscape. The incidence of foreign control in Canada is high among the industrialized nations of the world. American firms are predominant leaders in Canada, controlling 20% of corporate wealth.

Since 1988, foreign control of revenues has increased by almost 3%. In 1994, foreign-controlled companies earned 30% of total revenue. One reason for the growth in foreign control is that these companies were less affected than their Canadian counterparts by the recession. While Canadian business revenues increased 12%, foreign revenues rose twice as much: 25%.

SOURCES

Bank of Canada
Organisation for Economic Co-operation and Development
Statistics Canada

FOR FURTHER READING

Selected publications from Statistics Canada

- **Canadian Economic Observer**. Monthly. 11-010
- **National Income and Expenditure Accounts**. Annual. 13-201
- **Consumer Prices and Price Indexes**. Quarterly. 62-010
- **Canada's International Investment Position**. Annual. 67-202
- **Historical Labour Force Statistics**. Annual. 71-201
- **Labour Force Annual Averages**. Occasional. 71-529
- **Perspectives on Labour and Income**. Quarterly. 75-001E

Selected publications from other sources

- **Annual Financial Report of the Government of Canada**. 1994-95. Canadian Department of Finance. 1995.
- **Bank of Canada Review**. Bank of Canada. Quarterly.
- **OECD Economic Outlook**. Organisation for Economic Co-operation and Development. Twice yearly.

Legend

–	nil or zero	..	not available	x	confidential
--	too small to be expressed	...	not applicable or not appropriate		*(Certain tables may not add due to rounding)*

9.1 GROSS DOMESTIC PRODUCT (EXPENDITURE-BASED) AT MARKET PRICES

	Nfld.	P.E.I.	N.S.	N.B.	Que.	Ont.	Man.	Sask.	Alta.	B.C.	Y.T.	N.W.T.
						$ Millions						
Gross Domestic Product at market prices												
1983	5,767	1,234	10,251	7,756	91,204	152,046	14,667	15,927	56,911	47,070	427	1,420
1984	6,309	1,319	11,388	8,564	99,537	170,387	16,580	16,953	60,451	49,552	455	1,514
1985	6,485	1,361	12,382	9,030	107,244	185,625	17,771	17,738	64,664	52,781	459	1,599
1986	6,938	1,516	13,155	10,307	116,622	205,643	18,562	17,364	56,617	55,527	599	1,470
1987	7,484	1,627	14,231	11,360	128,379	226,798	19,775	17,864	58,431	62,073	828	1,566
1988	8,084	1,802	15,120	12,269	140,584	253,143	21,228	18,491	62,321	68,571	883	1,868
1989	8,525	1,911	16,052	12,967	148,144	276,073	22,442	19,524	65,711	74,808	961	1,962
1990	8,831	1,995	16,720	13,133	153,164	277,508	23,218	20,756	71,446	78,790	1,017	2,035
1991	9,189	2,098	17,411	13,498	155,575	278,463	23,011	20,686	71,306	81,453	913	1,957
1992	9,237	2,184	17,772	13,901	157,373	282,803	23,437	20,578	72,273	86,698	1,022	1,972
1993	9,501	2,325	17,952	14,624	161,720	288,569	23,778	21,753	77,770	91,228	838	2,038
1994	9,839	2,418	18,198	15,089	167,493	303,151	25,041	23,082	83,182	98,910	846	2,165
1995	9,958	2,591	18,760	15,833	174,422	315,069	26,333	24,281	85,411	103,433	947	2,323
1995												
Personal expenditure on consumer goods and services	7,466	1,666	13,133	10,345	106,597	183,149	16,916	14,692	45,332	65,226	498	895
Government current expenditure on goods and services	2,360	776	5,535	3,923	36,055	57,072	5,891	4,833	12,672	17,658	411	1,260
Government investment in fixed capital	290	83	496	508	3,779	6,332	751	476	1,493	2,821	156	231
Business investment in fixed capital	2,973	474	2,786	2,283	23,798	42,206	3,523	4,397	17,983	19,236	177	319
Government investment in inventories	–	–	1	1	12	10	1	1	2	2	–	–
Business investment in inventories	4	15	83	42	1,436	2,634	252	371	1,007	1,000	5	2
Net exports plus statistical discrepancy	-3,135	-423	-3,274	-1,269	2,745	23,666	-1,001	-489	6,922	-2,510	-300	-384
Final domestic demand	13,089	2,999	21,950	17,059	170,229	288,759	27,081	24,398	77,480	104,941	1,242	2,705

Source: Statistics Canada, CANSIM, matrices 2623–2631, 4997, 4998 and 6950.

9.2 GROSS DOMESTIC PRODUCT (INCOME-BASED) AT MARKET PRICES

	1985	1986	1987	1988	1989	1990	1991	1992	1993	1994	1995
						$ Millions					
Gross Domestic Product at market prices	477,988	505,666	551,597	605,906	650,748	669,467	676,477	690,122	712,855	747,260	776,299
Wages, salaries, and supplementary labour income	257,518	274,801	298,834	327,823	353,632	372,087	382,378	391,619	398,163	409,085	422,110
Corporation profits before taxes	49,490	45,355	56,571	64,667	60,093	44,814	34,829	35,060	42,135	56,611	64,015
Interest and miscellaneous investment income	40,302	39,289	39,967	45,207	52,735	59,524	56,211	55,457	53,530	56,637	57,934
Accrued net income of farm operators from farm production	2,808	3,946	2,890	4,275	3,042	2,065	1,644	1,730	2,544	1,642	1,930
Net income of non-farm unincorporated business, including rents	26,447	28,856	30,977	32,868	34,461	34,859	36,072	37,235	39,958	40,874	41,529
Inventory valuation adjustment	-1,760	-1,812	-3,187	-2,865	-1,580	-382	1,955	-2,556	-2,778	-5,316	-3,473
Net domestic income at factor cost	374,805	390,435	426,052	471,975	502,383	512,967	513,089	518,545	533,552	559,533	584,045
Indirect taxes less subsidies	47,212	53,827	59,719	67,790	76,214	76,662	79,878	84,389	88,731	92,492	95,113
Capital consumption allowances	55,926	60,595	64,116	68,128	72,352	78,594	82,331	85,305	87,904	92,925	96,234
Statistical discrepancy	45	809	1,710	-1,987	-201	1,244	1,179	1,883	2,668	2,310	907

Source: Statistics Canada, CANSIM, matrix 6627.

9.3 GROSS DOMESTIC PRODUCT (EXPENDITURE-BASED) AT MARKET PRICES

	1985	1986	1987	1988	1989	1990	1991	1992	1993	1994	1995
						$ Millions					
Gross Domestic Product at market prices	477,988	505,666	551,597	605,906	650,748	669,467	676,477	690,122	712,855	747,260	776,299
Personal expenditure on consumer goods and services	274,503	297,478	322,769	349,937	378,933	399,319	411,960	422,515	436,542	452,444	465,970
Durable goods	40,278	44,628	49,430	54,570	57,533	56,267	53,662	54,000	56,376	60,577	62,384
Semi-durable goods	28,147	30,604	33,148	35,220	37,068	37,997	37,692	37,974	39,143	41,555	42,489
Non-durable goods	79,959	83,597	88,019	93,646	99,736	104,561	109,506	111,310	114,364	115,152	117,458
Services	126,119	138,649	152,172	166,501	184,596	200,494	211,100	219,231	226,659	235,160	243,639
Government current expenditure on goods and services	95,519	100,129	105,836	114,472	124,108	135,157	144,885	150,390	152,158	150,593	150,834
Government investment in fixed capital	12,886	12,567	12,886	13,690	15,263	16,610	16,431	16,106	15,816	17,067	17,788
Government investment in inventories	-64	-35	-38	64	-3	67	-37	-40	-4	-1	30
Business investment in fixed capital	81,312	88,993	103,831	119,100	130,812	124,766	115,570	112,759	113,068	121,051	116,553
Residential construction	25,222	30,806	39,524	43,870	49,131	44,006	39,947	43,820	43,081	44,762	37,988
Non-residential construction	26,747	25,626	27,613	32,445	35,724	36,961	35,168	29,734	30,162	32,962	32,213
Machinery and equipment	29,343	32,561	36,694	42,785	45,957	43,799	40,455	39,205	39,825	43,327	46,352
Business investment in inventories	2,345	2,592	3,109	3,731	3,610	-2,902	-3,198	-3,661	1,107	3,994	6,996
Non-farm	1,997	1,745	3,552	4,319	3,029	-3,526	-3,250	-2,950	-146	4,144	6,720
Farm and grain in commercial channels	348	847	-443	-588	581	624	52	-711	1,253	-150	276
Exports of goods and services	134,919	138,119	145,416	159,309	163,903	168,917	164,849	181,189	209,370	250,877	290,325
Merchandise	119,061	120,318	126,340	137,779	141,514	145,556	140,233	155,403	181,251	217,936	253,821
Non-merchandise	15,858	17,801	19,076	21,530	22,389	23,361	24,616	25,786	28,119	32,941	36,504
Deduct: Imports of goods and services	123,388	133,369	140,502	156,384	166,079	171,223	172,805	187,254	212,534	246,455	271,291
Merchandise	102,670	110,374	115,119	128,862	135,455	136,858	136,616	149,201	171,929	203,001	225,431
Non-merchandise	20,718	22,995	25,383	27,522	30,624	34,365	36,189	38,053	40,605	43,454	45,860
Statistical discrepancy	-44	-808	-1,710	1,987	201	-1,244	-1,178	-1,882	-2,668	-2,310	-906
Final domestic demand	464,220	499,167	545,322	597,199	649,116	675,852	688,846	701,770	717,584	741,155	751,145

Source: Statistics Canada, CANSIM, matrix 6628.

9.4 GROSS DOMESTIC PRODUCT (EXPENDITURE-BASED) IN CONSTANT 1986 DOLLARS

	1985	1986	1987	1988	1989	1990	1991	1992	1993	1994	1995
	$ Constant 1986 (Millions)										
Gross Domestic Product at 1986 prices	489,437	505,666	526,730	552,958	566,486	565,155	555,052	559,305	571,722	594,990	608,835
Personal expenditure on consumer goods and services	284,923	297,478	310,453	324,301	335,284	338,717	333,396	337,619	342,858	352,913	357,827
Durable goods	41,961	44,628	48,226	51,442	51,983	50,252	47,741	48,045	49,465	51,883	52,520
Semi-durable goods	29,036	30,604	31,698	32,091	32,379	32,274	29,643	29,739	30,419	32,153	32,768
Non-durable goods	82,329	83,597	84,128	86,661	88,208	87,152	86,521	87,581	88,898	91,441	92,154
Services	131,745	138,649	146,401	154,107	162,714	169,039	169,491	172,254	174,076	177,436	180,385
Government current expenditure on goods and services	98,585	100,129	101,857	106,060	110,331	113,890	116,958	118,126	118,660	116,592	115,732
Government investment in fixed capital	12,776	12,567	12,849	13,311	14,477	15,470	16,231	16,217	16,334	17,376	17,852
Government investment in inventories	-67	-35	-37	62	–	63	-32	-35	-3	–	26
Business investment in fixed capital	82,863	88,993	99,693	110,794	117,153	111,492	107,005	105,202	105,761	111,969	111,305
Residential construction	27,184	30,806	35,843	36,855	38,610	34,864	30,511	32,908	31,517	32,089	27,240
Non-residential construction	27,129	25,626	26,400	29,301	30,848	31,005	30,212	25,730	25,861	27,443	25,895
Machinery and equipment	28,694	32,561	37,450	44,638	47,695	45,623	46,282	46,564	48,383	52,437	58,170
Business investment in inventories	2,229	2,592	3,259	2,453	3,778	-1,800	-2,395	-3,731	1,009	3,729	5,609
Non-farm	2,346	1,745	3,682	4,218	2,937	-3,084	-2,753	-2,611	58	3,822	5,449
Farm and grain in commercial channels	325	847	-423	-1,765	841	1,284	358	-1,120	951	-93	160
Exports of goods and services	132,218	138,119	142,942	156,528	157,799	164,312	166,687	179,426	198,093	227,120	254,269
Merchandise	115,681	120,318	124,665	136,247	137,830	144,162	146,479	158,332	176,016	201,959	227,129
Non-merchandise	16,361	17,801	18,277	20,281	19,969	20,150	20,208	21,094	22,077	25,161	27,140
Deduct: Imports of goods and services	123,935	133,369	142,678	162,385	172,584	175,960	181,831	192,000	208,856	232,871	253,082
Merchandise	102,132	110,374	117,271	133,877	141,072	141,597	146,042	156,411	173,703	197,804	217,275
Non-merchandise	21,956	22,995	25,407	28,508	31,512	34,363	35,789	35,589	35,153	35,067	35,807
Statistical discrepancy	-32	-808	-1,608	1,834	248	-1,029	-967	-1,519	-2,134	-1,838	-703
Final domestic demand	478,812	499,167	524,852	554,466	577,245	579,569	573,590	577,164	583,613	598,850	602,716

Source: Statistics Canada, CANSIM, matrix 6840.

9.5 GROSS DOMESTIC PRODUCT IMPLICIT PRICES INDICES

	1982	1983	1984	1985	1986	1987	1988	1989	1990	1991	1992	1993	1994	1995
	% Change in implicit prices from previous year													
Gross Domestic Product at market prices	8.7	5.0	3.1	2.6	2.4	4.7	4.7	4.8	3.1	2.9	1.2	1.1	0.6	1.8
Personal expenditure on consumer goods and services	10.2	6.3	3.9	3.7	3.8	4.0	3.8	4.7	4.3	4.8	1.2	1.8	0.7	1.6
Government current expenditure on goods and services	11.6	6.0	4.0	4.0	3.2	3.9	3.8	4.3	5.5	4.4	2.7	0.7	0.9	0.5
Government investment in fixed capital	7.1	2.4	2.8	1.9	-0.9	0.3	2.5	2.5	1.9	-5.8	-1.9	-2.5	0.3	0.8
Business investment in fixed capital	6.1	0.3	1.9	1.6	1.9	4.2	3.2	3.9	0.2	-3.5	-0.7	-0.3	0.7	-1.6
Exports of goods and services	2.0	0.6	3.5	1.0	-2.0	1.7	0.1	2.1	-1.1	-3.8	2.1	4.7	4.3	3.5
Deduct: Imports of goods and services	4.8	-0.3	5.2	2.7	0.4	-1.5	-2.2	-0.1	1.1	-2.4	2.6	4.4	3.7	1.3
Final domestic demand	9.5	5.1	3.5	3.3	3.1	3.9	3.7	4.5	3.6	3.0	1.2	1.2	0.6	0.8

Source: Statistics Canada, CANSIM, matrix 6841.

9.6 BALANCE OF INTERNATIONAL PAYMENTS

	1984	1985	1986	1987	1988	1989	1990	1991	1992	1993	1994	1995
						$ Millions						
Current Account												
Receipts	136,213	145,702	148,165	158,218	173,465	178,527	184,154	179,139	195,659	223,966	269,335	311,934
Merchandise exports	111,330	119,062	120,318	126,340	137,779	141,514	145,555	140,233	155,402	181,251	217,936	253,821
Non-merchandise	24,883	26,640	27,847	31,877	35,686	37,013	38,599	38,906	40,257	42,715	51,399	58,113
Services	14,705	15,857	17,801	19,076	21,530	22,387	23,361	24,615	25,788	28,118	32,941	36,504
Investment income[1]	7,974	8,516	7,026	9,719	10,288	10,749	11,130	10,240	10,208	9,980	13,645	17,147
Transfers	2,204	2,266	3,021	3,082	3,868	3,877	4,108	4,052	4,261	4,616	4,813	4,462
Payments	137,028	151,894	162,218	173,860	194,578	205,475	209,378	206,177	221,554	252,760	291,505	323,136
Merchandise imports	91,493	102,669	110,374	115,119	128,862	135,455	136,859	136,617	149,201	171,928	203,000	225,431
Non-merchandise	45,536	49,224	51,844	58,742	65,716	70,020	72,519	69,560	72,353	80,832	88,505	97,705
Services	19,139	20,718	22,995	25,383	27,522	30,623	34,363	36,189	38,055	40,606	43,454	45,860
Investment income[1]	23,962	25,946	26,086	30,205	34,621	35,800	33,974	29,427	30,207	36,049	41,124	47,762
Transfers	2,434	2,560	2,763	3,154	3,574	3,596	4,181	3,944	4,090	4,177	3,927	4,082
Balances												
Merchandise	19,838	16,392	9,944	11,222	8,917	6,059	8,696	3,616	6,201	9,323	14,935	28,390
Non-merchandise	-20,653	-22,584	-23,996	-26,865	-30,031	-33,007	-33,920	-30,654	-32,096	-38,118	-37,106	-39,591
Total current account	-815	-6,192	-14,053	-15,643	-21,114	-26,948	-25,224	-27,038	-25,895	-28,794	-22,170	-11,202
Capital Account[2]												
Canadian claims on non-residents, net flows	-11,021	-3,756	-10,265	-16,565	-17,365	-10,958	-10,630	-10,167	-2,547	-19,137	-16,882	-18,637
Canadian direct investment abroad	-4,772	-5,274	-4,864	-11,322	-4,738	-5,428	-5,522	-6,478	-4,459	-7,490	-10,157	-7,874
Portfolio securities												
Foreign bonds	-1,359	-750	-179	-874	-74	-1,549	-75	-1,161	-900	-4,070	525	-917
Foreign stocks	-714	-570	-2,065	-1,067	-2,914	-2,463	-2,521	-6,513	-7,387	-9,818	-9,335	-4,509
Government of Canada assets												
Official international reserves	1,092	112	-662	-4,461	-9,451	-346	-649	2,830	6,987	598	1,630	-3,529
Loans and subscriptions	-1,955	-867	-24	-596	-548	-982	-1,438	-1,785	-1,696	-286	-1,893	-661
Non-bank deposits abroad	-1,927	2,135	-2,301	968	-591	-304	-970	-386	1,636	-755	-1,976	-5,108
Other claims	-1,386	1,458	-169	789	951	113	546	3,326	3,272	2,685	4,324	3,961
Canadian liabilities to non-residents, net flows	18,012	16,249	27,013	35,357	39,065	37,275	37,495	40,197	27,048	57,090	37,088	25,292
Foreign direct investment in Canada[1]	6,156	1,774	3,864	10,660	7,951	5,941	9,163	3,148	5,392	6,425	9,945	14,713
Portfolio securities												
Canadian bonds	7,707	11,066	22,541	7,530	15,568	17,458	14,329	26,620	18,480	28,929	14,698	29,801
Canadian stocks	152	1,551	1,876	6,640	-2,379	3,885	-1,735	-990	1,036	12,056	6,412	-4,242
Canadian banks net foreign security transactions with non-residents[3]	532	311	-5,196	2,905	2,932	-2,613	2,454	5,378	-3,105	-251	390	-17,024
Money market instruments												
Government of Canada paper	1,514	-691	1,847	1,308	7,123	484	3,418	2,288	1,915	10,939	2,731	-2,865
Other paper	15	114	543	1,232	2,168	656	2,223	2,140	2,983	-1,643	-1,826	-544
Allocation of special drawing rights												
Other liabilities	1,935	2,124	1,537	5,082	5,703	11,464	7,643	1,613	346	635	4,739	5,453
Total capital account, net flow	6,990	12,492	16,748	18,793	21,700	26,318	26,865	30,030	24,501	37,953	20,207	6,654
Statistical discrepancy	-6,175	-6,300	-2,695	-3,150	-586	630	-1,641	-2,993	1,394	-9,159	1,964	4,547

1. From 1983, includes reinvested earnings accruing to direct investors.
2. A minus sign denotes an outflow of capital resulting from an increase in claims on non-residents or from a decrease in liabiities to non-residents.
3. When the banks' foreign currency position (booked in Canada) with non-residents is a net asset, the series is classified as part of Canadian claims on non-residents.

Source: Statistics Canada, CANSIM, matrix 2333.

9.7 CANADA'S INTERNATIONAL INVESTMENT POSITION[1]

	1983	1984	1985	1986	1987	1988	1989	1990	1991	1992	1993	1994	1995
							$ Millions						
Assets	95,250	110,055	121,256	136,441	152,639	171,289	187,786	208,617	229,691	243,095	272,490	310,981	333,364
Canadian direct investment abroad	42,318	50,092	57,224	61,497	70,641	76,169	84,273	91,462	101,761	107,451	114,860	131,394	142,347
Portfolio investment													
Foreign bonds	1,996	3,723	5,146	5,841	7,612	7,665	9,982	10,177	11,270	12,934	17,501	18,317	18,813
Foreign stocks	10,735	12,109	15,306	19,863	24,887	27,708	31,746	35,537	39,923	44,053	50,962	59,982	63,770
Other foreign debt	2,277	2,656	2,261	2,019	2,156	3,139	3,517	3,662	2,394	2,333	3,621	3,995	4,141
Official international reserves	5,232	4,206	4,580	5,654	10,658	19,317	19,456	21,551	19,530	15,135	16,882	17,487	20,767
Government of Canada loans and subscriptions	15,458	17,913	19,437	19,523	19,573	19,477	20,107	21,820	23,802	27,639	28,499	30,926	31,015
Other	17,233	19,356	17,300	22,043	17,112	17,814	18,707	24,408	31,011	33,550	40,166	48,881	52,511
Liabilities	238,540	261,219	293,671	323,796	354,160	379,047	412,688	455,374	495,015	536,893	595,344	648,431	672,641
Foreign direct investment in Canada	79,669	85,984	90,358	96,054	106,144	114,480	123,083	131,132	135,840	138,696	142,321	152,784	168,077
Portfolio investment													
Canadian bonds	82,984	93,578	111,921	136,714	144,882	149,284	162,776	181,146	208,280	236,440	275,271	304,485	329,839
Canadian stocks	12,325	13,041	15,134	16,249	18,202	18,073	20,563	20,598	17,590	17,952	23,638	31,088	32,074
Canadian money market instruments	14,881	16,481	18,172	17,192	20,078	21,441	28,267	30,553	32,673	35,257	34,198	34,066	31,942
Other Canadian debt	4,381	5,982	5,543	7,931	10,421	19,417	20,611	26,402	30,534	36,104	45,901	47,529	47,552
Canadian banks' net foreign currency position	25,280	27,511	29,726	24,289	26,033	26,734	24,287	28,699	34,005	34,330	34,794	36,997	19,282
Other Canadian liabilities	19,020	18,642	22,817	25,368	28,400	29,618	33,100	36,845	36,093	38,113	39,221	41,484	43,876
Canada's net international investment position	-143,290	-151,164	-172,415	-187,355	-201,521	-207,757	-224,901	-246,758	-265,324	-293,798	-322,854	-337,450	-339,278
Cumulative statistical discrepancy	35,185	41,360	45,735	45,355	43,845	42,081	37,608	39,249	42,242	40,847	50,006	46,049	40,010

1. At year-end

Source: Statistics Canada, CANSIM, matrix 4180.

9.8 PRIVATE AND PUBLIC INVESTMENT[1]

	1991	1992	1993	1994	1995	1996[2]
				$ Millions		
Canada	128,010.0	122,188.8	121,253.9	130,131.2	127,956.1	126009.4
Newfoundland	2,098.7	2,080.2	2,484.7	2,906.4	3,012.1	2729.5
Prince Edward Island	460.6	390.4	411.6	483.1	510.6	497.9
Nova Scotia	3,224.7	2,841.4	2,924.6	3,049.4	2,863.0	2707.1
New Brunswick	2,606.9	2,477.3	2,329.1	2,342.8	2,429.4	2569.8
Quebec	27,545.1	26,404.6	25,691.6	26,688.9	25,464.8	24693.6
Ontario	50,093.2	46,675.5	43,327.1	45,568.6	46,107.0	47255.1
Manitoba	3,423.0	3,333.3	3,517.0	3,489.5	3,926.4	3578.8
Saskatchewan	4,656.3	4,074.9	4,057.6	4,546.5	4,589.2	4728.5
Alberta	15,987.4	15,885.6	17,918.0	20,025.9	18,645.6	17530.9
British Columbia	17,215.9	17,367.5	18,005.9	20,402.6	19,656.0	19067.9
Yukon	249.0	242.4	190.4	215.3	302.6	225.3
Northwest Territories	449.1	415.6	396.3	412.1	449.4	425.0

1. Excludes repair expenditures.
2. Intentions.

Source: Statistics Canada, CANSIM, matrix 3114.

9.9 THE MONEY MARKET

	1982	1983	1984	1985	1986	1987	1988	1989	1990	1991	1992	1993	1994	1995
	$US per $Canadian													
Exchange rate	0.8105	0.8114	0.7722	0.7323	0.7197	0.7542	0.8125	0.8446	0.8571	0.8728	0.8273	0.7751	0.7322	0.7286
	%													
Selected interest rates														
Bank rate (last Wednesday of the month)	13.96	9.55	11.31	9.65	9.21	8.40	9.69	12.29	13.04	9.03	6.78	5.09	5.77	7.31
Prime business loan rate	15.81	11.17	12.06	10.58	10.52	9.52	10.83	13.33	14.06	9.94	7.48	5.94	6.88	8.65
Chartered bank typical mortgage rate														
1 year	16.85	10.98	12.00	10.31	10.15	9.85	10.83	12.85	13.40	10.08	7.87	6.91	7.83	8.38
3 years	17.83	12.52	13.21	11.54	10.88	10.69	11.42	12.15	13.38	10.90	8.95	8.10	8.99	8.82
5 years	18.04	13.23	13.58	12.13	11.21	11.17	11.65	12.06	13.35	11.13	9.51	8.78	9.53	9.16
Consumer loan rate	18.73	12.83	13.48	12.42	13.58	12.69	13.52	15.80	16.96	13.52	11.31	10.23	10.85	12.02
	$ Millions													
Money Supply (M1)	27,039	29,461	30,117	31,126	33,469	37,464	39,216	40,296	40,755	41,808	44,323	48,319	54,166	57,135

Sources: Statistics Canada, CANSIM, matrices 921, 926 and 2560; Bank of Canada, *Bank of Canada Review,* Ottawa.

9.10 CONSUMER PRICE INDEX

	1982	1983	1984	1985	1986	1987	1988	1989	1990	1991	1992	1993	1994	1995
	% Change in the index from previous year													
All-items	10.9	5.7	4.4	3.9	4.2	4.4	4.0	5.0	4.8	5.6	1.5	1.8	0.2	2.1
Food	7.2	3.7	5.6	2.8	5.0	4.4	2.7	3.6	4.1	4.8	-0.3	1.7	0.4	2.4
Shelter	13.5	7.3	4.1	3.6	2.8	4.5	4.6	5.9	5.6	4.7	1.8	1.4	0.4	1.1
Household operations and furnishings	10.6	5.4	3.3	2.6	3.0	2.9	3.8	3.7	2.0	3.9	0.5	0.9	0.3	1.9
Clothing and footwear	5.6	4.0	2.4	2.7	2.8	4.2	5.2	4.1	2.8	9.5	0.9	1.0	0.8	0.0
Transportation	14.0	5.0	4.3	4.8	3.2	3.6	1.9	5.2	5.6	1.8	2.0	3.2	4.5	5.2
Health and personal care	10.6	7.0	3.9	3.5	4.3	5.0	4.4	4.4	4.9	7.0	2.3	2.7	1.0	-0.1
Recreation, education and reading	8.7	6.4	3.4	4.4	5.2	5.0	5.6	4.5	4.2	6.8	1.2	2.5	2.9	3.9
Alcoholic beverages and tobacco products	15.5	12.7	8.1	9.6	11.9	6.7	7.4	9.2	8.7	17.2	6.0	1.6	-16.4	-0.1
Special aggregrates														
All-items excluding food	11.8	6.4	4.1	4.2	4.0	4.3	4.4	5.3	4.9	5.8	1.9	1.9	0.2	2.0
All-items excluding energy	9.9	5.6	4.2	3.7	5.2	4.6	4.3	5.1	4.4	5.7	1.6	1.9	0.2	2.3
Regulated prices	15.2	8.2	6.2	6.0	6.5	4.3	5.0	5.4	5.7	9.6	4.9	3.0	-3.7	0.9
Non-regulated prices	9.0	4.9	3.6	3.1	3.4	4.4	3.7	4.9	4.5	4.5	0.5	1.4	1.4	2.6

Source: Statistics Canada, CANSIM, matrix 7463.

9.11 RAW MATERIALS PRICE INDEX

	1983	1984	1985	1986	1987	1988	1989	1990	1991	1992	1993	1994	1995
	% Change from previous year												
All raw materials	4.3	3.0	1.2	-17.7	7.3	-3.3	3.3	4.1	-6.2	1.0	5.9	7.7	8.5
Vegetable products	4.5	8.1	-7.6	-1.6	-3.4	10.4	1.3	-7.7	-10.8	2.2	7.4	19.6	9.9
Animals and animal products	-2.3	5.8	-1.5	5.4	4.8	-4.9	1.4	4.5	-1.1	-0.2	5.0	-1.2	2.5
Wood	4.1	3.4	0.6	4.9	11.6	8.7	0.9	-0.5	1.6	10.7	32.9	10.4	9.1
Ferrous materials	1.6	9.3	1.7	0.7	-0.6	4.2	-3.4	-7.0	-3.4	3.6	12.1	13.6	2.9
Non-ferrous metals	4.4	-0.8	-5.8	3.7	14.1	17.2	-4.6	-10.1	-15.7	0.5	-3.0	27.1	19.7
Non-metallic minerals	3.0	3.2	5.0	2.7	-0.7	2.8	1.3	-0.1	0.2	-4.2	--	2.9	3.7
Mineral fuels	7.1	1.5	4.6	-36.5	9.7	-21.0	13.3	19.8	-8.9	-2.7	-5.1	1.3	8.4

Source: Statistics Canada, CANSIM, matrix 2009.

9.12 INDUSTRIAL PRODUCTS PRICE INDEX

	1983	1984	1985	1986	1987	1988	1989	1990	1991	1992	1993	1994	1995
	% Change from previous year												
All manufacturing industries	3.5	4.6	2.8	0.8	2.8	4.3	2.1	0.3	-1.0	0.5	3.3	5.8	8.1
Food	2.7	5.7	1.1	4.1	3.1	3.4	2.2	1.7	0.4	1.1	3.3	3.0	2.7
Beverages	6.7	4.2	3.6	5.7	2.8	3.8	5.8	3.0	3.3	1.3	1.8	1.2	1.7
Tobacco products	8.3	5.0	6.7	6.5	5.4	4.3	5.0	8.0	10.7	7.4	7.1	3.1	3.9
Rubber products	1.0	1.4	2.2	1.5	0.3	2.3	3.0	2.3	1.0	0.3	-0.1	2.7	5.3
Plastic products	3.1	4.6	2.2	4.2	3.6	10.4	3.5	-1.2	-1.3	-2.0	-0.1	4.2	10.0
Leather and allied products	3.0	5.3	2.3	4.2	5.9	6.2	3.6	3.8	2.2	1.0	1.9	3.9	3.9
Primary textiles	0.8	2.9	1.2	0.3	2.7	3.8	1.8	1.2	-0.5	-0.4	0.6	2.6	6.7
Textile products	2.8	3.7	2.3	3.0	1.9	3.7	2.4	1.1	1.0	-0.2	0.3	2.4	2.7
Clothing	3.2	2.4	1.9	2.6	3.6	2.9	2.6	2.4	1.2	0.5	0.3	1.3	2.1
Wood	10.3	-2.0	2.0	8.3	2.5	1.9	3.8	-0.6	-1.8	8.3	22.3	11.9	-1.3
Furniture and fixtures	4.2	4.5	2.9	4.0	4.6	4.0	4.1	3.6	1.0	-0.4	1.4	1.7	3.0
Paper and allied products	-3.3	11.3	1.3	4.2	9.3	9.6	3.2	-1.6	-9.6	-3.8	-0.8	10.3	37.1
Printing, publishing and allied	4.6	5.4	5.0	4.3	5.2	6.3	5.1	3.1	3.3	2.0	4.3	6.2	20.9
Primary metal	2.9	3.2	-1.6	2.1	6.0	18.2	-1.0	-9.6	-8.6	-2.6	-0.6	16.9	15.0
Fabricated metal products (excluding machinery)	3.0	3.9	3.5	3.3	2.5	4.2	2.9	0.8	0.1	-0.1	1.8	4.1	7.2
Machinery (excluding electrical machinery)	3.9	3.9	4.1	2.8	3.0	3.6	4.6	2.6	1.8	2.1	2.1	3.0	4.4
Transportation equipment	4.3	5.7	6.8	4.4	-0.1	-2.6	-0.3	0.5	2.1	5.1	5.9	5.5	3.7
Electrical and electronic products	3.4	4.3	2.2	2.4	1.9	3.7	3.5	-0.1	-0.6	0.3	1.1	2.2	2.5
Non-metallic mineral products	4.1	1.8	3.3	5.2	4.2	4.3	1.7	1.2	-0.7	-0.5	0.8	4.2	6.0
Refined petroleum and coal products	5.3	4.4	5.0	-19.7	-5.0	-7.2	1.5	12.7	-3.2	-8.0	0.1	0.2	5.7
Chemical and chemical products	3.4	4.3	1.8	1.3	3.1	11.0	1.8	-2.1	0.7	-1.5	2.2	6.6	8.6
Other manufacturing industries	7.0	1.1	2.5	5.8	4.2	3.1	2.4	1.0	1.4	0.7	2.5	3.4	3.3

Source: Statistics Canada, CANSIM, matrix 2008.

9.13 INTERNATIONAL ECONOMIC INDICATORS, 1994

	Growth in Real GDP	Unemployment rate	Consumer price inflation	Growth in Money Supply (M1)	Short-term interest rates	Long-term interest	Monetary unit	Exchange rates	Monthly averages Imports	Exports
			%					National currency units per $US	$US (billions)	
Canada	4.6	10.40	0.2	6.6	5.5	8.6	$	1.37	12.36	13.78
Australia	5.4	9.70	1.9	11.1	5.7	9.0	$A	1.37	4.14	3.95
Austria	2.7	6.60	3.0	6.0	5.1	6.7	S	11.42	4.59	3.74
Belgium	2.2	10.00	2.4	..	5.7	7.7	FB	33.46	10.50	11.44
Denmark	4.5	12.10	2.0	-5.4	6.2	7.9	DKr	6.36	2.99	3.49
Finland	4.0	18.40	1.1	8.9	5.4	8.4	Fmk	5.22	1.92	2.46
France	2.9	12.30	1.7	2.8	5.9	7.5	FF	5.55	18.38	19.61
Germany	3.0	10.60	2.7	5.2	5.4	6.9	DM	1.62	31.38	35.19
Greece	--	..	10.9	22.8	..	..	Dr	242.20	...	...
Iceland	2.8	4.80	1.5	10.8	4.9	5.0	ISK	70.00	0.12	0.14
Ireland	--	14.30	2.4	13.2	5.9	8.2	£ Ir	0.67	2.15	2.84
Italy	2.2	11.30	4.0	3.1	8.5	10.6	Lit	1,613.00	13.97	15.82
Japan	2.2	11.30	0.7	4.9	2.2	4.2	¥	102.20	22.91	33.01
Mexico	3.5	3.70	6.4	3.8	14.7	..	MN$	3.39	...	...
Netherlands	2.8	7.50	2.7	1.7	5.2	7.2	f.	1.82	11.65	12.92
New Zealand	4.1	8.20	1.7	6.0	6.7	7.7	NZ$	1.69	0.99	1.01
Norway	5.7	..	1.5	6.5	5.9	7.4	NKr	7.06	2.28	2.89
Portugal	0.7	6.90	5.2	7.3	..	10.4	Esc	166.00	2.16	1.42
Spain	2.0	24.20	4.8	7.2	8.0	9.7	Ptas	134.00	7.68	6.09
Sweden	2.2	8.00	1.4	0.3	7.4	9.5	SKr	7.72	4.31	5.09
Switzerland	1.2	4.70	0.8	5.5	4.0	5.0	FS	1.37	5.68	5.87
Turkey	-5.5	8.10	106.2	78.8	..	..	LT	29,778.00	1.91	1.54
United Kingdom	3.9	9.30	2.4	4.0	5.5	8.1	£	0.65	18.92	17.10
United States	4.1	6.10	2.5	1.7	4.6	7.4	$US	1.00	55.27	42.72

1. Some adjustments have been made to national statistics by the OECD to improve comparability. Data for Mexico have not been adjusted.

Source: Organisation for Economic Co-operation and Development. *Main Economic Indicators,* Paris, July 1995.

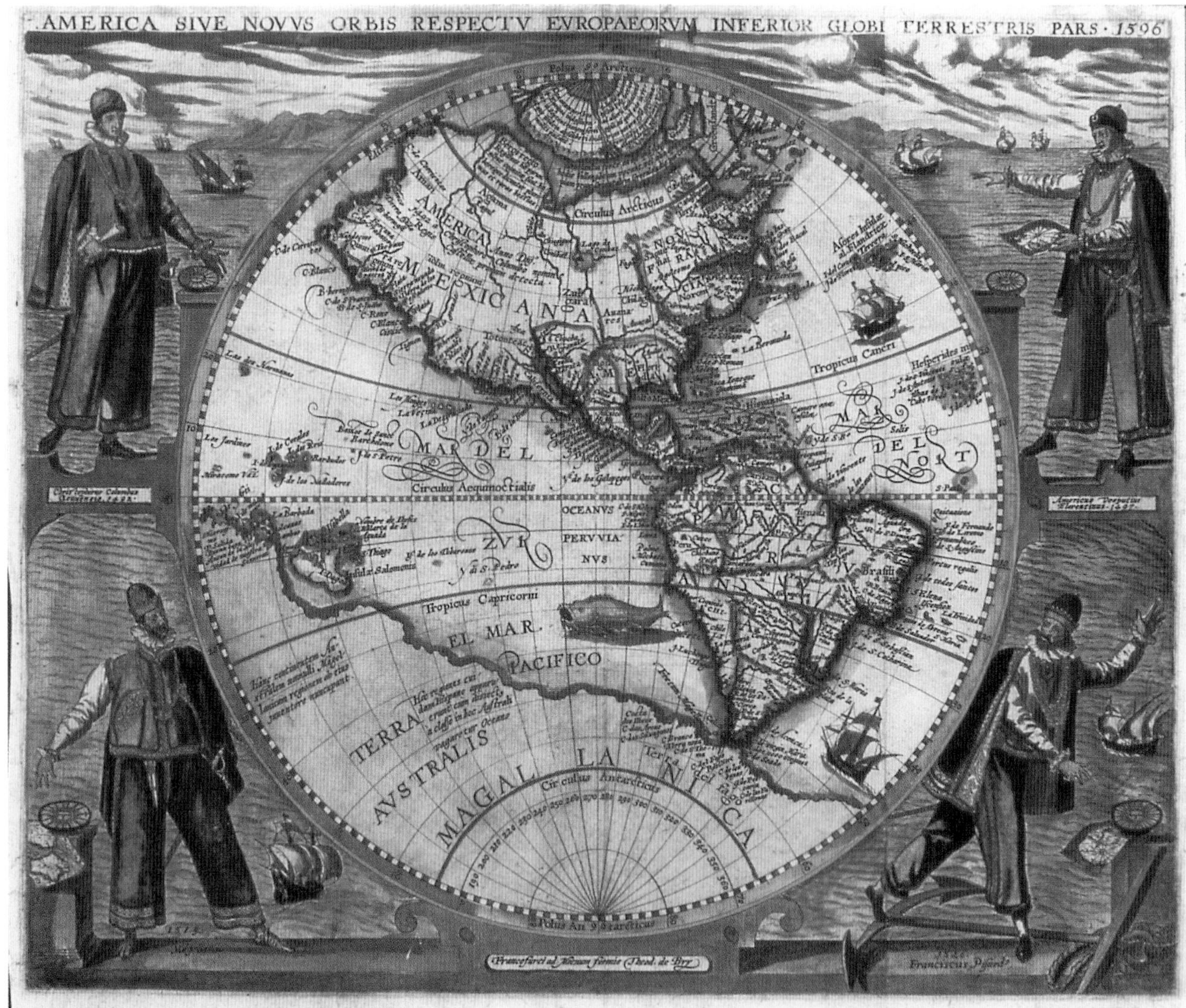

PETER PLANCIUS, NATIONAL ARCHIVES OF CANADA, NMC 27654

Chapter 10

CANADA IN THE GLOBAL ECONOMY

Photo by Carolyn Charlton

In 1815, the financier Nathan Mayer Rothschild used the latest in high-speed communications—carrier pigeons—to get a report on the Battle of Waterloo. Today, the electronic media would tell him the results within minutes, and his investment decisions would be relayed by computer to financial markets around the world in seconds or less.

But the decisions that are now carried out so quickly on international markets affect Canadians in different ways. Take the news that the value of our dollar has dropped sharply, for example.

A vacationer preparing to leave for Florida will be dismayed that costs are up for hotel bills, car rentals and other spending money. A Canadian ski resort operator will hope that more Americans choose snow over sand. Software manufacturers will be pleased that their products will be more competitive in other countries, while owners of self-directed RRSPs, will wonder if it's time to switch to foreign currency holdings.

In their different ways, these responses show the impact of the global economy on the lives of all Canadians. Our prosperity depends heavily on the decisions of foreign investors about our currency, stocks and bonds, and on our trade in goods and services.

Canada has a mid-sized, open economy. Our exports of goods and services represented 37% of our Gross Domestic Product (GDP) in 1995. We live next to an economic giant that constitutes our most important market, with extensive influence on our economic life. Ours is the western world's seventh largest economy, with membership in the G-7, and we are active members in international trading arrangements.

The General Agreement on Tariffs and Trade (GATT) and regional agreements such as the North American Free Trade Agreement (NAFTA) have promoted trade in goods and services across international boundaries. From 1993 to 1995 alone, Canada's exports of goods and services grew by 38%.

New information technologies have also helped transform the global economy in the last 10 years. The integration of financial markets has been matched by a worldwide trend toward freer trade and the rise of "global corporations." Together, these developments can be described as "globalization."

Money now travels around the world in larger quantities and at greater speeds than ever before. In 1973, daily trading in the world's foreign exchange markets totalled between $10 billion and $20 billion. In 1992, the most recent year for which figures are available, about $900 billion in currency was being traded each day. It has been estimated that the total annual value of trade in financial assets in world markets increased from $5 trillion in 1980 to $35 trillion in 1992, or twice the combined GDPs of all the member countries of the Organisation for Economic Co-operation and Development (OECD).

Not so long ago, it was relatively easy to identify a product as Canadian, American, or Japanese. With the rise of the global corporation, which spreads the design, production, marketing and distribution of products across a variety of countries, an increasing number of manufactured goods have multinational origins. Today, a dress might be designed on Queen Street in Toronto, sewn in Taiwan from cotton produced in India, marketed by an agency in London, England, and distributed by an American garment company.

This expansion of international commerce has not been steady and continuous. Over the past 30 years, there have been a series of global economic recessions and recoveries.

In 1995, however, much of the news about Canada's place in the global economy was good. The boom in Canadian exports that helped pull the country out of the recession of the early 1990s continued. Our exports of goods grew by 16% in 1995, while the amount of imported goods increased by 11%, leaving us with a positive balance for merchandise trade.

The successful completion of the Uruguay Round of GATT talks in April 1994 provided an orderly framework for trade liberalization, and for the first time included a multilateral framework for trade in services, and for the protection of trade-related intellectual property rights. At the beginning of 1994, the free trade agreement between Canada and the United States was expanded to include Mexico, as NAFTA came into effect.

While NAFTA created the largest free trade area in the world in terms of population and geographic size, even wider trade horizons were opened up at the Summit of the Americas in 1994, when 34 nations, including Canada, agreed to establish a free trade zone that will cover the entire Western Hemisphere by 2005. As one of the 18 member nations of the Asia–Pacific Economic Cooperation (APEC) group, Canada made a commitment to help create a Pacific Rim free trade area for APEC's developed members by 2010 and by 2020 for the rest.

Despite the immense potential of other markets, however, the size and proximity of the United States make it Canada's dominant trade partner, and link it inextricably to our economic performance.

While we had a record merchandise surplus in 1995, we still buy more services from other countries than we sell, and we pay out more interest to investors abroad than we earn on our own foreign investments. This deficit in non-merchandise trade—travel, freight, business, government and other services, as well as investment income and transfers—totalled $41.4 billion in 1995. About 80% of this amount went towards interest payments to foreign investors, reflecting Canada's long-standing reliance on foreign savings to fund our economic growth.

Balance of Payments

In personal finances, it's common sense that if you borrow or sell some of your assets, you can spend more than your current income. The same rule applies to a country's finances, as recorded in the Balance of Payments. Canada, like the United States and many other countries, has been borrowing heavily from abroad for many years; therefore, it spends more than it earns from abroad.

Canada's Balance of Payments is divided into a Current Account and a Capital Account. Imports and exports of goods and services, including everything from computers to interest payments on bonds of the company that makes them, are recorded in the Current Account. The Capital Account records capital payments, including direct investments such as Honda's new car plant in Ontario, or the purchase of stocks and bonds. These two accounts must always balance: if there is a deficit in the Current Account, for example, it is made up by an inflow of capital.

Canada's Current Account has shown a deficit almost every year for the last 40 years. Throughout this period, we have exported more goods than we have imported. However, we have bought far more services from other countries than we have sold, and we have paid more interest to foreign investors than we've received from our investments abroad. This deficit in non-merchandise trade has more than offset our surplus in merchandise trade. Net interest payments to investors in other countries is the largest contributor to our Current Account deficit. This is because over the years Canada has relied heavily on capital from the savings of foreign countries to finance its investment and spending.

Current Account

Canada has always been a trading nation. Our first representatives abroad were trade commissioners, not diplomats: the Trade Commissioner Service was created in 1894, well before the Department of External Affairs was founded in 1909.

Canada's trade has been with a series of dominant partners rather than a variety of countries. Our economy has also been characterized by strong government intervention—first by colonial, and then by national governments. The country was explored, developed and settled by two colonial powers; they used it as a source of raw materials and as a market for their own finished products.

Patrick Corrigan, Illustrator, National Archives of Canada, C-143313

In 1995, trade in goods boomed, with total exports worth $254 billion and imports, $225 billion.

Following Confederation, Canada attempted to reduce its dependence on the export of natural resources through the National Policy. This policy protected developing industries with tariffs, or duties, charged on imported manufactures. With the growing economic strength of the United States, and as a result of the National Policy, which encouraged American manufacturers to establish factories within the protective walls of Canada's tariffs, the U.S. became Canada's dominant foreign investment source and trade partner.

Today, Canada and the United States share the largest two-way trade in the world. In 1995, over three-quarters of Canada's merchandise exports went to the U.S., and the U.S. in turn supplied almost 70% of Canada's imports. Canada's other important trading partners are Japan, the United Kingdom, Germany, China and Mexico. Together, these countries account for 9% of our exported goods and 14% of our imports.

Natural resources are still important to Canada's trade, accounting for about one-third of total goods exported in 1994, but we have diverse non-resource manufacturing and

Maple Syrup Forever

Canada's indefatigable ambassador, the maple tree, has served Canadians for decades. It was the badge worn by Canadian soldiers in the First World War. It was incorporated into the Canadian Coat of Arms in 1921. For many years, it was a visual theme of Canada's unofficial national anthem, "The Maple Leaf Forever". Today, it is the central motif of our national flag.

But, the maple tree also provides another message of good will: maple syrup. In 1994, maple syrup farmers in Quebec and Ontario produced 19.5 million litres with a market value of $95 million. Canada, in fact, produces 75% of world supplies.

Prime consumers are, of course, the Americans, who generally buy 79% of our exports. But the Germans have also developed a taste. In 1995, they were our second-largest export market, with sales of almost $3.9 million. Australians like maple syrup, too. In 1994, they imported more than $672,000 worth.

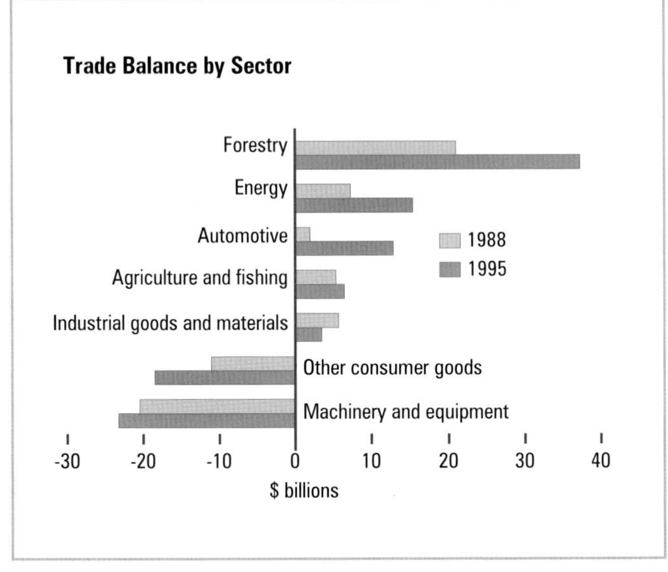

industrial sectors, responsible for the remaining two-thirds of our exports. Over 85% of our imports are manufactured end products: machinery, automotive products, industrial and electronic goods, computers and consumer items. In 1995, exchanges of services, including travel, freight, business, and government, accounted for about 15% of our total imports and exports of goods and services.

Merchandise Trade

In the first quarter of this century, the hot Canadian commodities in foreign markets were grains, minerals, timber and pulpwood. We still depend on our sales of raw and semi-finished goods, but machinery, equipment and automotive products are now our most important exports. Today, the space shuttle's Canadarm has somewhat more media cachet than, say, Marquis wheat. The variety and sources of our imports have changed too, as trade barriers have fallen in the last 20 years.

Our trade in goods boomed in 1995, with total exports worth $254 billion and imports, $225 billion. The resulting merchandise trade surplus of $29 billion was our highest ever. Our trade with the United States was the most important factor

In the not too distant future, Canadians who own a computer, a modem and a telephone line and who are on the Internet will be able to connect to the business of their choice, whether it is in Guelph or Madrid, rummage through each computer screen-load of merchandise, and make their purchase. The medium of exchange: electronic cash, or e-cash.

Citizens of Guelph, Ontario will be the first North Americans to shop with e-cash in 1996. This will be a one-year pilot in the use of smart card technology. Smart cards feature an embedded microchip which stores the electronic equivalent of cash. The card can be used to pay for goods and services at special merchant terminals in parking lots, vending machines and fast food outlets, to name just a few examples.

It's estimated that in 1994, some $27 million changed hands over the Internet. Much of this was likely business-to-business commerce, perhaps because consumers are currently wary of giving out their card numbers on the Internet until protection against theft is reasonably assured.

Unlike shopping with a credit card, though, shopping with e-cash can be private. There's no need for a name, a card number, an expiry date, a signature or an authorization. No bank records the purchase.

No credit card company logs the transaction. Merchants simply deposit the e-cash into their bank accounts and in the case of international transactions, exchange it later for local currency. In Guelph, merchants are actively supporting the launch of electronic cash, and the city of Guelph expects to use smart card technology in its own operations.

With expectations of lucrative fees, companies worldwide are competing to design the definitive digital currency. In Canada, about one-quarter of the 70 million transactions cleared each day in 1994 were electronic, that is, they did not involve cheques or other pieces of paper. A recent survey found 58% of Canadians expressing some likelihood of using an e-cash card.

As a result, banks are worried about the possibility of on-line service providers acting as banks. Traditionally, governments issue currencies though their central banks. E-cash, on the other hand, is issued by financial institutions, and is virtually outside the jurisdiction of most governments because it crosses borders electronically.

The financial sector is gearing up for a world of e-cash transactions. In 1995, more than 500 banks and financial institutions were on the Internet (albeit mostly for marketing purposes), while as recently as 1989, there were none. And in e-cash implementation, Canadian banks are ahead of those in most other countries.

in this surplus: in 1995, our surplus of $33 billion with our southern neighbour easily outweighed our merchandise trade deficits with all our other major trading partners except Japan.

Trade Products

Canada's single most important trade commodity is automotive products, which in 1995 accounted for 24% of our exports and 22% of our imports. The next two largest categories are machinery and equipment and industrial goods, which together made up 38% of our exports and 53% of our imports in 1995. These two categories include everything from aircraft to portable cassette players, as well as the parts to assemble them. Canada bought more consumer products than it sold in other countries in 1994; however, the opposite was true for our natural resources—we sold more than we bought. This contributed strongly to our growth in exports. Forestry, energy, agricultural and fishing products together made up 31% of our total exports in 1995.

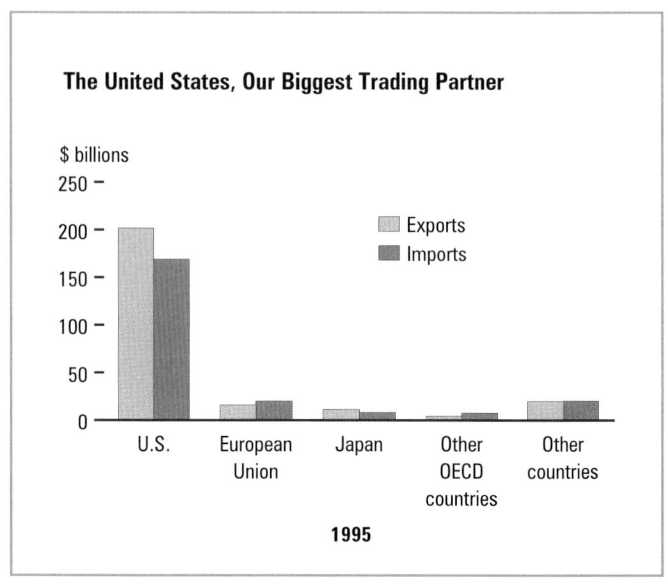

Trade Partners

Merchandise exports to our largest trading partner, the United States, have grown significantly in the last 10 years. In 1985, the U.S. accounted for 78% of our total exports, but by 1994 this share had grown to 82%. The years from 1992 to 1994 showed particularly strong growth as Canadian exporters responded to a revival of the American economy after the recession of the early 1990s. In 1995, however, our exports to the U.S. declined somewhat to 80% of the total. Our imports of goods from the U.S. remained stable at 69% of the totals for 1985 and 1994, but increased significantly to 75% of the total for 1995.

The only other major trading partner with which we have a merchandise trade surplus is Japan. In 1995, the value of our exports to Japan was $11.4 billion, while we imported goods worth $8.4 billion. Despite the trade surplus, our exports to Japan have actually declined in relative importance from their 1984 level of 5.1% of total merchandise exports, to 4.5% in 1994, while Japanese imports have increased from 4.1% of our total merchandise imports for 1984 to 4.5% in 1995. Our most significant imports from Japan are cars, electronic and computer equipment, and other machinery. The majority of our exports to that country are raw and semi-finished materials such as forestry, agricultural and petroleum products.

Our third-largest trading partner is the United Kingdom, which accounted for 1.5% of our merchandise exports and 2.4% of our imports in 1995. Our exports to the U.K. have declined from their 1984 level of 2.2%, while imports have remained comparable to their 2.5% share in 1984. We sell large quantities of minerals, metals, wood and paper products to the U.K., but manufactures such as machinery and electrical equipment are also important exports. Our single largest import from the U.K. is petroleum products, reflecting the importance of North Sea oil and gas.

Canadian trade with developing and newly industrialized countries, particularly those in the Pacific Rim, has boomed in the last 10 years. However, while our imports from these non-OECD countries more than doubled between 1984 and 1995, our sales to them as a percentage of total exports remained relatively constant.

David Seawell, First Light

Forestry exports made up more than 13% of the total value of Canada's merchandise exports in 1994.

Trade Agreements

Canada benefits from the lower tariffs of other countries because they reduce the cost of our exports in these countries. Lower Canadian tariffs help ensure access to more competitively priced goods for consumers, as well as for producers, who in turn can then be more competitive with their offerings. For this reason, the most important trading agreement for Canada since the Second World War has been the General Agreement on Tariffs and Trade. In 1948, Canada and 22 other countries became parties to this agreement, which provided for a sharp drop in tariffs, and set out rules to reduce other barriers to trade.

Since then, seven completed rounds of GATT negotiations have brought tariffs on industrial goods in developed countries down from an average of about 40% shortly after the Second World War, to a current average of about 5%. GATT has also been successful in establishing regulatory frameworks to control practices such as "dumping", by which a country sells products abroad for less than they are sold domestically.

NAFTA Update

The North American Free Trade Agreement, or NAFTA, links Canada, the United States and Mexico in what amounts to the largest free trade zone in the world. Together, these three countries include more than 360 million consumers.

The NAFTA entered into force in 1994, and is complemented by agreements in the areas of labour and the environment.

A reduction of tariffs and a generally better access to Mexican markets have contributed to an expansion of total trade between NAFTA partners. Since 1994, Canadian exports to the United States and Mexico have increased by more than 20%. In 1995, total foreign direct investment in Canada increased by 10% in areas such as transportation equipment, financial services and communications.

Using the terms of the NAFTA as a base, Chile and Canada are negotiating a free trade agreement to serve as a bridge for full Chilean access to the NAFTA.

In April 1994, the members of GATT successfully completed the Uruguay Round of negotiations after eight years of difficult debate. Under the new agreement, which also changed the name of GATT to the World Trade Organization (WTO), developed countries will reduce their current industrial tariffs by a further average of 38%. WTO economists estimate that the total value of world exports will be increased by $755 billion US annually by 2002.

The North American Free Trade Agreement took effect on January 1, 1994, linking Canada, the United States and Mexico in the largest free trade zone in the world. The three countries include some 363 million consumers (20 million more than the European Community [EC]), and have a combined GDP of nearly $7 trillion. The agreement will eliminate most restrictions on trade and investment between the three countries by 2003.

In 1995, Canadian exports to Mexico increased by 5% over the previous year. The actual value of Canadian exports to Mexico may be higher than recorded trade statistics, since most products are shipped through the United States, and final destinations are not always properly recorded.

In 1995, imports from Mexico increased by 18%. The most important items in our trade with Mexico are automotive products, machinery and electrical equipment. Together, these made up over one-quarter of Canada's total $1 billion in merchandise shipped to Mexico in 1995, and three-quarters of Mexico's $4.5 billion worth of goods shipped to Canada.

Our government is also eager to tap the potential of thriving markets in the Pacific Rim. In November 1994, Canada and the 17 other members of the Asia–Pacific Economic Cooperation forum agreed to the goal of free and open trade and investment in the Asia–Pacific region by 2010 for its developed members, and by 2020 for developing economies.

Trade in Services

Since 1950, excepting the year of Expo 67, Canada has bought more services from other countries than it has sold. In 1994, this services deficit dropped by an unprecedented $3.1

billion, standing at $9.4 billion at the end of the year. The most important factor in this drop was a decline in the travel deficit. Canadian travellers made fewer trips to the United States and spent less than during the early 1990s. In spite of this decline, Canadian travellers still spent $5.8 billion more abroad in 1994 than incoming travellers spent in Canada.

Business Services

There was also a decline of $0.3 billion in Canada's deficit on business services in 1994. This category includes payments for consulting and other professional services, such as engineering studies; research and development expenses; insurance and other financial services; and transportation-related expenses. Examples of such services include a company's purchase of consumer survey results for a product, or management expertise from abroad.

For many years, nearly all of Canada's deficit on business services has been with the United States. In 1993, purchases from the United States accounted for almost 70% of worldwide buying of business services. Two-thirds of these payments were made to affiliated companies, reflecting the large presence of U.S.-owned companies in Canada.

Tourism

Tourism is an important industry for Canada, contributing more than $25 billion each year to our economy. In 1994, American and overseas visitors spent $10.2 billion in Canada, an increase of more than 16% over the previous year. Although Canadian travellers spent about $5.8 billion more outside the country than visitors to Canada spent here, this deficit was the lowest since the late 1980s.

Where Do We Travel?

We Canadians may be living in a global economy that links countries together more than ever before, but we still like to travel within our own country. We generate nearly two-thirds of our own tourist revenues.

However, Canadians also adventure outside the country. In 1994, Canadians spent $15.9 billion travelling in the United States and other countries. We spent 9% less in the U.S. than we did in 1993, but 5% more in other countries. The number of Canadian visits to the United States declined for three consecutive years after 1991. This was probably due in part to the declining value of the Canadian dollar. We still like Florida, though. In 1993, Canadian visitors spent an estimated $2.1 billion in Canada's favourite sunspot, over one-quarter of our total tourist expenditures in the U.S. After the U.S., the most popular sunspot among Canadians was Mexico, which received 363,000 visits and $297 million from Canadians in 1993.

Who Visits Canada?

The United States is Canada's main source of foreign tourists, accounting for almost 80% of visitors staying one night or more in 1994. Americans paid a record 12.5 million visits to Canada in 1994: 58% of their trips were for pleasure, and 14% were for business. American visitors use cars more than any other form of transportation to get to Canada, and summer is the favoured time to visit. Ontario is the most-visited province, with British Columbia and Quebec coming in second and third. Toronto is the city most often visited by Americans in Canada. Even if they only spent 13% of their country's total travel expenditures in Canada, this still amounted to $5.7 billion in 1994.

After Americans, visitors from the United Kingdom rank a distant second, with 621,000 trips to Canada in 1994, followed by Japan, with 563,200 visitors. Together, these visitors spent just over $1 billion. The Japanese spent the most, about $1,140 a trip. Visits from the French have increased steadily over the last several years. Not surprisingly, visitors from the U.K. tend to visit Ontario, while travellers from France are more likely to visit Quebec.

Capital Account

"Close the 49th Parallel etc." urged the title of a 1970 collection of articles on American investment in Canada. At the time, large numbers of Canadians shared the authors' concerns about the extent of foreign investment—primarily American—in the Canadian economy. At the end of 1970,

"Travels," the writer Dorothy Duncan once suggested, "are dreams translated into action." Canadians must be very active dreamers. In 1994, we took 57.7 million trips outside Canada.

Since most large Canadian cities are within a day's drive of the Canadian–American border, it is not surprising that 68% of this travel involved day-trips to the United States and back. Depending on the value of the Canadian dollar relative to the U.S. dollar, cross-border shopping is a popular pastime for many Canadians.

Overnight stays of one or more nights in the United States accounted for another 26% of the trips. On the other hand, the number of Canadian visits to the U.S. has been dropping, probably due in part to the declining value of the Canadian dollar. For those of us who went, we mostly (67%) drove down; or took a plane (25%), or travelled by bus (4%). Our average stay was 7½ nights.

Only 6% of our trips were to other countries in 1994. About 16% of those were business trips, 20% were visits to friends or relatives, and the rest were for holidays, pleasure, recreation and other purposes.

Given the harshness of Canadian winters, it's easy to understand why our favourite American destination by far is Florida. In 1994, we stayed for a total of 41.3 million nights and spent $1.9 billion, more than a quarter of our $7.2 billion tourist expenditures in the United States. The next most frequent choices were California (seven million visit-nights and $568 million) and New York (6.9 million visit-nights and $558 million).

After the United States, the most popular destinations in 1994 were the United Kingdom (9.7 million visit-nights), Asian countries other than Hong Kong and Japan (6.3 million), France (5.2 million) and Mexico (four million). We spent about $4.5 billion in countries other than the U.S., and nearly half of that in Europe.

Canadians are even more enthusiastic travellers within Canada. We generate nearly two-thirds of our own tourist revenues of $25 billion each year.

On the other hand, we spent more when we travelled outside the country ($15.9 billion) than visitors to Canada spent ($10.2 billion) in 1994.

The United States is Canada's main source of foreign tourists, accounting for almost 80% of visitors staying one night or more in 1994. The 12.5 million American visits in 1994 were still fewer than the 14.9 million Canadian visits to the south. Americans spent only 13% of their country's total travel expenditure in Canada ($5.7 billion), significantly less than Canadians spent in the U.S.

Ontario is the most-visited province, with British Columbia and Quebec second and third.

In 1994, nearly 3.8 million foreign visitors other than Americans made trips to Canada. Travellers from the United Kingdom formed the largest contingent (621,000 trips) followed by Japan (563,200) and France (428,200). Together, these travellers spent $3.3 billion in Canada. Visitors from Africa spent the most, per trip, about $1,260, followed by Japanese travellers at $1,140.

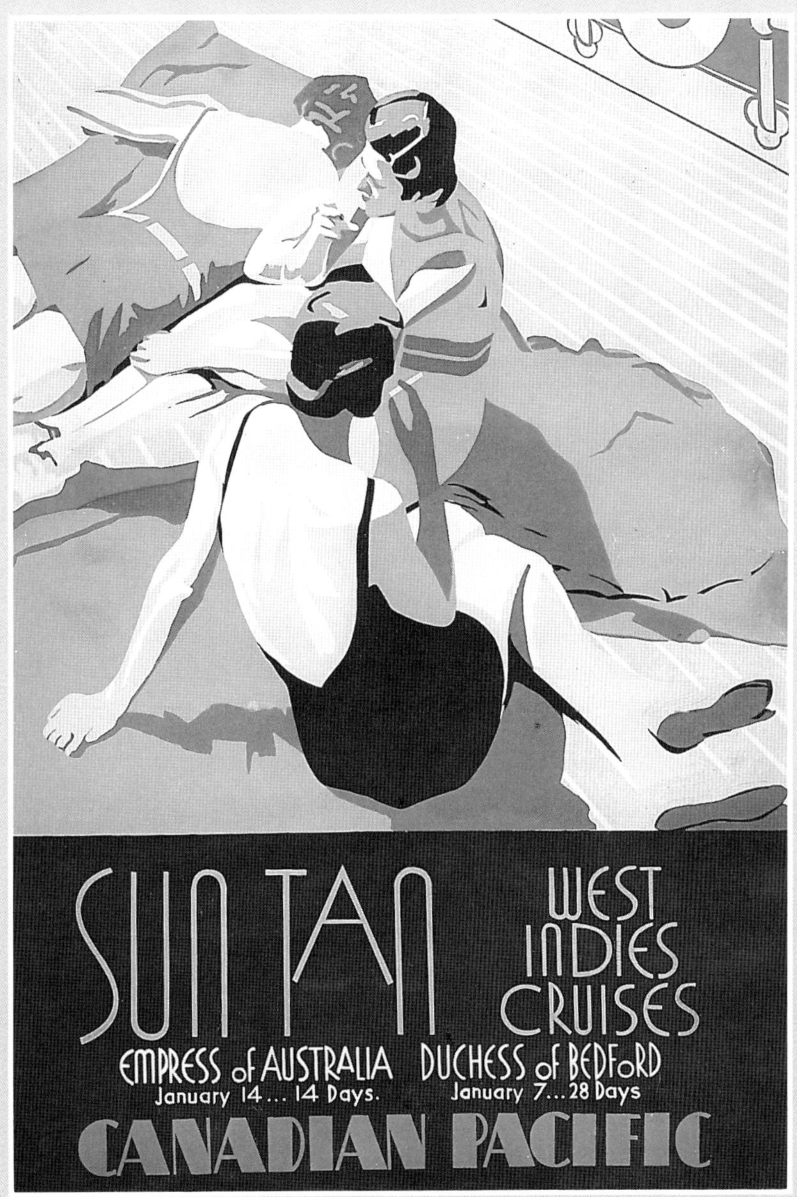

Canadian Pacific Limited, A6058

In 1994, Canadians spent nearly $16 billion travelling to other countries.

Bayne Stanley, Viewpoints West

Canada's Snowbirds.

non-residents controlled 76% of the money invested in the petroleum and natural gas industries, 70% in mining and smelting, and 61% in manufacturing.

For most of its history, Canada's borders have been open to foreign capital. In the 19th century, British investors made possible our economic growth and westward expansion by buying bonds to finance the building of canals and railways.

In the 20th century, British "portfolio investment," which did not carry ownership and control of the companies involved, was increasingly replaced by American "direct investment," which allows investors to influence or have a say in the management of a firm or enterprise. In short, foreign investors went from hands-off to hands-on involvement in our economy.

Widespread concern about the extent of American economic control led the federal government to set up the Foreign Investment Review Agency (FIRA) in 1974. Its mandate was to screen new foreign investment and to review foreign purchases of existing companies for significant benefit to Canada. This was followed in 1980 by the National Energy Program, which, among other things, also monitored the extent of foreign control in the energy industry.

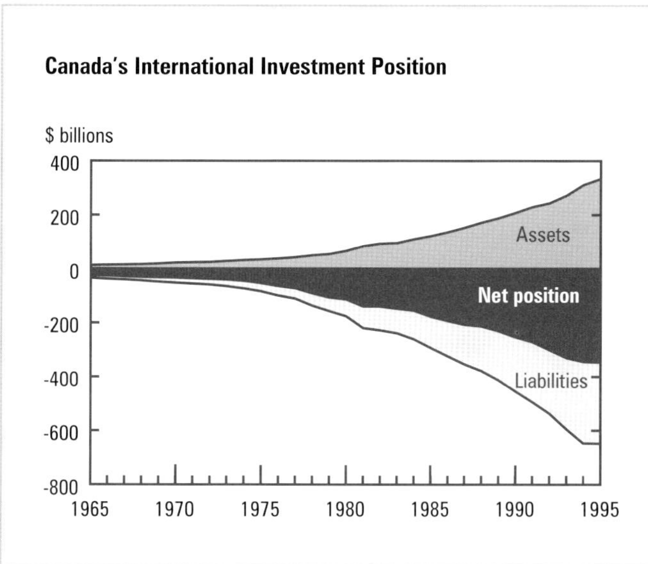

Foreign control of Canadian companies and assets dropped dramatically from a peak of 36% in 1971 to 23% in 1986, largely through Canadian takeovers of foreign-controlled companies. Following a change of government, FIRA legislation was replaced by the Investment Canada Act in 1985. This still provides for the review of major foreign investments to determine if they are likely to be of net benefit for Canada, but it also actively promotes investment by both foreigners and Canadians.

The United States is still the largest foreign investor in Canada, accounting for half of the capital invested here by other countries in 1995. However, this is down significantly from its 1984 share of 62%. Canada's relative dependence on American capital has been reduced in the last 10 years with the increasing economic strength of other countries and the globalization of financial markets.

Our second-largest creditor, the United Kingdom, increased its share of foreign investment in Canada from 7% to 14% between 1984 and 1995, while Japan went from 6% to 14%. Other countries of the European Community and of the OECD accounted for 28% of foreign investment in 1995.

Another major trend in recent years has been the relative shift back to portfolio investment: in 1970, direct investment accounted for 53% of all foreign investment, but by 1994 it made up only 25%. Canadian bonds accounted for nearly half of all foreign investment in 1995, up from 26% in 1975. Foreign investors clearly have confidence in the various levels of Canadian governments, and are willing to put their money in hands-off investments: more than three-quarters of the bonds they own were issued by our governments and their enterprises, such as provincial hydro companies.

At the end of 1995, 28% of the federal government's debt was owed to foreigners. United States investors buy the largest proportion of our bonds which accounted for 43% of the total in 1995, followed by Japanese investors with 13% of the total. The remainder was widely distributed among other countries.

As in the preceding three years, in 1995, the American share of direct investment in Canada increased, accounting for 67% of total foreign direct investment. However, this share is still significantly less than the 1984 high of 75%. The United Kingdom was the second largest foreign direct investor in Canada, with 10% of the total in 1995. The other countries of the European Community have also significantly increased their investment in Canada since the mid-1980s. The surge in economic development of the Pacific Rim countries, including Japan, Australia and Singapore, is reflected in their investments in Canada in recent years. These countries now own 7% of total foreign direct investment, more than double the percentage of the mid-1980s.

Canadian Investments Abroad

Increasingly, Canadians are looking outwards as far as investments are concerned. In 1995, our investments in other countries grew faster than foreign investments in Canada, for the third year in a row.

Since 1984, our foreign investments have more than doubled, reaching $333 billion in 1995. The majority of this amount is made up of direct investments and portfolio investments in stocks and bonds, but it also includes other assets, such as the federal government's international reserves, loans and subscriptions. Overall, however, we are still more debtors than creditors in international investment markets: for every dollar Canadians invested in other countries in 1995, foreigners invested about $2 in Canada.

Canadian direct investment abroad increased 8% to $142 billion in 1995. Most of this investment was in foreign subsidiaries of Canadian companies. The majority of our direct investment is in the United States, but its share of total foreign direct investment by Canadians declined from 69% in 1984 to 54% in 1995. Recently, Canadian companies have been increasing their investments in the U.K. and other EC countries: the share for these countries reached 20% in 1995, after almost doubling in the previous 10 years.

Canadian direct investment in Hong Kong continued to grow strongly in 1995 (up 38%), bringing the total for the Pacific Rim region to 10% of Canadian investment. In 1994, the first year of NAFTA, investment more than doubled in Mexico. The largest component of Canadian direct investment—about one-quarter—is in foreign financial industries, notably banking. Minerals and metal products are the second-largest sector, making up a 16% share in 1995.

Investments in foreign stocks and bonds have been increasing in recent years, reaching $83 billion in 1995, or one-quarter of our total foreign investments. Much of this increase is the result of investments by pension and mutual funds looking to global financial markets to diversify their portfolios. A 1991 law increasing the limit on investment allowed in foreign securities for pension purposes has encouraged this trend. While the bulk of Canadian foreign portfolio investments remain in the more traditional U.S. market, there has been a noticeable increase in overseas markets in recent years.

Recent immigrants, in large part from Hong Kong and Taiwan, have made a large contribution to Canadian investment abroad, holding a total of $29 billion in assets outside Canada in 1993. The federal government can also be considered a foreign investor, holding a significant amount of assets in the form of reserves and loans to countries and international agencies. Together, Canada's reserves and loans totalled $43.4 billion in 1994.

Globalization and Capital Flows

"I used to think that, if there was reincarnation, I wanted to come back as the president, or the Pope. But now I want to be the bond market: you can intimidate everybody." The remark by an advisor to American President Bill Clinton illustrates a common fear that governments are losing control over their national economies now that investors can move hundreds of millions of dollars around the globe with a few keystrokes.

All governments rely heavily on investments in their bonds, and when investors in the bond market become nervous about a country's economic or political situation, they tend to sell their holdings.

Some observers have argued that this fear is greatly exaggerated: governments have always been constrained by financial markets. What has changed, however, is the speed and severity with which globalized financial markets respond when they do not approve of government actions and policies. Canada's vulnerability to these markets has increased as a result of foreign investors' recent preference for Canadian bonds over direct investments.

The International Monetary Fund (IMF) plays a key role in co-ordinating international monetary issues. The IMF serves as a bank for its 181 member countries, including Canada. Member countries make deposits to the IMF, and with these it, in turn, makes loans to member countries whose financial commitments temporarily exceed their reserves. The IMF is also a forum for the development of rules on a variety of monetary issues, such as exchange rate intervention by national central banks.

Much of the attention focussed on the IMF in recent years has been on ways to prevent rapid fluctuations in exchange rates. As part of the Bretton Woods Agreement which set up the IMF, the industrial powers "pegged" the value of their currencies to the U.S. dollar, and were required to intervene in foreign exchange markets to keep their currencies' values within 1% of the fixed U.S. dollar rate.

This system began to fall apart in the late 1960s and early 1970s as governments found it increasingly difficult to maintain in the face of frequent changes in exchange rates. By 1973, most of the major industrial powers, including Canada, had "unpegged" their currencies and allowed their value to "float" in response to market forces. Incidents such as the Mexican peso crisis have led to calls for new systems to regulate currency values, including a proposal for a tax on those who buy and sell currencies in anticipation of shifts in exchange values. As yet, however, governments have not agreed on a solution.

The value of the Canadian dollar is critical to our economy. If the dollar were to suddenly drop by 10%, for example, Canadian exports would become 10% cheaper, unless those exports were priced in foreign currencies. As a result, there would be more sales of Canadian goods to foreign countries, with a beneficial effect on job creation and economic growth. However, the 10% drop would also make it more expensive to import goods not available in Canada, creating inflationary pressures. It would also be more expensive for provincial governments and corporations to pay back interest and principal on loans in foreign currencies.

The Bank of Canada intervenes in foreign exchange markets to help prevent dramatic shifts in the value of the dollar. It does this by selling Canadian dollars when they are in high demand, and buying dollars when their value is dropping. The intention is not to fix the currency at an artificial level, but to smooth the ups and downs in the market.

The World Bank

The World Bank, which also dates back to the Bretton Woods Agreement, is made up of two organizations, the International Bank for Reconstruction and Development (IBRD) and the International Development Association (IDA). The goals of both are to assist developing countries by providing loans, economic advice and technical assistance, and by serving as a catalyst to investment by others.

The World Bank's relative importance in funding development has dropped in recent years. About 10% of what developing countries receive from private foreign investment comes from the World Bank. In 1994, Canada contributed $335 million US to the Bank's lendable capital, or about 3% of the total disbursements.

The G-7 Summit

The G-7 Summit annually unites leaders of the seven major industrialized democracies and the European Community to discuss major economic and political problems. The first of these summits took place in 1975 between France, the Federal Republic of Germany, the United Kingdom, the United States, Italy and Japan. At the request of the United States, Canada became part of the summits in 1976, and the European Community followed in 1977.

In June 1995, Canada hosted the two-day G-7 Summit in Halifax. At the time, the leaders were preoccupied by the dangers of sudden currency fluctuations in the new global economy, and agreed to work towards an "improved early warning system" to prevent repetitions of the Mexican peso crisis. They also discussed the need for job creation and further reduction of international trade barriers.

OECD

The Organisation for Economic Development and Cooperation, located in Paris, was formed in 1961 to promote direct cooperation among industrialized economies in all economic, fiscal, monetary, trade and social policies. Its 27 members include Canada, the United States, Mexico, Eastern European countries, Japan, Australia, New Zealand and the European Commission, with the Czech Republic and Hungary as its newest members. Its new Secretary–General is the Honourable Don Johnston, a Canadian, who will serve a five-year term.

The OECD holds an annual ministerial meeting which is generally attended by ministers of foreign affairs, finance and trade who record their decisions in a communiqué which sets out agreed policy aims as well as the priorities for the work of the organization. These are based on the work of the 150 committees and working groups. The OECD may agree on decisions which are legally binding under international law (e.g. The Code of Liberalization of Capital Movements) or, alternatively, agree to recommendations which are an expression of political will to follow the policies set forth. The OECD is currently negotiating a Multilateral Agreement on Investment (MAI) which is expected to conclude by the June 1997 Ministerial meeting and will be open for signature by non-OECD members.

SOURCES

Statistics Canada

FOR FURTHER READING

Selected publications from Statistics Canada

- **Canadian Economic Observer**. Monthly. 11-010
- **Canadian International Merchandise Trade**. Monthly. 65-001
- **Exports, Merchandise Trade**. Annual. 65-202
- **Imports, Merchandise Trade**. Annual. 65-203
- **International Travel: Travel Between Canada and Other Countries**. Annual. 66-201
- **Canada's International Investment Position**. Annual. 67-202
- **Canada's International Transactions in Services**. Annual. 67-203
- **Canada's Balance of International Payments, Historical Statistics, 1926-1992**. Occasional. 67-508

Selected publications from other sources

- **The Economist**. The Economist Newspaper Limited.

10.1 IMPORTS OF GOODS[1] BY PRODUCT

	1988	1989	1990	1991	1992	1993	1994	1995	% of 1995 total
					$ Millions				
Imports	128,862.0	135,455.0	136,858.7	136,617.3	149,201.1	171,927.9	203,000.4	225,431.2	100.0
Agricultural and fishing products	7,557.6	8,256.3	8,739.0	9,003.7	9,736.4	11,013.5	12,578.9	13,370.5	5.9
Fruits and vegetables	2,576.3	2,729.1	2,911.8	3,078.5	3,249.2	3,520.6	3,641.6	3,897.5	1.7
Other agricultural and fishing products	4,981.2	5,527.3	5,827.2	5,925.3	6,487.2	7,493.0	8,937.3	9,473.0	4.2
Energy products	5,176.5	6,220.8	8,197.9	6,629.3	6,477.5	6,968.7	6,959.6	7,250.3	3.2
Crude petroleum	2,977.1	3,705.4	5,443.7	4,500.4	4,174.9	4,687.9	4,609.3	4,846.5	2.1
Other energy products	2,199.4	2,515.4	2,754.2	2,128.9	2,302.6	2,280.7	2,350.3	2,403.8	1.1
Forestry products	1,293.4	1,357.8	1,324.0	1,217.5	1,387.5	1,566.4	1,810.3	2,038.3	0.9
Industrial goods and materials	25,172.2	26,472.1	26,092.3	24,351.9	26,932.3	31,132.8	38,474.8	44,975.8	20.0
Metals and metal ores	7,801.4	7,570.9	7,052.3	5,915.0	6,359.0	7,058.5	9,350.4	11,484.2	5.1
Chemical and plastics	7,423.4	8,125.1	8,273.3	8,292.7	9,315.4	11,093.8	13,733.0	16,340.7	7.2
Other industrial goods and materials	9,947.4	10,776.1	10,766.7	10,144.1	11,257.9	12,980.4	15,391.4	17,150.9	7.6
Machinery and equipment	40,465.5	43,278.6	42,639.3	42,962.4	46,029.7	53,158.7	65,602.1	75,623.0	33.5
Industrial and agricultural machinery	12,875.7	13,528.0	12,578.7	11,140.0	11,357.0	13,832.9	17,937.5	20,523.7	9.1
Aircraft and other transportation equipment	5,965.6	5,505.3	4,821.5	5,565.4	5,050.8	5,202.5	5,665.7	7,538.2	3.3
Office machines and equipment	5,850.8	6,285.2	6,280.5	6,910.7	8,004.9	9,271.8	11,410.9	12,858.3	5.7
Other machinery and equipment	15,773.4	17,960.1	18,958.6	19,346.2	21,616.9	24,851.4	30,588.0	34,702.8	15.4
Automotive products	33,400.4	32,126.9	30,624.4	31,136.9	33,867.2	40,165.0	48,439.2	50,502.5	22.4
Passenger autos and chassis	12,164.2	11,833.9	10,717.8	11,665.8	11,680.5	11,856.2	13,785.8	13,256.4	5.9
Trucks and other motor vehicles	3,656.2	3,458.1	3,448.8	3,688.7	3,697.6	4,627.5	6,230.5	6,887.8	3.1
Motor vehicle parts	17,579.9	16,834.9	16,457.8	15,782.4	18,489.1	23,681.3	28,422.9	30,358.3	13.5
Other consumer goods	13,567.6	15,022.6	15,853.5	16,614.8	18,942.9	21,368.0	23,522.4	25,571.1	11.3
Apparel and footwear	3,106.6	3,473.6	3,746.0	3,462.2	3,914.9	4,370.1	4,680.6	5,146.0	2.3
Miscellaneous consumer goods	10,461.0	11,549.0	12,107.5	13,152.7	15,028.0	16,998.0	18,841.8	20,425.1	9.1
Special transactions trade	2,610.3	2,884.5	2,966.3	3,626.2	4,061.2	4,349.2	4,877.0	5,537.6	2.5
Unallocated adjustments	-381.5	-164.5	422.1	1,074.5	1,766.3	2,205.7	736.3	562.3	0.2

1. Balance-of-payments basis.

Source: Statistics Canada, Catalogue no. 65-001.

10.2 IMPORTS AND EXPORTS OF GOODS[1] BY COUNTRY

	United States		Japan		EU[2]		Other OECD[3]		Other countries[4]	
	$ Millions	%	$ Millions	%	$ Millions	%	$ Millions	%	$ Millions	%
Imports										
1991	94,361.7	69.1	8,678.8	6.4	14,043.2	10.3	4,490.0	3.3	15,043.6	11.0
1992	105,801.4	70.9	8,839.3	5.9	13,503.8	9.1	4,560.8	3.1	16,495.8	11.1
1993	125,843.1	73.2	8,408.6	4.9	13,855.5	8.1	4,607.2	2.7	19,213.5	11.2
1994	151,716.4	74.8	8,251.8	4.1	16,152.2	8.0	7,266.0	3.6	19,614.0	9.7
1995	168,985.4	75.0	8,361.0	3.7	20,006.8	8.9	7,814.6	3.5	20,263.4	9.0
Exports										
1991	105,801.9	75.4	7,114.9	5.1	11,476.8	8.2	2,511.6	1.8	13,328.1	9.5
1992	120,378.4	77.5	7,386.1	4.8	11,415.5	7.3	2,831.8	1.8	13,390.0	8.6
1993	144,907.7	79.9	8,213.4	4.5	10,995.0	6.1	3,132.7	1.7	14,002.5	7.7
1994	177,415.2	81.4	9,393.1	4.3	11,346.8	5.2	4,163.9	1.9	15,616.9	7.2
1995	202,038.3	79.7	11,499.0	4.5	15,922.2	6.3	4,337.1	1.7	20,024.2	7.9

1. Balance-of-payments basis.
2. European Union.
3. Organisation for Economic Co-operation and Development excluding the United States, Japan, and EU countries.
4. Countries not included in the EU or the OECD.

Source: Statistics Canada, Catalogue no. 65-001.

10.3 EXPORTS OF GOODS[1] BY PRODUCT

	1988	1989	1990	1991	1992	1993	1994	1995	% of 1995 total
					$ Millions				
Exports	137,779.6	141,514.0	145,555.2	140,233.2	155,401.8	181,251.3	217,935.9	253,820.8	100.0
Agricultural and fishing products	12,061.5	11,249.2	12,708.1	12,553.6	14,609.0	15,716.8	18,007.0	20,001.9	9.1
Wheat	3,537.4	2,506.3	3,209.0	3,182.2	3,808.1	3,167.4	3,518.4	4,393.3	2.4
Other agricultural and fishing products	8,524.1	8,742.8	9,499.1	9,371.3	10,800.9	12,549.4	14,488.5	15,608.5	6.7
Energy products	11,805.5	12,130.0	14,213.6	14,069.1	15,401.5	17,999.7	19,424.0	20,760.5	9.1
Crude petroleum	4,043.1	4,475.1	5,454.7	5,169.9	5,882.1	6,219.6	6,503.5	8,154.1	3.1
Natural gas	2,953.8	3,022.7	3,574.3	3,657.4	4,730.1	5,903.4	6,427.8	5,505.0	2.1
Other energy products	4,808.6	4,632.1	5,184.6	5,241.8	4,789.3	5,876.7	6,492.7	7,101.4	3.8
Forestry products	21,400.4	21,235.6	19,937.7	18,218.9	19,693.0	23,148.6	28,443.6	35,633.6	14.1
Lumber and sawmill products	7,021.7	7,089.3	6,587.2	6,188.6	8,000.3	11,275.8	13,678.2	13,613.8	5.3
Wood pulp and other wood products	6,354.1	6,788.1	5,928.4	4,752.9	4,655.7	4,152.7	5,865.9	9,759.9	3.3
Newsprint and other paper and paperboard	8,024.5	7,358.2	7,422.1	7,277.4	7,037.0	7,720.2	8,899.5	12,259.8	5.5
Industrial goods and materials	30,371.2	30,833.5	29,780.3	27,828.4	28,758.7	30,977.6	37,865.0	46,914.0	19.1
Metals and metal ores	5,058.1	5,370.2	5,290.5	4,432.5	4,125.6	3,653.5	3,952.2	5,279.4	3.4
Chemicals, plastics and fertilizers	7,007.1	6,549.9	7,161.5	6,916.9	7,590.4	8,331.9	10,590.6	13,834.8	4.0
Metals and alloys	12,541.3	13,428.1	11,896.9	11,398.3	11,469.9	12,524.2	15,266.0	18,056.8	7.4
Other industrial goods and materials	5,764.6	5,485.3	5,431.4	5,080.7	5,572.8	6,468.1	8,056.3	9,743.0	4.2
Machinery and equipment	21,344.5	23,676.8	28,378.2	28,401.1	31,397.3	36,485.1	46,604.1	56,266.8	15.8
Industrial and agricultural machinery	4,952.1	5,443.7	6,040.5	5,743.2	6,226.4	7,743.3	10,761.4	12,887.2	3.7
Aircraft and other transportation equipment	4,217.3	5,390.4	6,470.9	6,536.4	6,407.0	7,353.0	8,630.0	10,575.6	4.0
Other machinery and equipment	12,175.1	12,842.8	15,866.8	16,121.5	18,763.9	21,388.7	27,212.8	32,804.1	8.1
Automotive products	35,520.7	34,837.2	34,406.9	32,746.7	38,034.8	48,066.8	56,577.0	61,616.6	28.7
Passenger autos and chassis	16,649.7	16,040.0	16,196.1	16,367.2	17,793.8	24,344.3	30,328.0	34,338.3	14.5
Trucks and other motor vehicles	8,051.7	8,028.4	8,168.3	7,795.4	10,135.1	11,431.8	12,194.7	12,794.8	4.6
Motor vehicle parts	10,819.3	10,768.8	10,042.4	8,584.1	10,105.9	12,290.8	14,054.3	14,483.6	9.5
Other consumer goods	2,785.3	2,604.3	2,814.4	3,024.9	3,889.0	4,959.4	6,187.0	7,466.1	2.0
Special transactions trade	754.4	801.2	3,076.0	2,987.4	3,346.4	3,864.1	4,868.8	5,400.9	0.3
Unallocated adjustments	1,735.9	4,146.1	240.0	403.3	272.1	33.2	-40.8	-239.7	1.8

1. Balance-of-payments basis.

Source: Statistics Canada, Catalogue no. 65-001.

10.4 IMPORTS AND EXPORTS OF GOODS[1]

	Imports		Exports		Trade balance	Ratio of exports to imports
	Value	Change from previous year	Value	Change from previous year		
	$ Millions	%	$ Millions	%	$ Millions	Number
1988	128,862.0	11.9	137,779.6	9.1	8,917.6	1.07
1989	135,455.0	5.1	141,514.0	2.7	6,059.0	1.04
1990	136,858.7	1.0	145,555.0	2.9	8,696.3	1.06
1991	136,617.3	-0.2	140,233.2	-3.7	3,615.9	1.03
1992	149,201.1	9.2	155,401.8	10.8	6,200.7	1.04
1993	171,928.9	15.2	181,251.3	16.6	9,322.4	1.05
1994	203,000.4	18.1	217,935.9	20.2	14,935.5	1.07
1995	225,431.2	11.0	253,820.8	16.5	28,389.6	1.13

1. Balance-of-payments basis.

Source: Statistics Canada, CANSIM, Catalogue no. 65-001.

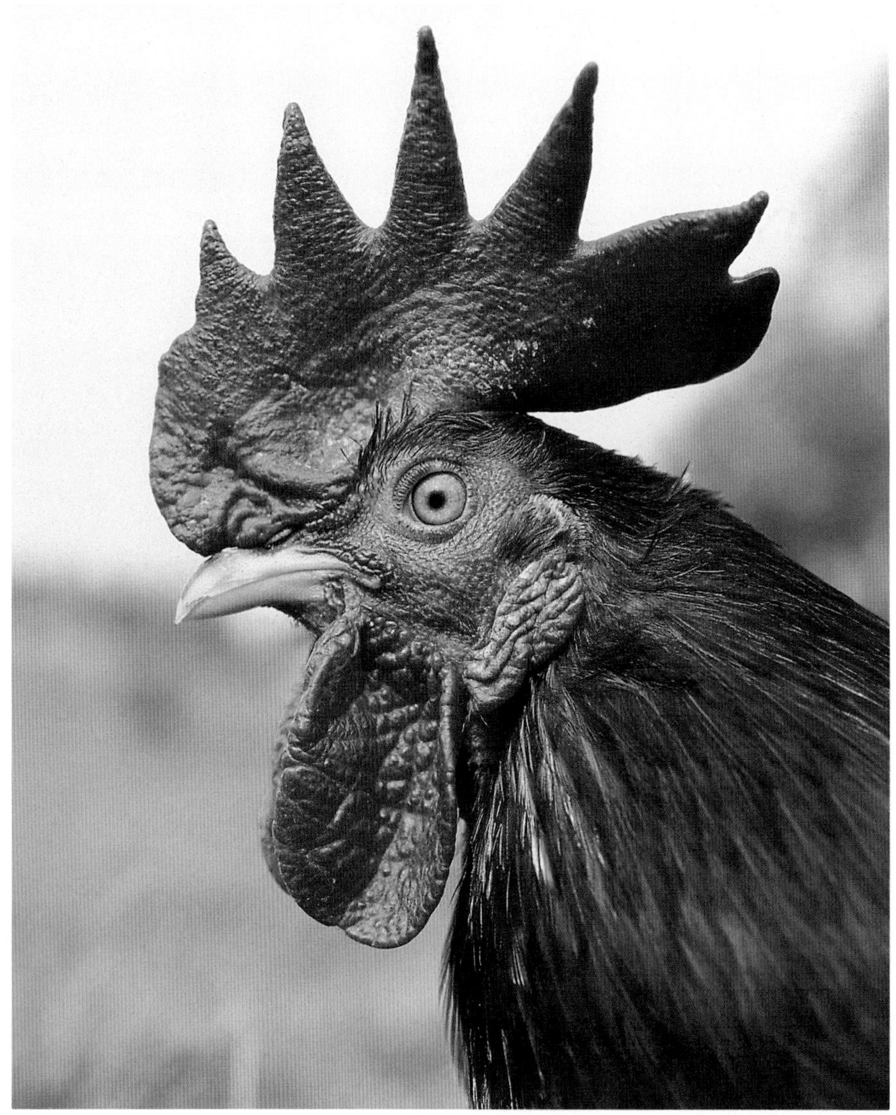

PHOTO BY **TIM WICKENS**

Chapter 11

PRIMARY INDUSTRIES

Photo by Robert Bourdeau

For generations the prosperity of Canadians has been based on harvesting the resources of the land and seas.

As early as 1608, Sir Francis Bacon considered our fish more valuable "than all the silver mines of Peru." Two years before that, Samuel Purchas had attributed the briskness of our winters to "the greatness of Forrests," which "doe hinder the Sunne from warming the ground."

The industries that find, develop and harvest our natural resources are called the primary industries for a good reason: they were the original foundations of Canada's economy.

A Wealthy Nation

Today, the four major sectors—agriculture, fishing and trapping, mining, quarrying and oil wells, and logging and forestry—contribute more than 7% to our national income each year. Canada's surface and subsoil assets, together with its relatively small population, are the main reasons why the average Canadian is the second-richest person in the world, according to a new system of wealth measurement devised by the World Bank.

For the individual worker, the primary industries pay relatively well. On average, employees in mining, quarrying and oil wells earned $50,171 in 1994, substantially higher than the national average of $29,490 for all Canadian workers. Forestry wages were also well above the average that year: about $38,000 annually. Individual farmers were closer

Liquid Asset

One of Canada's primary natural resources is water: Canadians have 9% of the world's fresh water, and each year use only 1.5% of the renewable supply.

Industries, households and governments all dip into Canada's water supply, and our primary industries do so in a big way. In 1991, of five water-using sectors, thermal power generation was the heaviest user, followed by manufacturing, municipalities and agriculture. Households, on the other hand, accounted for just 7% of water use.

Thermal power generation uses water both to cool condensers and to drive generators. This sector consumes about 63% of the water used in Canada. The result, however, is that in 1993, Canada generated more than half a million gigawatt-hours of electricity–enough to power urban Winnipeg for about 220 years.

Agriculture accounts for about 8% of water used, in this case for watering livestock and irrigating crops. Paper and allied products account for 6.4% of water use but recirculate almost 93% of it.

to the national average, but only if we include their income from both farming and off-farm work; in 1993, they averaged $30,162. Farm families fared better; in 1992, their average annual income was $49,982.

Job Prospects

In 1994, more than 700,000 Canadians depended on primary industries for jobs: a little over 5% of all workers employed in that year. Proportionally more jobs than ever before are being taken up by women in primary industries. The number of women working in the four main sectors (about 161,000) has been relatively constant over the five years from 1989 to 1994, and women now make up nearly a quarter of the work force in primary industries.

The number of jobs available to Canadians is related to the strength of the Canadian economy, which underwent some dramatic ups and downs between 1989 and 1994. In 1989, the economy reached a peak of expansion, and was followed by two years of severe recession in 1990 and 1991. The next two years produced relatively slow growth. Then, in 1994, a surge in economic activity resulted in the largest annual increase in jobs since 1987.

At the same time as the overall number of jobs in Canada has increased, the number of workers in primary industries has declined by more than 5% between 1989 and 1994. Nevertheless, the employment picture for primary industries was still better than in the goods-producing industries generally, which declined by nearly 10% over the same period.

This trend away from industrial jobs is continuing. Nearly three-quarters of Canadians with jobs worked in the service industries by 1994; in 1993, Canada had the highest proportion of service workers among all 25 nations in the Organisation for Economic Co-operation and Development (OECD).

While the value and importance of the primary industries increased dramatically in the decades after the Second World War, these industries continue to be sensitive to the boom-and-bust cycles that characterize the harvesting of natural resources. These cycles result from forces as varied as shifting consumer tastes, higher or lower commodity prices, the climate, the gradual depletion of mining ore, and declining fish stocks.

Jobs in the primary industries might seem to be more of a gamble, then, for an employee who is worried about steady employment. Or they may seem to have a faintly old-fashioned air about them—holdovers from the times when physical strength and endurance were the qualities most needed by Canadian workers. Yet a close look at the facts gives quite a different impression.

Sunrise Industries

The Gross Domestic Product (GDP) value of logging and forestry declined by more than 12% between 1989 and 1994, and fishing and trapping fell by 8%. However, agriculture was up 10%, and the GDP value of production of oil and mining rose a remarkable 15.6% during the same period.

Canada's primary industries represent a slightly larger proportion of our economy than they did only a few years ago. In 1989, a high point in the country's recent economic activity, the total value of all the goods produced and services provided was $505 billion. The primary industries contributed $34 billion, or 6.7% of the total. By 1994, after years of recession and recovery, that share had gradually risen to 7.1%. What is significant is not the size of the rise, but the fact that the value of the primary industries has increased over time.

New discoveries have contributed to this. Domestic industries based on oil and natural gas barely existed before the Second World War. But within a decade, drilling had transformed the economy of a whole province (Alberta).

Recent years have seen major oil and natural gas discoveries in the frontier areas of the north and off the coasts of the Atlantic provinces. Our known reserves of coal have increased nearly a third between 1985 and 1994.

The adaptability of Canadian workers has also made a difference. For instance, the East Coast fishing industry was devastated by severe declines in the Atlantic groundfish stocks of cod, pollock and haddock after 1991. Between 1989 and 1994, the number of fishermen remained at about 41,000; in 1995, their numbers dropped to about 33,000.

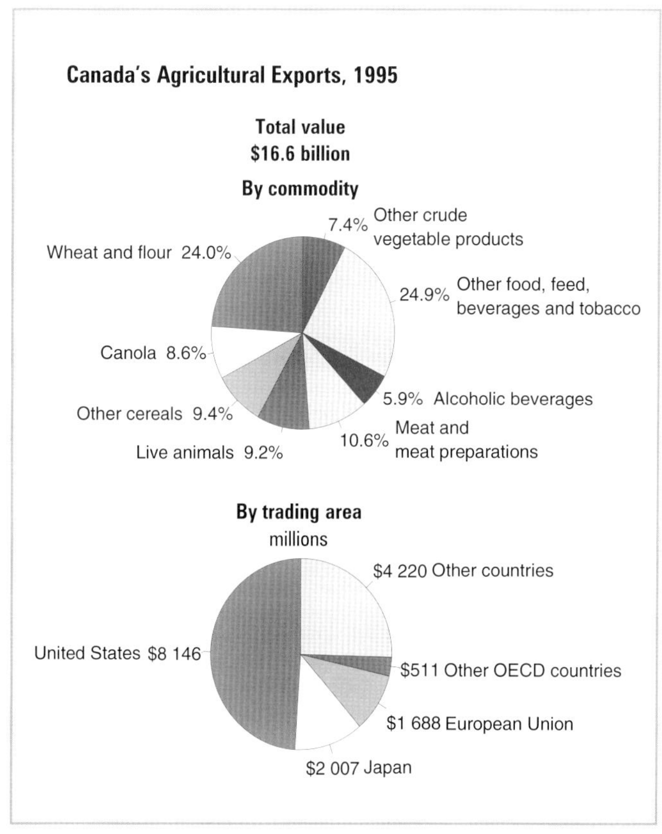

What happened? Well, many tried different catches, such as shellfish. Demand is strong from the United States and overseas for Canadian seafood and so we export more than 80% of our catches.

Indeed, Canada's natural resources sell well throughout the world, and international trade brings dollars into the country and creates employment. In 1994, the agricultural, energy and forestry sectors exported products worth nearly a third of the total value of goods exported in that year.

Yet, at the same time as primary industries are increasing in value, they are employing fewer people. Economists suggest that this situation indicates a gain in productivity, an important component of economic growth. In Canada, labour productivity rose between 1983 and 1989, declined slightly between 1989 and 1990, and was followed by three consecutive annual increases.

The gains are particularly noticeable in agriculture, where productivity almost quadrupled between 1961 and 1995. Similarly, the logging and forestry industries and the mining industry also experienced significantly increased productivity. Overall, labour productivity in the primary industries almost tripled over this period.

Among the four sectors, the largest in annual production, measured as a contribution to GDP, is mining, quarrying and oil wells, whose $24 billion in 1995 represented 61% of the total for all the primary industries. It was followed in economic importance by agriculture (29%), logging and forestry (8%) and fishing and trapping (2%). As a source of jobs, agriculture is overwhelmingly the largest: over 61% of workers in the primary industries in 1994 worked in agriculture.

Agriculture

"There must be hidden charms/ In North Canadian farms," Noel Coward once sang, but there are fewer and fewer Canadian farmers to appreciate them. In 1941, 27% of our population lived on farms; 50 years later the farm population was less than 3% of the total. In 1991, 390,870 operators were involved in running 280,040 farms. About one in three farming operations closes down every five years, replaced by a smaller number of new entrants.

Although the total number of farms continues to decline, the number of larger farms is increasing. For example, in 1993, there were 234,925 farms with operating revenues higher than $10,000, nearly a 2% increase over the year before. Smaller farms still predominate in Canada; those with annual operating revenues of less than $50,000 made up almost 46% of the total in 1993. But their number is decreasing, even though there are still more than 100,000 small farms; they declined by a little over 1% between 1992 and 1993.

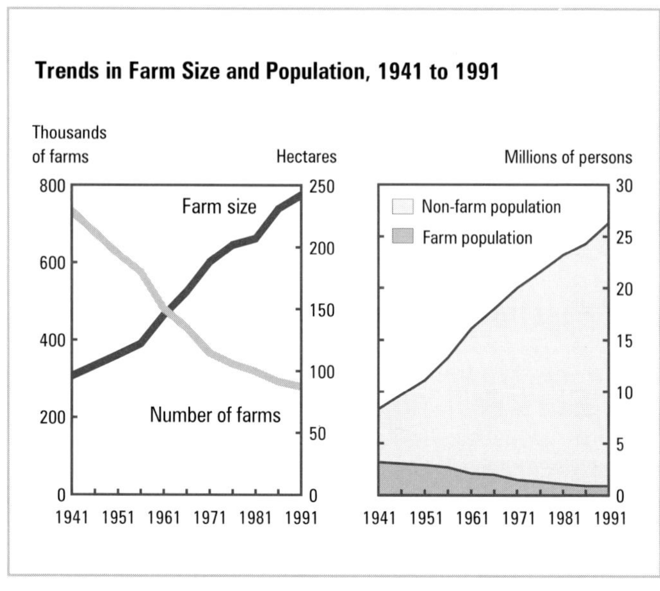

The big gains are coming from the expanding number of large farms: those with annual operating revenues of $100,000 or more. They increased by 7% between 1992 and 1993, when the 76,290 farms made up about 32% of the total. Although small farms are not necessarily less profitable than large farms, large farms are less likely to lose money because the rate of profit is applied to a larger scale of production.

Good farming land is comparatively scarce (only 7% of Canada's land mass, although still more than three times the land area of Great Britain). Farmers raise everything from wheat, vegetables and flowers, to cattle, hogs and chickens. Farms specializing in grains and oilseeds and cattle accounted for 70% of farms in 1993.

Miles of Wheat

In 1993, about 34.8 million hectares were planted in crops: 32 million in Western Canada and 2.8 million in the east. Wheat is by far the largest crop in hectares planted (12.8 million hectares in 1993), although the area planted and the amount of wheat harvested both declined between 1991 and 1993.

To manage hog farrowing, try Bacon Bits. To co-ordinate dairy herd breeding, install and run VAMPP. To predict weather variables and plan irrigation cropping, cast your weather eye not to the sky, but to Crystal Ball. You won't find these computer programs in the ***Farmers' Almanac****, but you'll find them up and running on the computers of increasing numbers of Canadian farmers.*

Although farmers have been using computers for years, the number of farmers using computers quadrupled between 1986 and 1991. The increased use of computers has been most impressive in larger operations where farmers are younger, more highly educated, and have higher farm sales than those farmers who do not yet use computers.

Signs are strong that high-tech farmers are finding their electronic almanacs improve the bottom line. In 1991, among large commercial farms earning between $50,000 and $250,000 a year, 13% relied on computers, compared with only 3% in 1986. Among farms with receipts greater than $250,000, one-third used computers in 1991, compared with just 12% in 1986.

It turns out that mushroom farmers are most likely to use computers, and maple syrup producers least likely—probably because typical mushroom farms are large, complex businesses with many employees, while sugar bushes remain the low-tech preserve of small family operations and hobby farmers.

Although they're among the latest signs, computers are far from the only technology to affect agriculture in recent years. Driven by trends that include larger farms, smaller farm families and rising labour costs, farmers are also investing in more powerful and efficient machinery to do their jobs.

For example, since the Second World War, when mechanical horsepower began replacing the animal variety, the number of tractors on Canadian farms has risen with every census count. Between 1961 and 1991, the average number of tractors on each farm more than doubled, from 1.4 to 2.9. Between 1986 and 1991, the largest increase of any type of equipment measured by the census was 56% among big four-wheel drive tractors in the 100- to 149-horsepower range.

As tractors get bigger and better, so do the implements they pull. For example, in the 1940s, early hay balers made rectangular bales that could fit into a bathtub. Weighing less than 30 kilograms, these bales had to be stacked by hand. In the past two decades, they have all but been replaced by new balers that make and move hay bales weighing close to a tonne apiece. Between 1986 and 1991, the number of small balers in Canada fell by 12%, while the number of big balers rose by 60%.

Western producers have made a major shift out of wheat and into newer crops like canola, dry peas, lentils and canary seed. This 1993 shift from wheat to other crops is unprecedented in western Canadian history. Diversification has often proven profitable; fewer farmers now specialize solely in traditional hard wheat.

Millions of Cattle

The number of cattle (13 million in 1993) and hogs (11 million) has been rising annually for the last decade, largely in response to increasing export sales and rising demand from the United States. While the number of sheep and lambs is small (less than a million in 1993), it too has been increasing, possibly to meet changing consumer tastes.

Livestock revenues rose by 10% in 1993, and those for crops by 7%, offsetting an 8% decrease in program payments or government subsidies. Cattle and hog sales were particularly strong in 1993, and grain and oilseed revenues increased by more than 10%. Average net farm operating income (before depreciation) for poultry and egg farms ($48,803) posted the strongest increase, up 21% over 1992, taking the lead from tobacco farms ($46,449). Dairy and potato farms were the only others to break the $40,000 mark. The average for all farms was $19,975. Livestock combination farms and fruit and vegetable farms came in well below the average.

Farming Inc.

Income from farming no longer provides a majority of the typical farmer's income. For individuals operating unincorporated farms with more than $10,000 gross revenue, off-farm income made up about 54% of the average farm operator's total income of $30,162 (before farm depreciation) in 1993.

The contribution of off-farm income is even more pronounced when the contribution of other family members is taken into account. In 1992, farm families earned an average of nearly $50,000 (before farm depreciation), up slightly from the year before. But they received only about a third of their income from farming. Off-farm employment contributed 43% to their total income; investment income, 10%, and pensions and other off-farm sources, 15%.

Historically, Canadian farmers have been independent businessmen and businesswomen, not employees. But that independence has also left them relatively weak in the face of large agri-food buyers and corporations, who were more interested in the prices they paid than in the farmers' costs of production.

To help stabilize their incomes, farmers first tried banding together in co-operatives. By the 1930s, the provincial and federal governments had stepped in with laws to control marketing through various boards, commissions and agencies. Currently such bodies oversee the production of dairy products, eggs, turkeys and chickens.

Agriculture continues to be big business in Canada. In 1994, the value of production was at least a billion dollars in each of Alberta, Saskatchewan, Ontario and Quebec. That year the value of agricultural production rose in every province except Saskatchewan, New Brunswick and Prince Edward Island.

Strong export sales are an important component of farm income in Canada. Taken together, agricultural and fisheries products exported in 1994 were worth $18 billion, a 40% increase over 1990. About half of Canada's agricultural exports are grains and the three main oilseeds: canola, soybeans and flaxseed. Wheat and flour were the leading exports in 1992, shipped mainly to the former Soviet Union, China, Korea and Japan. Most of our live-animal and meat exports were shipped to the United States and Japan.

Beef Down, Cukes Up

Of all the primary industries, agriculture is the most sensitive to shifts in consumer tastes, both abroad and at home. There is no doubt that Canadians have changed their eating habits in recent years. In general, we are consuming more vegetables, less butter and fewer eggs, and are switching from beef and pork to poultry meat.

Health concerns might underlie lower consumption of beef (down 16%) and pork (down 14%) between 1981 and 1991, as may a 31% rise in poultry consumption. Similarly, people are not eating as much butter (down 30%) or margarine (down 7%). Yogurt consumption went up by 95% between 1981 and

Photo by David Trattles

George and Francis, fishermen at North Rustico, P.E.I.

1991, while consumption of cheddar and variety cheeses rose by 40%. The mysteries of public taste may never be fully explained, for in the same period, cucumber consumption went up 28%, while tomatoes declined by 16%. Oranges, curiously, underwent a greater shift than either, down by 36%.

Fishing Jobs

Commercial fishing is not a significant factor in Canada's national economy. It was worth less than $3 billion in 1993; internationally we rank 15th in the world for the total weight of fish caught.

Nevertheless, the industry has been a major contributor to the economies of the coastal provinces and the North. On the Atlantic coast a quarter of the residents live in 1,300 fishing communities; before the recent collapse of the groundfish stocks, fully half these communities depended on fishing. In the North, where up to 90% of fishermen are Aboriginal peoples, fishing provides both food and a source of cash income where other employment is limited or non-existent.

Newfoundlanders have been particularly hurt over the past few years by the decline of fish stocks, which has idled fishermen and plant workers, and thrust many into retraining and relief programs. In 1994, fish landings fell 7% and fish processing dropped 16%. Both are now half the size they were in 1990. With the collapse of most groundfisheries, shellfish such as shrimps and crabs have become more important to the province's fishing industry; they now represent over 80% of the total catch.

The Atlantic fishery made up 64% of the value of production in 1993; the Pacific fishery 30%, and 6% came from inland fisheries. About 93% of the active Atlantic fishermen operated seasonally in 1993 from private boats; only 7% operated year-round from company-owned fishing trawlers. In the Pacific fishery, salmon accounted for more than 51% of the total landed value in 1993. The aquaculture industry is promising, although it is still small; the industry's output of $290 million in 1993 represented 17% of the landed value of Canadian fisheries.

Fur Trapping

Canada owes one of its national symbols to a European fashion for hats made of beaver fur: that industrious rodent, Roy Daniells called it, "whose destiny it was to furnish hats that warmed better brains than his own." The fur trade has long since nearly vanished, but a commercial wildlife industry is kept alive by fur farmers and trappers. Many trappers are Aboriginal peoples in the North, for whom fur provides scarce cash income. It may once more be Europe that determines their livelihood, ironically, for the European Union has threatened to ban the import of fur from animals caught by leg-hold traps.

The fur industry produced $31 million in ranch-raised pelts in 1994, a slight drop from the five-year high of $34 million in 1993. Mink is the most important species raised on fur farms, accounting for more than 90% of the value of production. Wildlife pelts from trapping were valued at $23 million in 1991-92, the highest in five years. The major wildlife species trapped were marten, beaver, mink and coyote (also called prairie wolf).

High Energy

Production of energy is a significant part of Canada's history, and part of our history has been patterned by the search for energy. Wood-fuelled iron smelting began in the New World by Norse settlers in 10th century Newfoundland; Samuel de Champlain built our first water-powered grist mill in 1607, in what is now Nova Scotia; and, coal has been mined in New Brunswick since 1639.

Climate, distance and scattered settlement all contribute to Canada's prodigious use of energy; Canada is one of the most energy-intensive nations in the world. In 1994, we used about 8.8 billion gigajoules. To put that into perspective, a 50-litre fill-up of gas gives a car about 72 gigajoules of energy; 1 million gigajoules' worth of gas would be enough energy to run about 13,800 average-sized cars for a year. Astonishing as it may seem, this means that in 1994, every Canadian used over 300 gigajoules of energy, in the form of petroleum (40%), natural gas (27%), coal and coke (12%), hydroelectric power (12%), and other sources such as nuclear power (9%).

Energy consumption for personal use is only a small part of Canada's energy picture. In fact, only about a fifth of the total energy we consume is used for our homes and farms. Most goes to industry, 35% in all, followed by transportation, and commercial and public administration uses.

Many of our industries, such as primary metals, and chemicals and petrochemicals, are heavy energy users. These industries depend on Canada's abundant supply of natural resources, which are energy-intensive to extract, transport and develop. As well, our relatively low energy costs and our proximity to the huge U.S. market have encouraged growth in these large, energy-intensive industries. Much that is produced by high-energy industries, such as pulp and paper, is exported.

Per capita energy consumption is highest in Alberta (664 gigajoules) followed by Saskatchewan (486 gigajoules). Much of this can be attributed to the energy-intensive industries in those provinces, particularly energy production in Alberta.

Paul Rand, National Gallery of Canada, Ottawa

Coal Diggers.

Acting on Exhaust

Government of Canada vehicles are driving towards a cleaner, more fuel-efficient future, thanks to a recent Act and other commitments that call for the greening of federal government vehicles by reducing fleet sizes, increasing fuel economy and burning cleaner fuels.

The 1995 Alternative Fuels Act commits the federal government to converting three-quarters of its 25,000 cars and light trucks to cleaner fuels by 2000. Alternative fuels covered by the Act include natural gas, propane, methanol, ethanol, hydrogen, and electricity.

Using alternative fuels will not only reduce pollution, it also has the potential to save the government money, and encourage vehicle manufacturers and Canadian car buyers to switch to vehicles not powered by gasoline.

Canada's energy industry already supplies several alternative fuels and fuel blends in larger Canadian cities. These fuels emit less carbon dioxide and fewer toxic substances than gasoline, and that means less atmospheric pollution.

Canada is the world's third-largest natural gas producer and 12th-largest crude oil producer. Although we account for less than 3% of world crude oil production and less than 8% of world natural gas production, Canadians sell energy products and services around the world and are significant participants in the international petroleum industry.

The value of energy products in 1994 generally increased from 1993: $13 billion in crude oil (up 6%), $9 billion in natural gas (up 21%), $1.5 billion in natural gas by-products (down 12%), and about $2 billion in coal (up 2%). Imports also increased by 7%.

Canadian companies and governments make very substantial investments in energy each year: $20 billion in 1994, or 16% of all government and business investment. In 1994, energy-related industries spent $10 billion in capital expenditures for exploration and production, and another $0.5 billion in refining and marketing.

In Reserve

The size of proven reserves will have long-term effects on the energy sector. Although Canada's crude oil reserves declined by about 4% between 1985 and 1994, increased exploration and improved extraction technologies could raise our proven reserves quite rapidly. About 70% of discovered oil in western Canada can't be exploited by conventional means.

Alberta's oil sands are potentially one of the world's largest petroleum reserves, comparable to the proven reserves of Saudi Arabia. Improved technology has allowed more cost-effective extraction of crude from the oil sands. As a result, this synthetic crude, a less costly source of energy, is becoming more popular. In 1994, synthetic crude accounted for 21% of total crude production.

Energy Fuels

Energy fuels are significant contributors to regional growth, particularly in western Canada. In British Columbia, natural gas production increased by 46% between 1990 and 1993, buoyed by strong demand from the United States. The energy sector has helped the province's economy out perform the national economy since 1987, even through the recession. In 1994, Alberta recorded the best growth among all provinces, thanks to the vibrant energy sector. Alberta's production of crude oil and natural gas has risen more than 24% over the last five years. In Saskatchewan, continuing high demand for crude petroleum by the United States sparked a 13% surge in output in 1994.

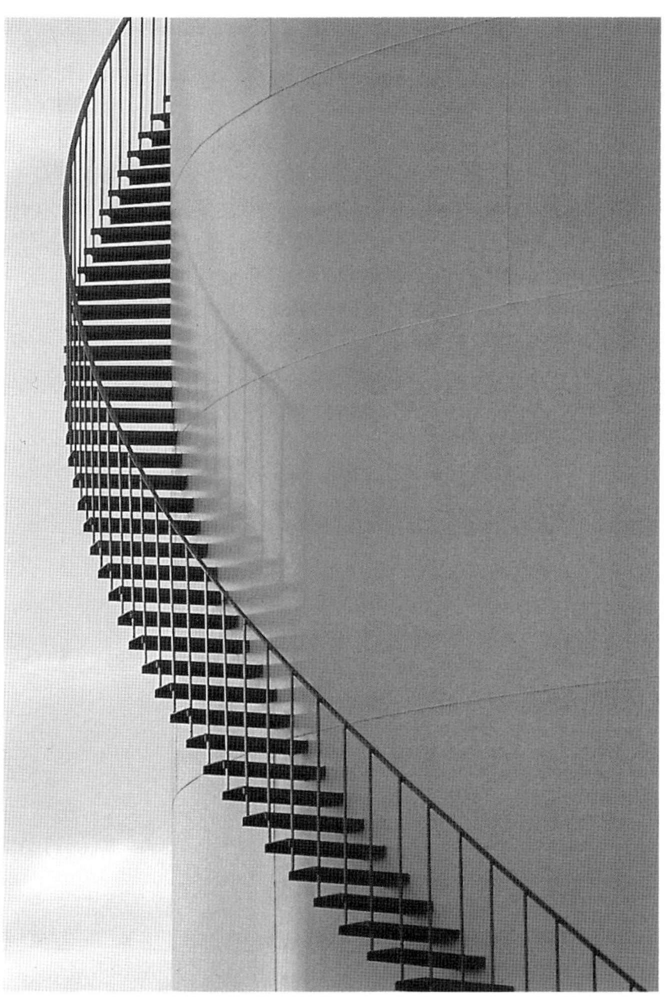

Photo by Lori Labatt

Oil storage tank.

In the Atlantic provinces, Nova Scotia experienced a 30% increase in crude oil production from offshore oil fields in 1994. Newfoundland's economy, hard hit by the collapse of the groundfisheries, was aided by continuing construction of the massive platform for the Hibernia offshore oil-drilling project.

Canada's energy exports have grown substantially over the past five years; in 1994, they were worth $22.5 billion. Crude oil, petroleum products, and liquid petroleum gases were the largest export products, followed by natural gas and coal. In 1994, Canada's trade surplus in energy alone was $15 billion.

Diamonds in Canada

Canada's Aboriginal peoples were making tools and weapons from copper in the central Arctic, in the Coppermine River area of the Northwest Territories and on the north shore of Lake Superior long before European settlers arrived. And Canada was associated with minerals in the earliest reports from the New World. Rock crystals near present-day Quebec City had Jacques Cartier fooled in 1535, leading to the tag "as false as a Canadian diamond."

Today, Canada is the world's largest producer of zinc, and one of the two largest producers of nickel; together with the Commonwealth of Independent States, we account for nearly 50% of world nickel production. Canada is the third-largest producer of copper, behind Chile and the United States, and one of the top three producers of potash, used mainly in the production of fertilizers. After South Africa, the United States and Australia, we are the fourth-ranked producer of gold.

In 1994, the mining industries—metal and non-metal mining, quarrying and coal mining—directly employed an estimated 57,000 workers. If we include mining, concentrating, smelting, refining, and the minerals and metals-based semi-fabricating and fabricating industries, about 2.5% of all jobs in Canada depend on the mineral industries.

For the first time in recent years, employment in 1994, in new and re-opened mines, exceeded employment lost by mine closures. But metal and non-metal mining companies reduced employment in 1994 for the fifth consecutive year. With increased shipments to Japan and the re-opening of some operations, employment of coal mine operators increased slightly after two years of decline. Quarries and sand-pit operators account for only a small number of employees, but they reported double-digit growth in employment in 1994.

Economics of Mining

The opening, expansion and closing of mines can have a profound effect on local communities, and even on the entire economies of smaller provinces and territories. In 1994, for example, the Yukon experienced the only decline in Gross Domestic Product among all provinces and territories. Following the Faro lead-zinc mine closure the previous year, its economy suffered a sudden 19% drop.

In the Northwest Territories, by contrast, the territorial economy moved ahead by more than 2% in 1994, its first increase in five years, in part because of higher production of metal ores. Drilling activities also grew in the Northwest Territories, as the race to locate diamonds—real diamonds, this time—and develop the first diamond operation in Canada stimulated exploration.

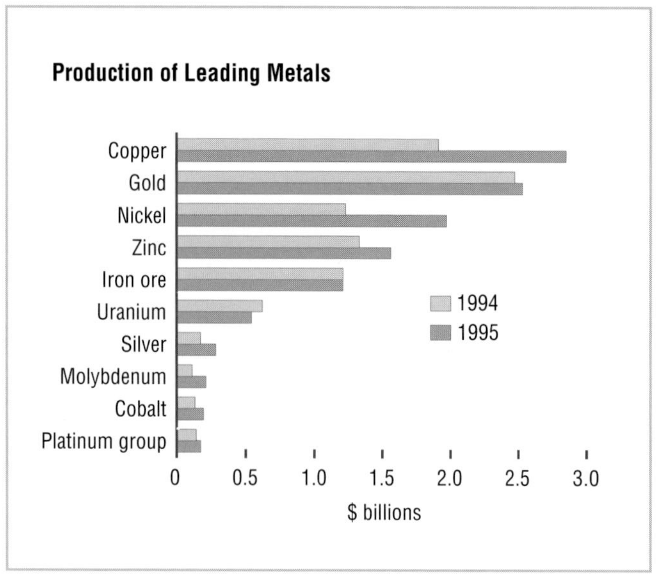

In 1994, the top six non-energy mineral commodities—based on the value of production—were gold ($2.4 billion), copper ($1.8 billion), zinc ($1.3 billion), potash ($1.2 billion), nickel ($1.2 billion) and iron ore ($1.1 billion).

Other notable mineral commodities produced in 1994 included uranium (Canada is the world's leading producer and supplier), asbestos, and salt, which we use extensively on our roads during winter. Because of expanded exports to the United States and increasing domestic construction in 1994, the value of structural materials ($2.5 billion) rose 8% over 1993. The major commodities contributing to the gain were clay products and cement.

Compared with 1993, estimated production of iron ore also increased in 1994, while it decreased for copper, gold, lead, nickel, silver and zinc. Despite the declines, the actual value of production for these metals increased. The estimated value of production of non-metals increased by 21% between 1993 and 1994, mainly because of potash and elemental sulphur. A record purchase of potash by China was particularly valuable to Saskatchewan in 1994.

Alberta's contribution to the value of total Canadian mineral output, including mineral fuels, represented the largest share of all provinces because of its dominant position in the fuels industry. In 1993, it held over 51%; Ontario ranked second (12%), followed by Saskatchewan (10%), British Columbia (10%), Quebec (7%) and New Brunswick (2%).

Canada is the world's largest exporter of minerals: excluding oil and coal, we sold $29 billion worth in 1994. Almost 80% of our minerals and mineral products are shipped to other parts of the world. The United States is the principal destination, purchasing about 80% of what we export, while the European Union and Japan buy about 11% of our mineral exports.

The 10 most valuable commodity exports in 1994 were: aluminum; precious metals and coins; iron and steel; inorganic chemicals; precious-metal compounds and radioactive

The Canadian poet, Robert Service, has written about the
"strange things done
in the midnight sun
By the men who moil for gold."

New moiling is going on in an unlikely site, up near Goose Bay on the coast of Labrador. Until 1993, Voisey Bay was a caribou hunting ground and home to a few Native coastal settlements. Today, geologists, drillers and prospectors are working around the clock to unearth one of the richest nickel, copper and cobalt deposits discovered in Canada.

The Voisey Bay discovery holds much promise. It is offering up immense amounts of ore, much of which is twice as pure as the ore found in other operating mines. The ore is also close to the surface, which allows open-pit mining at a lower cost, and, because Voisey Bay is near the ocean, this promises reduced transportation costs.

The Voisey Bay ore deposits were discovered by two diamond prospectors who were on a routine quest for new sites on behalf of Diamond Fields Resources Inc., a small Vancouver mining company. By mid-1995, however, more than 250,000 claims had been staked by 200 companies wanting a part of the action.

For Canada, this is good news. In the mid-1990s, international demand for nickel has been outpacing supply. Canada is already the world's second-largest producer of nickel. The Voisey Bay site alone may produce as much as 15% of current world production. Canada's share of world nickel production in 1994 was 17.2%.

For nearby Newfoundland, Voisey Bay has meant more jobs, and has injected new vigour into the economy. In 1995 alone, prospectors poured $55 million into the province, standing in line for hours to register their mineral claims.

Nickel, used to harden metals, is crucial to stainless steel production. It is a vital ingredient in many products, and is used to harden metals in everything from surgical instruments to aircraft propellers. Copper, which has traditionally been used in buildings and statues, and to make tools, has found new uses in the small electric motors in cars that power windows and operate windshield wipers. Cobalt is used to impart a blue colour to glass and ceramics, and is also used to treat cancer.

Analysts expect the Voisey Bay mine to be in full operation by 1999, although Native land claims and environmental issues must first be addressed.

elements; fertilizers; ores, slag and ash; copper; nickel; and sulphur, salts, earths, stone, plastering materials, lime and cement.

Nickel and Dimes

The extent of Canada's mineral reserves presents a continuing challenge to the mining sector. Since the beginning of the 1980s, most metal reserves have declined steadily. As of 1994, it is estimated that the apparent life of our nickel reserves is about 25 years, 17 years for lead, 12 years for copper, zinc and silver, 11 years for molybdenum (a metal used to strengthen alloys), and eight years for gold.

In 1993, three provinces dominated Canada's proven and probable mineral reserves. New Brunswick had half the lead reserves and 40% of the zinc and silver and Ontario had three-quarters of the nickel, 57% of the gold and 48% of the copper. British Columbia had all of the molybdenum and 35% of the copper.

But as a major find at Voisey Bay in Labrador demonstrated, exploration activities can change the reserve levels dramatically. In 1994, two Newfoundland prospectors sampled rock which led to the discovery of a very rich mineral deposit of nickel, copper and cobalt. This deposit is estimated to contain at least 100 million tonnes of ore, including 32 million tonnes of very high-grade massive sulphide—worth billions of dollars.

The mining industry is also faced with increased public concern over protection of the environment and sustainable development. In 1992, the Mining Association of Canada started the Whitehorse Mining Initiative, an agreement on economic and environmental sustainability among representatives of the industry, Aboriginal peoples, labour, governments, and the environmental community. For minerals and metals, the industry recognized that it must find, produce, use, re-use and recycle its products to create outputs that are more energy-efficient, require fewer resources to produce and can be more readily recycled.

Both the industry and the federal Department of Natural Resources are active in co-operative research on environmental issues, notably mine reclamation, mine tailings and effluents, and leaching of base metals from slag. Mine safety is another issue that receives widespread news coverage. The Department has introduced research programs on rockbursts, equipment safety, strata mechanics, ventilation, and emergency mine gas analysis.

Tides of Trees

Canada is a nation of forests. Some 49% of the country's land surface is blanketed by trees: about 10% of the world's total forest cover. The most recent figures show that in 1992, Canada was the world's largest producer of newsprint, the second-largest producer of pulp and the third-largest producer of sawn lumber.

About 64,000 Canadians had jobs in the logging and forestry industry in 1994, a 5% increase from the 61,000 employed in 1991. Strong demand for wood products, both domestically and internationally, boosted employment in logging in 1994. The value of forest products rose in six provinces and both territories in 1994, although it declined in British Columbia, which has Canada's most valuable forestry industry.

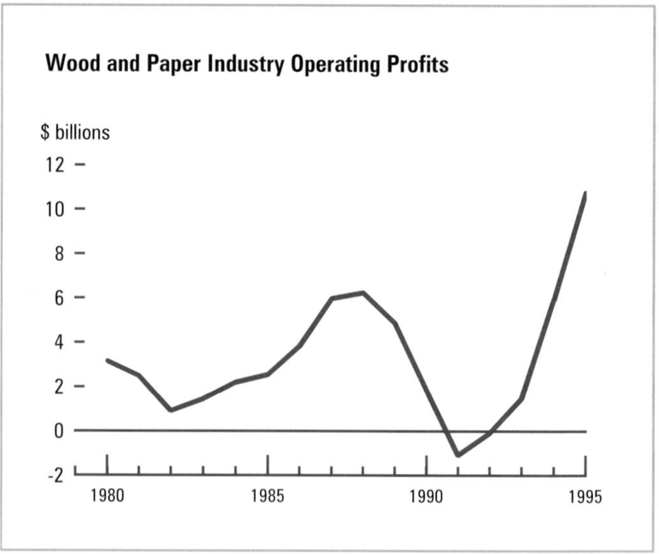

Photo by Lorraine Gilbert

Kerry, tree-planter, Princeton, British Columbia, 1988.

The real strength of our forestry industry lies in our export trade. We are by far the largest exporter of forest products in the world, with shipments equalling almost 20% of the $112 billion international market.

After minerals, the forest products sector continues to be the most important export sector among the primary industries. Forestry exports exceeded those of both agriculture and energy between 1990 and 1994. They made up more than 13% of the total value of all our merchandise exports in 1994.

In 1993, exports of paper were worth $10 billion; export sales increased every year between 1989 and 1993. Lumber exports came close to matching that total in 1993, and represented more than a 44% increase over 1992's exports. Yet pulp exports in 1993 were the lowest since 1986.

Although more than 245 million hectares of forest were inventoried as productive forest land in 1991, cutting down trees has become a source of controversy among many Canadians. Some object to clear-cutting methods of forestry, particularly in British Columbia. Strong protests in Clayoquot Sound received national attention in the 1990s.

Public concerns in recent years have helped galvanize the forestry industry, the federal and provincial governments, the universities, and Aboriginal, environmental and community groups. Sustainable forest development is the umbrella under which extensive research has begun into complex issues like the relationship between national parks and forests, the role of Aboriginal peoples and communities in regional resource management, the management of forests for endangered wildlife species, and reduction in the use of synthetic pesticides.

Governments have adopted high-visibility activities such as Tree Plan Canada, a community tree-planting program that has supported the planting of some 19 million trees in urban and rural communities across Canada. Since 1982, intergovernmental agreements have resulted in the planting of over two billion tree seedlings to renew commercially productive forests. Research laboratories have developed a virus to control the Gypsy Moth infestations of some forests, and governments are considering training and certification programs for forest workers.

SOURCES

Agriculture and Agri-Food Canada
Department of Fisheries and Oceans
Natural Resources Canada
Statistics Canada

FOR FURTHER READING

Selected publications from Statistics Canada

- **Provincial Gross Domestic Product by Industries**. Annual. 15-203
- **Agricultural Financial Statistics**. Annual. 21-205
- **Farming Facts**. Annual. 21-522E
- **Livestock Statistics**. Irregular. 23-603E
- **Canadian Forestry Statistics**. Annual. 25-202
- **Energy Statistics Handbook**. Monthly. 57-601
- **Perspectives on Labour and Income**. Quarterly. 75-001E
- **Canadian Agriculture at a Glance 1994**. Census. 96-301

Selected publications from other sources

- **Canadian Minerals Yearbook**. 1994. Natural Resources Canada. 1995.
- **1996-1997 Estimates, Part III**. **Department of Fisheries and Oceans**. 1996.
- **1996-1997 Estimates, Part III**. **Natural Resources Canada**. 1996.

Legend

–	nil or zero	..	not available	x	confidential
--	too small to be expressed	...	not applicable or not appropriate		*(Certain tables may not add due to rounding)*

11.1 FARM CASH RECEIPTS

	1986	1987	1988	1989	1990	1991	1992	1993	1994	1995
					$ '000					
Total farm cash receipts	20,578,256	21,270,824	22,350,972	22,854,856	21,933,844	21,928,209	23,632,176	24,167,017	25,761,568	26,680,861
Crops	7,875,484	7,341,863	8,291,082	8,764,329	8,873,334	8,726,252	8,540,837	9,007,051	11,482,732	12,826,343
Canadian Wheat Board payments	415,844	51,795	390,791	642,289	489,891	331,597	489,336	1,057,920	1,367,430	1,407,929
Wheat	2,454,956	2,551,048	2,573,448	2,167,671	2,694,083	2,743,923	2,232,798	1,751,357	2,436,290	2,791,240
Oats	48,826	48,200	117,617	145,025	81,083	53,801	97,900	144,663	144,889	225,940
Barley	740,413	491,518	514,206	685,954	545,047	472,485	386,377	402,605	507,270	712,099
Deferred grain receipts	65,153	-3,057	-176,055	102,718	77,475	103,634	9,144	-39,086	-416,748	-74,328
Canola	671,259	722,095	990,671	948,035	789,573	829,527	999,390	1,194,466	2,111,147	1,903,349
Other cereals and oilseeds	852,295	887,401	1,077,012	977,273	976,014	947,384	1,007,378	1,047,521	1,299,510	1,730,128
Other crops[1]	2,626,738	2,592,863	2,803,392	3,095,364	3,220,168	3,243,901	3,318,514	3,447,605	4,032,944	4,129,986
Livestock and products	10,248,452	10,618,888	10,697,839	10,843,186	11,210,310	10,854,358	11,329,858	12,275,726	12,493,516	12,670,679
Cattle and calves	3,602,786	3,809,603	3,968,178	3,964,333	4,024,410	3,878,114	4,457,228	4,967,529	4,845,565	4,651,229
Hogs	2,135,220	2,121,787	1,788,452	1,803,154	2,030,117	1,841,623	1,776,385	2,040,121	2,036,269	2,254,149
Hens and chickens	772,225	798,362	835,250	918,822	970,988	935,397	922,803	1,006,808	1,060,948	1,050,949
Dairy products	2,812,249	2,889,857	3,087,950	3,102,428	3,154,774	3,162,712	3,089,477	3,129,885	3,355,341	3,466,892
Other livestock and products	925,972	999,279	1,018,009	1,054,449	1,030,021	1,036,512	1,083,965	1,131,383	1,195,393	1,247,460
Payments	2,454,320	3,310,073	3,362,051	3,247,341	1,850,200	2,347,599	3,761,481	2,884,240	1,785,320	1,183,839
Gross Revenue Insurance Plan	–	–	–	–	–	837,656	1,389,629	1,370,363	543,052	177,581
Crop insurance	587,082	393,410	604,343	994,725	642,648	339,241	414,113	778,599	610,073	309,568
Provincial stabilization	326,795	115,720	348,037	344,094	234,998	359,676	359,126	261,553	300,466	308,234
Tripartite	3,061	1,169	136,453	486,146	148,573	107,891	371,031	21,204	27,419	22,393
Other payments	1,537,382	2,799,774	2,273,218	1,422,376	823,981	703,135	1,227,582	452,521	304,310	366,063

1. Ginseng not included in 1986.

Source: Statistics Canada, CANSIM, matrix 3571.

11.2 INCOME, FARM BUSINESSES

	1986	1987	1988	1989	1990	1991	1992	1993	1994	1995
					$ '000					
Total cash receipts	20,578,256	21,270,824	22,350,972	22,854,856	21,933,844	21,928,209	23,632,176	24,167,017	25,761,568	26,680,861
- Operating expenses after rebates	15,102,617	15,320,464	16,054,999	17,134,647	17,262,007	17,387,127	17,926,783	18,779,649	20,126,456	21,010,249
= Net cash income	5,475,639	5,950,360	6,295,973	5,720,209	4,671,837	4,541,082	5,705,393	5,387,368	5,635,112	5,670,612
+ Income in kind	196,075	196,862	194,610	194,138	190,484	185,017	189,309	216,908	229,782	221,171
- Depreciation charges	2,749,582	2,711,654	2,770,246	2,893,485	2,989,153	2,994,996	3,011,819	3,086,607	3,271,113	3,500,062
= Realized net income	2,922,132	3,435,568	3,720,337	3,020,862	1,873,168	1,731,103	2,882,883	2,517,669	2,593,781	2,391,721
+ Value of inventory change	601,961	-242,682	-1,123,077	781,216	1,332,730	248,977	-451,039	1,092,509	498,260	543,301
= Total net income	3,524,093	3,192,886	2,597,260	3,802,078	3,205,898	1,980,080	2,431,844	3,610,178	3,092,041	2,935,022

Source: Statistics Canada, CANSIM, matrix 263.

11.3 FARM PRODUCT PRICE INDEX

	1986	1987	1988	1989	1990	1991	1992	1993	1994	1995
Total index	100.0	99.0	105.0	110.7	107.1	100.9	101.2	108.7	113.0	116.7
Crops	100.0	92.6	113.8	126.1	111.4	98.5	100.7	105.2	118.5	134.5
Cereals	100.0	86.9	112.1	129.8	108.9	91.0	95.3	97.0	111.9	136.1
Oilseeds	100.0	90.5	131.5	124.2	117.3	100.4	101.9	117.5	138.6	148.5
Fruits	100.0	98.8	92.4	96.9	99.1	110.5	115.8	110.4	112.7	115.4
Vegetables (excluding potatoes)	100.0	108.5	112.8	112.8	107.4	115.6	116.7	117.6	117.7	115.4
Potatoes	100.0	134.1	118.0	163.3	151.6	136.3	126.7	139.7	174.5	163.2
Livestock and animal products	100.0	103.0	99.6	101.2	104.5	102.4	101.5	110.9	109.7	105.8
Cattle and calves	100.0	109.9	108.1	107.5	108.4	107.3	106.6	122.3	118.2	104.3
Hogs	100.0	97.4	76.1	76.6	90.6	81.2	74.5	86.6	82.8	85.6
Poultry	100.0	94.5	97.3	106.9	106.3	102.1	99.9	101.4	96.5	95.0
Eggs	100.0	92.7	98.2	103.4	96.3	97.4	101.9	103.9	106.3	111.5
Dairy	100.0	101.6	105.3	108.3	110.4	111.4	113.2	117.1	121.5	122.6

Source: Statistics Canada, Catalogue no. 21-603.

11.4 CENSUS FARMS[1] BY TYPE, 1991

	Canada	Nfld.	P.E.I.	N.S.	N.B.	Que.	Ont.	Man.	Sask.	Alta.	B.C.
Census farms	256,182	525	2,144	3,300	2,686	35,600	61,432	23,883	58,651	53,443	14,518
Cattle	66,280	48	488	1,011	822	6,583	16,853	5,071	9,037	22,143	4,224
Small grains (excluding wheat)	47,459	2	60	13	23	2,423	11,432	6,303	14,183	12,659	361
Wheat	42,988	–	3	–	–	94	529	6,479	29,777	6,015	91
Dairy	28,910	72	498	633	512	12,952	9,757	1,195	754	1,379	1,158
Miscellaneous specialty	22,933	126	144	543	404	5,355	7,312	1,041	914	3,730	3,364
Field crops, other than small grains	11,861	32	530	82	376	1,903	3,535	1,032	945	2,540	886
Hogs	10,464	14	203	99	71	2,308	3,830	1,242	790	1,653	254
Fruits and vegetables	10,030	112	80	652	269	2,091	3,746	142	46	142	2,750
Mixed farms											
Livestock combination	7,034	19	83	92	69	405	1,921	727	1,423	1,775	520
Other combinations	4,012	53	28	58	62	574	934	340	642	995	326
Poultry	4,211	47	27	117	78	912	1,583	311	140	412	584

1. Census farms with sales of $25,000 or more.

Source: Statistics Canada, Catalogue no. 93-348.

11.5 LIVESTOCK AND LIVESTOCK PRODUCTS, 1995

	Canada	Nfld.	P.E.I.	N.S.	N.B.	Que.	Ont.	Man.	Sask.	Alta.	B.C.
Cattle and calves ('000 head)[1]	14,689	8	94	127	105	1,477	2,226	1,422	2,825	5,540	865
Pigs ('000 head)[2]	12,183	5	118	133	84	3,410	3,330	1,869	907	2,115	213
Sheep and lambs ('000 head)	860	6	5	26	6	127	227	33	83	264	83
Poultry (tonnes)	860,697	10,081	2,800	29,071	21,816	237,349	301,877	39,143	23,131	75,416	120,013
Eggs ('000 dozen)	482,635	6,701	2,365	17,498	12,997	82,800	182,689	52,332	22,183	41,782	61,288
Milk and cream ('000 kilolitres)	7,022	31	95	170	122	2,768	2,383	281	207	573	573

1. As of July 1995.
2. As of October 1994.

Sources: Statistics Canada, CANSIM, matrices 1150, 1166, 9500–9510; Catalogue nos. 23-001 and 23-202.

11.6 FIELD CROPS

	1991	1992	1993	1994	1995	1991	1992	1993	1994	1995
	Area seeded '000 hectares					Production '000 tonnes				
Wheat										
Canada	14,213.2	14,394.8	12,984.6	11,001.4	11,392.5	31,945.6	29,878.5	27,231.5	23,122.1	25,432.1
Prince Edward Island	4.6	5.6	9.2	11.5	12.9	15.4	22.9	25.2	37.2	41.2
Nova Scotia	1.5	1.2	1.8	2.2	2.9	3.3	4.9	6.9	7.4	9.6
New Brunswick	2.3	1.6	2.5	3.1	3.4	6.9	4.8	7.6	5.9	9.2
Quebec	39.0	42.5	38.8	42.0	32.2	107.8	121.8	111.5	105.1	88.2
Ontario	190.2	305.5	224.6	307.5	311.6	623.1	1,330.8	680.3	1,260.1	1,435.6
Manitoba	2,175.1	2,173.0	2,077.2	1,661.2	1,626.7	4,806.3	5,807.7	3,637.3	3,696.6	3,404.7
Saskatchewan	8,603.2	8,557.1	7,588.0	6,428.4	6,628.7	18,501.2	16,192.1	15,031.2	12,300.0	12,946.5
Alberta	3,152.8	3,259.8	2,994.7	2,505.0	2,723.5	7,772.7	6,327.6	7,620.2	5,592.7	7,337.3
British Columbia	44.3	48.5	47.8	40.5	50.6	108.9	65.9	111.3	117.1	159.8
Canola (rapeseed)										
Canada	3,140.5	3,235.5	4,172.3	5,797.1	5,348.0	4,224.2	3,872.4	5,524.9	7,232.5	6,436.4
Ontario	26.0	14.2	20.2	22.3	36.4	45.4	29.5	38.6	45.4	68.0
Manitoba	507.8	647.5	752.7	1,031.9	951.0	796.1	986.6	907.2	1,485.5	1,227.0
Saskatchewan	1,359.4	1,375.9	1,881.8	2,670.9	2,509.1	1,723.7	1,474.2	2,381.4	3,175.1	2,653.5
Alberta	1,206.8	1,153.4	1,477.1	2,023.4	1,800.9	1,621.6	1,349.4	2,154.6	2,472.1	2,426.7
British Columbia	40.5	44.5	40.5	48.6	50.6	37.4	32.7	43.1	54.4	61.2
Barley										
Canada	4,524.4	4,086.7	4,559.2	4,330.4	4,656.3	11,617.3	11,031.5	12,972.1	11,690.0	13,034.7
Prince Edward Island	34.1	35.2	32.8	30.4	32.4	97.0	141.2	91.7	86.9	93.7
Nova Scotia	5.3	4.5	4.8	4.9	5.7	10.1	14.3	13.5	14.4	16.7
New Brunswick	12.8	14.2	16.2	14.2	16.6	32.7	51.4	45.6	34.9	44.3
Quebec	157.4	164.0	155.0	147.0	130.0	454.0	560.0	435.0	340.0	350.0
Ontario	197.0	178.1	170.0	141.6	133.5	548.7	631.4	500.8	446.3	418.0
Manitoba	544.5	455.3	465.4	445.2	485.6	1,426.1	1,567.6	1,241.0	1,328.1	1,328.1
Saskatchewan	1,343.2	1,254.5	1,618.7	1,537.8	1,740.1	3,069.9	3,157.0	4,245.6	3,919.0	4,354.5
Alberta	2,187.1	1,942.5	2,063.9	1,983.0	2,084.1	5,878.6	4,855.3	6,314.0	5,464.9	6,335.8
British Columbia	43.2	38.4	32.4	26.3	28.3	100.2	53.3	84.9	55.5	93.6
Specialty crops										
Canada	726.7	840.4	1,279.6	1,705.6	1,606.4	1,108.5	1,176.0	1,741.1	2,568.1	2,329.2
Peas										
Manitoba	51.6	50.6	80.9	85.0	72.8	84.4	108.9	85.7	168.7	147.0
Saskatchewan	79.3	141.6	303.5	449.2	546.3	160.6	244.9	585.1	898.1	868.2
Alberta	67.6	80.9	121.4	161.9	188.2	164.7	151.0	299.4	374.2	412.3
Lentils										
Manitoba	54.0	66.8	52.6	46.5	20.2	64.0	79.4	24.1	49.9	28.5
Saskatchewan	179.2	192.2	303.5	335.9	297.4	272.2	254.0	315.2	381.0	381.9
Alberta	4.9	20.2	16.2	16.2	16.2	6.6	15.6	9.4	19.5	21.5
Canary seed										
Manitoba	8.1	7.3	4.9	10.1	10.1	7.3	7.3	3.1	13.6	12.2
Saskatchewan	87.0	87.0	121.4	194.2	133.5	93.0	116.8	124.7	226.8	137.9
Mustard seed										
Manitoba	6.6	4.0	4.0	4.0	4.0	8.9	3.5	3.8	4.1	2.6
Saskatchewan	82.0	97.1	161.9	283.2	222.6	81.7	109.7	180.0	278.9	190.6
Alberta	24.2	18.3	24.3	36.4	46.5	30.5	20.1	32.1	36.3	60.3
Sunflower seed										
Manitoba	73.8	64.7	50.6	56.7	30.4	124.3	55.3	47.2	86.6	43.5
Saskatchewan	7.1	8.1	32.4	24.3	16.2	8.2	8.4	29.0	25.9	18.4
Alberta	1.2	1.6	2.0	2.0	2.0	2.1	1.1	2.3	4.5	4.3

11.6 FIELD CROPS (concluded)

	1991	1992	1993	1994	1995	1991	1992	1993	1994	1995
	Area seeded					Production				
	'000 hectares					'000 tonnes				
Oats										
Canada	1,233.0	1,663.4	1,724.5	1,839.2	1,571.4	1,793.9	2,828.5	3,549.1	3,637.6	2,857.5
Prince Edward Island	7.1	8.1	4.0	5.3	5.7	14.0	25.4	9.3	12.3	12.4
Nova Scotia	4.3	4.5	4.0	3.5	2.4	3.9	13.9	8.6	6.6	5.8
New Brunswick	8.8	12.1	10.9	10.5	9.3	13.7	31.6	21.7	19.7	17.5
Quebec	96.3	109.0	101.0	96.0	87.0	178.0	276.0	220.0	183.0	173.0
Ontario	75.4	80.9	66.8	48.6	40.5	137.3	177.4	141.1	100.2	86.4
Manitoba	155.4	230.7	242.8	303.5	303.5	222.1	555.2	493.5	663.2	624.6
Saskatchewan	335.7	485.6	607.0	728.4	607.0	385.6	663.2	1,079.5	1,388.0	1,110.4
Alberta	520.2	688.0	647.5	607.0	485.6	786.5	1,036.4	1,465.1	1,187.5	771.1
British Columbia	29.6	44.5	40.5	36.4	30.4	52.8	49.4	110.3	77.1	56.3
Flaxseed										
Canada	499.0	297.4	528.1	732.4	876.1	635.0	336.6	627.4	960.1	1,097.3
Manitoba	250.1	149.7	232.7	279.2	313.6	330.2	208.3	243.9	373.4	403.9
Saskatchewan	220.4	129.5	271.1	424.9	526.1	266.7	109.2	342.9	546.1	640.1
Alberta	28.5	18.2	24.3	28.3	36.4	38.1	19.1	40.6	40.6	53.3
Rye										
Canada	290.6	222.1	238.4	237.2	210.9	338.7	278.4	318.6	396.7	299.5
Prince Edward Island	1.5	–	–	–	–	3.2	–	–	–	–
Nova Scotia	–	–	–	–	–	–	–	–	–	–
Quebec	4.6	5.0	1.2	2.5	2.5	3.4	1.3	0.8	1.7	2.0
Ontario	38.4	26.3	22.3	32.4	30.4	43.2	25.4	26.7	45.7	45.7
Manitoba	44.5	32.4	28.3	16.2	28.3	61.0	66.0	43.2	35.6	48.3
Saskatchewan	128.3	85.0	133.6	129.5	101.2	147.3	109.2	165.1	221.0	139.7
Alberta	71.0	70.8	50.6	54.6	46.5	76.2	75.0	81.3	88.9	61.0
British Columbia	2.4	2.6	2.4	2.0	2.0	4.4	1.5	1.5	3.8	2.8
Soybeans										
Canada	597.9	643.6	728.7	820.1	821.0	1,459.9	1,455.3	1,851.3	2,250.7	2,279.0
Prince Edward Island	2.4	3.6	7.7	5.3	4.5	5.9	8.5	16.5	12.3	7.8
Quebec	25.3	33.0	33.0	56.0	80.0	66.0	86.0	93.0	170.0	230.0
Ontario	570.2	607.0	688.0	758.8	736.5	1,388.0	1,360.8	1,741.8	2,068.4	2,041.2
Grain corn										
Canada	1,104.8	1,081.3	1,007.6	961.6	1,002.5	7,412.5	4,882.6	6,501.2	7,042.9	7,250.9
Nova Scotia	1.5	2.0	2.4	2.8	2.2	7.7	11.4	9.5	11.0	13.2
Quebec	293.8	308.0	295.0	283.0	280.0	1,870.0	1,430.0	1,870.0	2,000.0	2,000.0
Ontario	765.5	720.3	688.0	647.5	700.1	5,308.8	3,400.0	4,572.2	4,902.4	5,131.0
Manitoba	40.5	48.6	20.2	26.3	18.2	205.7	35.6	36.8	116.8	94.0
Alberta	3.5	2.4	2.0	2.0	2.0	20.3	5.6	12.7	12.7	12.7
Tame hay										
Canada	5,845.4	6,410.1	6,508.5	6,913.2	6,649.0	29,192.4	27,672.9	29,658.7	31,830.8	27,064.4
Newfoundland	4.9	5.4	5.4	5.5	5.5	25.2	34.8	34.5	34.5	44.5
Prince Edward Island	51.0	48.6	49.0	49.0	49.8	192.3	411.5	307.5	252.2	245.8
Nova Scotia	67.5	69.6	71.0	71.2	70.4	323.9	474.6	390.5	560.6	505.3
New Brunswick	64.6	64.7	64.7	64.3	62.7	257.6	380.1	377.4	317.5	352.0
Quebec	869.3	880.0	930.0	920.0	870.0	3,990.0	4,300.0	6,350.0	5,800.0	5,800.0
Ontario	1,041.0	991.5	1,072.4	1,060.3	1,031.9	7,257.5	6,713.2	7,711.1	6,985.3	6,803.9
Manitoba	697.9	789.1	768.9	789.1	801.3	3,538.0	3,374.7	2,966.5	2,993.7	2,086.5
Saskatchewan	945.6	1,133.1	1,133.1	1,315.2	1,193.8	3,719.5	3,002.8	2,540.1	4,263.8	2,177.2
Alberta	1,754.9	2,084.1	2,063.9	2,286.5	2,266.2	8,164.7	7,620.4	7,348.2	9,162.6	7,620.4
British Columbia	348.8	344.0	350.1	352.1	297.4	1,723.7	1,360.8	1,632.9	1,460.6	1,428.8

Source: Statistics Canada, CANSIM, matrices 3541, 3545–3547, 3553, 3555–3559, 3561, 3563 and 3565.

11.7 USE OF FARM LAND

		Total area of farms	Improved land			All other land
			Under crops	Improved pasture[1]	Summer fallow[2]	
		km²				
Canada	1981[3]	658,889.2	309,658.1	44,047.3	97,019.1	208,168.6
	1986	678,257.6	331,812.4	35,592.2	84,990.2	225,862.9
	1991	677,537.0	335,077.8	41,412.2	79,209.5	221,837.5
Newfoundland	1981	334.5	47.4	41.5	3.6	242.1
	1986	365.6	48.8	38.2	3.9	274.8
	1991	473.5	62.7	46.1	1.5	363.3
Prince Edward Island	1981	2,830.2	1,582.8	362.3	30.3	854.9
	1986	2,724.3	1,565.0	226.2	30.3	854.9
	1991	2,588.8	1,541.0	192.8	10.0	845.0
Nova Scotia	1981	4,660.2	1,127.8	461.1	51.5	3,020.0
	1986	4,165.1	1,095.1	362.4	39.1	2,668.5
	1991	3,970.3	1,062.3	307.2	11.9	2,588.9
New Brunswick	1981	4,378.9	1,305.3	414.8	51.8	2,607.1
	1986	4,088.9	1,294.8	272.0	42.9	2,479.3
	1991	3,756.3	1,222.5	250.5	15.5	2,267.9
Quebec	1981	37,791.7	17,560.4	4,435.6	530.8	15,266.1
	1986	36,388.0	17,444.0	3,011.3	318.0	15,614.7
	1991	34,296.1	16,384.5	2,709.2	147.1	15,055.2
Ontario	1981	60,392.4	36,327.3	6,570.1	633.1	16,862.9
	1986	56,465.8	34,579.7	4,312.9	803.4	16,769.9
	1991	54,513.8	34,116.7	3,902.1	636.6	15,858.4
Manitoba	1981[3]	76,159.3	44,203.7	3,525.1	5,983.4	22,447.2
	1986	77,402.3	45,193.4	2,749.4	5,092.1	24,367.3
	1991	77,249.9	47,610.5	3,412.9	2,970.0	23,256.5
Saskatchewan	1981[3]	259,470.9	117,408.6	9,753.6	67,044.6	65,264.0
	1986	265,993.6	133,258.1	8,787.3	56,582.5	67,365.7
	1991	268,654.9	134,589.2	10,756.6	57,128.3	66,180.9
Alberta	1981[3]	191,085.1	84,412.4	15,814.4	22,054.7	79,783.3
	1986	206,553.4	91,625.2	13,768.1	21,270.1	79,889.9
	1991	208,110.0	92,920.4	17,424.8	17,714.0	80,050.9
British Columbia	1981[3]	21,786.0	5,682.4	2,668.8	635.3	12,800.6
	1986	24,110.6	5,708.4	2,064.3	811.7	15,526.2
	1991	23,923.4	5,568.0	2,410.0	574.8	15,370.7

1 The 1986 and 1991 Censuses included a separate question on unimproved land for pasture, resulting in more accurate reporting of improved pasture.

2. The data for summerfallow have been overstated for all five censuses in geographic areas where the practice is not common. However, a question added to the 1991 questionnaire on the use of weed control methods on summerfallow land significantly reduced the extent of this over-reporting of improved pasture.

3. In 1981, the area of unimproved land was under-reported in the four Western provinces, which affected the area for "all the other land" category and the total area of farms for each of the Western provinces and Canada.

Source: Statistics Canada, Catalogue no. 93-348.

11.8 FISH CATCHES

	1991						1994					
	Canada		Atlantic coast		Pacific coast		Canada		Atlantic coast		Pacific coast	
	Quantity[1]	Value	Quantity[1]	Value	Quantity[1]	Value	Quantity[1]	Value	Quantity[1]	Value	Quantity[1]	Value
	Tonnes	$'000	Tonnes	$'000	Tonnes	$'000	Tonnes	$'000	Tonnes	$'000	Tonnes	$'000
All fisheries	1,558,298	1,466,352	1,192,531	1,012,768	316,587	380,181	1,034,284	1,671,409	717,454	1,123,315	280,830	473,094
Inland fisheries	49,180	73,403	...	...	...	...	36,000	75,000	...	...	...	...
Sea fisheries	1,509,118	1,392,949	1,192,531	1,012,768	316,587	380,181	998,284	1,596,409	717,454	1,123,315	280,830	473,094
Groundfish	786,714	497,336	624,177	396,411	162,537	100,925	291,737	224,504	144,303	123,503	147,434	101,001
Cod[2]	320,941	233,078	309,031	227,014	11,910	6,064	25,803	31,366	22,719	29,605	3,084	1,761
Haddock	21,957	30,711	21,957	30,711	–	–	6,955	13,965	6,955	13,965	–	–
Redfish	115,992	41,805	92,570	24,889	23,422	16,916	65,677	28,304	50,774	15,716	14,903	12,588
Halibut	6,347	30,780	2,036	9,009	4,311	21,771	6,590	41,566	1,264	7,948	5,326	33,618
Flatfish	72,127	40,975	64,236	35,151	7,891	5,824	21,439	22,376	15,187	17,998	6,252	4,378
Greenland Turbot	22,474	18,237	20,187	17,636	2,287	601	13,158	14,847	11,036	14,409	2,122	438
Pollock	43,360	24,629	40,780	24,029	2,580	600	19,210	12,036	15,584	10,884	3,626	1,152
Hake[3]	162,980	37,517	63,925	22,128	99,055	15,389	118,488	23,783	14,656	9,003	103,832	14,780
Cusk	4,419	3,217	4,419	3,217	–	–	1,692	1,400	1,692	1,400	–	–
Catfish	1,389	344	1,389	344	–	–	485	182	485	182	–	–
Other groundfish	14,727	36,045	3,646	2,285	11,081	33,760	12,240	34,679	3,951	2,393	8,289	32,286
Pelagic and other finfish	434,878	295,188	305,897	71,100	128,981	224,088	356,768	335,008	250,051	73,725	106,717	261,283
Herring	255,285	78,737	215,544	29,316	39,741	49,421	246,091	91,336	206,777	27,677	39,314	63,659
Mackerel	25,876	7,548	25,876	7,548	–	–	20,614	6,980	20,612	6,978	2	2
Tuna	678	8,386	535	8,044	143	342	1,242	11,140	608	9,696	634	1,444
Alewife	7,552	1,939	7,552	1,939	–	–	5,825	1,624	5,825	1,624	–	–
Eel	980	4,198	980	4,198	–	–	752	3,260	752	3,260	–	–
Salmon	86,161	174,727	481	2,287	85,680	172,440	65,534	195,870	135	685	65,399	195,185
Skate	1,382	293	1,134	243	248	50	6,740	2,467	6,362	2,249	378	218
Smelt	1,241	1,174	1,241	1,174	–	–	1,399	1,807	1,396	1,799	3	8
Capelin	49,892	7,244	49,892	7,244	–	–	2,249	574	2,249	574	–	–
Other finfish	5,832	10,942	2,663	9,107	3,169	1,835	6,322	19,950	5,335	19,183	987	767
Shellfish	251,362	582,198	226,992	535,919	24,370	46,279	317,111	1,005,188	290,709	911,580	26,402	93,609
Clams/quahaugs	17,658	25,378	12,729	11,847	4,929	13,531	30,052	64,394	26,097	27,034	3,955	37,360
Oysters	6,382	6,780	1,900	3,316	4,482	3,464	7,880	8,803	2,630	4,603	5,250	4,200
Scallops	79,538	81,359	79,538	81,359	–	–	91,509	139,196	91,402	138,692	107	504
Squid	2,616	785	2,616	785	–	–	5,943	3,158	5,778	2,972	165	187
Mussels	3,646	4,801	3,646	4,801	–	–	6,118	6,496	6,118	6,496	–	–
Lobster	48,492	277,453	48,492	277,453	–	–	41,411	354,227	41,411	354,227	–	–
Shrimps	44,690	97,981	40,464	85,836	4,226	12,145	52,846	114,782	48,661	99,205	4,185	15,577
Crab, queen	35,161	68,971	35,161	68,971	–	–	60,399	270,137	60,398	270,136	1	1
Crab, other	2,985	9,107	1,098	419	1,887	8,688	10,149	26,830	4,505	2,673	5,644	24,157
Other shellfish	10,194	9,582	1,348	1,131	8,846	8,451	10,804	17,165	3,709	5,542	7,095	11,623
Other marine life	36,163	18,227	35,464	9,338	699	8,889	32,668	31,708	32,391	14,507	277	17,201
Marine plants	32,931	3,619	32,931	3,619	–	–	30,201	2,279	30,201	2,279	–	–
Lumpfish roe	2,297	4,976	2,297	4,976	–	–	1,579	8,206	1,579	8,206	–	–
Miscellaneous	936	9,633	237	744	699	8,889	888	21,223	611	4,022	277	17,201

1. Quantity in tonnes, live weight.
2. Pacific cod includes grey cod only.
3. Hake catches include over-the-side sales to foreign vessels.

Source: Department of Fisheries and Oceans, Economic and Policy Analysis Directorate.

11.9 FOREST HARVEST

	1990		1991		1992		1993	
	Total harvested	Clearcut	Total harvested	Clearcut	Total harvested	Clearcut	Total harvested	Clearcut
	Hectares							
Canada	892,869	821,098	856,403	769,909	905,755	794,707	968,584	844,365
Newfoundland	22,100	22,100	18,661	18,661	18,391	18,391	20,640	20,640
Prince Edward Island	2,317	917	2,091	1,116	2,550	1,345	2,976	1,451
Nova Scotia	39,310	39,310	37,566	37,566	33,932	33,932	42,780	42,780
New Brunswick	80,109	73,769	91,916	68,537	103,335	77,966	100,650	69,902
Quebec	253,325	232,965	236,725	214,965	248,491	212,864	311,623	269,496
Ontario	238,213	209,507	199,720	178,064	190,676	172,804	206,000	186,000
Manitoba	10,349	10,349	8,518	8,518	11,414	11,414	10,993	10,993
Saskatchewan	16,538	16,538	17,522	17,522	18,471	18,471	19,456	19,456
Alberta	48,387	48,387	49,213	49,213	55,852	55,852	44,565	44,565
British Columbia	181,530	166,565	193,654	174,930	221,599	190,624	207,748	177,929
Yukon	366	366	350	350	639	639	634	634
Northwest Territories	325	325	467	467	405	405	519	519

Source: Statistics Canada, CANSIM, matrix 6086.

11.10 ENERGY SUMMARY

	1986	1987	1988	1989	1990	1991	1992	1993	1994
	Petajoules[1]								
Primary production	9,736.2	10,250.4	11,175.4	11,349.7	11,392.6	11,789.0	12,239.9	13,034.3	13,941.3
Net supply[2]	7,210.0	7,382.7	7,830.2	8,090.3	7,865.6	7,764.5	7,929.7	8,190.7	8,417.6
Producers' own consumption	759.9	815.6	849.7	910.6	906.0	878.4	921.3	932.2	976.2
Non-energy use	609.3	664.3	676.9	676.9	638.4	665.8	679.5	735.1	744.9
Energy use	5,867.0	5,918.4	6,309.0	6,499.1	6,321.2	6,221.0	6,328.1	6,523.0	6,696.8
Industrial	1,940.0	2,011.9	2,121.8	2,127.6	2,043.6	2,021.7	1,989.6	2,034.8	2,086.0
Transportation	1,621.6	1,709.3	1,839.4	1,870.5	1,821.3	1,785.0	1,870.1	1,916.8	2,027.0
Agriculture	175.7	167.1	180.4	200.5	204.7	195.3	223.6	198.5	194.5
Residential	1,108.8	1,072.6	1,146.0	1,224.4	1,197.1	1,166.2	1,179.4	1,257.4	1,277.0
Public administration	136.0	134.7	140.2	145.9	144.0	136.8	135.5	133.1	144.9
Commercial and institutional	884.9	822.8	881.2	930.3	910.5	915.9	929.8	982.4	967.3

1. A 30-litre gasoline fill-up contains about one gigajoule of energy. A petajoule is one million gigajoules.
2. Net supply of primary and secondary sources.

Source: Statistics Canada, CANSIM, matrix 7977.

11.11 PRIMARY ENERGY PRODUCTION[1]

	1986	1987	1988	1989	1990	1991	1992	1993	1994
					Petajoules				
Primary sources									
Production	9,736.2	10,250.4	11,175.4	11,349.7	11,392.6	11,789.0	12,239.9	13,034.3	13,941.3
Exports	3,121.7	3,484.7	4,108.3	4,138.0	4,188.2	4,802.0	5,203.4	5,630.6	6,347.1
Imports	1,219.3	1,339.4	1,551.4	1,599.2	1,698.6	1,610.5	1,561.0	1,628.9	1,743.2
Adjustments[2]	74.3	21.3	33.1	-96.2	195.8	-70.7	-202.4	100.7	126.1
Available	7,817.4	8,105.4	8,639.6	8,923.0	8,779.2	8,632.8	8,760.3	9,047.5	9,360.0
Transformed to other energy forms[3]	4,120.3	4,338.8	4,590.5	4,725.4	4,620.1	4,446.7	4,470.6	4,528.6	4,720.7
Coal									
Production	1,382.1	1,393.9	1,614.2	1,718.4	1,669.3	1,748.0	1,545.8	1,651.3	1,735.3
Exports	759.0	738.0	875.7	997.8	943.0	1,036.1	830.9	860.0	964.9
Imports	399.1	415.3	506.5	420.7	408.7	359.2	371.9	243.4	265.6
Adjustments[2]	-19.1	-55.5	45.2	-57.6	69.2	-36.1	-48.3	-3.7	-57.7
Available	1,040.0	1,117.7	1,200.3	1,197.8	1,077.2	1,104.4	1,137.1	1,044.0	1,086.4
Transformed to other energy forms[3]	980.4	1,059.4	1,138.8	1,139.0	1,020.1	1,056.1	1,090.9	996.7	1,036.0
Crude oil[4]									
Production	3,531.2	3,690.9	3,877.9	3,769.3	3,734.8	3,729.4	3,884.9	4,070.7	4,299.9
Exports	1,307.1	1,387.3	1,588.9	1,446.0	1,462.5	1,703.7	1,876.4	2,051.8	2,219.0
Imports	792.4	903.9	1,002.6	1,087.8	1,198.1	1,214.7	1,146.2	1,323.9	1,405.0
Adjustments[2]	4.3	21.8	40.9	26.7	38.3	24.5	-14.6	-37.4	-5.3
Available	3,038.1	3,155.3	3,339.0	3,401.7	3,463.0	3,248.5	3,174.8	3,462.0	3,604.1
Transformed to other energy forms[3]	3,049.5	3,008.6	3,153.9	3,155.3	3,210.9	3,275.9	3,316.3	3,339.0	3,352.2
Natural gas[5]									
Production	3,135.6	3,402.0	3,921.7	4,152.5	4,261.6	4,486.3	4,960.1	5,348.0	5,831.3
Exports	796.8	1,059.3	1,360.4	1,432.3	1,537.2	1,804.0	2,195.3	2,395.3	2,752.6
Imports	9.8	3.5	14.6	29.2	24.2	12.1	17.1	30.9	40.0
Adjustments[2]	51.5	6.0	4.0	-17.4	75.4	-22.9	-146.8	-51.5	-8.9
Available	2,316.9	2,358.5	2,592.7	2,789.9	2,701.9	2,705.4	2,862.7	2,885.7	3,010.3
Transformed to other energy forms[3]	58.6	54.7	54.1	57.0	59.0	62.4	67.0	68.8	84.8
Natural gas liquids[6]									
Production	306.2	347.2	371.0	377.9	404.9	416.7	434.8	484.7	528.9
Exports	118.7	129.4	160.7	181.6	179.8	169.9	187.3	197.8	227.3
Imports	0.1	4.2	5.4	14.8	3.6	2.7	2.6	3.6	7.4
Adjustments[2]	33.1	44.7	8.9	-12.9	0.8	5.6	-31.0	-13.1	-12.3
Available	163.7	215.9	217.2	235.6	216.7	232.1	261.7	274.9	271.4
Transformed to other energy forms[3]	40.8	67.1	43.9	45.1	43.9	54.7	69.8	16.1	18.0
Electricity[7]									
Production	1,352.9	1,393.0	1,377.7	1,310.2	1,306.0	1,388.1	1,401.7	1,472.8	1,542.0
Exports	140.2	170.7	122.6	80.4	65.7	88.3	113.5	125.9	183.3
Imports	17.8	12.4	22.4	46.7	64.0	21.9	23.3	27.2	25.2
Adjustments[2]	–	–	–	–	–	–	–	–	–
Available	1,230.6	1,234.7	1,277.5	1,276.5	1,304.3	1,321.7	1,311.5	1,374.1	1,383.9
Transformed to other energy forms[3]	–	–	–	–	–	–	–	–	–

1. The quantities of crude oil and natural gas shown here include an estimate of producers' own consumption in the synthetic crude and crude bitumen sectors.
2. Includes stock variation, interproduct transfers and other adjustments.
3. For electricity and steam generation, coal coke production and refined petroleum products.
4. The general terms "crude oil" or "crude oil and equivalent" comprise conventional crude, condensate, pentanes, synthetic crude oil and crude bitumen.
5. Gross production, including reinjection and shrinkage.
6. Gas plant natural gas liquids include butane, propane and ethane.
7. Hydro and nuclear only.

Source: Statistics Canada, CANSIM, matrix 7977.

11.12 ENERGY USE[1]

	1986	1987	1988	1989	1990	1991	1992	1993	1994
					Petajoules				
Primary and secondary energy									
Producers' own consumption	759.9	815.6	849.7	910.6	906.0	878.4	921.3	932.2	976.2
Non-energy use	609.3	664.3	676.9	676.9	638.4	665.8	679.5	735.1	744.9
Energy use–final demand	5867.0	5918.4	6309.0	6499.1	6321.2	6221.0	6328.1	6523.0	6696.8
Industrial	1940.0	2011.9	2121.8	2127.6	2043.6	2021.7	1989.6	2034.8	2086.0
Transportation	1621.6	1709.3	1839.4	1870.5	1821.3	1785.0	1870.1	1916.8	2027.0
Agricultural	175.7	167.1	180.4	200.5	204.7	195.3	223.6	198.5	194.5
Residential	1108.8	1072.6	1146.0	1224.4	1197.1	1166.2	1179.4	1257.4	1277.0
Public administration	136.0	134.7	140.2	145.9	144.0	136.8	135.5	133.1	144.9
Commercial and institutional	884.9	822.8	881.2	930.3	910.5	915.9	929.8	982.4	967.3
Coal, coke and coke oven gas									
Producers' own consumption	3.2	3.8	4.6	3.9	4.4	5.0	2.7	3.9	3.9
Non-energy use	13.1	15.6	17.6	16.9	15.0	10.0	6.2	6.5	9.4
Energy use–final demand	228.1	223.2	230.0	219.8	177.6	185.3	187.1	179.8	166.0
Industrial	223.5	219.2	226.7	217.4	174.9	183.1	185.1	177.9	164.3
Transportation	–	–	–	–	–	–	–	–	–
Agricultural	–	–	–	–	–	–	–	–	–
Residential	4.0	3.6	2.8	2.2	2.5	2.1	2.0	1.8	1.5
Public administration	0.1	0.0	0.2	0.2	0.2	0.1	–	–	0.2
Commercial and institutional	0.5	0.4	0.3	–	–	–	–	–	–
Crude oil and petroleum products									
Producers' own consumption	207.6	210.2	225.7	235.0	238.9	230.6	239.4	346.1	346.9
Non-energy use	349.6	371.1	340.4	344.2	335.2	338.6	355.2	367.9	369.1
Energy use–final demand	2416.7	2432.5	2559.5	2638.6	2550.4	2408.3	2421.5	2473.5	2577.8
Industrial	312.8	303.7	315.3	326.6	314.6	284.0	259.1	273.5	289.4
Transportation	1515.5	1579.0	1674.6	1700.3	1647.8	1594.7	1634.0	1666.3	1762.6
Agricultural	118.9	115.7	122.5	137.7	139.8	132.5	157.5	126.8	131.1
Residential	205.1	181.3	189.6	203.3	185.4	161.9	138.0	172.5	163.0
Public administration	71.2	71.6	75.2	78.1	79.8	71.9	68.3	63.2	63.7
Commercial and institutional	193.3	181.2	182.2	192.5	183.0	163.4	164.4	171.3	167.9
Natural gas									
Producers' own consumption	419.5	469.7	477.1	521.2	530.0	505.8	540.9	447.1	478.0
Non-energy use	148.2	149.7	168.6	168.1	148.9	168.7	165.7	168.9	188.2
Energy use–final demand	1713.4	1697.2	1883.1	1957.3	1929.9	1943.7	2021.1	2114.1	2170.7
Industrial	724.0	781.3	857.4	869.6	854.8	834.6	831.6	850.7	876.4
Transportation	78.6	96.4	124.4	131.6	135.7	150.5	194.7	205.1	217.3
Agricultural	18.3	18.2	20.8	22.0	23.2	23.2	25.1	31.2	23.6
Residential	480.7	457.7	507.0	538.2	528.4	531.9	553.3	593.5	632.1
Public administration	20.5	17.9	18.6	20.6	19.0	17.9	19.9	22.4	32.7
Commercial and institutional	391.4	325.6	354.9	375.2	368.8	385.6	396.5	411.2	388.6
Natural gas liquids									
Producers' own consumption	2.5	1.2	1.0	1.8	2.5	0.7	4.0	2.9	3.5
Non-energy use	98.4	127.9	150.3	147.7	139.2	148.5	152.5	191.8	178.1
Energy use–final demand	80.0	85.6	95.3	99.9	90.7	88.3	88.0	119.6	127.1
Industrial	15.5	13.7	31.3	28.3	23.8	28.2	23.5	29.0	28.5
Transportation	17.5	23.2	28.3	26.4	25.9	28.9	29.2	32.4	33.9
Agricultural	5.9	5.5	5.6	8.2	7.1	5.2	6.8	6.2	4.9
Residential	26.5	28.2	12.3	13.1	12.5	9.1	14.2	11.8	9.8
Public administration	0.8	0.9	1.8	0.0	0.0	0.0	0.0	0.2	0.9
Commercial and institutional	13.8	14.2	16.0	23.9	21.3	16.9	14.3	39.9	49.1

11.12 ENERGY USE[1] (concluded)

	1986	1987	1988	1989	1990	1991	1992	1993	1994
					Petajoules				
Electricity									
Producers' own consumption	127.0	130.6	141.4	148.7	130.1	136.2	134.4	132.3	143.9
Non-energy use	–	–	–	–	–	–	–	–	–
Energy use–final demand	1396.6	1452.2	1524.7	1559.0	1551.6	1570.7	1593.6	1625.1	1640.2
Industrial	632.6	666.7	675.1	661.6	654.7	667.4	673.4	693.1	712.8
Transportation	10.1	10.7	12.1	12.1	11.8	11.0	12.3	13.1	13.3
Agricultural	32.6	27.7	31.4	32.5	34.7	34.3	34.1	34.1	34.8
Residential	392.6	401.8	434.2	467.5	468.3	461.2	471.9	477.7	470.7
Public administration	43.1	44.2	44.2	46.8	45.0	47.0	47.3	47.0	47.1
Commercial and institutional	285.5	301.2	327.6	338.5	337.2	350.0	354.6	360.0	361.6

1. Net primary and secondary energy.

Source: Statistics Canada, CANSIM, matrix 7977.

11.13 COAL, SUPPLY AND DEMAND

	1986	1987	1988	1989	1990	1991	1992	1993	1994
					Kilotonnes				
Supply	71,124	75,556	88,062	85,050	82,444	03,555	78,444	77,419	81,979
Production	57,812	61,211	70,644	70,529	68,331	71,138	65,610	69,027	72,805
Bituminous	32,199	32,652	38,585	38,794	37,673	39,915	32,563	35,319	36,640
Sub-bituminous	17,331	18,540	19,910	20,919	21,252	22,243	23,020	23,662	25,479
Lignite	8,282	10,019	12,149	10,816	9,406	8,980	10,027	10,046	10,686
Imports	13,312	14,345	17,418	14,521	14,113	12,417	12,834	8,392	9,174
Demand	70,436	76,881	86,192	86,611	80,046	84,375	80,064	77,847	84,458
Domestic demand	44,532	50,140	54,467	53,784	49,037	50,263	51,967	49,534	52,861
Newfoundland	...	...	...	...	...	...	...	...	...
Prince Edward Island	...	...	...	...	...	...	...	...	...
Nova Scotia	2,408	2,398	2,313	2,144	2,196	2,314	2,359	2,441	2,927
New Brunswick	470	526	654	614	409	426	471	389	350
Quebec	642	692	748	753	716	478	484	524	607
Ontario	15,868	18,834	20,161	19,502	16,077	16,375	15,761	12,466	10,116
Manitoba	296	647	980	516	460	328	349	291	264
Saskatchewan	6,977	7,894	8,871	8,640	7,644	7,738	8,591	8,892	9,370
Alberta	17,719	19,076	20,540	21,409	21,339	22,480	23,752	24,194	28,206
British Columbia	152	74	114	115	108	124	200	194	163
Exports	25,904	26,741	31,725	32,827	31,009	34,112	28,097	28,313	31,597

Source: Statistics Canada, Catalogue no. 57-601.

11.14 ENERGY PRODUCTION AND CONSUMPTION, INTERNATIONAL COMPARISONS, 1993

	Coal		Crude oil		Natural gas		NGLs		Electricity	
	Production	Consumption	Production	Consumption	Production	Consumption	Production	Consumption	Production	Consumption
	('000 tonnes)		('000 tonnes)		(terajoules)		('000 tonnes)		(gWh)	
Canada	72,673	4,505	84,761	..	5,234,352	2,228,541	15,979	..	527,386	431,387
Australia	228,792	8,265	24,438	..	970,880	428,562	2,216	..	163,751	136,758
Austria	3,093	2,303	1,155	..	58,776	159,469	40	..	52,675	44,529
Belgium	4,000	5,014	–	..	178	361,014	–	..	70,845	63,481
Denmark	–	597	8,265	..	183,896	67,497	–	..	33,738	30,621
Finland	7,861	4,664	–	..	–	61,073	–	..	61,172	62,326
France	16,872	10,350	2,752	..	134,147	1,310,440	453	..	472,004	332,298
Germany	313,076	34,190	3,064	..	639,745	2,104,486	–	..	525,721	446,066
Greece	54,857	2,094	537	..	4,325	2,633	25	..	38,396	31,179
Iceland	–	68	–	..	–	–	–	..	4,727	4,082
Ireland	5,447	2,643	–	..	100,312	54,296	–	..	16,396	13,549
Italy	5,559	6,617	4,620	..	729,510	1,531,580	20	..	222,788	224,305
Japan	51,145	42,295	778	10	90,394	56,653	–	2,833	906,705	796,599
Luxembourg	–	1,070	–	..	–	22,070	–	..	1,067	4,376
Mexico	8,557	2,404	140,099	..	1,123,746	758,048	15,152	..	126,566	102,210
Netherlands	2,879	2,434	2,672	..	2,936,245	1,157,581	576	..	76,992	78,724
New Zealand	3,101	2,082	1,842	..	204,265	45,425	184	..	33,624	29,929
Norway	267	1,203	111,854	..	1,126,696	–	2,617	..	120,004	101,750
Portugal	465	956	–	..	–	–	–	..	31,205	25,982
Spain	31,504	4,227	874	15	27,726	251,096	–	..	156,529	130,683
Sweden	2,164	1,725	–	..	–	16,383	–	..	145,975	120,918
Switzerland	–	–	–	..	90	88,150	–	..	61,070	47,239
Turkey	51,270	20,804	3,892	..	7,660	96,646	–	..	73,808	56,746
United Kingdom	74,667	16,431	93,949	..	2,536,581	2,039,309	6,136	..	323,029	285,747
United States	878,729	50,376	338,152	..	20,087,149	17,028,646	51,332	..	3,411,281	2,873,867

Source: International Energy Agency, *Energy Statistics of OECD Countries,* 1992-93.

11.15 ELECTRICITY, GROSS SUPPLY AND DEMAND

	1986	1987	1988	1989	1990	1991	1992	1993	1994
	Gigawatt hours								
Supply	473,549.0	499,805.7	510,590.3	506,636.9	495,725.5	506,981.6	518,882.2	529,621.8	551,173.9
Production	468,592.3	496,334.8	504,284.7	497,890.2	480,427.4	505,069.8	517,141.7	527,033.2	550,332.8
Imports	4,956.7	3,470.9	6,305.2	12,723.6	17,778.7	6,282.9	6,476.3	7,369.9	8,279.6
Demand	473,549.1	499,805.7	510,590.3	506,636.9	495,725.5	506,981.6	518,882.2	529,621.8	558,612.4
Domestic demand	434,614.7	452,378.9	476,561.4	484,548.4	477,597.2	482,367.2	487,332.9	494,774.1	507,600.9
Producer consumption	46,682.6	48,985.2	53,020.8	55,460.0	49,064.8	50,432.6	49,406.8	48,135.4	51,980.8
Transportation	2,798.9	2,967.2	3,365.6	3,366.4	3,273.9	3,055.6	3,406.7	3,629.2	3,684.2
Farm and residential	118,135.6	119,313.1	129,355.8	138,883.3	139,708.9	137,618.1	140,554.7	142,187.2	140,395.8
Public and commercial	91,280.0	95,921.4	103,281.4	107,033.9	106,173.9	110,255.3	111,646.9	113,074.2	113,548.1
Manufacturing	152,611.4	161,360.6	159,264.7	155,150.6	152,074.2	156,269.7	158,088.9	163,942.5	168,256.4
Mining	23,105.6	23,830.6	28,272.8	28,632.2	29,782.8	29,106.7	28,965.3	28,587.8	29,735.8
Exports	38,934.4	47,426.8	34,028.9	22,088.5	18,128.3	24,614.4	31,549.3	34,847.7	51,011.5

Source: Statistics Canada, Catalogue no. 57-601.

11.16 ENERGY TRADE

	1986	1987	1988	1989	1990	1991	1992	1993	1994
					$ Millions				
Energy imports	5,337	5,680	5,014	6,515	8,864	6,784	6,652	6,979	7,486
Petroleum	4,422	4,809	4,051	5,329	7,504	6,085	5,767	6,261	6,654
Crude oil	2,916	3,180	2,524	3,514	5,409	4,497	4,145	4,484	4,843
Petroleum products[1]	1,309	1,465	1,426	1,684	1,959	1,469	1,520	1,658	1,704
Liquid petroleum gases[2]	197	164	101	132	135	119	102	118	106
Natural gas	–	--	–	–	1	32	50	47	85
Coal and coal products	874	843	828	779	687	529	645	484	523
Electricity	9	9	59	297	558	70	77	85	44
Uranium[3]	31	18	76	110	116	68	114	102	182
Energy exports	12,138	13,338	13,339	13,491	15,971	16,310	17,490	20,138	22,487
Petroleum	5,866	7,029	6,620	7,015	9,467	9,632	9,797	10,934	11,587
Crude oil	3,774	4,855	4,040	4,508	5,710	6,055	6,685	6,919	7,438
Petroleum products[1]	1,406	1,511	1,933	1,971	2,980	2,762	2,366	2,713	2,719
Liquid petroleum gases[2]	686	663	647	536	777	816	746	1,302	1,430
Natural gas	2,483	2,527	2,955	3,017	3,267	3,512	4,608	5,778	6,717
Coal and coal products	1,869	1,696	2,068	2,194	2,276	2,204	1,880	2,070	2,289
Electricity	1,080	1,200	881	659	538	554	708	857	1,273
Uranium[3]	841	886	815	606	423	409	497	499	621
Energy trade balance	6,802	7,658	8,325	6,976	7,107	9,526	10,838	13,159	15,001
Petroleum	1,444	2,220	2,569	1,686	1,963	3,547	4,029	4,673	4,933
Crude oil	858	1,675	1,516	994	300	1,558	2,540	2,434	2,594
Petroleum products[1]	98	45	507	287	1,021	1,292	846	1,055	1,015
Liquid petroleum gases[2]	489	500	546	404	642	697	644	1,184	1,324
Natural gas	2,483	2,527	2,954	3,017	3,267	3,480	4,558	5,731	6,633
Coal and coal products	995	852	1,241	1,416	1,589	1,675	1,236	1,586	1,767
Electricity	1,071	1,191	821	361	-19	484	632	772	1,229
Uranium[3]	809	868	739	496	307	341	383	397	439

1. Includes ethane products in 1986 and 1987.
2. Includes ethane products, 1988-1994.
3. Includes chemicals, medicinal products and other non-energy amounts prior to 1988.

Source: Statistics Canada, Catalogue no. 57-601.

11.17 ENERGY CONSUMER PRICE INDICES

	1986	1987	1988	1989	1990	1991	1992	1993	1994
					(1986 = 100)				
All energy	100.0	102.6	103.2	106.8	117.4	123.2	123.5	125.1	125.8
Motor gas	100.0	104.8	103.8	110.3	126.6	124.7	120.2	118.4	117.0
Fuel oil	100.0	95.0	97.9	96.8	115.2	124.6	120.0	122.0	120.5
Natural gas	100.0	97.8	96.1	91.7	87.0	95.4	99.1	102.9	111.5
Electricity	100.0	104.2	108.2	112.6	119.3	136.4	145.3	151.4	152.3

Source: Statistics Canada, Catalogue no. 57-601.

11.18 PETROLEUM SUPPLY AND DEMAND

	1986	1987	1988	1989	1990	1991	1992	1993	1994
					Cubic metres (thousands)				
Supply	132,093.5	142,240.5	151,146.5	152,752.5	153,482.5	155,198.0	158,191.0	169,360.0	175,857.0
Domestic production									
Crude and equivalent	91,359.5	95,411.0	100,119.5	97,236.0	96,725.0	96,725.0	100,740.0	105,886.5	110,047.5
Refined products	83,475.5	87,490.5	91,651.5	93,440.0	94,863.5	89,863.0	88,001.5	92,527.5	95,046.0
Motor gasoline	33,288.0	34,200.5	35,660.5	36,500.0	36,792.0	36,500.0	36,354.0	37,157.0	37,996.5
Aviation turbo fuel	4,489.5	4,964.0	4,927.5	5,329.0	5,292.5	4,489.5	4,599.0	4,234.0	4,307.0
Diesel fuel	15,147.5	16,279.0	17,702.5	18,140.5	19,235.5	18,323.0	17,155.0	17,374.0	19,381.5
Light fuel oil	8,358.5	8,468.0	8,504.5	9,015.5	8,504.5	8,541.0	8,687.0	10,950.0	10,110.5
Heavy fuel oil	6,643.0	7,008.0	8,066.5	8,614.0	9,015.5	8,577.5	7,957.0	7,701.5	7,154.0
Gas plant ethane, propane and butane	13,103.5	15,074.5	15,914.0	16,352.0	17,228.0	18,177.0	19,089.5	20,951.0	21,973.0
Imports									
Crude and equivalent	20,586.0	23,469.5	25,951.5	28,251.0	31,098.0	31,536.0	29,674.5	34,383.0	36,098.5
Refined products	6,825.5	8,030.0	8,869.5	10,256.5	8,285.5	8,614.0	8,577.5	7,993.5	7,519.0
Ethane, propane and butane	182.5	219.0	292.0	657.0	146.0	146.0	73.0	109.5	255.5
Demand	135,269.0	141,474.0	156,366.0	156,293.0	156,475.5	160,308.0	165,746.5	173,411.5	179,653.0
Domestic demand									
Refined products	82,417.0	84,205.5	87,819.0	90,666.0	88,585.5	83,329.5	84,169.0	85,884.5	87,417.5
Motor gasoline	32,886.5	33,215.0	34,054.5	34,821.0	33,945.0	32,813.5	33,178.5	34,054.5	35,003.5
Aviation turbo fuel	4,380.0	4,672.0	5,037.0	5,183.0	5,000.5	4,453.0	4,635.5	4,453.0	4,708.5
Diesel fuel	15,001.5	15,804.5	16,644.0	17,191.5	16,863.0	15,877.5	15,841.0	16,680.5	18,286.5
Light fuel oil	7,044.5	6,314.5	6,643.0	6,862.0	6,424.0	5,730.5	5,767.0	5,949.5	5,767.0
Heavy fuel oil	7,117.5	7,482.5	8,942.5	10,804.0	10,621.5	9,015.5	9,088.5	8,395.0	7,555.5
Ethane, propane and butane[1]	5,876.5	6,679.5	7,993.5	8,796.5	8,942.5	10,293.0	11,972.0	11,789.5	12,483.0
Exports									
Crude and equivalent	33,945.0	36,025.5	41,172.0	37,558.5	37,960.0	44,238.0	48,581.5	53,290.0	57,013.0
Refined products	8,541.0	9,855.0	13,432.0	12,373.5	13,979.5	15,768.0	13,797.0	14,636.5	13,687.5
Ethane, propane and butane	4,964.0	5,365.5	6,570.0	7,190.5	7,081.0	6,679.5	7,263.5	7,884.0	9,125.0

1. Includes adjustment.

Source: Statistics Canada, Catalogue no. 57-601.

11.19 NATURAL GAS SUPPLY AND DEMAND

	1986	1987	1988	1989	1990	1991	1992	1993	1994
					Cubic metres (millions)				
Supply	82,317.7	88,828.6	102,664.5	109,171.0	111,900.6	117,794.4	130,374.9	141,826.2	153,372.5
Indigenous supply	82,057.3	88,735.3	102,280.0	108,399.2	111,259.7	117,475.4	128,716.0	141,013.4	152,334.1
Gross new production[1]	108,297.9	116,081.6	131,626.4	136,655.3	138,630.4	144,987.2	158,037.0	171,004.7	183,467.2
Injected and stored	14,144.4	14,175.1	15,122.6	14,855.9	13,237.0	13,029.0	12,169.3	13,558.1	14,554.1
Net production	94,153.5	101,906.5	116,503.8	121,799.4	125,393.4	131,958.2	145,867.7	157,446.6	168,913.1
Transformed to LPGs and C5+[2]	12,263.7	13,056.1	14,107.3	13,884.8	14,058.1	14,511.9	15,208.5	15,999.6	17,418.8
Adjustment	-167.4	115.1	116.6	-484.6	75.6	-29.2	1,943.1	433.6	-839.8
Imports	260.4	93.3	384.5	771.8	640.9	319.0	1,658.9	812.8	1,038.4
Demand	81,215.3	88,849.6	102,833.9	109,937.7	110,285.3	118,239.5	132,114.7	141,188.9	152,142.0
Domestic demand	60,125.2	60,840.8	66,921.1	72,026.0	69,596.5	70,551.6	74,217.5	78,172.4	80,738.8
Exports	21,090.1	28,008.8	35,912.8	37,911.7	40,688.8	47,687.9	57,897.2	63,016.5	71,403.2

1. Includes an estimate of producers' own consumption in the synthetic crude and heavy oil sectors.
2. Liquid petroleum gases (includes propane and butane) and C5+ (pentanes).

Source: Statistics Canada, Catalogue no. 57-601.

11.20 NATURAL GAS SALES IN CANADA

	1986	1987	1988	1989	1990	1991	1992	1993	1994
	Cubic metres (millions)								
Domestic sales	48,806.3	47,790.3	52,681.7	56,869.0	54,471.8	54,670.9	56,865.8	59,559.0	60,998.7
Industrial	25,498.5	24,779.4	25,522.3	27,306.8	25,783.9	24,958.0	24,606.5	25,075.7	24,635.0
Residential	12,192.1	11,462.9	12,748.3	13,871.4	13,515.3	13,645.9	14,235.4	14,861.7	15,546.1
Commercial	10,362.2	9,728.2	10,737.1	11,496.1	11,200.6	11,258.6	11,455.7	11,535.0	11,533.7
Direct sales	753.5	1,819.7	3,673.9	4,194.8	3,972.0	4,808.4	6,568.1	8,086.7	9,283.9

Source: Statistics Canada, Catalogue no. 57-601.

11.21 ELECTRICITY RATES AND BILLS, MONTHLY AVERAGES

	1986	1987	1988	1989	1990	1991	1992	1993	1994
	Cents per kilowatt hour								
Rates									
Residential (1,000 kWh)	5.17	5.39	5.62	5.89	6.32	7.25	7.76	8.09	8.14
Commercial (500,000 kWh)	4.42	4.58	4.78	4.98	5.29	6.04	6.49	6.79	6.83
Industrial (3,100,000 kWh)	3.66	3.70	3.84	4.04	4.19	4.42	4.79	4.96	5.24
	$ per month								
Bills									
Residential (750 kWh)	39.52	41.46	43.15	45.12	47.04	53.54	58.35	61.77	62.50
Commercial (25,000 kWh)	1,576.45	1,643.50	1,717.51	1,777.05	1,861.70	2,065.31	2,309.88	2,572.03	2,062.35
Industrial (400,000 kWh)	16,975.18	17,788.92	18,756.51	19,666.36	20,375.85	23,423.09	25,054.26	26,585.34	26,630.93

Source: Statistics Canada, Catalogue no. 57-601.

11.22 NUCLEAR POWER PLANTS

	1986	1987	1988	1989	1990	1991	1992	1993	1994
Number of reactors	18	18	18	18	19	19	20	22	22
Capacity									
Gross capacity (mW)	11,663.0	12,528.0	12,593.0	12,603.0	13,538.0	13,538.0	14,513.0	16,383.0	16,383.0
Net capacity (mW)	10,984.0	11,799.0	11,857.0	11,867.0	12,794.0	12,794.0	13,675.0	15,437.0	15,437.0
Production									
Gross production (gWh)	71,267.0	77,261.5	82,866.6	79,871.6	72,966.8	84,929.6	80,582.3	93,937.1	107,833.9
Net production (gWh)	67,233.0	72,888.2	78,176.0	75,350.6	68,836.6	80,122.3	76,021.0	88,620.0	101,730.1
Percent of total electricity generated (net)	14.8	15.1	16.0	15.6	14.8	16.4	15.2	17.3	19.1

Source: Statistics Canada, Catalogue no. 57-601.

11.23 VALUE OF MINERAL PRODUCTION BY MINERAL CLASS

	1987	1988	1989	1990	1991	1992	1993	1994	1995
					$ Millions				
All minerals	36,361	36,955	39,333	40,778	35,190	35,414	36,545	41,151	43,368
Metals	10,962	13,608	13,982	12,500	10,462	10,210	8,871	9,750	11,994
Industrial minerals	5,125	5,574	5,566	5,289	4,783	4,473	4,459	5,193	5,450
Mineral fuels	20,274	17,773	19,785	22,990	19,945	20,731	23,214	26,209	25,924
Other minerals	–	–	–	–	–	–	–	–	–

Source: Natural Resources Canada, *Canadian Minerals Yearbook, Ottawa, 1995.*

11.24 VALUE OF MINERAL PRODUCTION, CANADA, THE PROVINCES AND TERRITORIES

	1989	1990	1991	1992	1993	1994	1995
				$ Millions			
Canada	39,333	40,778	35,190	35,414	36,564	41,150	43,368
Newfoundland	897	866	772	706	699	837	906
Prince Edward Island	2	3	3	2	1	1	1
Nova Scotia	442	459	460	523	558	610	566
New Brunswick	859	878	671	910	772	862	1,002
Quebec	2,878	3,037	2,930	2,694	2,692	2,956	3,082
Ontario	7,308	6,446	5,101	4,776	4,535	4,921	5,833
Manitoba	1,668	1,311	1,125	1,082	862	820	1,052
Saskatchewan	3,017	3,183	2,863	3,158	3,238	4,225	4,634
Alberta	16,456	19,111	16,373	16,885	18,925	21,085	20,830
British Columbia	4,123	3,954	3,840	3,500	3,538	4,066	4,523
Yukon	534	542	349	496	141	86	185
Northwest Territories	1,149	988	703	681	603	680	753

Source: Natural Resources Canada, *Canadian Minerals Yearbook, Ottawa, 1995.*

11.25 VALUE OF CANADIAN MINERAL PRODUCTION, BY MINERAL CLASS, CANADA, THE PROVINCES AND TERRITORIES, 1995

	Total		Metals		Industrial minerals		Mineral fuels	
	$ '000	% of total	$ '000	% of total	$ '000	% of total	$ '000	% of total
Canada	43,367,774	100.0	11,993,625	100.0	5,450,304	100.0	25,923,845	100.0
Newfoundland	906,051	2.1	867,137	7.2	38,915	0.7	–	–
Prince Edward Island	1,181	–	–	–	1,181	--	–	–
Nova Scotia	565,815	1.3	–	–	200,809	3.7	365,006	1.4
New Brunswick	1,001,964	2.3	679,841	5.7	298,023	5.5	24,100	0.1
Quebec	3,082,140	7.1	1,995,184	16.6	1,086,956	19.9	–	–
Ontario	5,832,874	13.4	4,371,931	36.5	1,369,467	25.1	91,476	0.4
Manitoba	1,052,139	2.4	887,618	7.4	71,166	1.3	93,354	0.4
Saskatchewan	4,634,051	10.7	475,904	4.0	1,343,547	24.7	2,814,600	10.9
Alberta	20,829,984	48.0	349	--	576,280	10.6	20,253,356	78.1
British Columbia	4,523,240	10.4	2,036,413	17.0	438,564	8.0	2,048,263	7.9
Yukon	184,981	0.4	159,508	1.3	7,000	0.1	18,474	0.1
Northwest Territories	753,352	1.7	519,740	4.3	18,396	0.3	215,216	0.8

Source: Natural Resources Canada, *Canadian Minerals Yearbook, Ottawa, 1995.*

11.26 PRODUCTION OF CANADA'S TEN LEADING MINERAL COMMODITIES

	1989	1990	1991	1992	1993	1994	1995
Zinc (t)	1,272,854	1,179,372	1,083,008	1,195,736	990,727	976,309	1,093,541
Copper (t)	704,432	771,433	780,362	761,694	709,650	590,784	704,603
Gold (kg)	159,494	167,373	175,282	160,351	153,129	146,428	149,026
Nickel (t)	195,554	195,004	188,098	177,555	178,529	141,974	166,842
Natural gas (million m^3)	96,117	98,771	105,244	116,664	128,817	138,856	148,481
Crude petroleum ('000 m^3)	90,641	90,279	89,788	93,256	97,306	110,452	114,802
Coal ('000 t)	70,527	68,332	71,133	65,612	69,029	72,824	74,720
Iron ore (kilotonnes)	39,445	35,670	35,421	31,582	33,228	36,416	37,130
Natural gas by-products ('000 m^3)	23,055	23,863	24,919	26,735	30,163	22,666	24,917
Potash (kilotonnes)	7,014	7,345	7,087	7,040	6,880	8,517	8,848

Source: Natural Resources Canada, *Canadian Minerals Yearbook, Ottawa, 1995*.

11.27 LEADING MINERALS, 1995

	Production	Value
		$ Millions
Metals		
Gold (kg)	149,026.5	2,534.9
Copper (kilotonnes)	704.9	2,648.4
Zinc (kilotonnes)	1,093.5	1,556.1
Nickel (kilotonnes)	166.8	1,964.6
Iron ore (kilotonnes)	37,130.1	1,212.0
Uranium (tU)	10,093.8	539.0
Silver (t)	1,194.7	276.1
Platinum group (kg)	15,108.8	173.3
Cobalt (kilotonnes)	2.1	187.3
Lead (kilotonnes)	203.3	172.6
Non-metals		
Potash (kilotonnes)	8,847.3	1,462.4
Salt (kilotonnes)	10,772.1	267.9
Asbestos (kilotonnes)	510.8	233.7
Peat (kilotonnes)	1,010.2	143.6
Sulphur (kilotonnes)	7,977.3	206.9
Structural materials		
Cement (kilotonnes)	10,722.0	876.5
Sand and gravel (kilotonnes)	239,870.5	860.1
Stone (kilotonnes)	92,223.6	558.6
Lime (kilotonnes)	2,515.7	210.1
Clay products (kilotonnes)	..	104.5
Mineral fuels		
Petroleum, crude ('000 m^3)	114,802.4	15,424.5
Natural gas (million m^3)	148,481.4	6,845.6
Natural gas by-products ('000 m^3)	24,917.1	1,751.2
Coal (kilotonnes)	74,720.0	1,902.6

Source: Natural Resources Canada, *Canadian Minerals Yearbook, Ottawa, 1995*.

11.28 GROSS DOMESTIC PRODUCT AT FACTOR COST, PRIMARY INDUSTRIES

	1983	1984	1985	1986	1987	1988	1989	1990	1991	1992	1993	1994	1995
						$ Constant 1986 (Millions)							
Primary industries	29,712.8	31,755.1	32,246.7	32,674.1	32,945.1	34,338.2	34,480.1	34,845.5	34,559.0	34,261.4	36,192.3	38,086.8	39,362.8
Agricultural and related services industries	10,141.9	9,814.2	9,404.1	11,056.7	9,965.8	9,451.7	10,231.4	10,838.4	10,712.1	10,030.1	10,742.9	11,257.7	11,491.5
Fishing and trapping industries	852.4	776.7	945.3	980.2	885.5	946.3	1,023.0	1,129.4	1,023.4	991.7	1,020.1	937.0	815.8
Logging and forestry industries	2,759.7	3,042.1	2,978.4	3,041.9	3,370.0	3,404.5	3,509.8	3,212.8	2,821.8	2,827.8	3,004.9	3,133.2	3,312.4
Business sector logging and forestry industries	2,419.9	2,720.2	2,635.3	2,691.0	3,008.2	3,044.2	3,128.8	2,865.2	2,450.6	2,449.1	2,604.7	2,738.9	2,912.3
Non-business sector forestry services industry	339.8	321.9	343.1	350.9	361.8	360.3	381.0	347.6	371.2	378.7	400.2	394.3	400.1
Mining, quarrying and oil well industries	15,958.8	18,122.1	18,918.9	17,595.3	18,723.8	20,535.7	19,715.9	19,664.9	20,001.7	20,411.8	21,424.4	22,758.9	23,743.1
Business sector mining industries	3,884.9	5,256.4	5,197.5	5,158.0	5,888.8	6,353.9	6,211.1	6,044.8	6,201.4	5,921.1	5,661.2	5,637.3	6,070.6
Gold mines	610.1	679.1	740.1	880.6	987.1	1,213.8	1,541.6	1,676.7	1,778.3	1,603.4	1,549.3	1,507.3	1,541.6
Iron mines	379.4	444.5	585.7	452.7	505.1	568.5	607.2	437.5	431.9	419.9	391.0	457.8	461.3
Other metal mines	1,761.9	2,516.4	2,382.4	2,346.5	2,734.0	2,708.7	2,272.1	2,139.7	2,210.3	2,326.6	2,080.1	1,863.7	2,149.5
Coal mines	505.7	807.6	825.1	755.3	849.8	1,012.7	987.7	1,029.2	998.8	810.2	881.8	948.5	1,040.6
Other non-metal mines	610.3	774.9	691.4	723.0	812.8	850.2	802.6	761.7	782.2	761.0	759.0	860.0	877.6
Non-business sector mining industries	122.0	94.9	93.5	93.1	92.3	113.4	94.6	94.6	94.4	83.0	80.4	78.3	73.6
Crude petroleum and natural gas	9,587.4	9,899.3	10,594.0	9,762.6	10,379.4	11,449.2	11,208.7	11,320.4	11,605.0	12,429.7	13,243.3	13,990.4	14,747.2
Quarry and sand pit industries	407.7	470.7	541.3	643.7	687.7	721.4	685.9	550.4	439.5	414.9	423.8	454.1	478.2
Services related to mineral extraction	2,136.2	2,473.7	2,663.2	1,937.9	1,675.7	1,897.8	1,515.6	1,654.8	1,661.3	1,563.1	2,015.7	2,598.8	2,373.5

Source: Statistics Canada, CANSIM, matrix 4670.

11.29 PRIVATE AND PUBLIC INVESTMENT,[1] PRIMARY INDUSTRIES

	1991	1992	1993	1994	1995	1996[2]
				$ Millions		
Total private and public investment in Canada	128,010.0	122,188.8	121,253.9	130,131.2	127,956.1	126,009.4
Primary industries	10,684.9	9,071.4	12,529.4	17,774.2	17,105.5	16,300.7
Agriculture and related services	2,432.1	2,710.5	3,250.1	3,326.0	3,406.0	3,266.1
Fishing and trapping	145.1	136.5	133.9	131.9	117.5	120.4
Logging and forestry	101.8	117.4	175.0	463.2	454.8	408.3
Mining, quarrying and oil wells	8,005.9	6,107.0	8,970.4	13,853.1	13,127.2	12,505.9
Gold	328.5	294.2	298.8	652.8	697.4	546.6
Iron	224.0	137.3	84.4	124.1	180.8	222.8
Other metal mines	720.9	653.4	716.9	603.1	1,129.8	1,302.4
Peat	5.5	8.7	4.2	13.7	11.7	7.9
Gypsum	10.2	12.4	12.2	13.4	20.8	34.5
Potash	101.8	77.5	90.2	83.9	72.0	113.7
Other non-metal mines	73.4	81.5	110.8	92.0	71.7	60.7
Coal	390.8	172.7	264.4	218.5	329.9	403.2
Crude petroleum and natural gas	6,084.4	4,607.3	7,308.6	11,787.8	10,427.0	9,682.9
Quarrying and sand pit	25.8	27.8	36.4	121.7	87.4	62.8
Services incidental to mineral extraction	40.6	34.1	43.4	142.1	98.6	68.4
				%		
Investment in primary industries as a percent of total investment	8.3	7.4	10.3	13.7	13.4	12.9

1. Excluding repair expenditures.
2. Intentions

Source: Statistics Canada, CANSIM, matrix 3101, 3102 and 3114.

11.30 EMPLOYMENT, PRIMARY INDUSTRIES

	1985	1986	1987	1988	1989	1990	1991	1992	1993	1994	1995	Average annual growth rate 1985 to 1995
						Employees[1] '000						%
All industries[2]	9,651.1	9,927.2	10,329.1	10,659.0	11,054.7	11,146.1	10,549.5	10,246.9	10,271.4	10,447.1	10,673.6	0.9
Logging and forestry	64.5	59.5	66.2	65.3	67.0	61.3	60.6	59.4	63.0	63.9	66.5	0.3
Logging	50.2	45.2	50.9	48.8	49.6	43.3	43.6	41.1	43.2	44.6	46.9	-0.6
Forestry services	14.2	14.3	15.4	16.5	17.4	18.0	17.0	18.3	19.8	19.4	19.6	3.0
Mining, oil wells and quarrying	161.7	151.5	151.8	158.1	155.3	152.3	145.2	128.5	119.7	130.4	128.9	-2.0
Mining	69.0	66.2	66.3	67.5	67.5	65.5	58.8	54.5	50.7	50.2	51.6	-2.6
Metal mines	46.8	44.0	44.7	45.8	46.0	43.8	38.0	36.2	33.2	32.5	33.5	-3.0
Non-metal mines (except coal)	11.7	11.3	11.8	11.3	11.2	11.0	10.1	9.8	9.7	9.7	9.7	-1.7
Coal mines	10.4	11.0	9.9	10.4	10.3	10.7	10.7	8.5	7.8	8.0	8.4	-1.9
Crude petroleum and natural gas	44.0	41.8	40.5	42.6	43.7	43.9	44.5	40.2	33.2	35.8	35.8	-1.9
Quarries and sand pits	4.7	4.4	5.9	6.2	7.5	8.8	7.8	7.1	7.6	8.6	8.9	6.0
Stone quarries	1.4	1.4	1.9	2.1	2.4	3.0	2.6	2.6	2.1	2.8	2.6	5.8
Sand and gravel pits	3.3	3.0	4.0	4.1	5.1	5.7	5.1	4.5	5.5	5.9	6.4	6.2
Services related to mineral extraction	44.0	39.1	39.1	41.8	36.6	34.2	34.1	26.6	28.2	35.8	32.6	-2.7

1. Excludes owners or partners of unincorporated business and professional practices, the self-employed, unpaid family workers, persons working outside Canada, military personnel and casual workers for whom a T4 is not required.
2. Excludes agriculture, fishing and trapping, private household services, religious organizations and the military.

Source: Statistics Canada, Catalogue no. 72F0002.

11.31 EARNINGS, PRIMARY INDUSTRIES

	1984	1985	1986	1987	1988	1989	1990	1991	1992	1993	1994	1995	Earnings in 1995 as a % of all industry earnings
							Average weekly earnings[1] $						%
All industries[2]	398.10	412.02	424.25	440.26	459.75	483.31	505.14	528.60	547.01	556.76	567.11	572.49	100.0
Logging and forestry	515.93	519.84	539.60	568.45	584.13	626.06	643.46	679.83	697.27	709.99	730.83	732.50	127.9
Logging	536.47	545.68	568.25	589.66	615.05	655.53	671.70	693.67	725.64	731.75	762.87	764.59	133.6
Forestry services	440.17	428.71	449.28	498.20	492.66	542.11	575.42	644.42	633.53	662.49	657.15	655.86	114.6
Mining, oil wells and quarrying	661.52	698.52	716.46	728.68	775.13	819.69	863.29	908.78	935.10	956.81	964.83	997.71	174.3
Mining	634.11	661.68	687.38	703.16	762.60	806.66	849.63	893.99	934.52	946.41	972.67	1,013.75	177.1
Metal mines	644.45	670.98	689.93	714.36	778.77	829.83	876.74	928.68	972.31	988.59	1,018.75	1,068.15	186.6
Non-metal mines (except coal)	563.43	581.59	611.88	626.85	657.14	689.50	723.67	760.42	795.46	802.00	830.51	845.53	147.7
Coal mines	669.56	710.09	754.63	743.63	805.82	831.03	867.60	897.50	933.84	946.45	956.98	990.84	173.1
Crude petroleum and natural gas	775.38	834.10	847.98	873.20	919.80	986.20	1,043.34	1,110.13	1,098.68	1,148.77	1,165.58	1,202.52	210.1
Quarries and sand pits	544.51	538.86	519.85	548.85	579.58	601.68	621.74	650.78	672.02	640.86	669.64	724.13	126.5
Stone quarries	508.92	526.18	532.00	559.68	564.91	560.73	640.08	653.33	702.55	700.59	680.10	789.13	137.8
Sand and gravel pits	560.73	544.44	514.04	543.62	586.87	620.96	612.03	649.47	654.25	617.86	664.73	697.95	121.9
Services related to mineral extraction	602.44	637.50	646.87	649.34	676.70	689.77	719.89	730.13	759.19	834.75	824.28	822.17	143.6

1. Excludes owners or partners of unincorporated business and professional practices, the self-employed, unpaid family workers, persons working outside Canada, military personnel and casual workers for whom a T4 is not required.
2. Excludes agriculture, fishing and trapping, private household services, religious organizations and the military.

Source: Statistics Canada, Catalogue no. 72F0002.

FREDERICK B. TAYLOR, *HULL RIVETTING,* CANADIAN WAR MUSEUM

Chapter 12 MANUFACTURING AND CONSTRUCTION

Canadian Space Agency

In the summer of 1995, visitors and residents at Borden, P.E.I. were able to watch a thirty-storey-high floating crane lift gigantic slabs of precast concrete—each as long as two football fields and as heavy as two naval destroyers—and place them into the waters of Northumberland Strait, which separates Prince Edward Island from New Brunswick. Eventually these pieces of concrete will form part of a bridge joining Prince Edward Island with the rest of Canada. The concrete slabs were made on the site from 400,000 tonnes of washed concrete stone and 160,000 tonnes of cement—both manufactured in Nova Scotia—and another 340,000 tonnes of Quebec-manufactured concrete sand.

Later in 1995, the world watched astronaut Chris Hadfield in outer space using the Canadarm to help join the Space Shuttle Atlantis with the Russian space station Mir as the two vehicles orbited the earth at speeds of about 29,000 kilometres per hour. The Canadarm, a robot limb known in technical circles as the Shuttle Remote Manipulator System, was designed and manufactured in Canada by the Canadian Space Agency and Spar Aerospace.

These spectacular achievements of engineering and technology are examples of what is produced in the Canadian manufacturing and construction sectors. These two sectors are a vital link in the bridge between the natural world—the elemental world of rock, water, minerals, wood—and the material features of our modern society: from the cars we drive, to the roads we drive on, to the food we eat, to the houses in which we live.

The Numbers

The two sectors are formidable in number terms as well. Together, manufacturing and construction contributed to 24% of Canada's Gross Domestic Product (GDP) in 1995. They employed 2.7 million Canadians in 1995, about 19% of the total work force. What happens in these two sectors reflects, and to a certain extent determines, what happens in the wider economy.

Over the last few years there has been much talk of structural change in the Canadian economy, especially where employment is concerned. Following the recession of the early 1990s, the shift strengthened from blue-collar factory and construction jobs to information-based services. Between 1989 and 1995, employment in manufacturing dropped 7.8%, and in construction, 10.5%. At the same time, employment in community, business, and personal services increased 15.7%; and in finance, insurance, and real estate, 5.2%. In 1995, service jobs made up 66% of the total labour force, up from 65% in 1989.

But despite this shift in employment toward services, manufacturing and construction remain strong. In addition to a general increase in the value of manufacturing shipments over the last few years, Canadian manufacturers have become more productive and competitive. Exports of manufactured goods, destined mainly for the United States, have increased, helped by a weak Canadian dollar and a strong American economy. As well, a steady growth in both non-residential and residential construction over the past few years has boosted the construction sector as a whole, a reversal of the trend in the mid- to late 1980s, when residential building played the stronger role.

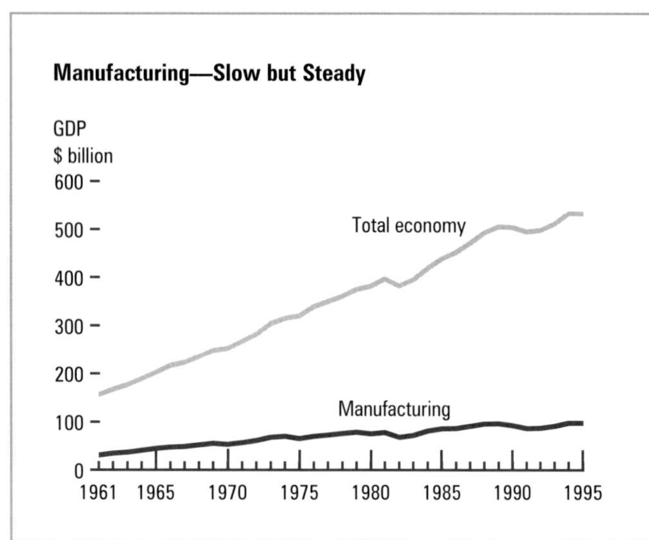

Manufacturing

Because of the tangible things it produces, the manufacturing sector shares a complex network of relationships with the wider economy—a network that extends well beyond the doors of the manufacturing plant. Manufactured goods need to be transported by truck, rail, ship, or pipeline to their markets. They also need to be packaged, stored, paid for, and distributed.

These requirements create and sustain a whole world of spin-off industries that naturally broaden the range of economic activity. The shipping, storage, packaging, and wholesale and retail trade industries rely directly and indirectly for their livelihoods on manufacturing, as do international currency brokers, insurers, and banks. To give an example, Canadian manufacturers purchased more than $5.8 billion worth of containers and other packaging products.

From Plywood to Car Parts

Manufacturers in Canada produce everything from cars and parts, to processed food, to gasoline and heating oil, to lumber and plywood, to computers. In 1995, the combined activities of this sector accounted for almost 19% of Canada's GDP. The sector employed two million people (15% of the national work force) and exported more goods than any other sector.

Of the 22 major industry groups in manufacturing, the largest is transportation equipment (the lion's share of which is automobiles and automobile parts). In 1995, this group accounted for over 22% of all manufactured goods produced

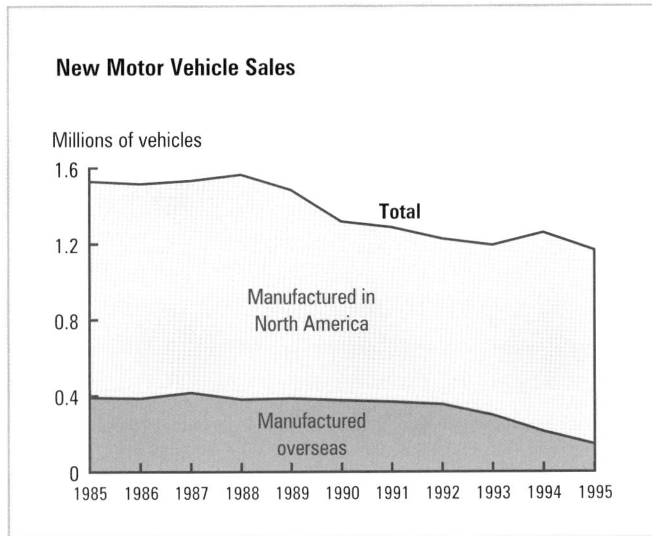

in Canada. In fact, transportation equipment, and the manufacturing sector's next four largest industries—food products, paper and allied products, electrical and electronic products, and chemicals—produced well over half of the sector's total output in 1995. In that year, manufacturers in these five industries shipped nearly $190 billion worth of goods.

Growth Patterns

Manufacturing has been growing steadily since the early 1980s. The value of shipments (a measure of activity in the manufacturing sector) has risen since 1978, with the exception of the recessions of the early 1980s and early 1990s. Growth also stalled in 1995. The sector's "value-added output" (a measurement of what manufacturers actually produced, minus the materials and energy they used) rose during the same period.

While shipments since the late 1970s are up, the sector's share of Canada's GDP declined slightly over the same period, from some 21% in 1978, to just about 19% in 1995. This drop, together with increasing shipments, has been influenced by the rise of the services sector in Canada. In 1978, the goods-producing side of the economy (which includes manufacturing) contributed 38% of GDP, while services contributed 62%. In 1995, goods producing declined to 34%, while services went up to nearly 66%.

The number of people working in manufacturing also declined over the same period. Most workers are concentrated in firms employing between 100 and 499 people, but the number of people working for larger firms (those employing 500 or more people) has declined by almost 150,000 since 1978. On the other hand, the number of people working for firms employing between 20 and 99 has increased by nearly 50,000.

The three industry groups with the strongest value-added growth have been the chemical products industry, printing and publishing, and plastics. The growth in plastic products may reflect the increasing number of applications that have been found for these products (it isn't hard these days to find a plastic bag in your home, whereas 10 years ago such items were somewhat more scarce).

The three industries with the weakest value-added growth over the same period have been non-metallic mineral products, clothing, and leather products. The non-metallic minerals group declined because of the slow performance of the construction sector, which uses much of what this group produces. Leather products declined mainly because of the rise of substitutes for leather, such as plastics products and fabrics. The clothing industry, which is fairly labour intensive, has suffered from foreign competition, mainly from developing countries where labour costs are lower.

In terms of jobs, the three industry groups with the biggest increases between 1984 and 1995 have been those that experienced strong growth: plastic products, wood, and transportation equipment. On the other hand, the three industry groups with the largest declines were leather products, refined petroleum and coal, and tobacco. Declining employment in the tobacco industry may be partly due to the effects of automation; this industry led the manufacturing sector in spending on computer-assisted processing equipment.

When the first Asiatic nomads arrived in what is now Canada, they built their shelters out of the materials nature readily offers: animal hides, snow, and wood. Today, as we head into the twenty-first century with our modems, VCRs, and fuel-injected automobiles, we still build our homes with readily available natural materials; but these days, instead of animal hides and snow, we use mainly wood.

Wood is the most versatile and widely used residential building material in Canada. A huge proportion (over 95%) of our low-rise housing stock was, and continues to be, built using wood in one form or another: whether it is standard dimensional lumber, plywood, oriented strandboard, or particleboard.

To get an idea of the huge role wood plays in the construction of our homes, consider that, of the 110,933 housing starts recorded by Canada Mortgage and Housing Corporation in 1995, more than 70,000 were single and semi-detached homes—the type of housing most likely to have been built with high proportions of wood.

According to the Canadian Wood Council, to build an average 1800 ft² Canadian home, you need nearly 11,000 board feet of lumber and 5,400 ft² of plywood or oriented strandboard. This means that to build those 70,000 single and semi-detached homes, Canadian builders used over 760 million board feet of lumber and nearly 390 million ft² of plywood and oriented strandboard. And that was just for one year.

There are few building materials which combine beauty with strength as successfully as wood does. From an aesthetic point of view, wood has an allure that is as tangible as it is hard to describe. Not only is it straight and strong, it can be relatively easy to harvest and cut to convenient sizes, especially in the case of softwoods like spruce, pine, fir, and cedar.

And if a tree isn't straight or large enough for standard dimension lumber, it can be used to make composite wood products. Manufacturing processes have been developed which make use of trees of any shape or size. These products include plywood, oriented strandboard, and particleboard. Plywood is made of thin layers of wood veneer which are peeled from logs and then pressed together with the grain of each alternate layer at a right angle to that of its neighbours; the latter two are made of wood pieces which are sliced, chipped, or ground up (often as the byproduct of lumber and plywood manufacturing), then glued and compressed into panels of remarkable strength and durability.

Because of its importance as a building material, wood is also a significant component of our economy. In 1994, Canadian wood products manufacturers shipped $14.3 billion worth of wood products.

The economic importance of wood, together with its undeniable aesthetic appeal and the fact that it is, if harvested responsibly, a wholly renewable natural resource, make it unique as a building material. Others might be as useful—concrete and steel, for example—but few materials are as close to our hearts and minds. In the words of American author and woodworker Bruce Hoadley, "the psychological appeal of wooden objects develops through the interaction of two vital elements working together: nature and mankind."

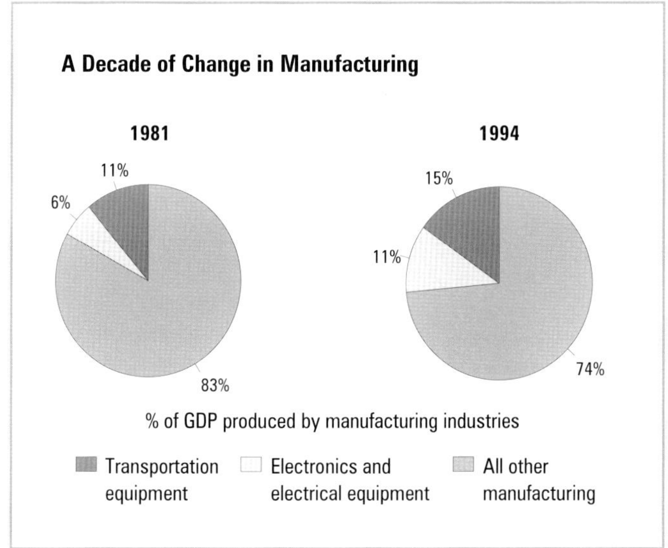

A Decade of Change

During the 1980s, shipments in the manufacturing sector grew almost continuously, increasing in every year except for 1981, and reaching a peak of $309 billion in 1989. Considering that shipments were worth less than $129 billion in 1978, this was impressive growth—especially given that prices levelled off after 1987.

But after seven years of very strong growth following 1983, manufacturing suffered a major setback during the 1990-91 recession. After shipments peaked at $309 billion in 1989, they dropped to $277 billion the next year as the economy headed into recession. In 1991, shipments fell even further to $263 billion, and it wasn't until 1993 that they returned to pre-recession levels.

Between 1989 and 1993, almost 400,000 people in the manufacturing sector lost their jobs—by far the biggest job loss recorded in any sector of the economy.

Since 1992, however, the sector has performed well. In 1993, manufacturing accounted for about three-quarters of all GDP growth. In 1994, it broke its 1989 shipments record with a $353 billion performance, while accounting for nearly

The Art of Building

*In this passage from **Looking Around**, Canadian author and architect Witold Rybczynski offers insightful guidance to the worth and character of an old Canadian building:*

"Works of art stand apart from time; buildings, like people, have a life, perhaps even a soul. They age and weather and show the marks of human habitation and prolonged use. In the process, they acquire character, a quality that embellishes and amplifies the architect's original intention. My office at McGill University, for example, is in a stately Montreal greystone building designed ninety-six years ago and originally intended to house the chemistry department. The massive walls, which once enclosed laboratories where white-coated scientists balanced retorts over Bunsen burners, now contain architecture students hunched over drawing tables. The interior has undergone some modifications, but the building's character is unmistakable: a crusty Victorian gent, willing to change with the times (up to a point) but holding fast to prescribed conventions; a little stuffy, a little formal; built for comfort, not for speed."

Photo by Kate Williams

Intersecting gears.

two-thirds of GDP growth between August and December. The sector's overall "capacity utilization rate," which tells how close an industry is to making full use of all its plant and equipment, increased from about 75% in 1991 to 83% in 1994.

Exports

The export picture was equally strong. In 1994, the manufacturing sector exported $146 billion worth of products—a 12.7% increase over 1993. The biggest exporters were in the automotive products industry; they shipped more than $57 billion worth of goods to foreign (mostly American) markets in 1994. In the same year, the paper and allied products industry exported nearly $16 billion worth. The electrical and electronic products industry was also important, exporting $14 billion worth of goods in 1994.

But the real success story in Canadian manufacturing exports has been in automobiles and softwood lumber. Fuelled by a cheap Canadian dollar, the Canadian auto industry (located largely in Ontario) had an excellent 1994, mainly because of strong U.S. demand for automobiles and parts. Softwood exports also performed well, due to a healthy American housing market. In fact, the exports of these two industries contributed greatly to Canada's balance of trade surplus in 1994.

The Job Shift

There have been some significant changes in the manufacturing sector over the last few years. One of the most noticeable is the dramatic change in the employment situation. Prior to the recession of 1990-91, just over two million people worked in this sector. In 1993, there were fewer than 1.6 million—a decline of around 400,000. By 1995, the situation had improved somewhat, with 96,000 additional jobs, but it was still below the pre-1990 levels. Automation, economic fluctuations, and the drive for increased productivity were all factors in this.

On the other hand, employment in the paper products industry, concentrated largely in Quebec, declined steadily between 1989 and 1994 before increasing slightly in 1995. Over 28,000 employees in this industry lost their jobs between 1990 and 1994. This was primarily due to increased automation as Canadian paper products manufacturers, who export nearly two-thirds of what they produce, improved their international competitiveness.

The electrical and electronics products industry also showed a decline in employment, linked to increased productivity. Over 42,000 people in this industry lost their jobs between 1989 and 1994, as did many in the refined petroleum and coal products industry, and the chemical products industry.

In 1991, this overall decline in manufacturing employment might have been attributed to cyclical downturn, with the full expectation that employment would soon return to pre-recession levels. But despite its strong performance since then, employment in the sector still has not fully recovered.

More with Less

There are strong signs that Canadian manufacturers are becoming more productive; that is, that they are able to produce more with a smaller labour force. Certainly, the sector's "output per person-hour" (a measure of labour productivity) increased between 1992 and 1994, and declined only marginally in 1995. This has coincided with a trend toward modernizing and upgrading equipment in the sector. It would appear that Canadian companies are on a push to become more competitive, especially those with large traffic in exports.

Manufacturers in the transportation equipment industry have been particularly active. In 1994, there was a 5.5% increase in employment and an 8% increase in value-added output. Paper and allied products manufacturers have increased output while employment in the industry has actually decreased. Makers of electrical and electronic products have also increased productivity in every year between 1990 and 1994, again with declining employment.

The rise in productivity in the auto sector is affected by the amount of money auto manufacturers spend on what is called "capital investment." This type of investment relates to new facilities, machinery, and equipment and is an indicator of an industry's confidence in its future prospects.

In 1995, the auto industry's capital spending plans were heavily weighted toward upgrading or replacing machinery and equipment: of the nearly $1.7 billion manufacturers in this industry planned to spend on capital projects in 1995, over 78% was earmarked for machinery and equipment.

Manufacturers in the paper and allied products industry had similar investment intentions, only they planned to spend even more: some $3.6 billion on new machinery and equipment. Again, this relates both to their need to become more competitive in the international marketplace (paper manufacturers export nearly two-thirds of what they produce), and to replace or repair equipment.

Manufacturers' spending on modernizing and upgrading machinery and equipment has steadily increased since the 1970s, and particularly since the mid-1980s. Between 1984 and 1992, the ratio of spending on machinery and equipment to that on building and repairing facilities climbed sharply; in 1995, manufacturers announced intentions to invest over $16 billion, nearly 88% of which was for machinery and equipment.

The surge of investment in machinery and equipment also seems to have helped Canadian manufacturers become more competitive in the global marketplace: it coincides with a rise in exports in recent years. It also creates room for a non-inflationary expansion in the sector; meaning that, in times of increasing demand, manufacturers can expand production without having to raise their prices.

Demand Up

There has been a strong and growing demand for Canadian manufactured goods, especially between 1991 and 1995. At the same time, Canadian manufacturers have steadily increased the use of their production facilities: in 1991, the sector's capacity utilization rate was almost 75%; in 1994, over 83%. This is a reflection of increased demand.

Ironically, imports of comparable goods to Canada have also increased steadily since 1992. (Imports of the same type of goods a domestic industry produces are another indicator of demand in that industry.) This has put pressure on Canadian manufacturers to become more competitive. It also may explain why some manufacturers have relocated to countries where labour is cheaper.

Manufacturing Centres

The location of manufacturing in Canada is really the story of two provinces: Ontario and Quebec. Together, they account for more than three-quarters of total manufacturing output. The remainder is shared by the western provinces (led by British Columbia), the Atlantic provinces, and the territories.

In 1995, Ontario led shipments in 15 of the 22 major industry groups in the sector, including four of the five largest categories (transportation equipment, food products, chemical products, and electrical and electronic products.) Quebec led in the production of primary textiles, textiles, clothing, and paper products. British Columbia produced the most wood products, the bulk of which consisted of softwood lumber which was exported to the United States.

Manufacturing facilities in Canada tend to be located close to the markets for the finished products, that is, where the majority of Canada's population lives. For example, the majority of petroleum refineries in Canada are nowhere close to where oil is pumped from the ground, but thousands of kilometres away—in southern Ontario and Quebec, near large urban centres. Similarly, Ontario and Quebec, with their large populations, are the centres of food processing, accounting for 64% of Canada's capacity in this industry.

However, in other cases, when the raw materials that go into making manufactured goods are highly perishable (like fish) or difficult and costly to transport over long distances (like western red cedar and hemlock), manufacturing facilities are located relatively close to where the raw materials are extracted. The Atlantic provinces' fish processing plants and the sawmills of British Columbia (which account for nearly 49% of Canada's lumber shipments) are good examples of this.

Investment

In addition to such indicators as shipments, employment, and GDP share, investment intentions across the country roughly reflect how well manufacturers are doing in their respective areas.

Investment expenditures, or intended expenditures, give an idea of the market conditions in which manufacturers operate and of the confidence they have in the economic prospects of their industries. If capital investment intentions rise year over year, as they have done in manufacturing since 1993, this indicates an expected rise in construction activity and installation of new plant and machinery, as well as growing demand for manufactured goods.

While spending on machinery and equipment in the sector as a whole grew in 1994 and 1995, province by province the picture is different from what one might expect. In 1995, planned expenditures in Newfoundland, the province with the weakest growth in manufacturing, increased by over 27%—the biggest jump in the country. Spending in New Brunswick, British Columbia, and Manitoba was also well above the national average.

In spite of slightly declining shipments (mainly due to weaker U.S. demand for automobile exports), Ontario manufacturers were optimistic enough to revise their investment plans sharply upwards in the middle of 1995. This optimism was strongest in the automobile industry, in which $1.3 billion of capital expenditures were intended for machinery and equipment—an 8.3% increase over what automakers planned to spend in 1994.

Western provinces were also confident: though they contributed 24% of Canada's GDP, they accounted for over 30% of total investment intentions. In 1996, nearly $3.7 billion of these intentions were in the manufacturing sector, and 87% of this amount was planned for machinery and equipment. The Atlantic provinces intended to invest $850 million, 90% of which was earmarked for machinery and equipment.

Quebec manufacturers felt the future looked promising; they upwardly revised their planned expenditures on machinery and equipment by 13%.

Small Manufacturers

Small manufacturing firms in Canada have had a good record of job creation over the last 20 years.

A 1994 study showed that job creation in firms of fewer than 100 employees was much stronger than in larger firms. Over the last 20 years, small producers have hired more people than they have laid off, contrary to the trend set by larger manufacturers. Nor has the increasing importance of small manufacturers come by default; small producers have been actively expanding the number of their plants.

Construction

The construction sector creates the physical foundation—the houses, apartments, and office buildings—in which we live and work. It also creates what we call "infrastructure": roads, bridges, highways, canals, pipelines, hydro dams, and power lines.

These buildings and structures are as diverse as human activity itself. They can be for pure fun and excitement, like the recently renovated Calgary SaddleDome (home of the Calgary Flames of the National Hockey League), or they can be merely functional, like the Combined Sewer Overflow tank begun in Hamilton in 1995. They can combine utility with beauty, like the 1995 project to convert a Moncton, New Brunswick, landfill into an urban parkland. They can also be the houses and apartments in which Canadians live.

Because the construction sector creates structures often designed to last for at least several decades, there is a permanence to its products not typically seen in manufacturing (what car lasts even two decades with regular use). Most construction projects require significant amounts of capital to get started, so it is a sign of confidence when builders and contractors say they are going to invest increasing amounts in construction activities. In mid-1995, investors in Ontario and the western provinces did just that, upwardly revising their investment plans for non-residential construction.

Since the early 1980s, construction activity in Canada has followed the economic cycle, although with some prolonged lags, particularly in residential construction. The value of construction work increased through the 1980s, except in 1983 when the economy was in recession. Similarly, after the value of work done in the sector reached more than $102 billion in 1990, it plunged to $94 billion the following year as the latest recession took hold. It fell even further in 1992.

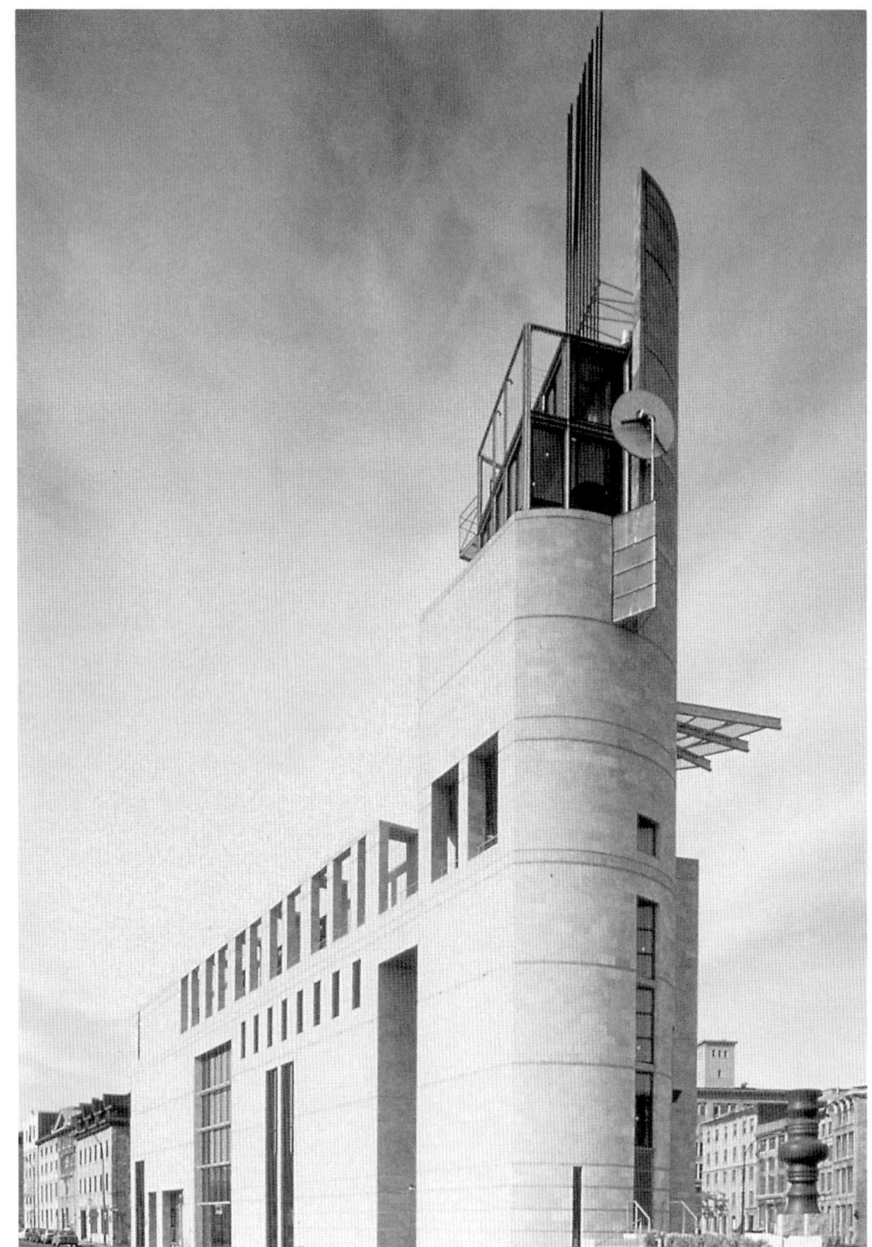

Photo by Michel Brunelle

Montréal Archeology and History Museum, Pointe-à-Callière.

Since then, construction growth in Canada has been relatively weak. Most of this has been due to a downturn in residential construction, the largest sub-category in the sector. In 1987, residential construction accounted for nearly 44% of the value of all construction work; in 1993, its value of $38 billion represented just under 41%. Indeed, demographic trends would suggest that Canada's aging population is likely to generate slower demand for new housing. Because of this, Canada Mortgage and Housing Corporation (CMHC) has predicted slow residential growth until the year 2025.

Non-residential Construction

Non-residential construction includes all building construction intended for industrial, commercial, and institutional use. This includes shopping malls, movie theatres, hospitals, and warehouses. The $110 million Library Square complex in downtown Vancouver, completed in 1995, is an example, as is the new $180 million expansion of the Metro Toronto Convention Centre.

Unlike residential building, which is determined in large part by the home buying habits of Canadians, non-residential building is more directly affected by the business cycle. For example, retailers open new stores when they feel confident that people will shop in them. Similarly, manufacturers will build new facilities if they think orders for their products will increase.

Non-residential construction activity has a somewhat similar growth pattern to that of the manufacturing sector: strong growth since the mid-1980s, except during the recession of the early 1990s. After a sharp decline in 1992, the value of non-residential construction rebounded in 1993 but remained below the peak year of 1990.

In 1995, it seemed that non-residential builders were optimistic that this growth would continue: there was an increase in the number of non-residential building permits issued. (While not an exact indicator of construction activity, a rise or fall in the number of building permits issued does indicate rising or falling intentions on the part of builders.) In addition, the value of non-residential permits in 1995 was higher than in 1994.

Bridging the Gap

By late 1997, it should be possible to get to Canada's only island province by car. One of the world's longest ever bridges is currently being constructed to connect mainland Canada to Prince Edward Island.

At an anticipated cost of $840 million, the Northumberland Strait Bridge is being built to last literally 100 years. Mainly concrete and steel, it will be 11 metres wide and stand as high as 60 metres off the water. Piers supporting the bridge will descend 35 metres into the water.

Despite the bridge's watery location, more than 80% of project work is taking place on dry land. For example, a 30-storey-high crane floating on water is currently in use—it can lift the combined weight of two modern destroyers (8,700 tonnes). In this way, bridge components will be individually built, then carried and placed directly onto the Strait.

The Builders

Over the last five years, the most money in non-residential construction has been spent on electric power construction and building and maintaining electric power stations and lines, street lighting, and electric transformer stations.

The large retail and entertainment organizations have also been active in plans to build, renovate, and relocate. In 1995, Canadian Tire Corporation planned to renovate or relocate 40 of its stores, and Price Club planned to build eight new stores and a large distribution centre. Entertainment giant Famous Players Theatres planned to build 12 new movie theatres across the country.

It seems that private investors were slightly more optimistic than public investors (which include the federal government, provincial governments and municipalities). Both intended to invest slightly more than $20 billion in 1996.

At the beginning of 1996, Canadian investors from both the private and public sectors planned to spend $43.7 billion on construction—a slight decrease from what they had spent in 1995.

Infrastructure Projects

Since the early 1980s, growth in non-residential construction was strongest in the "engineering construction" category, which includes mainly infrastructure projects. Infrastructure consists largely of roads, bridges, water supply, electrical transmission lines and pipelines. In many ways, it provides the physical platform on which Canada's economy rests.

In 1995, infrastructure construction in Canada took the shape of a $1 billion project to build the Highway 407 bypass around Toronto, and a 780-person crew working around the clock to build 277 kilometres of natural gas pipeline in northern Alberta. Also in 1995, over 12,000 projects were begun under the umbrella of the Canada Infrastructure Works program, a $6 billion joint federal–provincial–municipal initiative to upgrade municipal infrastructure.

Residential Construction

In his book *The Most Beautiful House in the World*, Witold Rybczynski writes that ". . . a small house is not easier to design than a large one, and an inexpensive cottage is in some ways a greater challenge than a mansion." Ideally, the design of a house should combine functionality with beauty, but the difficulty is that everyone has a different idea of what beauty and functionality are.

When it comes to our homes, the private and personal spaces in which we and our families live and dream, Canadians are united on one point: home—whether it's a detached three-storey house or a humble bachelor apartment—is the most important building in our lives.

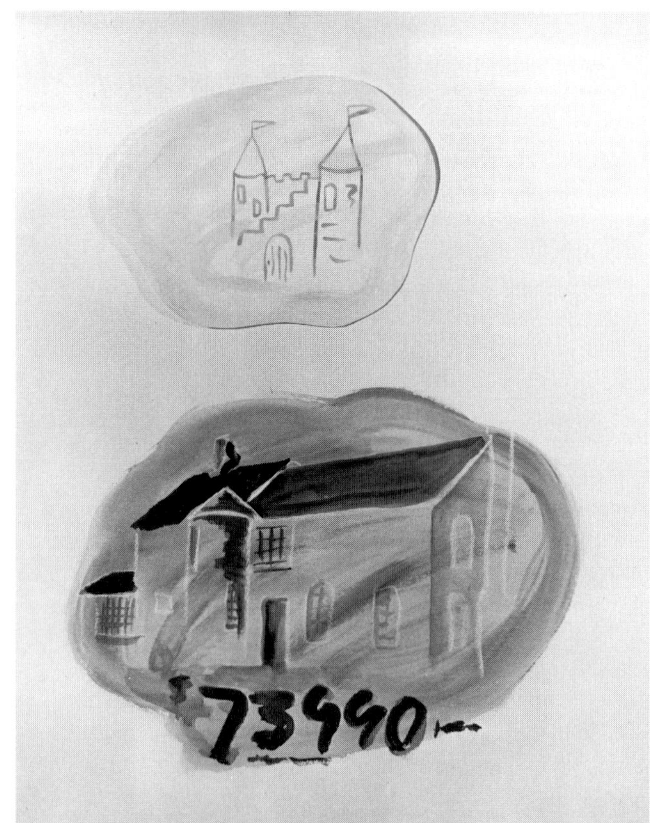

Shirley Wiitasalo, Collection of Carmen Lamanna, Courtesy of Susan Hobbs Gallery

***The Price,* 1981.**

In Canada, residential construction is very important to the economy. Simple arithmetic supports this: in 1993, Canadians spent more than $38 billion on residential structures. With over 30 million Canadians living in more than 10 million households, which are constantly changing as children grow up and as lifestyles evolve, there will always be demand for new housing.

In 1993, almost 63% of all buildings erected in Canada were intended for residential use, and over 40% of construction work—including office buildings, shopping malls, and all infrastructure—was in residential building.

Prospects

Demographic trends may well provide a clue to the long-term prospects of the residential construction market in Canada. The largest housing market segment of the Canadian population is occupied by the baby boomer generation (people between the ages of 31 and 51), who make up 42% of the population. Baby boomers, who are more likely to buy homes in the next few years, and have the highest incomes, are nevertheless an aging group. Their successors will be a much smaller pool of potential home-buyers.

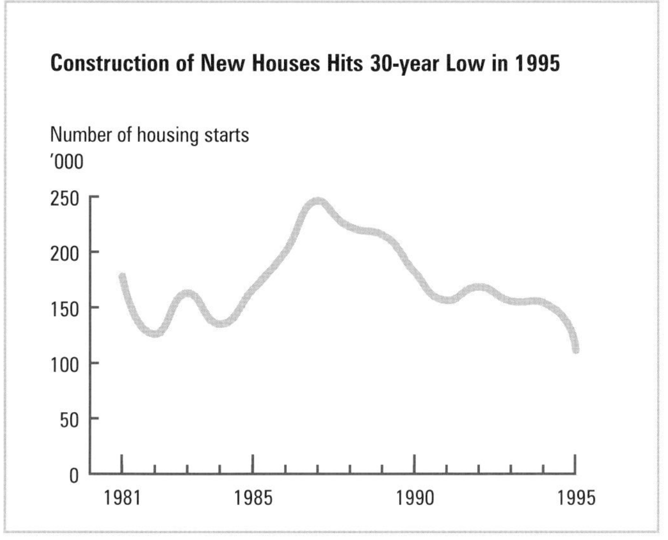

Constructs of Wind and Water

In Canada, where thousands of immigrants come from other lands every year, the idea that a home should combine beauty with functionality has taken on different dimensions. New ways of doing and looking at things are being superimposed on existing practices in many areas of life, and particularly in the construction of homes.

In Vancouver, for example, where one out of five residents is of Asian origin, almost a third of all business immigrants in 1992 came from Hong Kong and Taiwan.

These new immigrants are often looking for homes which comply with the energy-balancing principles of Chinese geomancy, or feng shui (literally "wind and water").

Feng shui is based on the belief that harmonizing the yin and yang energies in a given environment will favourably influence the health and destiny of the people who live in it. It is further based on a body of rules which governs the interior and exterior of inhabited spaces, taking into account many factors, from the alignment of doors to the location of trees and the placement of staircases.

Most Canadians would be surprised to learn that such everyday objects as the electric organ, the laser sailboat and the paint roller were invented by some of their compatriots. In fact, many Canadian inventions are at the root of thriving industries around the world.

Both artistic and scientific creations are often inspired by the places where they are born. For example, the vastness of our country probably has something to do with our ingenuity in communications. Several names stand out, of course: Alexander Graham Bell, a Scottish-Canadian who developed the telephone; Reginald A. Fessenden, who invented the wireless radio; and Armand Bombardier, the creator of the snowmobile.

In Yarmouth, Nova Scotia, in 1833, John Patch figured out how to use an Archimedean screw for propulsion, a discovery that revolutionized marine transportation. Wallace Rupert Turnbull, also a Maritimer, gained an international reputation in the 1920s for his aeronautical research, especially his variable-pitch propeller, still widely used today.

In 1838, Charles Fenerty developed a process for making paper out of wood pulp. This discovery gave an enormous boost to the printed word in general and newspapers in particular. In cinematography, an Ontarian by the name of William Chester Shaw developed the IMAX process in the 1960s, which today is at the leading edge of cinema projection technology.

Our climate has also stimulated our genius for inventions: what would we do without such familiar and indispensable inventions as the snowblower, frozen food, and the rotary shovel which is used to remove snow from railway tracks?

Some remarkable thinkers have nurtured the chemical industry: one of them was Thomas L. Willson, who in the 1890s discovered calcium carbide and acetylene, multi-purpose chemicals which played a huge role in the development of modern industry. In 1858, James Miller Williams dug the world's first oil well in the township of Enniskillen, Ontario.

But what about women inventors? Well, they have been few and for between, disadvantaged both by the social role imposed on them and by the **Patent Act**, *which in many cases required that their husbands co-sign for their inventions. For instance, even though the carpet-sweeper was invented by Anna Sutherland Bissell, it was her husband's name which became the household word. Between 1965 and 1975, about 500 women were granted patents in Canada. A century before, there had been less than two dozen.*

Today, the world of inventions is no longer the purview of the individual, male or female. Today, teams of researchers, engineers and designers are at the centre of product development. For example, the Canadarm is the invention of hundreds of talented individuals who have been working in concert towards the same goal. Another example is the modular Vista telephone from Nortel.

In addition, residential construction does not follow the business cycle the way non-residential construction does. Unlike other categories such as industrial and engineering construction, which closely follow the normal business cycle (albeit with a lag of about a year), the level of residential construction activity is influenced in the short to medium term by such intangible factors as Canadians' confidence in the long-term prospects of the economy, and especially in their prospects of having—and keeping—a job.

The majority of respondents to a CMHC survey in 1994 believed that uncertain job prospects are an obstacle to strong economic growth. Most Canadians were generally pessimistic about the performance of the economy in the short term, although they expected the situation to improve over the long term.

Residential construction activity is also influenced by more measurable things like interest rates and the affordability of housing. Yet in spite of optimal conditions in the borrowing market in 1991—with interest rates, especially mortgage rates, at 10-year lows—the value of residential construction work done, including repairs and renovations, actually declined by $6 billion.

Similarly, the steady decline in both land and housing prices through 1995 failed to produce an increase in the number of housing starts.

In fact, in 1995, the residential housing market in Canada was in an almost continuous slump with housing starts at their lowest level in 35 years. Residential building permits were also far lower than in 1994.

Residential construction activity grew considerably through the 1980s, from nearly $14 billion in 1980 to almost $43 billion in 1989—a threefold increase in nine years. After 1990, however, residential activity declined, dropping to $35 billion in 1991 before slowly recovering.

The bulk of spending since 1980 has been on repairs and renovations to existing residential structures. In 1993, the amount of money spent on repairs and renovations came to over $20 billion, nearly twice the amount spent on building new single-detached houses—an indication of the importance of the renovation and retrofit industry in Canada.

Photo by Chuck Russell

In 1993, Canadians spent about $20 billion on renovations and repairs.

SOURCES

Canada Mortgage and Housing Corporation
Statistics Canada

FOR FURTHER READING

Selected publications from Statistics Canada

- **Canadian Economic Observer**. Monthly. 11-010
- **Industrial Monitor**. 15F0011
- **Monthly Survey of Manufacturing**. Monthly. 31-001
- **Manufacturing Industries of Canada: national and provincial areas**. Annual. 31-203
- **Private and Public Investment in Canada, intentions**. Annual. 61-205
- **Private and Public Investment in Canada, revised intentions**. Annual. 61-206
- **Construction Canada**. Annual. 64-201

Selected publications from other sources

- **Heavy Construction News**. Maclean Hunter. Monthly.

Legend

–	nil or zero	..	not available	x	confidential
--	too small to be expressed	...	not applicable or not appropriate		*(Certain tables may not add due to rounding)*

12.1 GROSS DOMESTIC PRODUCT AT FACTOR COST, MANUFACTURING AND CONSTRUCTION

	1985	1986	1987	1988	1989	1990	1991	1992	1993	1994	1995
	$ Constant 1986 (millions)										
Manufacturing and construction industries[1]	113,171.0	114,930.7	120,711.8	126,458.0	129,014.3	125,315.6	116,439.6	115,894.0	119,493.3	127,376.7	130,217.0
Manufacturing industries	86,218.0	86,848.8	91,025.3	95,643.1	96,511.8	92,919.3	86,353.7	87,471.7	91,636.2	98,026.5	102,359.8
Food industries	9,588.2	9,531.5	9,600.6	9,559.4	9,250.9	9,421.9	9,643.3	9,792.6	9,829.5	10,082.1	10,192.5
Beverage industries	2,446.0	2,319.8	2,358.6	2,437.8	2,465.9	2,362.3	2,130.1	2,358.7	2,450.3	2,530.6	2,554.4
Tobacco products industries	667.5	630.1	670.7	684.2	629.4	608.4	591.6	538.9	544.7	624.4	580.5
Rubber products industries	1,166.9	1,019.1	1,067.4	1,120.5	1,084.5	1,057.7	950.9	1,187.3	1,372.5	1,542.1	1,586.8
Plastic products industries	1,643.0	1,649.4	1,852.2	1,898.7	1,958.3	1,871.1	1,777.6	1,849.1	1,993.2	2,195.4	2,175.7
Leather and allied products industries.	551.1	550.5	510.1	474.8	459.6	399.3	315.1	308.0	316.8	325.3	309.5
Primary textile and textile products industries	2,019.9	2,233.2	2,297.9	2,260.0	2,195.0	1,991.0	1,863.3	1,797.7	1,830.8	1,981.3	1,997.9
Clothing industries	2,489.8	2,599.4	2,694.2	2,636.4	2,604.4	2,478.1	2,244.7	2,145.6	2,152.8	2,184.7	2,198.7
Wood industries	4,611.9	4,625.6	5,338.9	5,442.4	5,337.2	4,897.7	4,384.1	4,730.5	5,022.5	5,187.8	5,075.1
Furniture and fixture industries	1,643.4	1,735.1	1,731.1	1,687.5	1,669.1	1,565.0	1,290.7	1,289.0	1,341.5	1,442.1	1,615.9
Paper and allied products industries	7,171.1	7,556.6	8,012.8	8,042.4	7,740.0	7,483.6	7,167.3	7,198.7	7,434.9	7,763.1	7,855.0
Printing, publishing and allied industries	5,323.4	5,452.9	5,443.1	5,703.2	5,855.5	5,764.3	5,150.7	4,803.8	4,612.9	4,611.0	4,378.1
Primary metal industries	6,351.7	6,127.8	6,773.2	7,130.8	6,922.1	6,438.0	6,459.2	6,658.8	7,394.9	7,554.9	7,543.1
Fabricated metal product industries	5,999.2	6,144.3	6,509.6	6,654.1	6,890.6	6,482.2	5,703.1	5,395.4	5,455.7	6,068.8	6,408.3
Machinery industries	3,422.5	3,546.9	3,476.8	3,880.9	3,919.1	3,621.1	2,920.4	2,727.2	3,081.1	3,402.3	3,765.2
Transportation equipment industries	11,704.4	11,406.9	11,355.9	13,470.5	14,224.8	13,372.1	12,031.3	12,276.7	13,648.8	14,742.8	15,627.0
Electrical and electronic products industries	6,183.3	6,459.3	7,147.9	7,710.8	8,179.7	8,192.6	8,003.5	8,505.6	8,788.4	11,000.6	13,461.6
Non-metallic mineral products industries	2,845.2	2,970.9	3,256.9	3,307.9	3,230.5	2,896.3	2,411.7	2,387.9	2,461.8	2,598.5	2,562.1
Refined petroleum and coal products industries	1,746.1	1,731.6	1,823.9	1,870.7	1,952.1	2,074.8	2,045.9	1,993.8	2,062.3	2,102.9	2,123.5
Chemical and chemical products industries	6,345.0	6,375.0	6,825.2	7,298.2	7,568.8	7,580.6	6,901.7	7,213.4	7,523.5	7,679.5	7,856.6
Other manufacturing industries	2,322.7	2,123.6	2,220.4	2,328.4	2,316.7	2,298.7	2,299.1	2,263.2	2,267.4	2,356.6	2,442.2
Non-business sector manufacturing industries	67.9	59.5	57.9	43.6	57.6	62.6	68.5	49.9	49.9	49.7	50.1
Construction industries	26,953.0	28,081.9	29,686.5	30,814.9	32,502.5	32,396.3	30,085.9	28,422.3	27,857.1	29,350.2	27,857.2
Residential construction	7,080.5	8,219.9	9,016.6	8,904.8	9,213.5	8,608.2	7,232.7	7,474.3	7,174.0	7,494.1	6,390.9
Non-residential building construction	6,119.4	6,229.3	6,807.4	7,164.8	7,578.2	7,565.1	6,740.6	5,725.5	5,212.6	5,449.7	5,438.8
Other construction activities	13,767.7	13,632.8	13,862.5	14,745.4	15,710.7	16,223.0	16,112.6	15,222.5	15,470.5	16,406.4	16,028.0

Source: Statistics Canada, CANSIM, matrix 4670.

12.2 PRIVATE AND PUBLIC INVESTMENT,[1] MANUFACTURING AND CONSTRUCTION

	1991	1992	1993	1994	1995	1996[2]
			$ Millions			
Private and public investment in Canada	128,010.0	122,188.8	121,253.9	130,131.2	127,956.1	126,009.4
Total manufacturing and construction	19,216.6	15,910.6	15,658.7	16,534.2	18,495.0	18,854.3
Manufacturing	17,523.3	14,146.7	13,777.6	14,529.0	16,609.1	17,079.7
Food and beverages	1,555.9	1,569.3	1,438.1	1,390.8	1,370.4	1,249.8
Tobacco products	x	x	x	x	x	x
Rubber products	219.1	288.1	186.8	155.5	207.1	259.4
Plastic products	290.2	263.6	275.0	380.8	374.7	305.2
Leather and allied industries	x	x	x	x	x	x
Textiles products	182.1	128.0	170.5	172.1	189.3	273.0
Clothing	104.8	112.3	75.9	145.6	95.2	69.4
Wood	475.2	459.2	692.6	1,134.5	1,418.4	971.1
Furniture and fixtures	64.9	65.2	81.7	100.5	112.1	111.9
Paper and allied products	3,547.8	2,704.0	2,241.4	2,100.4	3,499.2	3,379.6
Printing, publishing and allied	714.6	477.3	501.1	503.5	433.3	573.4
Primary metals	2,801.2	1,430.2	1,009.0	670.3	1,194.3	1,470.9
Metal fabricating	377.6	359.3	369.9	470.3	512.5	535.7
Machinery	291.5	219.0	253.3	484.1	362.8	421.6
Transportation equipment	2,248.7	2,509.0	2,991.9	3,507.8	3,818.4	4,180.6
Electrical products	785.2	628.0	719.5	714.0	700.7	548.1
Non-metallic mineral products	377.1	225.7	236.2	358.0	363.7	391.3
Petroleum and coal products	1,029.8	631.4	393.4	323.0	368.2	589.7
Chemical and chemical products	2,053.9	1,701.1	1,723.0	1,310.8	1,132.1	1,306.4
Other industries	250.7	228.0	237.6	416.1	249.9	251.1
Construction industry	1,693.3	1,763.9	1,881.1	2,005.2	1,885.9	1,774.6
			%			
Investment in manufacturing and construction as a percentage of total investment	15.0	13.0	12.9	12.7	14.5	15.0

1. Excluding repair expenditures.
2. Intentions

Source: Statistics Canada, CANSIM, matrices 3101 and 3103.

12.3 MANUFACTURING SHIPMENTS, ORDERS AND INVENTORIES

	1986	1987	1988	1989	1990	1991	1992	1993	1994	1995[1]
						$ Millions				
Shipments	253,411	271,627	297,540	308,805	298,919	280,191	286,043	309,675	352,835	390,029
New orders	254,814	272,613	302,569	308,414	294,396	277,585	286,156	312,744	355,780	390,032
Unfilled orders	23,703	24,409	28,583	30,131	28,002	25,585	25,355	27,836	32,034	34,761
Inventories	34,039	34,702	37,058	39,012	39,628	37,280	35,375	35,081	38,725	44,263
						Number				
Inventory-to-shipment ratio	1.6	1.5	1.5	1.5	1.6	1.6	1.5	1.4	1.3	1.4

1. Data for 1995 are annual totals from the Monthly Survey of Manufacturing.

Source: Statistics Canada, Catalogue no. 31-203 and 31-001.

12.4 EMPLOYMENT IN MANUFACTURING AND CONSTRUCTION

	1985	1986	1987	1988	1989	1990	1991	1992	1993	1994	1995	Average annual growth rate 1985-1995
							Employees[1] '000					%
All industries[2]	9,651.1	9,927.2	10,329.1	10,659.0	11,054.7	11,146.1	10,549.5	10,246.9	10,271.4	10,447.1	10,673.6	0.9
Manufacturing	1,775.3	1,836.1	1,918.7	1,966.2	2,004.3	1,885.4	1,691.5	1,599.2	1,596.7	1,631.6	1,675.9	-0.5
Non-durable goods	836.7	867.8	901.6	907.4	915.8	880.1	806.1	748.1	758.1	752.9	757.7	-0.9
Durable goods	938.6	968.4	1,017.1	1,058.8	1,088.5	1,005.4	885.4	851.1	838.6	878.7	918.2	-0.2
Food	186.0	190.1	203.8	207.7	202.7	197.4	187.8	184.0	179.6	181.0	182.7	-0.2
Beverages	33.4	33.4	32.4	32.5	31.5	31.2	26.7	24.7	24.6	25.8	25.1	-2.6
Tobacco products	6.6	6.3	5.7	5.3	5.1	4.8	4.8	4.8	4.7	4.5	4.4	-3.6
Rubber products	20.3	21.1	22.0	21.0	20.7	20.1	17.3	16.0	19.2	20.4	20.3	0.0
Plastic products	40.4	43.7	51.1	55.2	63.2	62.4	60.8	42.5	47.6	50.3	52.0	2.3
Leather and allied products	29.4	27.6	24.5	22.3	20.7	18.8	14.4	15.4	12.8	11.8	11.9	-7.9
Primary textiles	24.6	24.8	25.1	24.9	22.9	20.4	18.2	19.0	17.2	18.8	19.7	-2.0
Textile products	30.1	31.6	33.0	33.7	31.8	27.8	26.4	24.7	27.6	28.1	25.8	-1.4
Clothing	113.3	120.6	120.7	120.8	116.2	110.2	90.6	75.8	85.1	83.8	84.3	-2.7
Wood	99.4	100.6	115.8	119.8	122.2	114.7	98.1	96.0	99.7	114.6	115.5	1.4
Furniture and fixtures	53.5	61.1	60.3	61.9	66.3	57.8	51.5	44.8	42.3	46.0	45.9	-1.4
Paper and allied products	114.5	117.7	122.2	124.8	126.5	121.7	112.9	104.1	100.1	98.1	98.2	-1.4
Printing, publishing and allied industries	131.2	142.9	154.8	149.6	160.2	152.2	139.6	136.6	144.7	138.3	142.7	0.8
Primary metals	103.8	99.8	100.5	103.3	102.2	91.3	84.5	80.2	80.0	80.8	84.6	-1.8
Fabricated metal products	150.5	158.6	164.8	169.4	175.4	165.3	141.4	135.4	131.4	137.6	141.7	-0.5
Machinery	78.3	79.6	79.1	84.9	94.8	80.0	66.1	64.3	64.9	74.9	83.6	0.6
Transportation equipment	192.2	198.4	210.4	221.9	230.1	218.9	198.4	194.5	195.1	205.8	211.6	0.9
Electrical and electronic products	132.0	137.2	143.5	149.7	152.9	139.9	120.2	114.6	111.1	108.7	114.1	-1.3
Non-metallic mineral products	48.2	49.6	53.6	55.2	54.8	52.2	44.0	42.7	41.2	41.8	44.9	-0.6
Refined petroleum and coal products	23.2	23.3	21.1	21.5	21.3	19.4	17.7	17.3	13.9	13.1	12.1	-5.7
Chemical and chemical products	84.0	84.8	85.2	88.0	93.0	93.6	89.1	83.2	80.9	78.6	78.4	-0.6
Other manufacturing	80.6	83.3	89.0	92.7	89.7	85.4	81.1	78.7	73.0	68.4	76.3	-0.5
Construction	455.8	483.1	508.4	535.3	587.7	578.9	483.0	441.4	423.4	433.4	437.9	-0.4
Building developing and general contracting	105.6	115.2	117.1	129.8	153.1	139.2	110.1	105.5	99.2	98.0	94.0	-1.1
Residential building and development	73.9	80.1	80.3	89.2	105.4	95.5	74.5	75.4	72.0	68.4	66.3	-1.0
Non-residential building and development	31.7	35.0	36.8	40.6	47.7	43.7	35.6	30.2	27.2	29.7	27.7	-1.2
Industrial and heavy (engineering) construction	59.2	61.5	66.8	71.5	79.1	78.4	70.3	61.7	59.2	62.3	63.3	0.6
Trade contracting	270.5	285.4	301.7	311.4	332.0	337.6	282.0	257.6	249.3	257.1	261.8	-0.3
Services incidental to construction	20.4	21.0	22.6	22.6	23.5	23.8	20.6	16.6	15.6	15.9	18.9	-0.7
						% of total employment						
Manufacturing	18.4	18.5	18.6	18.4	18.1	16.9	16.0	15.6	15.5	15.6	15.7	...
Construction	4.7	4.9	4.9	5.0	5.3	5.2	4.6	4.3	4.1	4.1	4.1	...

1. Excludes owners or partners of unincorporated business and professional practices, the self-employed, unpaid family workers, persons working outside Canada, military personnel and casual workers for whom a T4 is not required.
2. Excludes agriculture, fishing and trapping, private household services, religious organizations and the military.

Source: Statistics Canada, Catalogue no. 72F0002.

12.5 EMPLOYMENT IN MANUFACTURING AND CONSTRUCTION, CANADA, THE PROVINCES AND TERRITORIES, 1995

	Canada	Nfld.	P.E.I.	N.S.	N.B.	Que.	Ont.	Man.	Sask.	Alta.	B.C.	Y.T.	N.W.T.
							Employees[1] '000						
All industries[2]	10,673.6	147.8	43.4	299.5	240.4	2,574.0	4,180.9	404.6	314.0	1,041.8	1,392.1	12.0	23.2
Goods-producing industries[2]	2,438.2	27.9	7.9	58.4	55.2	621.9	1,028.8	76.4	51.2	225.9	279.3	1.7	3.7
Logging and forestry	66.5	1.8	x	2.4	4.8	14.8	9.7	..	1.0	2.5	28.7	x	x
Mining, quarrying and oil wells	128.9	2.5	..	3.5	3.1	14.0	21.0	3.4	8.9	58.5	12.0	x	x
Manufacturing	1,675.9	11.6	4.0	36.8	31.7	463.6	798.6	53.2	24.9	92.4	158.6	x	x
Non-durable goods	757.7	8.8	3.2	22.9	19.1	238.5	313.9	25.3	12.8	44.8	68.1	x	x
Durable goods	918.2	2.8	0.9	13.9	12.6	225.1	484.7	27.9	12.1	47.6	90.5	x	x
Construction	437.9	9.0	3.4	12.8	12.0	95.3	149.2	13.1	11.8	60.2	69.1	0.7	1.4
Service-producing industries	8,174.9	119.0	35.3	239.9	184.3	1,935.9	3,129.5	326.4	261.5	810.1	1,103.4	10.2	19.4
Transportation, communication and other utilities	849.1	13.8	2.9	22.0	22.3	208.8	295.2	43.1	29.3	86.7	121.2	1.3	2.5
Trade	2,033.2	30.3	7.8	59.1	47.6	483.9	788.0	74.5	65.6	204.6	267.3	1.5	2.9
Finance, insurance, and real estate	641.5	6.2	1.9	16.2	10	144.6	276.2	24.7	21	56.3	82.9	..	1.1
Community, business and personal services	4,091.7	55.0	17.3	116.3	85.8	968.6	1,570.2	162.9	127.6	408.5	566.9	4.5	7.9

1. Excludes owners or partners of unincorporated business and professional practices, the self-employed, unpaid family workers, persons working outside Canada, military personnel and casual workers for whom a T4 is not required.
2. Excludes agriculture, fishing and trapping, private household services, religious organizations and the military.

Source: Statistics Canada, Catalogue no. 72F0002.

12.6 EARNINGS IN MANUFACTURING AND CONSTRUCTION

	1984	1985	1986	1987	1988	1989	1990	1991	1992	1993	1994	1995	Earnings in 1995 as a % of all industry earnings
	Average weekly earnings[1]												
	$												%
All industries[2]	398.10	412.02	424.25	440.26	459.75	483.31	505.14	528.60	547.01	556.76	567.11	572.49	100.0
Manufacturing	466.37	486.65	500.09	521.31	543.69	570.18	598.97	624.39	652.54	668.95	685.07	693.91	121.2
Non-durable goods	444.67	463.92	479.12	495.29	517.89	545.30	571.27	597.31	619.47	631.49	640.36	650.08	113.6
Durable goods	486.10	506.91	518.87	544.37	565.80	591.11	623.23	649.04	681.62	702.83	723.38	730.08	127.5
Food	403.29	414.12	435.04	450.29	468.93	487.80	512.51	533.62	542.05	560.48	568.74	575.58	100.5
Beverages	543.29	555.33	576.62	610.28	633.96	653.48	670.64	690.01	711.56	755.62	769.65	755.81	132.0
Tobacco products	593.50	653.09	683.41	735.03	790.48	844.04	891.97	958.03	996.97	1027.06	1141.55	1153.45	201.5
Rubber products	451.74	462.40	479.90	506.74	517.28	545.17	581.24	634.12	679.70	689.96	713.30	703.55	122.9
Plastic products	410.05	436.94	446.13	454.46	490.04	502.66	528.69	554.61	561.74	562.31	573.53	576.39	100.7
Leather and allied products	327.87	342.92	363.31	375.81	386.74	402.87	423.50	403.11	396.01	410.33	420.15	435.75	76.1
Primary textiles	397.59	415.55	432.98	452.60	476.76	498.69	522.56	562.08	608.83	631.48	655.56	681.59	119.1
Textile products	371.06	384.76	386.93	405.57	413.23	442.63	461.84	466.10	493.30	492.06	462.14	495.66	86.6
Clothing	289.29	311.17	318.54	313.16	319.05	342.51	361.44	374.63	378.24	375.24	382.74	397.82	69.5
Wood	450.58	468.24	467.44	492.21	502.82	529.03	560.10	577.95	594.90	608.52	619.01	633.74	110.7
Furniture and fixtures	374.53	377.32	390.79	408.74	411.26	449.19	463.01	471.71	498.27	509.30	529.47	529.13	92.4
Paper and allied products	573.71	604.00	630.06	654.46	683.72	718.20	745.89	795.13	828.16	846.78	871.60	900.98	157.4
Printing, publishing and allied	426.75	452.48	463.14	481.29	506.20	534.40	555.14	576.52	605.39	618.51	612.83	625.28	109.2
Primary metals	589.94	616.18	630.30	665.05	692.51	726.64	758.81	786.82	831.75	864.33	876.10	896.15	156.5
Fabricated metal products	453.39	465.87	481.50	516.53	532.76	561.78	589.01	612.09	634.24	632.58	648.22	666.67	116.5
Machinery	473.32	498.77	510.08	553.79	574.35	591.90	629.14	647.02	689.32	695.84	721.22	737.18	128.8
Transportation equipment	539.04	572.90	592.26	608.04	641.10	656.66	687.60	722.56	760.62	803.52	845.04	849.45	148.4
Electrical and electronic products	483.95	505.00	525.75	547.46	570.60	593.68	645.29	675.68	728.80	744.12	753.40	736.66	128.7
Non-metallic mineral products	498.12	515.59	541.20	561.39	585.08	611.75	630.53	660.78	695.08	698.31	702.76	719.06	125.6
Refined petroleum and coal products	787.87	806.20	805.14	860.90	907.47	957.99	991.00	916.66	877.55	1055.05	1090.97	1108.76	193.7
Chemical and chemical products	530.37	559.71	582.99	611.27	639.18	667.49	703.67	728.62	768.49	790.88	810.18	803.28	140.3
Other manufacturing	408.53	425.02	421.70	445.26	462.14	497.45	526.41	544.37	542.58	569.97	600.35	588.22	102.7
Construction	486.91	502.33	512.23	535.64	559.42	591.52	622.96	635.38	637.40	639.74	657.87	675.50	118.0
Building developing and general contracting	440.04	448.60	466.00	502.94	524.54	552.81	595.60	608.49	596.88	594.84	619.07	615.01	107.4
Residential building and development	403.94	410.46	428.02	463.45	482.67	507.75	542.06	542.13	536.71	545.12	559.78	567.16	99.1
Non-residential building and development	524.81	537.58	552.90	589.07	616.58	652.52	712.64	747.25	747.13	726.54	755.77	729.32	127.4
Industrial and heavy (engineering) construction	572.86	608.92	614.96	635.36	665.38	689.78	749.43	739.76	771.95	783.46	804.57	834.98	145.9
Trade contracting	479.87	492.67	498.43	518.94	544.17	583.01	607.44	624.22	623.07	626.51	637.60	659.59	115.2
Services incidental to construction	549.29	599.20	651.95	632.93	634.25	633.29	586.88	575.67	617.56	591.32	650.28	662.64	115.7

1. Excludes owners or partners of unincorporated business and professional practices, the self-employed, unpaid family workers, persons working outside Canada, military personnel and casual workers for whom a T4 is not required.
2. Excludes agriculture, fishing and trapping, private household services, religious organizations and the military.

Source: Statistics Canada, Catalogue no. 72F0002.

12.7 SHIPMENTS OF GOODS OF OWN MANUFACTURE BY INDUSTRY

	1987	1988	1989	1990	1991	1992	1993	1994	1995[1]
					$ Millions				
Manufacturing industry	271,627.0	297,539.8	308,805.3	298,918.5	280,190.7	286,043.3	309,674.9	352,834.7	390,028.6
Food	36,042.3	37,116.1	38,015.7	38,582.5	38,214.0	38,948.2	40,292.1	42,809.5	44,427.9
Beverage	5,323.6	5,865.4	5,779.6	5,620.6	5,800.5	6,293.4	6,563.7	6,713.2	6,856.6
Tobacco products	1,706.8	1,778.6	1,817.9	1,883.3	1,963.3	2,046.5	2,006.5	2,471.5	2,548.4
Rubber products	2,509.7	2,694.7	2,675.8	2,557.9	2,542.4	2,665.5	3,086.9	3,412.1	3,659.9
Plastic products	5,063.1	5,893.1	6,289.3	5,996.8	5,648.8	5,766.3	6,192.8	7,102.2	7,741.6
Leather and allied products	1,316.1	1,293.3	1,289.5	1,162.3	940.6	888.7	930.5	1,006.3	1,029.1
Primary textile	3,123.4	3,173.3	3,146.2	2,779.6	2,693.5	2,689.7	2,733.3	3,072.7	3,244.6
Textile products	3,253.0	3,411.0	3,478.1	3,363.6	3,042.0	2,796.1	2,875.7	3,170.1	3,286.5
Clothing	6,457.4	6,656.7	6,948.1	6,831.3	6,156.2	5,853.7	5,933.3	6,147.0	6,283.3
Paper and allied products	23,073.1	25,661.1	25,847.5	24,026.3	21,003.4	20,824.7	21,232.6	25,647.8	35,470.0
Printing, publishing and allied	11,180.4	12,525.7	13,531.1	13,703.9	13,045.9	12,875.3	12,840.0	13,495.6	14,545.0
Refined petroleum and coal products	16,438.9	14,273.8	14,958.7	18,569.5	18,066.4	17,450.3	17,244.4	17,535.5	17,321.3
Chemical and chemical products	20,267.1	22,775.3	23,667.7	23,117.9	21,297.4	21,489.4	22,609.5	25,598.0	28,556.1
Wood	14,611.0	15,322.2	15,843.2	14,805.9	13,165.7	15,059.8	19,082.9	22,906.7	21,851.6
Furniture and fixtures	4,389.5	4,619.7	4,902.8	4,661.9	3,939.4	3,771.1	3,988.2	4,522.8	5,079.5
Primary metal	19,153.7	22,715.4	22,884.5	19,243.8	17,851.2	18,045.2	19,810.5	23,441.8	26,232.5
Fabricated metal products	16,750.2	17,946.3	19,154.3	17,876.9	15,924.4	14,960.9	15,404.1	17,814.5	19,518.8
Machinery	8,724.8	10,012.3	10,995.5	10,396.1	8,904.0	8,755.8	10,089.6	12,374.7	14,333.9
Transportation equipment	43,332.6	51,178.1	53,783.3	51,654.9	48,179.7	52,785.1	64,112.8	76,132.1	85,937.3
Electrical and electronic products	15,831.1	18,191.7	19,488.8	18,474.8	19,494.0	20,142.6	20,299.2	23,862.3	27,862.5
Non-metallic mineral products	7,444.4	7,803.6	7,983.7	7,391.6	6,251.6	5,980.2	6,226.7	6,698.4	6,970.0
Other manufacturing	5,635.1	6,092.3	6,324.0	6,217.2	6,066.2	5,954.7	6,119.7	6,899.8	7,772.1

1. Data for 1995 are annual totals from the Monthly Survey of Manufacturing.

Source: Statistics Canada, Catalogue no. 31-203, 31-001.

12.8 SHIPMENTS OF GOODS OF OWN MANUFACTURE, CANADA, THE PROVINCES AND TERRITORIES

	1987	1988	1989	1990	1991	1992	1993	1994	1995[1]
				$ Millions					
Canada	271,627.0	297,539.8	308,805.3	298,918.5	280,190.7	286,043.3	309,674.9	352,834.7	390,028.6
Newfoundland	1,655.1	1,726.0	1,653.6	1,551.8	1,447.9	1,279.6	1,324.1	1,422.6	1,540.5
Prince Edward Island	362.5	391.7	417.3	396.4	435.7	501.4	510.8	538.0	615.1
Nova Scotia	4,745.6	4,790.6	5,181.4	5,150.5	5,281.8	5,119.7	5,268.9	5,413.1	5,929.2
New Brunswick	5,634.7	5,627.7	5,884.6	5,865.5	5,476.7	5,786.3	6,296.1	7,081.2	7,656.4
Quebec	66,454.1	73,631.4	75,465.1	73,973.6	69,958.5	69,220.4	74,675.4	85,133.0	94,363.4
Ontario	143,394.9	157,675.5	163,713.1	155,995.2	145,148.0	150,257.1	163,248.1	184,923.1	204,226.3
Manitoba	6,248.1	6,671.0	6,984.1	6,739.5	6,161.4	6,228.4	6,650.1	7,542.7	8,409.9
Saskatchewan	3,285.9	3,380.1	3,748.7	3,786.0	3,546.7	3,487.6	3,643.2	4,409.6	4,719.1
Alberta	16,421.8	18,078.8	19,111.0	20,048.8	19,477.1	19,241.6	20,951.2	25,260.1	28,306.9
British Columbia	23,368.9	25,510.1	26,580.2	25,335.9	23,192.7	24,853.3	27,060.1	31,046.1	34,168.8
Yukon	8.8	14.2	16.6	19.3	16.6	19.6	12.5	14.0	13.2
Northwest Territories	46.6	42.7	49.7	56.1	47.6	48.4	34.3	51.0	79.9

1. Data for 1995 are annual totals from the Monthly Survey of Manufacturing.

Source: Statistics Canada, CANSIM, matrices 9550, 9570-9582.

12.9 VALUE OF CONSTRUCTION WORK

	1983	1984	1985	1986	1987	1988	1989	1990	1991	1992	1993
						$ Millions					
Total value of construction	55,947.8	56,574.5	67,983.2	71,700.6	81,971.5	90,871.4	100,412.1	102,367.0	94,154.9	91,861.2	94,411.3
Building construction	30,752.7	31,411.6	41,459.0	47,426.9	57,907.7	63,885.4	71,238.3	70,046.9	60,900.7	59,948.0	61,315.2
Residential	16,851.4	16,647.3	24,144.7	28,885.3	35,825.3	38,935.9	42,729.6	41,012.1	34,767.7	37,314.8	38,432.5
Single detached	6,372.7	6,044.6	7,152.8	9,827.3	13,279.0	13,564.1	15,405.0	13,408.3	10,205.9	11,129.9	12,802.0
Semi-detached, including duplexes	352.2	302.8	346.0	440.1	517.1	516.5	545.3	603.0	634.1	840.5	723.1
Apartments, including row housing	2,444.4	2,338.6	2,626.6	3,392.5	5,259.2	5,599.3	5,868.9	6,026.2	4,403.3	4,873.5	4,795.3
Other	7,682.0	7,961.2	14,019.4	15,225.4	16,770.0	19,256.0	20,910.4	20,974.4	19,524.3	20,470.9	20,112.0
Industrial	2,449.8	2,708.0	3,470.1	3,201.3	3,243.9	3,841.9	4,487.6	4,344.0	3,641.8	2,776.9	2,594.2
Commercial	6,482.4	7,129.1	8,697.1	10,119.1	12,378.0	14,115.7	16,192.6	16,574.2	13,436.2	11,184.9	11,146.5
Warehouses, storehouses, refrigerated storage, etc.	585.4	571.0	593.5	729.2	840.5	1,011.8	1,107.2	1,039.2	790.2	659.1	669.2
Hotels, clubs, restaurants, cafeterias and tourist cabins	540.0	637.0	721.5	881.2	1,087.8	980.6	1,213.8	1,252.9	917.9	576.0	524.5
Office buildings	3,191.4	3,186.1	3,937.0	4,731.5	5,924.5	6,393.1	7,705.6	8,971.7	7,779.5	6,522.1	6,343.7
Stores, retail and wholesale	1,075.3	1,308.5	2,036.7	2,392.9	2,859.4	4,088.4	4,218.7	3,665.8	2,263.1	1,931.5	1,868.1
Garages and service stations	325.9	395.4	472.7	453.2	505.2	533.9	720.6	592.3	651.0	560.1	707.5
Theatres, arenas, amusement and recreational buildings	554.5	837.5	817.9	855.8	1,090.7	1,055.5	1,179.5	987.6	963.2	885.6	957.3
Other commercial	209.9	193.6	117.8	75.4	69.9	52.5	47.2	64.7	71.1	50.4	76.1
Institutional	3,064.5	2,924.2	3,119.3	3,565.2	4,313.6	4,540.0	5,110.6	5,535.5	5,844.7	5,964.2	6,205.4
Schools and other educational buildings	1,275.2	1,202.5	1,292.4	1,513.4	2,080.1	2,421.7	2,571.3	3,034.5	3,478.0	3,569.2	3,735.2
Churches and other religious buildings	140.5	152.5	151.3	159.1	150.8	184.0	187.4	163.2	126.0	103.7	79.1
Hospitals, sanatoria, clinics, first-aid stations, etc.	1,114.3	1,010.7	1,009.0	1,055.3	1,169.9	1,137.5	1,288.6	1,377.6	1,291.7	1,351.6	1,371.7
Other institutional buildings	534.5	558.5	666.7	837.3	912.8	796.8	1,063.3	960.2	949.0	939.8	1,019.3
Other building construction	1,904.5	2,003.0	2,027.7	1,656.0	2,147.0	2,451.8	2,717.8	2,581.2	3,210.3	2,707.2	2,936.8
Engineering construction	25,195.1	25,162.9	26,524.2	24,273.8	24,063.7	26,986.1	29,173.8	32,320.0	33,254.2	31,913.2	33,096.1
Marine construction	425.9	474.1	379.4	335.1	316.5	503.6	614.3	586.5	553.5	556.0	575.9
Road, highway and aerodrome construction	4,325.7	4,276.2	5,179.2	5,192.9	5,433.2	5,721.4	6,199.3	6,462.9	6,334.2	6,373.9	6,799.7
Waterworks and sewage systems	2,229.6	2,170.1	2,481.2	2,377.3	2,304.0	2,477.3	2,569.2	2,925.1	2,659.6	2,700.8	3,025.8
Dams and irrigation	290.8	272.3	282.5	242.7	307.4	398.0	469.4	456.2	398.8	306.1	333.7
Electric power construction	4,396.8	3,663.4	3,314.2	3,370.3	3,615.7	4,198.0	5,153.0	6,132.3	6,859.0	7,866.8	7,645.0
Railway, telephone and telegraph	2,469.0	2,723.9	2,787.1	2,752.9	2,922.4	3,089.6	3,511.3	3,611.7	3,134.9	3,052.6	3,069.8
Gas and oil facilities	8,127.7	8,551.7	9,207.2	6,727.8	6,030.0	7,287.6	7,402.8	8,325.2	9,628.6	7,790.5	8,080.7
Other engineering construction	2,929.7	3,031.2	2,893.5	3,274.9	3,134.7	3,310.6	3,254.4	3,820.2	3,685.7	3,266.6	3,565.5

Source: Statistics Canada, CANSIM, matrix 2855.

12.10 VALUE OF BUILDING PERMITS BY TYPE

	1982	1983	1984	1985	1986	1987	1988	1989	1990	1991	1992	1993	1994	1995
								$ Millions						
Canada	12,788.8	14,571.3	15,501.6	19,523.9	24,690.0	30,980.9	34,829.2	39,318.4	32,130.5	28,468.0	26,995.1	25,586.3	27,636.7	24,594.7
Residential	6,132.9	8,859.2	8,513.2	10,883.1	14,218.9	18,832.5	20,118.7	21,268.4	17,424.4	16,631.7	17,160.8	16,432.5	17,590.2	13,241.7
Non-residential	6,655.9	5,712.1	6,988.4	8,640.8	10,471.1	12,148.4	14,710.5	18,050.0	14,706.2	11,836.3	9,834.3	9,153.8	10,046.5	11,353.0
Industrial	1,096.3	939.6	1,367.2	1,885.5	1,899.4	2,806.1	3,046.3	5,492.2	3,392.7	2,119.8	1,643.3	1,755.6	2,250.2	2,822.8
Commercial	3,485.2	2,760.8	3,715.3	4,639.8	6,151.8	7,038.9	8,755.8	9,666.0	7,975.0	5,905.9	4,918.2	4,267.8	4,993.2	5,441.4
Institutional and government	2,074.4	2,011.7	1,905.9	2,115.6	2,419.8	2,303.4	2,908.4	2,891.8	3,338.4	3,810.6	3,272.8	3,130.4	2,803.1	3,088.9

Source: Statistics Canada, Catalogue no. 64-203.

12.11 VALUE OF BUILDING PERMITS, CANADA, THE PROVINCES AND TERRITORIES

	1982	1983	1984	1985	1986	1987	1988	1989	1990	1991	1992	1993	1994	1995
							$ Millions							
Canada	12,788.8	14,571.3	15,501.6	19,523.9	24,690.0	30,980.9	34,829.2	39,318.4	32,130.5	28,468.0	26,995.1	25,586.3	27,636.7	24,594.7
Residential	6,132.9	8,859.2	8,513.2	10,883.1	14,218.9	18,832.5	20,118.7	21,268.4	17,424.4	16,631.7	17,160.8	16,432.5	17,590.2	13,241.7
Non-residential	6,655.9	5,712.1	6,988.4	8,640.8	10,471.1	12,148.4	14,710.5	18,050.0	14,706.2	11,836.3	9,834.3	9,153.8	10,046.5	11,353.0
Newfoundland	102.3	144.9	153.6	183.6	207.5	235.5	272.9	346.8	312.6	275.0	242.5	255.4	262.7	201.7
Residential	42.5	95.3	90.2	115.8	119.8	124.5	162.1	198.9	203.8	160.0	160.6	166.9	174.9	131.1
Non-residential	59.9	49.7	63.4	67.8	87.7	110.9	110.8	148.0	108.9	115.0	81.8	88.5	87.8	70.5
Prince Edward Island	49.3	74.4	77.8	87.4	106.9	123.6	173.1	148.3	158.5	121.1	132.1	112.5	112.7	96.1
Residential	18.0	32.4	37.1	43.7	65.9	72.0	86.2	73.8	75.7	60.5	69.8	69.0	61.9	52.3
Non-residential	31.4	42.0	40.6	43.7	41.0	51.5	87.0	74.5	82.8	60.6	62.3	43.5	50.8	43.9
Nova Scotia	323.9	469.3	561.5	667.8	755.6	773.9	833.5	880.2	782.9	634.3	604.9	594.9	669.2	619.6
Residential	181.4	320.6	334.2	441.5	471.9	458.2	478.9	500.0	466.5	390.7	422.6	420.9	454.0	425.6
Non-residential	142.5	148.6	227.3	226.3	283.7	315.7	354.6	380.2	316.4	243.6	182.4	174.0	215.3	194.1
New Brunswick	180.4	277.3	293.2	372.7	461.1	516.7	502.2	593.5	493.3	413.9	453.7	427.4	440.5	487.9
Residential	65.0	144.9	158.0	204.1	229.3	235.8	256.3	273.0	267.7	219.7	255.5	259.7	249.5	209.2
Non-residential	115.4	132.4	135.2	168.5	231.8	280.9	245.8	320.5	225.6	194.2	198.2	167.7	191.0	278.7
Quebec	2,128.0	3,068.9	3,610.9	4,474.7	5,886.7	8,102.2	7,748.3	8,557.9	7,089.7	6,241.6	5,245.2	5,375.6	5,898.4	4,938.9
Residential	1,160.9	2,096.3	2,247.7	2,406.0	3,618.1	4,907.1	4,353.2	4,005.0	3,677.9	3,702.3	3,307.1	3,193.0	3,370.8	2,154.6
Non-residential	967.1	972.6	1,363.2	2,068.7	2,268.6	3,195.2	3,395.1	4,552.9	3,411.7	2,539.3	1,938.1	2,182.5	2,527.7	2,784.4
Ontario	4,211.1	5,349.9	6,274.3	8,392.6	11,359.5	14,833.7	17,280.8	19,558.9	14,024.9	11,997.8	9,962.9	8,774.7	10,001.3	9,192.1
Residential	2,084.9	3,250.5	3,360.6	4,886.4	6,648.9	9,377.6	10,564.5	10,873.2	7,414.5	7,018.9	6,362.0	5,528.4	6,434.5	4,946.2
Non-residential	2,126.3	2,099.4	2,913.7	3,506.2	4,710.6	5,456.1	6,716.2	8,685.7	6,610.4	4,978.9	3,601.0	3,246.3	3,566.8	4,245.9
Manitoba	266.1	432.5	528.5	696.4	809.8	862.7	789.2	836.9	731.5	561.1	541.2	528.6	685.3	525.4
Residential	137.4	277.8	320.4	424.2	520.6	515.7	475.1	394.2	344.0	251.6	307.1	306.1	318.5	254.8
Non-residential	128.7	154.8	208.1	272.1	289.2	347.0	314.1	442.7	387.5	309.6	234.2	222.5	366.8	270.7
Saskatchewan	430.5	613.5	569.6	548.3	741.5	666.1	524.4	502.7	453.9	327.5	323.1	326.8	372.3	478.2
Residential	238.4	356.9	272.4	284.4	359.0	302.3	242.5	144.6	123.5	90.8	155.2	154.7	158.5	161.0
Non-residential	192.1	256.5	297.2	263.9	382.5	363.8	281.9	358.0	330.4	236.7	167.8	172.1	213.7	317.2
Alberta	2,911.0	1,871.0	1,386.3	1,798.1	1,840.7	1,860.0	2,440.1	2,557.9	2,991.1	2,639.3	3,105.6	2,713.5	2,740.5	2,506.6
Residential	1,059.3	809.2	501.7	669.1	644.8	886.8	933.3	1,336.6	1,657.2	1,359.2	1,881.1	1,839.6	1,747.0	1,407.6
Non-residential	1,851.7	1,061.8	884.6	1,129.0	1,196.0	973.1	1,506.7	1,221.2	1,333.9	1,280.1	1,224.4	873.9	993.5	1,099.0
British Columbia	2,161.1	2,237.8	2,003.6	2,190.4	2,420.3	2,906.1	4,149.6	5,216.0	4,975.8	5,131.5	6,255.5	6,389.2	6,317.9	5,414.5
Residential	1,134.9	1,462.8	1,176.9	1,378.2	1,508.1	1,906.8	2,502.2	3,407.9	3,143.6	3,328.2	4,173.1	4,445.4	4,546.4	3,443.1
Non-residential	1,026.1	775.0	826.6	812.3	912.2	999.3	1,647.4	1,808.1	1,832.2	1,803.3	2,082.5	1,943.8	1,771.5	1,971.4
Yukon	18.0	15.2	23.8	31.0	57.5	49.8	45.2	50.5	56.5	73.7	71.2	42.2	51.0	74.0
Residential	4.8	5.5	5.7	8.4	11.8	22.8	18.9	29.7	26.8	27.2	44.3	30.5	30.7	23.7
Non-residential	13.3	9.7	18.2	22.6	45.7	27.0	26.3	20.9	29.7	46.5	26.9	11.7	20.2	50.3
Northwest Territories	7.0	16.8	18.5	80.8	42.9	50.7	69.9	68.7	59.8	51.2	57.1	45.7	84.9	59.6
Residential	5.4	7.1	8.2	21.2	20.9	22.9	45.5	31.4	23.1	22.6	22.5	18.4	43.5	32.5
Non-residential	1.6	9.7	10.4	59.6	22.0	27.8	24.5	37.3	36.7	28.5	34.6	27.4	41.4	27.1

Source: Statistics Canada, Catalogue no. 64-203.

12.12 NEW HOUSING PRICE INDEX

	1986	1987	1988	1989	1990	1991	1992	1993	1994	1995
						1986=100				
Canada	100.0	113.8	125.6	142.2	144.3	134.3	134.3	136.0	136.1	134.5
House only	100.0	115.6	125.7	135.9	135.3	125.2	124.5	125.5	125.5	124.2
Land only	100.0	109.9	126.5	159.7	169.3	160.6	163.7	168.6	169.4	167.6
St. John's	100.0	105.0	107.4	113.2	117.3	125.8	126.8	126.9	127.4	127.6
Halifax	100.0	103.3	107.2	109.2	109.5	109.3	110.5	113.7	116.9	120.3
Saint John - Moncton - Fredericton	100.0	104.8	107.8	111.6	113.2	114.2	115.3	115.2	115.3	115.2
Quebec City	100.0	108.9	118.4	126.6	130.8	134.5	135.5	135.1	134.4	135.4
Montreal	100.0	115.0	126.0	130.2	133.7	134.6	134.7	135.8	136.5	137.5
Ottawa - Hull	100.0	105.7	112.7	119.1	123.8	123.3	123.4	122.8	123.0	120.8
Toronto	100.0	126.2	147.2	180.2	173.3	147.2	140.7	137.3	137.0	137.9
Hamilton	100.0	116.8	130.3	141.3	144.5	136.0	131.0	127.6	127.2	125.7
St. Catharines - Niagara Falls	100.0	112.5	119.9	130.0	139.0	134.2	130.9	126.8	121.8	120.8
London	100.0	116.1	125.1	137.3	145.1	145.9	146.2	146.1	146.4	142.5
Kitchener - Waterloo	100.0	114.4	124.7	137.5	140.2	129.3	125.4	126.5	123.1	122.3
Windsor	100.0	106.7	112.3	122.3	127.7	127.7	127.6	126.9	127.0	128.5
Sudbury - Thunder Bay	100.0	x	118.1	125.8	132.9	133.4	132.8	135.3	137.2	137.6
Winnipeg	100.0	105.9	107.1	106.6	108.7	108.5	108.4	112.2	116.1	117.8
Regina	100.0	103.6	105.2	106.9	108.9	111.4	116.6	123.0	127.9	131.9
Saskatoon	100.0	104.2	106.1	106.9	107.6	106.7	107.2	110.9	112.5	113.5
Calgary	100.0	104.0	113.0	121.1	136.2	132.5	133.3	137.5	140.7	141.8
Edmonton	100.0	104.2	109.5	118.6	137.5	140.6	141.9	146.9	148.3	146.3
Vancouver	100.0	104.5	109.9	127.1	134.4	124.7	135.7	146.1	145.2	137.7
Victoria	100.0	97.7	104.8	115.2	123.3	121.5	127.5	131.3	130.1	118.9

Source: Statistics Canada, CANSIM, matrix 2032.

12.13 HOUSING STARTS

	Canada	Nfld.	P.E.I.	N.S.	N.B.	Que.	Ont.	Man.	Sask.	Alta.	B.C.
						Starts					
All housing											
1981	177,973	3,210	203	3,715	2,188	29,645	50,161	2,824	5,972	38,470	41,585
1982	125,860	2,793	248	3,691	1,680	23,492	38,508	2,030	6,822	26,789	19,807
1983	162,645	3,281	673	5,697	4,742	40,318	54,939	5,985	7,269	17,134	22,607
1984	134,900	2,720	643	4,598	2,873	41,902	48,171	5,308	5,221	7,295	16,169
1985	165,826	2,854	788	6,923	4,142	48,031	64,871	6,557	5,354	8,337	17,969
1986	199,785	2,883	1,110	7,571	4,045	60,348	81,470	7,699	5,510	8,462	20,687
1987	245,986	2,682	933	6,460	3,716	74,179	105,213	8,174	4,895	10,790	28,944
1988	222,562	3,168	1,151	5,478	3,621	58,062	99,924	5,455	3,856	11,360	30,487
1989	215,382	3,536	815	5,359	3,681	49,058	93,337	4,084	1,906	14,712	38,894
1990	181,630	3,245	762	5,560	2,683	48,070	62,649	3,297	1,417	17,227	36,720
1991	156,197	2,836	553	5,173	2,872	44,654	52,794	1,950	998	12,492	31,875
1992	168,271	2,271	644	4,673	3,310	38,228	55,772	2,310	1,869	18,573	40,621
1993	155,443	2,405	645	4,282	3,693	34,015	45,140	2,425	1,880	18,151	42,807
1994	154,057	2,243	669	4,748	3,203	34,154	46,645	3,197	2,098	17,692	39,408
1995	110,933	1,712	422	4,168	2,300	21,885	35,818	1,963	1,702	13,906	27,057
Single detached	64,425	1,165	364	3,040	1,722	13,428	20,124	1,564	1,341	10,096	11,581
Semi-detached	7,536	72	20	417	127	2,264	2,306	45	86	592	1,607
Row	11,887	40	18	72	51	1,046	6,175	121	60	1,340	2,964
Apartment	27085	435	20	639	400	5147	7213	233	215	1878	10905

Source: Statistics Canada, CANSIM, matrix 988.

12.14 HOUSING STOCK, 1995

	Canada	Nfld.	P.E.I.	N.S.	N.B.	Que.	Ont.	Man.	Sask.	Alta.	B.C.	Y.T./N.W.T.
	Dwelling units											
Housing stock	10,993,406	193,138	46,957	342,750	265,575	2,894,768	4,036,152	421,540	382,554	975,313	1,405,555	29,104
Owned	6,806,643	148,708	33,465	236,245	192,776	1,590,368	2,557,421	279,912	263,815	617,221	875,009	11,703
Rented	4,186,763	44,430	13,492	106,505	72,799	1,304,400	1,478,731	141,628	118,739	358,092	530,546	17,401
Occupied	10,737,016	186,400	45,400	334,000	259,600	2,828,000	3,951,000	412,000	365,700	946,100	1,380,300	28,516
Owned	6,704,342	146,005	32,890	234,097	191,337	1,579,303	2,506,258	277,276	259,549	607,636	858,424	11,567
Rented	4,032,674	40,395	12,510	99,903	68,263	1,248,697	1,444,742	134,724	106,151	338,464	521,876	16,949
Vacant	256,390	6,738	1,557	8,750	5,975	66,768	85,152	9,540	16,854	29,213	25,255	588
For sale	102,301	2,703	575	2,148	1,439	11,065	51,163	2,636	4,266	9,585	16,585	136
For rent	154,089	4,035	982	6,602	4,536	55,703	33,989	6,904	12,588	19,628	8,670	452
Single detached dwellings	6,277,597	146,328	35,286	239,456	196,959	1,295,703	2,305,329	291,368	292,431	635,707	820,213	18,817
Owned	5,615,770	133,154	31,946	216,503	180,010	1,193,665	2,078,485	261,021	252,595	553,554	704,066	10,771
Rented	661,827	13,174	3,340	22,953	16,949	102,038	226,844	30,347	39,836	82,153	116,147	8,046
Occupied	6,193,661	142,914	34,324	236,904	194,895	1,285,062	2,266,909	287,035	285,400	627,889	813,689	18,640
Owned	5,563,311	131,481	31,406	214,872	178,914	1,187,397	2,051,553	258,906	248,869	549,403	699,773	10,737
Rented	630,350	11,433	2,918	22,032	15,981	97,665	215,356	28,129	36,531	78,486	113,916	7,903
Vacant	83,936	3,414	962	2,552	2,064	10,641	38,420	4,333	7,031	7,818	6,524	177
For sale	52,459	1,673	540	1,631	1,096	6,268	26,932	2,115	3,726	4,151	4,293	34
For rent	31,477	1,741	422	921	968	4,373	11,488	2,218	3,305	3,667	2,231	143
Multiple dwellings	4,715,809	46,810	11,671	103,294	68,616	1,599,065	1,730,823	130,172	90,123	339,606	585,342	10,287
Owned	1,190,873	15,554	1,519	19,742	12,766	396,703	478,936	18,891	11,220	63,667	170,943	932
Rented	3,524,936	31,256	10,152	83,552	55,850	1,202,362	1,251,887	111,281	78,903	275,939	414,399	9,355
Occupied	4,543,355	43,486	11,076	97,096	64,705	1,542,938	1,684,091	124,965	80,300	318,211	566,611	9,876
Owned	1,141,031	14,524	1,484	19,225	12,423	391,906	454,705	18,370	10,680	58,233	158,651	830
Rented	3,402,324	28,962	9,592	77,871	52,282	1,151,032	1,229,386	106,595	69,620	259,978	407,960	9,046
Vacant	172,454	3,324	595	6,198	3,911	56,127	46,732	5,207	9,823	21,395	18,731	411
For sale	49,842	1,030	35	517	343	4,797	24,231	521	540	5,434	12,292	102
For rent	122,612	2,294	560	5,681	3,568	51,330	22,501	4,686	9,283	15,961	6,439	309

Source: Statistics Canada, CANSIM, matrices 4079–4090.

PHOTO BY **MIKE BEEDELL**

Chapter 13 COMMUNICATIONS, TRANSPORT AND TRADE

Wanda Koop, *Satellite Dish*, 1986, Winnipeg Art Gallery

Canada "holds the ghosts of the pioneers," Canadian author Douglas Coupland has written, "ghosts who [must] stare at the blinking communication towers across the land and wonder at the modern luxury of freedom of travel and instantaneous thought transmission."

Yet Canada's pioneers began with little more than the earth on which they stood, a survival instinct, and a desire to build a future for themselves. Today, that future has been realized: Canada boasts a sophisticated communications network, and transport, trade and utilities industries that together account for nearly one-quarter of the country's Gross Domestic Product (GDP), the economy's total output.

Communications

With almost 30 million people spread out over 10 million square kilometres, it's fitting that Canada would be a world leader in communications. Canadians can embark on the ultimate road trip and drive for days on the 8,000 kilometre-long Trans-Canada Highway from St. John's, Newfoundland to Victoria, British Columbia. They can travel the same distance in a matter of seconds on the "information highway"—a network of networks of wires, telephone cables and satellites that links computers, telephones and other devices in homes, businesses and institutions.

The ease of electronic communication has opened borders, and increased traffic in business and information between Canada and the rest of the world. It has also pervaded every sector of Canada's economy as firms use research and the resulting knowledge to boost their productivity, gain a competitive edge and penetrate global markets. Nearly three-quarters of goods manufactured in Canada come from companies that use computer-based technology for inspection and communications.

Canadian businesses are latching onto electronic communications gadgets, using computer modems, fax machines, cellular phones and pagers. Households are catching up. In 1995, nearly three in 10 Canadian homes had a computer, and four out of 10 home computers were hooked up to a modem, a device that uses ordinary telephone lines to exchange information between computers. Many Canadians use modems for electronic mail, giving rise to a new catch phrase, "Did you get my e-mail?"

Technology is revolutionizing the way Canadians work and play. In 1994, nearly six in 10 adults said they knew how to use a computer. The revolution, which began in the business world, seems to be spearheaded by young people. The computer literacy rate among 15- to 24-year-olds was 81%, compared with just 10% of those 65 and older.

Cable TV firms want to offer telephone service. Phone companies want to use their fibre optic cables to send video and computer data. Magazines, radio and TV stations are publishing on the Internet. Network television wants in on the cable TV business. Quite simply, the distinctions between communications companies are beginning to blur.

With the explosion in computers and other high-tech ways to produce, disseminate and use information, communications firms are doing well. In the second quarter of 1995, these companies as a whole had an 18% profit margin, nearly three times the average rate of return among all industries.

Technology is expanding the professional middle class. More people are working in this field than ever before. Employment in communications reached a new high in the second quarter of 1995, at 331,000 people. The number of people working in broadcasting, telecommunications and computer services grew twice as fast as the number in other industries between 1984 and 1994. Needless to say, workers in these sectors are highly educated and well paid. Almost 30% have a university degree, compared with 18% of the total work force. These people earn, on average, about $7,000 more a year than the average worker.

Surfing the Net

At the touch of a button, computer users can check on the stock market, read a front-page newspaper story, even look for a job. Anyone with a computer and a modem can go "surfing"—the term used to describe browsing the Internet, the international computer network, and its World Wide Web, which displays text with graphics, photos, and even sound and motion.

By mid-1995, an estimated 3.4 million Canadians—17% of the population—were using the Internet. More than one-third of them were surfing on their home computers. Much of the information is free, with most users paying a fee to hook up their computer modem to the Internet.

There's a sense of speed and increasing immediacy with these new technologies. In Halifax, Canada's first public computer network delivered through television cables is 1,000 times faster than conventional telephone lines. Telesat Canada, using its Anik satellites, now beams information through the air at a speed more than 100 times faster than that of traditional modems. Telephone companies are working with fibre optic cables to create faster computer networks.

Speed aside, there is the issue of Internet content. In 1995, a government-appointed advisory council and the federal Canadian Radio-television and Telecommunications Commission (CRTC) urged competition on the information highway and recommended, among other things, that the government move to protect and encourage Canadian content. The government wants to ensure that all Canadians have Internet access, either through free or inexpensive connection services or terminals available in public places in all regions.

Canadian companies are in the forefront of the telecommunications revolution. In 1995, more than 70 Canadian firms had exhibits at the world's largest telecommunications trade show held in Geneva, Switzerland. These companies signed hundreds of deals worth nearly $1 billion. Between 1985 and 1995, Canadian firms increased spending on research and development in this area from less than $80 million to nearly $150 million.

But it's the telephone, invented by Alexander Graham Bell in 1876, that is the grandfather of them all. And it's the telephone that still holds its own as a communications method. Almost 99% of Canadian households have a telephone; that's about 57 phone lines for every 100 Canadians.

In 1993, Canadians spent $5.4 billion in local service charges, and another $6.9 billion on long-distance calls. According to the Organisation for Economic Co-operation and Development (OECD), Canada has the fifth-cheapest basic phone service in the industrialized world.

In addition, increased competition in the telephone business has lowered some long-distance rates for consumers. While phone companies on average were making money in the early 1990s, profits were falling. These firms earned $1.6 billion in 1993, down nearly 10% from the year before.

Companies offering cheaper long-distance rates have not done as well as they had hoped. In 1994, the long-distance carrier Unitel laid off 1,000 workers. Sprint Canada, another long-distance rival of the provincial phone companies, bought out a struggling competitor, STN, the Smart Talk Network. Even Canada's largest telephone company, Bell Canada, planned to cut 10,000 jobs by the end of 1997 and its profits dropped almost by half between 1992 and 1995, partly due to competition in long-distance.

Dial *00

In 1995, residents of Regina became the first in the world to use a voice-activated dialing service that works without speakers and recognizes many words. Callers simply press *00 and speak the name of a business that must subscribe to the service, and the telephone makes the connection. Phone companies are adding services like this to stay ahead of competition from new technologies.

A new breed of devices, called Personal Communications Services (PCS), will allow people to communicate anytime, anywhere. Using a radio frequency, PCS telephones are expected to have all the mobility of cellular phones. They also promise to be cheaper, better-sounding, and capable of sending faxes, e-mail and computer data. Mobile phones that now use satellites work all over North America—unlike conventional cellular phones, which reach only 20% of Canada's land mass.

Almost as fast as it can send information, Canada's telecommunications industry is constantly changing and evolving. Firms must keep up with technology, consumers and regulators to create products and services that will fill a need and boost their bottom line.

Cable Canada

Traditional broadcasting—Canada's 484 radio and 108 television stations—is losing ground as Canadians embrace new media such as the Internet and cable specialty channels.

The biggest money-maker in broadcasting is cable television. In 1994, its net profits more than doubled, reaching $259.5

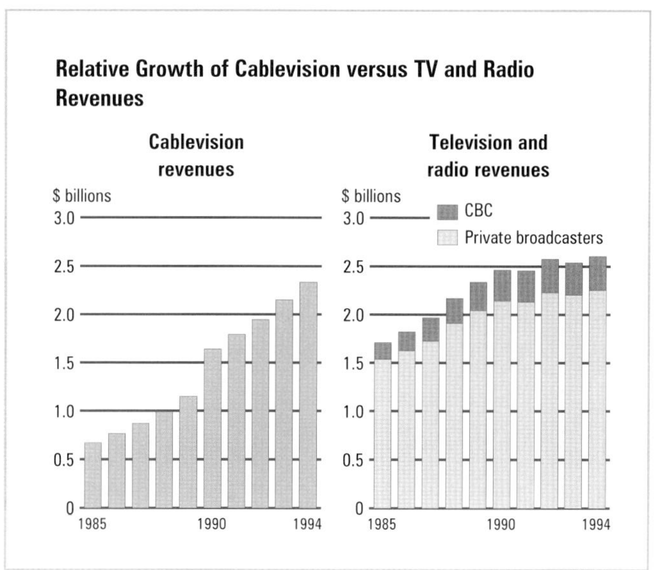

Earth's largest and most spectacular recurring meteor shower, called the Leonids, comes every 33 years, around the 17th of November. The Leonids are named after the constellation Leo since they appear to originate from a point in that constellation. During their last visit in 1966, the Leonids showered about 150,000 bits of sand and ice into our atmosphere, just in one half-hour period, although the spectacle went on for several hours.

In 1999, a repeat performance is expected, but the consequences could be quite dramatic on the relatively new population of satellites in space. Since 1972, when Canada launched Anik A-1, the world's first domestic communications satellite, more than 250 satellites have been launched into orbit.

Current Anik satellites carry dozens of channels, including all of Canada's major TV networks. These channels, in turn, carry data for Canada's electronic banking, credit card verification and airline and travel reservation systems. Some satellites back up land-based communications networks. If the Leonids knock them out, every Canadian would soon know about it.

Damage, should it occur, won't be confined to Canadian satellites. Leonids could also harm the American Hubble space telescope, the Russian space station Mir, and possibly the Space Station Freedom, in which Canada is a partner. Even small meteoroids are destructive. In 1995, a pebble the size of a grain of sand dinged a window on the American shuttle Discovery, causing $100,000 damage. But fortunately, physicists say the odds are against Leonids hitting most of our orbiting space hardware.

Meteoroids can travel at up to 70 kilometres per second, so if they collide with anything, it vaporizes. The resulting plasma cloud carries an electrical charge akin to interplanetary lightning which in turn can overload a spacecraft's electrical circuits.

The Leonids should provide a spectacular show when they arrive, with a possibility of up to 50 meteors a second streaking radially from one spot in the sky in a colourful, cosmic rain. The last such show was over the southwestern United States on November 17, 1966. The next should occur on November 17, 1999, with the best viewing to be had in India and central Europe. It's also likely that the Leonid display will continue into the year 2000, appearing over Canadian and central U.S. skies.

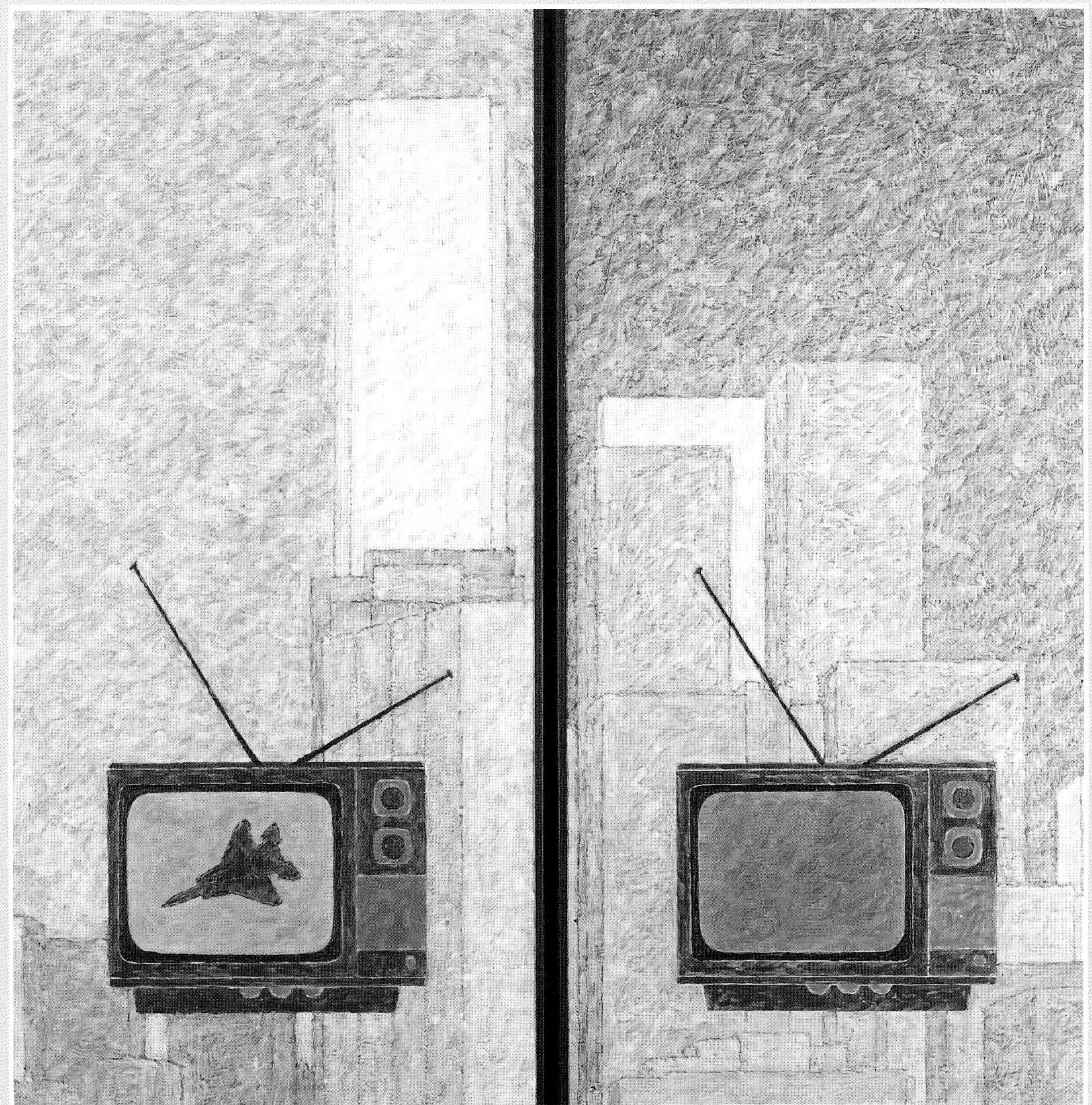

Peter Dykhuis, Carleton University Art Gallery

Simulated Picture.

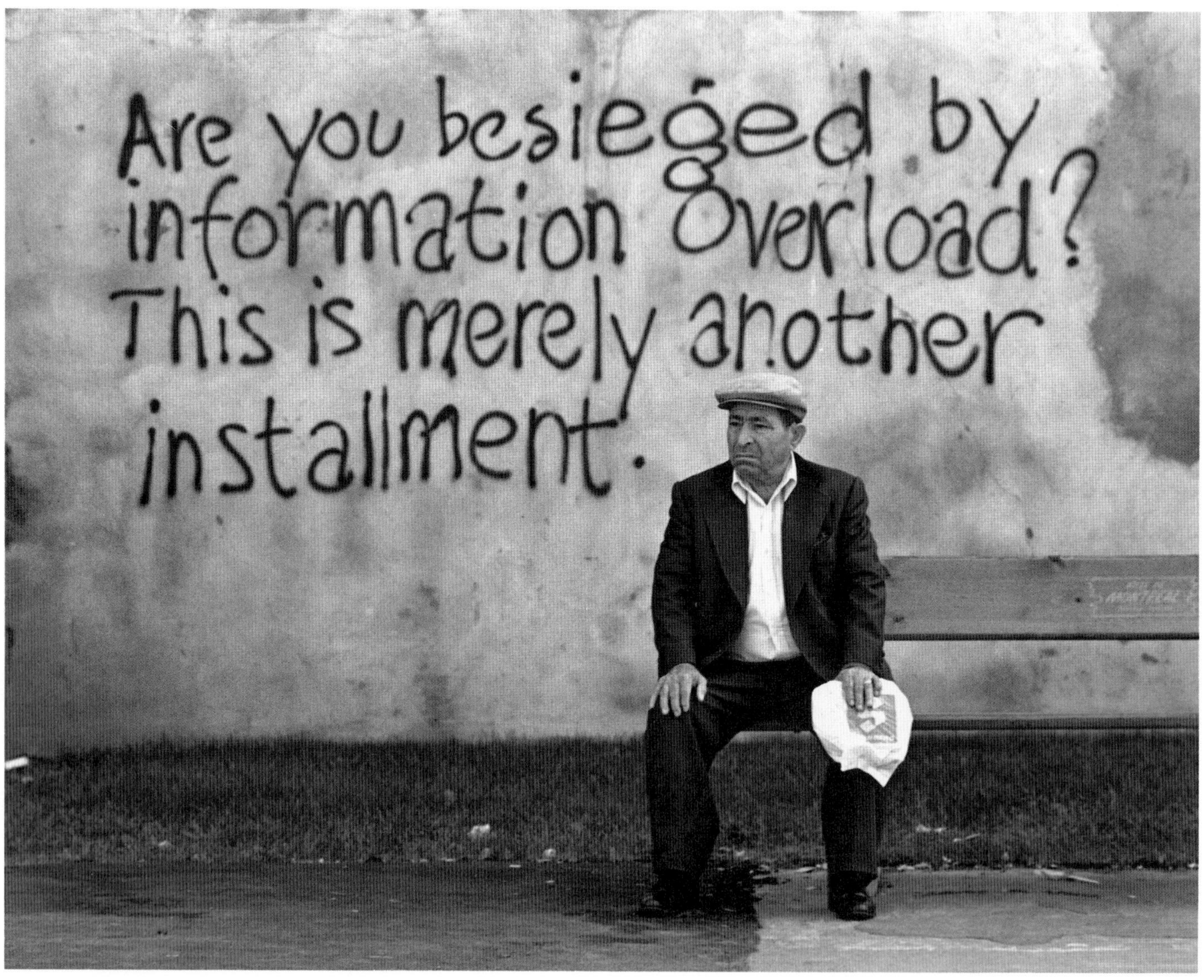

Photo by Andrew Clyde Little

Montreal graffiti.

million. Private television broadcasters headed in the other direction. That year, their profits fell more than one-third. Radio has been in the red for several years. Between 1991 and 1994, Canada's private radio stations lost a total of $156.8 million.

Virtually every Canadian home has a television set (99%), and three-quarters of those homes subscribe to a cable service. Through a cable hooked up to their television set, subscribers receive dozens of channels—both stations normally available for free, and channels showing programs such as movies, music videos, documentaries, current affairs, Parliamentary debates, and sports, that are usually available only through paying a fee to a cable company.

Some cable TV companies plan to switch to digital transmission by late 1996, meaning subscribers will need an electronic box to convert the signals to analog so their TV sets can receive them. The new technology will allow cable TV companies to offer 200 or more channels by the year 2000, compared with the 60 or 70 offered now.

Canadian companies are poised to start offering direct-to-home (DTH) television service. Consumers install a satellite dish on their roof and pay a fee to receive programs directly from the broadcaster. Cable TV companies know they'll face stiff competition from DTH, but they're banking on the strength of their community programming, which DTH does not offer.

New Radio Waves

Canada's private radio stations hope what will put them in the black again is digital radio, a new technology that broadcasts compact disc-quality sound. Listeners must buy new "smart" interactive radios that can pick up the digital signal, and can also display advertisements and information on traffic, weather and songs. A pilot project in 1995 saw successful digital radio transmission in Vancouver, Toronto, Montreal and Ottawa. Until the digital broadcasting takes hold, radio stations say it will be simulcast for several years with AM and FM signals.

But radio stations face competition from pay audio programming. Some radio broadcasters are forming partnerships with cable TV companies who want to use digital satellite technology to transmit compact disc-quality music through cable television and direct-to-home satellites. As the 1997 *Canada Year Book* was going to press, the CRTC was examining proposals from several broadcasters, including the CBC, to offer up to 30 different commercial-free audio channels. Canadians who subscribe to cable TV would pay about $10 a month to receive the channels.

"Canadian Radio for Canada"

Without a public broadcasting system, private radio stations in Canada would "certainly pass into the United States orbit." That's what editorial writers at the Ottawa *Citizen* predicted on June 16, 1936. Later that year, the Canadian Broadcasting Corporation was born. Sixty years later, the CBC is firmly rooted in the Canadian psyche.

But its tenure is increasingly shaky. Federal government cutbacks threaten the corporation. In late 1995, CBC President Perrin Beatty announced the corporation may have to cut as much as $350 million from its budget by the 1997-98 fiscal year. While some of the cuts involved the corporate head office in Ottawa and other administrative staff, $131 million had been earmarked to go from the programming budgets of English and French radio and TV. As many as 1,800 people were to be let go by the end of the 1995-96 fiscal year, with another 1,000 layoffs possible for the following year.

In 1994-95, the CBC's operating budget was more than $1.5 billion. Advertising revenues from its TV networks and its all-news cable channels—Newsworld in English, Le Réseau de l'information in French—increased nearly 3% in 1995. (CBC's radio networks are commercial-free.) CBC is selling more commercials although it's losing viewers to more specialty cable TV channels.

Canadians travelling abroad can hear news from home, thanks to Radio Canada International (RCI), the CBC's international radio network. It beams more than 200 hours of programming a week in eight languages (English, French, Ukrainian, Russian, Arabic, Spanish, Chinese and Creole) to five continents.

About one-third of all RCI Programming is designed for Canadians abroad, often consisting of the CBC's most popular shows at home. RCI also broadcasts news and entertainment (even hockey games) via satellite radio and shortwave for Canada's soldiers and peacekeepers serving in areas such as the former Yugoslavia, the Golan Heights and Somalia.

Benjamin Franklin's Canadian Posting

Benjamin Franklin, the American statesman, scientist and philosopher, is famed for proving that lightning is electricity. Less well known is that he began Canada's postal service.

In 1763, Canada had come under British control. The following year, the British government appointed Franklin Deputy Postmaster General of its colonies in North America, and he became responsible for the newly-acquired territory north of the St. Lawrence River.

As no organized postal system existed, Franklin established post offices in Quebec, Trois Rivières and Montreal, and organized a monthly mail service between Canada, New York and England. He also increased postal service revenue, remitting the money to London, much to the displeasure of the colonists.

Franklin, in fact, sympathized with the colonial people. The British government soon questioned his loyalty and, in 1774, as tensions increased in colonial America, British authorities forced him to resign.

A Letter a Day

Canada's largest retail chain doesn't sell blankets or toothpaste—it sells stamps! Canada Post Corporation has about 18,500 outlets across the country. In 1994-95, the Post Office processed 11.6 billion pieces of mail—that's more than 400 items for every Canadian, and an increase of 700 million pieces from the year before. Despite increased revenues, the corporation lost $69 million that year. Canada Post hopes to turn itself around, aiming for a $26 million profit in 1996.

In 1995, the Post Office raised the cost of a first-class domestic letter by two pennies to 45¢, and increased most other postage rates. Still, Canada Post says the basic letter rate has been kept well below inflation, rising by 43% from 1982 to 1994, while the overall cost of living increased 56% in that time. Canada's domestic letter rate is one of the lowest among major industrialized countries.

Transport

Canada's transportation industry is reinventing itself to compete in the new marketplace. The buzzwords of the 1990s now include "deregulation," "commercialization" and, of course, recession. The government is moving away from its traditional role of operating and subsidizing transportation to focus more on policy development and safety regulation.

In 1995, Canada and the United States signed an "Open Skies" agreement that allows Canadian and American airlines almost unlimited access to cross-border flights between any two cities in the two countries. Canada's airports are changing hands. By late 1995, the government had signed 44 letters of intent with local authorities to commercialize airports. Transport Canada believes the local authorities will upgrade the airports and attract new businesses to the sites.

The government is moving to cut red tape for the transport industry, especially for the railways, which face the toughest regulation in the transport industry. New rules would make it easier for railways to sell uneconomical branch lines to independent operators. In late 1995, the government privatized Canadian National Railways (CN) by selling public shares, the largest such offering in Canadian history. Railways no longer receive subsidies to move western grain to market, paving the way for western trucking companies to ship more grain. Via Rail, Canada's national passenger railway, has faced cuts in subsidies for several years, resulting in pared-down service.

Marine transport is also affected by the government's new approach. In 1995, Transport Canada announced a new marine policy aimed at modernizing the marine transport sector. Plans announced in 1996 include the commercialization of the Great Lakes-St. Lawrence Seaway system, ferry and pilotage services, and the Canadian port system.

Trucking, rail and marine companies shipping goods within and from Atlantic Canada no longer receive subsidies. Instead, the government is giving money to the provinces to upgrade highways and help shippers adjust to the new marketplace.

Transport firms are forging new alliances to ship goods by more than one method, called "intermodal services." Railways are forming partnerships with other railways, marine shippers and trucking firms.

NAFTA

The North American Free Trade Agreement (NAFTA) between Canada, the United States and Mexico has expanded north–south shipping routes by all modes of transport. The value of goods exported to the United States in 1994 jumped at least 23% for each of the four major shipping modes: truck, rail, marine and air. Railways, whose tracks run east–west, have been scrambling to catch up to the truckers, who have the flexibility to travel north–south.

Trucking is key to shipping merchandise to and from the United States, Canada's biggest trading partner. In 1992, truckers moved about 80% of the total value of imports from the United States, and a little more than half the value of goods shipped south of the border. Canadian trucks can now enter Mexico, allowing them to pick up and drop off U.S. freight on the way to and from Mexico. But NAFTA works the other way as well. In 1994, the number of American truckers operating in Canada increased 10%.

Highway 16/5 Illumination
by Tom Wayman

Canadian poet Tom Wayman has written about Free Time in a so-named collection. He captures the feeling of living for "the moments in which we are as free as possible to be ourselves" in this poem called ***Highway 16/5 Illumination:***

South-east of Edmonton, on the road that leads
to Vermilion, Lloydminster, and the
Saskatchewan border
I feel coming into me again like
a song about a man born in the country
the joy of the highway: the long road

that reaches ahead through these wooded rises,
the farms
that spread their fields out around themselves
flat to the sun, the odor of hay filling the cabin
of the car

mile by mile, border after border, horizon
to horizon. The highway stretches away
in all directions, linking and connecting
across an entire continent

and anywhere I point the front wheels
I can go.

DRIVING FACTS

Number of vehicles built in Canada in 1994: 2.2 million.

Total vehicles registered in Canada in 1994: 13 million.

Total kilometres Canadians drove in 1994: 228.6 billion.

Percentage of all Canadian retail activity generated by sales of motor vehicles, parts and associated services in 1993: 27%.

Percentage of all energy consumed throughout a vehicle's life that goes into manufacturing it: 20%.

Number of kilometres Canadians travel in automobiles for every 100 kilometres they travel: 82.

Total length of all highways in Canada, 1991: 879,000 kilometres.

Percentage more than residents of other G-7 countries that Canadians travel in autos: 10%.

Number of tonnes of rubber particles emitted into the atmosphere by tire wear in 1990: 36,650.

Percentage of nitrogen oxides emitted in Canada that autos accounted for in 1990: 17%.

Average fuel efficiency of Canadian auto, 1973: 16 litres per 100 kilometres.

Average fuel efficiency of Canadian autos, 1995: 8 litres per 100 kilometres.

Proportion of urban motor travel that urban transit accounted for in 1994: less than 5%.

Canadian ship captains are realigning their compasses. In 1994, the weight of marine shipments between Mexico and Canada nearly tripled from four years earlier, while marine exports to the United States increased 18% from the year before.

Air Traffic

It's not a made-in-Canada problem. Airlines worldwide suffered during the recession. From 1990 to 1993, scheduled airlines lost more than US$20 billion, according to the International Civil Aviation Organization. In the same period, Canada's major commercial airlines lost more than $2 billion. In 1994, Canadian airlines returned to profitability, earning total net incomes of $142 million.

Canadians love a bargain, and it's showing up in revenues for the charter commercial airlines. While overall passenger traffic decreased in 1993, the number of people flying with charter airlines in search of lower fares jumped 21%.

Scheduled air travel between Canada and the United States declined by 3% in 1994 from the year before. That same year, the number of people taking scheduled flights between Canada and Florida dropped 10%, and there were 15% fewer passengers flying charters to the "Sunshine State." Overnight travel to the United States by all modes of transit has been dropping since December 1991, partly because of the Canadian dollar's falling value against the American dollar.

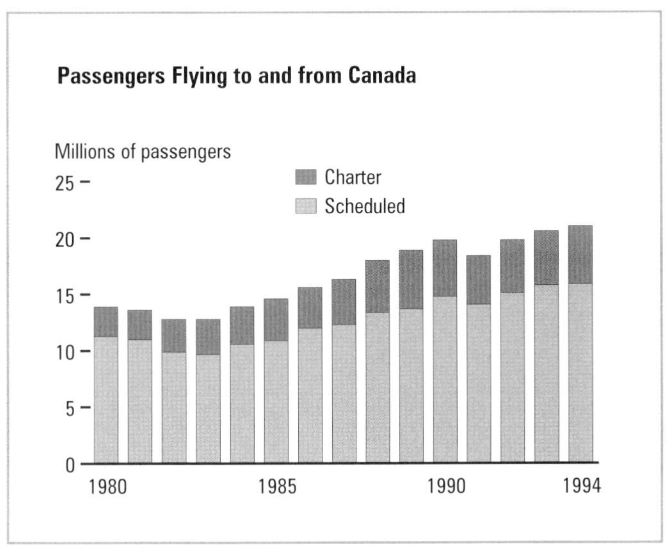

Railway Trips

The railways have been hit hard by the recession, competition from truckers and American railways, and the move away from an economy based on resources to one based on manufacturing and services. Between 1988 and 1993, Canada's railways reduced their work force by nearly one-quarter. During the decade ending in 1995, the share of goods shipped by rail fell 20%.

To compete better, Canada's largest railways, Canadian Pacific (CP) and Canadian National, have abandoned tracks and branch lines that don't fit in to their main operations. Both have created North American systems with U.S. subsidiaries. CN opened a tunnel under the St. Clair River in 1995 to carry trains between Ontario and Michigan, slicing 24 hours off the old travel time.

In 1994, CP enlarged its tunnel under the Detroit River to handle larger freight cars that previously took 12 hours to be shipped by barge between Windsor and Detroit, the threshold crossed by more than one-quarter of the goods shipped between Canada and the United States.

Canadian railways are also making partnerships with trucking firms so that tractor–trailer containers can be loaded onto flatbed cars, offering more flexibility. This intermodal service is key to the railways' marketing strategy and may save both the rail and trucking industries.

In 1995, Canada's railways carried less grain, one of the largest commodities transported by rail. CP Rail attributed the drop in Western grain shipments to cuts in the federal government's Crow subsidy, a subsidy designed to lower railway transportation costs for many western grains on their way to market.

Pudlo Pudlat, National Gallery of Canada, Ottawa. Courtesy of the West Baffin Eskimo Co-operative Ltd., Cape Dorset, N.W.T.

Airplanes in the Settlement.

Since Via Rail drastically reduced services and abandoned some routes in 1990, the railway has been steadily losing passengers. Canadians take just 1% of their overnight trips by rail, compared with 3% by bus, 6% by air, and 88% by car.

Trucking

Trucking's flexibility makes it attractive to manufacturers and wholesalers, and it is grabbing a greater share of Canada's transport market. In 1986, trucking accounted for just over 30% of the transport industry's GDP; by 1994, that had risen to nearly 40%.

Trucking firms are building partnerships with railways, marine shippers, and airlines, to offer faster service on short-haul trips, and door-to-door delivery. Truckers have also been deregulated, and now offer clients warehouse storage and courier services. Despite this diversification, trucking was held back by the recession. The industry's profit margin in 1992 was just 2.4%.

Shipping

Goods shipped through Canada's 2,400 ports and harbours bring in around $2.5 billion in revenues each year. In 1993, Canadian-based for-hire marine carriers made $100 million. Transport Canada is trying to streamline the marine carrier system, saying there are more ports than the traffic can support.

More international traffic is passing through Canadian ports as foreign trade increases, especially natural resources exports. From 1993 to 1995, shipments to and from foreign countries were rising, while traffic within Canada was falling. That's partly because exports to Europe were declining, and so fewer goods such as wheat were shipped eastwards down the St. Lawrence Seaway, using domestic ports. More goods were transported by rail to western ports to be transferred to ships heading to the Pacific Rim. In the first nine months of 1995, Vancouver—Canada's busiest port—accounted for more than one-quarter of international shipments handled at Canadian ports, fuelled by a strong demand for coal in Japan.

Canadian ports also handle trans-shipments, foreign cargoes that pass through Canada en route to or from another country.

Shipwrecked Inland

Hundreds of miles inland from the storms and gales of the Atlantic Ocean, lying at the bottom of the Great Lakes and the St. Lawrence River west of Montreal, are 6,000 known shipwrecks. Most were lost to fires, storms and collisions during the age of sail, the years from 1750 to 1870. As many as 9,000 more lonely wrecks may await discovery, but nobody knows for sure.

Arguably, Canada's most famous shipwreck is the 729-foot freighter ***SS Edmund Fitzgerald****, which went down in Lake Superior on November 10, 1975, in a severe storm. All 29 hands perished. Also lying beneath the waves, in Lake Ontario, are the British warships,* ***Hamilton*** *and* ***Scourge****, both lost in a fierce storm during the War of 1812.*

In 1994, there were more than 1,000 ships plying their trade along the inland waterways of the Great Lakes and the St. Lawrence River. But in the same year, there was only one reported shipwreck, the ***Miss Stephanie II****, which sank in Lake Huron.*

In the first nine months of 1995, trans-shipments of crude petroleum from Europe to the United States helped Port Hawkesbury, Nova Scotia, handle a record 8.4 million tonnes of cargo, nearly double the amount for the same period the year before.

One of Canada's great shipping routes, the St. Lawrence Seaway—a series of locks, canals and rivers that link Lake Ontario and the Gulf of St. Lawrence—is in danger of losing its fleet. Vessels small enough to navigate the river are retiring at an alarming rate. The Crown corporation that administers the route, the St. Lawrence Seaway Authority, is looking for ways to reverse the trend. The Authority estimates that by the year 2000, there will be only 42 vessels in the world that can navigate the Seaway.

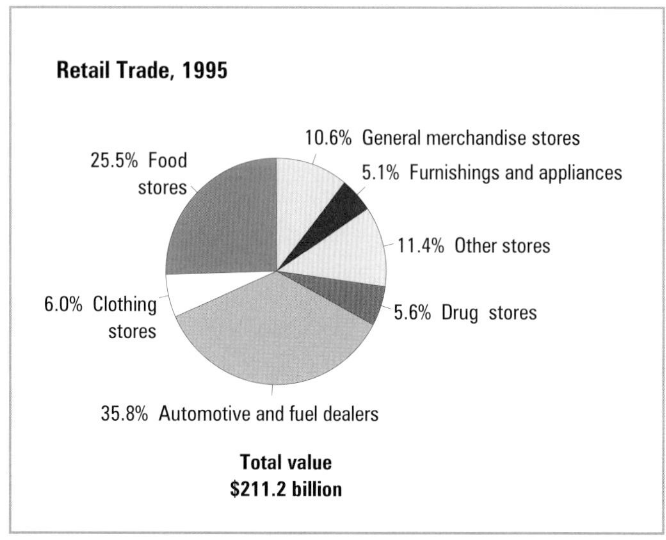

Ridership Down

Fewer Canadians are taking urban transit. From 1992 to 1994, ridership fell nearly 5%. In that same period, revenues fell while expenses rose. In 1994, Canada's urban bus systems travelled more than 776 million kilometres, a 3% increase from 1992. There are public transit systems in at least 84 Canadian cities.

Intercity bus companies have also been losing ridership. In 1994, buses carried 11.4 million people, a slight rebound from the year before, when the number of passengers dropped 27% to 10.9 million. Though 1994 saw a slight increase in ridership, the long-term trend was heading downward. In 1994, these carriers managed to earn a total of $31 million in profits before taxes.

In 1994, the number of employees in the motor carrier passenger industry, which includes urban transit, intercity, school and charter bus companies, fell almost 9%, a loss of more than 5,000 jobs. Almost half of the workers in the industry are employed by urban transit companies.

Trade

In his 1887 catalogue, retail tycoon Timothy Eaton had grand designs to expand his business from his downtown Toronto shop. Of the publication he produced to show Eaton's wares, he boasted: "This catalogue is destined to go wherever the maple leaf grows, throughout this vast dominion."

But the face of retail in Canada is changing. Shopping malls, which squeezed out many streetfront stores and revolutionized retailing in the 1950s and 1960s, are themselves facing a threat: the "big box" stores. These self-serve, warehouse-type stores of 9,000 square metres or more sell everything from groceries, clothes and prescription drugs to stereos and car parts. They can be anywhere from two to 10 times the size of their competition. In 1989, big box stores accounted for just under 3% of all retail sales. By 1994, they had grabbed nearly 8% of the market.

Mergers and buyouts mean survival of the fittest. In 1994 and 1995, there were several big mergers. The American retail giant Wal-Mart bought out Woolco and began converting more than 120 of its Canadian locations to Wal-Mart stores. Canada's two largest booksellers, Coles and SmithBooks, joined forces to form the Chapters chain. The women's clothing chain Reitmans bought out Dalmys.

While the bulk of retail sales comes from independent stores, chain stores have been steadily gaining ground. In 1950,

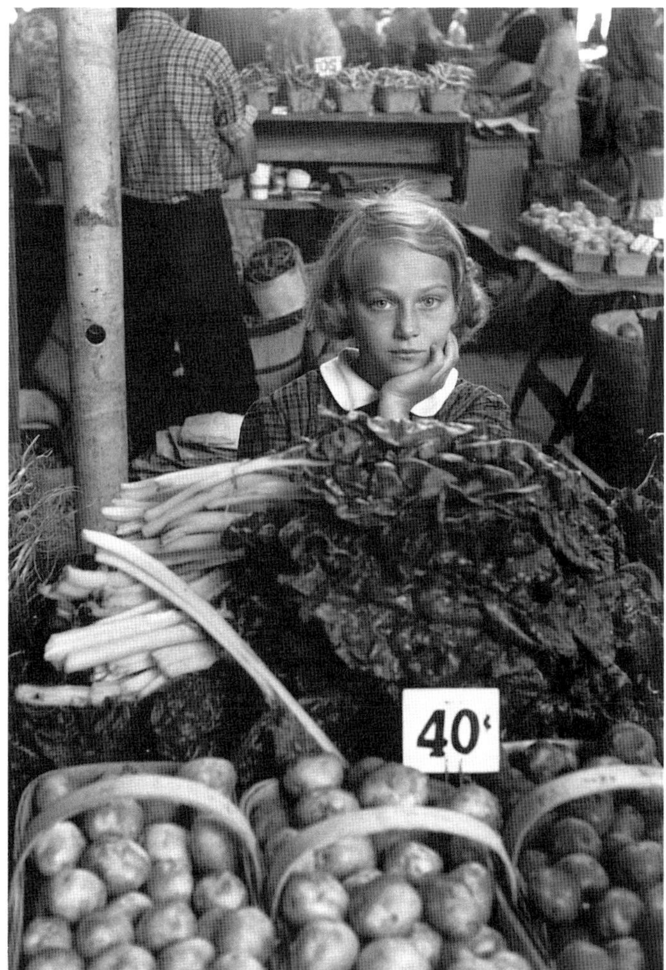

Photo by Michel Lambeth, CMCP

St. Laurence Market, Toronto.

chain stores accounted for around 18% of total retail sales. During the 1990s, their share rose to nearly one-third. Retail chains (firms with four or more stores) have experienced increased sales in the last few years, while department store sales have been falling. In fact, department stores' market share has been dropping steadily since at least 1989.

Even during the lean early 1990s, consumers continued to spend more in retail stores. In 1993, shoppers parted with 5.7% more money than in 1992, spending almost $200 billion. Consumers in British Columbia spent 10% more on retail items than the year before, partly due to an influx of immigrants from outside Canada and the province.

Retailers are threatened not just by their competitors, but by their customers and employees as well. A survey of store owners by the Retail Council of Canada showed that in 1993, people stole $2.25 billion worth of goods from stores. At that time, less than one-quarter of Canadian stores had no budget for loss prevention. But more retailers are installing anti-theft devices such as price tags that set off alarms when a stolen item leaves the store.

The Shoppers

With the swipe of a card, consider it sold. More than 100,000 retailers across the country have direct payment, allowing shoppers to use a machine at the check-out to deduct money from their bank accounts. Every month, Canadians use direct payment about 35 million times. In 1994, shoppers paid for more than $9.4 billion worth of goods and services using bank debit cards, mainly at supermarkets.

Another new trend literally allows people to shop 'til they drop. Retailers are staying open longer, although analysts say sales have not noticeably increased. Stores often stay open later so they don't lose business to competitors. To keep customers coming back, retailers offer another incentive: "loyalty programs" reward shoppers who buy items on a regular basis. Customers earn points to redeem for merchandise or airline tickets, or get an instant discount at the cash register.

When they're shopped out, Canadians can put their feet up and browse mail order catalogues or the Internet. In 1993, the value of goods bought by post increased 12%, to a total of nearly $1 billion. The next year, advertisers spent more than $1 billion on catalogues and direct mail ads, more than on any other medium except daily newspapers and television. Stores are gearing up for competition with retailers selling their wares on the Internet.

In 1993, more than 13% of all payrolls in Canada went to someone working in the retail industry. Store employees tend to be younger and are usually paid less than employees in other industries. In 1994, nearly one-quarter of people with part-time jobs worked in retail. Almost one-third of all retail workers were younger than 24 years of age. Retail employees earned nearly 40% less than the average weekly wages in the rest of the economy.

The Wholesalers

Most of us never see wholesalers, the firms that sell goods to other businesses—including to retailers who, in turn, sell the items to us. But wholesalers are doing a booming trade. Wholesalers and retailers account for 12% of Canada's GDP.

In 1993, wholesaling grew faster than the rest of the Canadian economy, thanks in part to strong imports and exports. Wholesalers earned a record $254 billion in sales that year, a 7.7% increase from 1992. Firms selling machinery, computers, and other equipment boosted sales by nearly 5%, partly due to the fact that Canadian factories and businesses were modernizing their plants and offices with new technology.

Wholesalers in British Columbia increased revenues by 15% in 1993, thanks in part to increased lumber exports. Manitoba firms did 7% more business that year. Analysts say revenues would have been higher if the wheat crop had been better. Wholesalers in the Atlantic region have not recovered from the early 1990s recession, largely due to dwindling fish stocks. Ontario has the lion's share of wholesale trade, accounting for 39% of the country's wholesale business. That's nearly double the second-place province, Quebec, which conducts 22% of Canada's wholesale trade.

Consumers have a watchdog in Industry Canada, which regulates retailers and wholesalers. It enforces consumer protection laws, such as the Competition Act, that can fine retailers hundreds of thousands of dollars for misleading advertising.

SOURCES

Canada Post
Canadian Broadcasting Corporation
Canadian Radio-television and Telecommunications Commission
National Transportation Agency of Canada
Statistics Canada
Transport Canada

FOR FURTHER READING

Selected publications from Statistics Canada

- **Air Passenger Origin and Destination, Canada – United States Report**. Annual. 51-205
- **Rail in Canada**. Annual. 52-216
- **Passenger Bus and Urban Transit Statistics**. 53-215
- **Trucking in Canada**. Annual. 53-222
- **Shipping in Canada**. Annual. 54-205
- **Radio and Television Broadcasting**. Annual. 56-204
- **Cable Television**. Annual. 56-205
- **Retail Chain and Department Stores**. Annual. 63-210
- **Wholesaling and Retailing in Canada**. Annual. 63-236
- **Household Facilities and Equipment**. Annual. 64-202

Selected publications from other sources

- **Annual Report 1994-95**. Canada Post. 1995.
- **Annual Report 1994-95**. Canadian Broadcasting Corporation. 1995.
- **Annual Report 1994-95**. Canadian Cable Television Association. 1995.
- **Canadian Retailer**. Retail Council of Canada. Monthly.

Legend

–	nil or zero	..	not available	x	confidential
--	too small to be expressed	...	not applicable or not appropriate		*(Certain tables may not add due to rounding)*

13.1 GROSS DOMESTIC PRODUCT AT FACTOR COST, COMMUNICATIONS, TRANSPORTATION AND TRADE

	1985	1986	1987	1988	1989	1990	1991	1992	1993	1994	1995
	$ Constant 1986 (millions)										
Communications, transportation and trade	99,222.8	102,991.0	109,363.2	114,625.2	117,596.7	117,048.0	115,176.5	116,693.9	120,942.5	128,889.3	132,009.5
Communications	12,699.9	13,310.6	14,203.9	15,299.2	16,910.6	18,122.0	18,800.9	19,350.8	19,896.1	21,422.0	22,896.4
Telecommunications	10,646.8	11,144.2	12,007.3	13,029.4	14,532.7	15,661.7	16,351.8	16,762.1	17,380.7	18,884.5	20,321.9
Postal and courier service	2,020.8	2,103.7	2,132.9	2,193.8	2,303.0	2,381.8	2,372.6	2,519.7	2,448.4	2,474.1	2,512.6
Non-business sector radio and television broadcasting	65.0	62.7	63.7	75.9	74.9	78.5	76.4	69.1	67.0	63.4	61.9
Transportation and storage	21,816.7	22,186.8	23,621.7	24,759.8	24,460.1	23,862.3	22,837.5	23,307.7	23,940.2	25,156.4	25,611.9
Transportation	17,033.7	17,493.1	18,538.8	19,296.8	18,955.2	18,417.2	17,267.1	17,406.5	17,669.6	18,686.9	19,077.7
Air transport and related services	2,810.7	2,921.4	2,867.2	3,005.3	2,888.1	2,581.3	1,997.6	2,068.2	1,981.4	2,028.9	2,103.9
Railway transport and related services	3,711.6	3,916.6	4,008.6	4,251.6	4,014.3	3,958.1	4,127.4	4,229.7	4,382.3	4,815.2	4,851.4
Water transport and related services	1,274.6	1,298.3	1,463.3	1,513.7	1,328.2	1,292.7	1,167.4	1,050.6	1,051.9	1,087.5	1,155.4
Truck transport	5,262.7	5,384.9	6,085.2	6,418.4	6,422.1	6,308.9	6,101.8	6,279.0	6,552.1	7,021.4	7,196.4
Other transportation	4,005.1	3,971.9	4,114.5	4,107.9	4,302.6	4,276.3	3,872.8	3,778.9	3,701.9	3,733.9	3,770.6
Pipeline transport	2,134.7	2,126.1	2,389.5	2,797.8	2,870.9	2,913.6	3,074.7	3,446.8	3,731.0	3,961.4	4,127.0
Storage and warehousing	605.7	634.7	731.7	661.5	577.0	592.1	628.7	565.3	593.5	632.7	629.6
Non-business sector transportation	2,053.2	1,932.9	1,961.7	2,003.6	2,057.0	1,939.4	1,867.0	1,889.0	1,946.1	1,875.4	1,777.6
Other utility industries	15,565.2	15,912.2	16,476.8	16,739.6	16,501.6	15,733.5	16,554.9	16,407.5	16,832.2	17,584.3	17,593.2
Electric power systems	12,721.5	13,165.8	13,773.7	13,844.5	13,407.5	12,679.1	13,361.2	13,149.7	13,446.9	14,082.3	14,035.3
Gas distribution systems	1,817.5	1,653.0	1,558.6	1,696.2	1,783.8	1,709.2	1,855.3	1,927.2	2,022.1	2,066.5	2,153.2
Non-business sector water systems	680.0	714.2	721.3	735.8	765.8	785.9	781.3	800.7	813.9	828.4	812.2
Other utility industries	378.9	379.2	423.3	463.2	544.5	559.3	557.1	529.9	549.3	607.1	592.5
Wholesale trade	21,765.8	23,312.0	25,131.6	26,971.7	28,111.3	28,435.0	27,691.6	27,984.5	29,519.0	32,211.1	33,097.3
Retail trade	27,375.2	28,269.4	29,929.2	30,854.9	31,613.1	30,895.2	29,291.6	29,643.4	30,755.0	32,515.5	32,810.7

Source: Statistics Canada, CANSIM, matrix 4670.

13.2 PRIVATE AND PUBLIC INVESTMENT,[1] COMMUNICATIONS, TRANSPORTATION AND TRADE

	1991	1992	1993	1994	1995	1996[2]
			$ Millions			
Private and public investment in Canada	128,010.0	122,188.8	121,253.9	130,131.2	127,956.1	126,009.4
Communications, transportation and trade	29,008.0	26,882.5	24,108.5	22,549.0	24,103.5	24,351.4
Communications industries	5,884.2	6,274.8	5,602.4	5,251.0	5,095.9	5,584.7
Telecommunications broadcasting	621.2	637.0	657.6	701.5	853.6	1,029.2
Telecommunications carriers	4,972.1	5,328.7	4,686.4	4,344.3	4,075.7	4,275.2
Other telecommunications industries	x	22.7	28.9	46.4	23.4	25.7
Postal and courier service	x	286.4	229.5	158.8	143.2	254.6
Transportation industries	3,992.9	2,925.1	2,707.4	3,607.0	4,202.2	4,566.0
Air transport	1,843.5	923.7	636.0	1,003.6	1,027.8	742.6
Railway transport	473.8	539.4	651.0	656.6	950.4	1,145.5
Water transport	262.1	373.8	229.8	233.1	329.5	463.1
Truck transport	351.9	416.1	434.7	709.2	624.0	502.8
Public passenger transit	740.7	612.1	703.2	786.5	886.7	1,243.5
Other transportation industries	0.0	15.1	9.0	7.3	7.9	8.6
Services incidental to transportation	35.1	44.9	43.7	210.7	376.0	459.8
Pipelines	2,546.2	2,431.9	2,046.5	2,081.2	1,766.7	1,275.6
Storage and warehousing	152.8	139.7	169.2	182.2	188.8	248.7
Grain elevators	108.4	94.7	142.9	138.2	110.8	189.8
Other storage and warehousing industries	44.3	45.0	26.3	44.0	78.0	58.9
Other utilities	13,808.6	12,807.2	10,662.7	8,417.0	8,775.4	8,815.7
Electric power	11,826.3	10,917.4	8,723.3	6,493.7	6,428.5	5,983.7
Gas distribution	775.0	898.5	970.8	953.1	981.5	942.7
Water systems	978.2	789.7	738.3	808.9	1,116.3	1,633.0
Other utilities	229.2	201.6	230.2	161.3	249.2	256.3
Trade	5,169.5	4,735.7	4,966.8	5,091.8	5,841.2	5,136.3
Wholesale trade	1,751.1	1,995.7	1,911.2	1,826.6	2,533.8	2,615.1
Retail trade	3,418.4	2,740.0	3,055.6	3,265.2	3,307.4	2,521.2
			%			
Investment in communications, transportation and trade as a percentage of total investment	22.7	22.0	19.9	17.3	18.8	19.3

1. Excludes repair expenditures.
2. Intentions.

Source: Statistics Canada, CANSIM, matrices 3105, 3106, and 3107.

13.3 EMPLOYMENT, COMMUNICATIONS, TRANSPORTATION AND TRADE

	1985	1986	1987	1988	1989	1990	1991	1992	1993	1994	1995	Average annual growth rate 1985-1995
	Employees[1] '000											%
All industries[2]	9,651.1	9,927.2	10,329.1	10,659.0	11,054.7	11,146.1	10,549.5	10,246.9	10,271.4	10,447.1	10,673.6	0.9
Transportation, communication and other utilities	833.8	834.4	836.1	851.5	886.0	902.2	860.4	851.5	841.3	849.9	849.1	0.2
Transportation and storage	474.0	471.9	468.1	475.8	495.5	502.9	462.9	456.4	455.0	458.5	455.3	-0.4
Transportation	451.4	450.5	447.2	453.7	471.6	481.4	441.7	433.4	431.1	434.6	430.8	-0.4
Air transport	45.0	47.8	49.2	53.6	58.3	61.0	55.5	52.8	50.5	52.9	53.0	1.5
Services incidental to air transport	6.7	7.3	8.1	7.6	7.6	7.2	6.3	5.6	5.8	8.2	7.9	1.5
Railway transport and related services	91.1	88.3	79.1	76.3	73.0	68.6	63.9	62.5	59.6	57.3	53.2	-4.8
Water transport	18.2	18.2	17.4	18.7	18.8	17.0	16.4	14.1	14.3	15.3	18.1	-0.1
Services incidental to water transport	10.7	10.2	11.0	10.3	10.7	10.5	9.8	9.0	10.4	11.6	11.7	0.8
Truck transport	140.6	136.5	139.4	142.7	150.8	144.9	127.3	127.2	127.7	131.4	135.8	-0.3
Public passenger transit systems	61.3	65.7	67.9	70.2	73.0	85.1	81.2	83.0	83.1	76.4	70.6	1.3
Other transportation	77.8	76.6	75.1	74.3	79.4	87.2	81.2	79.1	79.7	81.4	80.5	0.3
Pipeline transport	7.9	7.9	7.7	8.1	8.4	9.0	8.7	8.9	8.3	8.1	7.9	0.0
Storage and warehousing	14.7	13.4	13.2	14.0	15.5	12.5	12.5	14.0	15.5	15.8	16.6	1.1
Communication and other utilities	359.8	362.5	368.0	375.7	390.5	399.3	397.6	395.2	386.3	391.4	393.8	0.8
Communication	246.3	249.1	251.7	254.9	265.2	267.5	262.8	259.7	252.2	258.4	264.9	0.7
Telecommunication broadcasting	38.3	39.9	38.2	37.6	42.0	40.8	39.5	40.6	41.8	41.7	40.9	0.6
Telecommunication carriers	109.3	109.4	111.8	112.6	121.9	124.3	122.4	119.1	105.6	108.8	113.7	0.4
Other telecommunication	2.6	2.8	2.6	2.6	2.8	2.8	2.6	2.6	1.9	1.8	1.9	-2.8
Postal and courier service	96.0	97.1	99.1	102.2	98.6	99.6	98.2	97.5	102.9	106.0	108.3	1.1
Utilities (electric power, gas, water)	113.5	113.4	116.3	120.9	125.3	131.8	134.8	135.5	134.1	133.0	128.9	1.2
Electric power systems	82.3	82.1	83.8	86.6	88.8	94.6	97.6	98.4	95.0	90.8	87.7	0.6
Gas distribution systems	12.3	12.4	12.8	12.8	13.5	14.2	14.8	15.3	15.9	15.8	16.0	2.4
Water systems	8.4	8.5	8.5	8.4	8.5	8.8	8.9	8.7	8.7	8.7	8.2	-0.2
Other utilities	10.4	10.4	11.2	13.0	14.5	14.2	13.6	13.0	14.5	17.8	17.1	4.6
Trade	1,799.5	1,850.3	1,935.9	1,990.3	2,053.7	2,155.5	2,005.8	1,934.5	1,949.0	1,958.1	2,033.2	1.1
Wholesale trade	542.0	545.9	571.1	591.3	619.5	637.8	613.2	601.6	594.7	608.2	648.4	1.6
Farm products	13.3	16.0	15.6	14.5	16.3	19.2	17.6	15.6	10.9	11.1	11.1	-1.6
Petroleum products	28.6	24.2	23.0	25.2	25.2	27.9	26.3	26.2	27.8	26.1	25.1	-1.2
Food, beverage, drug and tobacco	85.3	86.7	90.8	93.9	97.1	96.4	95.8	98.2	94.8	93.5	99.3	1.4
Apparel and dry goods	23.0	25.2	21.6	24.5	19.5	20.2	18.3	20.2	15.4	16.7	19.2	-1.6
Household goods	18.2	19.8	21.7	18.9	22.5	18.6	16.7	20.5	19.0	19.2	16.6	-0.8
Motor vehicles, parts and accessories	55.3	56.4	61.0	58.6	65.1	60.9	59.1	55.7	57.7	57.2	64.2	1.4
Metals, hardware and building materials	93.9	97.2	101.9	107.8	113.7	114.6	100.3	100.5	97.8	103.2	111.1	1.5
Machinery, equipment and supplies	165.9	167.8	179.3	182.9	188.6	204.7	205.7	182.7	182.6	190.2	205.1	1.9
Other wholesale products	58.5	52.7	56.2	65.0	71.5	75.3	73.4	82.0	88.7	91.0	96.7	4.7
Retail trade	1,257.5	1,304.3	1,364.8	1,399.1	1,434.2	1,517.7	1,392.6	1,332.9	1,354.3	1,350.0	1,384.7	0.9
Food, beverage and drug	361.0	372.3	401.7	420.4	428.9	468.3	427.8	401.8	436.2	451.3	472.3	2.5
Shoes, apparel, fabric and yarn	121.5	131.2	143.8	150.0	153.5	160.4	140.4	130.7	127.0	132.4	136.9	1.1
Household furniture, appliances and furnishing	81.8	88.7	89.0	86.6	90.0	88.8	87.6	74.5	76.7	77.0	74.9	-0.8
Automotive vehicles, parts and accessories, sales and service	301.1	312.6	321.6	330.1	348.0	367.7	316.5	316.5	313.1	304.4	307.9	0.2
General retail merchandising	218.4	223.5	220.0	217.5	220.9	217.9	226.7	210.5	191.7	183.1	184.0	-1.5
Other retail stores	173.8	176.1	188.7	194.5	192.8	214.5	193.7	198.8	209.6	201.9	208.8	1.7
	% of total employment											
Transportation, communication and other utilities	8.6	8.4	8.1	8.0	8.0	8.1	8.2	8.3	8.2	8.1	8.0	...
Trade	18.6	18.6	18.7	18.7	18.6	19.3	19.0	18.9	19.0	18.7	19.0	...

1. Excludes owners or partners of unincorporated business and professional practices, the self-employed, unpaid family workers, persons working outside Canada, military personnel and casual workers for whom a T4 is not required.
2. Excludes agriculture, fishing and trapping, private household services, religious organizations and the military.

Source: Statistics Canada, Catalogue no. 72F0002.

13.4 EMPLOYMENT, COMMUNICATIONS, TRANSPORTATION AND TRADE, CANADA, THE PROVINCES AND TERRITORIES, 1995

	Canada	Nfld.	P.E.I.	N.S.	N.B.	Que.	Ont.	Man.	Sask.	Alta.	B.C.	Y.T.	N.W.T.
							Employees[1] '000						
All industries[2]	10,673.6	147.8	43.4	299.5	240.4	2,574.0	4,180.9	404.6	314.0	1,041.8	1,392.1	12.0	23.2
Goods-producing industries	2438.2	27.9	7.9	58.4	55.2	621.9	1028.8	76.4	51.2	225.9	279.3	1.7	3.7
Logging and forestry	66.5	1.8	x	2.4	4.8	14.8	9.7	..	1.0	2.5	28.7	x	x
Mining, quarrying and oil wells	128.9	2.5	..	3.5	3.1	14.0	21.0	3.4	8.9	58.5	12.0	x	x
Manufacturing	1,675.9	11.6	4.0	36.8	31.7	463.6	798.6	53.2	24.9	92.4	158.6	x	x
Construction	437.9	9.0	3.4	12.8	12.0	95.3	149.2	13.1	11.8	60.2	69.1	0.7	1.4
Service-producing industries	8,174.9	119.0	35.3	239.9	184.3	1,935.9	3,129.5	326.4	261.5	810.1	1,103.4	10.2	19.4
Transportation, communication and other utilities	849.1	13.8	2.9	22.0	22.3	208.8	295.2	43.1	29.3	86.7	121.2	1.3	2.5
Transportation and storage	455.3	6.2	1.9	10.8	12.8	109.0	142.5	26.2	16.0	51.0	76.7	0.7	1.5
Communication and other utilities	393.8	7.5	1.1	11.2	9.5	99.9	152.7	16.9	13.2	35.7	44.6	0.6	1.0
Trade	2,033.2	30.3	7.8	59.1	47.6	483.9	788.0	74.5	65.6	204.6	267.3	1.5	2.9
Wholesale trade	648.4	6.2	1.9	15.2	12.7	160.5	259.9	24.3	21.1	65.6	80.2	..	..
Retail trade	1,384.7	24.1	5.9	43.9	34.9	323.4	528.2	50.2	44.5	139.0	187.1	..	..
Finance, insurance, and real estate	641.5	6.2	1.9	16.2	10.0	144.6	276.2	24.7	21.0	56.3	82.9	..	1.1
Community, business and personal services	4,091.7	55.0	17.3	116.3	85.8	968.8	1,570.2	162.9	127.6	408.5	566.9	4.5	7.9

1. Excludes owners or partners of unincorporated business and professional practices, the self-employed, unpaid family workers, persons working outside Canada, military personnel and casual workers for whom a T4 is not required.
2. Excludes agriculture, fishing and trapping, private household services, religious organizations and the military.

Source: Statistics Canada, Catalogue no. 72F0002.

13.5 EARNINGS, COMMUNICATIONS, TRANSPORTATION AND TRADE

	1985	1986	1987	1988	1989	1990	1991	1992	1993	1994	1995	Earnings in 1995 as a % of all industry earnings
	Average weekly earnings[1]											
	$											%
All industries[2]	412.0	424.3	440.3	459.8	483.3	505.1	528.6	547.0	556.8	567.1	572.5	100.0
Transportation, storage, communication and other utilities	540.4	556.6	573.7	596.3	619.7	641.2	680.6	701.3	709.5	716.8	729.5	127.4
Transportation and storage	516.6	530.0	544.5	574.5	590.6	605.5	639.4	653.0	664.3	675.5	689.2	120.4
Transportation	514.4	526.5	540.9	571.7	590.1	601.4	634.8	647.1	659.3	670.5	684.3	119.5
Air transport	591.9	598.3	612.5	644.7	669.8	719.7	769.3	800.0	757.6	755.2	788.8	137.8
Services incidental to air transport	482.9	481.9	474.0	520.7	524.8	552.5	527.5	547.5	604.6	535.9	594.3	103.8
Railway transport and related services	588.3	627.7	631.4	695.1	725.5	770.3	820.8	844.2	890.4	911.5	940.7	164.3
Water transport	562.3	554.0	590.8	650.2	673.3	684.9	710.6	741.7	802.4	798.5	795.6	139.0
Services incidental to water transport	718.5	722.5	764.0	787.3	839.0	797.6	814.8	828.6	874.7	840.5	856.5	149.6
Truck transport	482.0	479.0	498.1	528.8	541.4	544.1	555.2	570.5	582.0	590.6	599.6	104.7
Public passenger transit systems	458.6	466.7	487.1	484.8	515.9	509.2	545.8	542.0	552.7	573.4	589.5	103.0
Other transportation	449.2	472.8	489.6	512.4	520.9	535.4	582.0	592.6	609.5	631.5	630.9	110.2
Pipeline transport	721.6	757.5	782.7	825.6	852.7	879.3	926.1	983.1	1,019.7	1,029.2	1,073.7	187.6
Storage and warehousing	472.6	513.2	529.5	519.4	464.4	566.2	600.6	623.5	610.7	630.1	634.7	110.9
Communication and other utilities	571.7	591.1	610.8	624.0	656.6	686.2	728.6	757.1	762.7	765.1	776.2	135.6
Communication	530.5	548.7	562.5	566.3	603.0	621.8	654.2	679.6	678.5	683.5	697.4	121.8
Telecommunication broadcasting	511.7	521.6	550.5	571.7	601.0	650.9	681.5	708.5	786.0	776.9	817.2	142.7
Telecommunication carriers	604.9	633.5	651.7	650.7	702.4	727.4	771.3	804.5	809.1	823.2	839.0	146.6
Other telecommunication	558.8	557.5	590.8	618.1	659.3	691.7	706.1	751.7	650.9	621.9	636.6	111.2
Postal and courier service	452.6	464.1	465.8	470.0	479.5	476.2	495.9	513.1	501.3	504.4	504.7	88.2
Utilities (electric power, gas, water)	661.1	684.1	715.4	745.6	769.9	816.9	873.5	905.6	921.1	923.5	937.9	163.8
Electric power systems	706.8	729.0	766.7	801.3	824.4	870.8	934.4	966.6	988.6	1,001.7	1,021.3	178.4
Gas distribution systems	597.4	621.9	642.5	666.8	707.0	748.9	793.4	837.3	855.7	866.1	859.1	150.1
Water systems	538.4	556.3	574.5	601.8	635.5	662.1	696.3	734.9	755.8	768.8	786.4	137.4
Other utilities	474.4	508.2	522.0	546.0	573.4	622.5	639.2	637.9	650.0	650.9	656.9	114.7
Trade	307.8	321.6	329.2	342.2	360.4	375.5	391.1	401.2	409.4	422.1	431.7	75.4
Wholesale trade	433.2	457.0	470.1	487.4	516.8	538.8	557.6	579.2	590.9	605.6	622.1	108.7
Farm products	382.7	413.1	449.2	443.5	445.6	387.6	475.7	485.8	438.5	481.0	521.0	91.0
Petroleum products	534.1	540.7	523.2	589.9	698.3	682.0	553.8	588.0	611.9	626.9	646.0	112.8
Food, beverage, drug and tobacco	428.5	450.7	450.6	450.4	459.8	492.9	514.9	526.6	545.6	576.8	560.9	98.0
Apparel and dry goods	378.8	437.1	445.1	431.9	485.6	471.0	489.5	500.7	467.8	527.0	496.8	86.8
Household goods	419.4	426.7	458.8	495.1	485.5	548.0	580.2	587.1	606.2	587.9	615.2	107.5
Motor vehicles, parts and accessories	433.9	442.7	477.0	502.9	527.1	550.5	551.1	575.4	591.7	589.7	612.4	107.0
Metals, hardware and building materials	401.3	417.6	436.9	441.3	483.6	498.4	523.0	540.7	536.3	547.5	573.4	100.2
Machinery, equipment and supplies	472.9	505.1	518.9	554.3	590.6	610.5	632.3	664.9	680.3	689.6	710.4	124.1
Other wholesale products	365.6	397.5	396.9	404.0	413.7	455.9	488.9	533.5	545.4	562.4	591.5	103.3
Retail trade	253.7	264.9	270.3	280.8	292.9	306.9	317.8	320.8	329.7	339.5	342.5	59.8
Food, beverage and drug	258.2	262.7	266.1	275.3	277.5	286.3	299.7	302.3	306.8	316.8	315.3	55.1
Shoes, apparel, fabric and yarn	207.8	218.3	220.5	226.4	230.3	240.9	253.8	249.7	258.6	266.3	262.5	45.9
Household furniture, appliances and furnishing	286.2	288.5	307.1	331.0	347.9	368.8	374.1	389.2	396.3	401.8	396.0	69.2
Automotive vehicles, parts and accessories, sales and service	296.7	319.6	326.8	341.1	372.6	393.8	416.0	409.8	425.8	446.9	457.0	79.8
General retail merchandising	222.0	229.3	233.1	239.7	241.2	259.9	260.0	271.8	280.6	278.8	279.7	48.9
Other retail stores	226.5	240.8	246.6	256.3	266.6	274.0	285.8	289.5	297.2	307.6	323.7	56.5

1. Excludes owners or partners of unincorporated business and professional practices, the self-employed, unpaid family workers, persons working outside Canada, military personnel and casual workers for whom a T4 is not required.
2. Excludes agriculture, fishing and trapping, private household services, religious organizations and the military.

Source: Statistics Canada, Catalogue no. 72F0002.

13.6 PRIVATE TELEVISION

	1988	1989	1990	1991	1992	1993	1994
				$ '000			
Operating revenues	1,188,057	1,275,978	1,364,988	1,377,788	1,460,496	1,464,467	1,490,061
Sales of air time	1,092,079	1,170,392	1,248,382	1,262,736	1,341,424	1,329,877	1,370,898
Local time sales	303,362	320,283	340,182	325,037	337,207	347,145	356,888
National time sales	613,907	665,167	734,069	750,850	787,570	796,530	788,773
Network time sales	174,810	184,942	174,131	186,849	216,647	186,202	225,236
Production and other	95,978	105,586	116,606	115,052	119,072	134,590	119,163
Operating expenses	1,069,990	1,206,634	1,374,221	1,394,013	1,407,197	1,386,806	1,413,233
Program	612,639	696,641	774,164	789,973	800,899	791,133	820,885
Technical services	62,757	71,116	74,084	70,164	71,865	71,566	71,520
Sales and promotion	120,262	135,806	149,799	147,222	148,085	156,002	154,202
Administration and general	187,659	200,150	226,131	223,063	220,131	212,367	220,629
Depreciation	46,739	51,027	54,499	54,068	55,709	54,992	56,066
Interest expense	39,934	51,894	95,544	109,523	110,508	100,746	89,930

Source: Statistics Canada, CANSIM, matrix 1810.

13.7 CABLE TELEVISION[1]

	1988	1989	1990	1991	1992	1993	1994
				$ '000			
Operating revenue	989,509	1,153,586	1,356,621	1,477,612	1,588,093	1,680,976	1,763,119
Operating expenses	805,471	931,761	1,173,569	1,298,424	1,342,858	1,497,559	1,538,734
Program origination	55,920	54,413	61,371	63,269	68,389	75,145	80,205
Technical services	243,295	309,573	448,611	504,995	532,011	539,885	567,563
Sales and promotion	36,165	40,051	45,286	42,512	43,990	44,929	49,662
Administration and general	235,165	259,822	296,915	298,574	322,359	343,440	357,545
Depreciation	148,542	166,708	197,815	232,907	242,841	265,720	275,713
Interest expense	86,384	101,194	123,571	156,167	133,268	228,440	208,045
				'000			
Number of subscribers	6,559	6,886	7,121	7,286	7,279	7,465	7,664
Households wired for cable service	8,344	8,770	9,097	9,241	9,270	9,514	9,722
				Km '000			
Cable length	138	146	153	157	168	169	180

1. All cable television systems licensed to operate in Canada by the CRTC are included. Master antenna television and pay television (such as First Choice or Superchannel) are not included.

Source: Statistics Canada, Catalogue no. 56-205.

13.8 CANADIAN AIR CARRIERS,[1] OPERATING REVENUES AND EXPENSES

	1988	1989	1990	1991	1992	1993	1994
				$ '000			
Operating revenues	7,136,850	7,860,686	8,271,245	7,602,801	7,548,389	7,535,257	8,376,995
Scheduled services	5,562,090	6,024,095	6,412,344	5,909,761	5,884,911	5,792,261	6,335,497
Passenger	4,957,333	5,413,265	5,765,908	5,299,925	5,280,370	5,180,855	5,705,202
Goods	604,757	610,830	646,436	609,836	604,540	611,406	630,294
Charter services	1,244,815	1,439,352	1,508,799	1,389,527	1,395,349	1,439,459	1,715,004
Passenger	1,079,129	1,269,029	1,332,238	1,232,354	1,239,915	1,237,154	1,485,332
Goods	165,686	170,324	176,561	157,173	155,434	202,305	229,671
Other flying services	41,806	45,129	37,319	46,172	33,389	55,796	66,743
Subsidies	4,285	4,743	6,077	5,350	6,185	2,481	1,227
Net incidental air transport related revenue	283,854	347,367	306,706	251,992	228,556	245,260	258,524
Operating expenses	6,879,902	7,777,510	8,273,002	7,852,869	7,784,349	7,548,483	7,965,126
Ground maintenance	96,693	110,012	107,880	98,130	185,543	177,787	224,037
Aircraft operations	2,375,143	2,827,637	3,029,675	2,771,063	2,678,847	2,703,104	2,879,241
Flight equipment maintenance	870,697	994,609	1,013,588	944,668	876,847	908,318	1,024,537
General services and administration	3,228,863	3,539,597	3,799,126	3,672,522	3,694,920	3,396,622	3,474,444
Depreciation	308,507	305,656	322,734	366,487	348,192	362,651	362,867

1. Level I-IV air carriers which, in each of the two calendar years immediately preceding the report year, realized annual gross revenues of $250,000 or more, transported 5,000 or more revenue passengers, or transported 1,000 or more tonnes of revenue goods.

Source: Statistics Canada, Catalogue no. 51-206.

13.9 CANADIAN AIR CARRIERS, OPERATING STATISTICS[1]

	1988	1989	1990	1991	1992	1993	1994
All air carriers							
Number of passengers ('000)	35,987	37,199	36,777	31,779	32,202	31,483	32,868
Cargo and mail carried (tonnes)	629,701	661,886	656,076	624,668	618,833	653,656	683,873
Passenger-kilometres ('000)	63,757,233	68,417,945	66,758,636	58,077,168	62,189,539	60,752,162	65,739,524
Goods tonne-kilometres ('000)	1,611,937	1,703,068	1,740,747	1,573,257	1,497,977	1,646,141	1,798,669
Hours flown ('000)	2,051	2,241	2,254	2,092	2,046	1,989	2,102
Scheduled services							
Number of passengers ('000)	30,176	30,734	30,351	26,105	26,254	25,348	26,110
Cargo and mail carried (tonnes)	471,813	490,865	500,764	479,075	474,519	522,326	516,712
Passenger-kilometres ('000)	48,737,033	50,390,650	50,117,748	42,774,558	45,069,463	43,887,217	47,196,369
Goods tonne-kilometres ('000)	1,389,474	1,462,549	1,560,326	1,403,829	1,410,503	1,564,809	1,661,866
Hours flown ('000)	1,153	1,256	1,278	1,193	1,238	1,167	1,193
Charter services							
Number of passengers ('000)	5,812	6,465	6,427	5,674	5,949	6,135	6,758
Cargo and mail carried (tonnes)	157,888	171,021	155,313	145,593	144,314	131,330	167,161
Passenger-kilometres ('000)	15,020,200	18,027,295	16,640,889	15,302,610	17,120,076	16,864,946	18,543,155
Goods tonne-kilometres ('000)	222,463	240,519	180,420	169,427	87,474	81,332	136,803
Hours flown ('000)	898	985	977	899	808	823	908

1. Levels I-IV.

Source: Statistics Canada, Catalogue no. 51-206.

13.10 RAILWAY CARRIERS, REVENUES AND EXPENSES

	1986	1987	1988	1989	1990	1991	1992	1993	1994
					$'000				
Operating revenues	7,570,483	7,899,255	8,003,139	7,446,645	7,068,378	7,156,652	6,909,544	6,992,827	7,510,192
Freight transportation	6,216,841	6,562,532	6,571,037	6,084,497	5,993,115	6,184,085	5,930,457	5,959,792	6,584,631
Passenger transportation	250,025	244,741	276,843	317,552	219,130	154,985	158,639	168,592	180,033
Services to VIA	243,327	181,447	145,142	129,174	84,976	67,472	67,434	65,474	62,874
Government payments	649,573	705,643	764,015	653,387	515,043	491,038	498,148	499,796	434,418
Other revenue	210,717	204,892	246,102	262,035	256,114	259,072	254,866	299,173	248,236
Expenses	6,787,364	6,838,334	6,979,010	7,080,291	6,716,893	6,849,456	7,785,996	6,604,944	6,677,161
Ways and structures	1,182,877	1,222,481	1,271,674	1,258,855	1,237,998	1,225,545	1,278,903	1,278,062	1,222,101
Equipment	1,759,826	1,811,269	1,799,923	1,826,355	1,672,911	1,598,890	1,546,689	1,524,928	1,553,111
Rail operations	2,330,982	2,305,853	2,362,856	2,315,022	2,288,248	2,255,963	2,297,247	2,269,402	2,396,098
General	1,513,679	1,498,731	1,544,557	1,680,059	1,517,736	1,769,058	2,663,157	1,532,552	1,505,851

Source: Statistics Canada, Catalogue no. 52-216.

13.11 RAILWAY EQUIPMENT IN SERVICE

	All railways	Class I			Classes II and III
		Canadian National	Canadian Pacific	VIA Rail	
Locomotives	3,324	1,681	1,185	111	347
Freight	2,546	1,324	932	–	290
Passengers	71	14	–	43	14
Yard	671	343	249	59	20
Associated equipment	36	–	4	9	23
Freight cars	116,510	62,263	38,753	–	15,494
Box	29,558	17,523	8,819	–	3,216
Hopper	40,463	21,325	17,885	–	1,253
Gondola	15,745	6,315	4,145	–	5,285
Refrigerator	171	130	25	–	16
Flat	25,495	12,958	7,555	–	4,982
Stock	28	2	26	–	–
Caboose	994	612	275	–	107
Other freight cars	4,056	3,398	23	–	635
Passenger cars	549	41	–	381	127
Head-end	44	–	–	31	13
Meal/lounge	72	–	–	61	11
Sleeping	80	–	–	78	2
Conventional	177	–	–	93	84
LRC[1]	109	–	–	109	–
Diesel	26	–	–	9	17
Commuter	41	41	–	–	–

1. Light rail cars.

Source: Statistics Canada, Catalogue no. 52-216.

13.12 RAILWAY TRACK LENGTHS, 1994

	All railways	Class I			Classes II and III
		Canadian National	Canadian Pacific	VIA Rail	
	km				
Track owned and operated	83,351	44,796	28,152	–	10,403
Track owned	69,021	40,796	20,937	–	7,289
Main line	32,718	18,827	8,959	–	4,931
Branch line	19,055	11,457	6,977	–	620
Yards	17,249	10,511	5,000	–	1,737
Track operated[1]	14,330	4,000	7,215	–	3,115
Main line	5,134	907	2,470	–	1,757
Branch line	3,060	35	2,737	–	287
Yards	6,136	3,057	2,008	–	1,070

1. Under lease, trackage rights or jointly owned.

Source: Statistics Canada, Catalogue no. 52-216.

13.13 DEPARTMENT STORE SALES

	1987	1988	1989	1990	1991	1992	1993	1994	1995
	$'000								
Canada	12,906,005	13,271,120	13,914,295	14,192,795	12,913,325	13,011,856	12,793,896	13,298,958	13,923,627
Newfoundland	150,603	160,068	166,033	207,477	183,185	180,480	180,996	201,955	x
Prince Edward Island	81,762	88,843	89,703	86,386	54,628	54,728	54,243	54,712	x
Nova Scotia	432,284	451,264	467,729	474,834	434,828	438,358	442,876	445,741	458,235
New Brunswick	285,874	299,225	311,646	316,298	289,517	297,524	297,759	328,130	344,271
Quebec	2,459,602	2,549,168	2,604,412	2,658,569	2,405,423	2,345,978	2,313,854	2,412,466	2,544,193
Ontario	5,207,070	5,495,461	5,795,838	5,832,635	5,297,682	5,396,775	5,385,283	5,586,889	5,812,769
Manitoba	599,158	572,958	585,971	604,166	534,552	537,233	530,852	553,603	592,910
Saskatchewan	394,976	394,740	392,970	411,987	368,846	368,306	362,942	393,300	437,424
Alberta	1,489,204	1,470,241	1,549,888	1,584,157	1,454,822	1,434,761	1,370,812	1,423,183	1,522,220
British Columbia	1,805,472	1,789,157	1,950,103	2,016,292	1,889,833	1,957,710	1,854,278	1,898,982	1,945,934

Source: Statistics Canada, CANSIM, matrix 112.

13.14 TYPES OF MOTOR VEHICLE REGISTERED

	1986	1987	1988	1989	1990	1991	1992	1993	1994
All motor vehicle registrations	15,336,350	15,794,050	16,336,261	16,719,558	16,981,130	17,223,039	17,388,000	17,586,041	17,794,703
Passenger automobiles	11,585,622	11,686,439	12,086,001	12,380,258	12,622,038	13,061,084	13,298,000	13,477,896	13,639,358
Trucks and truck tractors	3,156,387	3,516,892	3,706,032	3,826,963	3,867,385	3,679,804	3,624,000	3,647,963	3,697,792
Motorcycles	430,135	414,322	369,758	348,125	331,075	324,118	313,444	308,946	305,887
Buses	56,476	59,266	59,834	62,494	63,962	64,208	64,479	64,523	65,138
Moped	35,258	33,772	30,559	29,872	27,940	27,113	26,504	25,584	23,922
Other road motor vehicles	72,472	83,359	84,077	71,846	68,730	66,712	60,381	61,129	62,606

Source: Statistics Canada, Catalogue no. 53-219.

13.15 MOTOR VEHICLE REGISTRATIONS, CANADA, THE PROVINCES AND TERRITORIES, 1994

	All motor vehicle registrations	Passenger automobiles	Trucks and truck tractors	Motorcycles and mopeds	Buses	Other road motor vehicles
Canada	17,794,703	13,639,358	3,697,792	329,809	65,138	62,606
Newfoundland	322,652	216,760	91,018	7,343	1,517	6,014
Prince Edward Island	91,310	65,221	24,290	1,374	386	39
Nova Scotia	577,767	392,176	169,970	12,777	2,488	356
New Brunswick	519,581	328,112	175,856	9,963	–	5,650
Quebec	3,750,971	3,107,133	501,911	82,791	16,441	42,695
Ontario	6,304,626	5,069,383	1,097,588	109,326	28,330	–
Manitoba	796,368	556,752	229,427	9,932	161	96
Saskatchewan	721,309	420,817	284,167	4,470	4,179	7,676
Alberta	1,935,076	1,546,012	342,310	35,448	11,306	–
British Columbia	2,716,020	1,916,081	746,421	53,518	–	–
Yukon	32,301	11,329	19,944	808	217	3
Northwest Territories	26,721	9,582	14,890	2,059	113	77

Source: Statistics Canada, Catalogue no. 53-219.

13.16 NEW MOTOR VEHICLE SALES

	1987	1988	1989	1990	1991	1992	1993	1994	1995
New motor vehicles	1,533,637	1,565,501	1,483,875	1,317,852	1,287,790	1,227,419	1,192,934	1,260,056	1,166,535
Passenger cars	1,065,093	1,056,310	988,134	884,564	873,184	798,023	739,049	748,666	670,190
North American	700,930	724,733	675,340	580,397	573,297	503,460	493,759	573,361	553,265
Imports	364,163	331,577	312,794	304,167	299,887	294,563	245,290	175,305	116,925
Commercial vehicles	468,544	509,191	495,741	433,288	414,606	429,396	453,885	511,390	496,345
North American	417,189	459,777	422,398	361,386	347,671	370,422	402,112	475,444	469,590
Imports	51,355	49,414	73,343	71,902	66,935	58,974	51,773	35,946	26,755

Source: Statistics Canada, Catalogue no. 63-007.

13.17 FUEL SALES[1]

	1986	1987	1988	1989	1990	1991	1992	1993	1994
					Litres '000				
Canada	25,859,224	28,575,527	31,718,186	32,038,416	31,842,330	31,209,092	31,786,778	32,563,430	33,297,035
Newfoundland	521,886	535,421	568,172	583,386	572,472	573,614	578,270	585,091	591,489
Prince Edward Island	165,107	166,155	175,611	175,896	177,133	168,763	172,143	174,007	182,350
Nova Scotia	1,039,829	1,057,589	1,095,247	1,105,209	1,113,673	1,065,925	1,082,148	1,085,350	1,104,480
New Brunswick	914,122	956,130	999,483	970,293	956,257	904,505	929,763	961,131	1,001,020
Quebec	6,578,395	6,651,383	6,843,471	7,051,184	6,982,566	6,823,648	6,868,325	7,037,733	7,199,940
Ontario	11,715,600	11,978,200	12,368,600	12,660,325	12,129,200	11,887,265	11,982,500	12,255,200	12,530,021
Manitoba	1,296,202	1,308,123	1,339,359	1,341,072	1,298,488	1,250,175	1,244,457	1,253,892	1,278,402
Saskatchewan[2 3]	...	404,300	870,373	683,659	1,193,109	1,169,700	1,445,521	1,373,463	1,297,605
Alberta[2 3]	...	1,903,008	3,768,243	3,774,250	3,788,294	3,746,700	3,718,700	3,873,700	3,924,600
British Columbia	3,551,813	3,519,014	3,597,655	3,599,180	3,539,953	3,527,620	3,666,882	3,869,461	4,082,964
Yukon	54,591	57,018	60,661	60,155	57,932	59,047	65,358	61,276	66,373
Northwest Territories	21,679	39,187	31,310	33,807	33,253	32,130	32,711	33,126	37,791

1. Sales are net sales. They represent the amount of taxable fuel consumed on public roads and streets in Canada.
2. No figures available for 1986 because the road tax was removed.
3. Data in 1987 represents net sales from July to December.

Source: Statistics Canada, Catalogue no. 53-218.

13.18 PASSENGER AND URBAN TRANSIT BUS INDUSTRY

	1986	1987	1988	1989	1990	1991	1992	1993	1994
					$ Millions				
Revenues[1]	3,412.7	3,671.4	3,782.8	4,264.4	4,358.1	4,819.2	5,072.3	5,077.1	5,105.1
Scheduled intercity carriers	335.9	346.9	332.9	362.0	404.5	408.1	397.4	361.7	380.6
Urban transit	2,282.9	2,443.7	2,581.8	2,986.8	3,109.4	3,459.2	3,587.1	3,624.8	3,511.5
School buses	639.5	710.8	700.1	744.0	676.4	767.3	873.2	860.5	1,014.7
Charter and other passenger buses	154.4	170.0	168.0	171.6	167.8	184.6	214.6	230.1	198.3
Expenses	3,070.7	3,252.5	3,394.6	3,681.4	3,903.1	4,340.0	4,543.5	4,579.1	4,627.8
Scheduled intercity carriers	316.1	320.8	320.0	316.4	385.6	388.8	382.3	344.4	349.6
Urban transit	2,057.6	2,147.4	2,301.6	2,531.5	2,722.3	3,051.5	3,140.8	3,246.0	3,167.6
School buses	552.8	626.9	617.9	672.0	632.6	722.9	813.1	768.0	929.7
Charter and other passenger buses	144.2	157.4	155.1	161.5	162.6	176.8	207.3	220.7	180.9
					Millions				
Passengers carried[2]	1,545.2	1,492.0	1,533.3	1,537.6	1,545.4	1,466.0	1,445.9	1,407.4	1,372.1

1. Includes subsidies.
2. Only for intercity carriers and urban transit.

Source: Statistics Canada, Catalogue no. 53-215.

13.19 PASSENGER AND URBAN TRANSIT BUS INDUSTRY, REVENUES, 1994

	All services	Intercity	Urban	School bus	Charter and other
			$ Millions		
Total revenues	5,105.1	380.6	3,511.5	1,014.7	198.3
Operating revenues	3,112.5	380.6	1,518.9	1,014.7	198.3
Urban transit service	1,425.3	–	1,425.3	–	–
Intercity service	260.7	241.2	1.2	7.5	10.8
Charter/tours	212.0	37.9	3.3	54.2	116.6
School bus service	949.4	3.1	3.8	913.9	28.6
Other passenger bus service	52.5	–	4.9	17.1	30.5
Other revenues	212.6	98.5	80.4	21.9	11.8
Subsidies	1,992.6	–	1,992.6	–	–

Source: Statistics Canada, Catalogue no. 53-215.

13.20 OIL PIPELINE TRANSPORT

	1988	1989	1990	1991	1992	1993	1994
				Cubic metres (millions)			
Crude oil							
Canadian crude oil production	100.3	97.2	96.9	96.7	100.9	105.8	110.5
Pipeline imports	4.7	6.6	7.4	9.6	10.1	10.9	11.4
Pipeline exports	39.0	36.2	38.0	42.8	47.2	52.1	56.1
Net receipts of crude oil into pipeline	109.4	108.4	109.0	110.2	115.5	123.4	128.8
				Kilometres			
Pipeline distance							
Gathering[1]	9,137.5	10,288.3	10,376.7	10,895.8	10,997.7	11,112.3	10,795.1
Truck-crude	19,482.7	19,425.6	19,546.6	19,373.9	19,406.0	19,259.2	19,874.0
Product lines	5,107.6	5,148.7	5,150.0	5,455.5	5,627.5	5,969.2	5,991.5
Cubic metre kilometres (millions)	130,000.0	124,524.3	121,770.0	117,846.7	121,823.4	118,300.0	119,039.5
Average kilometres per cubic metre	761.7	724.6	705.3	679.0	676.5	618.0	593.4
				Number			
Compressor stations	247	257	246	250	252	252	262
				$ Millions			
Financial statistics							
Operating revenues	905.9	920.5	977.8	1,011.0	1,023.8	1,050.1	1,074.3
Operating expenses	398.8	424.7	466.1	497.9	514.5	534.2	547.6
Net income	284.8	283.6	258.7	607.2	221.6	201.9	216.7
Property account	3,265.2	3,450.9	3,657.2	3,802.3	4,024.2	4,187.4	4,543.3
Long-term debt	1,366.3	1,362.5	1,357.8	1,598.4	1,366.7	1,705.4	2,095.2

1. Excludes producers' gathering lines.

Source: Statistics Canada, Catalogue no. 55-201.

13.21 WHOLESALE MERCHANTS' INVENTORIES

	1985	1986	1987	1988	1989	1990	1991	1992	1993	1994	1995
					$ Millions						
All inventories	234,414.9	257,003.4	275,705.9	297,265.9	292,856.4	289,260.4	283,508.8	296,644.1	310,110.3	335,532.2	370,969.8
Food, beverage, drug and tobacco products	27,305.4	29,264.2	32,214.4	31,350.9	31,332.3	31,312.3	32,434.7	36,209.3	39,440.2	42,473.2	44,775.3
Apparel and dry goods	8,467.0	9,168.7	10,737.7	11,341.9	9,629.5	9,376.1	9,298.5	10,549.9	12,030.2	12,878.3	12,419.2
Household goods	12,174.8	13,098.1	13,681.9	14,197.3	14,365.4	14,065.6	12,693.1	14,170.2	15,197.2	15,732.6	18,104.2
Motor vehicles, parts and accessories	30,354.1	35,832.0	38,647.0	39,158.5	40,241.6	41,302.5	41,393.7	42,712.3	44,233.1	43,559.5	49,801.2
Metals, hardware, plumbing and heating equipment and supplies	19,871.2	21,691.9	23,076.9	25,804.6	24,997.9	22,904.9	23,747.2	25,363.1	26,613.0	30,432.1	34,326.9
Lumber and building materials	21,237.1	23,452.3	25,238.7	31,153.8	29,320.8	29,170.5	26,729.2	29,071.6	31,900.3	34,680.4	37,998.2
Farm machinery, equipment and supplies	21,464.8	21,038.9	21,164.3	20,970.9	19,492.7	18,317.9	16,502.6	16,377.7	14,868.2	17,741.3	18,523.7
Other machinery, equipment and supplies	59,168.6	67,050.8	71,838.0	82,640.5	87,990.8	85,962.8	84,228.3	84,887.8	85,065.5	92,537.5	101,120.0
Other products	34,371.8	36,406.4	39,106.9	40,647.6	35,485.4	36,847.8	36,481.5	37,302.2	40,762.7	45,497.2	53,901.2

Source: Statistics Canada, CANSIM, matrix 59.

13.22 WHOLESALE MERCHANTS' SALES

	1985	1986	1987	1988	1989	1990	1991	1992	1993	1994	1995
					$ Millions						
Canada, wholesale sales	143,816.4	156,214.8	175,251.8	190,211.2	188,767.7	182,822.4	176,843.1	190,330.0	204,591.1	230,712.5	242,926.0
Food, beverage, drug and tobacco products	35,264.1	37,816.8	40,995.1	40,736.0	41,833.3	42,984.2	45,116.2	49,428.7	53,523.1	55,704.0	56,873.4
Apparel and dry goods	3,907.9	4,574.3	4,888.0	5,180.4	4,854.5	4,227.2	4,239.7	4,708.3	5,364.4	5,507.3	5,368.8
Household goods	5,100.7	5,751.6	6,142.2	7,264.3	6,618.5	6,558.8	6,219.9	6,792.6	7,048.0	7,456.9	7,590.7
Motor vehicles, parts and accessories	15,780.9	17,273.0	18,884.7	20,392.1	21,385.5	20,801.1	20,744.5	20,875.9	22,388.9	26,563.6	26,544.9
Metals, hardware, plumbing and heating equipment and supplies	12,033.2	12,213.2	14,516.1	16,609.7	16,408.4	13,970.9	12,559.3	13,189.3	14,340.3	17,779.7	19,333.3
Lumber and building materials	13,384.9	15,700.0	18,666.9	19,866.9	19,251.2	17,646.0	15,863.9	17,523.7	19,384.1	21,090.9	20,533.3
Farm machinery, equipment and supplies	5,336.3	5,373.4	5,268.8	5,398.2	4,642.2	4,274.3	3,675.0	4,145.2	4,627.2	5,357.2	6,023.0
Other machinery, equipment and supplies	29,088.0	31,672.5	36,599.9	43,986.2	45,068.4	42,611.4	39,261.4	43,561.0	45,569.5	53,665.0	58,232.0
Other products	23,920.4	25,840.0	29,290.1	30,777.5	28,705.8	29,748.6	29,163.2	30,105.3	32,345.6	37,587.8	42,426.6
Newfoundland	1,525.5	1,569.4	1,790.5	1,930.1	2,026.3	1,996.2	1,960.1	1,995.0	2,083.9	2,182.9	2,237.4
Prince Edward Island	x	x	x	x	486.4	444.0	431.6	522.2	466.6	555.5	530.6
Nova Scotia	2,837.3	3,226.2	3,812.0	4,742.1	4,851.1	4,625.5	4,235.0	4,189.4	4,477.5	4,983.4	5,369.1
New Brunswick	2,328.0	2,557.2	2,800.3	3,306.5	3,499.6	3,220.7	2,906.8	2,882.3	2,835.5	3,173.1	3,454.9
Quebec	35,499.7	39,303.2	43,422.1	48,079.0	47,148.6	45,932.3	43,911.6	47,194.4	48,708.0	52,420.1	54,449.1
Ontario	58,015.1	65,229.2	75,844.2	78,747.2	76,749.6	73,523.8	72,999.5	79,145.7	84,825.9	97,452.3	105,697.5
Manitoba	5,974.8	6,155.4	5,995.5	6,188.5	6,206.5	6,015.4	5,841.0	6,571.2	6,975.3	7,637.5	8,112.9
Saskatchewan	5,279.5	5,397.3	5,278.1	5,750.0	6,270.8	6,178.5	5,785.0	5,629.7	6,301.9	7,124.4	8,118.5
Alberta	14,564.8	14,233.6	15,640.9	17,394.1	17,143.7	17,141.8	16,472.6	17,194.2	19,132.0	22,213.5	22,688.4
British Columbia	17,328.1	17,991.0	20,134.6	23,387.6	24,153.5	23,529.0	22,089.7	24,756.0	28,525.4	32,710.9	31,974.5
Yukon and Northwest Territories	x	x	x	x	231.5	215.2	210.0	250.0	259.2	258.8	293.2

Source: Statistics Canada, CANSIM, matrix 648.

13.23 RETAIL SALES

	1984	1985	1986	1987	1988	1989	1990	1991	1992	1993	1994	1995
						$ Millions						
Retail sales	127,413.3	142,211.8	153,785.7	168,893.6	181,651.8	189,301.7	192,558.3	181,208.2	185,049.3	193,815.0	206,861.6	211,522.3
Food	33,293.2	35,575.3	38,141.9	41,061.0	43,027.0	44,480.0	46,420.6	47,091.1	48,556.4	51,081.4	53,495.1	54,009.4
Supermarkets and grocery stores	30,923.5	33,005.6	35,270.2	37,969.5	39,708.9	40,740.6	42,474.7	43,511.9	45,444.8	47,695.8	49,772.9	49,855.7
All other food stores	2,369.7	2,569.7	2,871.7	3,091.5	3,318.1	3,739.4	3,945.9	3,579.2	3,111.6	3,385.6	3,722.2	4,153.7
Drug and patent medicine stores	5,237.7	5,944.0	6,737.6	7,428.5	8,310.6	8,965.3	9,476.4	9,795.4	10,721.6	11,889.2	12,036.0	11,943.7
Clothing	8,027.4	9,041.4	9,950.7	10,751.7	11,376.8	11,823.1	11,918.1	10,750.1	10,748.3	11,436.3	12,245.8	12,715.5
Shoe stores	1,276.6	1,404.0	1,551.3	1,626.6	1,737.9	1,819.3	1,825.5	1,590.2	1,506.3	1,614.0	1,769.7	1,708.1
Men's clothing stores	1,527.9	1,528.6	1,657.6	1,822.1	1,974.9	2,045.8	2,076.1	1,713.0	1,666.2	1,739.2	1,701.9	1,645.3
Women's clothing stores	2,792.3	3,237.8	3,535.3	3,784.1	3,925.6	4,002.5	3,999.6	3,690.6	3,671.8	3,819.2	4,034.2	4,097.3
Other clothing stores	2,430.6	2,871.0	3,206.5	3,518.9	3,738.4	3,955.5	4,016.9	3,756.3	3,904.0	4,263.9	4,740.0	5,264.8
Furniture	6,857.5	7,552.9	8,633.9	10,079.1	10,841.8	11,376.5	11,208.5	9,444.8	9,832.5	10,632.2	10,959.5	10,841.2
Household funiture and appliance stores	5,609.1	6,096.9	6,769.6	7,800.3	8,401.3	8,838.2	8,596.9	7,411.9	7,660.6	8,385.5	8,672.4	8,551.0
Household furnishings stores	1,248.4	1,456.0	1,864.3	2,278.8	2,440.5	2,538.3	2,611.6	2,032.9	2,171.9	2,246.7	2,287.1	2,290.2
Automotive	42,611.5	50,478.2	53,804.9	60,580.9	66,489.0	69,066.1	69,370.9	62,587.5	62,957.5	66,482.0	73,157.6	75,547.6
Motor vehicle and recreational vehicle dealers	24,339.5	30,361.9	33,361.9	37,555.6	41,978.1	42,893.5	41,695.1	37,689.3	38,501.3	41,365.2	47,089.6	49,591.6
Gasoline service stations	10,381.9	11,839.5	11,463.2	13,056.3	13,587.6	14,362.0	15,355.0	14,287.8	14,167.9	14,245.8	14,202.7	14,598.4
Automotive parts, accessories and services	7,890.1	8,276.8	8,979.8	9,969.0	10,923.3	11,810.6	12,320.8	10,610.4	10,288.3	10,871.0	11,865.3	11,357.6
General merchandise stores	16,872.7	18,001.5	18,925.4	19,301.9	19,871.2	20,532.8	21,353.8	20,682.9	20,859.8	20,494.5	21,530.6	22,664.9
Other retail stores	14,513.1	15,618.5	17,591.7	19,691.2	21,735.5	23,058.0	22,810.0	20,856.3	21,373.2	21,799.3	23,436.8	23,800.3
Other semi-durable goods stores	3,797.7	4,266.5	4,992.7	5,702.9	6,495.5	7,006.1	6,950.8	5,977.1	6,415.9	6,658.1	7,171.3	7,094.0
Other durable goods stores	3,334.0	3,659.0	4,242.1	4,793.4	5,237.7	5,572.1	5,474.8	4,876.3	4,935.3	5,207.0	5,614.4	5,504.2
All other retail stores	7,381.4	7,693.0	8,356.9	9,194.9	10,002.3	10,479.8	10,384.4	10,002.9	10,022.0	9,934.2	10,651.1	11,202.1
Newfoundland	2,122.8	2,312.0	2,469.4	2,828.8	3,168.0	3,356.1	3,527.4	3,393.9	3,359.1	3,327.7	3,408.9	3,478.2
Prince Edward Island	560.4	589.1	620.6	688.9	760.0	787.7	817.7	759.2	798.4	845.9	867.6	910.2
Nova Scotia	4,328.0	4,900.3	5,132.9	5,592.7	6,034.0	6,210.0	6,214.9	5,851.0	6,109.9	6,371.3	6,463.6	6,350.4
New Brunswick	3,136.0	3,398.1	3,730.2	4,063.3	4,418.4	4,621.3	4,776.7	4,595.4	4,763.0	4,960.9	4,932.1	5,082.8
Quebec	32,446.1	35,567.1	38,703.4	43,456.4	46,583.3	47,192.0	47,578.3	44,850.1	45,078.4	47,298.8	50,363.7	49,597.9
Ontario	47,565.9	53,728.1	58,554.7	64,729.9	69,791.1	72,567.8	72,568.4	67,159.6	68,704.4	71,290.2	76,044.2	78,424.9
Manitoba	4,785.9	5,515.2	5,772.5	6,127.4	6,336.7	6,599.0	6,596.4	6,276.7	6,392.9	6,666.3	6,948.9	7,339.5
Saskatchewan	4,481.8	4,865.5	5,171.5	5,416.1	5,677.3	5,757.7	5,688.6	5,308.1	5,378.7	5,739.5	6,266.7	6,598.2
Alberta	13,030.4	14,887.9	15,762.4	16,351.8	17,563.2	18,874.8	20,023.0	18,949.8	19,440.4	20,350.5	21,854.5	22,196.3
British Columbia	14,570.9	16,015.8	17,416.4	19,160.4	20,802.0	22,790.6	24,199.8	23,537.4	24,432.8	26,347.6	29,032.2	30,855.4
Yukon and Northwest Territories	385.3	432.6	451.6	478.1	518.3	544.9	567.0	526.8	590.8	616.7	679.1	688.7

Source: Statistics Canada, CANSIM, matrix 2299.

KAJ SVENSSON, VIEWPOINTS WEST

Chapter 14 FINANCE AND SERVICES

Robert Lankinen, First Light

The Canadian financial sector is one of the most efficient and stable in the world, not to mention one of the largest; for example, with $335.1 billion of trading activity in 1993, the Toronto Stock Exchange stands sixth world-wide. The solidity of this sector has also become one of the ascribed traits of Canadians themselves.

"The Canadian character is solid. Cautious and thrifty, Canadians are a nation of accountants," wrote an American journalist in the late 1980s. "In Canada there are 6.4 million more savings accounts than there are people."

When this American journalist was writing, the deposits held by the Canada Deposit Insurance Corporation (CDIC) totalled $511 billion. The CDIC insures deposits held by Canada's banks, trust and loan companies, and credit unions. In 1994, this figure reached $645 billion, an average of about $22,000 per adult Canadian. Most of these deposits were with Canada's largest financial institutions, the chartered banks, whose worldwide revenues totalled $27.3 billion in 1995.

Dominating the chartered banks are the so-called "Big Six": the Bank of Montreal, the Bank of Nova Scotia, the Canadian Imperial Bank of Commerce (CIBC), the Toronto Dominion Bank (TD), the Royal Bank of Canada and the National Bank. Together, these six banks control almost 90% of Canada's banking assets.

No other country in the world has a network of bank branches and automated banking machines (ABMs) as extensive as ours, with 8,301 branches and 12,808 ABMs in 1995. This means that customers in Inuvik have the same services as residents of Vancouver, 6,000 kilometres away. In 1993, our ratio of one full-banking branch for every 3,584 people was higher than that of any other major industrialized nation except Japan.

In 1993, about half a million Canadians worked in the finance sector, a sector that accounted for about 25% of all the equity invested in Canadian private business. The only sector in which Canadians have invested more was the petroleum and natural gas industry.

The Four Pillars

Four key areas or "pillars" dominate finance: banks, trust companies, insurance companies, and securities activities (those involving stocks and bonds). Together, these four types of institutions safeguard our deposits; lend them, in turn, to individuals and businesses; offer financial security through insurance; and help Canadians invest in the stock market.

But if solid and cautious have been the traditional traits of the financial sector in Canada, there is also a sense of change and movement. Certain mutations have altered this landscape of distinct and predictable pillars. Currently, the barriers that separate bank from insurance company and insurance company from trust company are breaking down. There's been a blurring of roles.

One of the primary reasons has been the change in the legislation covering these industries. In 1992, Canada's Bank Act and three other acts were completely overhauled; one of the major changes allowed banks to own trust firms and insurance companies. This considerably narrowed the difference between banks and trust companies, and was largely the inspiration for numerous acquisitions and mergers during the 1990s. Since the legislation was passed, many trust and loan companies have been purchased or merged with other companies and several others have ceased operations.

Both businesses and ordinary Canadians have been directly affected by these changes. There's now more choice and variety; stock market advice is available at the bank, as well as from a stockbroker. A single institution can, and does, offer a complete range of financial services.

Another force altering the landscape of the financial sector has been the tremendous revolution in technology, which Canada has embraced. Institutions can now transfer money instantaneously anywhere in the world. Canadians can bank on the Internet. World stock markets can be scanned in an instant on a computer screen. As well, globalization, with its lowering of trade barriers, and the shift from national markets to world markets, has made it easier for money to cross borders.

As a result, international financial activity, especially securities trading, has increased rapidly, as has the stock of worldwide financial assets. Since 1980, the stock of these worldwide assets has increased 2½ times faster than the Gross Domestic Product (GDP) of rich industrial countries. For the first time ever, the amount of money changing hands around the world is far more than is required to finance the world's business, trade and investment transactions.

Some have argued that this extraordinary mobility of money has come at a cost, however, claiming it has weakened the ability of governments to control their financial markets. In Canada, we are now much more vulnerable to international trends; indeed, the sheer volume of market activity has made macroeconomic and fiscal policy less effective than in the past.

Recession

Nonetheless, Canada's financial sector was not immune to the recession of the early 1990s. From 1990 to 1994, 139 financial institutions closed down.

The fall in interest rates certainly played its part. Canadians were hesitant to invest in deposit instruments such as term deposits or guaranteed investment certificates (GICs), which are linked to interest rate performance. But banks and trust companies rely heavily on these services for their money; they found themselves with a significant shortfall of business.

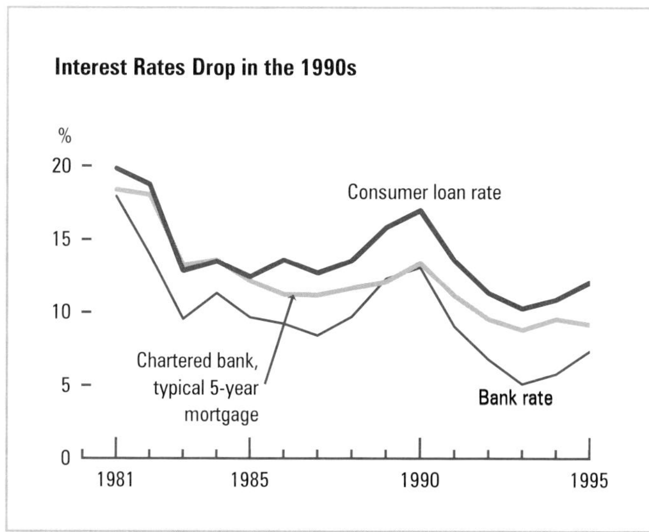

The decline in commercial real estate was also ever-present during the recession. Between 1989 and 1994, the value of commercial real estate fell some 40%. The real victims here were the trust and insurance companies that had issued large loans believing that real estate values would increase.

Financial Institutions Reform

Historically, there is little consensus as to just how the four "pillars" came to be. One thing is certain, however. The rule traditionally has been to prevent cross-ownership; that is, where one type of financial institution buys another. In this way, no one financial service has been able to dominate the sector.

Since the 1960s, the range of services provided by each sector has begun to broaden and overlap. For example, banks, which in 1967 had been allowed to do mortgage lending (traditionally reserved for trust companies), wanted to get into the fiduciary business. The other three pillars wanted to provide securities advice.

As well, companies were realizing that, to compete in the new era of globalization, they had to be large and diversified.

One international event in particular set an example. In October, 1986, Great Britain witnessed what became known as the "Big Bang" when British banks, for the first time, were allowed onto the floor of the London stock exchange to participate in securities transactions. For the banks, it was a euphoric day indeed.

In 1985, the Canadian government had already begun a sweeping reform of financial sector legislation with the intention of allowing financial institutions to expand their business activities. The first Canadian "bang" came in 1987 when banks, trust and insurance companies were permitted to buy securities firms or start their own. A second and bigger "bang" came in 1992 when four acts, including the Bank Act and the Trust and Loan Companies Act, were completely revamped.

Thirteen hundred pages and 2,400 clauses later, banks, trust, loan and insurance companies were allowed to enter into each other's type of business directly or to purchase subsidiaries that could do this.

Ownership rules were relaxed. Banks could now own trust companies. Banks and trust companies could own insurance companies and insurance companies could own bank or trust companies. However, life insurance companies still cannot take deposits, and banks and trust companies cannot finance auto leasing or sell insurance products through their branches.

Financial institutions, however, want these few limitations removed. The legislative package is to be reviewed in 1997. Already, banks are lobbying the government for the right to sell insurance while insurance companies want access to the Bank of Canada's payments system.

Deposit-Taking Institutions

When Canadians have more money than they need for immediate purposes, they generally either place it in a deposit-taking institution or invest it directly in securities.

Rumours have persisted for more than 200 years about what lies buried deep underground on a small Nova Scotian island. "It's Captain Kidd's hidden booty," say some. "It's Marie Antoinette's jewels," say others. Some have speculated that the treasure is Mayan, or maybe even the Holy Grail. Treasure hunters have tried to excavate the island, but a mysterious, booby-trapped pit has stalled them. Even 20th-century engineers haven't outwitted the technology of Oak Island's ancient traps.

The search for treasure on Oak Island has become one of the world's longest-running and most costly treasure hunts. To date, the Oak Island Exploration Company alone has spent more than $3.5 million dollars seeking the treasures. Groups of adventurers have included a young Franklin Roosevelt, Hollywood actor John Wayne and Errol Flynn.

The hunt began in 1795, when a teenage boy walking across the uninhabited island spied an odd, circular depression in the ground right beneath the sawed-off limbs of an oak tree. Having heard local rumours of Captain Kidd and buried treasure, he returned with friends and began digging. Two feet down, they found a massive layer of stone covering a circular shaft. Ten feet down, they struck oak logs crisscrossing the shaft. They dug those out, but after encountering more log platforms, they grew discouraged and gave up.

In 1803, the first organized group continued where the teenagers had left off. At a depth of 90 feet, searchers found a large flat stone covered with an indecipherable inscription. Believing they were now close to treasure, they brought the rock to the surface. In the process, they tripped a booby-trap that flooded the shaft with sea-water. Later, treasure hunters discovered that ingenious underground tunnels linked the shaft to the ocean. Continued flooding has made modern-day explorations treacherous.

In 1995, the hunt for the elusive Oak Island treasure resumed. The Oak Island Exploration Company invited scientists from the Woods Hole Oceanographic Institution in Massachusetts, who explored the site using the same camera probes and hi-tech equipment used to explore the ***Titanic*** *and the* ***Bismarck****.*

Although search parties haven't yet found the mythic treasure, they have made other discoveries. Among these have been scissors, dating back to before 1850, of Spanish American origin, and coconut fibres—although the nearest coconut tree is 2,400 kilometres away. Go figure.

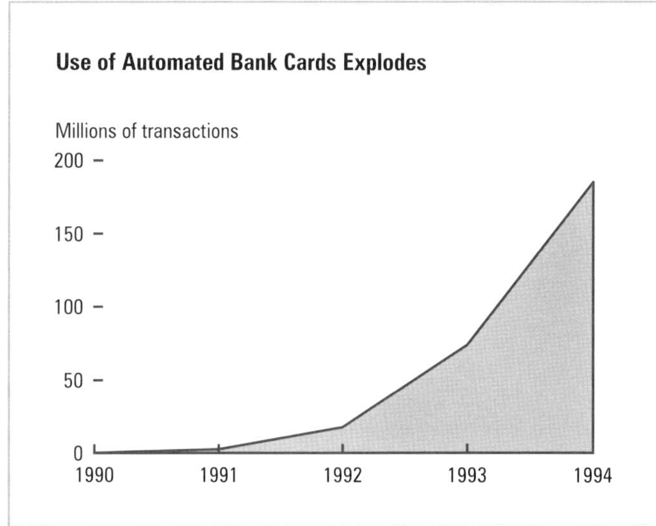

Canada's deposit-taking institutions are its chartered banks, trust and loan companies, credit unions and various provincial institutions. Here, money accumulates interest, but is readily available. In turn, the institution can use it to issue loans, or for its own investment purposes.

The protection of this money in Canada is the responsibility of the Canada Deposit Insurance Corporation, a federal Crown corporation set up in 1967. The CDIC's avowed maxim is to give "as much confidence in a Canadian dollar on deposit in a bank or trust company as in a dollar in its wallet." To do so, it insures depositors' funds to a maximum of $60,000 per depositor in the federal and provincial deposit-taking institutions that are its members.

In 1994 and 1995, the CDIC was required to make good on its word as two of its members failed: Confederation Trust, Canada's fourth largest trust company, and Income Trust. As a result, CDIC paid insurance amounts of $679 million and $194 million respectively. Consequently, the CDIC's accumulated deficit has grown to $1.75 billion in 1995.

In addition to the CDIC, the Office of the Superintendent of Financial Institutions (OSFI) maintains public confidence in the financial system. The OSFI, established in 1987, supervises and regulates banks, and federally incorporated trust, loan and insurance companies. While the roles of these two agencies can overlap, they are different: OSFI is the supervisor and CDIC is the insurer; CDIC relies on OSFI for reports on the financial health of its member institutions.

Both agencies monitor member institutions that are showing signs of financial difficulty more closely, and try to resolve problems early before they become a risk to the institution's solvency.

Banks

The Canadians employed by our banks—170,808 in 1993—are finding the nineties the best of times and the worst of times. On the one hand, banks have shown large profits as the decade progresses. In 1995, the total profit of the six largest banks was $5.2 billion, 21% higher than in 1994. Two banks have earned profits of more than a billion dollars, and one bank set a profit record for all Canadian banks. Indeed, the chartered banks are experiencing the largest rate of growth in the entire financial sector.

On the other hand, some depositors, who provide banks with 94% of their capital base, are experiencing high levels of unemployment and bankruptcy.

Ever since the 1920s, the Big Six have dominated our banking industry. They now control more than 90% of the total banking assets in the country, which is the highest concentration by far among the G-7 countries. However, the Big Six represent only about 10% of our 55 chartered banks (nine of these, including the Big Six, are domestically owned and 46 are foreign bank subsidiaries).

To bank critics, this concentration means the Big Six are becoming a monopoly across the business sector. With a monopoly there is little competition, which means consumers have less choice regarding their bank and the fees they pay. In turn, bank power has increased since legislation has allowed banks to purchase other financial institutions.

Canadians use banks every day. Some see them as "public institutions," in a position of responsibility; to a degree the

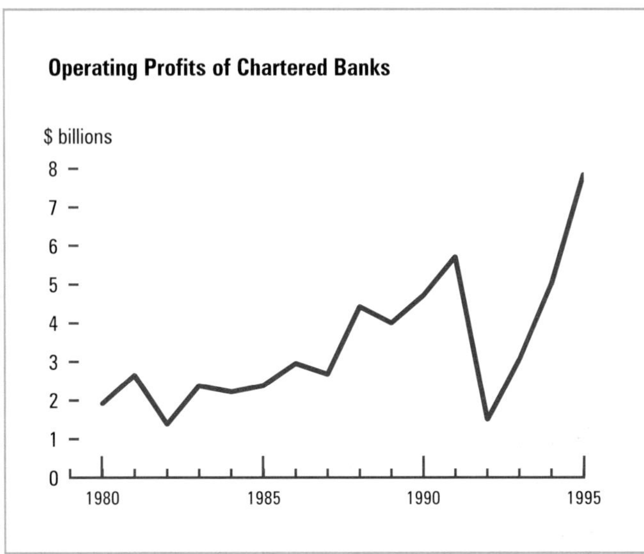

government has put banks in charge of managing the money supply and giving out credit. From this perspective, some say it is inappropriate for banks to be making large profits.

From another perspective, Canadians should be proud. The history and dominance of the Big Six have made our banking system one of the most stable, efficient and respected in the world. Fee revenue—the money collected through services to customers—is 67% higher in American banks than it is in Canadian banks. Banks rate third after hospitals and the construction industry in terms of employment, and exceed all other sectors in amounts of corporate and employee charitable donations ($41.4 million in 1994).

As well, the profits attract new shareholder investment, including international investors. Over half of Canadians own bank shares, if not directly, through RRSPs and other savings instruments. Compared with other private companies, the profits of banks are modest. For the first half of the 1990s, the Bank of Montreal's average return on equity was 14.4%, while the figure for Rothmans Inc. was 32.7% and for CanWest Global Communications, 50.5%.

The banks' growth is due in part to the generally improving performance of Canada's economy. There are now fewer loan losses. The move into new areas, with the new legislation, has also meant profitable business growth in consumer banking.

Retail

The activities of Canadian banks fall into four categories: retail, commercial and corporate, investment, and international banking.

Retail banking refers to the accounts of individual Canadians and small businesses and is the largest single deposit category in both number and amount. It also includes loans such as mortgages and bank-issued credit cards.

Canadians own 24 million credit cards; that's about two per adult, one of the highest rates in the world. The average credit card interest rate in Canada in 1994 was 16.35%, much lower than rates in the United Kingdom and the United States (21.75% and 17.44% respectively). Still, nearly half of Canadian cardholders avoid interest charges by paying off the full balance within the grace period.

Retail banking has seen numerous initiatives recently, many of them driven by technology. There are five banks with sites on the Internet and this has made Canada one of the world leaders in Internet banking. Some banks now offer home banking—your telephone or personal computer can access your bank account.

Debit cards (bank cards that are used to pay for goods and services directly) have gained popularity quickly. Between 1993 and 1995, their use increased by a mighty 1,600%. The next step toward a supposedly cashless society is the "smart card," whose computer chip increases security. It will also allow users to "stock up" large amounts of money and information.

Commercial and Corporate

Commercial and corporate banking refers to the services banks offer to businesses and large corporations. Small and medium-sized businesses, for example, often require loans to get "off the ground." Small businesses now constitute 90% of

It was no small change. The two-dollar coin issued in 1996 became Canada's first mass-circulation coin to be made with two metals and the second denomination in recent years to be transformed from paper currency.

The two-dollar coin joins the loon, the beaver, the schooner, the maple leaf and the caribou (otherwise known as the dollar, the nickel, the dime, the penny and the quarter). With a production cost of 16 cents and an expected lifespan of 20 years, the coin is considerably cheaper to use over the long term. A two-dollar bill, for example, which cost six cents to print, has a lifetime of only one year. The government expects the coin's relative longevity will save $250 million during the next 20 years.

Deciding the look of the coin was highly public. Opinion polls were conducted in 2,000 households across the country, and 65% of those polled favoured a wildlife theme.

Picking out the actual image, however, was an epic task. An estimated 19,000 suggestions poured in from enthusiastic Canadians. A children's contest on TVOntario alone collected more than 10,000 suggestions. High-school students in Montreal and Vancouver joined in the unveiling ceremony by sending their ideas to the mint on video tape. Students from Inuksuk High School in the Northwest Territories shared their ideas via a live two-way satellite link.

Patiently, staff at the Royal Canadian Mint surveyed the 19,000 suggestions, which included everything from a Blue Jay and the CN Tower to perogies and turbot. There was even a bid made for two male deer posing as "two bucks." In the end, the government chose the polar bear, giving respected wildlife artist Brent Townsend the go-ahead to illustrate Canada's newest coin.

The next question was what to call the new coin. Again, Canadians rose to the challenge. Proposals included the "toonie," the "broonie," the "bogey" and the "bear buck." They also included the "two-tone," the "nanook" and the "polar doubloonie." There were also comments on the coin's value, for instance, the "bearly nothing." At the time of publication, Canadians were calling the two-dollar coin the "dublooney," the "dubloon," the "toonie," and, in Quebec, the "polar."

This is not the only entertainment Canadians have enjoyed for their two dollars over the years. During the 1800s, the two-dollar bill had a brazen reputation for being the amount spent by railway workers on nightly carousing. The Americans had a habit of calling it a "deuce"—a euphemism for the devil.

The government plans to circulate many two-dollar coins—more, in fact, than they did two-dollar bills. That's because of Canada's "sock-drawer syndrome," in which Canadian coins are either lost or squirreled away in households across the country. The same rationale resulted in four loonies for every previous dollar bill when the one-dollar coin came out in 1987. During the first 18 months of the dublooney's circulation, the government plans to produce more than 300 million coins at its Winnipeg-based mint.

banks' commercial customers. The increased attention is due partly to the Small Business Act which was amended in 1993 to enlarge the extent to which banks can lend to these businesses. In 1994, banks had $27 billion in loans outstanding to small businesses, up from $24 billion in 1992.

Investment

Banks are in the business of making money as well as safeguarding it.

When a bank takes the money that Canadians confide in it and invests it in Canadian stocks, government treasury bills and other securities, this is one aspect of investment banking. This also includes the money banks generate through trading in foreign currencies. In 1995, banks used more than $97 billion of their Canadian assets for their own investment purposes.

Investment banking also refers to the investment services banks can now offer their customers due to changes in the Bank Act. Through banks, customers can buy and sell stocks, bonds, mutual funds, and other retirement and investment products. Banks also provide money-management advice for these products.

The ability of banks to sell mutual funds other than their own (which they could sell prior to 1992) has contributed to the rapid growth in the mutual fund market. The total value of Canadian funds increased almost fourfold between 1990 and 1994 (from $35 billion to $130 billion). Between 1973 and 1995, the number of registered mutual funds in Canada went from 66 to over 895.

International

Our major banks are considered significant international players. Canada has almost 300 foreign branches in almost 60 countries, which account for 30% of our major banks' revenue. This ensures financial support for Canadian businesses wanting to deal abroad. It means activities with foreign clients, which lead to new investments in Canada. It also means Canadian travellers can obtain cash at over 100,000 automated banking machines in 50 different countries.

Other Deposit-Taking Institutions

Savings and loan services are also available from credit unions (caisses populaires in Quebec) and from various provincially run financial institutions such as the Ontario Savings Office.

Credit unions are co-operative financial institutions that operate for a particular membership. In fact, they go back to 1900 when Alphonse Desjardins founded the first co-operative in Quebec. Credit unions enjoyed strong growth in the West in the 1930s and 1940s during the heyday of the union movement.

There are two types of credit unions: local and central. An example of a local credit union is the Ottawa Women's Credit Union. Each province (except Quebec) has at least one central credit union that regulates credit union activity in the province; for example, the Credit Union Central of Alberta.

At the end of 1995, Canada's 2,500 local credit unions and 13 central credit unions had total assets of $124.4 billion, up from $117.6 billion in 1994. More than half of these were from caisses populaires, which are generally more active than co-operatives in other provinces.

Trust and Loan Companies

There is an old saying that trust companies are for those fortunate enough to have money to put in trust for family members, or unfortunate enough to die. Even with the 1992 reforms, trust companies are still associated with their traditional areas: deposit and loan services, and fiduciary business (the administering of wills and estates, pension plans and trust funds).

However, since the 1992 reforms, the overlap between the activities of trust and loan companies and banks has caused many to refer to them as one pillar: the deposit-taking pillar. The one difference is that trust companies don't have access to the Bank of Canada as a lender of last resort.

Trust companies accept deposits and issue loans much the way chartered banks do. However, more than 25% of these deposits are held in items like registered retirement savings plans, and are tax-deferred until withdrawn. As well, trust companies tend to specialize in the residential mortgage industry.

Prior to 1992, fiduciary business was the exclusive domain of trust companies. However, most other financial institutions can now carry out fiduciary business through their trust company subsidiaries.

Mortgage loan companies lend money in the form of mortgage loans. For this reason, many of them are affiliated with a trust company or chartered bank.

The recession took its toll on Canada's trust companies; in the early 1990s, more than half a dozen failed. Since 1992, several of the biggest, such as Royal Trust Corporation, General Trust Company and Montreal Trust Company, have been acquired by banks.

The remaining independents have felt the competition. Their total assets are less than two-thirds what they were in 1992: $73 billion compared with $134 billion. On the other hand, at the end of 1994, trust companies as a sector were on the upswing.

The Bond Market

Bonds, stocks, and treasury bills (short-term government bonds) all fall under the broad heading of securities. Securities are investments that can be readily converted into cash by selling them on the bond market, stock exchange or other financial market.

A bond is a certificate that acts as proof that the issuer of the bond owes the holder of the bond a certain amount of money. By issuing the bond, the issuer promises to pay the holder a specified amount of interest for a specific time period (usually from five to 20 years), and to repay the loan on the bond's maturity date.

Financial institutions, Crown corporations and all three levels of government issue bonds for the purpose of raising long-term capital. Although Canada Savings Bonds may be listed in denominations of $100, most bonds are issued in amounts of $1,000 or more.

For investors, bonds provide assured return because they are secured with the assets of the issuer. For this reason, bonds are seen as low-risk investments. Also, if a company goes bankrupt, the bondholders get paid before the shareholders.

The bond exchange is not like the stock exchange. The bond exchange does not have its own building, but there is a huge phone and screen network called the bond market. Linked into this market are investors, investment dealers (who buy securities and resell them for a profit) and bond traders, all of whom hope to profit from the effect of interest rates on a bond's market value. As interest rates fall, the value of the bond increases and vice versa.

While the securities industry is overseen by the securities commission of the province in which securities are issued, the five exchanges and the national Investment Dealers' Association act as self-regulating organizations, regulating the compliance and behaviour of various players in the industry.

The Stock Market

There is an old adage in the investment world that the greater the risk, the greater the reward. Stocks are relatively high-risk investments. Dividends—payments to shareholders that are tied to the company's profits—are high when profits are high and low when business is poor. In contrast, interest payments on bonds are almost always fixed. With stocks, if the company goes bankrupt, or if the stock market "crashes" as it did in 1987, shareholders lose considerably.

In general, the 1990s have seen extraordinary growth in securities in Canada due mainly to the decline in interest rates and the issuing of new securities. In 1993, companies issued $21 billion in common stock.

Robert Teteruck Photography

Pillars of the CIBC Bank Building, King St. East and Jarvis, Toronto.

In 1995, the Canadian dollar, however, was undervalued due to concerns about both the federal government's debt (currently $546 billion) and Canada's overall political stability, given the results of the Quebec referendum in October, 1995. This affected the growth of securities, especially from international buyers.

The majority of stocks are traded in marketplaces called stock exchanges where prices are established by supply and demand. Each exchange has seats that are owned by stockbrokers who bring together buyers and sellers for a commission. Canada's five stock exchanges are located in Montreal, Toronto, Vancouver, Winnipeg and Calgary.

The Bank of Canada

Canada's central bank, the Bank of Canada, is at the heart of the Canadian financial system. The Bank of Canada was established in 1934 and was given responsibility for regulating "credit and currency in the best interests of the economic life of the nation." The bank does not carry out ordinary banking business, nor does it accept deposits from the general public. But its actions influence the economic circumstances of businesses and individuals across the country.

Through its responsibility for monetary policy, the Bank of Canada promotes overall economic performance in the best way it can—by seeking to preserve confidence in the value of money. But the Bank of Canada's functions involve a good deal more than monetary policy. The bank acts as the federal government's banker and fiscal agent and is the sole issuer of Canadian bank notes.

The Bank of Canada's board of directors plays a central role in governing the Bank of Canada. The board is composed of the Governor, the Senior Deputy Governor, 12 directors and the Deputy Minister of Finance (who has no vote). The 12 directors are appointed for three-year terms by the Minister of Finance. Coming from every province and with experience in fields as diverse as farming, business and law, they are an important link between the Bank of Canada and their respective regions.

Bank of Montreal

Canada's oldest chartered bank was born out of necessity. In the early 19th century, Upper and Lower Canada were British colonies. Since 1791, they had possessed elected legislatures, but government was ultimately in the control of London. Neither colony had a currency of its own, and most transactions were conducted under a system of barter.

In 1817, nine Montreal traders formed the Bank of Montreal, which thus became British North America's first institution to offer full banking services.

In the 1820s, the provincial governments of the day granted several banks charters. The first charter was granted in 1820 to the Bank of New Brunswick, based in Saint John, which merged with the Bank of Nova Scotia in 1913. The Bank of Montreal received its charter in 1822. In its articles of association, it capped the interest rate for all transactions at 6%.

The Bank of Montreal's early history was a story of firsts, issuing notes for its first public works financing—the Lachine Canal in the 1820s, and its first railway (Champlain and St. Lawrence) in the 1830s.

The bank also became involved in construction to improve St. Lawrence–Great Lakes navigation, and in the 1850s, provided financing for the building of the Grand Trunk Railway from Quebec to Sarnia.

The major role of the directors is to ensure that the bank is being managed competently. They are responsible for appointing or reappointing the Governor and Senior Deputy Governor (with the approval of Cabinet), and for appointing other Deputy Governors. The board approves the corporate objectives, plans and annual budget of the bank.

Directors are not expected to be experts in economics. Senior management at the Bank of Canada formulates and implements monetary policy and reports to the board at regular meetings. In the Bank of Canada Act, Parliament has defined the relationship between the bank and the government and has placed the bank in a position to carry out its responsibilities independently. For most purposes, the bank's accountability as a public institution is through its board of directors, but there are special arrangements for monetary policy.

The Minister of Finance and the Governor meet regularly to discuss monetary policy. If a profound disagreement were to occur over monetary policy that the bank planned to follow, the government could issue a public, written directive to change the policy. This provision makes it clear both that the government must take the ultimate responsibility for monetary policy and that the Bank of Canada must accept immediate responsibility so long as a government directive is not in effect.

In December, 1993, the federal government and the Bank of Canada set a target path for inflation extending from the end of 1995 to the end of 1998. The objective is to keep inflation inside a range of 1 to 3% during that period. By 1998, a decision will be taken on a future target range that would be consistent with price stability.

Monetary Policy

Monetary policy is about money. The Bank of Canada is concerned with how much money circulates in our economy and how much that money is worth. The bank seeks to protect the value of our currency and provide money that can be used with confidence—money whose value is not eroded by inflation—by influencing the pace of monetary expansion.

Inflation creates uncertainty, distorts economic decision-making, and imposes costs unequally on society's members, such as individuals on fixed incomes. (For example, with inflation at 4.5% per year, money loses half of its value in about 15 years.) By fostering price stability, the bank's monetary policy goal is to promote, in the best way it can, good overall economic performance and hence enhance the standard of living of Canadians.

The bank is able to exert influence on the pace of monetary expansion in the economy because it is the source of the ultimate means of payment in the economy, that is, bank notes and the settlement balances of financial institutions. Because the bank can control the supply of settlement balances, the central bank can influence the willingness of banks and other financial institutions in turn to expand the supply of money and credit. This is the fundamental leverage, or monetary policy instrument, that the Bank of Canada has at its disposal to influence developments in the Canadian economy.

The bank affects the amount of liquidity in the financial system in a variety of ways. Its primary method involves the transfer of Government of Canada deposits between the government's account at the Bank of Canada and its accounts at financial institutions. Typically, a transfer of deposits from the government's account at the bank to the financial institutions will provide more liquidity than is desired by the financial institutions. This will tend to put downward pressure on very short-term interest rates. The bank can also influence short-term interest rates by its purchase or sale of Government of Canada securities.

Changes in short-term interest rates lead to changes in a broad range of interest rates, and in the foreign exchange rate. Movements in these various rates influence the rate of expansion of money and credit, and the growth of spending in the economy. The pressure from spending in turn determines the ease with which prices can be increased.

Movements in the exchange rate also directly affect the cost of imported and exported goods and the incentive for Canadian producers competing against foreign firms to contain their costs. Over time, too-rapid growth in spending will result in increased inflation, while growth in spending that does not put pressure on prices is much more likely to be sustainable.

Banking Services

The Bank of Canada is at the centre of the nation's financial system. Each day, masses of cheques are written by the general public and governments on accounts with Canadian financial institutions; at the end of each day those claims must be settled. The total claim of one institution on another is calculated and a transfer of funds takes place to settle accounts—a transfer that occurs on the books of the Bank of Canada. This is called the payments clearing and settlement process. The Canadian Payments Association, established by an act of Parliament in 1980, manages Canada's payments system.

The Bank of Canada provides very short-term, secured loans to financial institutions to cover overnight shortfalls in liquidity in their settlement accounts at the Bank of Canada arising from the clearing and settlement of payment items.

In addition, the bank may make "extraordinary" loans to institutions that are solvent but have persistent cash flow difficulties. In this way, the Bank of Canada ensures that liquidity problems at individual financial institutions do not threaten their viability or undermine public confidence in the entire financial system.

Fiscal Agent

The Bank of Canada helps the Government of Canada manage its debt. The government's debt includes treasury bills, which are auctioned weekly, Canada Savings Bonds, and other marketable bonds. The bank also acts as an adviser and agent for the Government of Canada in managing the nation's foreign reserves (including gold reserves), held in the government's Exchange Fund Account.

Canada's paper currency is the Bank of Canada's best-known product. In fact, the signatures of the Governor and Senior Deputy Governor appear on every note. The bank has sole responsibility for issuing bank notes, and is actively involved in their design, production and distribution.

Before the Bank of Canada was established, paper money was issued by a number of banks, other institutions and the Government of Canada. When the bank began operations, it assumed responsibility for all government (Dominion) notes and started issuing its own notes. A little more than a decade later, on January 1, 1945, the right of chartered banks to issue paper money was revoked. The banks paid the Bank of Canada an amount corresponding to their outstanding note liabilities, and the Bank of Canada assumed responsibility for these notes as of January 1, 1950.

Although both these chartered bank notes and Dominion notes remain legal tender, they are taken out of circulation when they are returned to any financial institution. Gradually, the Bank of Canada has replaced the confusing kaleidoscope of notes which once circulated in Canada with Bank of Canada notes. As of March 1996, bank notes held by the public amounted to $23.4 billion.

The bank stays in close contact with law enforcement agencies to keep more than a few steps ahead of counterfeiters. Paper bills are designed to be difficult to forge and, in recent years, the bank has pioneered the use of an optical security device, which changes colour when tilted. This started on high denomination bills, but will now be applied to $20 notes.

Insurance

If insurance buys peace of mind, Canadians must surely sleep well. At the end of 1993, Canadians and Canadian businesses owned more than $1.4 trillion worth of life insurance. Almost half of this was individual insurance ($701.8 billion), an average of about $89,900 per Canadian, more than triple the amount in 1980.

Insurance companies provide protection against various types of risk. Canadians and their businesses generally buy two types of insurance: property and casualty insurance; and life insurance, which includes individual and group pensions, and accident and sickness insurance.

The 1990–91 recession resulted in considerable consolidation of the insurance industry; companies have either withdrawn, been acquired by larger institutions or have failed. Eventually, only a few—the best and the largest companies—will remain. At least in theory, that means competition for business will be high and consumers should experience lower prices and improved service.

In 1995, there were 163 federally registered life insurance companies in Canada. In 1994, the return on shareholders' equity reached 7.22%. This is still below the 1989 figure of almost 15%.

In 1994, another 231 federally registered property and casualty insurers provide insurance in the case of damage or theft. Automobile insurance accounted for $7.1 billion, which is more than half of all insurance in this area. Unlike the life insurance sector, property and casualty insurers earn their money through investments rather than premiums. In 1993, net profits in this sector fell from $917 million to $658 million, due to a drop in investment gains.

Community, Business and Personal Services

There is a sense of the intangible about the service sector in Canada. In the manufacturing sector, the results of a day's work are visible. Cars, toothpaste, plastic wrap and bridges are all products that are tangible. In the service sector, a product can be a trip on a bus, or the action of a waiter: perhaps you have been served duck à l'orange. It can also be a visit to the doctor. In the service sector, the product is the service.

Services exist in all sectors of society; buses are a transportation service, universities an educational service. Specifically, community, business and personal services account for 50% of all service industry employees—that's a little more than five million Canadians.

Membership in this group is wide-ranging—everything from personal services like cat-sitting and beauty salons to leisure services such as bowling centres and movie theatres. Business services include computer companies, accounting services, advertising agencies and lawyers, consultants and engineers. You'll also find community services such as hospitals, schools, museums, day-care facilities, optometrists and blood banks.

Growth Trends

These services, especially the exploding area of business services, have contributed to the astonishing growth that has occurred in the services sector over the last two decades. Between 1974 and 1994, community, business and personal services, as a group, experienced employment growth of 86%. In the same time period, just in the business services sector, the number of full-time jobs more than doubled, accounting for 6% of total employment in 1994.

The tremendous growth in part-time employment in Canada over the last 20 years has also occurred largely in the services sector, particularly the community, business and personal services industry, which accounts for three-quarters of the total increase in part-time employees.

Compared with the goods-producing sector, the services sector suffered only marginally in the 1990 recession. Community and personal services played a role here: they are non-commercial sectors and the demand for them continues—even increases —during a recession. This is partly because community services grow when unemployment is high.

Also, services in general don't tend to experience the temporary layoffs that plague the goods-producing sector. This is because services are consumed at the point of production and tend to be used immediately. The upshot of this is no accumulation in inventories or cutbacks in production, both of which cause layoffs in goods-producing industries.

Business Services

Of all this sector's areas of activity, business services is the most dynamic. Business services generally mean services

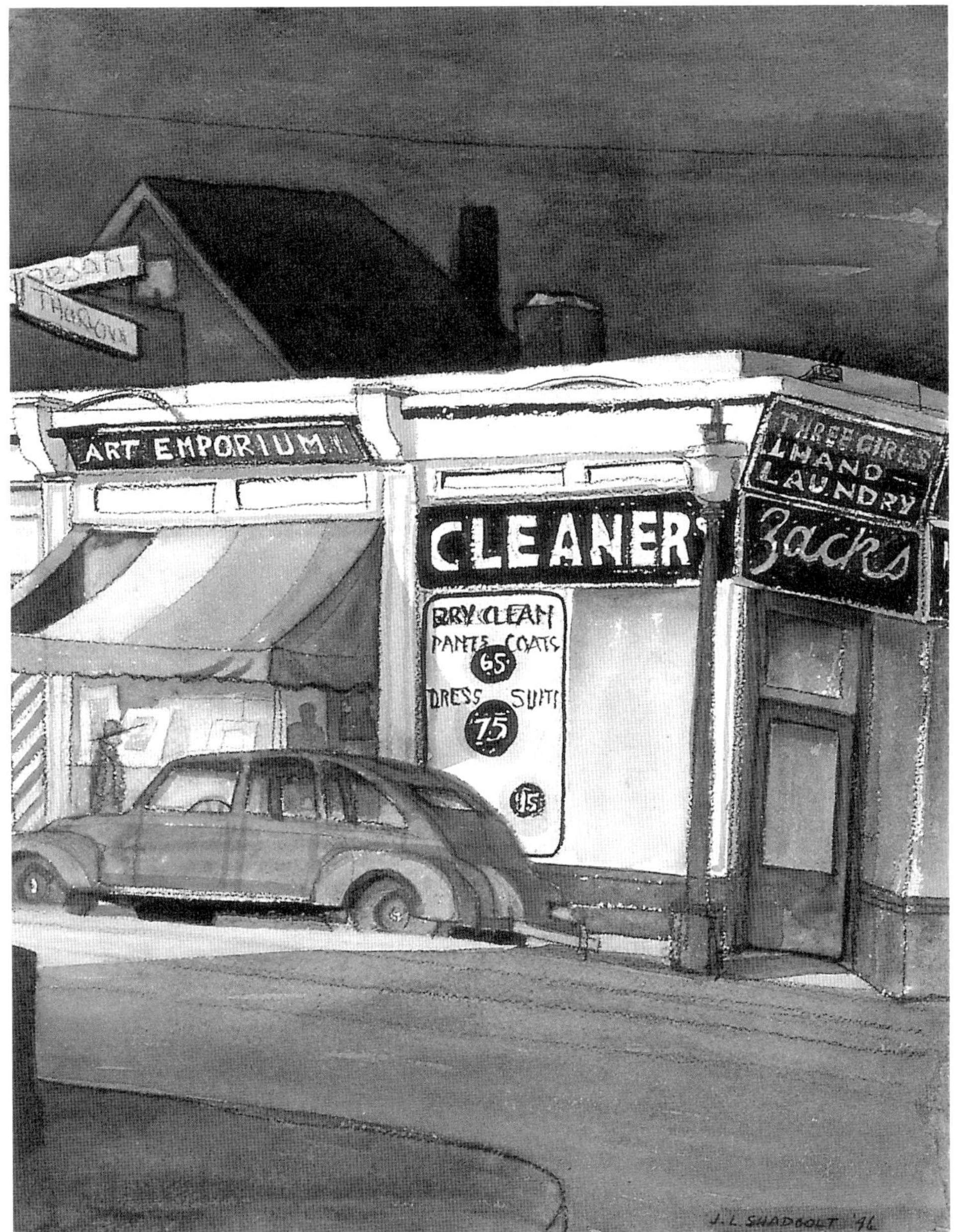

Jack Shadbolt, National Gallery of Canada, Ottawa

***Zack's Cleaners, Robson and Thurlow*.**

Night Unfurls Its Splendour

To Canada's tourism industry, the splendour of musicals like ***The Phantom of the Opera*** *and* ***Show Boat*** *has been their great impact on tourism and, of course, the local economy.*

For example, since it opened in Toronto in 1989, ***The Phantom of the Opera*** *has generated an estimated $200 million per year in direct and indirect economic spinoffs for the local economy. About $82 million of that has come from out-of-town visitors. Production alone directly provides the equivalent of 2,250 full-year jobs. In turn, the musical generates about $64 million in wages and salaries for performers and crew, and for those working in related services such as hotels, restaurants and stores.*

During ***Show Boat's*** *20-month run in Toronto, it created about $185 million in economic benefits.*

It has been estimated that about 40% of theatregoers in Toronto are tourists, with many coming from south of the border.

provided to the business community rather than the general public. (These include computer services, accounting services, architectural and engineering firms, advertising agencies, lawyers, and consulting firms.)

Since 1976, jobs in business services have increased by 150%, from 297,000 to 768,000. This growth rate has outpaced the economy's average growth rate (33.2% since 1976) by a huge margin. The business service sector's percentage of the overall employment picture doubled from 3% in 1976 to 6% in 1994. Even at a time when corporate profits in Canada fell to their lowest level since the 1930s, business services have endured.

A success story of women entrepreneurs belongs to this area. Between 1976 and 1994, there was a 920% increase in the

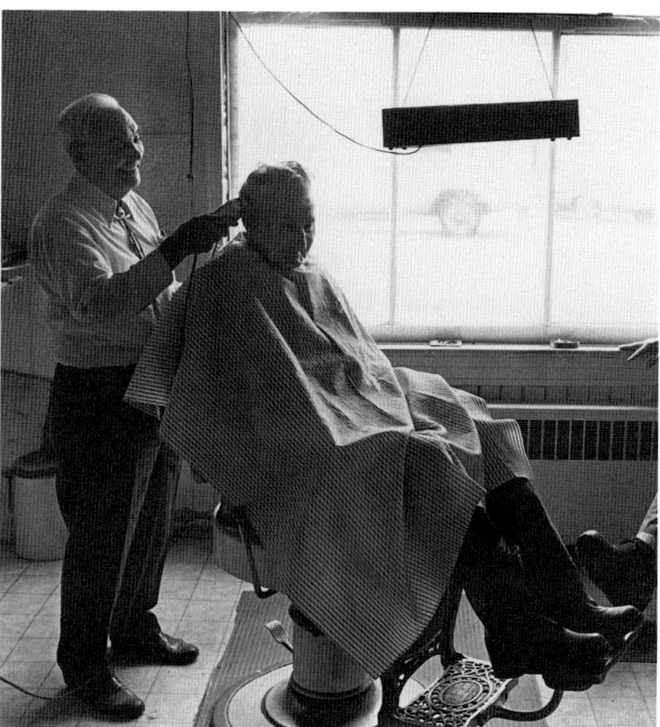

Photo by Kate Williams

In the services sector, a product can be a trip on a bus, or a haircut.

numbers of women setting out on their own in the business services area. Moreover, business studies have shown that the businesses started by these women tend to survive the first five years better than those started by men.

The rise in self-employment is most pronounced in the business services sector. Between 1976 and 1994, self-employment in this area grew by a factor of five and now exceeds 30% of total employment in the business services sector—a higher proportion than for the economy as a whole.

Business services employees are better educated than average; more than 90% have a high school diploma and more than one-third have at least one university degree. Generally, one in four employees working in Canada has not finished high school.

These people also earn more than the average employee; in 1992, business services employees earned on average \$30,406—\$37,447 if they were on a salary. (The averages across the economy were \$28,590 and \$35,934 respectively.)

Most business services are in Ontario and Quebec, and most employees are urbanites. In 1992, more than eight in 10 were located in metropolitan areas. Toronto stands out with the largest percentage of business services employees (29.7% or 161,000 people) and Montreal is next (18.2% or 99,000 people) followed by Vancouver and Ottawa.

Computer Services

Computer services have certainly stimulated job growth in the business services sector. Between 1976 and 1994, employment went up 639%, despite job losses of 20,000 in 1992.

This huge growth rate is due to the entry of new firms, outsourcing activity and the introduction of new products and services. To appreciate the success of computer services, consider that employment growth in business services greatly outpaced the economy's average and computer services led this growth.

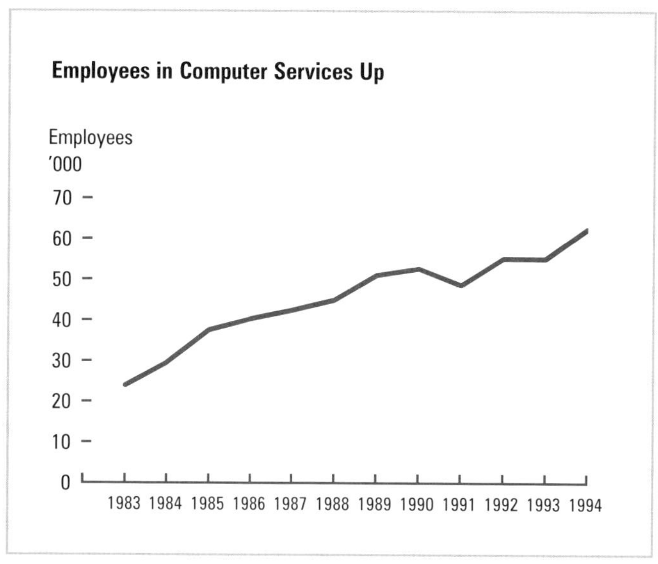

Second to computer services in terms of employment growth were management consulting services (including lobbyists and public relations companies), which grew by 416%.

Hospitality

The restaurant sector was one of the major casualties of the recession. It's also been one of the slowest to recover. According to the Canadian Restaurant and Foodservices Association, eating out is the last item in discretionary spending to come back into someone's personal budget.

Although consumers are eating out more, they're not splurging. This explains the success of casual taverns and take-out and delivery establishments, compared with places for fine dining. (Between 1993 and 1994, sales increased 8.6% for pubs, taverns and lounges, and 11.7% for take-out and delivery, compared with 2.6% for licensed restaurants.)

As real disposable income rises, growth in food and beverage services (5.7% in 1994) is expected to accelerate along with our inclination for upscale, licensed restaurants.

In the world of hotels and motels, the recession of the early 1990s, combined with a generally depressed tourist market, brought about myriad business failures, mergers and acquisitions. Recovery seems imminent however; in 1993-94, all members of this group—hotels and motor hotels—reported an increase in both occupancy rates and average room revenue.

Canadians seem to prefer motels near airports or highways, and hotels that are close to airports and downtown areas. For all types of accommodation, business is consistently better west of Ontario. In Alberta and the Northwest Territories, for example, profit margins were 7% and 6% in 1993-94. In Quebec and Ontario, accommodation businesses suffered losses of 6% and 7%.

Leisure and Personal Services

In 1992, theatricals and other staged entertainment had the highest revenue growth of all this sector's members. This is where blockbusters like *The Phantom of the Opera*, *Miss Saigon*, and *Sunset Boulevard* come in. *Phantom*, Canada's longest running musical, broke the Canadian record for ticket sales before opening: $24 million worth prior to its debut in Toronto in 1989. Revenues increased slightly from the production and distribution of movies and audio and video products. Yet the movie theatres industry still lost $73 million between 1990 and 1992.

On the other hand, revenues were up for funeral services, golf courses, and sports and other recreation services.

SOURCES

Canada Deposit Insurance Corporation
Canadian Bankers Association
The Canadian Securities Institute
Department of Finance Canada
Investment Dealers Association
Office of the Superintendent of Financial Institutions Canada
ScotiaMcLeod Incorporated
Statistics Canada

FOR FURTHER READING

Selected publications from Statistics Canada

- **Services Indicators**. Quarterly. 63-016
- **Computer Service Industry**. Annual. 63-222
- **Business Services Part 2: The Human Side**. George Sciadas. 63F0002 no.2
- **Labour Force Annual Averages, 1989-1994**. Occasional. 71-529
- **Perspectives on Labour and Income**. Quarterly. 75-001E

Selected publications from other sources

- **Annual Report**. 1994-95. Canada Deposit Insurance Corporation. 1994.
- **Annual Report**. 1994-95. Office of the Superintendent of Financial Institutions Canada. 1995.
- **Bank Facts 1994**. Canadian Bankers Association. 1995.
- **Developments in the Financial Services Industry since Financial Sector Reform**. Background document prepared by the Department of Finance for the Senate Committee on Banking, Trade and Commerce. 1994.
- **The Economist**. The Economist Newspaper Limited. Monthly.

Legend

–	nil or zero	..	not available	x	confidential
--	too small to be expressed	...	not applicable or not appropriate		*(Certain tables may not add due to rounding)*

14.1 GROSS DOMESTIC PRODUCT AT FACTOR COST, FINANCE AND SERVICES

	1986	1987	1988	1989	1990	1991	1992	1993	1994	1995
	$ Constant 1986 (millions)									
Finance and services industries	201,243.3	208,499.4	217,165.9	223,958.6	226,451.6	228,368.8	230,754.6	233,987.3	237,597.9	241,000.1
Finance, insurance and real estate industries	69,515.1	72,827.2	75,671.5	77,712.3	78,491.1	80,462.1	81,284.7	83,214.2	85,246.9	86,721.3
Finance and real estate industries	33,234.9	34,465.6	35,209.0	35,633.4	34,594.1	34,694.5	34,648.0	35,010.9	35,415.1	35,515.3
Banks, credit unions and other deposit accepting institutions	8,203.0	8,530.2	8,919.5	9,182.1	9,218.3	9,106.4	9,085.4	9,217.9	9,711.6	10,180.1
Trust companies and other finance and real estate industries	25,032.0	25,935.4	26,289.5	26,451.3	25,375.8	25,588.1	25,562.6	25,793.0	25,703.5	25,335.2
Insurance industries	2,936.7	3,029.6	3,202.7	3,085.3	2,937.2	3,080.7	2,869.2	2,919.8	2,999.1	2,993.9
Non-business sector insurance and other finance industries	481.4	895.8	949.8	1,011.8	1,018.1	1,043.2	1,049.6	1,070.5	1,091.5	1,112.5
Government royalties on natural resources	3,849.0	4,075.9	4,452.0	4,393.8	4,455.0	4,551.2	4,778.6	5,156.8	5,546.6	5,857.2
Owner occupied dwellings	29,013.1	30,360.3	31,858.0	33,588.0	35,486.7	37,092.5	37,939.2	39,056.2	40,194.6	41,242.4
Community, business and personal services	100,362.7	104,254.1	109,588.3	113,686.0	114,701.4	114,206.1	115,380.5	116,957.7	118,992.6	121,588.5
Business service industries	17,042.3	19,056.3	21,150.0	22,552.6	22,618.3	22,340.9	22,394.6	23,023.1	23,918.2	25,345.7
Educational service industries	25,607.6	25,788.1	26,143.5	26,784.8	27,334.1	27,640.0	28,219.7	28,525.8	28,502.5	28,386.8
Health and social services industry	28,024.0	28,846.5	29,815.1	30,917.7	31,918.1	32,603.2	32,758.8	32,602.2	32,651.7	33,191.3
Accommodation and food service industries	11,608.7	11,879.3	12,111.7	12,635.0	12,232.6	10,929.1	11,074.1	11,312.6	11,729.3	11,847.3
Personal and household services industries	7,495.2	7,701.8	8,140.4	8,516.5	8,658.4	8,393.0	8,307.0	8,447.8	8,595.7	8,573.9
Amusement, recreational and other services	10,585.0	10,982.1	12,227.6	12,279.5	11,939.7	12,300.0	12,626.1	13,046.2	13,595.2	14,243.5
Government service industries	31,365.5	31,418.1	31,906.1	32,560.3	33,259.1	33,700.6	34,089.4	33,815.4	33,358.4	32,690.3
Defence services	4,220.6	4,248.0	4,251.3	4,259.6	4,281.4	4,204.7	4,163.9	4,039.4	3,926.4	3,626.7
Federal government services	10,042.6	9,848.3	9,877.4	10,093.4	10,267.5	10,503.8	10,666.1	10,613.3	10,633.7	10,458.2
Provincial government services	9,552.1	9,654.7	9,852.3	10,092.9	10,401.6	10,566.3	10,694.3	10,577.3	10,281.8	10,117.2
Local government services	7,550.2	7,667.1	7,925.1	8,114.5	8,308.7	8,425.8	8,565.1	8,585.4	8,516.5	8,488.2

Source: Statistics Canada, CANSIM, matrix 4670.

14.2 PRIVATE AND PUBLIC INVESTMENT,[1] FINANCE AND SERVICES

	1991	1992	1993	1994	1995	1996[2]
	$ Millions					
Private and public investment in Canada	128,010.0	122,188.8	121,253.9	130,131.2	127,956.1	126,009.4
Finance and insurance industries	5,154.8	5,002.2	5,695.3	7,054.8	7,887.9	8,435.5
Deposit accepting intermediaries	1,527.6	1,251.1	1,383.0	1,309.0	1,459.3	1,839.9
Consumer and business financing	3,254.9	3,392.9	3,998.4	5,508.6	5,920.1	6,158.0
Insurance industries	372.3	358.2	313.9	237.2	508.5	437.6
	%					
Investment in finance and investment industries as a percentage of total investment	4.0	4.1	4.7	5.4	6.2	6.7

1. Excludes repair expenditures.
2. Intentions.

Source: Statistics Canada, CANSIM, matrix 3108.

14.3 EMPLOYMENT, FINANCE AND SERVICES

	1985	1986	1987	1988	1989	1990	1991	1992	1993	1994	1995	Average annual growth rate 1985-1995
						Employees[1]						
						'000						%
All industries[2]	9,651.1	9,927.2	10,329.1	10,659.0	11,054.7	11,146.1	10,549.5	10,246.9	10,271.4	10,447.1	10,673.6	0.9
Finance, insurance and real estate	591.1	621.0	646.2	684.8	698.9	708.7	696.0	672.8	664.2	643.2	641.5	0.7
Finance and insurance	420.0	435.8	452.8	478.2	487.1	493.9	490.9	482.0	478.2	462.9	460.5	0.8
Deposit accepting intermediaries	237.4	245.8	251.0	261.8	271.1	287.9	292.7	280.6	278.8	271.7	269.5	1.2
Banks	162.5	166.6	170.9	177.9	184.4	196.2	197.9	195.7	194.8	193.7	193.0	1.6
Trust companies	26.8	27.6	28.6	30.3	31.8	34.1	34.6	33.5	27.7	25.3	22.8	-1.5
Deposit accepting mortgage companies	1.7	2.4	1.0	0.7	2.5	2.0	0.7	0.6	0.5	0.2	0.2	-17.7
Credit unions	46.1	49.0	50.2	52.5	52.1	55.2	59.1	50.5	55.5	51.7	53.4	1.3
Other deposit accepting intermediaries	0.3	0.3	0.3	0.3	0.3	0.3	0.3	0.3	0.3	0.7	0.2	-3.6
Consumer and business financing intermediaries	20.5	20.2	20.3	21.5	21.7	21.7	20.4	20.8	19.8	17.8	15.9	-2.3
Investment intermediaries	51.5	51.4	57.3	66.5	65.0	56.1	48.1	53.2	45.5	46.7	50.3	-0.2
Insurance (excluding agencies)	86.2	90.7	91.0	92.4	93.2	98.2	102.8	101.1	105.2	97.2	93.1	0.7
Other financial intermediaries	24.4	27.6	33.1	36.1	36.1	30.1	26.8	26.2	28.9	29.5	31.7	2.4
Real estate operators and insurance agencies	171.2	185.2	193.4	206.6	211.8	214.8	205.1	190.8	186.0	180.3	181.0	0.5
Business services	465.8	482.3	508.5	520.0	567.6	585.5	540.9	511.0	528.8	560.1	602.9	2.4
Employment agencies and personnel suppliers	44.1	46.5	50.8	56.2	67.1	59.2	50.7	42.9	55.3	64.3	74.0	4.8
Computer and related services	37.6	40.3	42.4	44.9	51.0	52.7	48.6	55.2	55.1	62.5	68.9	5.7
Accounting and bookkeeping services	41.5	44.8	46.7	47.5	51.5	55.1	55.5	53.2	55.8	52.4	53.1	2.3
Advertising services	33.1	34.8	37.5	37.5	43.2	39.5	30.2	29.2	26.0	24.3	31.2	-0.5
Architecture, engineering and other scientific and technical services	77.6	77.1	87.6	90.7	99.8	111.0	111.9	93.8	95.3	105.9	114.9	3.6
Offices of lawyers and notaries	59.4	60.5	61.4	63.5	64.9	63.0	59.8	54.2	57.4	60.0	54.1	-0.8
Management consulting services	64.2	72.0	69.4	60.3	76.6	80.6	65.2	69.4	67.9	68.7	76.4	1.6
Other business services	108.4	106.3	112.7	119.4	113.4	124.4	118.9	113.1	116.0	122.1	130.4	1.7
Educational and related services	765.4	779.7	812.2	838.4	863.8	888.1	905.7	916.3	932.2	933.3	933.6	1.8
Health and social services	933.5	970.0	1,010.6	1,064.3	1,092.5	1,128.0	1,135.8	1,135.3	1,138.9	1,145.3	1,187.1	2.2
Accommodation, food and beverage services	655.0	694.6	741.9	763.1	810.5	793.2	732.6	721.4	748.1	741.2	770.1	1.5
Accommodation services	168.3	171.6	184.8	193.7	212.8	198.2	178.0	181.6	172.3	163.2	160.8	-0.4
Food and beverage services	486.8	522.9	557.1	569.5	597.8	595.0	554.5	539.8	575.8	578.0	609.4	2.1
Miscellaneous services	486.6	489.0	524.4	540.9	575.9	604.8	573.5	556.1	556.0	593.9	597.9	1.9
Amusement and recreational services	134.9	139.5	144.1	156.9	154.2	167.6	158.5	160.0	163.0	172.1	177.9	2.5
Personal services (excluding private households)	83.6	82.6	94	95.9	102.0	108.3	107.8	98.1	98.2	104.0	105.8	2.2
Barber and beauty shops	41.3	39.1	40.9	42.1	45.5	47.2	45.7	44.3	47.1	47.3	48.3	1.4
Laundries and cleaners	20.3	20.0	23	23.1	24.0	30.1	33.2	27.7	25.5	28.9	28.6	3.2
Funeral services	5.4	5.0	5.3	5.3	6.8	8.6	9.5	10.6	9.5	10.2	12.2	7.7
Other personal services (excluding private households)	16.5	18.5	24.8	25.3	25.8	22.4	19.4	15.6	16.1	17.6	16.7	0.1
Membership organizations	88.7	89.7	93.5	91.1	100.2	99.3	94.2	96.8	93.3	93.7	91.7	0.3
Other services	179.5	177.2	192.8	197.0	219.4	229.6	213.0	201.2	201.5	224.1	222.5	2.0
Automobile and truck rental and leasing	87.1	82.1	85.7	83.0	95.1	106.0	107.3	95.5	91.4	104.3	99.6	1.2
Photographers	11.0	12.1	13.5	13.0	15.6	17.9	14.7	11.8	12.1	14.1	14.9	2.8
Services to buildings and dwellings	8.0	7.6	9.7	7.7	7.9	5.9	4.2	3.8	4.7	4.9	5.4	-3.5
Travel services	55.2	58.6	62.5	68.3	74.8	72.6	66.1	66.3	67.0	70.7	71.4	2.4
Other services	18.2	16.8	21.4	25.0	26.0	27.2	20.6	23.8	26.3	30.1	31.1	5.0
Public administration	663.1	675.7	668.4	680.8	691.5	702.2	718.5	719.5	710.2	703.6	688.4	0.3

14.3 EMPLOYMENT, FINANCE AND SERVICES (concluded)

	1985	1986	1987	1988	1989	1990	1991	1992	1993	1994	1995
	% of total employment										
Finance, insurance and real estate	6.1	6.3	6.3	6.4	6.3	6.4	6.6	6.6	6.5	6.2	6.0
Business services	4.8	4.9	4.9	4.9	5.1	5.3	5.1	5.0	5.1	5.4	5.6
Educational and related services	7.9	7.9	7.9	7.9	7.8	8.0	8.6	8.9	9.1	8.9	8.7
Health and social services	9.7	9.8	9.8	10.0	9.9	10.1	10.8	11.1	11.1	11.0	11.1
Accommodation, food and beverage services	6.8	7.0	7.2	7.2	7.3	7.1	6.9	7.0	7.3	7.1	7.2
Miscellaneous services	5.0	4.9	5.1	5.1	5.2	5.4	5.4	5.4	5.4	5.7	5.6
Public administration	6.9	6.8	6.5	6.4	6.3	6.3	6.8	7.0	6.9	6.7	6.4

1. Excludes owners or partners of unincorporated business and professional practices, the self-employed, unpaid family workers, persons working outside Canada, military personnel and casual workers for whom a T4 is not required.
2. Excludes agriculture, fishing and trapping, private household services, religious organizations and the military.

Source: Statistics Canada, Catalogue no. 72F0002.

14.4 EMPLOYMENT, FINANCE AND SERVICES, CANADA, THE PROVINCES AND TERRITORIES, 1995

	Canada	Nfld.	P.E.I.	N.S.	N.B.	Que.	Ont.	Man.	Sask.	Alta.	B.C.	Y.T.	N.W.T.
	Employees[1] '000												
All industries[2]	10,673.6	147.8	43.4	299.5	240.4	2,574.0	4,180.9	404.6	314.0	1,041.8	1,392.1	12.0	23.2
Goods-producing industries	2,438.2	27.9	7.9	58.4	55.2	621.9	1,028.8	76.4	51.2	225.9	279.3	1.7	3.7
Logging and forestry	66.5	1.8	x	2.4	4.8	14.8	9.7	..	1.0	2.5	28.7	x	x
Mining, quarrying and oil wells	128.9	2.5	..	3.5	3.1	14.0	21.0	3.4	8.9	58.5	12.0	x	x
Manufacturing	1,675.9	11.6	4.0	36.8	31.7	463.6	798.6	53.2	24.9	92.4	158.6	x	x
Construction	437.9	9.0	3.4	12.8	12.0	95.3	149.2	13.1	11.8	60.2	69.1	0.7	1.4
Service-producing industries	8,174.9	119.0	35.3	239.9	184.3	1,935.9	3,129.5	326.4	261.5	810.1	1,103.4	10.2	19.4
Transportation, communication and other utilities	849.1	13.8	2.9	22.0	22.3	208.8	295.2	43.1	29.3	86.7	121.2	1.3	2.5
Trade	2,033.2	30.3	7.8	59.1	47.6	483.9	788.0	74.5	65.6	204.6	267.3	1.5	2.9
Finance, insurance, and real estate	641.5	6.2	1.9	16.2	10.0	144.6	276.2	24.7	21.0	56.3	82.9	..	1.1
Finance and insurance	460.5	4.4	1.4	11.1	6.5	107.6	202.4	19.3	15.3	36.1	56.0	..	..
Community, business and personal services	4,091.7	55.0	17.3	116.3	85.8	968.8	1,570.2	162.9	127.6	408.5	566.9	4.5	7.9
Business services	602.9	4.6	..	11.2	8.7	135.0	266.0	16.8	11.0	60.0	87.5	..	..
Educational and related services	933.6	15.7	4.2	30.8	20.9	228.5	354.7	38.9	31.6	86.1	118.4	1.1	2.6
Health and social services	1,187.1	20.3	4.7	37.2	28.7	303.1	436.1	54.1	43.2	109.1	147.5	0.9	2.2
Accommodation, food and beverage services	770.1	7.9	..	22.6	16.7	169.5	270.5	30.9	26.3	91.0	127.6	1.4	1.3
Miscellaneous services	597.9	6.5	..	14.5	10.8	132.7	242.9	22.2	15.5	62.3	85.8	..	..
Public administration	688.4	16.7	5.7	29.4	22.1	164.1	250.2	27.2	22.6	66.3	76.0	2.6	5.4

1. Excludes owners or partners of unincorporated business and professional practices, the self-employed, unpaid family workers, persons working outside Canada, military personnel and casual workers for whom a T4 is not required.
2. Excludes agriculture, fishing and trapping, private household services, religious organizations and the military.

Source: Statistics Canada, Catalogue no. 72F0002.

14.5 EARNINGS, FINANCE AND SERVICES

	1985	1986	1987	1988	1989	1990	1991	1992	1993	1994	1995	Earnings in 1995 as a % of all industry earnings
	Average weekly earnings[1]											
	$											%
All industries[2]	412.02	424.25	440.26	459.75	483.31	505.14	528.60	547.01	556.76	567.11	572.49	100.0
Finance, insurance and real estate	420.94	445.33	477.92	507.91	541.92	542.75	565.01	596.68	627.40	638.39	651.11	113.7
Finance and insurance	444.96	467.96	500.54	516.21	544.26	566.55	599.19	626.86	668.49	670.14	687.33	120.1
Deposit accepting intermediaries	412.79	419.99	436.96	458.76	482.48	506.54	532.81	557.91	570.56	585.60	602.06	105.2
Banks	431.62	440.19	455.49	478.56	504.72	529.58	555.05	578.25	593.40	599.51	623.31	108.9
Trust companies	402.02	409.32	425.47	446.96	471.37	493.43	522.44	537.17	544.49	569.84	583.49	101.9
Deposit accepting mortgage companies	142.84	78.14	388.95	372.98	158.15	162.19	586.83	561.69	580.25	589.13	682.51	119.2
Credit unions	361.90	372.83	380.67	399.23	425.73	444.82	463.06	491.73	502.32	537.31	532.12	92.9
Other deposit accepting intermediaries	511.21	586.96	553.43	540.25	568.87	599.32	667.93	728.44	769.95	857.56	843.52	147.3
Consumer and business financing intermediaries	466.97	473.26	503.96	515.23	590.68	600.81	652.46	695.23	726.67	729.80	762.78	133.2
Investment intermediaries	476.23	561.02	588.30	560.74	534.33	576.93	598.37	660.19	706.17	652.81	698.88	122.1
Insurance (excluding agencies)	482.05	498.52	532.39	574.73	618.66	655.42	675.95	681.89	711.41	728.73	744.99	130.1
Other financial intermediaries	542.44	617.31	740.44	701.73	806.06	806.73	989.91	1,031.03	1,357.88	1,246.48	1,187.65	207.5
Real estate operators and insurance agencies	362.01	392.06	424.98	488.70	536.55	488.01	483.25	520.44	521.78	556.88	558.97	97.6
Community, business and personal services	343.71	352.01	366.56	383.97	402.79	428.31	455.89	474.08	481.25	488.09	490.96	85.8
Business services	381.50	390.32	412.89	449.24	490.61	533.59	557.60	583.53	586.14	607.24	623.29	108.9
Employment agencies and personnel suppliers	247.23	249.12	244.84	275.37	327.40	350.03	364.82	398.80	389.26	392.11	385.38	67.3
Computer and related services	460.02	448.05	521.31	560.20	616.18	677.03	721.40	738.44	727.74	795.61	800.95	139.9
Accounting and bookkeeping services	370.90	399.87	408.20	453.48	477.48	525.68	541.03	539.76	530.55	563.63	575.72	100.6
Advertising services	422.51	414.87	416.92	477.31	490.92	477.36	510.89	551.37	604.22	626.57	657.98	114.9
Architecture, engineering and other scientific and technical services	533.66	526.55	536.98	575.37	633.28	689.67	733.72	765.51	784.36	785.60	818.33	142.9
Offices of lawyers and notaries	378.18	382.98	401.44	448.91	509.17	559.00	552.51	570.07	590.63	613.45	618.91	108.1
Management consulting services	313.86	373.49	408.85	455.42	502.01	553.46	576.47	612.97	645.17	640.73	678.95	118.6
Other business services	333.37	334.94	360.75	380.04	392.61	416.49	418.81	444.45	435.68	462.51	472.82	82.6
Educational and related services	499.38	513.02	532.05	557.98	576.76	605.91	640.33	667.74	674.05	671.41	669.37	116.9
Health and social services	346.82	359.19	375.44	392.39	411.97	435.37	466.91	485.06	498.45	504.63	503.44	87.9
Accommodation, food and beverage services	181.67	178.38	188.71	191.89	195.96	206.38	209.49	215.84	217.77	227.19	231.80	40.5
Accommodation services	223.97	218.90	239.43	237.23	238.54	262.39	266.41	276.43	282.01	294.06	302.77	52.9
Food and beverage services	167.04	165.08	171.89	176.47	180.80	187.72	191.21	195.46	198.54	208.31	213.08	37.2
Miscellaneous services	274.87	289.87	299.85	305.97	328.95	343.50	361.59	366.96	377.46	381.34	387.97	67.8
Amusement and recreational services	258.03	264.18	276.15	283.18	310.77	336.78	347.77	354.03	357.52	367.26	369.95	64.6
Personal services (excluding private households)	222.43	231.34	240.27	240.78	265.82	287.97	292.68	305.58	309.44	312.53	322.22	56.3
Barber and beauty shops	214.08	219.61	225.12	227.16	260.25	273.01	272.46	286.31	276.33	287.39	288.90	50.5
Laundries and cleaners	265.56	280.24	282.47	264.34	274.20	317.47	319.43	325.50	339.28	341.60	335.90	58.7
Funeral services	275.82	310.92	338.79	367.52	391.32	388.69	417.24	431.26	501.38	472.87	537.79	93.9
Other personal services (excluding private households)	172.69	181.90	204.94	215.20	234.86	241.10	233.34	239.70	245.29	239.93	237.44	41.5
Membership organizations	309.40	342.29	357.44	366.60	411.83	423.39	444.43	444.32	479.50	446.80	460.92	80.5
Other services	294.92	310.84	318.66	327.84	333.22	340.05	370.10	369.96	379.51	396.72	403.57	70.5
Automobile and truck rental and leasing	357.75	375.52	448.80	527.86	483.15	484.32	507.19	521.57	527.22	498.06	496.29	86.7
Photographers	221.26	221.12	228.09	253.07	227.46	277.63	311.43	356.10	309.00	338.54	355.83	62.2
Services to buildings and dwellings	235.78	266.80	284.73	272.89	265.36	273.75	264.13	282.58	279.80	299.00	313.78	54.8
Travel services	254.28	263.04	221.01	232.19	269.34	284.50	378.41	410.55	481.88	489.36	502.78	87.8
Other services	339.75	350.89	357.61	377.30	388.28	378.89	417.26	402.36	407.35	425.21	425.70	74.4
Public administration	524.02	543.20	571.84	592.97	636.52	689.12	701.92	727.64	746.59	752.88	749.83	131.0

1. Excludes owners or partners of unincorporated business and professional practices, the self-employed, unpaid family workers, persons working outside Canada, military personnel and casual workers for whom a T4 is not required.
2. Excludes agriculture, fishing and trapping, private household services, religious organizations and the military.

Source: Statistics Canada, Catalogue no. 72F0002.

14.6 CHARTERED BANKS[1]

	1989	1990	1991	1992	1993	1994	1995
				$ Millions			
Assets	549,564	608,135	634,340	676,620	753,992	841,037	912,058
Canadian dollar assets	378,444	408,701	435,030	453,975	521,868	572,666	610,757
Canadian dollar liquid assets	28,084	32,099	46,535	57,865	82,181	87,238	91,959
Bank of Canada deposits, notes and coin	6,289	6,581	7,153	5,880	5,916	5,042	4,669
Treasury bills (amortized value)	17,125	17,979	26,529	33,295	36,761	36,035	35,086
Government of Canada direct and guaranteed bonds	3,451	6,488	11,819	17,388	32,829	42,291	49,286
Call and short loans	1,219	1,051	1,033	1,302	6,676	3,870	2,918
Other	33	–	-	-	-	-	-
Less liquid Canadian dollar assets							
Loans in Canadian dollars	269,299	290,814	305,814	323,996	357,878	393,063	417,981
Federal government, provinces and municipalities	1,352	1,510	1,638	1,801	1,605	2,028	1,944
Personal, business and other loans	168,314	175,809	177,818	179,147	185,888	201,132	216,729
Residential mortgages	89,614	102,660	114,548	130,195	153,647	173,330	184,499
Non-residential mortgages	6,910	7,505	9,051	10,073	14,942	14,820	13,011
Leasing receivables	3,109	3,330	2,760	2,780	1,795	1,754	1,797
Canadian securities	16,597	18,545	22,554	24,372	27,815	34,682	38,095
Provincial and municipal	2,965	3,230	6,029	6,765	8,066	11,124	11,078
Corporate	13,632	15,315	16,525	17,607	19,749	23,559	27,017
Canadian dollar deposits with other regulated financial institutions	7,303	9,355	9,930	8,347	8,927	13,920	11,129
Other Canadian dollar assets	57,160	57,888	50,196	39,395	45,068	43,763	51,593
Foreign currency assets	171,120	199,434	199,310	222,645	232,125	268,371	301,301
Liabilities	549,564	608,135	634,340	676,620	753,992	841,037	912,058
Canadian dollar liabilities	370,250	401,107	421,509	439,331	502,805	551,606	599,442
Canadian dollar deposits	274,630	297,995	311,952	339,085	377,231	406,349	433,614
Personal savings deposits	184,228	202,597	216,515	228,732	263,766	280,291	297,559
Non-personal term and notice deposits	63,798	68,342	70,147	81,831	80,765	90,885	94,120
Gross demand deposits	24,526	23,830	23,214	27,115	30,260	32,396	35,744
Government of Canada	2,078	3,225	2,077	1,407	2,439	2,777	6,190
Advances from Bank of Canada	261	428	1,069	132	46	394	481
Bankers' acceptances	43,666	44,109	36,151	21,970	26,171	26,607	30,701
Liabilities of subsidies other than deposits	3,729	4,027	4,578	2,960	3,072	4,588	3,370
Other liabilities	19,884	23,253	32,353	39,713	58,918	72,932	88,159
Shareholders' equity							
Capital stock							
Common	11,926	12,802	13,308	14,131	15,351	16,532	16,659
Preferred	4,444	4,642	6,378	6,126	5,802	5,659	5,114
Contributed surplus	219	263	258	222	209	209	216
Retained earnings	11,490	13,588	15,463	14,992	16,004	18,336	21,130
Foreign currency liabilities	179,314	207,028	212,830	237,290	251,187	289,431	312,616

1. As of December 31.

Source: Statistics Canada, CANSIM, matrix 914.

14.7 MORTGAGES

	1983	1984	1985	1986	1987	1988	1989	1990	1991	1992	1993
						Loans					
New housing	98,148	79,548	102,749	107,738	116,759	147,552	113,399	119,953	113,174	108,835	103,898
NHA[1] mortgages	57,332	43,462	43,866	25,437	34,379	33,930	32,771	31,120	45,381	52,580	53,982
Single detached housing	19,953	17,771	12,658	11,037	12,808	13,264	14,781	13,007	16,332	19,981	21,852
Multiple unit housing	37,379	25,691	31,208	14,400	21,571	20,666	17,990	18,113	29,049	32,599	32,130
Conventional mortgages	40,816	36,086	58,883	82,301	82,380	113,622	80,628	88,833	67,793	56,255	49,916
Single detached housing	31,760	27,838	44,849	56,935	57,277	71,887	50,855	54,988	41,016	36,847	29,836
Multiple unit housing	9,056	8,248	14,034	25,366	25,103	41,735	29,773	33,845	26,777	19,408	20,080
Existing housing	5,340	4,822	6,258	7,207	9,103	12,704	10,366	11,348	10,813	10,930	10,355
NHA[1] mortgages	2,941	2,572	2,496	1,647	2,433	2,691	2,923	2,943	4,581	5,546	5,889
Single detached housing	1,185	1,154	858	777	1,009	1,148	1,328	1,212	1,640	2,173	2,468
Multiple unit housing	1,757	1,418	1,638	870	1,424	1,543	1,595	1,731	2,941	3,373	3,421
Conventional mortgages	2,398	2,249	3,762	5,561	6,670	10,014	7,443	8,405	6,231	5,384	4,466
Single detached housing	2,067	1,924	3,158	4,368	5,140	7,124	5,509	5,929	4,588	4,144	3,386
Multiple unit housing	331	325	604	1,192	1,530	2,890	1,934	2,477	1,643	1,240	1,080
						$ Millions					
New housing	451,716.0	388,894.0	559,440.0	644,993.0	599,295.0	624,302.0	681,704.0	621,439.0	849,210.0	939,084.0	789,135.0
NHA[1] mortgages	121,687.0	121,146.0	121,826.0	107,420.0	110,414.0	117,421.0	125,868.0	106,060.0	137,961.0	202,323.0	233,653.0
Single detached housing	74,009.0	76,994.0	89,494.0	77,243.0	81,661.0	84,161.0	91,340.0	74,576.0	95,163.0	135,977.0	135,185.0
Multiple unit housing	47,678.0	44,152.0	32,332.0	30,177.0	28,753.0	33,260.0	34,528.0	31,484.0	42,798.0	66,346.0	98,468.0
Conventional mortgages	330,029.0	267,748.0	437,614.0	537,573.0	488,881.0	506,881.0	555,836.0	515,379.0	711,249.0	736,761.0	555,482.0
Single detached housing	180,805.0	145,636.0	256,874.0	305,247.0	294,986.0	332,626.0	370,847.0	352,341.0	479,358.0	516,391.0	381,023.0
Multiple unit housing	149,224.0	122,112.0	180,740.0	232,326.0	193,895.0	174,255.0	184,989.0	163,038.0	231,891.0	220,370.0	174,459.0
Existing housing	17,383.7	15,285.1	23,888.0	30,212.7	34,253.4	41,572.2	49,447.4	44,100.7	59,246.7	72,003.2	61,308.0
NHA[1] mortgages	5,009.6	5,224.3	5,864.3	5,688.5	6,430.6	7,415.3	8,531.7	7,249.8	10,788.3	17,473.3	19,329.9
Single detached housing	3,539.0	3,792.1	4,649.1	4,337.3	5,041.0	5,660.7	6,590.8	5,503.3	8,093.6	12,710.6	12,748.8
Multiple unit housing	1,470.6	1,432.2	1,215.1	1,351.2	1,389.6	1,754.6	1,940.9	1,746.5	2,694.8	4,762.7	6,581.1
Conventional mortgages	12,374.1	10,060.8	18,023.8	24,524.2	27,822.8	34,156.9	40,915.7	36,850.9	48,458.4	54,529.9	41,978.1
Single detached housing	9,580.7	7,745.9	14,125.3	18,578.2	21,187.0	27,039.9	32,720.8	30,085.6	39,061.4	44,487.4	34,218.9
Multiple unit housing	2,793.4	2,314.9	3,898.5	5,946.0	6,635.8	7,117.0	8,194.9	6,765.3	9,396.9	10,042.6	7,759.1

1. National Housing Act.

Source: Statistics Canada, CANSIM, matrix 425.

14.8 TRUST AND MORTGAGE LOAN COMPANIES[1 2]

	1989	1990	1991	1992	1993	1994	1995
				$ Millions			
Assets	236,603	260,834	271,530	258,950	240,269	234,422	222,953
Cash and gross demand and notice deposits	2,622	1,676	3,584	3,946	12,261	15,256	6,457
Term deposits	2,441	2,268	2,167	3,348	1,327	1,979	740
Government of Canada treasury bills	8,894	10,817	11,423	10,321	9,736	8,527	7,687
Other short-term paper and bankers' acceptances	8,218	8,152	5,318	3,901	5,836	5,092	4,847
Canadian bonds							
Government of Canada direct and guaranteed	1,377	1,647	2,862	2,633	4,416	4,483	4,655
Provincial and municipal	904	1,116	1,833	2,170	1,238	1,373	1,126
Corporate	3,017	2,023	1,614	1,355	695	1,215	523
Residential mortgages	152,150	169,326	179,019	172,499	157,659	151,955	157,928
Personal loans	16,000	16,092	15,033	12,971	11,884	11,192	11,709
Non-residential mortgages	19,290	22,661	24,451	23,619	19,146	15,816	13,016
Other loans	5,150	6,300	6,503	6,852	4,894	3,066	2,280
Leasing contracts	2,058	2,462	2,412	1,872	1,171	953	816
Other assets	14,483	16,294	15,312	13,464	10,006	13,514	11,171
Liabilities	236,603	260,797	271,530	258,950	240,269	234,422	222,953
Deposits	209,397	231,368	237,779	226,483	207,205	200,651	193,097
Savings deposits	67,445	71,237	68,583	60,035	53,371	44,639	40,668
Term deposits, guaranteed investment certificates and debentures	141,953	160,131	169,196	166,448	153,834	156,012	152,429
Bank loans, promissory notes and debentures	3,744	3,513	4,691	4,748	4,229	5,002	3,717
Other liabilities	12,904	14,239	17,022	16,518	17,594	19,581	16,969
Shareholders' equity	4,483	5,253	5,743	5,509	6,857	5,826	5,951

1. Including subsidiaries of banks.
2. As of December 31.

Source: Statistics Canada, CANSIM, Matrices 2530 and 2531.

14.9 LIFE INSURANCE SALES

	1988	1989	1990	1991	1992	1993	1994
Number of policies sold	1,004,171	915,135	873,240	750,578	726,005	808,777	754,795
				$ '000			
Annualized premium sales	554,580	559,952	578,544	532,233	523,121	562,968	538,778
Face amount sales	81,863,922	81,250,586	80,559,008	74,213,582	73,673,802	79,582,819	77,404,785
				$			
Premiums per $1000 insurance	81	83	86	86	85	85	84
Average policy size	979,319	1,066,563	1,108,539	1,187,845	1,216,516	1,182,162	1,232,169
Premium per policy	6,637	7,346	7,946	8,510	8,634	8,362	8,581

Source: Statistics Canada, CANSIM, matrix 148.

14.10 LIFE INSURANCE PREMIUMS AND CLAIMS

	1988	1989	1990	1991	1992	1993	1994
				$ Millions			
Canadian companies							
Net premiums	23,665	24,309	27,926	29,199	28,857	30,248	30,659
Claims incurred	15,138	16,852	18,273	19,399	23,315	27,940	28,865
Foreign companies							
Net premiums	3,345	3,508	4,293	4,205	4,088	4,371	4,065
Claims incurred	2,023	2,368	2,835	2,724	2,884	3,320	3,811

Source: Office of the Superintendent of Financial Institutions, *Summary Financial Data,* Ottawa.

14.11 LIFE INSURANCE BENEFIT PAYMENTS

	1989	1990	1991	1992	1993	1994	1995
				$ Millions			
All payments	13,068.47	13,591.40	14,521.63	15,819.87	18,708.33	21,730.79	23,313.29
Life insurance	4,342.64	4,216.74	4,663.54	4,903.57	4,926.43	4,932.78	5,635.36
Death and accidental death claims	2,112.09	1,982.57	2,250.93	2,520.56	2,538.78	2,379.36	2,860.54
Disability payments	45.89	66.36	51.41	38.15	48.98	37.20	37.19
Matured endowments	89.89	72.43	69.69	72.48	73.52	79.00	73.09
Surrender values	888.47	838.93	991.91	948.19	994.78	1,116.43	1,348.18
Dividends to policy holders	1,206.30	1,256.45	1,299.60	1,324.20	1,270.38	1,320.77	1,316.35
Annuities	8,725.84	9,374.65	9,858.10	10,916.29	13,781.90	16,798.02	17,677.93
Individual policies	7,621.35	7,891.04	8,681.58	9,610.43	11,385.88	14,339.52	13,199.67
Group policies	5,447.12	5,700.35	5,840.05	6,209.43	7,322.47	7,391.27	10,113.62

Source: Statistics Canada, CANSIM, matrix 56.

14.12 PROPERTY AND CASUALTY INSURANCE PREMIUMS AND CLAIMS

	1988	1989	1990	1991	1992	1993	1994
				$ Millions			
Canadian companies							
Net premiums	7,896	8,353	8,883	9,236	9,639	9,902	10,342
Claims incurred	5,882	6,469	6,918	7,136	7,573	7,483	7,745
Foreign companies							
Net premiums	3,220	3,224	3,485	3,401	3,260	3,305	3,644
Claims incurred	2,407	2,627	2,614	2,646	2,458	2,464	2,614

Source: Office of the Superintendent of Financial Institutions, *Summary Financial Data,* Ottawa.

DESIDERANTES MELIOREM PATRIAM
A MARI USQUE AD MARE

SECTION 4

THE NATION

PIERRE ST. JACQUES, GEOSTOCK

Chapter 15

THE GOVERNMENT

Ron Watts, First Light

Canada's diverse peoples and vast and varied land mass are an odd foundation for a country. Canadian author Andrew Malcolm has said that "beset by political handicaps, a harsh climate, and a divisive geography, a disparate Canada set out to build a modern, independent country . . . The fact that it accomplished this task at all denotes an impressive amount of skill and grace."

On the evening of October 30, 1995, the nation eagerly awaited the results of Quebec's sovereignty referendum. The final tally: 50.6% of Quebecers supported the "No" (federalist) side, while 49.4% favoured separation from the rest of Canada. This was an emotional time, and a signal that Canadians' "skill and grace" would continue to be tested in the struggle for national consensus and a national identity.

In April 1999, the map of Canada will change dramatically, as Nunavut, a third territory, is created. The result of an established trend towards increased self-government and autonomy of Aboriginal peoples, Nunavut will likely be governed mostly by the Inuit. Although the land mass of Nunavut will be very large, its population of 25,000 will be about the size of a small Ontario city.

Governments of all levels in Canada are facing the same problem: the need to deal with rising debt levels. Throughout the 1990s, they have been responding to the problem by centralizing, and in some cases decentralizing, privatizing and deregulating services. Often, the burden has been transferred to taxpayers through higher local taxes, new user and licence fees, and cutbacks to programs and services.

As governments try to allocate shrinking funds to the services and structures people need and want, Canadians may notice their very infrastructure beginning to crumble, as some bridges, roads, sidewalks and sewers fall into disrepair from lack of routine—but expensive—maintenance.

Any Canadian government must envy Alberta for its budget surplus. The Alberta government has privatized many key services, from provincial parks and licences (drivers', marriage, birth) to roads and liquor stores. Sweeping cuts to health care, strict new welfare rules, large funding cuts to all levels of education, public service layoffs, new user fees, high oil and natural gas sales, and corporate taxes from the energy industry all helped the government eliminate its deficit early in 1996.

Ontario is pursuing fiscal restraint by finding savings in its own operations and by asking municipalities and boards of education to do the same. Social assistance and subsidies for businesses have been reduced. At the same time, personal income tax rates have fallen by 30%.

The federal government's big-ticket items—social programs and the public service—have become the targets of unprecedented and massive cuts. There have been billion dollar cuts in federal transfers to the provinces for health, welfare and postsecondary education.

Pillars of Canada's social safety net, such as Unemployment Insurance and the Canada Pension Plan (CPP), have become targets of much discussion and reform. As the baby boomers age, they will put an ever-increasing strain on the country's health and social programs. In particular, some fear that the CPP may face a funding crisis as the working population shrinks and the retiree population expands.

In addition, the government is clearly moving away from direct ownership and the provision of services when these can be better provided by the private sector or other agents, or in partnerships. There have been some high-profile privatizations, including those of Petro Canada, Canadian National Railway and the Air Navigation System. And as airport operations are being transferred to local governments, Transport Canada is moving away from its role of providing services while maintaining its role as policy-maker and regulator. Business subsidies have dropped by 60% and there is less federal involvement in mega-projects.

Yet, while the federal government struggles to keep the country together, Parliament continues to uphold the motto on Canada's coat of arms: *Desiderantes meliorem patriam* (they desire a better country), within the long-established structure of the Canadian federal system.

Power and Process

Canada is a constitutional monarchy, a federation and a parliamentary democracy. In Canada, as in most democratic countries, federal power is shared by the government's legislative, executive and judicial branches. As a constitutional monarchy, all three powers flow from the Crown.

Her Majesty Queen Elizabeth II of Great Britain and Northern Ireland is the Queen of Canada and our constitutional head of state. She delegates her duties, which are mainly ceremonial, to her representatives in Canada: the Governor General and the provincial lieutenant-governors. Formally, the prime minister and cabinet advise the Queen. Practically, however, cabinet holds the power and the Governor General usually acts on cabinet's advice. By convention, the Governor General and the lieutenant–governors have mainly formal and ceremonial roles.

The legislature's elected representatives adopt laws and vote on taxes and other administrative matters. The prime minister and cabinet ministers, who are members of Parliament, exercise the Crown's executive powers by proposing legislation, presenting budgets to the legislature and implementing laws. The independent judiciary is the final interpreter of these laws.

Federation

The Canadian government is a federation, meaning that the broad powers of government are distributed between a central (federal) government and 10 provincial governments. Each exercises its own powers, as outlined in the Constitution. The Northwest Territories and Yukon however, are governed under federal legislative jurisdiction. The territories exercise delegated power, not constitutionally-granted power.

In a parliamentary system, the prime minister is the chief minister and head of the executive—he or she leads the

Photo by Duncan Cameron, National Archives of Canada, PA-136154

A.Y. Jackson's proposal for a flag design, October 1964.

government. Normally, the prime minister is the leader of the party holding the majority of seats in the House of Commons. (If an election fails to produce a clear majority, or when the government resigns, the Governor General may ask a minority party to form a government.)

The prime minister is formally appointed by the Governor General. Although the prime minister's position and responsibilities are not defined by law or in a constitutional document, the federal government leader is, and has always been, the most powerful figure in Canadian politics.

As chair of cabinet, the prime minister controls discussion at Cabinet meetings, where government policies are determined. The prime minister usually selects cabinet ministers from the governing party's elected members of Parliament, although senators may also be named to cabinet. These ministers are then formally appointed—or dismissed—by the Governor General. Ministers usually head government departments, although some may be assigned special parliamentary duties, or may act as ministers of state.

In 1945, Canadian author Hugh MacLennan wrote a dramatic account of two peoples living within a single nation. "Two Solitudes" became a classic, and its title entered the language as a metaphor for the differences between the English and French in Canada. More than half a century later, MacLennan's metaphor found renewed meaning in the Quebec Referendum of October, 1995.

In this referendum, Quebecers were once again asked whether they wished to remain in the Canadian federation, or to sever the bonds that have kept Quebec a part of Canada since 1867. The final result showed that while 2,362,648 people voted NO to separation, 2,308,360 voted YES. The turnout was exceptionally high at 94%; the NO side thus won by 54,288 votes—a narrow margin of 1.2%.

The last referendum of this kind was held in May of 1980. During that vote, Quebecers revealed a more decided wish to remain within Canada. In fact, 60% of voters rejected the concept of sovereignty-association.

The French presence in Canada dates to 1605, when Samuel de Champlain founded Port Royal as the first permanent French settlement in North America. But full-fledged Quebec separatism didn't begin until the Rebellions of 1837-38, when a few thousand French-Canadians in Lower Canada, supported by prominent anglophones such as Wolfred Nelson, led an armed rebellion against unpopular British rule. The rebels' manifesto primarily sought government reform but included a call for sovereignty. This short-lived uprising was one of the few times that Canada has almost had a civil war.

In the late 1950s, the Quebec separatist movement re-emerged as a political force and became, in the 1960s, a focus of tremendous social, economic and political change. Although the push to separate from Canada has historically been tied to a small percentage of the Quebec population, in recent years increasing numbers of Quebecers have voted in referendums to establish a sovereign Quebec.

The issues that have propelled the Quebec separatist movement surround the safeguarding of the French language and culture in Quebec. Much of the debate on Quebec's place in Canada has therefore centred on constitutional issues and the sharing of powers between the provincial and federal governments.

The people of Canada have been challenging and changing the Canadian Constitution ever since 1867, when the Constitution Act brought together, into one federal state, the provinces of Ontario, Quebec, Nova Scotia and New Brunswick. Six provinces later joined the original four: Manitoba (1870), British Columbia (1871), Prince Edward Island (1873), Alberta and Saskatchewan (1905), and Newfoundland (1949).

Recent milestones in Canada's constitutional evolution include the Canada Act, 1982, and the Constitution Act 1982, which patriated the Constitution from Great Britain, created Canada's Charter of Rights and Freedoms, and put in place a general amending formula. An important milestone in federal legislation was the Official Languages Act, 1969, which declared English and French to be Canada's two official languages.

When the Constitution was patriated in 1982, Quebec was the only province that refused to give its consent to the agreement reached. In 1987, the Meech Lake Accord was presented to meet Quebec's concerns but died in 1990 when the legislatures of Manitoba and Newfoundland failed to give their unanimous approval. The failure of the Charlottetown Accord in a national referendum in 1992 highlighted the fundamental division between Quebec and the other provinces.

In early 1996, the federal government, led by Prime Minister Jean Chrétien, passed a bill giving five regions of Canada—including Quebec—the power to veto any future constitutional changes and recognizing Quebec as a distinct society within Canada. The bill was federal, rather than constitutional, law.

The speech from the throne in February 1996 stated: "as long as the prospect of another Quebec referendum exists, the Government will exercise its responsibility to ensure that the debate is conducted with all the facts on the table, that the rules of the process are fair, that the consequences are clear, and that Canadians, no matter where they live, will have their say in the future of the country."

Ted Grant, Ted Grant Photography Ltd.

Parliament Hill.

The prime minister recommends various appointments to the Governor General: those of ministers, Privy Councillors, lieutenant-governors, speakers of the Senate, chief justices, senators, and deputy ministers in the public service. The prime minister also recommends a Governor General for the Queen's appointment. The Prime Minister's Office, the Privy Council Office (PCO) and the Federal-Provincial Relations Office all support the prime minister.

On November 4, 1993, the Right Honourable Jean Chrétien became Canada's 20th prime minister—and the eighth Liberal prime minister—following an October general election. Canadian voters withdrew support from the governing Progressive Conservatives and sent a clear message for change as they elected a Liberal majority. Support for the New Democratic Party fell in a similarly dramatic fashion, as the party retained only about one-fifth of its seats.

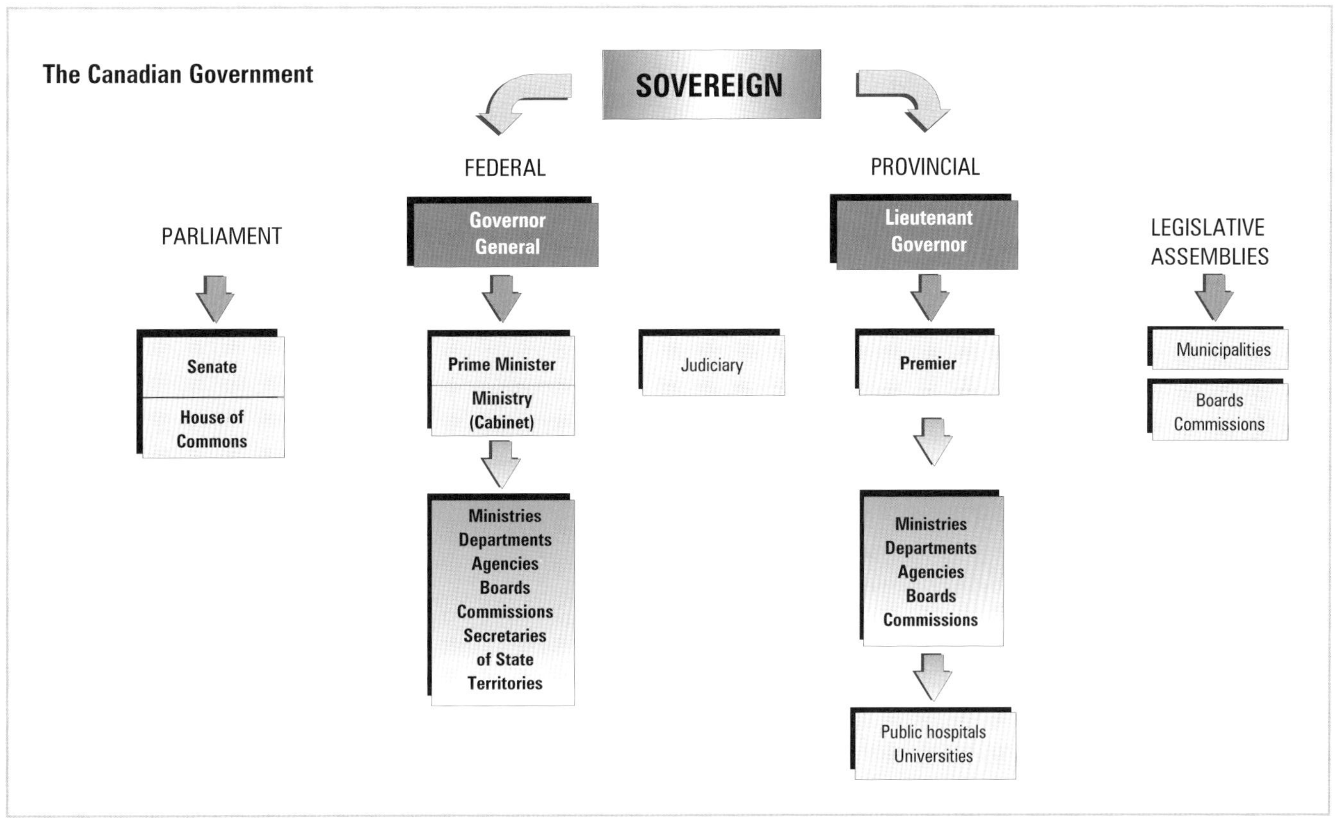

The separatist Bloc Québécois, which won 54 seats in Quebec, became the Official Opposition, while the Reform Party, which was strong in Western Canada, saw the number of its seats increase from one to 52.

The Privy Council Office

The Privy Council Office supports the prime minister and cabinet in their role as government decision-makers. The PCO provides advice, information and services to the prime minister. The prime minister heads the PCO program, helped by the clerk of the Privy Council (secretary to the cabinet) and by a chief of staff.

One of the PCO's many responsibilities is to prepare and distribute documents and reports for the cabinet and cabinet committees. Several activities fall under the program, including commissions of inquiry and task forces, which cover a broad range of issues. In 1995, for example, the Commission of Inquiry into the Deployment of Canadian Forces to Somalia and the Commission of Inquiry on the Blood System in Canada were among those in progress.

Privy Councillors are appointed to lifetime membership by the Governor General on the prime minister's recommendation. Members include mostly present and former federal cabinet ministers and chief justices of Canada, provincial premiers, and former speakers of the Senate and the House of Commons. Other distinguished Canadians may also be honoured with appointments; for example, long-time parliamentarians. Cabinet ministers must be sworn into the Privy Council.

The cabinet acts as the Committee of the Privy Council. It has no legal or statutory basis; therefore, its formal authority is obtained through legal instruments called orders-in-council, which are explicit, written executive or legislative actions. These are issued by the Governor General in the role of Governor-in-Council acting on the advice of the cabinet.

The Legislature

By definition, a legislature is "a group of persons having the duty and power to make laws for a country, province, or state." Members may be elected—as in all provincial legislatures and the House of Commons—or appointed, like members of the Senate. The federal legislative body is composed of the Queen and these two federal houses.

The House of Commons

The House of Commons is Canada's elected federal legislative body: it represents the people of Canada. Although many decisions are made in the House, in addition to its primary law-making role, its function is mainly one of review, approval and criticism. Canada is divided into electoral districts (also called constituencies or, more informally, ridings) and one member of Parliament is elected for each district.

The number of seats in the House of Commons is based on representation by population according to a constitutional formula. That is, every 10 years, after the decennial census, the number of seats is adjusted and ridings are redrawn to reflect population changes. As of the 1993 federal election, there were 295 constituencies.

Canada has a multi-party system in which one party usually dominates. Each party selects a leader to speak on its behalf both within and outside the House of Commons. Throughout Parliament's history, many different viewpoints and parties have been represented.

Elections

According to the Charter of Rights and Freedoms, "Every citizen of Canada has the right to vote in an election of members of the House of Commons or of a legislative assembly and to be qualified for membership therein." In Canada, federal elections are governed by the Constitution Act and the Canada Elections Act.

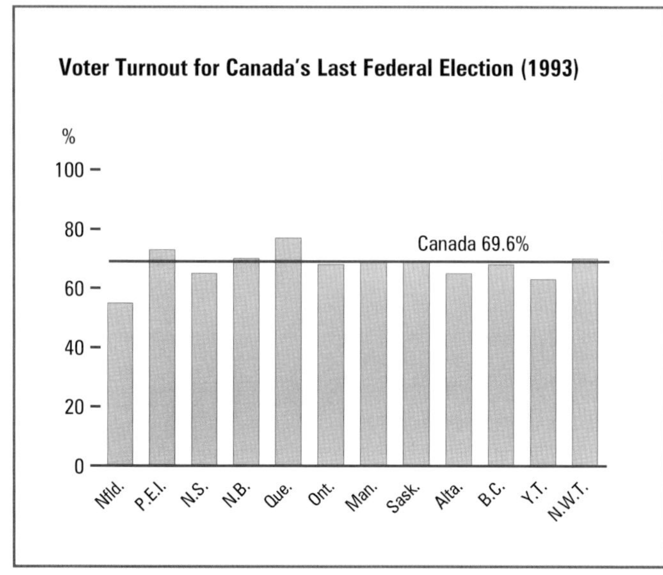

All Canadian citizens who are at least 18 years old, are resident in Canada, and whose names appear on the official list of voters are eligible to vote. There are some exceptions, including electoral officers. Special voting rules apply to some; for example, members of the Canadian Forces and federal public servants posted abroad. Advance polls and proxy voting accommodate those who can't vote on election day.

The prime minister has the power to advise the Governor General to dissolve Parliament, the first step in calling an election. The Governor General sets the election date. Because all those involved in a federal election—candidates, parties and election officials—need time to organize, the date of the poll must be at least 47 days away from the time the election is called.

According to the Constitution, Parliament's mandate can last no longer than five years, but it is unusual for a government

How much does an election weigh?

About 763 tonnes. That's Elections Canada's estimate of the amount of election supplies required for the federal general election held on October 25, 1993.

The nearly 29 million items produced for the election included 65,195 ballot boxes for more than 54,000 polling stations in ridings across the country.

Elections Canada is the non-partisan federal agency responsible to the House of Commons for administering federal elections and referendums. During an election, the agency's staff of fewer than 60 increases nearly overnight to about 185,000 enumerators, returning officers and other people essential to running an election.

Arrangements are also made for voting by special ballot. In 1993, the arrangements accommodated everyone from the 1,000 Canadian peacekeepers in the United Nations Protection Force in Bosnia to the 41 members of the crew of an icebreaker in Frobisher Bay, Northwest Territories. Enquiries officers answered more than 420,000 telephone calls from Canadians inside and outside the country.

On election day, 13,835,018 Canadians cast their ballots and Canada had a new government.

to last its full term. Generally, federal elections are held every four years. Sometimes an election may be held earlier; this may happen if the government resigns.

Election results are simply determined in Canada: the candidate who receives the most votes is declared elected. This is often referred to as the "first-past-the-post" system, which means that if more than two candidates run, the winner may actually be elected on a minority of votes. All provincial and federal elections in Canada follow this system.

The Senate

The Senate is often described as the chamber of "sober second thought." Also known as the upper house of the legislature, it was established partly to protect the interests of the less populous regions of Canada. For this reason, membership is based on regional representation and not representation by population.

Although the Senate is not as powerful as the House of Commons—it cannot introduce or raise the amounts in money bills, for example—it does have three basic functions. In its main role, the Senate is responsible for reviewing government bills. In an investigative role, special committees of the Senate look into major social and economic issues or proposed legislation. In its deliberative role, the Senate is a national forum for debating public issues and airing regional concerns.

Senators are appointed in the Queen's name by the Governor General on the advice of the prime minister. Before 1965, senators were appointed for life; now they must retire at age 75. The Senate has 104 seats: Newfoundland, 6; Maritime Provinces Division, 24 (10 each from Nova Scotia and New Brunswick and 4 from Prince Edward Island); Quebec Division, 24; Ontario Division, 24; the Western Provinces Division, 24 (6 each from Manitoba, Saskatchewan, Alberta and British Columbia); and the Yukon and Northwest Territories, 1 each. As of January 1996, all but three senators were affiliated with a political party.

The Judiciary

The judiciary interprets the laws created by Parliament; judges determine whether laws have been broken or whether they are unconstitutional (for example, if they are contrary to the Charter of Rights and Freedoms or if they fall outside the jurisdiction of Parliament or provincial legislatures). Canada's judiciary is independent: it is not controlled by cabinet or Parliament, which leaves it to carry out its duties impartially. It also means that the government cannot revoke court appointments.

The Creation of a Law

The principle of the legislative process is that a bill, or a proposed law, becomes law by passage through a legislature. Canadian legislation can originate in the House of Commons or the Senate. In Canada, money bills (those dealing with spending or raising money) must be introduced by a cabinet minister in the House of Commons. After it has been introduced, legislation can be removed or withdrawn, defeated, amended, passed, or it may "die on the Order Paper" when the legislature recesses. Bills must pass through three readings in both the House of Commons and the Senate. It is the Governor-General who completes the process by giving royal assent.

Cabinet

The cabinet is the decision-making body where ministers determine the policy for proposed legislation. The government house leader is responsible for the order and manner in which bills are considered in Parliament. Government bills are identified by numbers (for example, C-199), according to the order in which they are introduced in the legislature, but they may be considered in any sequence. After a bill is passed it is given a name, although some well-known laws may continue to be referred to by number; for example, Quebec's language law is often referred to as Bill 101.

Public bills apply to everyone in the country. There are two types of public bills: those introduced and sponsored by a minister (government public bills) and those sponsored by a member of Parliament (private members' public bills). Government public bills are normally introduced by the sponsoring minister; a private member's public bill is one introduced by any individual member, embodying policy proposals of concern to him or her. There is also another class of government bill—very few are introduced in any parliamentary session—known as private members' private bills. Such bills benefit a particular individual or group; a recent example allowed two religious groups to amalgamate.

Readings

First reading is a formality, after which the bill is printed and distributed to members of the House of Commons. A sponsor may sometimes give a brief explanation of the bill.

At a later sitting, the sponsoring member, usually a minister, moves that the bill be given second reading and referred to an appropriate House of Commons committee. There is usually much debate on the general principles of the bill at this stage, as the House decides if the bill is actually needed and, if so, if it is sound.

If the bill is approved in principle, the next step begins as a designated House committee considers the bill clause by clause, calling on expert witnesses, if necessary. When the study is completed, the committee refers the bill—with or without amendments—back to the House of Commons. Then, the House decides whether it will accept the bill or amend it further.

Finally, at third reading, amendments that do not contradict the principle of the bill may be considered and the minister moves that the bill be passed. If the vote is favourable, the bill is introduced in the Senate, where it goes through a similar process.

The Senate's consent should not be taken for granted, however. The Senate does not fall under cabinet control, and the majority of its members may have quite different party affiliations from those of the majority of the house. For example, in late 1995, the Liberal party's controversial gun control legislation was narrowly approved by the Conservative-dominated Senate after several months of

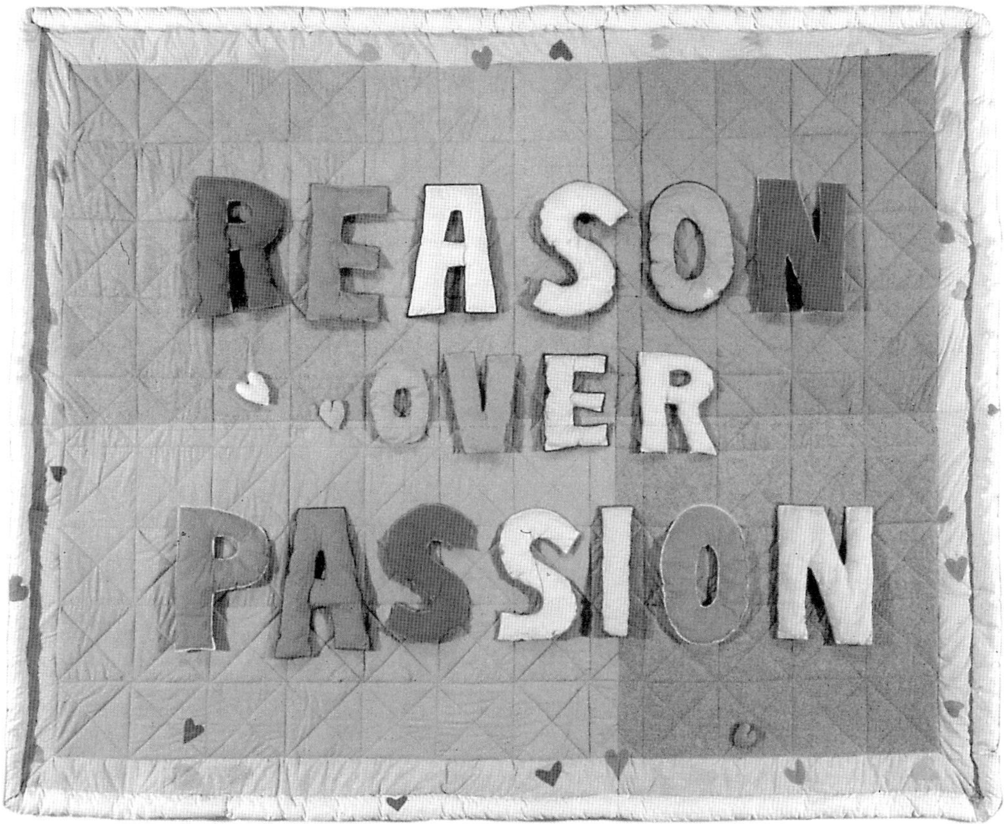

Joyce Wieland, National Gallery of Canada, Ottawa

Reason over Passion.

Senate committee hearings and much debate over proposed Conservative amendments. Finally, the bill was passed; it became law in late 1995.

Before becoming law, a bill must also receive royal assent, given by the Governor General. This is usually a formality: in Canada, royal assent to federal legislation has never been denied. The bill then comes into force, unless it includes a provision for becoming law at a later date. Money bills that make changes to taxes are usually retroactive to the day they were announced in the House of Commons.

Provincial and Local Governments

In addition to the federal government, Canada has two further levels of government: provincial and local. However, only the federal and provincial levels have constitutional standing; that is, powers as outlined in the Constitution Act, 1867. The territories fall under federal administration. While defence and external relations, criminal law, money and banking, trade, transportation, citizenship and native affairs are federal concerns, the provinces are responsible for education, health and social services, civil law, natural resources and local government.

In each province, a lieutenant governor, who is appointed by the Governor General, represents the Queen. The lieutenant governor acts on the advice of a ministry or executive council responsible to the provincial legislature. All provincial legislatures are unicameral; that is, they have one legislative body. Paralleling the federal system, the provincial assembly is elected for a term of up to five years, and may be dissolved by the lieutenant governor on the advice of the premier. Provincial assemblies function much like the House of Commons.

Local services are usually provided through the municipal, metropolitan and regional governments created by the provincial and territorial governments. The roles of local governments may vary considerably across Canada. They may provide services such as police and fire protection, road maintenance and snow removal. Education is normally administered separately. Local governments may also supply electricity and gas. Special agencies or joint boards and commissions are often created to provide certain services, such as public transit, for groups of municipalities.

Legislative assemblies govern the territories, led by commissioners who perform duties similar to those of the lieutenant–governors. These territorial bodies report to the Minister of Indian Affairs and Northern Development, who has jurisdiction over the territories and Indian and Inuit affairs.

Aboriginal Peoples

Indian and Northern Affairs Canada administers the Indian Act and other legislation relating to status Indians. The department fulfils the federal government's legal obligations to Aboriginal peoples. It supports Indian and Inuit economic development and self-sufficiency, and negotiates for increased autonomy for status Indian communities and settlement of Aboriginal land claims.

The Constitution Act, 1982 defines Canada's Aboriginal peoples as including Indians, Inuit and Métis peoples. The Charter of Rights and Freedoms recognizes and confirms the rights of our Aboriginal peoples in Canada. The term "Indian" includes: status Indians—those recorded in the Indian Act register and usually belonging to a band; non-status Indians—those with Indian ancestry who are not registered; and treaty Indians—those who are registered members of, or who can prove descent from, a band that signed a treaty (most are also included in the register as status Indians).

Inuit refers to those people who have descended from the indigenous peoples who lived in the northernmost parts of the Northwest Territories, Quebec and Labrador. Métis are persons of Indian and European ancestry.

The Royal Commission on Aboriginal Peoples—the largest royal commission ever—was launched in April 1991, with a broad mandate to review the fundamental place and role of Aboriginal peoples in contemporary Canada. The commission continued its work through 1995 and is expected to present its recommendations in 1996.

Status Indians

In 1995, Canada's total status Indian population was 593,050 (347,919 on reserves and 245,131 outside reserves), spread out over 608 Indian bands. There are 2,370 status Indian reserves in Canada. In northern and outlying regions, many bands follow a traditional lifestyle—hunting, fishing and trapping.

Inuit

Most of Canada's 36,215 Inuit, as identified in the Aboriginal Peoples Survey, live in the Northwest Territories, northern Quebec, Newfoundland and Labrador. While some still follow a traditional lifestyle, the Inuit have gained much more control over their own affairs in recent years. In 1992, the Inuit signed a historic land claim package with the Canadian government, which will create a third territory, Nunavut. Inuktitut for "our land," Nunavut will be formally established in April 1999, recognizing the Inuit's belief that their ancestors' land is an extension of their being.

This new region—what is now the eastern two-thirds of the Northwest Territories—covers about 2.2 million square kilometres, an area twice the size of British Columbia. Although the area is vast, the population is small: around 25,000, roughly the size of Val d'Or, Quebec. As about 80% of Nunavut's population will be Inuit, they are expected to control the government, with its legislative assembly, cabinet, territorial court and civil service. Eastern Arctic voters have chosen the Baffin Island town of Iqaluit (formerly Frobisher Bay) as the capital.

Social Support for Aboriginal Peoples

The Department of Indian Affairs and Northern Development (DIAND) works closely with Aboriginal governments to meet the needs of native Canadians living on reserves. Recently, however, the department has begun transferring more of its responsibilities to the Aboriginal groups themselves. By 1994-95, these communities controlled 82% (up from 77% in 1992-93) of all funding from Indian and Inuit Affairs. These funds are used to provide housing, education, economic development, child, family and adult care services, and other social services.

Federal funding for Aboriginal peoples is currently about $5 billion annually. In addition to DIAND and the Department of Health, 10 other departments have programs directed to Aboriginal peoples, including Industry Canada and the Canada Mortgage and Housing Corporation.

Government Structure and Finance

While our politicians formulate the country's goals and develop policy, this side of government would be powerless without administrative support. The public service, or the bureaucracy, provides that support.

A Shrinking Public Sector

Since 1992, all three levels of government have laid off thousands of public servants as one means of reducing deficits. In fact, after peaking in 1992, total public sector employment, which includes governments and government business enterprises, began declining at faster rates each year. About 2.3 million Canadians were government—federal, provincial/territorial or local—employees in 1994, down 1.6% over 1993.

At the provincial-territorial level, employment also declined for the third consecutive year, to just over one million employees in 1994, down 2.0%, or 20,800 employees, over 1993. Although public hospitals accounted for just over half (53%) of total provincial and territorial government employment in 1994, cutbacks in health care have begun to take their toll, as the number of hospital employees has dropped by 1.8%. In 1994, local government employment declined for the first time since 1990, dropping by 6,000 employees, or 0.7%.

In 1994, only 17.1% of Canada's public servants were in federal jobs; local governments accounted for 38.9%, and the largest proportion of public servants, 44.0%, worked for the provinces. Indeed, the federal government continues to shrink in proportion to Canada's total working population. Only 3.2% of paid workers were with the federal government in 1994; provincial and territorial and local governments accounted for 8.4% and 7.5%.

Also in 1994, the public sector represented 19.1% of all paid workers in Canada and accounted for 23.5% of all salaries and wages paid. Public servants earned a total of $84.5 billion in 1994, of which 40.7% was paid to provincial and territorial employees, 39.7% to local government workers and 19.6% to federal public servants.

In 1994, a total of 330,400 employees worked for federal, provincial, territorial and local government business enterprises, which are commercial operations included in the public sector. Employment in this sector dropped for the fourth consecutive year, as the provincial and territorial governments continued to downsize and privatize their public enterprises.

Employment in local government business enterprises dropped by 1% in 1994 to 51,600 employees. Traditionally, government business enterprises have competed with similar operations in the private sector, or they have monopolized markets that would otherwise belong to the private sector.

Federal government employment dropped by 2.8% in 1994, following declines of 1.2% in 1992 and 1.7% in 1993. Most of this decrease can be attributed to massive cuts in the military.

By 1999, further restructuring calls for a reduction of more than 33,000 military, reserve and civilian employees. Many air, navy and army command offices across the country will be closed. The government will also be looking at which of its functions can be privatized or contracted out.

Financial Administration

The Constitution Act, 1867 set out the basic principles guiding the government's financial affairs: no tax shall be imposed and no money spent without the authority of Parliament; and expenditures must be in accordance with the conditions authorized by Parliament.

The government introduces all money bills and exercises financial control through a budgetary system that fixes the government's financial needs annually, outlining the current and prospective condition of the public treasury. The government's fiscal year ends on March 31.

The Budget

The minister of finance presents a budget speech each year, usually in February. The speech addresses the state of Canada's economy and reviews the government's financial operations during the preceding fiscal year. The budget presents the government's fiscal plan, with revenue projections and spending plans. The minister also introduces proposed changes in taxation; changes in sales taxes or excise duties usually take effect immediately.

Public Monies

The Financial Administration Act outlines procedures for controlling and accounting for revenues and expenditures. All public money must be paid into a central fund in the name of the receiver general for Canada.

On top of collecting and disbursing public money, the government receives and pays out substantial sums in connection with the public debt. To finance the deficit and to redeem securities as they mature, the government issues and sells securities. The Bank of Canada acts as the government's agent in the management of public debt.

Under the Financial Administration Act, the president of the Treasury Board and the minister of finance decide how the accounts of Canada and of individual departments will be kept. The public accounts are prepared by the receiver general and tabled in the House of Commons every fall.

The Treasury Board controls government department budgets and financial administration in general. The board makes annual budgetary allotments to each department after it has analyzed the multi-year operational plans submitted by the departments for the Main Estimates. In the current climate of cutbacks, Treasury Board will focus on providing a more efficient management framework for the public service.

Transfer Payments

The provinces, territories and municipalities receive federal government funding to provide health care, postsecondary education, social assistance and other public services. In 1957, equalization (transfer) payments were introduced to allow the less well-off provinces to provide comparable public services at reasonably comparable taxation levels.

The payments are calculated using a formula outlined in federal legislation, to arrive at a standard per capita revenue level. The provinces with financial resources below that standard receive funding from the federal government to make up for the shortfall. Seven provinces currently receive equalization payments: Newfoundland, Prince Edward Island, Nova Scotia, New Brunswick, Quebec, Manitoba and Saskatchewan. British Columbia, Alberta and Ontario do not receive equalization payments because they are relatively more prosperous. Equalization has been renewed to the end of the century.

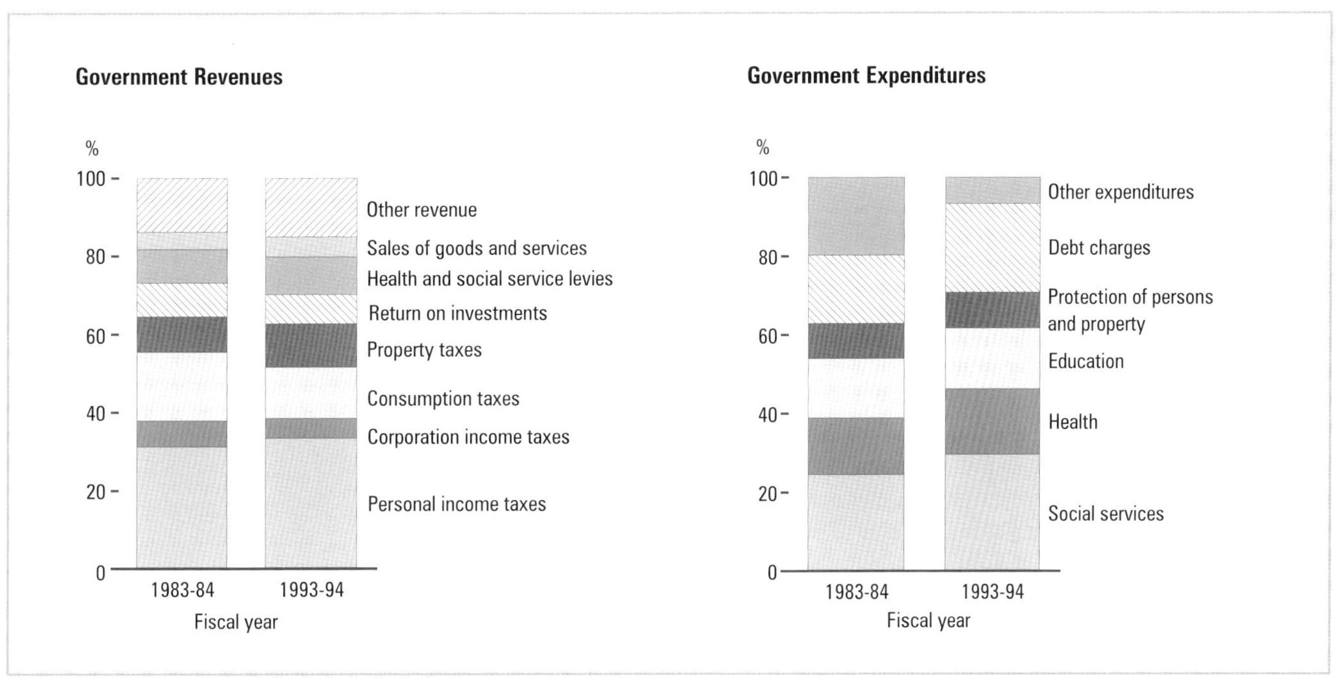

In 1994-95, the federal government transferred about $27 billion to provincial, territorial and municipal governments. Most of this funding fell under two other major programs: Established Programs Financing (EPF) and the Canada Assistance Plan (CAP). EPF was introduced in 1977: it is the main federal program providing provinces with support for health care and postsecondary education. It is also the largest single federal transfer to provinces, accounting for about $10 billion in 1994-95. Through CAP the federal government pays half the cost of provincial social assistance and welfare services; in 1994-95, this amounted to $7.3 billion.

Decentralizing Government

Beginning in the 1996-97 fiscal year, the government will adopt the Canada Health and Social Transfer (CHST), replacing EPF and CAP. This will give each province a lump sum to spend on major health and social programs. This move away from the traditional way of transferring federal money will give the provinces more scope to manage and reform their own programs. During the first year (1996-97), the CHST will be apportioned along the same lines as the current system, until a new formula is determined.

Although the territories receive EPF and CAP transfers along with the provinces, the equalization program does not apply to the governments of the Northwest Territories and the Yukon. They receive formula financing to help them provide a range of public services comparable to those offered by the provinces. Transfers to the territories are calculated as the difference between territorial governments' expenditure requirements and their revenue means. Such agreements will expire on April 1, 1999, to coincide with the creation of Nunavut.

Other smaller transfers provide funding to the provinces and territories. For example, grants to municipal governments in lieu of taxes, which ensured that the federal government contributes to local services much like any other property owner and employer, fell into this "other transfers" category.

The house that was to become the prime minister's official residence is, appropriately enough, almost the same age as Canada. A grey stone cliffside mansion overlooking the Ottawa River, it was built in 1868 by lumber baron Joseph Currier as a wedding present to his wife. The original name of Sussex Place was "Gorffwsfa," which is Welsh for "place of peace."

This "place of peace" is actually one of seven official residences in Canada. Of these, six are located in the National Capital Region and one is in Quebec City.

The six in the capital area are Rideau Hall, 24 Sussex Drive, Stornoway, 7 Rideau Gate, Harrington Lake and the "Farm" at Kingsmere. The latter two are situated in Gatineau Park, just north of Ottawa in Quebec. The other Quebec-based property is the Citadel in Quebec City.

Canada's Governor General resides in the 175-room Rideau Hall, which is across the street from Sussex Drive, and while in Quebec, he stays at the Citadel, an old walled fortress overlooking the St. Lawrence River.

The leader of the Opposition generally inhabits Stornoway, in Rockcliffe Park, a village adjoining Ottawa, while the Speaker of the House of Commons lives at the "Farm". This latter dwelling is part of the Mackenzie King estate in Gatineau Park, a few kilometres north of Ottawa. King bequeathed the estate to the Canadian people when he died in 1950.

Since 1966, distinguished guests of the country have sojourned at 7 Rideau Gate which is located between Rideau Hall and 24 Sussex Drive.

The National Capital Commission, the Crown corporation that plans Canada's capital, cares for six of these residences. The exception is the Citadel, which the federal government maintains. In fiscal year 1994-95, upkeep for all seven cost $2.8 million.

All these stately homes have been acquired over time. At first, Canada saw fit to provide housing only for the Governor General, the Queen's representative to Canada. To prepare for the arrival of Viscount Monck in 1865, the then-colonial government leased Rideau Hall, an 11-room home nicknamed "MacKay's Castle," after the Scottish stonemason who built it in 1838.

The castle was intended to be a temporary residence, but by 1868, Monck had enlarged it to about four times the original size. In that year, the federal government purchased it and the 32 hectares of surrounding property for $82,000.

Unlike the Governors General, elected leaders have fended for themselves in the housing market until 1950.

In 1943, the federal government began proceedings to expropriate 24 Sussex from a subsequent owner to prevent its possible commercial use. It gained possession for $104,000 in 1946, and for a brief period the Australian Embassy occupied the property.

Four years later, 24 Sussex became the prime minister's official residence. The prime minister of the day, Louis St. Laurent, agreed to live there only on the condition that he pay rent, a practice which his successors continued until 1971.

Harrington Lake, which is the Prime Minister's secondary residence, was acquired in 1951, as part of the federal government's plan to create Gatineau Park. It was in 1959 that the country's prime minister began to use it as a second residence.

Stornoway is a two-and-a-half storey stucco home built in 1913. As a private home, its most famous occupant was Princess Juliana of the Netherlands, who took refuge there during the Second World War. In 1950, a private trust fund established to buy a house for the leader of the Opposition purchased Stornoway for $44,000. The fund maintained the house for many years, but began to diminish in the late 1960s. In 1970, the government agreed to buy Stornoway for $1.

But such payments were frozen in the 1994 budget as part of overall fiscal restraint.

Financial Challenges

The federal government plays the lead role in managing the nation. It sets federal tax rates, regulates industry and trade and influences the country's interest and exchange rates through the Bank of Canada. And, along with the provinces, it helps fund basic services, such as education and health care. Federal, provincial and local governments provide roads, bridges, sidewalks, sewers, and other services.

In recent years, governments at all levels have been struggling to allocate shrinking funds to the services and structures people need and want. But huge debts mean that governments have less to spend and make it difficult for them to borrow. Deficit reduction and debt management have become critical targets for governments across Canada.

The wide range of government services carries an extremely high price tag. In 1994, total government taxation revenue amounted to more than $235 billion—just over $9,000 for every Canadian. In Canada, the government pays many of its bills by collecting taxes on our income. Personal income tax continues to be the most important source of federal revenue, accounting for close to half of the total. Sales and excise taxes, which include the Goods and Services Tax (GST), make up the second-largest revenue source. Unemployment insurance premiums, corporate income tax, and other revenues (Bank of Canada profits and interest income, for example) follow.

Provincial and territorial revenue for 1994-95 totalled $154 billion. Expenditures amounted to $174 billion, for a deficit of $20 billion. Health remained the largest expense, accounting for just over one-quarter of total expenditures. Social services, the second-largest expense, represented about 19%; education expenditures accounted for 18%. The rest went towards general services and other programs.

Local government revenue amounted to $71 billion in 1993; expenditures stood at $73 billion. The major revenue source for local government was property and related taxes, which

On Guard For Thee

Across the Ottawa River from the nation's capital is a building engineered to last 500 years. Located about 12 kilometres from Ottawa, Canada's new high-tech National Archives building is a building of the future, but intended to preserve the past.

For years, the National Archives' collections have been stored in more than a dozen buildings across Ottawa, many of which threatened rather than protected the nation's archival heritage. The new facility in Gatineau, Quebec, will preserve Canada's collective memory from the four enemies of every archivist—fire, flood, vermin and fluctuations in temperature and humidity.

The new building covers 32,000 square metres; it is, in fact, big enough to accommodate two 747 jets. The lower three floors form a concrete bunker divided into 48 enormous climate-controlled vaults, each designed to hold some 12,000 boxes of archival material. Here will rest Canada's most treasured drawings, prints, maps, manuscripts, books, records, photographs, oil paintings, medals, postage stamps and other keepsakes. The National Archives building will be completed by November 1996 at a cost of $89 million.

amounted to over two-thirds of the total. Fines, surplus funds from local enterprises, as well as sales of goods and services, licences and permits, concessions and franchises, provide revenue, along with transfer payments from other levels of government. Education is the largest expense; it represented 40% of total expenditures. Other sizeable expenditures included transportation and communications, social services, health, and protection of persons and property.

Fundamental Challenges

The federal government has been spending more than it collects in revenues for about 25 years. In late 1995, the federal finance minister stated that the government's fundamental challenge is a debt that is growing faster than the economy. In fact, paying interest on the debt has crowded out all other spending.

Roughly 30% of total spending goes to pay debt charges, leaving about 70% for programs. By contrast, in the mid-1970s, only 10% of spending was on debt charges.

In the 1994-95 fiscal year, the deficit did actually shrink a little, after growing for several years. The shortfall between what the government spent ($160.8 billion) and what it took in ($123.3 billion), resulted in a $37.5 billion deficit.

Each year's deficit is tacked onto previous years' deficits to form the federal debt. To finance the current and past deficits, the government must borrow to keep the country going. As of March 31, 1995, Canada's federal net debt amounted to $545.7 billion, almost $18,000 for every Canadian, up from just over $17,000 the previous year.

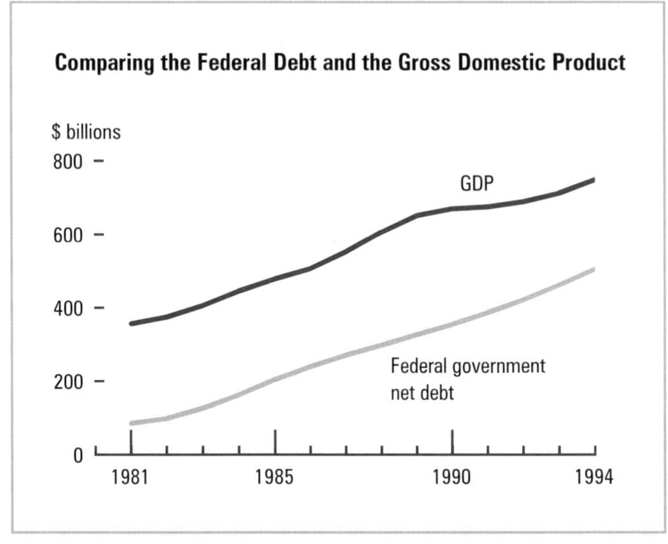

The relationship between the growth in our debt and the growth in our economy is known as the debt-to-GDP ratio. This measures the level of debt (what the country owes) as a percentage of GDP (what the country produces). This level of debt now stands at around 3:4, or 75%, close to four times higher than it was 20 years ago.

Canada does have a high debt burden; in fact, it has the second-highest of the world's seven largest economies. However, even countries with much lower ratios (France, Germany and the United Kingdom) now see their debts as excessive. Canada is not alone in its struggles to reduce the debt and get the country back on track.

SOURCES

Department of Finance Canada
Elections Canada
Indian and Northern Affairs Canada
Privy Council Office
Revenue Canada
The Senate
Statistics Canada
Treasury Board of Canada

FOR FURTHER READING

Selected publications from Statistics Canada

- **Federal Government Enterprise Finance**. Annual. 61-203
- **Provincial Government Enterprise Finance**. Annual. 61-204
- **Public Sector Finance**. Annual. 68-212
- **Public Finance Historical Data 1965/66-1991/92**. Occasional. 68-512
- **Public Sector Employment and Wages and Salaries**. Annual. 72-209

Selected publications from other sources

- **Democratic Government in Canada**. R. MacGregor Dawson and W.F. Dawson. 1989.
- **The Language of Canadian Politics**. John McMenemy. 1980.

Legend

–	nil or zero	..	not available	x	confidential
--	too small to be expressed	...	not applicable or not appropriate		*(Certain tables may not add due to rounding)*

15.1 GOVERNMENT TRANSFER PAYMENTS TO PERSONS

	1983	1984	1985	1986	1987	1988	1989	1990	1991	1992	1993	1994
						$ Millions						
All government levels	49,947	53,536	57,995	61,596	66,222	71,205	76,847	85,199	98,029	107,173	112,759	113,174
Federal	28,079	29,699	31,738	33,191	34,266	36,050	38,047	42,334	49,816	53,420	56,620	55,160
Family and youth allowances	2,303	2,393	2,492	2,524	2,552	2,595	2,634	2,711	2,824	2,870	37	37
Pensions—World Wars I and II	598	625	637	653	676	702	738	822	844	920	907	909
War veterans' allowances	424	468	519	505	475	448	436	432	439	443	441	417
Unemployment insurance benefits	10,062	9,859	10,118	10,394	10,369	10,781	11,445	13,119	17,323	18,648	17,592	15,012
Pensions to government employees	1,602	1,769	1,961	2,168	2,400	2,626	2,845	3,000	3,453	3,724	3,984	4,129
Old age security fund payments	10,137	10,999	12,150	13,148	14,006	14,801	15,718	16,705	17,955	18,776	19,479	20,170
Scholarships and research grants	377	442	459	492	495	521	555	665	691	726	727	780
Adult occupational training payments	–	–	–	–	–	–	–	–	–	–	–	–
Other transfer payments	2,476	3,041	3,270	3,244	3,293	3,576	3,676	4,880	6,287	7,313	13,453	13,706
Provincial	16,409	17,426	18,874	20,019	21,613	23,300	25,498	27,750	30,680	33,593	33,888	34,231
Direct relief	4,077	4,509	4,888	5,120	5,363	5,584	5,891	6,617	7,960	9,371	10,059	10,343
Old age and blind pensions	663	673	706	727	813	845	828	870	882	816	418	411
Mothers' and disabled persons' allowances	204	254	265	295	290	280	294	310	364	410	438	447
Workers compensation benefits	1,894	2,144	2,294	2,675	2,947	3,054	3,304	3,706	3,724	3,835	3,712	3,922
Pensions to government employees	733	781	923	1,097	1,292	1,493	1,613	1,299	1,450	1,570	1,514	1,273
Grants to postsecondary educational institutions	4,199	4,345	4,581	4,687	4,825	5,234	5,581	5,874	6,283	6,390	6,458	6,260
Grants to benevolent associations	3,592	3,471	3,716	3,776	4,314	4,855	5,930	6,912	7,782	8,660	8,701	9,002
Other transfer payments	1,047	1,249	1,501	1,642	1,769	1,955	2,057	2,162	2,235	2,541	2,588	2,573
Local	752	812	866	964	1,065	1,141	1,275	1,747	2,726	3,382	3,890	4,095
Canada Pension Plan	3,485	4,045	4,676	5,349	6,948	8,095	9,137	10,199	11,298	12,886	14,197	15,249
Quebec Pension Plan	1,222	1,554	1,841	2,073	2,330	2,619	2,890	3,169	3,509	3,892	4,164	4,439

Source: Statistics Canada, CANSIM, matrix 5067.

15.2 HOUSE OF COMMONS SEATS[1]

	All seats	Liberal Party of Canada	Bloc Québécois	Reform Party of Canada	New Democratic Party	Progressive Conservative Party of Canada	Independent and other
Canada							
1980	282	147	–	–	32	103	–
1984	282	40	–	–	30	211	1
1988	295	83	–	–	43	169	–
1993	295	177	54	52	9	2	1
1993							
Newfoundland	7	7	–	–	–	–	–
Prince Edward Island	4	4	–	–	–	–	–
Nova Scotia	11	11	–	–	–	–	–
New Brunswick	10	9	–	–	–	1	–
Quebec	75	19	54	–	–	1	1
Ontario	99	98	–	1	–	–	–
Manitoba	14	12	–	1	1	–	–
Saskatchewan	14	5	–	4	5	–	–
Alberta	26	4	–	22	–	–	–
British Columbia	32	6	–	24	2	–	–
Yukon	1	–	–	–	1	–	–
Northwest Territories	2	2	–	–	–	–	–

1. Following general elections.

Source: Chief Electoral Officer of Canada, *Thirty-fifth General Election 1993: Official Voting Results,* Ottawa, 1993.

15.3 VOTING IN FEDERAL GENERAL ELECTIONS

	1980	1984	1988	1993	1980	1984	1988	1993	1980	1984	1988	1993
	Electors on the lists				Total ballots cast				Voter participation			
									%			
Canada	15,890,416	16,775,011	17,639,001	19,906,796	11,015,514	12,638,424	13,281,191	13,863,135	69.3	75.3	75.3	69.6
Newfoundland	346,281	370,219	384,236	419,635	204,092	242,491	257,793	231,424	58.9	65.5	67.1	55.1
Prince Edward Island	83,976	87,215	89,546	99,645	66,558	73,801	75,986	72,973	79.3	84.6	84.9	73.2
Nova Scotia	592,992	613,964	644,353	707,202	424,055	462,885	481,682	457,610	71.5	75.4	74.8	64.7
New Brunswick	473,972	491,169	508,741	562,128	337,544	379,850	386,201	391,247	71.2	77.3	75.9	69.6
Quebec	4,395,389	4,575,493	4,740,091	5,025,263	2,994,202	3,485,815	3,562,777	3,873,050	68.1	76.2	75.2	77.1
Ontario	5,597,683	5,882,320	6,309,375	7,266,097	4,018,101	4,461,416	4,706,214	4,918,819	71.8	75.8	74.6	67.7
Manitoba	687,702	704,585	729,281	791,374	477,282	516,053	544,756	543,339	69.4	73.2	74.7	68.7
Saskatchewan	639,649	673,289	675,160	704,248	457,239	524,566	525,219	488,755	71.5	77.9	77.8	69.4
Alberta	1,315,770	1,479,675	1,557,669	1,851,822	797,394	1,022,274	1,167,770	1,206,871	60.6	69.1	75.0	65.2
British Columbia	1,718,562	1,853,110	1,954,040	2,420,709	1,213,030	1,437,904	1,538,628	1,640,614	70.6	77.6	78.7	67.8
Yukon	14,046	15,056	16,396	20,565	9,698	11,731	12,849	14,471	69.0	77.9	78.4	70.4
Northwest Territories	24,394	28,916	30,113	38,108	16,319	19,638	21,316	23,962	66.9	67.9	70.8	62.9

Source: Chief Electoral Officer of Canada, *Thirty-fifth General Election 1993: Official Voting Results,* Ottawa, 1993.

15.4 CONSOLIDATED FEDERAL, PROVINCIAL, TERRITORIAL AND LOCAL GOVERNMENT REVENUE AND EXPENDITURE[1]

	1985-86	1986-87	1987-88	1988-89	1989-90	1990-91	1991-92	1992-93[2]	1993-94[2]	1994-95[3]
						$ Millions				
Revenue	179,423.7	191,062.8	216,248.4	234,223.7	259,806.9	275,494.8	276,733.6	283,051.6	288,477.1	303,005.0
Own source revenue	178,718.6	190,357.2	215,487.8	233,397.3	258,908.9	274,528.9	275,740.4	282,010.4	287,407.3	301,924.3
Income taxes	70,891.0	79,361.1	92,824.8	98,801.1	111,177.9	118,810.3	117,993.4	113,815.6	114,497.1	122,057.4
Personal income taxes	56,593.8	63,895.5	75,589.7	79,263.0	90,098.9	100,255.2	102,385.9	100,026.9	98,365.3	102,487.7
Corporation income taxes	13,243.2	14,109.6	16,073.1	17,960.1	19,718.3	17,183.1	14,346.5	12,597.8	14,860.8	18,179.9
Taxes on payments to non-residents	1,054.0	1,356.0	1,162.0	1,578.0	1,360.6	1,372.1	1,261.0	1,190.9	1,271.0	1,389.8
Property and related taxes	15,606.9	16,746.8	18,050.1	22,067.7	24,607.3	27,018.1	29,146.8	31,375.1	32,375.0	33,468.6
Real property taxes	12,842.0	13,793.8	14,920.7	16,259.9	18,082.2	20,425.1	22,144.5	24,375.8	25,362.7	26,127.7
Other property and related taxes	2,764.9	2,953.0	3,129.3	5,807.8	6,525.1	6,593.0	7,002.3	6,999.3	7,012.4	7,340.9
Consumption taxes	34,800.1	40,005.7	45,062.6	50,359.3	54,670.6	53,736.5	54,883.5	56,236.3	58,095.5	61,466.8
General sales taxes	21,134.7	25,025.4	27,368.5	32,349.6	35,758.6	34,981.9	33,930.4	35,620.5	37,917.4	42,146.2
Motor fuel taxes	4,034.0	4,776.0	6,501.1	6,754.1	6,935.1	7,128.9	8,482.1	9,071.4	9,566.2	10,017.3
Alcoholic beverages and tobacco taxes	4,488.6	4,673.5	4,930.5	5,035.9	5,474.8	5,909.5	7,356.1	6,766.2	5,822.5	4,766.5
Customs duties	3,975.0	4,191.0	4,390.0	4,526.9	4,591.8	4,004.9	3,999.4	3,811.4	3,652.0	3,575.0
Other consumption taxes	1,167.8	1,339.8	1,872.5	1,692.9	1,910.2	1,711.3	1,115.5	966.7	1,137.3	961.8
Health and social insurance levies	15,614.1	17,282.0	19,109.8	20,891.6	20,815.0	21,724.8	24,396.3	26,943.9	27,890.0	29,362.4
Petroleum and natural gas taxes	3,489.0	467.0	-13.0	–	–	–	–	-15.4	–	–
Miscellaneous taxes	2,770.3	3,190.0	3,672.8	2,140.5	2,688.3	4,699.2	4,901.3	5,111.3	5,107.5	5,309.6
Natural resource revenues	7,924.0	4,437.8	5,727.6	5,364.5	5,520.0	5,684.4	4,676.3	4,977.4	6,283.5	7,604.4
Privileges, licences and permits	2,568.1	2,951.3	3,255.7	3,428.5	3,646.5	3,873.0	4,119.9	4,336.6	4,652.7	4,906.9
Sales of goods and services	7,789.3	8,756.4	9,867.2	10,365.6	11,385.2	12,237.7	12,650.2	13,397.9	14,052.2	13,692.7
Return on investments	14,938.3	14,821.1	15,541.9	18,364.4	20,604.0	23,041.4	20,787.4	21,853.2	21,508.3	19,861.5
Other revenue from own sources	2,327.4	2,338.0	2,388.4	1,614.2	3,794.3	3,703.6	2,185.4	3,978.6	2,945.5	4,194.1
Transfers	705.1	705.6	760.6	826.4	897.9	966.0	993.2	1,041.3	1,069.8	1,080.7
Transfers from other levels of government	–	–	–	–	–	–	–	–	–	–
Transfers from government enterprises	705.1	705.6	760.6	826.4	897.9	966.0	993.2	1,041.3	1,069.8	1,080.7
Expenditure	224,495.7	234,060.4	250,232.0	266,723.2	293,259.9	317,560.7	339,995.7	349,187.7	351,403.4	357,568.5
General services	12,692.1	13,238.2	14,650.8	15,205.5	16,564.5	18,158.6	18,749.8	18,665.7	18,961.6	18,236.7
Protection of persons and property	17,918.8	18,381.5	19,895.8	20,685.0	22,536.1	24,118.5	24,665.2	25,101.5	25,684.6	24,476.5
Transportation and communications	12,461.5	12,512.8	12,943.4	13,804.4	14,627.6	15,329.7	15,493.4	14,976.4	15,227.2	15,689.3
Health	27,726.3	30,403.6	32,545.9	35,088.3	38,574.7	41,822.7	45,391.7	46,958.7	46,641.8	47,100.5
Social services	46,461.5	49,403.4	51,946.6	55,171.4	60,900.7	68,406.4	79,151.2	85,719.9	87,257.8	85,783.1
Education	28,502.1	28,910.3	30,780.8	33,215.5	35,930.8	38,910.9	42,298.8	44,192.4	44,364.9	43,919.6
Resource conservation and industrial development	15,297.3	14,596.3	14,720.3	14,787.9	15,177.4	13,665.9	16,606.4	14,827.0	14,198.1	14,119.3
Environment	4,194.3	4,284.5	4,584.2	5,375.9	6,211.7	7,134.7	7,127.6	7,040.4	7,043.3	8,040.0
Recreation and culture	4,685.0	4,898.8	5,277.4	5,596.0	6,319.4	7,056.7	7,355.9	7,368.1	7,097.0	7,214.9
Labour, employment and immigration	1,731.1	1,799.6	1,776.1	2,390.1	2,563.7	2,831.3	3,031.4	3,277.7	3,390.7	3,310.8
Housing	2,526.9	2,299.5	2,350.5	2,704.4	2,844.6	3,288.9	3,545.5	3,589.3	3,866.9	3,827.6
Foreign affairs and international assistance	2,050.0	2,896.0	3,271.0	3,632.5	4,120.1	3,513.7	3,912.6	4,245.6	3,916.0	4,933.6
Regional planning and development	1,144.9	1,259.2	1,285.3	1,417.8	1,583.1	1,719.7	1,714.9	1,709.5	1,612.9	1,614.8
Research establishments	–	–	–	–	–	–	–	–	–	–
General purpose transfers to other levels of government	1,310.8	1,342.6	1,387.4	1,377.4	1,613.0	1,854.0	2,025.0	2,328.8	2,099.7	2,072.8
Transfers to own enterprises	5,269.3	5,028.1	6,080.5	4,701.6	4,989.1	5,593.1	4,910.0	5,467.8	4,508.2	5,112.7
Debt charges	40,164.9	42,466.1	46,342.2	51,090.7	58,474.9	63,542.4	63,491.5	63,600.1	65,264.2	71,325.0
Other expenditures	359.0	339.8	393.9	478.7	228.3	613.5	524.8	118.7	268.5	791.2
Surplus (deficit)	(45,072.0)	(42,997.7)	(33,983.6)	(32,499.5)	(33,453.1)	(42,065.9)	(63,262.1)	(66,136.0)	(62,926.2)	(54,563.5)

1. From April 1 of one year to March 31 of the next year.
2. Figures shown are revised estimates.
3. Figures shown are estimates.

Source: Statistics Canada, CANSIM, matrix 2820.

15.5 FEDERAL GOVERNMENT REVENUE AND EXPENDITURE[1]

	1984-85	1985-86	1986-87	1987-88	1988-89	1989-90	1990-91	1991-92	1992-93	1993-94[2]	1994-95[2]	1995-96[3]
						$ Millions						
Revenue	78,055	83,060	90,145	103,089	109,505	120,747	127,112	129,170	132,210	129,365	136,982	145,453
Own source revenue	78,020	82,990	90,050	102,978	109,419	120,610	126,986	129,036	132,080	129,232	136,887	145,373
Income taxes	41,484	45,028	50,821	59,399	61,386	69,766	73,903	74,334	71,865	68,920	75,002	81,475
Personal income taxes	31,083	34,764	39,580	47,359	48,078	55,384	60,805	63,714	62,396	58,205	62,008	65,602
Corporation income taxes	9,380	9,210	9,885	10,878	11,730	13,021	11,726	9,359	8,278	9,444	11,604	14,350
Taxes on payments to non-residents	1,021	1,054	1,356	1,162	1,578	1,361	1,372	1,261	1,191	1,271	1,390	1,523
Consumption taxes	14,465	17,260	20,979	23,927	26,335	28,760	27,552	27,974	29,123	29,868	31,951	33,265
General sales taxes	7,729	9,383	12,022	12,984	15,744	17,768	17,061	15,461	17,236	18,317	20,957	22,130
Motor fuel taxes	405	770	1,491	2,671	2,542	2,414	2,472	3,438	3,454	3,639	3,820	4,180
Alcoholic beverages and tobacco taxes	2,164	2,639	2,676	2,832	2,706	3,032	3,173	4,450	4,005	3,406	2,931	2,892
Customs duties	3,796	3,975	4,191	4,390	4,527	4,592	4,005	3,999	3,811	3,652	3,575	3,270
Other consumption taxes	371	493	599	1,050	816	954	841	626	617	854	668	793
Health and social insurance levies	7,617	8,783	9,633	10,554	11,252	10,646	12,682	15,361	17,493	18,233	18,928	19,520
Petroleum and natural gas taxes	6,140	3,489	467	-13	111	56	-1	5	-15	–	–	–
Miscellaneous taxes	462	438	440	490	683	642	642	602	571	447	508	504
Natural resource revenues	181	224	56	52	56	67	64	54	47	58	42	45
Privileges, licences and permits	114	153	169	199	216	249	276	320	353	410	534	559
Sales of goods and services	2,346	2,291	2,837	3,288	2,854	3,070	3,315	3,396	3,783	3,944	3,425	3,523
Return on investments	4,529	4,334	3,871	4,190	5,577	5,843	7,554	6,031	7,435	6,149	5,024	4,952
Other revenue from own sources	682	990	777	892	949	1,511	999	959	1,425	1,203	1,473	1,530
Transfers	35	70	95	111	86	137	126	134	130	133	95	80
Transfers from other levels of government	–	–	24	38	45	94	81	85	81	79	38	38
Transfers from government enterprises	35	70	71	73	41	43	45	49	49	54	57	42
Expenditure	115,039	116,911	120,826	130,720	136,334	148,748	158,971	167,141	171,405	171,039	174,216	177,703
General services	4,843	4,979	5,303	5,751	6,012	6,350	7,383	7,163	7,437	7,562	7,532	7,633
Protection of persons and property	10,854	11,876	11,986	12,962	13,440	14,441	15,175	14,995	15,368	15,822	14,795	14,642
Transportation and communications	3,733	3,457	3,536	3,689	3,727	3,610	3,640	3,903	3,517	3,789	3,911	3,258
Health	7,060	7,134	7,465	7,462	7,685	7,780	7,354	8,048	9,771	8,331	8,895	8,286
Social services	33,203	34,445	36,193	37,887	39,280	43,210	48,593	55,271	58,864	59,458	57,050	57,276
Education	3,891	3,973	4,187	4,222	4,251	4,441	4,194	4,438	5,248	4,914	5,260	5,129
Resource conservation and industrial development	10,929	8,077	7,072	8,708	7,440	6,486	6,145	7,844	6,836	6,683	6,994	8,128
Environment	491	422	446	498	530	610	690	703	714	751	948	915
Recreation and culture	903	852	931	1,028	1,044	1,123	1,275	1,364	1,446	1,347	1,331	780
Labour, employment and immigration	1,364	1,277	1,364	1,393	1,790	2,000	2,151	2,272	2,523	2,689	2,579	1,632
Housing	2,098	1,491	1,456	1,553	1,598	1,736	1,979	1,905	1,980	2,135	2,123	2,026
Foreign affairs and international assistance	2,041	2,050	2,896	3,271	3,632	4,120	3,514	3,913	4,256	3,924	4,942	3,371
Regional planning and development	388	278	344	347	443	482	468	371	427	485	445	447
Research establishments	1,161	1,072	1,090	1,131	1,059	1,276	1,497	1,676	1,837	1,584	1,560	1,284
General purpose transfers to other levels of government	6,830	6,799	7,234	8,080	9,104	10,040	10,248	10,007	9,672	11,460	10,885	10,606
Transfers to own enterprises	2,816	3,310	2,702	3,718	2,125	2,250	2,159	2,123	2,211	1,973	2,202	1,981
Debt charges	22,428	25,417	26,617	29,016	33,167	38,771	42,484	41,139	39,289	37,982	42,298	47,800
Other expenditures	6	2	4	4	8	20	22	6	9	150	466	2,509
Surplus (deficit)	(36,984)	(33,851)	(30,681)	(27,631)	(26,829)	(28,001)	(31,859)	(37,971)	(39,195)	(41,674	(37,234)	(32,250)

1. From April 1 of one year to March 31 of the next year.
2. Figures shown are revised estimates.
3. Figures shown are estimates.

Source: Statistics Canada, CANSIM, matrix 2780.

15.6 PROVINCIAL AND TERRITORIAL GOVERNMENT REVENUE AND EXPENDITURE[1]

	1983-84	1984-85	1985-86	1986-87	1987-88	1988-89	1989-90	1990-91	1991-92	1992-93	1993-94[2]	1994-95[2]
						$ Millions						
Revenue	84,536.8	91,086.7	97,574.0	100,744.7	112,592.2	123,543.8	134,398.6	142,606.8	141,683.7	145,179.4	152,047.5	159,633.7
Own source revenue	65,708.3	71,035.9	76,977.2	79,832.2	89,928.1	99,496.3	109,186.1	115,985.6	114,816.4	115,031.5	123,024.6	129,006.2
Income taxes	22,009.2	23,373.1	26,114.5	28,804.3	33,713.9	37,415.1	41,411.8	44,907.2	43,659.5	41,950.8	45,577.1	47,055.6
Personal income taxes	19,020.9	19,727.4	22,081.3	24,579.7	28,518.8	31,185.0	34,714.9	39,450.4	38,672.4	37,630.5	40,160.3	40,479.7
Corporation income taxes	2,988.3	3,645.7	4,033.2	4,224.6	5,195.1	6,230.1	6,696.9	5,456.8	4,987.1	4,320.3	5,416.8	6,575.9
Property and related taxes	1,146.6	1,192.1	1,106.3	1,025.5	1,041.0	3,589.8	4,040.4	4,567.1	4,776.0	5,323.8	5,432.1	6,736.9
Consumption taxes	14,300.9	15,589.1	17,488.7	18,971.7	21,074.8	23,959.1	25,836.7	26,110.6	26,838.4	27,052.3	28,180.7	29,469.1
General sales taxes	9,058.5	10,194.8	11,727.1	12,976.2	14,354.6	16,528.7	17,949.4	17,878.8	18,427.7	18,343.8	19,556.4	21,145.1
Motor fuel taxes	3,229.4	3,179.9	3,264.0	3,285.0	3,830.1	4,211.7	4,521.4	4,656.6	5,044.4	5,617.4	5,927.2	6,197.8
Alcoholic beverages and tobacco taxes	1,449.1	1,607.8	1,849.6	1,997.5	2,098.5	2,373.2	2,442.8	2,736.8	2,905.7	2,761.7	2,416.5	1,835.1
Other consumption taxes	563.9	606.6	648.0	713.0	791.6	845.6	923.2	838.3	460.6	329.4	280.6	291.1
Health and social insurance levies	5,831.0	6,319.9	6,831.1	7,649.0	8,555.8	9,639.3	10,168.8	9,042.5	9,035.3	9,450.9	9,657.0	10,434.4
Miscellaneous taxes	1,769.0	2,136.0	2,262.0	2,649.4	3,050.6	1,213.0	1,862.5	3,932.4	4,181.1	4,391.1	4,523.5	4,676.4
Natural resource revenues	7,600.6	8,088.9	7,700.0	4,381.8	5,675.6	5,308.7	5,453.0	5,619.8	4,622.6	4,930.3	6,225.1	7,562.4
Privileges, licences and permits	1,930.8	2,131.4	2,169.1	2,500.8	2,715.6	2,847.7	2,983.0	3,222.0	3,432.6	3,591.4	3,853.8	3,969.9
Sales of goods and services	2,066.4	1,974.9	2,239.9	2,263.7	2,332.0	2,463.6	2,709.9	3,033.2	3,210.3	3,353.2	3,453.8	3,392.4
Return on investments	8,473.6	9,717.8	10,451.4	10,804.9	11,153.6	12,384.9	13,927.4	14,493.1	14,043.9	13,896.3	14,968.8	14,578.3
Other revenue from own sources	580.2	512.7	614.2	781.1	615.2	675.0	792.7	1,057.8	1,016.7	1,091.4	1,152.7	1,130.8
Transfers	18,828.5	20,050.8	20,596.8	20,912.5	22,664.1	24,047.5	25,212.5	26,621.2	26,867.3	30,148.0	29,022.9	30,627.5
Transfers from other levels of government	18,725.1	19,933.5	20,499.6	20,837.3	22,543.4	23,899.2	25,035.1	26,420.3	26,653.5	29,938.4	28,799.7	30,407.2
Transfers from government enterprises	103.4	117.3	97.2	75.2	120.7	148.3	177.4	200.9	213.8	209.6	223.2	220.3
Expenditure	92,192.2	97,758.0	107,707.1	112,845.4	118,507.0	128,604.2	139,303.1	151,418.2	165,132.6	171,725.1	172,371.6	175,434.5
General services	5,214.8	5,227.3	5,615.8	5,732.5	6,457.6	6,433.5	7,088.5	7,381.5	7,831.6	7,520.4	7,873.1	7,258.7
Protection of persons and property	2,802.6	3,075.6	3,183.6	3,523.2	3,948.5	3,943.2	4,466.8	4,937.3	5,287.8	5,199.2	5,126.6	5,004.0
Transportation and communications	5,941.5	5,449.8	6,041.3	5,761.6	5,758.4	6,097.7	7,002.7	7,293.7	7,364.3	7,195.3	7,127.1	7,343.7
Health	22,972.3	24,419.8	26,470.5	29,009.7	30,876.1	33,630.0	36,829.7	39,853.5	43,457.5	44,906.6	44,924.5	45,179.7
Social services	13,626.4	14,708.6	15,672.9	17,019.2	18,542.7	20,436.8	22,365.3	25,581.8	29,797.7	32,929.2	33,915.5	34,560.0
Education	19,524.9	19,547.4	22,311.9	22,375.6	23,131.9	25,448.6	26,412.6	28,821.2	30,995.4	32,543.8	31,045.9	32,017.4
Resource conservation and industrial development	5,995.5	6,437.6	7,667.3	7,589.9	6,510.7	7,435.4	8,466.4	7,897.6	9,506.9	8,576.0	7,899.3	7,417.8
Environment	1,022.1	1,195.1	1,432.2	1,216.8	1,300.2	1,504.4	1,760.7	2,027.2	2,098.9	1,944.6	1,883.6	1,973.2
Recreation and culture	1,303.6	1,307.9	1,410.4	1,453.4	1,415.2	1,539.4	1,738.0	1,861.0	2,009.3	1,841.5	1,663.0	1,632.0
Labour, employment and immigration	315.9	323.8	528.7	482.7	416.0	621.6	593.6	681.0	801.6	846.4	790.5	825.5
Housing	578.1	485.2	823.9	639.7	598.9	692.4	724.3	892.4	1,097.9	1,105.2	1,265.3	1,281.4
Regional planning and development	811.9	788.7	687.4	695.8	696.9	690.4	703.3	724.3	869.7	778.8	679.1	692.8
Research establishments	173.0	195.6	238.8	252.6	256.4	321.3	340.9	358.3	349.4	491.9	515.7	513.3
General purpose transfers to other levels of government	1,730.6	1,777.7	1,853.9	1,953.7	2,022.6	2,513.5	1,788.6	2,297.3	2,441.0	2,543.9	2,093.6	2,034.0
Transfers to own enterprises	1,166.7	1,485.4	1,133.1	1,429.6	1,429.8	1,627.0	1,696.3	2,298.6	1,549.4	1,789.9	1,074.3	1,485.3
Debt charges	8,911.3	11,218.0	12,608.4	13,690.0	15,143.7	15,667.2	17,312.9	18,481.3	19,633.5	21,504.7	24,487.8	26,209.7
Other expenditures	101.0	114.5	27.0	19.4	1.4	1.8	12.5	30.2	40.7	7.5	6.7	6.0
Surplus (deficit)	(7,655.4)	(6,671.3)	(10,133.1)	(12,100.7)	(5,914.8)	(5,060.4)	(4,904.5)	(8,811.4)	(23,448.9)	(26,545.6)	(20,324.1)	(15,800.8)

1. From April 1 of one year to March 31 of the next year.
2. Figures shown are revised estimates.

Source: Statistics Canada, CANSIM, matrix 2781.

15.7 PROVINCIAL AND TERRITORIAL GOVERNMENT REVENUE AND EXPENDITURE BY PROVINCE OR TERRITORY, 1994-95[1]

	Nfld.	P.E.I.	N.S.	N.B.	Que.	Ont.	Man.	Sask.	Alta.	B.C.	Y.T.	N.W.T.
						$ Millions						
Revenue	3,593.9	851.9	4,832.2	4,645.6	40,565.6	50,643.6	6,607.9	6,460.9	16,415.0	23,217.6	511.0	1,288.5
Own source revenue	1,958.4	503.9	2,875.0	2,975.2	32,729.1	42,890.9	4,712.5	4,948.2	14,371.6	20,635.5	125.8	280.1
Income taxes	529.5	125.2	1,001.4	843.2	14,097.7	18,145.0	1,382.9	1,229.5	3,877.0	5,700.1	41.5	82.6
Personal income taxes	475.9	105.6	906.0	690.5	12,821.0	15,290.5	1,232.0	1,074.8	3,050.7	4,741.5	31.5	59.7
Corporation income taxes	53.6	19.6	95.4	152.7	1,276.7	2,854.5	150.9	154.7	826.3	958.6	10.0	22.9
Property and related taxes	8.4	43.7	16.2	220.9	1,114.0	1,230.7	292.6	189.8	1,231.7	2,381.4	1.7	5.8
Consumption taxes	745.8	161.0	1,005.4	885.4	7,271.0	11,972.9	1,075.2	1,198.6	895.0	4,216.8	13.7	28.3
General sales taxes	553.8	112.9	741.5	686.0	5,683.0	9,116.4	686.6	713.0	–	2,851.9	–	–
Motor fuel taxes	125.5	26.2	193.6	159.5	1,365.0	2,447.1	214.5	339.2	525.0	784.1	6.2	11.9
Alcoholic beverages and tobacco taxes	66.5	20.9	60.1	37.0	208.0	324.2	118.0	146.4	330.0	500.1	7.5	16.4
Other consumption taxes	–	1.0	10.2	2.9	15.0	85.2	56.1	–	40.0	80.7	0.0	0.0
Health and social insurance levies	95.6	11.6	100.8	99.0	4,773.4	2,351.0	138.8	100.9	1,062.3	1,661.5	5.2	34.3
Miscellaneous taxes	85.4	8.7	33.5	29.6	361.6	3,179.3	292.4	240.3	259.0	185.0	0.6	1.0
Natural resource revenues	29.1	0.6	12.2	54.6	181.3	371.6	63.2	659.7	3,599.0	2,585.9	2.4	2.8
Privileges, licences and permits	90.0	12.0	84.4	77.6	1,416.1	1,426.1	77.6	121.3	282.4	375.3	2.9	4.2
Sales of goods and services	76.6	41.4	140.1	99.7	878.5	1,014.4	116.7	235.6	295.5	394.4	21.6	77.9
Return on investments	289.2	99.0	476.0	631.6	2,131.4	3,006.1	1,145.8	954.3	2,824.2	2,943.0	35.7	42.0
Other revenue from own sources	8.8	0.7	5.0	33.6	504.1	193.8	127.3	18.2	45.5	192.1	0.5	1.2
Transfers	1,635.5	348.0	1,957.2	1,670.4	7,836.5	7,752.7	1,895.4	1,512.7	2,043.4	2,582.1	385.2	1,008.4
Transfers from other levels of government	1,635.5	348.0	1,957.2	1,670.4	7,616.2	7,752.7	1,895.4	1,512.7	2,043.4	2,582.1	385.2	1,008.4
Transfers from government enterprises	–	–	–	–	220.3	–	–	–	–	–	–	–
Expenditure	3,634.7	864.8	5,087.1	4,629.0	47,810.8	59,021.4	6,951.9	5,886.4	16,523.1	23,190.6	480.5	1,354.2
General services	219.6	49.2	224.7	205.6	2,095.6	2,088.3	209.5	436.8	588.9	866.8	56.8	216.9
Protection of persons and property	130.4	24.7	153.2	100.1	1,274.3	1,726.6	203.2	171.5	420.2	698.3	32.2	69.3
Transportation and communications	220.1	76.3	252.4	323.4	1,687.0	2,583.1	213.9	204.4	741.9	861.6	92.0	87.6
Health	815.1	168.2	1,406.9	1,039.5	11,009.4	17,308.6	1,764.3	1,254.3	3,891.8	6,251.3	69.0	201.3
Social services	551.1	127.6	638.7	657.3	9,950.9	13,877.2	1,026.4	904.6	2,151.3	4,518.7	49.5	106.7
Education	733.2	164.1	974.4	915.7	9,809.6	8,110.0	1,081.9	773.8	3,762.9	5,357.3	82.4	252.1
Resource conservation and industrial development	180.6	88.2	213.0	144.2	2,083.1	1,241.0	374.3	419.0	1,523.9	932.7	34.6	183.2
Environment	80.4	17.0	49.9	46.8	647.3	471.0	45.0	67.9	229.7	288.6	9.6	20.0
Recreation and culture	27.1	9.2	37.7	32.5	511.6	380.7	164.4	72.8	197.2	153.9	10.9	34.0
Labour, employment and immigration	28.5	5.3	11.8	25.6	538.3	108.5	33.1	7.7	39.6	25.1	1.4	0.6
Housing	–	0.1	31.8	–	406.2	719.5	13.0	12.1	42.6	56.1	–	–
Regional planning and development	10.4	1.2	32.7	33.3	144.2	115.1	110.0	30.6	30.7	121.7	18.7	44.2
Research establishments	–	–	7.3	8.9	279.7	87.2	5.1	15.3	78.2	31.6	–	–
General purpose transfers to other levels of government	42.9	5.3	52.7	135.7	391.4	742.6	140.1	75.7	265.3	139.4	14.5	28.4
Transfers to own enterprises	21.0	3.8	1.6	62.9	101.3	594.0	34.5	27.9	108.3	415.9	7.4	106.7
Debt charges	574.3	124.6	998.3	897.5	6,874.9	8,868.0	1,533.2	1,412.0	2,450.6	2,471.6	1.5	3.2
Other expenditures	–	–	–	–	6.0	–	–	–	–	–	–	–
Surplus (deficit)	(40.8)	(12.9)	(254.9)	16.6	(7,245.2)	(8,377.8)	(344.0)	574.5	(108.1)	27.0	30.5	(65.7)

1. From April 1 of one year to March 31 of the next year.

Source: Statistics Canada, CANSIM, matrices 2782 to 2793.

15.8 LOCAL GOVERNMENT REVENUE AND EXPENDITURE[1]

	1985	1986	1987	1988	1989	1990	1991	1992	1993	1994
					$ Millions					
Revenue	41,052.4	43,562.3	47,031.6	50,790.8	55,687.4	60,767.3	65,529.8	69,250.0	70,214.8	70,458.0
Own source revenue	21,308.7	23,147.5	25,273.1	27,845.8	31,183.3	33,815.0	35,698.1	37,550.1	38,668.3	38,586.2
Property and related taxes	14,500.6	15,721.3	17,009.1	18,477.8	20,566.8	22,451.0	24,370.6	26,051.3	26,942.9	26,731.7
Real property taxes	11,735.7	12,768.3	13,879.7	15,153.4	16,898.1	18,471.9	20,045.2	21,806.6	22,673.1	22,449.2
Other property taxes	2,764.9	2,953.0	3,129.3	3,324.4	3,668.7	3,979.1	4,325.4	4,244.7	4,269.9	4,282.5
Consumption taxes	51.4	55.0	60.8	65.5	74.9	74.5	71.0	60.9	47.2	47.4
General sales taxes	24.6	27.2	29.9	33.7	41.2	42.5	41.6	41.2	44.0	44.3
Other consumption taxes	26.8	27.8	30.9	31.8	33.6	32.0	29.4	19.8	3.2	3.1
Miscellaneous taxes	70.3	100.6	132.2	132.2	128.0	125.2	112.4	148.8	137.0	124.7
Natural resource revenues	–	–	–	–	–	–	–	–	–	–
Privileges, licences and permits	246.0	281.5	341.1	364.7	414.3	374.8	367.5	391.9	388.8	403.1
Sales of goods and services	4,424.9	4,924.7	5,511.2	6,295.0	6,916.3	7,338.6	7,524.7	7,676.2	7,929.1	8,147.6
Return on investments	1,292.3	1,284.5	1,337.6	1,520.6	1,944.1	2,146.3	1,899.1	1,803.9	1,744.1	1,664.5
Other revenue from own sources	723.2	779.9	881.2	990.0	1,139.1	1,304.6	1,352.7	1,417.1	1,479.1	1,467.2
Transfers	19,743.6	20,414.8	21,758.5	22,945.0	24,504.1	26,952.3	29,831.7	31,699.9	31,546.5	31,871.8
Transfers from other levels of government	19,205.8	19,855.5	21,191.6	22,308.1	23,826.8	26,232.5	29,100.2	30,916.7	30,753.2	31,066.9
Transfers from government enterprises	537.9	559.4	566.9	636.9	677.3	719.8	731.5	783.3	793.3	804.9
Expenditures	41,878.5	44,348.1	47,702.7	51,402.3	56,237.5	62,163.4	67,370.1	69,645.6	71,142.6	71,986.7
General services	2,153.7	2,262.9	2,498.1	2,772.4	3,138.4	3,420.5	3,773.2	3,700.9	3,656.8	3,701.3
Protection of persons and property	3,406.9	3,620.9	3,816.2	4,121.5	4,507.5	4,974.7	5,379.1	5,586.7	5,769.9	5,750.4
Transportation and communications	4,292.5	4,523.0	4,905.2	5,248.0	5,736.5	6,231.0	6,127.9	6,061.5	6,244.5	6,609.2
Health	2,433.7	2,643.7	2,816.2	2,886.3	3,221.2	3,346.3	3,453.1	3,567.6	3,662.1	3,577.7
Social services	1,493.1	1,680.2	1,905.1	2,106.2	2,401.4	2,992.2	4,190.0	4,924.9	5,437.6	5,570.7
Education	17,031.7	17,858.6	19,154.7	20,568.3	22,396.8	24,625.3	27,224.5	28,384.9	28,991.3	28,341.0
Resource conservation and industrial development	440.0	538.4	569.5	585.1	723.9	781.8	795.4	762.1	735.6	684.5
Environment	2,980.4	3,360.7	3,689.2	4,061.4	4,614.2	5,288.5	5,303.0	5,304.2	5,294.1	6,181.4
Recreation and culture	2,621.1	2,707.6	3,019.4	3,240.5	3,673.7	4,135.4	4,237.4	4,310.6	4,321.1	4,485.2
Housing	226.1	239.1	219.1	484.2	479.5	559.3	751.9	736.3	696.4	655.5
Regional planning and development	358.1	391.1	464.2	572.0	614.1	753.3	692.6	651.3	604.5	647.4
Transfers to own enterprises	826.2	896.5	932.7	949.2	1,042.4	1,135.3	1,237.2	1,466.8	1,460.6	1,425.1
Debt charges	3,278.9	3,298.4	3,321.8	3,375.4	3,501.7	3,729.3	3,905.9	4,089.2	4,147.7	4,222.6
Other expenditures	336.1	327.1	391.3	432.0	186.4	190.6	298.7	98.9	120.4	134.8
Surplus (deficit)	(826.1)	(785.7)	(671.1)	(611.5)	(550.1)	(1,396.1)	(1,840.3)	(395.6)	(927.9)	(1,528.7)

1. From January 1 to December 31.

Source: Statistics Canada, CANSIM, matrix 2794.

15.9 CONSOLIDATED GOVERNMENT[1] ASSETS, LIABILITIES AND NET DEBT

	1988	1989	1990	1991	1992	1993
			$ Millions			
Assets	134,555	143,627	151,227	164,595	166,314	171,379
Cash on hand and on deposit	19,285	20,372	21,934	27,894	24,540	26,783
Receivables	11,992	13,066	14,820	17,333	19,111	20,093
Advances	49,568	52,127	50,225	55,180	55,126	53,986
Securities	48,779	52,027	56,629	56,014	60,463	62,381
Other financial assets	4,931	6,035	7,619	8,174	7,074	8,136
Liabilities	522,914	563,363	601,741	656,080	718,682	794,880
Bank overdrafts	5,862	6,372	7,291	8,665	7,221	8,278
Payables	32,298	34,554	37,165	37,940	38,969	40,150
Advances	9,031	8,681	10,083	11,503	12,225	12,233
Treasury bills	79,084	98,563	113,702	134,656	149,891	159,759
Savings bonds	56,812	51,023	44,121	37,454	39,078	39,719
Bonds and debentures	222,512	238,425	261,243	288,681	323,360	373,798
Other securities	21,552	20,713	22,177	21,516	22,526	28,786
Deposits	9,652	10,821	13,598	15,912	18,076	17,084
Other liabilities	86,111	94,211	92,361	99,753	107,336	115,073
Net debt	388,359	419,736	450,514	491,485	552,368	623,501

1. Data for the federal, provincial and territorial governments are as at March 31. The local governments' data are as at December 31 of the previous year.

Source: Statistics Canada, CANSIM, matrix 3254.

15.10 FEDERAL GOVERNMENT DEBT[1]

	1983	1984	1985	1986	1987	1988	1989	1990	1991	1992	1993	1994	1995
							$ Millions						
Gross federal debt	173,660	210,841	248,052	283,739	318,218	349,830	380,820	407,084	444,578	476,610	515,794	558,701	599,268
Total unmatured debt	115,476	142,126	172,797	201,518	229,492	252,058	277,625	295,985	325,212	352,905	383,798	414,942	441,991
Marketable securities	82,664	103,733	130,633	156,828	183,386	196,243	226,863	251,983	287,276	313,806	345,924	380,113	407,117
Marketable bonds	51,714	58,994	71,373	86,957	100,294	110,222	121,121	131,810	147,104	161,499	181,322	208,464	233,621
Treasury bills	29,125	41,700	52,300	61,950	76,950	81,050	102,700	118,550	139,150	152,300	162,050	166,000	164,450
Other marketable securities	1,825	3,039	6,960	7,921	6,142	4,971	3,042	1,623	1,022	7	2,552	5,649	9,046
Non-marketable securities	66,938	76,381	84,454	91,660	98,075	113,203	113,975	113,599	114,043	120,980	125,785	128,926	135,906
Canada savings bonds	32,641	38,204	41,959	44,245	44,310	53,323	47,756	40,929	34,444	35,598	34,369	31,331	31,386
Bonds issued to the Canada Pension Plan	171	189	205	445	1,796	2,492	3,006	3,073	3,492	3,501	3,505	3,498	3,488
Superannuation funds	34,126	37,988	42,290	46,970	51,969	57,388	63,213	69,597	76,107	81,881	87,911	94,097	101,032
Dominion notes	–	–	–	–	–	–	–	–	–	–	–	–	–
Other federal debt	24,058	30,727	32,965	35,251	36,757	40,384	39,982	41,502	43,259	41,824	44,085	49,662	56,245
Debt payable in foreign currencies	5,235	5,222	9,085	13,811	12,010	11,294	8,415	5,751	4,526	3,444	5,409	10,668	16,921
Net federal debt	125,625	162,250	204,108	239,888	270,873	298,103	326,484	354,848	386,785	421,316	461,685	503,766	541,128

1. As of March 31st.

Source: Statistics Canada, CANSIM, matrix 3199.

15.11 EMPLOYMENT, PUBLIC ADMINISTRATION

	1984	1985	1986	1987	1988	1989	1990	1991	1992	1993	1994	1995	Average annual growth rate 1984-1995
	Employees[1]												
	'000												%
Public administration	662.3	663.1	675.7	668.4	680.8	691.5	702.2	718.5	719.5	710.2	703.6	688.4	0.4
Federal administration[2]	264.9	264.4	265.1	256.9	257.8	259.9	264.1	272.7	272.1	266.1	264.7	252.1	-0.4
Provincial administration	209.7	214.5	222.0	221.9	227.5	235.6	236.0	238.5	236.4	236.9	231.7	228.9	0.8
Local administration	187.6	184.1	188.6	189.6	195.5	196.0	202.1	207.3	211.0	207.1	207.2	207.5	0.9
All industries[3]	9,311.9	9,651.1	9,927.2	10,329.1	10,659.0	11,054.7	11,146.1	10,549.5	10,246.9	10,271.4	10,447.1	10,673.6	1.2
	% of total employment												
Public administration	7.1	6.9	6.8	6.5	6.4	6.3	6.3	6.8	7.0	6.9	6.7	6.4	...

1. Excludes owners or partners of unincorporated business and professional practices, the self-employed, unpaid family workers, persons working outside Canada, military personnel and casual workers for whom a T4 is not required.
2. Excluding the military.
3. Excludes agriculture, fishing and trapping, private household services, religious organizations and the military.

Source: Statistics Canada, Catalogue no. 72F0002.

15.12 EARNINGS, PUBLIC ADMINISTRATION

	1984	1985	1986	1987	1988	1989	1990	1991	1992	1993	1994	1995	Earnings in 1995 as a % of all industry earnings
	Average weekly earnings[1]												
	$												%
Public administration	504.06	524.02	543.20	571.84	592.97	636.52	689.12	701.92	727.64	746.59	752.88	749.83	131.0
Federal administration[2]	554.78	571.05	595.68	631.68	650.40	688.79	740.42	747.83	786.13	809.62	811.50	811.63	141.8
Provincial administration	484.65	508.06	519.97	544.47	573.45	626.03	674.34	697.71	715.75	713.88	719.79	716.19	125.1
Local administration	454.15	475.08	496.77	522.79	539.96	579.82	639.36	646.37	665.52	703.00	714.99	711.85	124.3
All industries[3]	398.10	412.02	424.25	440.26	459.75	483.31	505.14	528.60	547.01	556.76	567.11	572.49	100.0

1. Excludes owners or partners of unincorporated business and professional practices, the self-employed, unpaid family workers, persons working outside Canada, military personnel and casual workers for whom a T4 is not required.
2. Excluding the military.
3. Excludes agriculture, fishing and trapping, private household services, religious organizations and the military.

Source: Statistics Canada, Catalogue no. 72F0002.

15.13 MILITARY PERSONNEL

	1982	1983	1984	1985	1986	1987	1988	1989	1990	1991	1992	1993	1994
	Annual average number of employees												
Canada	107,860	110,406	109,728	110,530	111,704	113,394	114,604	117,332	118,779	121,410	117,461	113,177	108,803
Newfoundland	1,645	1,738	1,732	1,768	1,780	1,870	1,969	2,088	2,201	2,350	2,438	2,464	2,369
Prince Edward Island	1,148	1,191	1,209	1,210	1,196	1,203	1,200	1,197	1,048	743	368	337	332
Nova Scotia	14,449	14,786	14,602	14,945	15,074	14,961	15,128	15,137	15,144	15,389	14,926	15,135	14,865
New Brunswick	5,685	5,780	5,683	5,575	5,790	5,950	5,906	5,852	5,884	6,042	5,945	5,895	5,773
Quebec	17,374	17,197	16,944	17,298	17,430	17,861	17,899	18,368	18,844	19,723	19,079	19,151	19,077
Ontario	32,366	32,978	32,830	32,835	32,827	33,553	34,109	35,718	36,215	37,316	36,990	36,150	35,211
Manitoba	4,897	5,201	5,335	5,414	5,573	5,457	5,470	5,307	5,417	5,531	5,247	5,252	5,059
Saskatchewan	2,416	2,481	2,436	2,452	2,331	2,216	2,156	2,266	2,316	2,465	2,468	2,395	2,315
Alberta	9,071	9,580	9,579	9,839	9,783	10,035	9,991	10,214	10,482	10,980	10,939	10,910	10,840
British Columbia	10,634	11,187	11,173	11,020	10,968	11,239	11,381	11,486	11,459	11,646	11,665	11,202	10,754
Yukon	7	7	8	7	8	8	7	7	6	2	4	3	8
Northwest Territories	500	523	533	387	199	96	79	76	71	77	77	80	83
Outside Canada	7,670	7,757	7,665	7,782	8,744	8,947	9,311	9,617	9,693	9,147	7,315	4,205	2,115
	Annual total of wages and salaries $ '000												
Canada	2,021,669	2,215,623	2,382,062	2,517,671	2,698,032	2,878,881	3,118,892	3,364,101	3,651,328	3,668,070	3,670,728	3,642,632	3,579,151
Newfoundland	23,321	26,140	28,583	30,723	33,133	36,958	42,749	48,815	54,702	56,512	60,918	63,309	63,213
Prince Edward Island	22,423	24,510	26,947	28,531	29,532	30,906	31,494	33,304	29,768	17,827	3,381	2,500	2,699
Nova Scotia	289,310	317,330	338,245	359,972	380,146	398,825	428,444	453,011	489,393	500,248	512,732	539,243	548,020
New Brunswick	99,937	107,677	115,101	118,575	128,988	139,567	146,468	152,155	162,925	163,503	167,570	173,373	175,770
Quebec	244,246	260,021	281,643	300,209	318,588	346,250	361,971	393,674	430,636	437,273	443,172	478,864	493,044
Ontario	610,273	666,424	722,876	761,591	795,983	848,395	941,690	1,046,247	1,129,695	1,135,534	1,161,535	1,182,273	1,182,735
Manitoba	92,904	106,588	117,799	124,922	132,627	136,620	147,060	152,431	165,871	165,181	161,714	170,758	167,331
Saskatchewan	39,804	43,711	46,686	49,362	48,614	46,241	46,439	52,386	56,682	59,099	61,178	61,101	61,209
Alberta	169,271	192,226	208,892	226,284	234,586	251,641	270,898	296,012	325,621	340,071	349,068	363,742	382,044
British Columbia	196,789	221,149	236,160	244,662	253,566	271,809	294,207	314,260	336,131	340,995	352,822	352,046	351,964
Yukon	201	239	276	257	299	297	272	292	284	105	223	139	429
Northwest Territories	13,523	14,761	15,897	12,192	6,905	3,715	3,344	3,748	3,939	4,242	4,439	4,571	5,010
Outside Canada	219,668	234,849	242,959	260,393	335,068	367,660	403,847	417,748	465,684	447,481	391,976	250,713	145,683

Source: Statistics Canada, CANSIM, matrix 2720.

PAUL COUVRETTE, PAUL COUVRETTE PHOTOGRAPHY

Chapter 16 THE LEGAL SYSTEM

Photo by Felix H. Man

"The law in Canada," Rudyard Kipling once mused, exists and is administered "as an integral part of the national character—no more to be talked about than one's trousers." Certainly, most Canadians seem to be instinctively comfortable with our reputation for an orderly society.

Our history is counter-revolutionary, and our Constitution calls for "Peace, Order, and good Government" rather than "life, liberty, and the pursuit of happiness" proclaimed in the American Declaration of Independence. One of our national symbols is a police constable, the Mountie.

Canadians are not complacent about our hard-won reputation for peacefulness. Canada is often cited as one of the safest countries in the world, but daily news reports on television, radio and in newspapers constantly highlight violent crime. According to the 1993 General Social Survey, one in four Canadians stated that they feel somewhat or very unsafe walking alone in their neighbourhoods after dark.

Good of the People

In 1992-93, governments spent more than $5.7 billion on policing, and a further $2.4 billion on adult and youth correctional services. Correctional agencies supervised an average of approximately 146,890 offenders on any given day during 1994-95.

Yet crime, policing and corrections are not necessarily the hallmarks of the kind of civilization and civil society that Canadians are building. As Cicero noted in ancient Rome, "the good of the people is the chief law," an aim that effectively summarizes the Canadian legal system. Some Canadians may think that a judge's gavel—concluding a decision from the bench in court—is the symbol of law in Canada, but they may have been watching too much American television. Canadian judges don't normally use gavels. Balance is the real hallmark of our system, symbolized by the scales of justice weighing all the factors of a case for the public good.

Our governments, courts and police—the makers, interpreters and enforcers of our laws—are dedicated to upholding the fundamental values of Canadian society, while at the same time addressing the needs of a constantly changing country. That ability to reconcile competing social, political and economic facts has given our legal system the power to be a civilizing force in Canada.

The legal system continues to face both old and new problems. The number of Canadians in prison is increasing steadily. Many Canadians fear that they will be victims of crime. Laws have not yet caught up with the rapid developments in technology and communications.

The cost of litigation (going to court) is rising sharply, crowded court schedules have led to prolonged delays, and the legal aid system may not be as affordable as it once was. Nevertheless, our legal system has shown flexibility in the past, and no doubt it will continue to evolve in response to these new pressures and trends.

Crime in Canada

Canada has one of the highest crime rates among the industrialized countries. Although our rate of violent crime is significantly lower than that of the United States, our level of property crime is actually very close to that of the U.S. In 1993, 24% of Canadians were victims of at least one crime or attempted crime.

In 1994, 2.6 million Criminal Code incidents were reported: about 12% were violent crimes, 58% were property crimes, and the remaining 31% included crimes such as arson, prostitution, and restricted weapons offences. Males

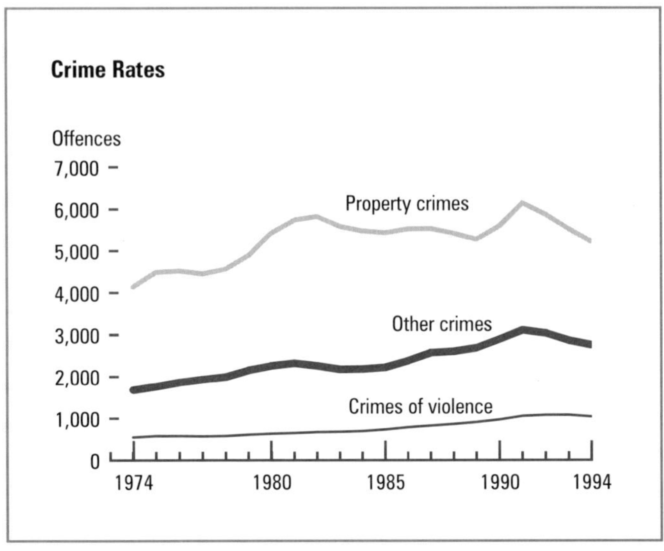

accounted for 82% of all persons charged with Criminal Code offences in 1994: 87% of those charged with violent crimes and 78% charged with property offences were males.

Crime is an act that is an offence against the state, against the people and against the public interest. The offences that our society considers criminal—everything from abduction to fraudulently practising witchcraft—are listed in the Criminal Code, Food and Drugs Act, the Narcotic Control Act and the Young Offenders Act. Our definitions of crime change over time; in the 19th century, theft was punishable by death. It is a popular misconception that Canada abolished the death penalty for all crimes in 1976; in fact, the National Defence Act still provides the death penalty for a long list of serious operational offences like spying for the enemy, espionage, and mutiny with violence.

From time to time new crimes, such as stalking, are added to the Criminal Code. A potentially lethal problem in the abuse of women, stalking was not considered a crime in Canada until the law was changed in 1993. The anti-stalking provisions were introduced to protect people from harassment by others who repeatedly follow or communicate with them, repeatedly watch their house or workplace, or directly threaten them or a member of their family. Further amendments to the Criminal Code tabled in 1996 proposed to strengthen anti-stalking provisions.

If a crime has been committed, the police (acting on behalf of the government) first investigate it. A Crown attorney (a lawyer also acting on behalf of the government) then appears in court to prosecute the person suspected of committing the crime. If the judge or jury finds the person guilty, the federal or provincial government may segregate, punish and rehabilitate the offender. Finally, in some circumstances, a criminal injuries compensation board may provide a financial award to an innocent victim of a violent crime.

The criminal law does more than protect victims and punish offenders; it also sends a clear message to the public that this type of behaviour will not be tolerated.

Violent Crimes

When we think about crime, we usually think about violent crimes. These are the ones that get the newspaper headlines and make the television news, leading many of us to think that the level of crime in our neighbourhoods has increased. The Criminal Code recognizes seven kinds of violent offences: homicide, attempted homicide, sexual assault, non-sexual assault, other sexual offences, abduction, and robbery.

But if we look beyond the headlines, we actually find that the level of all crime reported to the police decreased in Canada by 5% in 1994, the third consecutive year-to-year decline. The 1994 violent crime rate declined by 3%, the largest annual decline since crime statistics surveys began in 1962. But just as the headlines must be read with care, so must the statistics. Despite recent decreases, the overall 1994 crime rate was 8% higher than a decade ago. And the decline in violent crime followed 15 years of annual increases.

We really do not know the true level of crime in Canada because not all crimes are reported to the police. The likelihood of reporting varies from crime to crime, and reflects shifts in public perception about the seriousness of certain types of crime.

It is difficult to determine what proportion of the increase in violent crime over the past 15 years was due to actual increases in the level of violence. As well as changes in reporting behaviour by the public, factors such as police charging practices and policy and legislative changes may all have contributed to the increase. Much of the previous rise in violent crime may have been caused by increased reporting of minor assaults, both physical and sexual.

Assault is the most frequently reported kind of violent crime in Canada, accounting for six in 10 reported violent incidents in 1994. This increase may be attributable to changes to the Criminal Code, which allow police to act in cases of domestic violence and make it easier for them to lay charges.

In 1994, 75% of victims of assault knew their assailants: 18% were assaulted by a spouse, 6% by a former spouse, 3% by a parent, 6% by other family, 7% by a close friend, 8% by a business acquaintance and 27% by a casual acquaintance. Strangers committed 25% of assaults.

Sexual assaults accounted for 10% of all violent incidents in 1994. Approximately one-third of sexual assault victims were under 12 years of age, and approximately another third were aged 12 to 17. For sexual assault victims, 35% were assaulted by a casual acquaintance, 22% by a stranger, 11% by a parent, 13% by another family member, 8% by a close friend, 7% by a business acquaintance and 4% by a spouse or ex-spouse.

In 1994, homicides in Canada occurred at the lowest rate in 25 years: 596 incidents of first- and second-degree murder, manslaughter and infanticide (the murder of a child). British Columbia had the highest homicide rate in Canada in 1994 (3.1 per 100,000), and Newfoundland the lowest (0.7 per 100,000). Eight in ten homicides were solved by the police; a crime is considered solved when there is sufficient evidence to lay a charge against a suspect.

In homicides for which an accused person was identified, 40% of the victims were killed by a spouse or other family member, 46% by an acquaintance, and only 13% by a stranger. The family appears to be a dangerous place to be. During their first year of life, children face the greatest risk of being homicide victims. Of the 27 children killed in 1994, 20 were killed by a parent.

Courtroom dramas make exciting television shows, but an increasing number of Canadians are finding the real thing far too exciting. The emotional and financial stress of taking a dispute to court are causing consumers, lawyers and justice officials to look for other ways of settling legal problems.

Mediation and arbitration are the most common alternatives to launching a lawsuit. With combined mediation–arbitration and mini–trials, these procedures are called dispute resolution, or DR. Dispute resolution can include all possible processes for resolving a conflict, from consensual to adjudicative, from negotiation to litigation.

In a dispute resolution, the disputing parties usually hire an experienced neutral person to help find a solution to the problem. On the scheduled day they convene in an ordinary meeting room, rather than a courtroom. The parties may have their lawyers with them, and they can ask witnesses to appear.

An important aim of DR is to enable the disputants to settle the problem themselves, rather than using the ancient, time-consuming and costly adversarial techniques of lawyers battling it out by litigation in a courtroom. As the Minister of Justice, Allan Rock, has put it, "success would be freeing up the system from its present bias toward court-oriented procedures in favour of a more flexible, client-oriented and adaptive model in which procedure is the pliable servant of our purpose rather than its unforgiving master." In fact, several Canadian law schools are now beginning to teach mediation skills to new law students.

Although some lawyers estimate that only 5% of lawsuits actually end up before a judge, long delays are still caused by the number of cases waiting to go to trial. These delays in the traditional system, together with increasing costs to disputants and taxpayers alike, make DR's advantages appealing to justice officials.

The federal Department of Justice, for instance, has established a Dispute Resolution Project to co-ordinate efforts to make greater use of DR. These efforts include using DR in the federal government's own cases, including DR clauses in federal government contracts and training employees in DR processes.

Not all cases are suitable for dispute resolution. Some Canadian women's advocates point out that mediation should involve equally powerful parties, which may not be the case in many male–female relationships, especially when a spouse has been abused.

An evaluation of a federal–provincial pilot project in Toronto, involving 3,540 DR cases from September 1994 to early 1996, indicated that allowing litigants to participate in low-risk mediation increased their chances of settling a case before trial.

In commercial cases, the first survey of all 310 Ontario arbitrators in 1993 showed that arbitrations were much quicker and much less costly than comparable litigation. The 127 respondents noted that in comparison with a minimum wait of six months for a trial, 41% of arbitrations were resolved within four weeks. The estimated average cost of a complete commercial arbitration was $25,930 in 1992; the average arbitration lasted three days. In a courtroom trial, on the other hand, the legal fees for one party alone were estimated at $20,000 to $25,000 per day.

The survey also reported that the hearing process involved fewer witnesses, documents and lawyers than might have been expected in a trial, and that the disputing parties showed a high degree of control over the proceedings, co-operation with each other, and satisfaction with the process.

Youth Crime

Younger Canadians tend to commit more crimes than older Canadians. The Uniform Crime Reporting Survey found that 15% of individuals accused in violent incidents in 1994 were aged 12 to 17. The same age group accounted for 30% of those accused in property incidents, rather out of proportion to their numbers in the population; youths 12 to 17 represented approximately 8% of Canadians. Although the rate of property crime among youths decreased by 16% between 1986 and 1994, the rate of youth-perpetrated violent crimes more than doubled.

Youth crime—crime committed by 12- to 17-year-olds—is a growing concern for Canadians. Each year almost one in 10 youths comes into contact with police for violation of the Criminal Code or other federal statutes. Again, care must be taken when interpreting these statistics.

The numbers of youths charged in criminal incidents may be affected by screening procedures, for example. Many have argued that these procedures have resulted in more lenient treatment for youths. Police data, however, show that an increasingly higher proportion of youths arrested by police are formally charged than previously.

Most crimes committed by youth are not violent. Property offences (mostly breaking and entering) account for the largest proportion of all reported youth crime. In 1994, 58% of youths charged with Criminal Code offences were charged with property crimes, 18% with violent crimes (mostly minor assault), and 24% with other crimes. That same year, youths accounted for 11% of all those accused of committing homicide, somewhat higher than their share of the population.

Property Crimes

The rate of property crimes declined between 1984 and 1994. In 1994, Canadians committed 1.5 million property crimes such as theft, breaking and entering, fraud, and possession of stolen goods. The only significant increases occurred in 1990 and 1991, coinciding with the economic recession.

In 1994, thefts of $1,000 and under made up about half of the property crimes and more than a quarter of the total Criminal Code offences. Break-and-enter incidents accounted for about one-quarter of the 1994 property crimes; 59% of the targets were residences.

Motor Vehicle Crimes

According to the Uniform Crime Reporting Survey, the motor vehicle theft rate has continued to rise in recent years, from

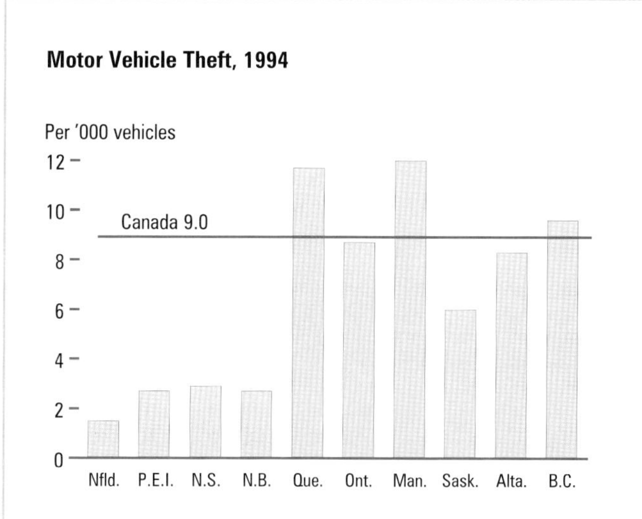

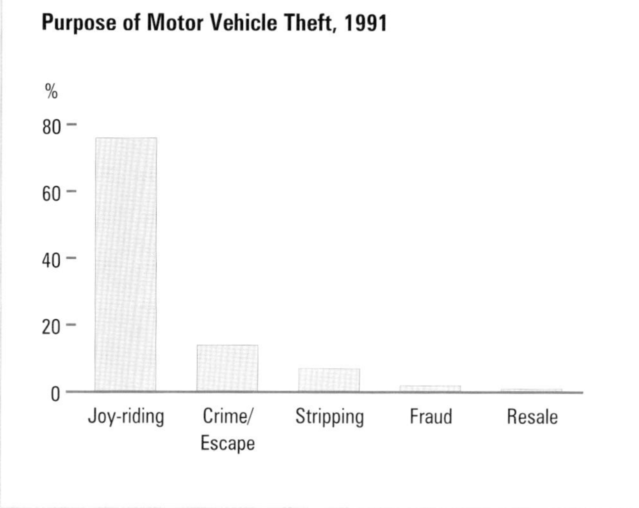

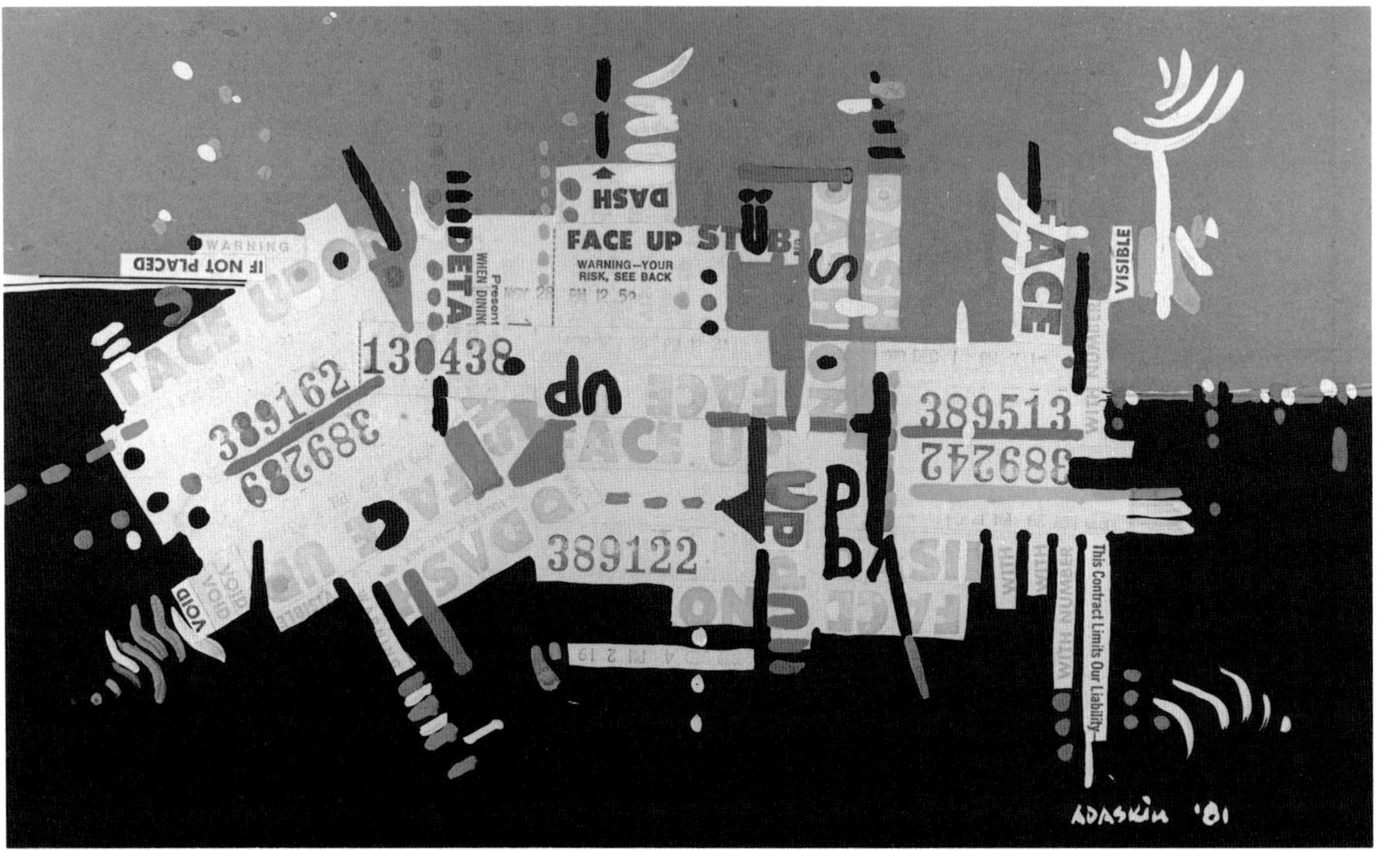

Gordan Adaskin. Courtesy of Murray and Dorothea Adaskin

***Parking Ticket Collage,* 1981.**

5.3 per 1,000 registered vehicles between 1980 and 1989 to 8.2 per 1,000 registrations between 1990 and 1994.

In 1994, Manitoba had the highest rate of stolen cars (12 per 1,000 registered vehicles), and Newfoundland the lowest (1.5 per 1,000). Across Canada, 159,633 motor vehicles were stolen, the highest yearly total since 1962.

The rate of property thefts from vehicles (including parts and personal property) increased slightly from 19.0 per 1,000 registered vehicles in 1980 to 19.8 in 1994. An international crime survey of 20 industrialized nations, published in 1992, found that Canadian car owners reported the highest rate of car vandalism (9.2% of owners), the third-highest rate of theft from their cars (7.2% of owners), but had the 11th-highest rate of stolen cars (1.1% of owners).

Drunk Driving

Canadians seem to be listening to the campaigns against drinking and driving, but contrary to popular belief, it is not young drivers who have the highest rate of drunk driving offences. Every province and territory reported a decrease in the number of people charged with impaired driving under the Criminal Code between 1987 and 1994. Prince Edward Island had the most striking decrease (48%), and the Yukon was at the other end of the scale (a 10% decrease).

The total number of people charged with impaired driving decreased by 41% between 1983 and 1994, and the number of fatally injured impaired drivers fell by 18% from 1987 to 1994.

In 1994, the 30 to 34 age group was the largest single group charged with impaired operation offences. Although this group represented only 9.1% of Canada's population in the 1991 Census, they were responsible for 18% of the charges, followed by 35- to 39-year-olds and 18- to 24-year-olds (both at 16% of charges). The vast majority of those charged were males—approximately 90%—although the proportion of females charged rose from 8% in 1987 to 10% in 1994.

Hate Crimes

Hate crimes strike at the heart of Canada's civil society, because they repudiate the basic principles of human rights guaranteed by our Constitution. An offender identifies the victim as a member of a group that he or she hates, based on the victim's race, religion, nationality, ethnic origin, gender, sexual orientation or disability. Since hate crimes are directed at both a group and an individual victim, they carry an element of harm that is not present in other kinds of offences.

Hate crimes may be among the most under-reported forms of criminality in Canada. Victims may fear additional victimization, victims of racially motivated crimes may fear that the criminal justice system will not respond to their reports adequately, and homosexual men and women may be concerned that reporting crimes directed at them may result in their being stigmatized by homophobia. One preliminary estimate suggests that, in 1994, approximately 60,000 hate crimes were committed in nine urban centres: Vancouver, Edmonton, Calgary, Regina, Winnipeg, Toronto, Ottawa, Montreal and Halifax.

Almost 1,000 hate crime incidents were recorded by police in 1993-94; of these, 61% were directed at racial minorities, 23% at religious minorities, 11% at the victims' sexual orientation, and 5% at ethnic minorities.

Policing

Canadian policing has come a long way from Sir Gilbert Parker's North-West Mounted policeman of the 1890s, Sergeant Fones, who had "the fear o' God in his heart, and the law of the land across his saddle, and the newest breech-loading at that." Canadian federal, provincial and municipal police are still on the front line, but with the latest paramilitary equipment, sophisticated communications, psychological and legal training, and criminal intelligence services.

Members of the federal Royal Canadian Mounted Police (RCMP) are in demand as trainers of new police forces around the world, and many have served as international peace-keepers. At the same time, some of the most effective crime prevention is being carried out by community-based women and men in uniform, working on bicycle patrols and from storefront stations.

Responsibilities for policing are divided among the federal, provincial, territorial and municipal governments. The RCMP handles the enforcement of most federal laws. In 1996 the force had 15,142 uniformed members, and 5,319 people working in administration.

Although the Constitution gives the provinces the responsibility for enforcing the Criminal Code, all provinces and territories (with the exception of Quebec and Ontario) have contracted with the RCMP to enforce criminal and provincial laws. The Ontario Provincial Police and the *Sûreté du Québec* provide provincial policing services. In Newfoundland, the Royal Newfoundland Constabulary shares provincial policing duties with the RCMP.

The provinces have delegated their policing powers to cities and towns. Depending on the province, towns larger than 500 persons must have their own police forces. Municipalities are usually given the option of creating their own municipal force, or contracting for services from the RCMP or the provincial force.

Between 1988-89 and 1992-93, expenditures on policing services accounted for about 60% of the costs of the criminal justice system; policing cost $5.8 billion in 1994-95. Adjusted

"Canada must be the only country in the world where a policeman is used as a national symbol," wrote Canadian author Margaret Atwood. Ironically, this may have something to do with the United States.

Between 1907 and 1975, Hollywood made 575 movies set in Canada and 256 of them featured the RCMP or the earlier North-West Mounted Police and Royal Northwest Mounted Police.

According to Canadian author Pierre Berton, who has noted this statistical anomaly, Hollywood's love affair with the force did not translate into a desire for accuracy. Rather, says Berton, American movie makers portrayed the Mounties as "hard-riding, hard-shooting cowboys from the American wild west, thinly disguised in scarlet and gold."

Nothing, in fact, could be further from the truth. The idea for a mounted police force was the brainchild of Sir John A. Macdonald, Canada's first prime minister. Mindful of the violence which had accompanied westward expansion in the United States, Macdonald conceived a force of mounted police who would establish friendly relations with the Aboriginal peoples and maintain peace as the settlers arrived.

The North-West Mounted Police was organized in 1873 and dispatched west the next year. A first task was to chase away whisky traders who had been disrupting the traditional values of the Aboriginal peoples. The force soon adopted the fitting motto: "Maintiens le droit".

In the 1890s, the Yukon Territory was invaded by tens of thousands of prospectors intent on getting rich in the Klondike gold rush. Violence and disorder threatened, but the presence of several hundred mounted policemen stopped lawbreakers in their tracks. In a less dramatic fashion, the Mounties ensured the orderly development of the western Arctic and Arctic Islands. The force averted trouble by being in place in advance of the newcomers from the south, and establishing strong relationships with the Aboriginal peoples.

In 1904, the force was given the title "royal" by King Edward VII, in recognition of its accomplishments. In 1920, the Canadian government extended its jurisdiction across Canada, making it a truly national police force. The new force absorbed the Dominion Police, which had enforced federal law in eastern Canada, and was renamed the Royal Canadian Mounted Police.

Today, the RCMP continues as Canada's national police force enforcing federal law across the nation. It also acts as the provincial police force in all provinces except Ontario and Quebec and the territorial police in the Yukon and the Northwest Territories, as well as the local police force for about 200 municipalities. The force is 22,000 strong, of which 16,000 are uniformed members and the remainder civilian employees.

for inflation, policing expenditures decreased for the first time since data collection started in the mid-1980s, by 0.3% from 1993-94 to 1994-95.

In 1994, Canada had 55,865 sworn police officers, a decrease of 1.8% from the previous year; this was the largest annual drop recorded since 1962. Both decreases reflect the budget reductions and restructuring that have taken place in many public sector areas. As a result, the ratio of police to civilians rose to one officer for every 523 Canadians, the highest ratio since 1973.

Aboriginal policing is an example of a distinctively Canadian approach to community policing. The First Nations Policing Policy, for example, is improving policing on First Nations' reserves by using officers trained in Aboriginal culture and beliefs. It is also encouraging each service to employ enough First Nations police officers to ensure that policing will be responsive and sensitive to First Nations' culture.

The criminal justice system has been changing to better respond to incidents of family violence; new sexual assault legislation and the policy of mandatory charging and prosecuting family violence cases are two responses. In violent incidents reported to police by the victim in 1992-93, 64% of victims reported that they were satisfied with the way that police responded. But the level of satisfaction depended on whether the victim was a woman or a man. For violent incidents involving male victims, 75% were satisfied, compared with 54% of incidents involving victims who were women.

Corrections

Punishment, pure and simple, was the original mandate of Canada's correctional system. In the 18th century we inherited the British "bloody code," so called because it relied almost exclusively on whipping and hanging to punish criminals.

Today, federal corrections officers are responsible for protecting society by actively encouraging and helping offenders to become law-abiding citizens, while exercising safe, secure and humane control. Modern correctional services face two seemingly incompatible pressures. Canadians are concerned

Res Ipsa Loquitur

The thing speaks for itself, or res ipsa loquitur, as many a lawyer has quipped. The expression could well be the guiding light for some of the more arcane laws still on the books in Canada's Criminal Code.

Here are some examples. In Canada, it is illegal for two people to fight with their fists or their hands, if they have previously arranged the encounter. According to the Criminal Code, this constitutes prize fighting. On the other hand, if the boxers wear gloves, amateur boxing matches are exempt, as are contests organized by provincially recognized athletic boards.

Pugilism aside, it's also technically a crime to take part in an "immoral, indecent or obscene (theatrical) performance." The definitions are not clear, but case law has shown that a play is not considered immoral solely if it is performed in the nude.

Anyone taking oysters from a marked bed can be found guilty of theft. Under the Criminal Code, oyster beds are the property of the person who has sufficiently marked them out or made it known that the oyster beds are claimed.

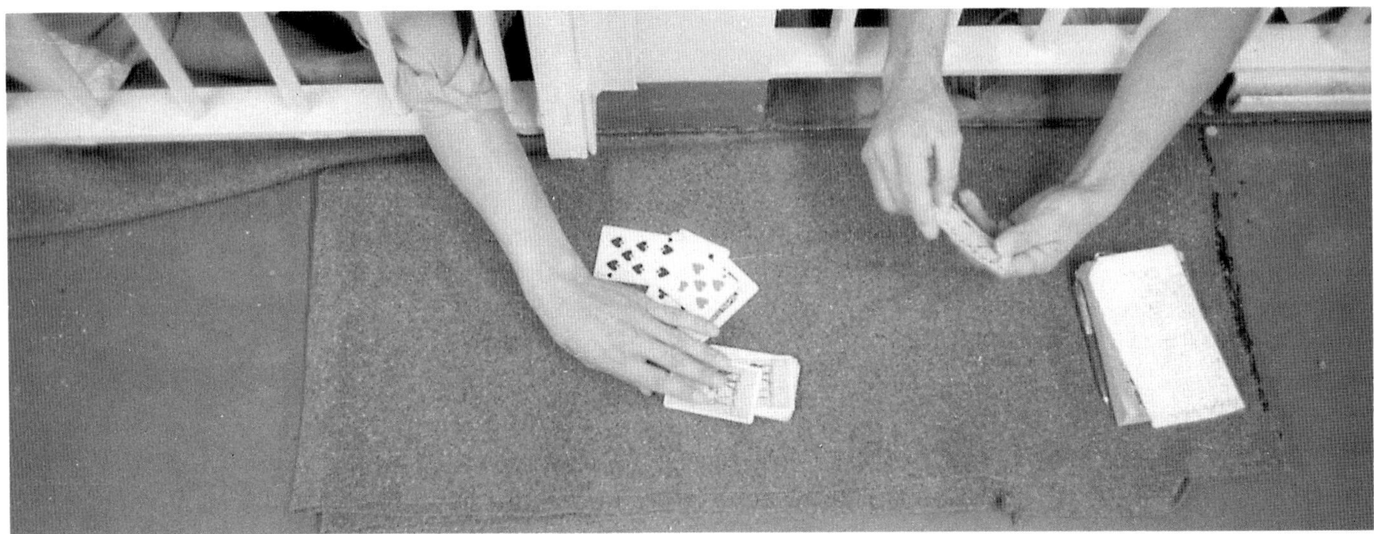

Ed Spiteri, National Archives of Canada, PA-128104

Prisoners playing cards in cellblock.

about violent crimes, creating a demand for more effective measures to deal with sexual and other violent offenders. At the same time, corrections agencies are experiencing escalating prison populations and associated workloads.

By the 1990s, Canada was jailing its population at a rate higher than that of any other western democracy except the United States.

In the five years between 1989-90 and 1993-94, the total federal and provincial caseload increased by 31%, from 117,571 to 154,106. Sentences of two years or more are served in federal penitentiaries, and of less than two years in provincial correctional centres.

In 1993-94, about 66% of those convicted were on probation, 12% were released into the community under various forms of conditional release, and 21% were incarcerated. On an average day in 1993-94, some 32,803 inmates were in custody; provincial inmates accounted for 59% and federal inmates for 41%.

Males made up 91% of sentenced offenders admitted to provincial institutions in 1993-94, and 97% of those admitted to federal facilities. Adult corrections costs rose 28% in current dollars from 1988-89 to 1993-94, reaching $1.9 billion. Between 1988-89 and 1992-93, youth custody and community service costs rose by 37% in current dollars to $485 million.

Prison sentences, while somewhat shorter than in the past, are being handed down by the courts more frequently. The number of people admitted to both provincial and federal institutions increased substantially from 1989-90 to 1993-94, relative to the number of offenders actually in prison at any given time.

Admissions to provincial facilities increased by 20% in that five-year period, while the average provincial inmate population grew by only 10%. In the same period, admissions to federal facilities increased by 32%, compared with a growth of 17% in the average federal inmate population.

The Canadian justice community is beginning to be concerned about the possibility of discrimination in the legal system. In 1996, a commission of judges and civic officials appointed by the government of Ontario concluded that systemic racism exists in the Ontario criminal justice system.

Aboriginal people are over-represented in the correctional system; while persons with Aboriginal ancestry accounted for about 4% of Canada's population, Aboriginal offenders in 1993-94 accounted for 17% of persons sentenced to provincial custody, 12% of those in federal custody, and 12% of those on probation.

The federal Department of Justice and the provinces have jointly instituted a Native Courtworkers Program to meet the counselling needs of Aboriginal people in conflict with the law, and to reduce the communication barriers between Aboriginal people and administrators of the criminal justice system; $10.2 million was spent in 1994-95.

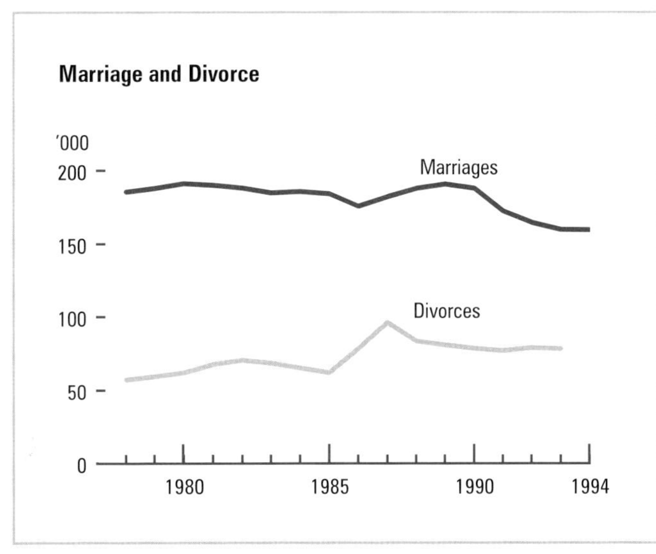

Private Law

Private law, like good manners, helps make life's frictions more bearable and fair. Unlike public law, which regulates our relations with the state, private or civil law concerns our relations with each other.

A significant trend in Canadian law over the past decades has been the growing power of the provincial legislatures and courts to regulate private law issues. Except for a list of exclusively federal powers, provincial property and civil rights laws cover most of the legal relationships between individuals in Canada, including law concerning the family, property, wills, contracts and torts (wrongs for which the law generally permits recovery of damages).

Much business activity, for example, is governed by statutory rules and the decisions of government officials; the courts have tended to assign this government intervention in the marketplace to the provinces if it doesn't clearly fall to the federal government.

With the increased complexity of modern business and personal life, the number of cases being filed with certain courts and agencies in some provinces is increasing. The volume of applications to resolve landlord and tenant disputes in Ontario, for instance, rose from about 28,000 to almost 44,000 from 1989-90 to 1993-94. Partly as a result, another trend in some provinces is a growing backlog of civil cases waiting to be tried before a judge.

From 1990 to 1994, the pending trial list in Ontario approximately doubled; in Toronto alone some 9,000 cases were waiting in 1994. Prime Minister William Ewart Gladstone of the United Kingdom once noted that justice delayed is justice denied; of the 23,300 civil cases awaiting trial in Ontario by the end of 1994, more than half had been waiting more than 12 months.

Officials in the provincial legal systems are now turning to methods of resolving disputes that do not involve the expense and delay of a full trial before a judge. Usually known as alternative dispute resolution, these methods include mediation, arbitration, negotiation, pre-trials and mini-trials. In most cases, an experienced neutral person helps the parties find a solution.

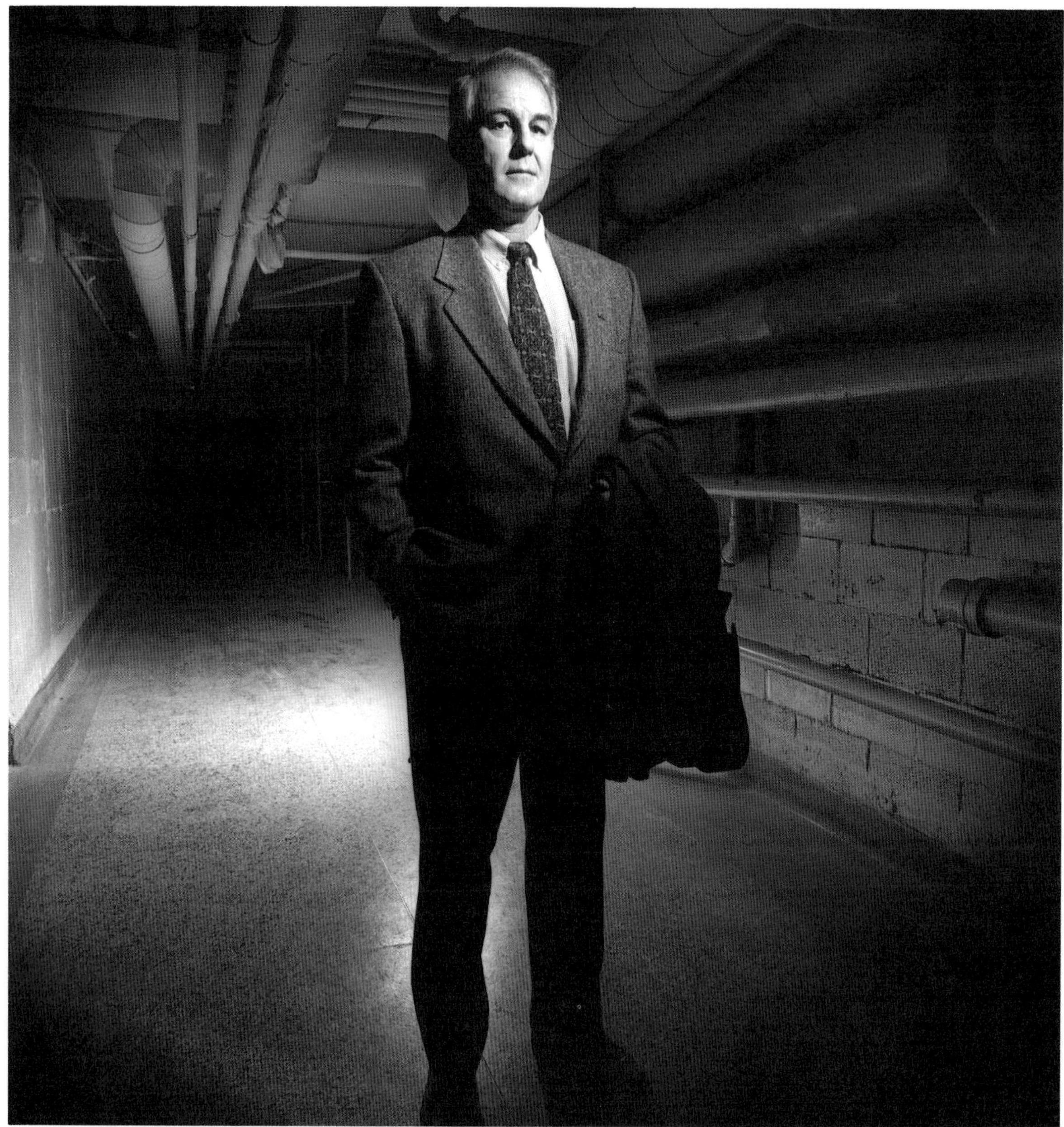

Photo by Tony Fouhse

Inspector Ron McKay, RCMP.

In Toronto, beginning in October 1994, 10% of all new civil cases were referred to an Alternative Dispute Resolution Centre. In the Ottawa region, about half of the disputes involving youths that were mediated by the Dispute Resolution Centre of Ottawa-Carleton from October 1993 to December 1995 were resolved within 10 days, and 71% within 30 days.

Few areas of civil law affect individual Canadians so directly and dramatically as family law: divorce, custody of children, maintenance and support of spouses and children, and adoption. Although about 60% of Canadians 15 years old and over were married by 1994, some 5.2% were divorced.

The 1968 federal Divorce Act liberalized the conditions for getting a divorce; in the 18 years after the Act became effective, the number of divorces rose from 1,367 for every 10,000 marriages annually to 3,908.

A new Divorce Act in 1986 reduced the amount of time that a couple had to be separated before a divorce could be granted, and in 1987 the number of divorces for every 10,000 marriages peaked at 4,789. The number then declined, and has remained stable since 1989, with 3,812 divorces for every 10,000 marriages in 1993. The decrease in the divorce rate in recent years is partly related to a decrease in marriages as couples increasingly choose to live together without being married.

A Canadian divorce is recognized across Canada; enforcement of a court order for maintenance is a provincial responsibility. All provinces and territories now have agreements for the reciprocal enforcement of maintenance orders.

Within provinces, various procedures are being introduced to help ensure that a divorced spouse doesn't become impoverished because his or her former partner failed to pay maintenance. In 1994, British Columbia passed a new Family Maintenance Enforcement Amendment Act and Alberta amended its Maintenance Enforcement Act.

Both Quebec and Nova Scotia passed legislation to improve their enforcement programs, in 1995 and 1996 respectively. Several provinces have assumed the authority to search government databases (such as motor vehicle registrations in seven provinces) to locate spouses who are trying to avoid payment.

Recent technological developments have affected civil law in Canada as much as they have public law. Intellectual property law, for example, was once concerned mainly with trademarks, patents, the names of corporations and the well-established principles of copyright.

Now intellectual property can involve industrial design based on new materials, business competition problems arising from major discoveries in science, and computer services, including licensing, software development, electronic data exchange, joint ventures and outsourcing arrangements.

The development of cheap photocopying in the 1960s led to worries about copyright infringement of authors' publications; the rise of international computer networks in the 1990s (notably the Internet) has opened up enormous questions about censorship, royalties, the security of information, and the ownership of authors' works—even works of art—in electronic form.

Canada revised the federal Copyright Act in 1988 for the first time since 1923, to strengthen the rights of creators such as composers, writers and visual artists. The next phase of revisions, aimed at users such as radio and television stations, cable television networks and the broadcasting industry, has yet to be introduced because of difficulties in defining and protecting the interests of consumers, business and government.

Computer-based communications have created a further civil law issue that worries many Canadians: personal privacy. Protecting privacy in the computer age is like trying to change the tires on a moving car. We face employee monitoring, government and private sector data matching, zealous telemarketing, surveillance cameras on street corners, smart cards, scanners, and sophisticated tracking devices.

The 1983 federal Privacy Act and specific legislation in all the territories and provinces except Prince Edward Island, form

ADOPTIONS IN CANADA

Every year, thousands of Canadians wait and hope to adopt a child. In 1990, for example, about 16,000 waited to adopt, either through provincial government agencies or through independent adoption agencies. The difference between the two methods is largely one of time and money. Public adoptions are paid for through taxes or provincial grants and may take up to six years. On the other hand, private adoptions are reported to cost from $4,500 to $5,900 and usually take 21 months on average.

In Canada, lengthy waits occur partly because few Canadian babies are put up for adoption. In 1990, there were at least seven applicants for every baby that was adopted publicly.

As a result, international adoptions are now the most common way for Canadians to reduce delays. In fact, they outnumber domestic infant adoptions three to two. Like domestic adoptions, international adoptions can be public or private. Canada's National Adoption Desk, a federal agency, provides the provinces with international adoption services and acts as an international coordinator and consultant.

Almost unheard-of in Canada before the Second World War, international adoptions have grown from fewer than 10 in 1970 to nearly 2,000 in 1995. In 1995, Canadians welcomed children from more than 70 countries into their families. The largest number of children—about 655—came from mainland China, followed by India (185), Haiti (148) and Romania (94).

International adoptions differ from domestic adoptions in several ways. The adopted children tend to be older (usually several months old and often older), and the process is often more expensive. But there is no shortage of children to adopt. Countries that have difficulty supporting their existing populations tend to have high birth rates, and thus more abandoned children.

Unfortunately, many countries that lack proper regulations for international adoptions also have problems with child abuse. In some countries, children have been sold for prostitution, pornography, labour—even for their vital organs. Instances of child abuse prompted the 1993 Hague Convention on Intercountry Adoptions. To protect children, the convention will secure recognition of adoptions between member countries. Delegates from 65 countries drew up the convention, and 10 have ratified it. Canada will ratify the convention once the provinces and territories have reached consensus.

the basis of privacy law in Canada. Each is directed at the public sector; only Quebec covers the private sector as well, including banks, the transportation companies, and the telecommunications industry.

The federal Privacy Commissioner and the various provincial commissioners or ombudsmen have varying authority over privacy violations, from making recommendations to issuing binding orders and taking violators to court. The Quebec Commissioner has the power to impose fines of up to $20,000 for non-compliance in the private sector.

Principles of Canadian Law

Whether we are dealing with public law, which regulates our relations with the state, or private law, which regulates our relations with each other, the idea of balance remains central to the Canadian legal system.

The scales of justice attempt to balance our individual rights with the needs of society as a whole, and the pivotal point is our recognition of the rule of law. The rule of law is a simple phrase that packs a powerful legal punch. The opposite of "might is right," it means that all members of society—government and private persons alike—must be equally responsible before the law. It recognizes the supremacy of our laws in controlling the powers of government and government officials.

Another fundamental principle of Canadian law is justice. In general, justice means giving every person his or her due, although to lawyers it also involves due process and rationality. That is, if a dispute is determined by fair procedures before an impartial tribunal, and the tribunal honestly tries to give consistent and rational reasons for its decision, then we can say that justice has been done.

Canadian law, like the country itself, is both unique and distinctive in having two legal traditions operating side by side: *le droit civil* and the common law. These two families of laws share a common heritage, come from identical political institutions, and are interpreted by similar courts.

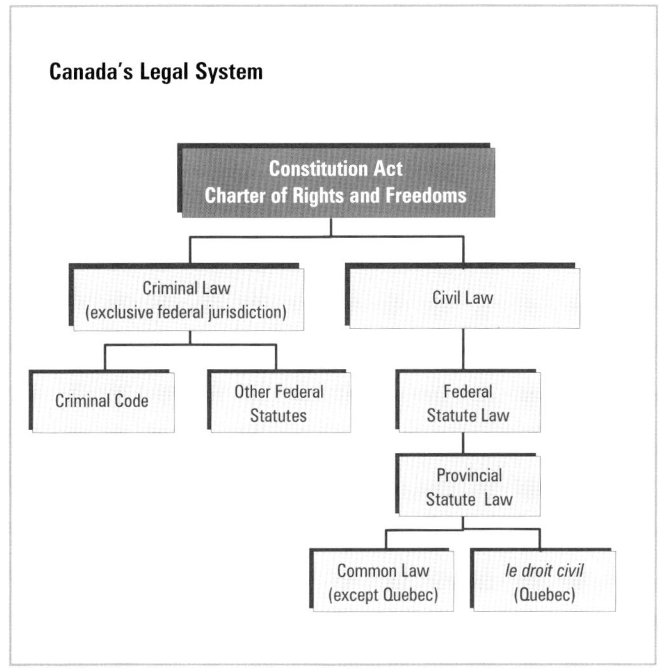

In Quebec, private law is based on the French and ancient Roman traditions of a written code of law, the Civil Code. Most of continental Europe, Scotland, Central and South America, some of the West Indies and many countries in Africa now use the civil code system, by which judges study the code to find the law that applies to the case at hand. A major revision and updating of the Civil Code came into force in Quebec in January 1994. The common-law tradition is at the root of all Canadian public law, and of private law outside Quebec; it is often called judge-made law because it relies on previous decisions made by the courts, or precedents.

Canada's Constitution

Canada's Constitution is our supreme law: the blueprint governing the way our governments work. It embodies the rule of law, placing absolute limits on what the state or any of its officials can do. Freedom of religion, expression and association, for example, are basic freedoms guaranteed by the

Charter of Rights. Government control of these freedoms extends only to "such reasonable limits prescribed by law as can be demonstrably justified in a free and democratic society."

The Canadian Constitution is a haphazard collection of (among other elements) common law, statutes, conventions, values and assumptions, all clustered around the Constitution Act, 1982.

The Constitution Act, 1982 defines the Constitution of Canada as including the Canada Constitution Act, 1982, 30 listed acts and orders and any amendments to these acts and orders. It includes the Constitution Act, 1867 (formerly known as the British North America Act, 1867), which was passed by the United Kingdom Parliament in 1867 to create the Canadian federation, the Canada Act 1982, which ended the United Kingdom's ability to pass laws affecting Canada, and the Canadian Charter of Rights and Freedoms.

The written elements of the Constitution establish many of the institutions we take for granted, setting out the basic principles of democratic government, distributing powers between the federal and provincial governments, providing the framework for the machinery of government (including the structure of Parliament and our courts), and recognizing Aboriginal and treaty rights. Unwritten laws, or conventions passed down through the generations, also form part of the Constitution. For example, the status of the Prime Minister as the head of our government is mentioned nowhere in the written Constitution. In the process of deciding constitutional issues, our courts also add to constitutional law.

Although Canada is one of the oldest continuous democracies in the world, our Constitution is one of the newest. It assumed its current form amidst much controversy after the federal government announced in 1980 that it intended to "patriate" the British North America Act, 1867 (to make it amendable in Canada rather than in the United Kingdom), and to add the Canadian Charter of Rights and Freedoms.

The Constitution Act, 1982 received the approval of Parliament and all provinces except Quebec. Later governments entered into further negotiations to secure Quebec's approval, from 1987 to 1990 (resulting in an agreement that was not approved by two other provinces) and 1991 to 1992 (resulting in an agreement that was defeated in a national referendum).

The referendum of 1992 was the first time that individual Canadians had had a direct voice in Canadian constitution-making. The existing Canadian Constitution is still a source of deep dissatisfaction for a substantial number of Canadians in Canada's second-largest province.

The Canadian Charter of Rights and Freedoms

A well-known element of the Canadian Constitution is the Canadian Charter of Rights and Freedoms, which has caused a legal revolution by changing some basic operations of governments and the courts.

The Charter guarantees a familiar list of rights, including the fundamental freedoms of conscience, religion, thought and expression, assembly and association. Certain democratic rights are itemized, such as the rights to vote and to regular elections, and mobility rights for Canadian citizens.

We are ensured the right to be free of arbitrary detention and of unreasonable search and seizure, to have a trial within a reasonable time, and to be presumed innocent. Canadians have the right to life, liberty and security of the person, and the right not to be deprived of them except in accordance with the principles of fundamental justice.

The Charter secures equality before the law for all Canadians, confirms the status of English and French as the official languages of Canada, and specifies certain minority language education rights. It also instructs judges to interpret the Charter "in a manner consistent with the preservation and enhancement of the multicultural heritage of Canadians."

All these rights are subject to three important limitations. First, the Charter applies only to the actions of the government. It is intended as an instrument for the protection of individuals from abuses of state power, and does not regulate behaviour between private individuals.

Second, the rights are guaranteed subject to "such reasonable limits prescribed by law as can be demonstrably justified in a free and democratic society." That is, if any limits are to be put on the rights, then the government must establish to the satisfaction of the courts that those limits can be justified in a free and democratic society.

Finally, there is an override provision by which Parliament or a provincial legislature may specifically declare that a law will operate notwithstanding certain provisions of the Charter. This "notwithstanding clause" has been used by Quebec, for instance, to retain a provincial act concerning the use of French on signs.

Since the introduction of the Charter, courts have been given the task of developing some kind of balance between the fundamental rights of citizens on the one hand and the rights and obligations of government on the other. For example, a municipal bylaw prohibiting posters on utility poles was struck down as an unjustifiable infringement on freedom of expression.

Surreptitious electronic recording of conversations by police was found to be unconstitutional, on the grounds that if the state were allowed complete discretion to record our private conversations, there would be nothing left of our basic right to exist free from state surveillance.

Canada's Legal Institutions

Canadian law has two main sources: legislation passed by the federal Parliament and provincial and territorial legislatures, and case law from decisions by judges in federal and provincial courts. The writing of legal scholars is sometimes considered a source; although such opinions may be influential, they have no legal authority.

Canada is a constitutional monarchy, and all government actions are taken in the name of the Crown. In Canada the "Crown" is the composite symbol of the institutions of state. The personal embodiment of the Crown is the Queen, whose representative is the Governor General of Canada; in each province the Queen is represented by a lieutenant-governor, appointed by the Governor General in Council. The Governor General retains the power to exercise prerogative power—in appointing a Prime Minister or declaring war, for example.

Canada's Final Court of Appeal

The Supreme Court of Canada is the highest court in the land, the last judicial resort for all litigants, whether governments or individuals. It was founded in 1875, but all appeals from its decision to the Privy Council in England were only abolished in 1949.

When the Supreme Court held its first sitting on January 17, 1876, in rooms borrowed from the Railway Committee at the House of Commons, there was not a single case to be heard. Today, the Supreme Court hears about 120 appeals a year from the provincial and territorial courts of appeal and from the Federal Court of Appeal. All sessions are open to the public.

The Supreme Court performs another special function. It considers important questions of law, such as the constitutionality or interpretation of federal or provincial legislation, or the division of powers between the federal and provincial levels of government, when such questions are referred to the Court by the federal government.

The Supreme Court consists of the Chief Justice of Canada and eight puisne (meaning ranked after) justices. Justices may hold office until they reach the age of 75. All Justices must live within 40 kilometres of the National Capital Region, since the Court sits only in Ottawa.

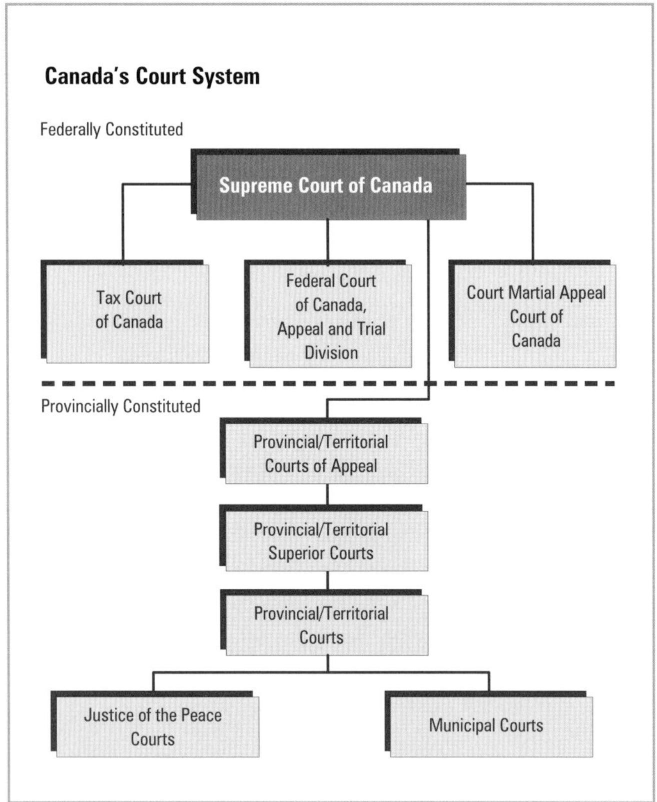

The Constitution establishes 11 law-making bodies in Canada: the Parliament of Canada (composed of the Governor General, the Senate and the House of Commons), and the 10 provincial legislatures. It divides up the authority to enact statutes; for instance, the federal government has exclusive powers over many issues that concern the entire country, such as criminal law, national defence, copyrights and currency.

The provinces legislate on matters of mainly local and private natures, such as property, education, and municipalities. The federal Parliament has the ultimate power over all matters in the two territories, but it delegates law-making powers to the territorial governments. Similarly the provinces delegate some of their powers to municipal councils, who enact municipal bylaws telling us, among many other things, where and when we can park our cars.

The responsibility for establishing and operating the courts is divided between the provincial and federal governments. Whatever the level of the court, judges must rule on the guilt or innocence of an accused person in a criminal trial, or must choose between the contending arguments of two parties, plaintiff and defendant, in a civil trial. The federal government is primarily responsible for criminal law and procedure across the country, but both federal and provincial courts hear civil and criminal cases.

The Supreme Court of Canada is at the apex of the system. Nine judges, three of whom must be from Quebec, hear selected appeals from federal or provincial appeal courts. To be heard, the issues must be of importance to the entire country.

In 1994, it heard 119 appeals: over 40% on criminal law issues, and 24% on Charter issues. The Charter has transformed the role of the court, expanding it from that of an interpreter to a full-fledged lawmaker, basically writing the constitutional law of Canada. The Federal Court of Canada is a specialized court that hears claims against or by the federal government. It also handles patent, copyright and admiralty cases.

Although the names of the courts may vary, most provinces and territories have a similar court structure, usually with two levels: provincial courts and superior courts. Provincial courts deal with less serious criminal law matters and civil matters with lower dollar value. The superior courts, in turn, include both trial and appeal levels. The trial levels have broad authority to hear all civil matters and serious criminal matters, such as murder.

Although certain cases may be appealed to the Supreme Court, appeal court decisions are normally final. Family, youth and small claims courts are also part of the provincial court system although more serious family and youth cases can find their ways into superior courts.

Administrative tribunals often have quasi-judicial powers in deciding on questions of administrative law, which concerns the powers of the federal and provincial governments. For example, administrative tribunals have been set up outside formal court procedures to deal with broadcasting licences, Unemployment Insurance and occupational safety.

SOURCES

Canadian Centre for Justice Statistics
Department of Justice
National Crime Prevention Council
Solicitor General Canada
Statistics Canada

FOR FURTHER READING

Selected publications from Statistics Canada

- **Juristat**. Irregular. 85-002
- **Policing in Canada**. Annual. 85-523

Selected publications from other sources

- **Civil Justice Review: First Report**. Ontario Court of Justice and Ontario Ministry of the Attorney General. 1995.

Legend

–	nil or zero	..	not available	x	confidential
--	too small to be expressed	...	not applicable or not appropriate		*(Certain tables may not add due to rounding)*

16.1 JUSTICE SPENDING[1]

	1988-89	1989-90	1990-91	1991-92	1992-93
			$ '000		
Justice spending[2]	7,162,959	7,781,333	8,661,139	9,119,262	9,569,655
Police	4,389,414	4,684,760	5,248,530	5,426,887	5,716,833
Courts[3]	639,891	..	766,334	..	867,006
Legal aid	300,312	341,388	412,072	513,953	603,434
Youth corrections	355,926	398,400	434,010	475,113	487,900
Adult corrections	1,477,416	1,653,785	1,800,193	1,893,309	1,894,482

1. Most municipal police forces report on a calendar year; all other data represent fiscal year reporting.
2. In order to provide total line comparisons from year to year, court expenditures for 1989-90 and 1991-92 have been estimated as a mid-point between the two years and included in the totals for these years.
3. Figures for courts are collected every second year.

Source: Statistics Canada, Catalogue no. 85-002.

16.2 CRIMES

	1964	1974	1984	1989	1990	1991	1992	1993	1994
All offences	960,917	2,009,886	2,713,946	2,992,632	3,170,185	3,438,550	3,269,850	3,149,371	3,027,636
Criminal Code	626,038	1,456,885	2,147,657	2,425,936	2,627,193	2,898,988	2,847,981	2,735,626	2,632,830
Crimes of violence	54,769	126,053	179,397	248,579	269,503	296,962	307,512	310,201	303,398
Murder	218	545	621	605	589	688	654	552	541
Attempted murder	121	521	922	830	905	1,044	1,054	984	918
Manslaughter	35	53	42	49	65	60	77	75	49
Robbery	5,666	16,955	23,310	25,722	28,109	33,236	33,201	29,955	28,888
Other violent crimes	48,729	107,979	154,502	221,373	239,835	261,934	272,526	278,635	273,002
Property crimes	414,048	946,793	1,408,663	1,443,048	1,554,348	1,726,769	1,674,773	1,599,037	1,524,931
Breaking and entering	97,224	233,362	356,912	348,430	379,364	434,602	427,153	406,421	387,877
Theft of motor vehicles	39,930	83,309	76,613	100,208	114,082	139,345	146,801	156,685	159,663
Theft	237,619	538,937	828,041	844,114	900,490	981,889	943,532	892,058	843,659
Possession of stolen goods	6,011	15,312	24,322	27,663	29,814	34,040	31,551	30,827	30,522
Frauds	33,264	75,873	122,775	122,633	130,598	136,893	125,736	113,046	103,210
Other crimes	157,221	384,039	559,597	734,309	803,342	875,257	865,696	826,388	804,501
Prostitution	2,054	3,249	1,024	9,717	10,273	10,567	10,137	8,517	5,588
Gaming and betting	2,656	3,264	1,701	1,587	1,405	1,385	739	704	422
Offensive weapons	2,939	10,812	16,019	17,148	18,061	19,687	17,704	18,584	18,919
Other Criminal Code	149,572	366,714	540,853	705,857	773,603	843,618	837,116	798,583	779,572
Federal statutes	33,791	102,979	91,837	106,901	92,336	93,719	103,552	105,099	101,086
Provincial statutes	248,772	368,716	378,656	360,852	349,241	343,263	318,317	308,646	293,720
Municipal by-laws[1]	52,316	81,306	95,796	98,943	101,366	102,580	..	..	..

1. Data not available after 1991.

Source: Statistics Canada, CANSIM, matrix 2200.

16.3 YOUTHS AND ADULTS CHARGED

	1986	1990	1991	1992	1993	1994
All persons charged	861,604	898,692	930,489	863,063	817,371	754,371
Adults charged	724,817	742,009	758,816	702,160	666,706	610,994
Male	624,965	628,956	640,794	587,651	556,623	512,858
Female	99,852	113,053	118,022	114,509	110,083	98,136
Youth charged	136,787	156,683	171,673	160,903	150,665	143,377
Male	113,318	127,826	139,398	128,148	119,178	114,161
Female	23,469	28,857	32,275	32,755	31,487	29,216
Criminal Code						
Violent crime	87,957	125,957	141,660	145,354	150,330	147,019
Adults charged	78,682	110,267	122,741	125,326	128,853	125,363
Male	71,082	98,919	109,817	111,693	114,144	110,079
Female	7,600	11,348	12,924	13,633	14,709	15,284
Youth charged	9,275	15,690	18,919	20,028	21,477	21,656
Male	7,547	12,405	15,059	15,734	16,381	16,753
Female	1,728	3,285	3,860	4,294	5,096	4,903
Property crime	268,243	272,332	295,947	280,944	256,201	230,936
Adults charged	189,381	188,591	204,291	197,341	181,220	161,891
Male	148,201	144,561	156,778	150,191	136,982	124,401
Female	41,180	44,030	47,513	47,150	44,238	37,490
Youth charged	78,862	83,741	91,656	83,603	74,981	69,045
Male	65,912	68,424	74,352	66,565	59,232	54,784
Female	12,950	15,317	17,304	17,038	15,749	14,261
Other Criminal Code offences	145,548	169,379	186,097	183,950	176,597	164,177
Adults charged	124,679	142,261	154,356	152,268	146,168	135,119
Male	108,493	121,448	130,993	128,361	122,822	114,631
Female	16,186	20,813	23,363	23,907	23,346	20,488
Youth charged	20,869	27,118	31,741	31,682	30,429	29,058
Male	17,737	22,942	26,509	26,041	24,954	23,996
Female	3,132	4,176	5,232	5,641	5,475	5,062
Federal statutes	49,282	53,767	54,032	58,091	56,539	55,607
Adults charged	45,261	49,161	49,442	53,026	50,443	48,167
Male	40,043	42,846	42,971	44,782	43,186	41,231
Female	5,218	6,315	6,471	8,244	7,257	6,936
Youth charged	4,021	4,606	4,590	5,065	6,096	7,440
Male	3,495	3,766	3,653	4,057	5,003	6,142
Female	526	840	937	1,008	1,093	1,298
Provincial statutes	280,383	243,270	223,018	194,724	177,704	156,632
Adults charged	258,114	219,527	200,272	174,199	160,022	140,454
Male	232,470	194,422	176,786	152,624	139,489	122,516
Female	25,644	25,105	23,486	21,575	20,533	17,938
Youth charged	22,269	23,743	22,746	20,525	17,682	16,178
Male	17,396	18,795	18,162	15,751	13,608	12,486
Female	4,873	4,948	4,584	4,774	4,074	3,692

Source: Statistics Canada, CANSIM, matrices 2198 and 2199.

16.4 YOUTH COURTS DISPOSITIONS[1]

	1991-92	1992-93	1993-94	1994-95
		Cases		
All dispositions	75,143	77,256	78,010	73,969
Secure custody	9,720	10,616	11,119	11,616
Open custody	12,578	13,427	14,483	13,596
Probation	31,268	31,246	30,361	35,627
Fine	5,959	5,469	5,381	4,472
Community service order	9,427	10,051	10,316	4,866
Absolute discharge	3,127	2,888	2,697	2,413
Other dispositions[2]	3,064	3,559	3,653	1,379

1. From April 1 of one year to March 31 of the next year.
2. Includes dispositions such as detention for treatment, compensation, pay purchaser, compensation in kind, restitution, prohibition, seizure, forfeiture, essays, apologies and counselling programs.

Source: Statistics Canada, Catalogue no. 85-522.

16.5 TRAFFIC OFFENCES

	1987	1988	1989	1990	1991	1992	1993	1994
Traffic offences	407,087	403,301	412,465	398,831	393,052	390,456	365,649	322,079
Criminal Code offences	241,429	235,855	236,602	227,201	226,070	219,693	197,825	185,641
Dangerous operation of a:								
Motor vehicle	5,926	6,018	6,219	5,676	5,364	5,284	5,548	5,526
Motor vehicle causing death	166	170	198	186	222	219	198	244
Motor vehicle causing bodily harm	583	599	683	684	609	589	582	642
Boat, vessel or aircraft	164	165	121	129	169	174	167	203
Boat, vessel or aircraft causing death	19	19	13	15	25	21	16	20
Boat, vessel or aircraft causing bodily harm	39	32	28	32	26	29	38	31
Impaired operation of a:								
Vehicle causing death	182	188	186	166	171	161	168	130
Vehicle causing bodily harm	7	13	22	15	7	21	14	16
Vehicle with BAC[1] over 80 mg	1,452	1,374	1,385	1,387	1,300	1,383	1,160	1,164
Boat, vessel or aircraft causing death	93	128	85	121	80	64	82	30
Boat, vessel or aircraft causing bodily harm	131,872	128,355	128,744	124,306	126,903	119,884	107,194	97,701
Boat, vessel or aircraft with BAC[1] over 80 mg	402	338	267	328	361	240	221	228
Failure or refusal to provide a breath sample	13,867	13,113	13,187	12,246	11,484	10,284	8,432	7,377
Failure or refusal to provide a blood sample	445	520	507	509	421	382	303	333
Failure to stop or remain at the site of an accident	77,916	75,466	75,418	70,702	65,974	67,053	60,066	60,124
Driving a vehicle while prohibited	8,572	9,811	10,413	11,006	12,647	12,959	13,182	11,641
Provincial statute offences	165,658	167,446	176,045	171,630	166,982	170,763	167,824	136,438
Failure to stop or remain at the site of an accident	88,607	90,006	97,468	98,664	95,950	89,714	93,525	79,421
Dangerous driving	49,363	48,192	49,759	41,640	37,712	39,970	36,937	27,024
Driving while licence suspended	27,688	29,248	28,818	31,326	33,320	41,079	37,362	29,993

1. Blood alcohol concentration.

Source: Statistics Canada, CANSIM, matrix 310.

16.6 INMATES IN FEDERAL CUSTODY[1]

	1989	1990	1991	1992	1993	1994
Canada	11,415	11,289	11,783	12,342	13,322	13,948
Atlantic	1,019	978	1,058	1,173	1,419	1,409
Quebec	3,369	3,271	3,431	3,646	3,748	3,825
Ontario	3,135	3,178	3,343	3,552	3,858	3,781
Prairie	2,250	2,291	2,372	2,422	2,773	3,041
Pacific	1,642	1,571	1,579	1,549	1,524	1,892

1. Average counts until 1993 were based on 52 weekly counts. In 1993, the count is based on a snapshot taken on March 31.

Source: Statistics Canada, CANSIM, matrix 313; Catalogue no. 85-211.

16.7 INMATES IN PROVINCIAL CUSTODY

	1985	1990	1991	1992	1993	1994
Canada	16,178	17,944	18,944	19,367	19,481	19,934
Newfoundland	295	294	354	410	380	393
Prince Edward Island	77	105	108	115	96	95
Nova Scotia	396	379	396	395	436	439
New Brunswick	399	404	416	464	466	429
Quebec	2,621	3,168	3,344	3,556	3,545	3,553
Ontario	5,978	6,853	7,381	7,421	7,254	7,282
Manitoba	805	987	959	939	893	941
Saskatchewan	1,154	1,316	1,315	1,198	1,214	1,240
Alberta	2,254	2,324	2,430	2,584	2,718	2,712
British Columbia	1,907	1,771	1,895	1,927	2,113	2,361
Yukon	66	91	84	80	73	69
Northwest Territories	226	252	259	278	293	420

Source: Statistics Canada, CANSIM, matrix 312.

16.8 POLICE PERSONNEL

	Police personnel	Police officers	Civilian personnel	Police/civilian ratio	Population per police officer	Criminal Code incidents per police officer[1]
1974	57,361	45,276	12,085	3.75	505	32
1979	63,991	48,990	15,001	3.27	496	38
1984	67,513	50,010	17,503	2.86	514	43
1989	73,332	54,233	19,099	2.84	505	45
1990	75,364	56,034	19,330	2.90	496	47
1991	75,763	56,768	18,995	2.99	495	51
1992	76,606	56,992	19,614	2.91	501	50
1993	76,409	56,901	19,508	2.92	509	48
1994	74,902	55,865	19,037	2.93	524	47

1. Data exclude Criminal Code traffic offences.

Source: Statistics Canada, Catalogue no. 85-002.

REGIONAL REFERENCE CENTRES

Telecommunications Device for the Hearing Impaired 1-800-363-7629.

Toll Free Order Only Line (Canada and the United States) 1-800-267-6677.

National Enquiries Line: 1-800-263-1136

National Capital Region Internet: infostats@statcan.ca.

ATLANTIC REGION

Serving the provinces of Newfoundland and Labrador, Nova Scotia, Prince Edward Island and New Brunswick.

STATISTICS CANADA
Advisory Services
1770 Market Street
HALIFAX, Nova Scotia
B3J 3M3

Local calls: (902) 426-5331
Fax: (902) 426-9538

QUÉBEC REGION

STATISTICS CANADA
Advisory Services
200 René Levesque Boulevard West
East Tower, 4th Floor
MONTREAL, Quebec
H2Z 1X4

Local calls: (514) 283-5725
Fax: (514) 283-9350

NATIONAL CAPITAL REGION

Statistical Reference Centre

STATISTICS CANADA
R.H. Coats Building Lobby
Holland Avenue
OTTAWA, Ontario
K1A 0T6

Local calls: (613) 951-8116
Fax: (613) 951-0581

ONTARIO REGION

STATISTICS CANADA
Advisory Services
Arthur Meighen Building
25 St. Clair Avenue East, 10th Floor
TORONTO, Ontario
M4T 1M4

Local calls: (416) 973-6586
Fax: (416) 973-7475

PRAIRIE REGION

STATISTICS CANADA
Manitoba
Advisory Services
344 Edmonton Street, MacDonald Building, Suite 300
WINNIPEG, Manitoba
R3B 3L9

Local calls: (204) 983-4020
Fax: (204) 983-7543

STATISTICS CANADA
Saskatchewan
Advisory Services
2002 Victoria Avenue,
Avord Tower, 9th Floor
REGINA, Saskatchewan
S4P 0R7

Local calls: (306) 780-5405
Fax: (306) 780-5403

STATISTICS CANADA
Northern Alberta and
Northwest Territories
Advisory Services
10001 Bellamy Hill,
Park Square, 9th Floor
EDMONTON, Alberta
T5J 3B6

Local calls: (403) 495-3027
Fax: (403) 495-5318

STATISTICS CANADA
Southern Alberta
Advisory Services
138 Fourth Avenue South East,
First Street Plaza, Room 401
CALGARY, Alberta
T2G 4Z6

Local calls: (403) 292-6717
Fax: (403) 292-4958

PACIFIC REGION

Serving the province of British Columbia and the Yukon Territory.

STATISTICS CANADA
Advisory Services
Library Square Tower
Suite 600-300 West
Georgia Street
VANCOUVER, British Columbia
V6B 6C7

Local calls: (604) 666-3691
Fax: (604) 666-4863

METRIC CONVERSION

In view of the degree of metric conversion in Canada, almost all quantities in this edition of the Canada Year Book appear only in the International System of Units (SI) metric or in neutral units such as dollars or dozens.

It is a requirement in SI metric to use spaces instead of commas to separate groups of three digits; a space is optional with a four-digit number. In all Statistics Canada publications, a period is used as a decimal marker.

Relative weights and measures:
SI Metric, Canadian Imperial and United States units

AREA

1 sq. km (square kilometre) = 0.3861022 square miles
1 ha (hectare) = 2.471054 acres
= 10000 sq. m
100 ha = 1 sq. km

LENGTH

1 m (metre) = 39.37 inches
= 3.28 feet
= 1.09 yards
1 km (kilometre) = 0.6213712 statute miles = 3,280.840 feet
= 0.5399568 nautical miles = 2,850.972 feet

VOLUME AND CAPACITY

1 L (litre) = 0.0353147 cubic feet
= 0.4237760 board feet (for lumber)
= 0.0274962 Canadian bushels (for grain)
= 0.2199692 Canadian gallons
= 35.1951 fluid ounces
= 0.8798774 quarts
= 1.75975 pints
= 0.264172 U.S. gallons
= 1.05669 U.S. quarts
= 2.11338 U.S. pints

1 cu. m (cubic metre) = 6.289811 barrels (oil barrel: 42 U.S. gallons)
= 0.3531466 register tons (in shipping)*
= 35.31466 cubic feet
= 1000 cu. dm

MASS WEIGHT

1 g (gram) = 0.03527396 ounces (avoirdupois)
= 0.03215075 ounces (troy or apothecary)
1 kg (kilogram) = 2.20462262 pounds (avoirdupois)
1 t (metric tonne) = 1.10231131 tons (short)
= 0.98420653 tons (long)

LENGTH AND MASS

1 t-km (tonne-kilometre) = 0.6849445 short ton miles

VOLUME AND MASS

1 cu. m of water weighs 1 tonne (approximate)

TEMPERATURE

Fahrenheit temperature = 1.8 (Celsius temperature +32)
Celsius temperature = 5/9 (Fahrenheit temperature -32)
At sea level, water freezes at 0°C (32°F) and boils at 100°C (212°F) (approximate).

ENERGY

1 kJ (kilojoule) = 0.947086 British thermal units (BTU) (mean)
1 MJ (megajoule) = 0.3722506 horsepower-hours
1 MJ = 0.277778 kilowatt-hours
1 PJ = 1 000 000 000 MJ

* *Please see footnote on the next page.*

The following weights and measures are used in connection with the principal field crops and fruits:

Crops	Pounds per bushel	Kilograms per bushel	Bushels per 1 000 kg (1 t)
Wheat, potatoes and peas	60	27.215 5	36.743 7
Wheat flour	43.48	19.722 2	50.704 3
Oats	34	15.422 1	64.841 8
Barley and buckwheat	48	21.772 4	45.929 6
Rye, flaxseed and corn	56	25.401 2	39.368 3
Mixed grains	45	20.411 7	48.991 6
Rapeseed, mustard seed, pears, plums, cherries, peaches and apricots	50	20.679 6	44.092 5
Sunflower seed	24	10.886 2	91.859 3
Apples	42	19.050 9	52.491 0

Strawberries and raspberries: 1 kg = 1.47 quarts in British Columbia
= 1.76 quarts in all other provinces.

To produce 100 kg of flour it takes 138 kg of wheat (approximate).

Conversion example

If converting from metres to feet where:
1 m = 3.281 feet
multiply the number of metres by 3.281 to get the number of feet.
10 metres = 10 times 3.281or 32.81 feet.

If converting from feet to metres where:
1 m = 3.281 feet
divide the number of feet by 3.281 to get the number of metres.
10 feet = 10 divided by 3.281 or 3.05 metres.

* *Gross register tonnage of ship, as used by Lloyd's Register of Shipping, is a measurement of the total capacity of the ship and is not a measure of weight. Net register tonnage equals gross register tonnage minus space used for accommodation, machinery, engine area and fuel storage, and so states the cargo-carrying ability of the ship.*

APPENDIX C

COVER

John de Visser, Masterfile
A view of the Rockies
from Hope–Princeton Highway, B.C.

Richard Desmarais
A view of the Atlantic Ocean
taken at Fort Louisbourg,
Cape Breton Island.

SECTION 1

Mark Tomalty, Masterfile
Barred Owl, Mount Bruno
Provincial Park, Quebec.

Chapter 1
Darwin Wiggett, First Light
Round bales near Leduc, Alberta.

J. David Andrews, Dynamic Light Productions
Aspen trees.

Chapter 2
Thomas Kitchin, First Light
Calgary City Centre, Bow River, skyline, Alberta.

Unknown artist, National Archives of Canada, C-126252
Poster entitled *Sowing, April, Great Britain*, 1926-1934.

SECTION 2

Pete Ryan, GeoStock
Football stadium spectators.

Chapter 3
David Trattles
Ashley MacIsaac fiddles.

Mike Beedell
Inuit boy from Pond Inlet.

Chapter 4
Mike Beedell
A woman kayaking with her dog.

Denis Boissavy, Masterfile
Baby photo.

Chapter 5
Kennon Cooke, Valan Photos
Arts Building and Moyse Hall, McGill University, Montreal.

Mike Pinder
Dan Aykroyd receiving honorary
degree at Carleton University, Ottawa, 1995.

Chapter 6
Photo by Lawrence Cook, The Indian Art Centre,
Department of Indian and Northern Affairs, Canada
National Pastimes 1991. Artist: Jim Logan.

David Trattles
Laundry at Port-aux-Basques.

Chapter 7
National Gallery of Canada, Ottawa
Longshoremen, Miller Brittain.

Glenbow Collection, Calgary, Canada
Factory, Laurence Hyde.

Chapter 8
Fine Arts Committee, The Toronto Hospital, Western
Division. Gift of Mrs. E.R. Wood, Toronto, 1927.
Algoma Hill, Lawren Harris. Image courtesy of the National
Gallery of Canada, Ottawa.

Gift of G. de B. Robinson to the University Art Collection,
University of Toronto.
Untitled pen drawing, by Percy J. Robinson, c. 1919-21, to
illustrate a poem, also by the artist, entitled *The Georgian Bay*.
Image courtesy of the National Gallery of Canada, Ottawa.

SECTION 3

Kaj Svensson, Viewpoints West
Western sandpipers, Boundary Bay, B.C.

Chapter 9

Irwin Barrett, First Light
Balancing rock, Long Island, Newfoundland.

Felix H. Man, National Archives, PA-145951
Observation platform at the end of the CPR Transcontinental train, 1933.

Chapter 10

Peter Plancius, National Archives, NMC 27654
A 16th century map that shows the extent of European knowledge relating to North and South America in the late 1500s.

Carolyn Charlton
Two people standing by relief map.

Chapter 11

Tim Wickens
Rooster.

Robert Bourdeau
Gatineau Park, Quebec.

Chapter 12

Photo by William Kent, Canadian War Museum, Cat. No. 72047.
Hull Rivetting. Artist: Frederick B. Taylor.

Canadarm, as first seen through Space Shuttle Columbia's cabin window, during Mission STS-2, November 1981, Canadian Space Agency.

Chapter 13

Mike Beedell
Yellow train in Churchill, Manitoba.

Photo by Sheila Spence, Winnipeg Art Gallery
Satellite Dish, 1986, from the *Northern Suite Series.*
Artist: Wanda Koop.

Chapter 14

Kaj Svensson, Viewpoints West
World currencies.

Robert Lankinen, First Light
Loon.

SECTION 4

The Arms of Canada.

Chapter 15

Pierre St. Jacques, GeoStock
Canada Day, 1989.

Ron Watts, First Light
Legislature details, Winnipeg, Manitoba.

Chapter 16

Paul Couvrette, Paul Couvrette Photography
Members of the Supreme Court of Canada, 1996.

Felix H. Man, National Archives, PA-145953.
Royal Canadian Mounted Police, Banff, Alberta. 1933.

LAST IMAGE

Mike Beedell
Northern explorer holding Canadian flag.

Selected quotes were printed with permission from the following sources:

From *The Canadian Encyclopedia Plus* by McClelland & Stewart. Used by permission of McClelland & Stewart, Inc., Toronto, *The Canadian Publishers.*

From *Canadian Literary Landmarks*, reprinted with permission from Hounslow Press.

From *Colombo's Canadian Quotations* by John Robert Colombo. Used by permission of McClelland & Stewart, Inc., Toronto, *The Canadian Publishers.*

Dictionnaire des citations québécoises, by Gilbert Forest. Used by permission of Éditions Québec/Amérique, Montréal.

Free in the Harbour and Northwest Passage © 1981 – Stan Rogers, Fogarty's Cove & Cole Harbour Music Ltd. Used by permission.

"If I had $1,000,000" by Steven Page and Ed Robertson. © 1988 WB Music Corp. & Treat Baker Music. All rights administered by WB Music Corp. All rights reserved. Used by permission.

La Petite Poule d'eau, by Gabrielle Roy. © Fonds Gabrielle Roy.

From *The Politics of Canadian Broadcasting, 1920-1951*; *Timothy Eaton and the Rise of his Department Store;* and *Naming Canada: Stories about Place Names from Canadian Geographic*, all reprinted with permission from University of Toronto Press.

From *The Roaring Girl*, Greg Hollingshead, Somerville House Books, Toronto, 1996. Reprinted with the permission of Stoddart Publishing Co. Limited, Don Mills, Ont. M3B 2T6.

From *Understanding Wood* by R. Bruce Hoadley. Used with permission of The Taunton Press, Inc. 63 South Main Street, P.O. Box 5506, Newtown, CT 06470. © 1980 The Taunton Press, Inc. All rights reserved.

INDEX

Please note: If a page number is followed by "g," the information sought is contained only in a graphic. However, if the information is contained in both the text and the graphic, no letter follows the page number. If a page number is followed by the letter "t," the reference is to a table.

Q

R

S

T

Y

Z

ARCTIC OCEAN
Approximate Limit of Permanent Polar Ice
40°
110°
80°
QUEEN ELIZABETH ISLANDS
AXEL HEIBERG ISLAND
Eureka
Grise Fiord
MELVILLE ISLAND
DEVON ISLA
Resolute
Parry Channel
Beaufort Sea
BANKS ISLAND
Sachs Harbour
Amundsen Gulf
DISTRICT OF FRANKLIN
VICTORIA ISLAND
Holman
Paulatuk
Cambridge Bay
Gjoa Haven
Spence Bay
Pelly Bay
Coppermine
NORTHWEST TERR
Bering Strait
ALASKA
ARCTIC CIRCLE
(UNITED STATES OF AMERICA)
Yukon River
Old Crow
Aklavik
Tuktoyaktuk
Inuvik
Fort McPherson
YUKON TERRITORY
Dawson
Mayo
Carmacks
Faro
Pelly River
Haines Junction
WHITEHORSE
Teslin
Cassiar
Watson Lake
Fort Good Hope
Mackenzie River
Fort Franklin
Fort Norman
Great Bear Lake
Echo Bay
Wrigley
DISTRICT OF MACKENZIE
Back R
Fort Simpson
Rae
YELLOWKNIFE
Fort Providence
Great Slave Lake
Hay River
Pine Point
Fort Resolution
Fort Smith
Slave River
Liard R
Fort Nelson
DISTRICT OF KEEWATIN
Thelon R
Baker Lake
Rankin Inlet
Eskimo Point
Churchill
Stewart
Masset
Prince Rupert
Kitimat
BRITISH COLUMBIA
PACIFIC OCEAN
Peace River
Dawson Creek
Grande Prairie
Fort McMurray
Lake Athabasca
La Loche
Reindeer Lake
Brochet
Lynn Lake
Churchill
Prince George
Ocean Falls
Port Hardy
VANCOUVER ISLAND
Williams Lake
Fraser River
ALBERTA
Athabasca
North Saskatchewan
EDMONTON
Thompson
Nelson R
MANITOBA
Flin Flon
Prince Albert
Saskatchewan
SASKATCHEWAN
Red Deer
Kamloops
Kelowna
Columbia R
Nanaimo
VICTORIA
Vancouver
New Westminster
Calgary
South Saskatchewan R
Saskatoon
Lake Winnipegosis
Swan River
Dauphin
Lake Manitoba
Lake Winnipeg
Severn R
Sandy Lake
Red Lake
Moose Jaw
REGINA
Weyburn
Brandon
WINNIPEG
Kenora
Fort Frances
UNITED STATES OF AMERICA

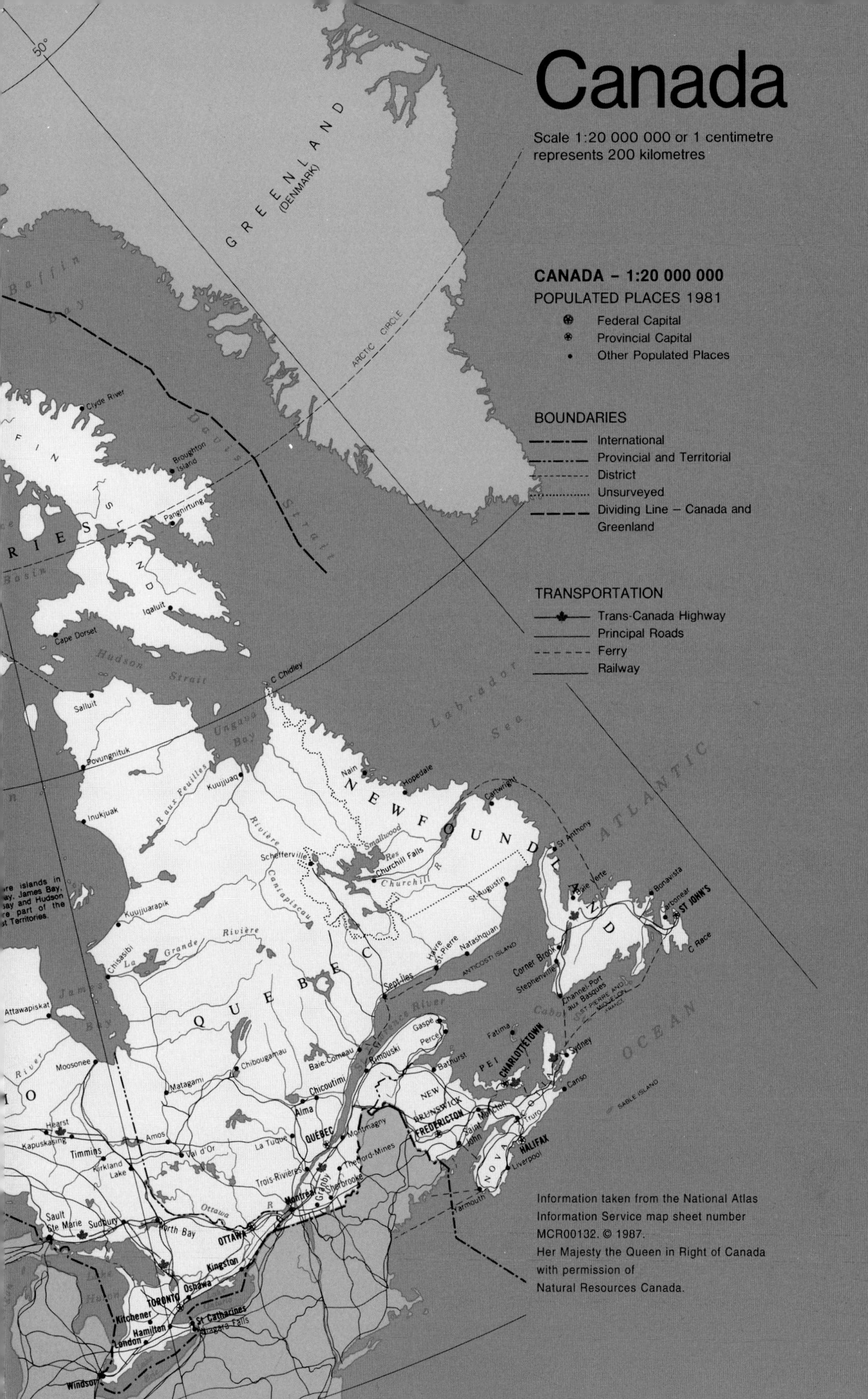
Canada
Scale 1:20 000 000 or 1 centimetre represents 200 kilometres
CANADA – 1:20 000 000
POPULATED PLACES 1981
Federal Capital
Provincial Capital
Other Populated Places
BOUNDARIES
International
Provincial and Territorial
District
Unsurveyed
Dividing Line – Canada and Greenland
TRANSPORTATION
Trans-Canada Highway
Principal Roads
Ferry
Railway
GREENLAND (DENMARK)
ARCTIC CIRCLE
Baffin Bay
Davis Strait
Clyde River
Broughton Island
Pangnirtung
Iqaluit
Cape Dorset
Hudson Strait
C Chidley
Ungava Bay
Labrador Sea
ATLANTIC OCEAN
Salluit
Povungnituk
Kuujjuaq
Inukjuak
Nain
Hopedale
Cartwright
NEWFOUNDLAND
Smallwood Res
Churchill Falls
Churchill R
Schefferville
St Anthony
Baie Verte
Bonavista
Carbonear
ST JOHN'S
C Race
St-Augustin
Natashquan
Havre St-Pierre
ANTICOSTI ISLAND
Corner Brook
Stephenville
Channel-Port aux Basques
ST PIERRE AND MIQUELON (FRANCE)
Kuujjuarapik
Chisasibi
La Grande Rivière
QUEBEC
Sept-Îles
Gaspé
Percé
Fatima
CHARLOTTETOWN
PEI
Sydney
Canso
SABLE ISLAND
Attawapiskat
James Bay
Moosonee
Chibougamau
Baie-Comeau
Rimouski
Bathurst
Matagami
Chicoutimi
Alma
NEW BRUNSWICK
FREDERICTON
Moncton
Saint John
Truro
NOVA SCOTIA
HALIFAX
Liverpool
Yarmouth
Hearst
Kapuskasing
Timmins
Amos
Val d'Or
La Tuque
QUÉBEC
Montmagny
Thetford-Mines
Kirkland Lake
Trois-Rivières
Sherbrooke
Granby
Montréal
Ottawa R
Sault Ste Marie
Sudbury
North Bay
OTTAWA
Kingston
Oshawa
TORONTO
Kitchener
Hamilton
St Catharines
Niagara Falls
London
Windsor
Lake Huron
Information taken from the National Atlas Information Service map sheet number MCR00132. © 1987.
Her Majesty the Queen in Right of Canada with permission of Natural Resources Canada.